CHARIOTS, SWORDS AND SPEARS

CHARIOTS, SWORDS AND SPEARS

IRON AGE BURIALS AT THE FOOT OF THE EAST YORKSHIRE WOLDS

edited by

MARK STEPHENS

with contributions by
Sophia Adams, Michelle Alexander, Diane Alldritt, Anwen Cafell, Thomas G.B. Fox,
Melanie Giles, Peter Halkon, Derek Hamilton, Matthew Hitchcock, Malin Holst, Yvonne Inall,
Rod Mackenzie, Nicholas Patterson, Paola Ponce, Dominic Powlesland, Jane Richardson,
Kerry L. Sayle, Katharine Steinke, Max Stubbings and Paula Ware

OXBOW | books
Oxford & Philadelphia

Published in the United Kingdom in 2023 by
OXBOW BOOKS
The Old Music Hall, 106–108 Cowley Road, Oxford, OX4 1JE

and in the United States by
OXBOW BOOKS
1950 Lawrence Road, Havertown, PA 19083

Hardback Edition: ISBN 978-1-78925-542-3
Digital Edition: ISBN 978-1-78925-543-0 (epub)

A CIP record for this book is available from the British Library

Library of Congress Control Number: 2022946056

Printed in Malta by Melita Press

Typeset in India by Lapiz Digital Services, Chennai.

For a complete list of Oxbow titles, please contact:

UNITED KINGDOM
Oxbow Books
Telephone (01865) 241249
Email: oxbow@oxbowbooks.com
www.oxbowbooks.com

UNITED STATES OF AMERICA
Oxbow Books
Telephone (610) 853-9131, Fax (610) 853-9146
Email: queries@casemateacademic.com
www.casemateacademic.com/oxbow

Oxbow Books is part of the Casemate Group

Front cover: Two horses from Chariot Burial in Barrow 85, Burnby Lane, Pocklington.
Back cover: Left: Chariot Burial with Upright Horses in Grave 3613, The Mile, Pocklington; Right: The outer face of the shield
(photogrammetric image by M. Abbott)

Contents

List of figures

List of tables

List of contributors

DR SOPHIA ADAMS
Honorary Research Fellow, Scottish Universities Environmental Research Centre (SUERC)

DR MICHELLE ALEXANDER
Senior Lecturer in Bioarchaeology, Department of Archaeology, University of York

DR DIANE ALLDRITT
Manager, Archaeobotanical Services, Glasgow

DR ANWEN CAFELL
Research Fellow, Durham University

THOMAS G. B. FOX
University of York

DR MELANIE GILES
Senior Lecturer in Archaeology, University of Manchester

PETER HALKON
Senior Lecturer in Archaeology, University of Hull

PROFESSOR DEREK HAMILTON
Senior Research Fellow, Scottish Universities Environmental Research Centre (SUERC)

MATTHEW HITCHCOCK
PhD student, University of Manchester, focusing on British Iron Age shields

MALIN HOLST
Managing Director, York Osteology and Lecturer in Osteology, Department of Archaeology, University of York

DR YVONNE INALL
Research Consultant and former Research Assistant at University of Hull

DR ROD MACKENZIE
Visiting Scholar, Department of Material Science and Engineering, University of Sheffield

DR NICHOLAS PATTERSON
Senior computational biologist, Program in Medical and Population Genetics at the Broad Institute, Mass., USA

DR PAOLA PONCE
Associate Lecturer in Osteology, Department of Archaeology, University of York

DOMINIC POWLESLAND
Director of Landscape Research Centre and Visiting Professor at the universities of York, Leeds, Huddersfield and Vienna

DR JANE RICHARDSON
Archaeological Services Manager, West Yorkshire Archaeological Services

DR KERRY L. SAYLE
Post-doctoral Research Assistant, Scottish Universities Environmental Research Centre (SUERC)

DR KATHARINE STEINKE
Tutor and Demonstrator, Department of Archaeology, University of Edinburgh

MARK STEPHENS
Project Manager, MAP Archaeological Practice Ltd

MAX STUBBINGS
Project Officer/Surveyor, MAP Archaeological Practice Ltd

PAULA WARE
Managing Director, MAP Archaeological Practice Ltd

Summary

MAP Archaeological Practice carried out a series of archaeological excavations at a multi-period site on the eastern side of Burnby Lane, Pocklington, East Yorkshire. The work was carried out in several phases between August 2014 and March 2017 and covered two separate housing developments (separated by a hedge); these are treated as the same archaeological excavation in this report. In addition, the results of the excavation of two Iron Age barrows at The Mile, on the northern edge of Pockington, are included in this report.

East Yorkshire is the heartland of the 'Arras Culture', whose associated burials, often under square barrows, and often richly furnished (sometimes with chariots), have led to the suggestion of a link with northern France. It is also one of the few areas in Britain with evidence of burial customs in the middle Iron Age. The excavation of the Burnby Lane cemetery was the largest examination of middle Iron Age burials in Britain since the Garton and Wetwang Slack excavations, which took place from 1963 to 1989 (Dent 2019, 33–46).

The excavations examined and recorded a landscape of activity that began with a scatter of Neolithic pits and a late Neolithic hengiform enclosure, followed by a small group of Bronze Age round barrows which acted as a focus for burials in the Iron Age. The Iron Age cemetery consisted of two separate groups of square and round barrows, one at the west and the other to the east, with additional isolated individual barrows to the south and east; it also included 'flat' graves. The most notable burials were associated with a chariot complete with associated ponies (the first excavation in modern times), spears, a shield and a sword. Other grave goods consisted of a moderate quantity of brooches (those from B2 and B42 being exceptionally rare examples) and bracelets, as well as a complete pottery vessel. A number of the burials were placed within wooden structures, perhaps best described as timber 'cists' rather than coffins.

Following the abandonment of the square barrow cemetery, a series of Roman-period landscape boundaries were cut across the northern edge of the western barrow group. Subsequently, the disused western barrow group became a focus for Anglian burial. Some of the Anglian graves were notable for the inclusion of knives, brooches, and groups of beads and other items of personal adornment. Weapons were scarce and consisted of two spears. (The Anglian remains will be reported on in a separate volume.)

The scars of ridge and furrow show that the site formed part of the medieval arable landscape, which was subdivided into a series of fields in post-medieval times.

The excavation of the landscape site at The Mile, on the northern edge of Pocklington, recorded two more Iron Age barrows, one square and the other circular. The area defined by the ditches of the square barrow contained a unique 'intact' chariot burial complete with upright ponies, and the inhumation of a mature adult male, who lay on a richly decorated shield, itself an exceptionally rare find from excavation. The circular barrow contained the burial of a young man who was also accompanied by a shield, plus a set of iron and bone spearheads. The 'satellite' burial of a young woman was situated a short distance to the south-east of the circular barrow.

Acknowledgements

The excavations were directed and supervised by the Mark Stephens, with a core team consisting of John Bendicks, Zara Burn, Alistair Cross, Zech Jinks-Frederick, Martyn King, Peter Makey, Sergio Quintero-Cabello and John Stephens. Kelly Hunter supervised the excavation of Barrows 46, 47 and 49–55, and the machining-stripping of the southern field. Nick Bartlett, Steve Cooper, Simon Cosage, James Dodds, Lauren Ferrero, Steve Kennedy, Sarah Paris, Charlie Puntero (*nee* Stodart), Emma Samuels, Max Stubbings, Amy Talbot, Rianca Vogels, Cat Whitehouse (*nee* Chapman) and Luke Yates worked at the site for shorter periods.

The Burnby Lane chariot was excavated by the writer, Sergio Quintero-Cabello, John Stephens and Owain Wells. The benefit of insights from previous chariot excavations in East Yorkshire by Tony Brewster, John Dent and Ian Stead, and by Angela Boyle at Ferry Fryston, is readily acknowledged.

The figures were prepared by Max Stubbings, with initial digitising of the burials by Max Greaves. Jennifer Jackson produced the finds illustrations for Chapters 8, 9, 10 and 11 and Sergio Quintero Cabello illustrated the pottery for Chapter 12. The finds were managed by Sandra Garside-Neville, who was succeeded by Cat Chapman and Max Greaves. The environmental samples were processed by Damian Carr and Carl Stockhill.

Maggs Felter (York Archaeology) carried out the conservation of objects from both sites, and also led the lifting of the wheels of both chariots and the shield at The Mile. Steven Allen (YA) illustrated the shield from The Mile chariot burial as well as identifying the wood remains preserved on the finds. Sophia Adams reported on the Iron Age brooches and bracelets. Derek Hamilton (Scottish Universities Environmental Research Centre) and Sophia Adams analysed the dating evidence and took the samples from those skeletons associated with brooches; Derek and Sophia were responsible for the stable isotope analysis, along with Thomas G.B. Fox, Michele Alexander, Kerry L. Sayle and Katherine Steinke. Malin Holst and Anwen Caffell (York Osteology) reported on the Burnby Lane osteology, with Paola Ponce also reporting on burials from The Mile. Jane Richardson examined the animal bone. The carbonised plant remains were reported on by Jane Richardson. Yvonne Inall examined the weapons form Burnby Lane. Dominic Powlesland undertook the 3-D modelling of the chariot from The Mile.

Paula Ware and Sophie Coy took good care of the vital administration and behind the scenes management of the project and helped in many ways with the report. They also liaised with the developers, Barratt-David Wilson Homes (Burnby Lane) and Persimmon Homes (The Mile).

Many colleagues contributed with support, advice and assistance to the project, including John Dent, Terry Manby, Ian and Sheila Stead, and Pete Wilson. The support and input from Peter Halkon and Malcolm Lillie from the University of Hull was invaluable; Malcolm also facilitated the DNA analysis of individuals from Burnby Lane which was carried out at the Harvard Medical School by David Reich and his colleagues, who kindly shared the results in advance of the publication of their research.

Thanks are extended to all the staff of the East Yorkshire SMR, including Ruth Atkinson and Dave Evans in the early stages of the project, and latterly Lucy MacCarthy and her colleagues at the Humber HER.

The work could not have taken place without the support and co-operation of Barrett–David Wilson Homes, who funded the work at Burnby Lane, with particular thanks to John Birkin, Lee Kilby, Peter Morris, the late Paul Newman, Dean Oades (the Site Manager) and Paul Stones. Thanks also go to Andy Galbraith and staff of Norcon, the site contractors, who carried out the machining. The Mile excavation was funded by Persimmon Homes and MAP extends thanks to Simon Usher for his support with the project.

Peter Halkon would like to thank Terry Manby and Andrew Sefton for information for the Neolithic and Bronze Age sections, Paula Ware of MAP for inviting him to advise on the Pocklington project and for supplying data, and Tony Hunt of YAA Mapping for the drone photography.

Finally, thanks are due to Catrina Appleby for her many constructive comments, patience and dedication as editor.

Abbreviations and glossary

Flexed: the legs are at an angle greater than 90° to the spine.

Crouched: the legs are angled at less than 90° to the spine.

Contracted: the legs are approximately parallel to the spine.

Extended: the torso and limbs are out straight.

Supine: the burial is laid on its back.

Prone: the burial is laid on its front.

Flat Grave: a grave not enclosed by a barrow ditch, suggesting that there was not a mound covering it.

Terms used in describing skeletal pathology

CO: cribra orbitalia (fine pitting in the orbital roof likely caused by anaemia, vitamin C deficiency or chronic infection)

DDD: degenerative disc disease

DJC: degenerative joint change

Endocranial lamellar bone: new bone formation on the inside of the cranium as a reaction to a range of conditions such as meningitis, tuberculosis and anaemia

HFI: hyperostosis frontalis interna (associated with hormonal changes from the pituitary gland)

Lamellar bone: changes to the bone resulting from a healed infection

OA: osteoarthritis

Pilasterism: bending of the femoral shaft due to vitamin D deficiency

Sk: Skeleton

1

Introduction

Mark Stephens

A series of archaeological excavations was carried out by MAP Archaeological Practice Ltd at an Iron Age cemetery east of Burnby Lane, Pocklington, East Yorkshire (Figs 1.1 and 1.2; SE 801 486 centre), in advance of residential development by Barratt-David Wilson Homes (who funded the work). A Desk-based Assessment was carried out by MAP for the entire area (plus the area to the north-east), but each phase of the development had its own programme of geophysical survey, trial trenching and open-area excavation. The first phase concentrated on Nine Acres, the area of land immediately south of Pinewood Close, and the second phase concerned the two fields immediately to the south of Nine Acres. The archaeological work was carried out according to a series of Written Schemes of Investigation that were prepared by MAP Archaeological Practice Ltd at the request of Barratt-David Wilson Homes and agreed by the Humber Archaeology Partnership.

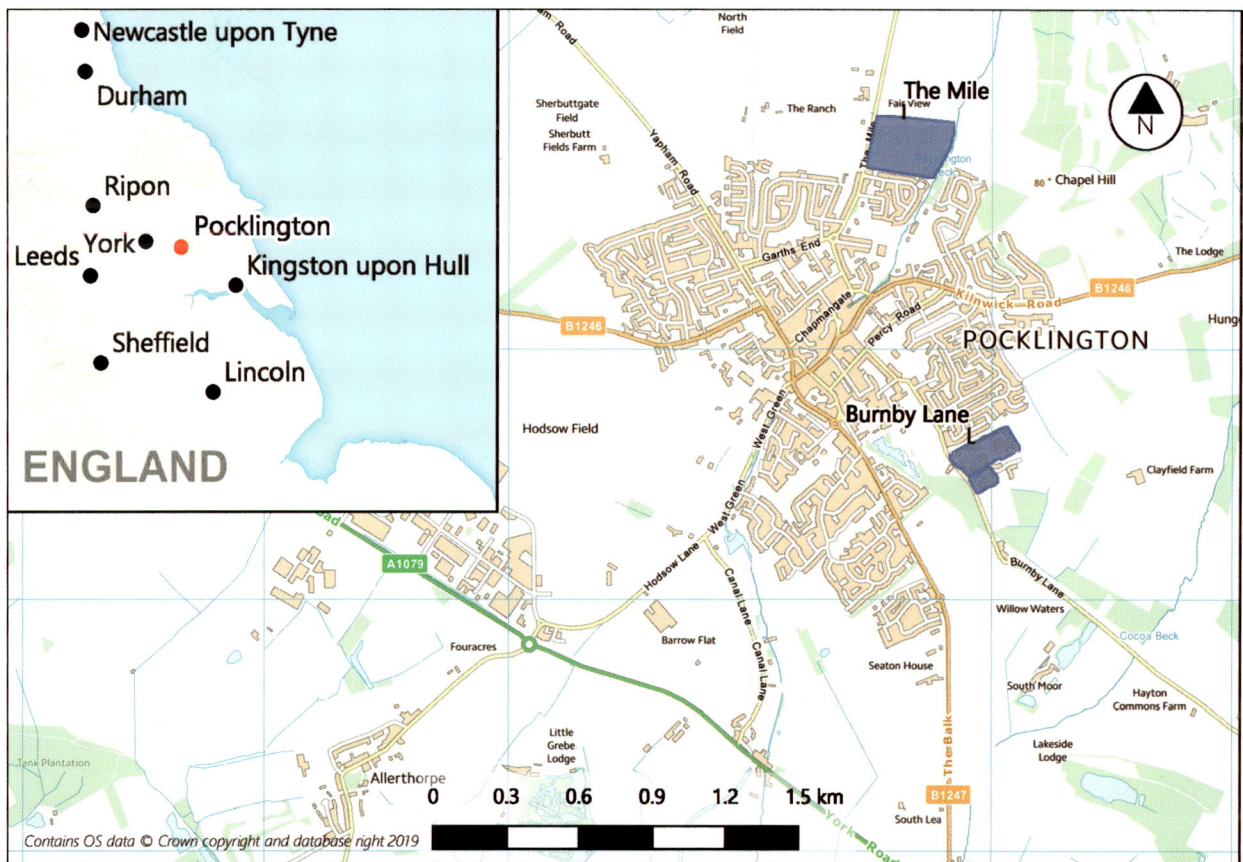

Figure 1.1 Site location

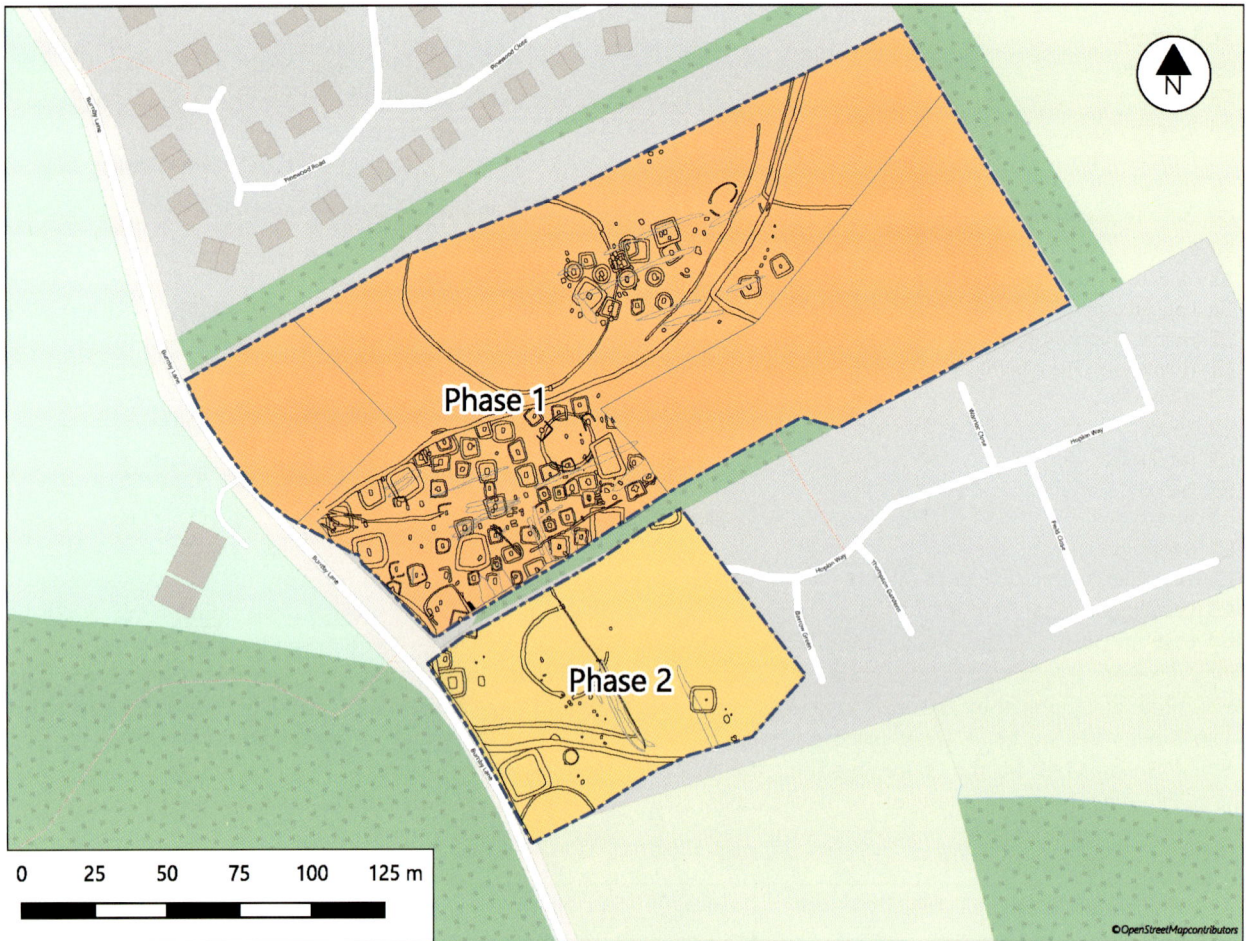

Figure 1.2 Site plan of Burnby Lane

The excavation of a square barrow and a circular barrow at The Mile, on the northern edge of Pocklington, on behalf of Persimmon Homes, is described in Chapter 6.

This report has been written in advance of the complete scientific analysis and dating of the human remains, which should add much detail to our understanding and interpretation of both the cemetery and the wider landscape. Certainly, the work on the isotopes and radiocarbon-dating, plus some DNA analysis, described in this report is a major achievement. Further radiocarbon-dating of the skeletons will add to our understanding of the development of the cemetery, and it is hoped that additional DNA and isotope analysis will provide more insight into the lives and origins of those buried within it. It is intended that detailed reporting on the other phases at the site will be published in a forthcoming volume which will include catalogues of the pottery, flint and other finds from those phases. For the moment, the chronology for the burials laid out below uses the physical evidence, information provided by the finds, and the available radiocarbon dates. One problem that cannot be overcome is the acidic nature of the soils at the site,

which left most of the burials in a fragile condition and hampered the skeletal analysis.

Burnby Lane: site description

The site is situated in Pocklington civil parish, within the East Riding of Yorkshire (centred at SE 801 486). The total development area, which was approximately 6.2ha in size (Fig. 1.2), lies immediately east of Burnby Lane, *c*. 900m south-east of the centre of the market town of Pocklington. Immediately prior to the excavations, the northern part of the site consisted of a grassed field and a 1960s' bungalow (Nine Acres) with its associated garden and paddock; the two fields to the south were under arable cultivation. The site had a mean elevation of *c*. 33m AOD and dipped slightly to the south-east.

Geology and soils

The soils at the site consist of permeable calcareous and non-calcareous loams of the Landbeach Association, which overlie chalky glaciofluvial gravels of variable

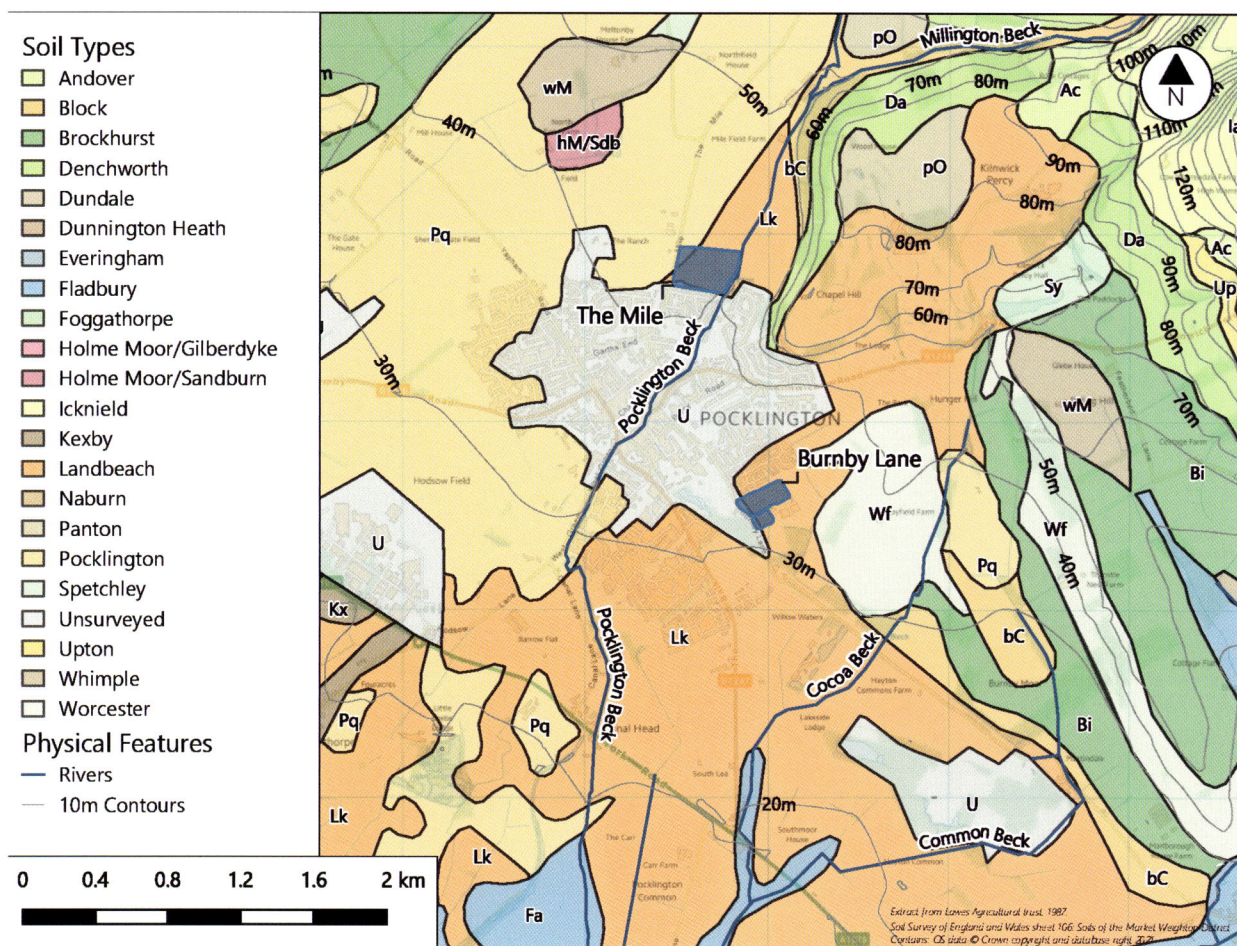

Figure 1.3 The physical geography and soils of the Pocklington area

thickness (King and Bradley 1987, 512b; Fig. 1.3). This soil is permeable and either well-drained or only occasionally waterlogged. The underlying bedrock is of the Mercia Mudstone Group ('Keuper Marl') of the Triassic period (British Geological Survey online).

The Burnby Lane site is situated on the western edge of an area of soils of the Landbeach Association, which can be occasionally waterlogged. The Worcester Association soils 400m to the east are generally poorly drained and prone to waterlogging. Further again to the south-east, large areas consist of slowly permeable Brockhurst and Wickham Association soils, and very poorly drained Fladbury soils. The site is therefore situated on a relatively dry and tractable area adjacent to land that would have been unsuitable for arable agriculture in the prehistoric period; this has significant implications for the character of human exploitation of the land through time.

Archaeological and historical background

The Burnby Lane site lies within a rich archaeological landscape dating to the prehistoric and later periods

(Fig. 1.4). The broader landscape of Eastern Yorkshire includes many previously excavated sites of the Arras culture (Fig. 1.5), while the archaeology of the site's immediate area is illustrated by aerial photographs of cropmarks on the two plots of land immediately north of the site and both within and beyond its southern sector (see Stoertz 1997, map 3 for RCHME plot). The cropmarks in the area to the north (now under Pinewood Close) showed two double-ditched boundaries or trackways on parallel south-west to north-east alignments *c.* 200m apart (Fig. 1.4). The western 'trackway' passed through a group of four square barrows with a larger, circular feature on the eastern side. The eastern 'trackway' had a square enclosure on its western side and a group of eight probable square barrows on its eastern side. In the southern part of the site, and immediately to the south, the cropmarks consisted of an east–west-aligned double-ditched 'trackway' along with at least 12 square barrows and circular features on both sides, plus other linear features.

Iron Age activity has been revealed by several archaeological excavations on the southern side of Pocklington

Figure 1.4 Sites in Pocklington mentioned in the text and cropmarks from RCHME survey (Stoertz 1997)

(Fig. 1.4). Four linear ditches dating to the late Iron Age/ Romano-British period were recorded during a Watching Brief at The Balk (Parry 2001), which is situated *c.* 250m south-west of Burnby Lane. Iron Age ditches, postholes and finds were located *c.* 700m west of Nine Acres at Cemetery Lane, Pocklington by Humber Field Archaeology (Fraser 2007). On-Site Archaeology excavated 13 trial trenches and carried out a Watching Brief at Hodsow Lane, *c.* 800m west of Burnby Lane (OSA 2009), recording an Iron Age/Romano-British enclosure, field boundaries and ditches, plus two 'flat' inhumations, a ritual animal burial and a possible dwelling. Northern Archaeological Associates excavated a site for Yorkshire Water at Canal Lane, Pocklington, *c.* 1.2km south-west of Burnby Lane (Tabor 2009), the earliest activity there consisting of a scatter of Neolithic Grooved Ware pits, along with a substantial flint assemblage. Two Iron Age inhumations that are particularly relevant to the Burnby Lane site were radiocarbon-dated to 380–160 cal BC and 360–50 cal BC

respectively. There was also a Romano-British enclosure dating to between the 2nd and 4th centuries AD.

On-Site Archaeology also carried out a programme of archaeological work on land to both west and east of The Balk, Pocklington, between May 2013 and October 2015 in advance of residential development. At Mayfields, west of The Balk, work identified a round barrow, five large square barrows, many postholes, Romano-British and medieval ditches, and medieval postholes. None of the barrows had surviving burials. On-Site's archaeological work in Balk Field, which lies *c.* 400m south of the Burnby Lane site, revealed a shallow-ditched circular feature *c.* 10–12m in diameter (OSA 2015a). None of the features suggested by the cropmarks, which implied the presence of an Iron Age cemetery and pits, survived within the excavated areas at Balk Field. One suggestion is that these survived as shallow features at the time of the aerial survey (Stoertz 1997) but subsequent ploughing had removed them. Fortunately, the strip of land abutting The Balk showed considerable archaeological activity in the form of Romano-British enclosures and a trackway, albeit truncated by ploughing.

Moving to Pocklington's later history, the town was recorded in the 1086 Domesday Survey as a Royal Manor with 15 burgesses, a church, a priest, and three watermills; it had been held by Earl Morcar in the time of Edward the Confessor. The place-name means '*Pocela's* farm' (Smith 1937).

The medieval town flourished due to its involvement in the wool trade and revenues from corn milling. The Burnby Lane site lies outside the core of the medieval settlement, *c.* 900m south-east of the parish church, and in the medieval period lay within Clay Field, one of the Open Fields of Pocklington (indications of which were shown by the furrows revealed by the excavation). After the Enclosure of Pocklington's Open Fields in 1757, the area was subdivided into smaller units, as illustrated in the 1854 First Edition Ordnance Survey map. The 1854 map calls the field immediately north of the site *White Bread Hills*; it is tempting to conjecture that this refers to formerly upstanding features, perhaps even the barrows that were subsequently recorded as cropmarks.

Nine Acres, the dwelling that existed in the western part of the site until demolition at the end of August 2014, was constructed prior to 1972.

In response to the planning application at the site, Archaeological Services WYAS carried out a geophysical survey of the northern area in July 2014 (ASWYAS 2014), identifying eight major anomalies (A-I) (Fig. 1.6). Anomaly A was a WSW–ENE linear feature running parallel to the modern north and south site boundaries and represented a former field boundary present on the 1854 First Edition Ordnance Survey map; B was a possible boundary relating to the same field system. C was an

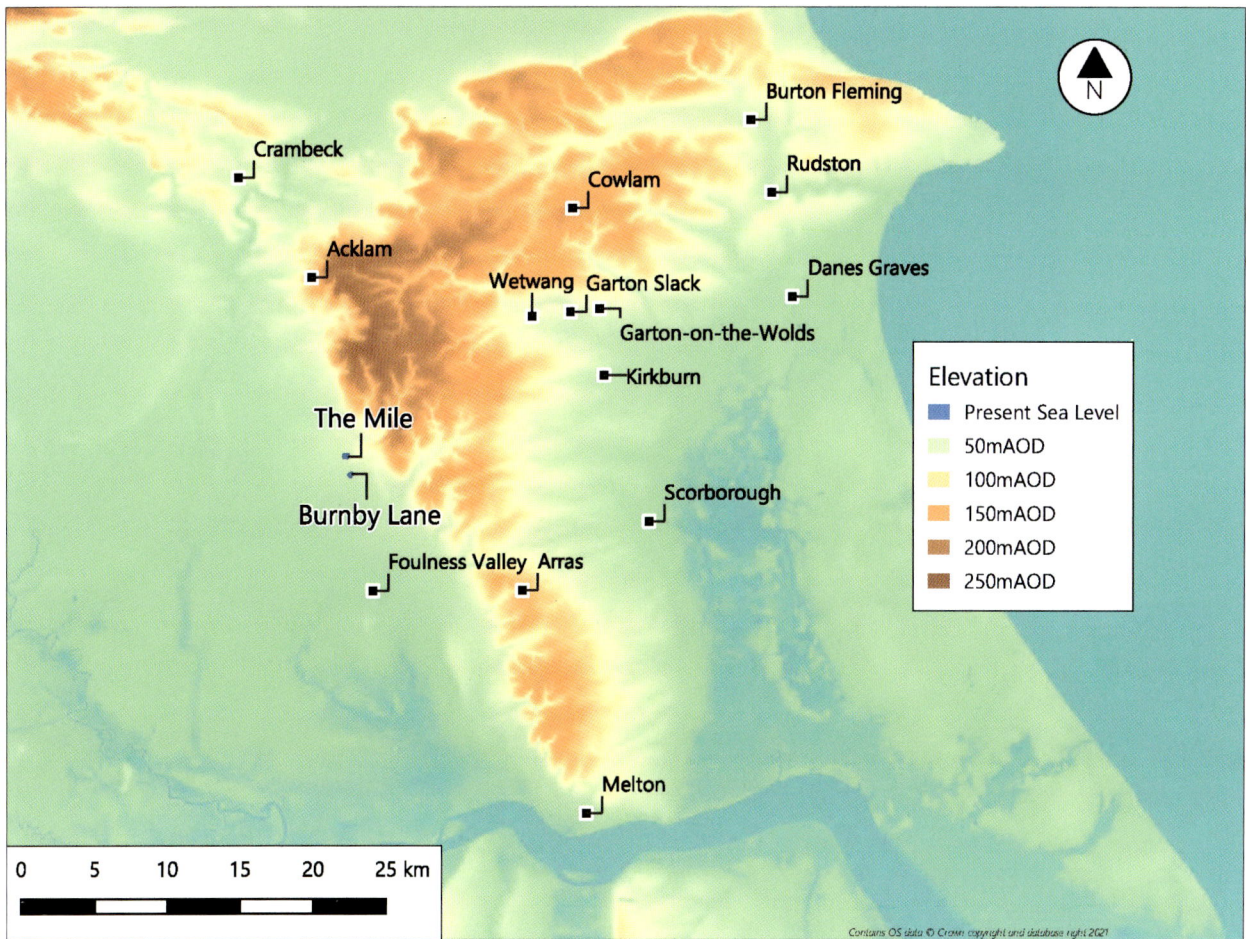

Figure 1.5 Other Yorkshire barrow sites mentioned in the text

intermittent linear anomaly that appeared to relate to the cropmarks in the area immediately north of the site, and D was the south-west continuation of C, which skirted round the southern edge of E, a circular ditched enclosure measuring *c.* 70m in diameter. F and G were possible square barrows, *c.* 8m and 15m across respectively. H was a rectangular anomaly of possible modern origin (in fact this almost certainly relates to the soak-away pit of the former bungalow). Finally, Anomaly I was a curvilinear feature of possible archaeological origin, partly masked by magnetic disturbance from the modern bungalow.

Using this previous geophysical survey of the site as a guide, MAP Archaeological Practice excavated 15 trial trenches in August to September 2014 (MAP 2014). The presence of the trackway and circular enclosure were confirmed but the square anomalies (F and G) proved elusive. Additionally, a previously unrecognised square barrow was excavated that enclosed the grave of an adult. Other gullies and ditches were interpreted as parts of additional square barrows.

In May 2015, On-Site Archaeology carried out a geophysical survey on the southern development area (OSA 2015b) which provided some correlation between cropmarks identified from the air and responses from the geophysical survey, the latter consisting of several positive linear features, linear trends and isolated positive responses (Fig. 1.6).

Subsequent trial trenching within the two fields forming the southern development area consisted of 13 trial trenches covering an area of 1400m² (MAP 2015). Archaeological remains were recorded in four of the trenches; those in Trenches 10, 11 and 13 corresponded to cropmark anomalies, but an additional ring gully and associated rubbish pit within Trench 8 had not been highlighted by either cropmark or geophysical surveys. Plough furrows were revealed across the full extent of the examined area and Trenches 6, 7 and 12 had signs of deep plough scarring, indicating heavy truncation by modern ploughing.

The confirmation of a significant archaeological landscape at Burnby Lane – square barrows, boundaries and enclosures of Iron Age to Anglian date – led to the various stages of open-area excavation described in this report.

The archives will be deposited with East Riding Museum Service under Accession numbers; Burnby Lane ERYMS 2022.37 and The Mile ERYMS 2022.38.

Figure 1.6 Geophysical survey Phases 1 and 2 plan

The landscape and archaeological background to the excavations at Burnby Lane and The Mile, Pocklington

Peter Halkon

Geology, soils and topography

The town of Pocklington is conveniently situated between the lowlands of the Vale of York and the western escarpment of the Yorkshire Wolds. The topography of the area is largely determined by the underlying geology. The bedrock immediately to the east of Burnby Lane as it approaches the present town comprises red and grey marls of the Triassic and Rhaetic, in the Mercia Mudstone Group (British Geological Survey 2019a). This was clearly visible during the digging of the foundations for the Burnby Lane housing estate and accompanying drainage works. Above this, over most of the site and indeed much of the local landscape, are superficial deposits of gravel and sand in the Pocklington Gravel Formation (BGS 2019b). The soils are classified by the Soil Survey of England and Wales (now the National Soil Resources Institute) as being in the Landbeach Soil Series and are described as being permeable calcareous coarse loamy soils, affected by groundwater over chalky gravel (Cranfield University 2019). Understanding the qualities of the soil is very important, firstly in terms of past human landscape interaction and secondly in terms of the facility of these soil types to show cropmarks in dry years, such as in the summer of 2018, when many new sites were revealed in the region. This was particularly the case along The Mile, to the west of the main area of the excavation, where loamy soils over gravel predominate (Fig. 2.1).

Further to the east of the Burnby Lane site, the land slopes gently upwards from the 30m contour until it rises to a prominent ridge, formed from rocks of the Jurassic and Lower Lias, which runs northwards from the River Humber to the south of Kilnwick Percy. The soils here are a reddish fine loam over clayey soils, which are slowly permeable and are seasonally waterlogged in the Brockhurst 2 Soil Series (Cranfield University 2019), hence Clayfield Lane and Clayfield Farm. Beyond this to the north and east are the Yorkshire Wolds, with Solid

Geology comprising Cretaceous chalk in the Ferriby, Welton and Burnham Formations (Whitham 1991). The shallow soils here are well-drained calcareous silts in the Andover 1 soil series on the hilltops, with similar but deeper, more humose soils in the valley bottoms in the Icknield Soil Series (Cranfield University 2019).

In characterising the soil types around Pocklington, it was found that those in the Landbeach and Andover series both scored highly in terms of workability and drainage qualities and the Landbeach soils in particular, in terms of fertility, suitable for the growing of all crops (Halkon 2008). The wetter clay soils in the Brockhurst 2 series and the calcareous flinty soils of Icknield Soil Series in the dry valleys would be suitable for contrasting pastoral regimes (King and Bradley 1987), chalk upland being particularly favoured for sheep, whereas the wetter soils encourage a lusher growth more favoured by cattle.

To the west of the present town the terrain (Fig. 2.2) is generally flat at around 30m OD, sloping gently eastwards to reach 44m OD at The Mile before rising steeply to 86m OD to the east of Pocklington Beck, on a prominent ridge known as Chapel Hill, the northern part of which is presently occupied by the Kilnwick Percy golf course. To the south, towards the Burnby Lane site, the land drops down to around 40m OD.

Drainage and water sources

An aquifer forms at the junction between the Lias and Jurassic rocks and the chalk, and at the mouths of valleys around Pocklington there are many springs which feed the White Keld, Ridings and Millington becks (Lewin 1969). Millington Beck to the north changes its name to Pocklington Beck as it crosses the parish boundary and continues to run roughly south-westwards through the town centre until it turns towards the south and finally joins Missick Beck near the village of Bielby.

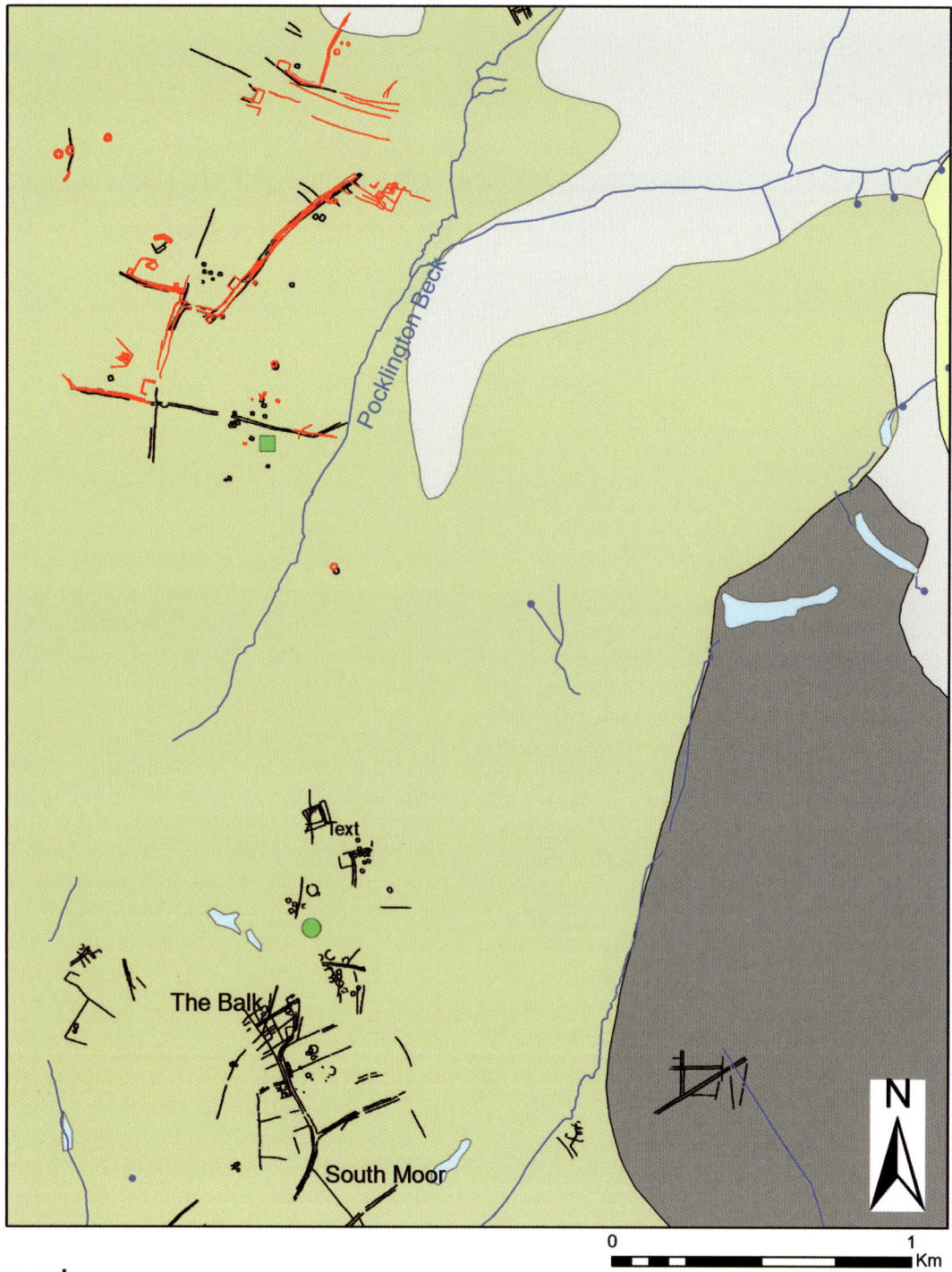

Legend

▢	CLAY (SEASONALLY WET)	🟢 Burnby Lane site	🟩 The Mile site
▨	LOAM/GRAVEL		
▨	LOAMY CLAY/SHALE (SEASONALLY WET)		
▢	SILT/CHALK		
▢	OPEN WATER		
•	Springs		
—	watercourses		
—	Cropmarks (Stoertz 1997)		
—	Cropmarks (Halkon/Hunt 2018)		

Figure 2.1 Cropmarks and soils around Pocklington (P. Halkon after Cranfield University)

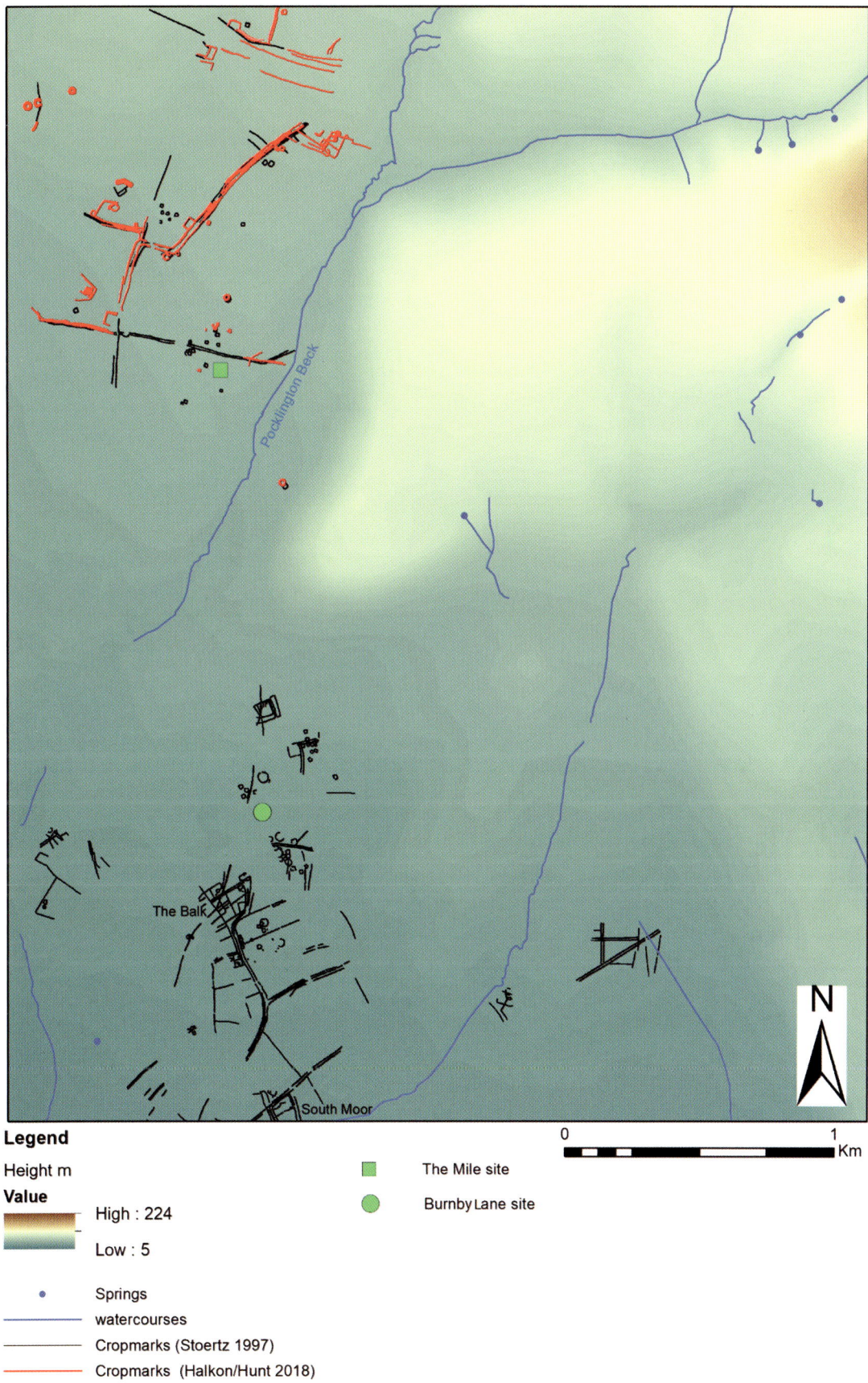

Figure 2.2 Cropmarks against the topography around Pocklington (P. Halkon based on DTM EDINA Digimap Ordnance Survey Service 2021)

It is clear that as it runs southwards from Millington into Pocklington parish, the beck is very significant in the distribution of archaeological sites visible as cropmarks, which lie along the 'grain' of the landscape, in particular a droveway which runs broadly parallel to it along The Mile. The cropmarks will be discussed in more detail below. A similar distribution pattern of cropmarks can be seen between the nearby villages of Burnby and Hayton where excavation has confirmed that enclosures and linear features, also of Iron Age date, that were aligned along the beck named after the villages through which it runs, continued in use in the Roman period (Halkon, Millett and Woodhouse 2015).

Cocoa Beck, its name morphed from Caukey or Cawkeld Beck, meaning a chalk stream, is around 880m to the south-east of the Burnby Lane site and provides a reliable water supply. It is likely that prior to large-scale extraction for domestic and agricultural purposes the water table was considerably higher and springs more plentiful than at present (Younger and McHugh 1995; Halkon 2008). This would particularly be the case along the ridge to the east of the Burnby Lane site. In wet winters such as 2018, for example, springs were rejuvenated to the extent that a number of roads in the area were flooded.

In summary, the range of soils suitable for a variety of agricultural purposes, its position between the lowlands of the Vale of York and the Wolds, a plentiful water supply, all of which coalesce to provide ecological diversity, make the landscape around Pocklington an ideal location for a wide range of past human activities.

Previous archaeological discoveries around Pocklington

Despite the dearth of upstanding archaeological features due largely to intensive arable regimes, aerial photography, fieldwork and casual finds have resulted in the discovery of much archaeological evidence around Pocklington; the focus here, however, will be on those in the vicinity of The Mile and Burnby Lane excavations.

Palaeolithic/Mesolithic

Considerable evidence for earlier prehistoric activity has been found in and around Pocklington, the earliest being a lower Palaeolithic ovate quartzite handaxe found in a potato field near Pocklington (Manby 2021, 35). At Sherbuttgate, Pocklington the metacarpal bones of an auroch (*Bos primigenius*) were discovered in May 1974 and subsequently identified by Dr Juliet Jewell, Mammal Section British Museum (Natural History) (Sefton 2019). Although this remains undated, such animals may have provided quarry for hunter-gather groups, as a Mesolithic scraper was found in the vicinity of Pocklington (item presently in the archives of Pocklington School) and late Mesolithic microliths are also recorded in the Hull Museum collections from Ousethorpe (Manby 2021, 75),

around 1.5km to the north of The Mile excavation. It seems highly likely that these are associated with activity around Millington Beck and can be broadly paralleled with that along the River Foulness to the south of Holme-on-Spalding Moor (Halkon *et al*. 2009). Mesolithic flints were also found in the Pocklington Wastewater Treatment Works excavation in Barmby Moor parish, 1.25km from the centre of Pocklington, which were almost certainly residual (Makey 2008).

Neolithic

The soils around Pocklington were particularly attractive to the first farmers of the Neolithic and evidence for activity within the landscape at this time has been found in a number of locations. The Pocklington School collection contains part of a Neolithic sickle and an arrowhead (Mackay 1979; Gilbank 2011). A further leaf-shaped flint arrowhead was found unstratified during a watching brief at Pocklington School, West Green, along with a late Neolithic or early Bronze Age core (Tabor 2005; Cardwell 2006). Although it is uncertain whether they represent clearance of woodland by early farmers or simply woodland management, there is a distinct cluster of Neolithic polished stone and flint axe heads recorded from the Pocklington area (Radley 1974, 16). A further example was found at South Moor (Radley 1974), a Group 1 axe head, probably of Cornish origin, although a source at Carrock Fell in the Lake District may be possible (Halkon 2009). There are polished axe heads made of green tuff, probably of Group VI from Cumbria, found at Pocklington in the Hull and East Riding Museum in Hull and in the Yorkshire Museum, York (Radley 1974, 16). Part of a Neolithic polished stone axe, flint arrowheads, scrapers and a blade are also recorded from Sherbuttgate (Moorhouse 1978). Polished stone axe heads have also been discovered around a kilometre to the north of The Mile excavations at Ousethorpe, including one of Group VII type from Graig Lywd, North Wales (Manby 2021, 75).

Middle Neolithic pottery of Peterborough and Mortlake styles dated to *c*. 3600–3200/3100 cal BC (Manby *et al*. 2003) was found during the MAP excavation at The Mile, where pits containing sherds of later Neolithic flat-bottomed decorated Grooved Ware of Durrington Walls type were also discovered. At Burnby Lane, Hayton, 4km to the south-east of Pocklington, sherds from jars and bowls of Grooved Ware in the Woodlands tradition were associated with hazelnut shells radiocarbon-dated to 2880–2490 cal BC (Beta-223632) and 2930–2690 cal BC (Beta-223633). The pits also contained struck flint along with cereal grains and cattle bones, suggesting a mixed farming economy had already developed here (Halkon *et al*. 2010). A similar group of five pits, also containing cattle bone and Grooved Ware pottery in the Durrington Walls style, was found at Barrow Flats, Barmby Moor, during the construction of the Pocklington Wastewater Treatment Works 1.25km from the centre of Pocklington (Tabor 2008).

Figure 2.3 Hengiform and square barrow at The Mile (orthomosaic June 2018, Tony Hunt YAA Mapping)

Grooved Ware pottery is broadly contemporary with the construction of henges and hengiforms, the classic ritual monuments of this period of the Neolithic and the drought of early summer 2018 revealed cropmarks of several hengiforms close to The Mile excavation. On raised ground to the east of Pocklington Beck, the cropmark of a circular feature 23m in diameter was clearly visible. Although the cropmark of the ditch was somewhat blurred at the edges, it was around 3m across. There were amorphous features within the circle, but these may well be geological in origin. Although vague, there may be an entrance to the north-west. Around 500m to the north of The Mile excavation, a further circular feature was visible in the crop (Fig. 2.3). At 22m in diameter, with a *c.* 3m wide ditch, it had opposed entrances aligned WNW–ESE and although considerably smaller, closely resembles the group of Class 2 henge monuments in the Vale of Mowbray, particularly those around Thornborough (Harding 2013). There are vestiges of a concentric inner circular feature *c.* 13m across with a narrow ditch inside the main enclosure. A square barrow is clearly visible 40m to the east of this feature.

It is clear then, that by the later Neolithic the valley of Pocklington Beck around The Mile had become a focus for ritual activity of some kind.

Bronze Age

As well as the hengiform monuments discussed above, the 2018 drone photography on The Mile revealed other circular features some 11m across which are most likely to be the ring ditches of round barrows dating from the Bronze Age, although they may be the ring gullies of roundhouses. It is noticeable that the main droveway

Figure 2.4 The Mile droveway and ring ditches of possible round barrows (orthomosaic June 2018, Tony Hunt YAA Mapping)

which runs broadly parallel with Pocklington Beck was deliberately positioned to curve round the easternmost of a pair of ring-ditched features. The corner of its almost right-angled bend also lies between the two ring ditches, the implication being that the droveway both respected and was aligned on these features (Fig. 2.4). A similar relationship between droveways and round barrows can be observed at a number of locations in eastern Yorkshire, for example at Wetwang/Garton Slack, where a droveway goes round a pre-existing monument (Dent 2010).

In addition to the flints from Pocklington School referred to above, early Bronze Age finds have also been made at a number of locations around Pocklington.

During developer-funded excavations on Yapham Road by MAP a burial containing a Beaker was found. A flat axe in copper alloy from the early Bronze Age is recorded in the Portable Antiquities Scheme (McIntosh 2010). An unusual later short-flanged adze was also found at Hayton, resembling Schmidt and Burgess (1981, 92–114) later short-flanged axes and dating from the middle Bronze Age, *c*. 1500–1150 cal BC (Manby *et al*. 2003). For the later Bronze Age, a hoard of Yorkshire-type looped copper alloy socketed axe heads was found in the grounds of Pocklington School (Moorhouse 1973). A looped copper alloy spearhead was also discovered at South Moor (Radley 1967).

Iron Age

Although it is possible that some of the later Bronze Age finds around South Moor may relate to a complex of cropmarks extending from Pocklington Grange Farm to the present town covering over 2km (Fig. 2.5) (Stoertz 1997), typological comparison suggests that these features are more likely to be Iron Age in date. At the heart of the South Moor complex is a double-ditched droveway or linear earthwork which runs roughly parallel to Pocklington Beck in a north-easterly direction. To the north of South Moor the droveway forks to the east, the northern branch eventually turning almost at right-angles eastwards into a complex palimpsest of features which run towards the Burnby Lane site. One of the most obvious features is a rectilinear enclosure 101 × 60m in size, within a further rectilinear enclosure, situated between Willow Rise and Cocoa Beck, attached to a droveway which runs SW–NE. It is subdivided into unequal sections, the larger, southernmost portion, containing the ring ditch of a roundhouse over 20m in diameter, its entrance facing south (Fig. 2.6). The single linear features in the area around this enclosure are likely to demarcate fields.

The Iron Age sees the introduction of square barrows, the classic monument of the Arras culture of eastern Yorkshire and a major topic covered by this volume. These consist of a square ditched enclosure surrounding a grave which is then mounded over with the spoil from the ditch to form a low platform. It is highly likely that this burial tradition derived from the near Continent, as it extends from Dorset to the Czech Republic, but is concentrated in eastern Yorkshire, the Champagne and Marne regions of France, and the Hunsrück-Eifel areas of Germany (Stead 1979). The square-barrow tradition appears sometime in the later 5th century BC. The vast majority of square barrows in eastern Yorkshire have been erased by ploughing and are only visible as cropmarks, but there are surviving above ground examples at Scorborough, Beverley Westwood, and Dane's Graves, near Kilham.

Square barrows can be categorised into three main groups: Group 1, thought to be the earliest, consists of ditched enclosures often with rounded corners, usually 12–15m square with no surviving central burial. Group 2

are generally 8–11m square, with shallow, medium depth or occasionally deep graves; and Group 3, which are generally smaller, are usually the latest in the sequence (Dent 2010). There are also small circular barrows in some cemeteries, including Pocklington, and it is noticeable that many of these contain significant burials, for example at Garton Station and Kirkburn (Stead 1991a). The square barrow cemeteries range in size from a few dispersed barrows to large ones such as Burton Fleming/Makeshift (346 burials) and Carnaby (over 300 burials) (Stoertz 1997). At Wetwang/Garton Slack, 450 burials have been excavated (Dent 2019). At Arras, recent research has shown that this cemetery originally consisted of well over 200 burials, the majority of which are those with no visible central grave (Halkon *et al*. 2019). The excavations here between 1815 and 1817 (Stillingfleet 1847; Stead 1979; Halkon *et al*. 2019) resulted in the discovery of three chariot burials, the so-called King's Barrow, consisting of a male accompanied by two horses and portions of either pork or wild boar, being of particular relevance as both Pocklington chariot burials contained complete horse skeletons, and in the case of The Mile chariot burial, the bones of pigs also.

At Nunburnholme Wold, high up on the western escarpment of the Yorkshire Wolds above Pocklington, there is a square barrow cemetery of around 50 barrows, discovered through aerial photography and geophysical survey. It is associated with a palimpsest of enclosures connected by droveways running up through valleys in three directions from the lowlands of the Vale of York. The droveways lead into an ovoid open area some 250 × 150m, at the hilltop's highest point, with a pair of ditches forming a funnel at its eastern end (Halkon 2019a). The results of the excavations here in 2014, 2015 and 2018, combined with its prominent location, suggest that it may best be interpreted as a central meeting place for a whole region. Like the square barrow cemeteries at Pocklington, there was evidence of earlier ritual and burial activity in the form of the parallel ditches of what is likely to be a Neolithic mortuary enclosure, a hengiform feature or large round barrow, and a group of the penannular ring ditches of round barrows, revealed through geophysical survey. One of these was partially excavated in 2016 and a rim sherd of a Collared Urn was discovered (Halkon and Lyall 2016).

In 2014 (Halkon *et al*. 2014), a square barrow was excavated which contained the skeleton of a female aged at least 45 years, tightly crouched with her head to the north, and placed in a box-like wooden structure with the remains of a suckling pig at her feet. This burial was radiocarbon-dated to 197–47 cal BC (Beta-516926). Some 7m to the north of the 2014 burial, a further square barrow row was excavated in 2015; this contained the skeleton of a male aged 17–22 (Halkon, Lillie and Lyall 2015). Like the 2014 burial, the body had been placed inside some kind of wooden box or shuttering. Crouched

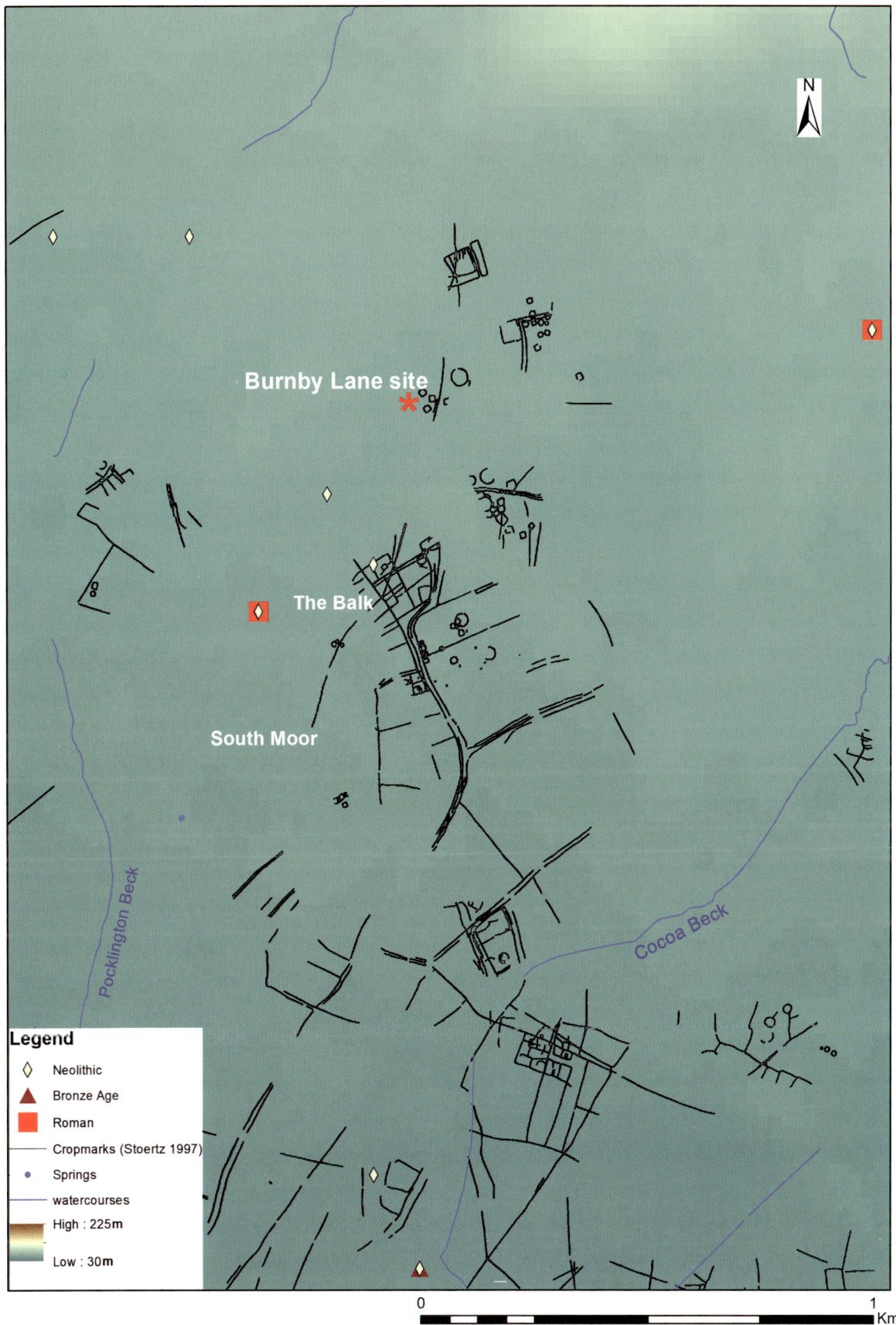

Figure 2.5 Cropmarks (after Stoertz 1997) against the topography of the Southmoor area (P. Halkon based on DTM EDINA Digimap Ordnance Survey Service 2021)

Figure 2.6 Aerial photograph of South Moor looking north towards Pocklington (P. Halkon, July 1992)

with his head to the north and facing east, part of a young pig had been laid across his lap. The corpse had been buried on its back and his knees may have been raised. The skeleton was radiocarbon-dated to 195–42 cal BC (Beta-520210). Apart from a relationship with earlier Bronze Age ritual and burial monuments, both burials shared similarities with the Pocklington Burnby Lane cemetery, in regard to the box-like structures in some of the burials.

There does seem to be a strong relationship between barrow cemeteries and movement through the landscape, as the larger cemeteries at Arras, Warter and North Dalton, like Garton and Wetwang, are all associated with major valleys which are likely to have formed route-ways through the Wolds. The Arras cemetery lies at the head of Sancton Dale, which leads down to the lowlands and the head of a former tidal estuarine inlet of the River Humber that eventually became Walling Fen (Halkon 2008). Created by a marine transgression and sea-level rise sometime between 800–500 BC, this inlet is of great significance in understanding the Iron Age in the region, as it provided access to the iron-producing lowlands of the Foulness Valley and to the Humber estuary and beyond. In a similar way, Garton/Wetwang Slack leads down to the headwaters of the River Hull near Elmswell (Congreve 1938) where iron smelting also took place, probably in the Iron Age. In the case of The Mile, square barrows and the earlier ritual and burial monuments ran along the grain of the landscape parallel to Pocklington Beck.

Several of the enclosure complexes close to Pocklington have been excavated prior to housing development, particularly in the blocks of land to the west of The Balk, in Balk Field (Parry 2001) (Fig. 2.5). The linear ditches here were found to date from the later Iron Age

and early Roman period, with finds including sherds of later Iron Age pottery and a small sherd of samian ware. Of particular interest, given the discovery of the Burnby Lane chariot burial, is a piece of iron slag and vitrified hearth or furnace lining from some form of iron working or possibly manufacture, identified as being of Iron Age date, which according to Cowgill (2001) resembled slag from the Iron Age iron industries of the Foulness Valley (Halkon and Millett 1999; Halkon 2012).

In 2014–15, excavation prior to housing development on land north of Mayfield by On-Site Archaeology, to the west of The Balk, provided further evidence of Iron Age and Roman activity in the form of pits and a complex of ditches (OSA 2018). The pottery assemblage included an almost complete decorated wheel-thrown butt beaker dating from the mid-1st century AD, substantially earlier than the majority of the other Roman pottery found there.

To the east of The Balk, immediately to the south of the more northerly of the two eastern branches of the main droveway feature, is a cluster of circular features likely to be Bronze Age round barrows, surrounded and cut by Iron Age square barrows revealed in the cropmark plots and confirmed by geophysical survey (Gaffney 1995). Further square barrows are attached to the droveway itself, close to the point where it bends to the east. The burial monuments are isolated from a complex of rectilinear and linear features which lie under the present playing field and possibly represent settlement-related activity associated with the Burnby Lane cemetery. It is almost certain that this complex continues under Primrose Wood, as a narrow single linear cropmark aligns with a similar feature now under housing (Stoertz 1997). Immediately to the east of the Burnby Lane site is a further cluster of ring ditches, probably of Bronze Age date, and some square barrows of Group 1 (Dent 2010; Halkon 2013) which are relatively large, have rounded corners and no obvious central grave pit. It is clear, therefore, that the cemetery at Burnby Lane, although it is separated from settlement activity, is by no means isolated, but is part of a complex later prehistoric landscape.

Reference has been made above to cropmarks appearing along The Mile, particularly in the dry early summer of 2018 (Fig. 2.7). The most prominent of the features is a droveway over a kilometre in length with a ditch on each side, which conventional aerial photography by the writer and orthophotographs taken by Tony Hunt of YAA Mapping shows has been slightly realigned or recut on a number of occasions. At around 600m south, the droveway turns sharply to the west for around 100m before resuming in a southerly direction (Fig. 2.8). As has been noted above, its diversion may be due to the possible hengiform structure, and the corner of the bend itself is positioned between two ring ditches, likely to be the remains of round barrows.

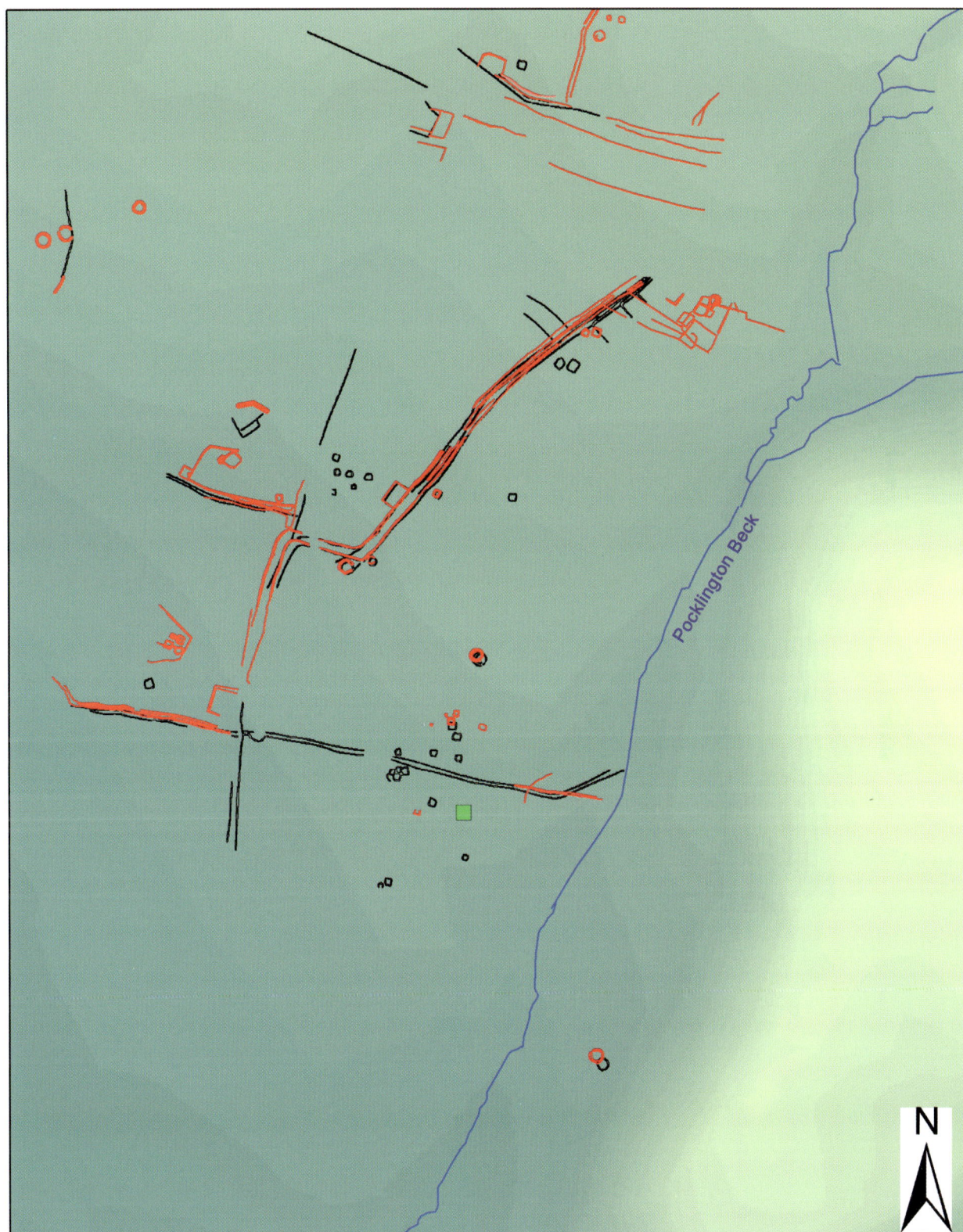

Figure 2.7 Cropmarks against the topography around The Mile (P. Halkon based on DTM EDINA Digimap Ordnance Survey Service 2021)

Figure 2.8 The main droveway and appended enclosure on The Mile (orthomosaic June 2018, Tony Hunt YAA Mapping)

Unlike the droveways at Arras and elsewhere, which have appended enclosures along their length that are known as ladder settlements (Halkon 2019a), The Mile droveway has only two rectilinear enclosures attached to it. The largest of these is 38m by 25m in size but contains no obvious features. There is a scatter of square barrows, mainly of Group 1, along The Mile on the same orientation as the main droveway and one group, around 100m to the west of the droveway, which appear to be surrounded by a trapezoidal enclosure.

Conclusion

While not previously regarded as a particularly significant area for prehistoric archaeology, this survey has demonstrated the considerable density of activity in Pocklington and its environs. Its well-drained productive soils, plentiful water supply and its position between the lowlands of the Vale of York and the Wolds uplands provided opportunities for differing modes of past human exploitation. Although the discovery of the chariot burials came as somewhat of a surprise, the Yorkshire Wolds crop-mark survey mapped dense Iron Age activity, particularly to the south of the present town (Stoertz 1997). The Iron Age square barrow cemeteries were by no means the first burial or ritual monuments in the area, as the cemeteries at both Burnby Lane and The Mile were constructed in the vicinity of earlier prehistoric monuments, perhaps deliberately as some form of claiming ownership or legitimacy for new arrivals. Although the Stoertz survey (1997) provided hints as to the presence of some form of ritual landscape, the dry summer of 2018 revealed further features along The Mile, reinforcing the significance of Pocklington Beck to site distribution.

3

The early prehistoric landscape

Mark Stephens

Late Neolithic/early Bronze Age

A scatter of pits and gullies containing sherds of Peter-borough and Grooved wares, Beaker and Food Vessel and associated flintwork was present across the site (Fig. 3.1).

A group of three pits (18378, 18392 and 18406) and a gully (18380) were recorded in the eastern area of the site; these pre-dated Period 4 (Romano-British), 18392 and 18406 being truncated by Ditch D. These features are grouped together because of their proximity and early stratigraphical position; however, only one dateable sherd was associated with them – a sherd of Peterbor-ough (Mortlake) ware from the fill of 18392 (18391). In addition, the southern end of the 3m-long gully (18380) was cut away by the northern edge of Ditch D and was attributed to this phase.

A further group of three pits (16641, 16655 and 16682) was excavated in the north-eastern part of the site. These pits were sub-circular and had similar sequences of filling, with brown upper fills and darker primary fills. Associated finds consisted of a flint graver/burin and a utilised core rejuvenation flake, both in very fresh condition and late Neolithic/early Bronze Age in date.

Towards the west of the site, the well-defined sub-cir-cular Pit 17187 contained a late Neolithic/early Bronze Age flint flake in 'very fresh' condition (Makey 2017). In the north-west of the site, Pit 15814 lay close to the north-west circuit of Enclosure E and contained Grooved Ware sherds, plus five worked flints and six flint chunks (manufacturing debris) including a 'fresh' Neolithic flint blade (SF 36), a late Neolithic/early Bronze Age flake, plus a residual serrated edged flake (SF 37) and two conjoining flakes of the same date. It is likely that this flint group was deposited close to where it was originally used. The burnt plant remains within the pit consisted of trace amounts of cereal grain and fragments of hazelnut shell.

Two pits (16542 and 16544) were cut by the ditch of Barrow 37 within the eastern barrow group, the former containing Grooved Ware sherds. To the south, Pit 16546 pre-dated Barrow 37, and although it contained no datable material, it may belong with Pits 16542 and 16544. Pit 16164, also within the eastern barrow group, pre-dated the central burial of Barrow 32 and contained probable Beaker sherds and animal bone (16133).

To the south of the eastern barrow group, two pits were identified (16012 and 16014), their fills containing large amounts of oak charcoal and heat-cracked flints, making it possible that these were general waste or cooking pits. The pits also contained animal bone fragments and sherds of Grooved Ware.

Two pits containing Grooved Ware sherds were situated in the vicinity of the later Barrow 79, Pit 077 to the east, and Pit 138 to the south, between Ditches J and K.

Hengiform Enclosure E

Enclosure E was a sub-circular feature around 60m in diameter, its size and form suggesting a hengiform enclo-sure earlier than, and unlike, the three Period 2 round barrows (see below). Only a very narrow entranceway was identified in the excavated area, a gap *c*. 0.5m wide in the eastern circuit of the ditch (the north-west section of the enclosure lay beyond the excavated area). The enclosure ditch was relatively insubstantial and had a variable profile that averaged *c*. 1.00m in width and 0.50m in depth, with a gravel-rich primary fill and a silty sand fill at the top. Enclosure E pre-dated Square Barrows 30 and 38.

Four vertically sided postholes (1008, 6008, 8008 and 8010) were identified within Enclosure E during the Trial Trenching stage, but were not necessarily contemporary with it, and the general lack of associated 'domestic' features, rules out a domestic function for the enclosure.

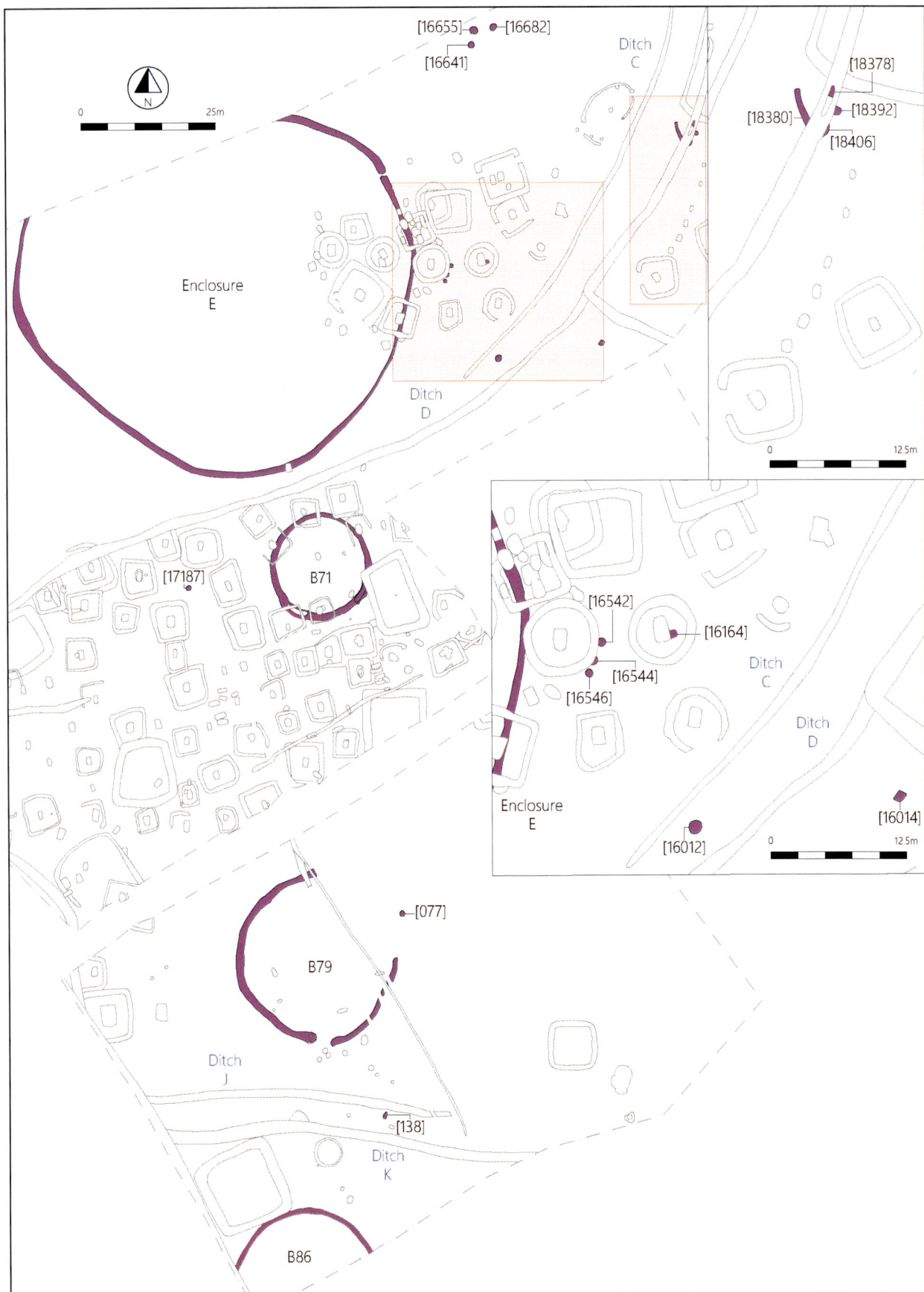

Figure 3.1 Location of Neolithic and Early Bronze Age features at Burnby Lane

Early Bronze Age barrows

Three round barrows (Barrows 71, 79 and 86 – distinct from the smaller Iron Age round barrows) represented the second period of activity.

Barrow 71

Located *c*. 8m south of Enclosure E, Barrow 71 was sub-circular and around 19m in diameter externally. It had a relatively insubstantial ditch with a narrow, 0.5m-wide 'causeway' across it on the north-east side (segments 17136 and 17248). The ditch had a rounded V-shape profile and was *c*. 1.10m wide and 0.45m deep.

A grave excavated approximately at the centre of the barrow contained an Iron Age burial (17102 – Sk 122) and was therefore not directly connected to the barrow (see below). Barrow 71 was also overlain by six later square barrows (Barrows 52, 53, 54, 55, 57 and 68) that were dug into its northern and south-western margins.

Barrow 79

This was another sub-circular barrow, albeit larger with an approximate external diameter of 29m. It was situated *c*. 60m south of Barrow 71 in the southern field. There appeared to be two opposed entrances on the north-east and south-west sides, but it is possible that these are the result of truncation from ploughing or perhaps accentuated by the plough. The north-eastern entrance was 15.0m wide, but the south-western entrance was much narrower, at 2.5m. The ditch had a shallow, trough-shaped profile and was between 1.2m and 1.9m wide, the depth varying between 0.12m and 0.25m; it had a yellowish silty sand fill.

A shallow pit (fill 013, cut 014) situated within the western part of the enclosed area contained a quantity of rye grain, along with trace amounts of oak and conifer charcoal, perhaps intrusive from hearth waste. A fragment from an iron key shows that this was a later feature and unrelated to the barrow.

Three possible postholes (023, 025 and 038) were identified under the western terminal of the south-west entrance, and a group of five small oval pits (47, 49, 51, 53 and 56) may also have been associated.

A north–south-aligned grave (cut 010, fill 008) was recorded in the western part of the area enclosed by the barrow ditch; this contained the very poorly preserved and extremely fragmented skeleton (009 – Sk 160) of a young juvenile aged 5–6 years. A late Neolithic or early Bronze Age flint knife (SF 1), complete and in moderate condition, was found alongside the skeleton. The relationship of the grave to the barrow is uncertain, but as the flint knife was in good condition, it is likely that it was deliberately placed with the burial, suggesting the grave is contemporary with the barrow.

Barrow 86

Barrow 86 was situated at the south-west of the site, around 30m south-west of Barrow 79, and extended beyond the excavated area. The barrow was sub-circular, with a slightly sinuous ditch giving a diameter of *c*. 26m. The ditch had a round-based V profile, between 0.70m and 0.90m wide and 0.45m deep. There was a yellowish-brown sandy gravel primary fill, with darker sandy silt at the top.

4

The Iron Age cemetery at Burnby Lane

Mark Stephens

The Iron Age cemetery was the third period of activity at the site, following the Neolithic Grooved Ware occupation and hengiform structures, and Bronze Age round barrows. There was an expansion in the funerary use of the landscape during the Iron Age, represented by both square and circular barrows, along with 'flat' unenclosed graves. The Iron Age barrows formed two groups, a larger one to the west (Fig. 4.1) and a smaller one to the east (Fig. 4.2), plus several outliers (Fig. 4.3). The barrows are described below in the order in which they were excavated and the various ditch segments comprising individual barrows are listed clockwise starting at the north-western segment. The ditch fills were completely excavated after the section had been drawn. A summary of all the barrows is presented in Table 4.1.

No attempt is made in this report to present the varied Iron Age barrows and burials in sequence, except where stratigraphic relationships were present, as full radiocarbon-dating of the skeletons was not available at the time of writing. Any stratigraphic relationships that did exist between individual barrows or burials are mentioned in the following descriptions of barrows and burials.

The specialist summaries of the human bones and various categories of artefacts can be found in the following chapters:

8 – the spears and sword from Burnby Lane
9 – other Iron Age weaponry from Burnby Lane and The Mile
10 – chariot fittings from Burnby Lane and The Mile
11 – brooches and bracelets from Burnby Lane and The Mile
12 – other Iron Age finds from Burnby Lane and The Mile
13 – human osteology at Burnby Lane and The Mile
14 – animal bone from Burnby Lane and The Mile
15 – carbonised plant remains from Burnby Lane

Barrows

Barrow 1

Summary

Barrow 1 was a square barrow measuring 7m by 7m internally (Fig. 4.4); it was located at the north-west corner of the western barrow group (Fig. 4.1). Seven ditch segments were excavated (15107, 15116, 15035, 15045, 15096, 15102 and 15090 – the north-west corner being truncated), the ditch having a rounded-V profile and measuring *c.* 1.00m wide and 0.50m deep. The primary ditch fills were rich in gravel, with brownish sandy silt at the top. Finds were limited to an Iron Age sherd from the fill of the eastern side (15034) and a Neolithic flint core-rejuvenation flake with a serrated edge from the primary fill of the western side (15101). The north side of Barrow 1 was cut away by the later Ditch D, and a group of gullies that cut across the centre of the barrow which contained a few Roman sherds.

Skeleton/Grave

No associated burial or grave survived for Barrow 1.

Barrow 2

Summary

Situated immediately south of Barrow 1, Barrow 2 was *c.* 8m by 8m internally (Fig. 4.5). Seven ditch segments were excavated (15122, 15086, 15175, 15121, 15185, 15201 and 15099 – the south-west corner lay outside the excavated area). The ditch had a rounded-V profile and averaged 1.80m in width and 0.80m in depth, with gravelly primary fills and darker sandy silt at the top. The primary fill of the north-east corner (15085) contained both Iron Age sherds and animal bone fragments, and the secondary fill of the south-east corner (15118) also contained an Iron Age sherd. The uppermost fill of the south-east corner (15117) contained a piece of iron strip (SF 366).

Figure 4.1 Barrow location plan, Western Group

Table 4.1 Summary of barrows

B No.	Shape	N–S (m)	E–W (m)	Diam.	Rel. ?	Primary	Sk no.	Aligned	Facing	Posture
1	Sq.	6.5	5.5		<D	x				
2	Sq.	11.5	12			15176	2	N–S	W	Flexed
3	Sq.	5.5	5.5			15187	3	N–S	E	Flexed
4	Sq.		5.5			15219	5	N–S	E	Cr.
5	Sq.	6.5	6.5			15223	6	N–S	W	Cr.
6	Sq.?	5.5	5.5			15300	12	N–S	W	Cr.
7	Sq.	.5.5	5.4		<D	15331	7	N–S	E	Cr.
8	Sq.	6	6.5			15399/400	18/19	N–S	U	U
9	Sq.	4	4		<D	15327	13	S–N	U	Fl.
10	Sq.	10	>7.5		<D	x				
11	Sq.	6.5	7.5			17004	117	N–S	E	Cr.?
12	Sq.	7.5	7.5		<D	15394	16	N–S	E	Cr.
13	Sq.	4.5	4.5		>B14	15476	21	N–S	E	Flexed
14	Sq.	11.5	11.5		<B13	x				
15	Sq.	5.5	5.5		<D	15496	25	N–S	E	Cr?
16	Sq.	5.5	6			15494	24	N–S	E	Flexed
17	Sq.	6.5	6.5			15630	28	N–S	E	Cr.
18	Sq.?	c.4	c.4			15622	27	N–S	E	Flexed
19	Sq.	6	6		<B20	15733	36	N–S	E	Cr.
20	*Trap.*	*12.5*	*12*		*<B22 >19*					
21	Sq.	5	5			15724	34	N–S	W	Prone, Fl
22	Sq.	4.5	4		>B20	15710	33	S–N	?W	?Cr.
23	Sq.?	4.5	4.5			15728	35	S–N	W	Cr.
24	Sq.	4	4.4			15846	43	S–N	W	Cr.
25	Rect.	4	7			15851	44B	N–S	W	Contr.?
26	Sq.	5	4.5			15856	45	N-S	W	Cr.
27	Sq.	4.5	3.8			x				
28	Sq.?	5.5	7.5			15909	48	N–S	E	Fl.
29	Sq.	5.5	4.5			15974	54	S–N	E	Cr.
30	Sq.	6.8	6.2		>E	16001	55	N–S	W	Cr.
31	Sq.	5.5	4.5			16069	58	S–N	W	Cr.
32	Circ.			6.4	>16164	16072	59	N–S	E	Fl. Prone
33	Circ.			4.2	>16287	16018	56	NW-SE	E	Cr.prone

(Continued)

Table 4.1 (Continued)

B No.	Sex	Age	Grave goods	Structure	Organics	Comments	Dating	Radiocarbon date (cal BC)
1								
2	F	46+	Y			Bracs 3–4; Fib. 5	2Ba brooch: 3rd cent. BC	94.5% 389–347, 319–207
3	M	26–35?						
4	F?	36+				Animal bone nr. l. leg		
5	M?	18–35						
6	U	18–35		Y				
7	/	6.5/8.5			Y			
8	U	18+?				15399=15400		
9	U	36–45	Br. SF10				2Cb: mid-3rd–early 2nd cent.?	380–341,327–204
10								
11	U	18+						
12	F	17–20				also 15402 32–40 wks		
13	/	14.5/16.5		Y				95% 390–200
14								
15	M	36–45?			Y			
16	M?	18–25						
17	U	25+			Y			
18	M	36–45	Br. SF24				2C: 3rd–2nd cent. BC	95.4% 362–201
19	F	26–35	Brac.SF32	Y		Disturbed? = 15656		
20						*Anglian Burial*		
21	U	18–35				Rounded corners		
22	U	36+		Y				
23	M?	36+		Y		Part ditch only		
24	U	26–35?			Y	Wrapped?		
25	M?	36+				Part only of sk		
26	M?	18–25	Fe SF 45				2Ca: 3rd–2nd cent. BC	95.4% 381–341, 327–209
27						Empty grave? 15884		
28	U	18–25	SF57,268		Y	Head-rest? 15870		
29	M	26–35				Prone		
30	F	26+	SF 74		Y	Antler toggle		
31	M?	36+		?	Y	Rounded corners		
32	M	18–25	SF 75 Fe			SFI + BFI to head		
33	M	26–35			Y	> grave <16285>	2Ab: mid-IA ?3rd cent. BC	failed – insufficient carbon

(Continued)

Table 4.1 Summary of barrows (Continued)

B No.	Shape	N–S (m)	E–W (m)	Diam.	Rel. ?	Primary	Sk no.	Aligned	Facing	Posture
34	Circ.			5.5	>B36	16027	57	N–S	E	Cr.
35	Circ.			5.8		16109	61	N–S	E	Flexed
36	Sq.	5.5	5.8		<B34	16159	63	N–S	U	Cr.
37	Circ.			6.5		16370	78	N–S	E	Fl.
38	Sq.	5.7	5.7		>B39+40	16373	80	N–S	E	Cr.
39	Sq.	6.8	6.5		<B38	x				
40	Sq.	6.4	5.7		<B39, 38	16493	89	N–S	U	?contr.
41	?circ.			c.4.8		16278	66	E–W	S	Cr.
42	Sq.	7.5	7.5			16443	82	N–S	E	Cr.
43	Sq.	6.6	6.8		>B44	16466	85	N–S	E	Cr.
44	Sq.	>5.7	5.8		<B43	16470	86	N–S	E	Fl.
45	Sq.	6.4	6.4			16491	88	N–S	U	U
46	Sq.	6.3	6.1		<B47	17081	119	N–S	E	Cr.
47	Rect.	5.4	3.6		>B46+48	17001	116	N–S	U	Cr.
48	Sq.	6.2	6.2		<B47	16678	93	N–S	E	Cr.
49	Rect.	6.4	5.4			4012	A	S–N	W	Cr.
50	Rect.	6.6	5.6			17090	121	N–S	E	Cr.
51	Sq.	5.3	4.8		<D	17078	118	N–S	E	Cr.
52	Sq.	>4.3	5.5		>B71	17105	123	N–S	E	Cr.
53	Sq.	5.3	4.4		>B71, ?55	17135	124	S–N	E	Flexed
54	Sq.	5.5	5.6		>B71	17172	125	?	U	U
55	Sq.	6.2	5.8		>B71	17175	126	S–N	W	Flexed
56	Sq.	5.8	6.5			16745	99	N–S	E	Cr.
57	Sq.	>5.2	6.4		>B71	16783	102	N–S	E	Cr.
58	Sq.	4.3	3.5			16728	95	N–S	E	Cr.
59	Sq.	>4.5	>4.2			16780	101	N–S	E	Cr.
60	Sq.	4	4			16747	100	N–S	E	Cr.
61	Sq.	4.4	4.2		>B65	16883	107	N–S	E	Cr.
62	Sq.	5.8	5.5			16896	109	N–S	E	Flexed
63	Sq.	7.5	5.8		<lin.16831	18173	143	N–S	E	Cr.
64	Sq.	5.5	5			16990	113	N–S	E	Cr.

(Continued)

Table 4.1 (Continued)

B No.	Sex	Age	Grave goods	Structure	Organics	Comments	Dating	Radiocarbon date (cal BC)
34	M	18–25?	SFs 68–73	Y	Y	Sword + spears		
35	M	26+						
36	F	18+				V. shallow grave		95.4% 188–39
37	M	36–45?	Multiple	Y	Y	Shield burial		
38	F	18+		Y	pig bone	5 IA secondaries		
39						>B40		
40	U	18+			Y	N. side bowed		95.4% 727–396
41	F	26–35?				SW arc of ditch only		
42	F??	26+	Br. SF84	Y?			C 1st BC.	95.4% 351–306, 210–88, 76–58
43	M	36+			Y?	Secs 16450 + 16473		
44	M	36+						
45	U	36+	SF 85+86			W causeway; pot		
46	F	46+	Br. SF91				2Cb: mid 3 - early 2?	95% 359–275, 261–164
47	M	17–19						
48	F	46+		Y	Y			
49	F	26–35						
50	F	26+	SFs 93–5			Bracelet, Fib, bead		95.4% 488–362
51	U	18–35						
52	U	26+	SF 92 Br.				Penann. C3-1 BC?	
53	M??	26+				Severely truncated		
54	U	12+ ?adult				Burial truncated		
55	U	15–17	SF96 Fe			Fe bow brooch	mid-3rd-early 2nd	insufficient carbon
56	Ind.	36+		?	Y	NE corner curved		
57	/	2–3 yrs.			Y			
58	F	18–35						
59	U	18–25?				Badly truncated		
60	F	26–35?				Rounded corners		
61	F	36+				Well-defined grave		
62	F	18–25				Ang secondary 16881		insufficient carbon
63	U	26–35?		Y		Anglian secondaries		
64	M	26–35				Anglian secondary		

(Continued)

Table 4.1 Summary of barrows (Continued)

B No.	Shape	N–S (m)	E–W (m)	Diam.	Rel. ?	Primary	Sk no.	Aligned	Facing	Posture
65	Sq.	6	4.5		<B61	18013	129	N–S	E	Cr.
66	Sq.	5.5	6.5		<B65,>67	18224	148	N–S	E	Cr.
67	Sq.	6.2	5.2		<B66	18164	142	N–S	E	Cr.
68	Sq.	5.3	5.3		>B71	18272	151	N–S	E	Cr.
69	Sq?	>9	9		<lin.16831	x				
70	Circ.			4.5		18111		N–S		Supine, legs flexed
71	Circ.			17	Sq.Brws	17102?		N–S	E	Cr.
72	Rect.	14.5	9.3		>B71	18004?	127	U	U	U
73	Sq.	5.3	6.4		<lin18324	18303	153	S–N	W	Flexed
74	Sq.	5.5	6			18348	158	N–S	W	Cr.
75	Sq.	>4	>4		<lin16831	18329	155	S–N	W	Cr.
76	Sq.	4.5	>3.5			18346	157	N–S	U	Cr. Supine
77	Sq.	7.5	7.5			18441	159	S–N	U	U
78	Sq.	6	>4.5			16	161	N–S	E	Cr.
79	Circ.			c. 28						
80	Circ.			c.4.3		x				
81	Sq.	>3	>4.5			x				
82	Sq.	c. 8.2				x				
83	Sq.	15	15			x				
84	Sq.	9	9			x				
85	Sq.	8.5	>8.5			394	165	N–S	E	Cr?
86	Circ.									
87	Sq.	5.8	>3.8			15782	41	N–S	E	Cr.

(Continued)

Grave 15172

The primary burial (15176) survived within a shallow rectangular grave (15172) which measured 2.50m in length, 1.02m in width and 0.20m in depth.

Skeleton (15176 – Sk 2)

The poorly preserved and extremely fragmentary skeleton was that of a mature adult female (46+ years), in a flexed posture, aligned north to south and lying on the right side, with the head to the north facing west. The pathological conditions of this woman consisted of DDD, DJC and OA of the spine, additional DJC to the right tempero-mandibular joint, left scapula and right hip joint, and a suspected vertebral artery aneurysm in her neck. She was a 2nd- or 3rd-degree relative to the female primary burials of B58 and B48 (Patterson *et al.* 2022) and was radiocarbon-dated to the period 390–200 cal BC (SUERC-83069).

Grave goods

An impressive suite of grave goods consisted of two copper alloy bracelets (SFs 3 and 4 – one with coral mounts; Figs 11.6 and 11.7) and a 3rd-century BC Adams Type 2Bh copper alloy bow brooch with coral inlay (SF 5; Fig. 11.3). A small number of animal bone fragments were recovered with the burial.

Table 4.1 (Continued)

B No.	Sex	Age	Grave goods	Structure	Organics	Comments	Dating	Radiocarbon date (cal BC)
65	M	46+?			Y	'Ring' around Sk		
66	U	18–35		Y	Y	Anglian secondary		
67	M	36+		Y				
68	U	36–45?				Irregular W. side		
69						Anglian secondaries		
70	M	45+?	SFs 297–9	18114	Y	Northern arc only	Anglian	
71	/	9.5–11				Grave approx.central	Bronze Age	
72	U	16+				Arm bones in centre		
73	M??	18–35				Anglian secondary		
74	F?	18–25?	SF 559, CuA bracelet			Anglian secondary		
75	F	26–35				Anglian secondary		
76	U	26+				Poor preservation		
77	U	12+adult?				Isolated, truncated		
78	M	36–45				Sub-rect. Grave		
79						Gaps at NE and SW	Bronze Age	
80						Continuous ring		
81						Only part dug		
82						Only part dug		
83						>B86		
84						No grave surviving		93.% 205–51 pony
85	M		chariot					
86							Bronze Age	
87	U	36+		Y		Only partial ditches		

Barrow 3

Summary

Barrow 3, which lay close to the south-east corner of Barrow 2, was square, with an internal measurement of 4.2m (Fig. 4.6). The eastern ditch did not survive. The apparently plough-truncated ditches (segments 15123 and 15137) were shallow (*c.* 0.15m) and fragmentary, *c.* 0.80m wide and with a U-shaped profile; they were filled with sandy gravel.

Grave 15188

The central grave (15188) was sub-rectangular and measured 1.6m in length, 0.70m in width and 0.30m in depth. The grave fill (15186) contained an Iron Age sherd, and trace amounts of bread wheat and six-row barley, probably intrusive from nearby burning (see Chapter 15).

Skeleton (15187 – Sk 3)

The very poorly preserved and moderately fragmented skeleton of a male, aged 26–35 years, was flexed, lying on the left side, with the head to the north facing east. This man had a DJC of the spine plus soft tissue trauma to the right femur; he also had CO.

Barrow 4

Summary

This was another relatively small square barrow, situated immediately south-west of Barrow 3, with which it had

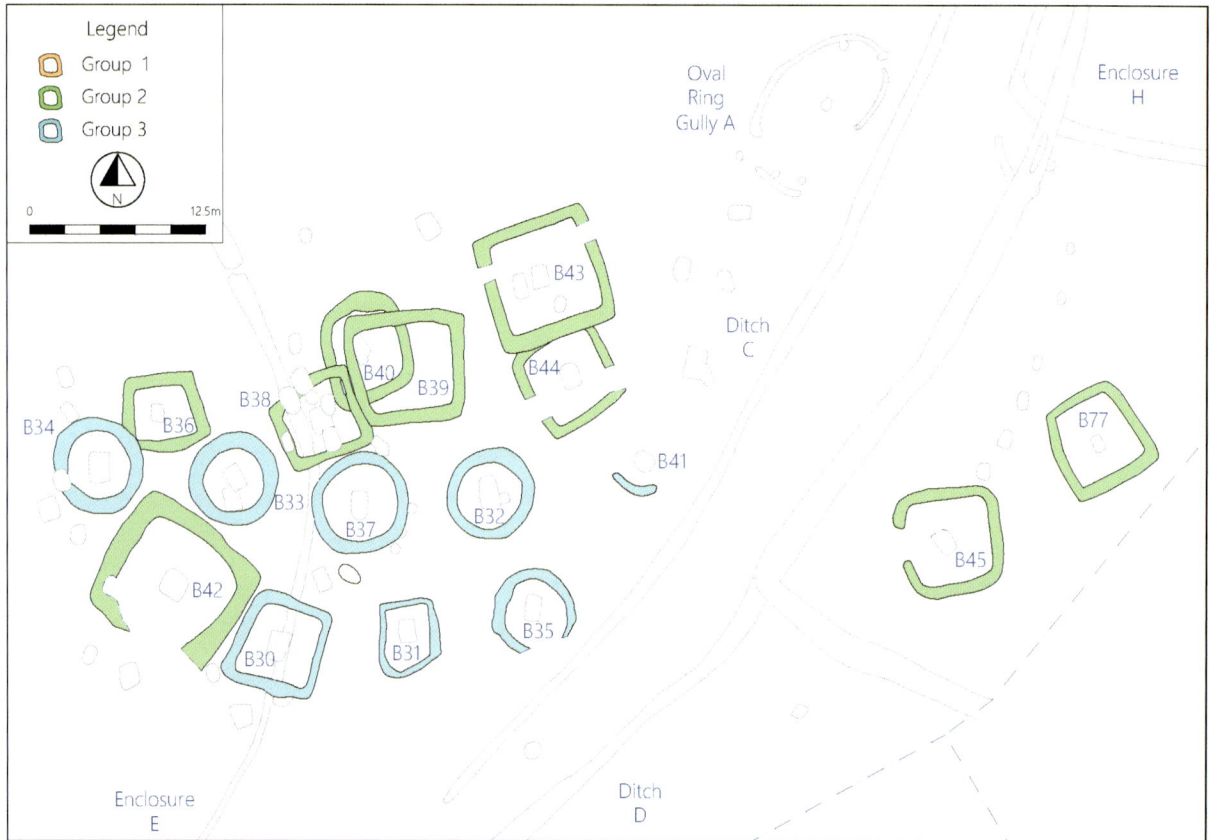

Figure 4.2 Barrow location plan, Eastern Group

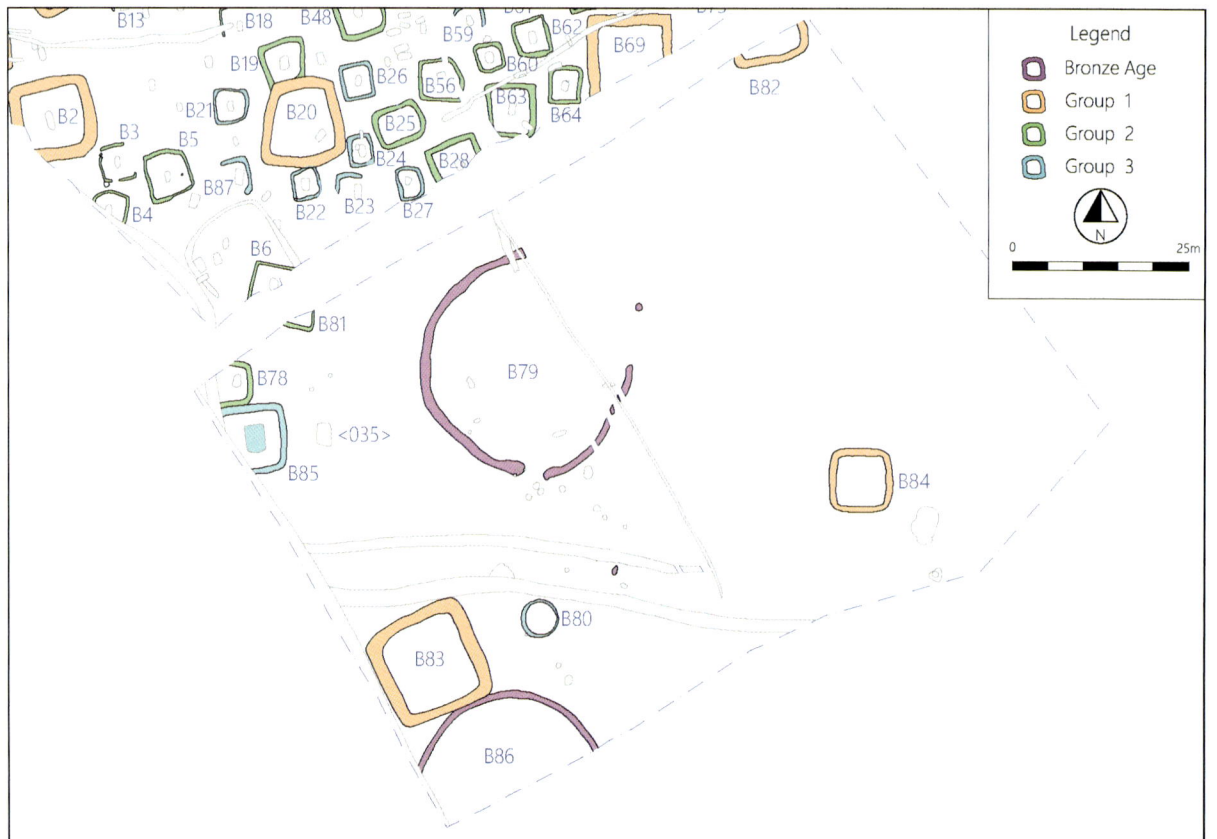

Figure 4.3 Barrow location plan, Southern Area

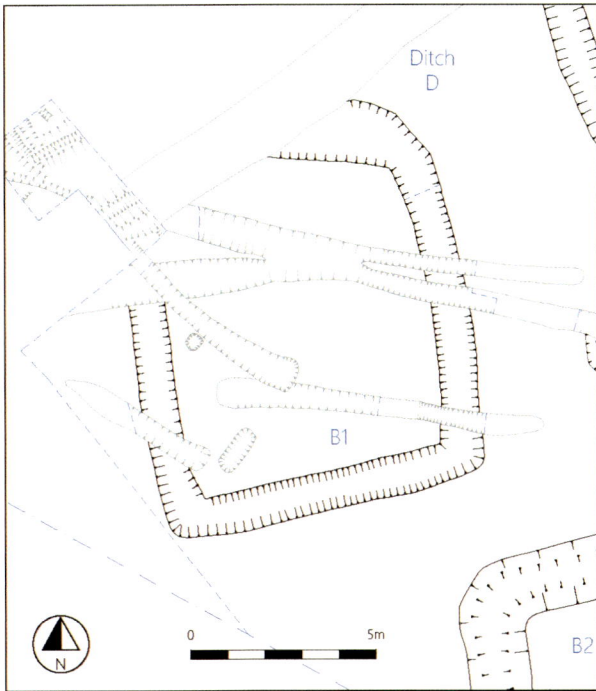

Figure 4.4 Plan of Barrow 1

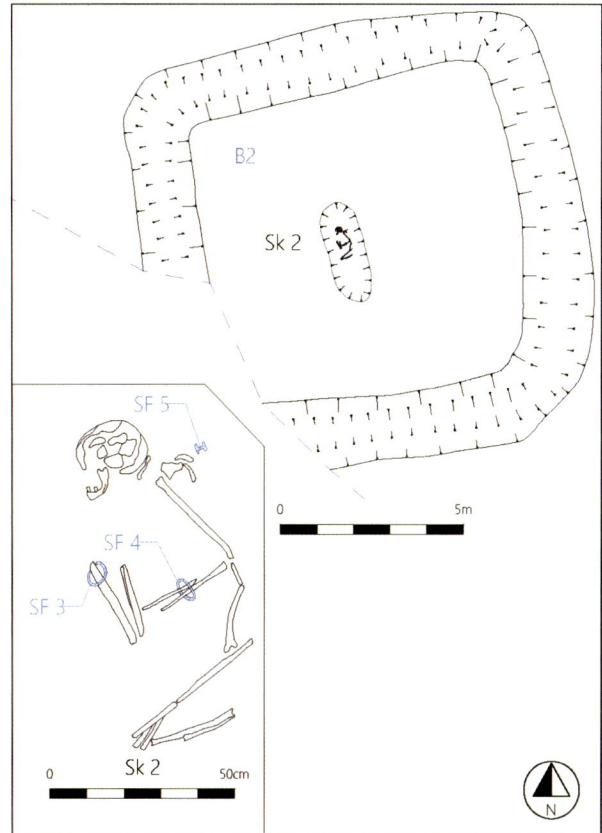

Figure 4.5 Plan of Barrow 2 and Skeleton 2 <15176>

a skewed alignment (Figs 4.1 and 4.7). It measured 4.5m across internally. The ditch was excavated in five segments (15170, 15194, 15196, 15198 and 15180 – the western side of the barrow was missing) and was 0.75m wide and 0.20m deep, with a U-shaped profile, filled with sandy gravel. The west side of Barrow 4 was cut away by a later ditch (15168 and 15178) that ran parallel to Burnby Lane.

Grave 15220

The central grave (15220) was sub-rectangular, with a length of 1.40m, a width of 0.90m and a depth of 0.20m. The grave fill (15216) contained a 1st–2nd-century oxidised sherd (probably intrusive from the truncating later ditch). A small amount of fragmentary animal bone was recovered along with the human burial.

Skeleton (15219 – Sk 5)

This was the very poorly preserved and extremely fragmented skeleton of a 36+ year-old probable woman, crouched with the head to the north, lying on the left side and facing east.

Barrow 5
Summary

This square barrow lay immediately east of Barrow 4 and measured 5.5m across internally (Figs 4.1 and 4.8). The complete circuit of the ditch survived (excavated as segments 15209, 15211, 15213, 15215, 15217, 15203,

15205 and 15207), and measured up to *c.* 0.50m wide and 0.10m deep. Flat grave 15428 (Sk 20) lay immediately to the south-east of the barrow.

Grave 15222

The central grave (15222) was shallow and sub-rectangular, measuring 1.50m in length, 0.70m in width and 0.06m in depth.

Skeleton (15223 – Sk 6)

This was the very poorly preserved and extremely fragmentary skeleton of a male aged 18–35 years, crouched on the right side, with the head to north facing west.

Barrow 6
Summary

Barrow 6 was a square barrow situated 15m south-east of Barrow 5; it was excavated in several stages due to factors associated with the development schedule. It was truncated along its western edge, so that the surrounding ditch was excavated in two segments (15227 and 16341). Barrow 6 was *c.* 5.5m wide internally, and the ditch was 1.00m wide and *c.* 0.40m deep with a flat-based V profile (Fig. 4.9). The ditch fills consisted of gravelly primary fills with darker sandy silt at the top. Context

Mark Stephens

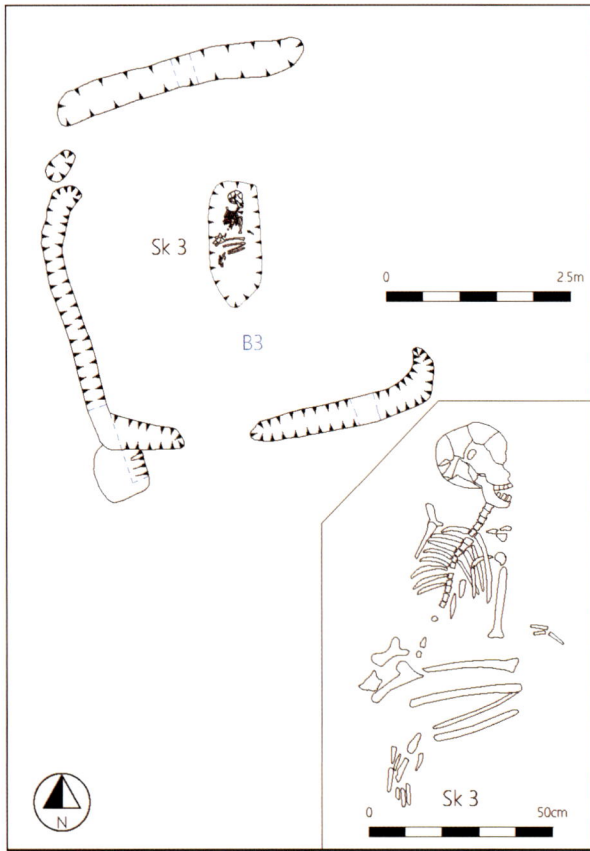

Figure 4.6 Plan of Barrow 3 and Skeleton 3 <15187>

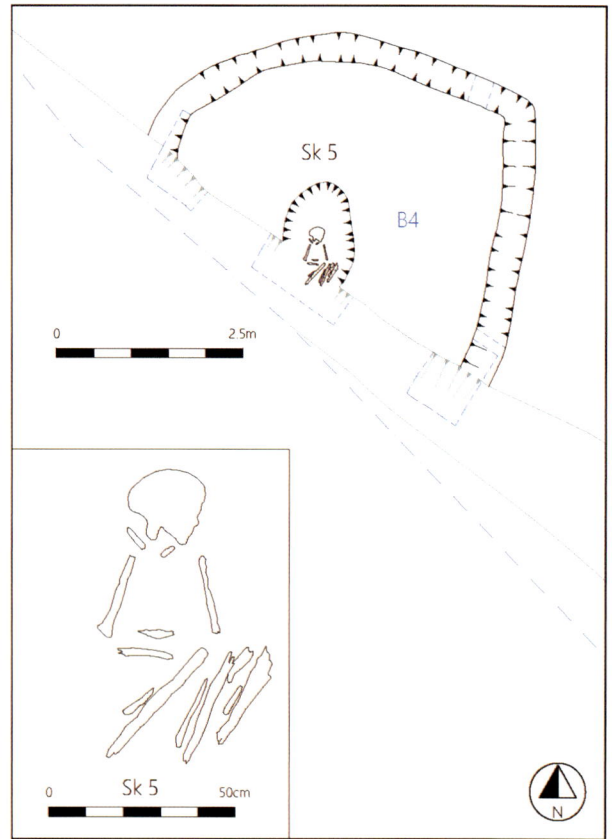

Figure 4.7 Plan of Barrow 4 and Skeleton 5 <15219>

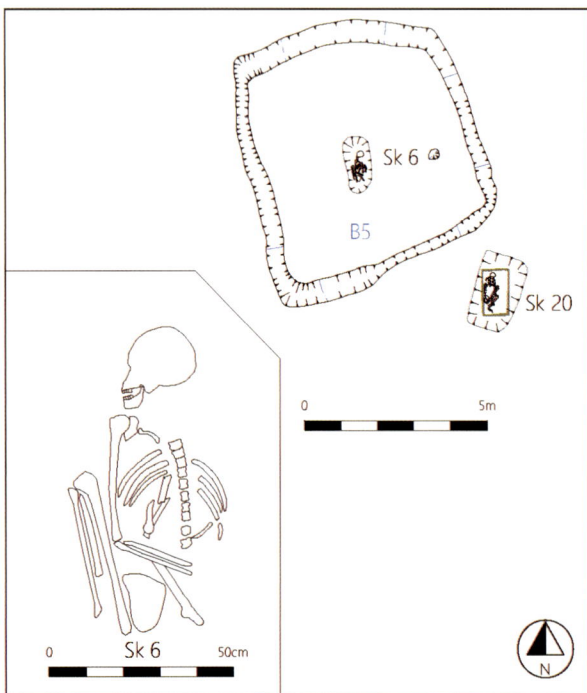

Figure 4.8 Plan of Barrow 5 and Skeletons 6 <15223> and 20 <15428>

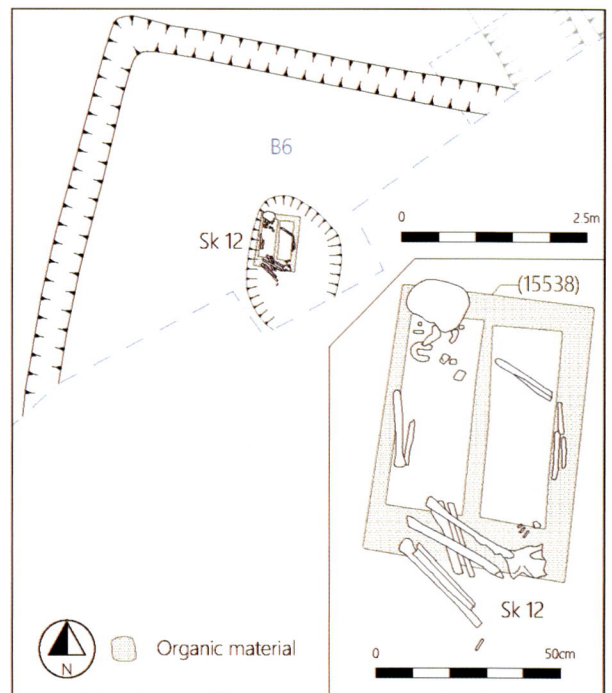

Figure 4.9 Plan of Barrow 6 and Skeleton 12 <15300>

15226 contained an Iron Age sherd along with poorly preserved barley grains. Barrow 6 was probably part of the adjacent Barrow 81 that was excavated in the southern field (Fig. 4.3).

Grave 15361

The central grave was an oval, vertically sided cut (15361) measuring 1.80m in length, 1.25m in width and 0.37m in depth. A residual crude flint flake and a flint chunk, both undiagnostic, were found in the fill (15360). The grave contained the remains of a structure (15358) against the north-west edge.

Skeleton (15300 – Sk 12)

Structure 15358 (below) contained the poorly preserved and extremely fragmentary skeleton of an individual of unknown sex aged 18–35 years, apparently supine with the legs flexed and the head to the north. The position of the pelvis indicated that it could have rotated in a void, which hints that the structure may originally have been lidded (although there were no physical traces of a lid).

Structure 15358

This was rectangular, with its longest axis to the north, and measured 1.25m by 0.52m, and at least 0.09m in height. There were two traces of lining to the northern part of the structure, consisting of 15355 at the base and 15354 above; these were dark sandy silt deposits around 0.10m wide, 15354 having a square cross-section and containing fragments of undiagnostic iron corrosion (SF 13). The structure itself was filled with two distinct gravelly deposits (15357 and 15356) and was surrounded by a more general backfill deposit (15359). A wedge of yellowish gravel (15363) overlay the top of the western edge of the structure, and the remaining upper part of the grave was filled by dark sandy silt (15352).

Barrow 7

Summary

Barrow 7, situated 65m north-east of Barrow 6 on the northern edge of the western barrow group, was a square barrow measuring 4.40m across internally (Figs 4.1 and 4.10). The northern edge was missing (having been truncated by Ditch D) but the remainder was excavated in four segments (15268, 15278, 15303 and 15287). The ditch was 0.80m wide and 0.50m deep, with a flat-based V profile. It was filled with gravel at the base and darker, siltier material at the top. The only find was an abraded Iron Age sherd from the primary fill of the south-east corner (15277). The lower fill at the north-east corner (15301) contained a grain of barley, along with indeterminate grains, suggesting cooking or cereal drying in the vicinity.

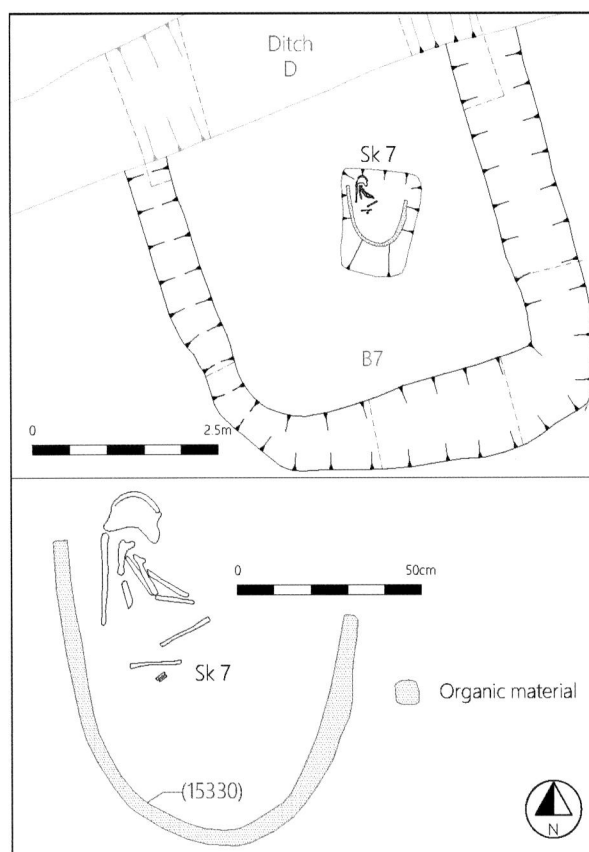

Figure 4.10 Plan of Barrow 7 and Skeleton 7 <15331>

Grave 15332

The central grave was a relatively shallow sub-rectangular cut (15332), measuring 1.35m in length, 0.95m in width and 0.28m in depth.

Skeleton (15331 – Sk 7)

The grave contained the very poorly preserved and severely fragmented skeleton of an older juvenile aged 6½ to 8½ years, apparently crouched and lying on the left side facing east, with the head to the north.

Structure 15330

A U-shaped deposit of dark silt surrounded the west, south and east of the skeleton; this probably represented the base of a structure. This survived to 0.96m in length, 0.80m in width, and between 0.05m and 0.13m in height.

Barrow 8

Summary

Barrow 8, which lay immediately west of Barrow 7, was a square barrow measuring 5.5m across internally (Fig. 4.11). The ditch was excavated in seven segments (15351, 15346, 15387, 15384, 15374, 15377

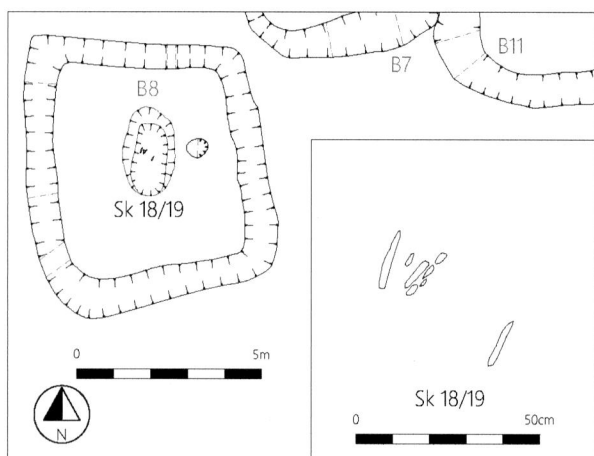

Figure 4.11 Plan of Barrow 8 and Skeleton fragments 18/19 <15399/15400>

and 15381), showing it to be *c.* 0.45m wide and up to 0.90m deep, with a rounded-V profile. Gravel filled the base of the ditch, with darker silty sand above (15375); this contained medieval sherds and undiagnostic slag fragments. The primary fill of the south-west corner (15339) contained 17 sherds from the same Anglian jar. The primary fill (15383) of the south-east corner had two Iron Age sherds, and another Iron Age sherd came from the primary fill of the east ditch (15386). The central grave was truncated by an Anglian secondary burial (15391).

Grave 15401

The central grave (15401) was of rounded rectangular form and was skewed north-eastwards from the axis of the barrow; it was 2.10m in length, 1.45m in width and 0.40m in depth. The lower grave fill (15399) contained a late Neolithic/early Bronze Age flint flake in 'fresh' condition. A small number of animal bone fragments was associated with the burial.

Primary skeleton (15399/15400 – Sk 18/19)

The primary burial consisted of the extremely poorly preserved and extremely fragmentary remains of a probable adult of unknown sex, consisting of parts of the right arm and un-sided leg bones.

Barrow 9
Summary

Barrow 9 lay *c.* 9m west of Barrow 7 and was *c.* 4m square internally (Fig. 4.12). Ditch D had truncated the northern barrow ditch, but the surviving remains were excavated in five segments (15294, 15318, 15321, 15325 and 15271). The ditch had a flat-based V profile and measured *c.* 0.50m

wide and 0.30m deep; it was filled with gravel at the base and a darker silt above.

Grave 15328

The central grave (15328) was of rounded rectangular form and steep-sided, with a length of 1.70m, a width of 0.95m and a depth of 0.72m.

Skeleton (15327 – Sk 13)

The burial was very poorly preserved and severely fragmented with only the limb bones present. This was an individual of unknown sex aged 36–45 years, flexed, and with the (absent) head to the south. There was pilasterism to both femora. The skeleton was radiocarbon-dated to the period 390–190 cal BC (SUERC-83070).

Grave goods

An iron Hull and Hawkes 2Cb involuted bow brooch (SF 10) of mid-3rd to early 2nd-century BC date was found in the area of the left shoulder.

Barrow 10
Summary

This was a dubious square barrow represented by a ditch that wrapped around the northern and eastern ditches of Barrow 9 (Fig. 4.12). Barrow 10's ditch was cut through by Ditch D to the north and destroyed by a furrow to the west. The barrow ditch was excavated in four segments (15308, 15397, 15310 and 15312), showing it to have a flat-based V profile, around 0.70m wide and 0.20m deep.

Grave

No associated grave survived for this barrow, but much of the area enclosed by the barrow ditch was completely truncated by Ditch D.

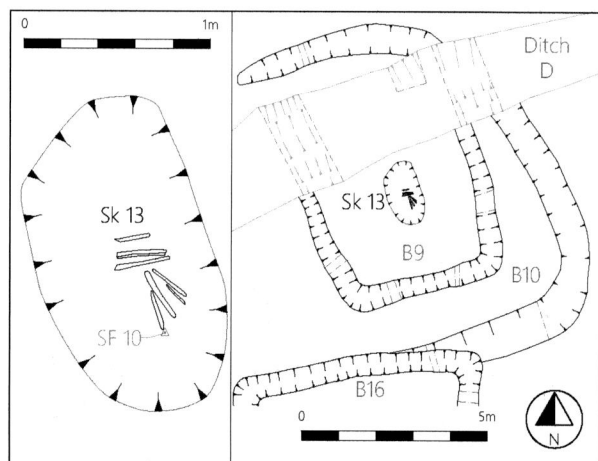

Figure 4.12 Plan of Barrows 9 and 10 and Skeleton 13 <15327>

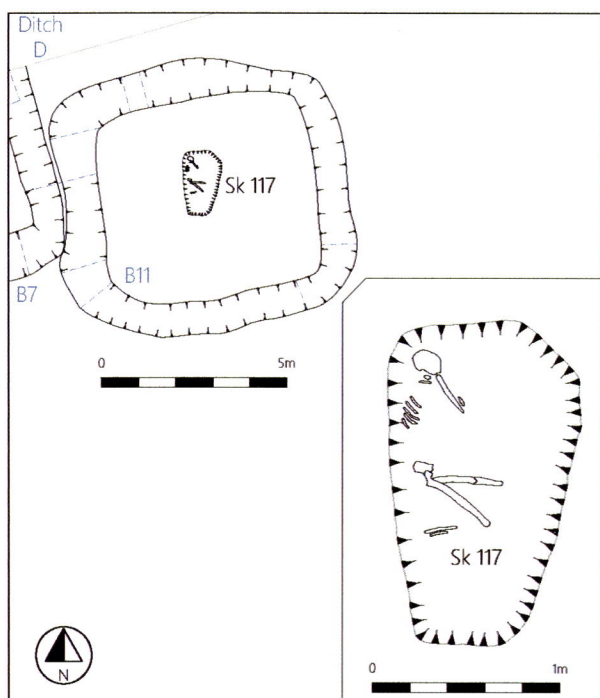

Figure 4.13 Plan of Barrow 11 and Skeleton 117 <17004>

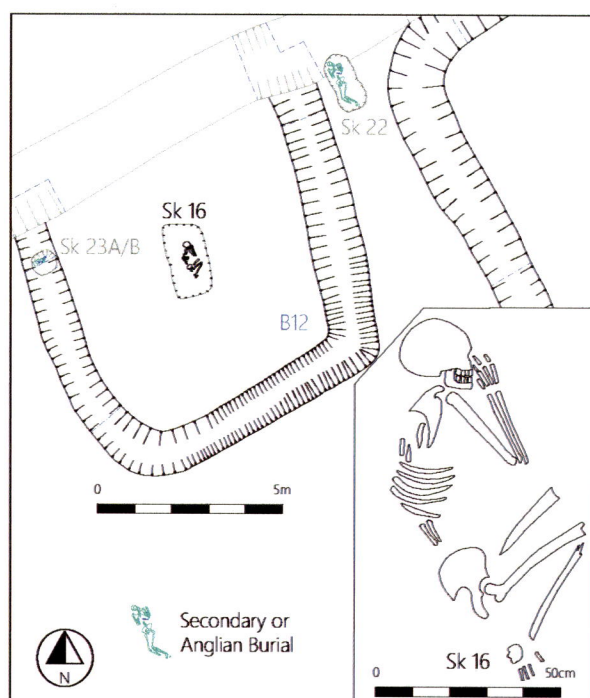

Figure 4.14 Plan of Barrow 12 and Skeleton 16 <15394>

Barrow 11

Summary

Barrow 11 was situated on the eastern side of Barrow 7; the two barrows slightly overlapped, but not sufficiently to establish any firm relationship between them (Fig. 4.13). This barrow was of rectangular form, the internal measurements being 5m from north to south and 6m from east to west. The ditch, which was excavated in seven segments (15370, 17047, 17051, 17049, 15364, 15283 and 15367), was 0.80m wide and 0.35m deep, with a U-shaped profile. There was a gravelly primary fill and a darker, siltier upper fill. Five Iron Age sherds were found in the fill of the eastern ditch (17046); the single grains of rye and six-row barley from the western ditch (17048) were probably intrusive.

Grave 17005

The central, sub-rectangular grave (17005) was 1.76m long, 0.99m wide and 0.23m deep.

Skeleton (17004 – Sk 117)

This was the very poorly preserved and severely fragmented skeleton of an adult of unknown sex, flexed and lying on the left side, with the head to the north, facing east.

Barrow 12

Summary

Barrow 12 lay at the north-west of the western barrow group, immediately east of Barrow 1 (Figs 4.1 and 4.14).

The northern ditch of the barrow was cut away by Ditch D, but it was presumably square in shape and around 6.5m across internally. Seven segments were excavated into the ditch (15450, 15512, 15545, 15492, 15508, 15524 and 15413). The ditch was *c.* 1.40m wide and 0.70m deep, with a rounded-V profile. Perhaps because the barrow and its ditch were larger than average for the site, the filling history of the ditch was more complex than usual; to take the western ditch (15524) as an example, it was filled at the base with a gravelly silty yellow sand, with successive bands of silty material (15522 and 15520) separated by brown silts (15521 and 15481). Finds from the fills of the south-west corner consisted of residual flint flakes from each of the lower fills (15505–6), plus an early Bronze Age flint scraper and an Anglian sherd from the secondary fill (15504). The lower fill of the southern ditch (15491) contained Roman sherds.

Grave 15395

The grave (15395) was a centrally placed sub-rectangular cut measuring 1.94m by 1.20m, and 0.24m deep. The grave fill (15393) contained an undiagnostic slag fragment.

Skeleton (15394 – Sk 16)

This was the poorly preserved and moderately fragmented skeleton of a female aged 17–20 years. It was flexed and lying on the left side, with the head to the north, facing east. This woman suffered from sacroiliitis (inflammation of the sacro-iliac joints) which is likely to have contributed both to her death, and that of her unborn (32–40 weeks

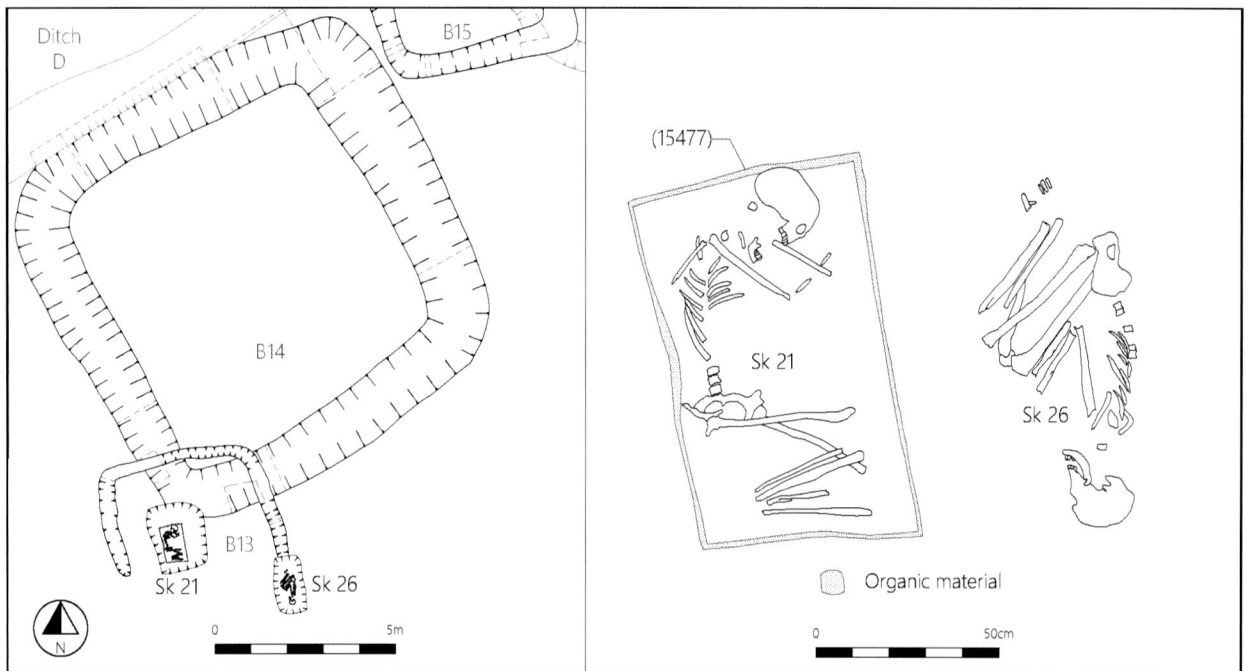

Figure 4.15 Plan of Barrows 13 and 14 and Skeletons 21 <15476> and 26 <15514>

in utero) baby (15402 – Sk 17), whose bones were found in the pelvic area.

Anglian secondary burial

A secondary burial (15486) of Anglian date was cut into the western ditch.

Barrows 13 and 14, Burial 15514

Summary

These two barrows and an isolated flat burial formed a significant sequence and were located to the east of Barrow 12 (Figs 4.1 and 4.15).

Barrow 14

This was a large square barrow *c.* 8m by 8m internally; the later Ditch D clipped its northern ditch. The barrow ditch was excavated in eight segments (15614, 15531, 15617, 15589, 15586, 15540, 15593 and 15560) and generally had a gravelly primary fill with dark silt above. The upper fill of the west ditch (15590) contained three undiagnostic slag fragments, the upper fill of the north 15556 (=15609) a Roman rim sherd and an Iron Age body sherd, the primary fill of the north ditch (15613) a residual late Neolithic/early Bronze Age flint bladelet, and the lower fill of the east side (15616) a gritstone quern fragment. A fragment of disarticulated human adult left femur was recovered from ditch fill 15556. There were also medieval and post-medieval sherds from the upper fill (15584) of the southern ditch. The primary fill (15613) of the north ditch contained a grain of bread wheat, a cleavers seed and

a garden pea, and that of the east ditch (15616) another stray grain of bread wheat; these remains were probably from adjacent burning or cooking events. No associated burial survived with Barrow 14.

Barrow 13

This barrow, which cut across the south-western corner of Barrow 14, was represented by a horseshoe-shaped ditch, open-ended to the south, measuring *c.* 4m across internally. The ditch (segment cuts 15538, 15595, 15602 and 15604) was narrow and slot-like, with a width varying between 0.25m and 0.40m, and a depth of less than 0.10m. The ditch fill consisted of uniform brown sand.

Barrow 13 – grave 15478

There was a large, slightly off-centre rectangular grave, measuring 2.00m long, 1.40m wide, and 0.38m deep. The grave fill (15474) contained single grains of oat and six-row barley, plus a garden pea, which were probably intrusive from later nearby burning.

Barrow 13 – skeleton (15476 – Sk 21)

This was the poorly preserved and severely fragmented skeleton of an unsexed adolescent aged 14½–16½ years. This individual was tightly placed within Structure 15478, lying on the left side, with the head to the north, facing east. Endocranial new bone was present, plus lamellar bone on both legs. Two radiocarbon dates are available from this skeleton (SUERC-78039 and -79413) which combine to form mean date of 2241±23 BP; this calibrates to 390–200 cal BC.

Barrow 13 – structure 15477

Structure 15478 was represented by a dark narrow stain which formed a rectangle around 1.02m long and 0.62m wide. The interior was filled with gravelly brown sand, with yellowish-brown sand and gravel (15474) in the remainder of the grave.

Isolated burial 15514 – Sk 26

Grave 15515 lay at the south-east terminal of Barrow 13. The grave was sub-rectangular and vertically sided, measuring 1.37m long, 0.88m wide and 0.20m deep. It contained the poorly preserved and severely fragmented skeleton *(15514 – Sk 26)* of a male aged 36–45 years, in a flexed posture, lying on the left side, but with the head to the south and facing west. This man had OA in the spine and right wrist, DJC in both tempero-mandibular joints, and maxillary sinusitis. This skeleton was radiocarbon-dated to the period 410–230 cal BC (SUERC-78040).

Barrow 15

Summary

Barrow 15 was situated immediately east of Barrow 14, with its northern ditch truncated by Ditch D (Fig. 4.16). This was a square barrow that measured *c.* 4.5m across internally. The ditch was excavated in seven segments (15419, 15406, 15470, 15465, 15466, 15461 and 15435) and measured 0.60m wide and 0.25m deep, with a U-shaped profile. The ditch fills consisted of gravel-rich sand in the base with darker silt above. The upper fill of the north-west corner (15433) contained two Iron Age sherds, the primary fill (15405) of the east ditch another Iron Age sherd, with further Iron Age sherds in the upper fill of the west ditch (15433); the upper fill of the south-east corner (15467) contained a fragment of a possible forged iron off-cut. The primary fill at the north-east corner (15418) contained four bread wheat grains plus a single grain of barley; radiocarbon-dating showed the bread wheat to be medieval and therefore intrusive. The upper fill of the north-west corner (15434) contained a few indeterminate grains. The primary fill (15405) of the east ditch was cut by a shallow oval pit filled with a dark silt (cut 15457, fill 15456) that was subsequently covered over by the ditch's upper fill (15404). Pit fill 15456 contained the largest group of burnt debris to be found at the site, mainly oak charcoal, probably indicating that it was a fire pit. A fragment of oak charcoal suggests the feature might date from 750–400 cal BC (SUERC-78050), though since the sample was not identified as sapwood or as short-lived roundwood, this date should be regarded as a *terminus post quem* for the feature.

Grave 15423

The central sub-rectangular grave (15423) was slightly skewed in relationship to the alignment of the ditches, and at 0.44m was relatively deep.

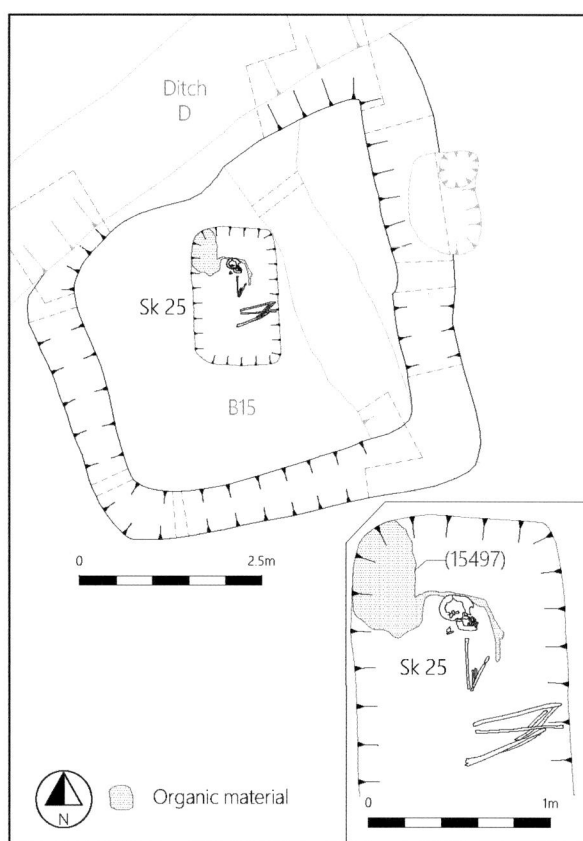

Figure 4.16 Plan of Barrow 15 and Skeleton 25 <15496>

Skeleton (15496 – Sk 25)

This was the very poorly preserved and severely fragmented skeleton of a male aged 36–45 years, laid in a flexed posture on the left side facing east, with the head to the north. He had CO, endocranial new bone and pilasterism of both femora.

Probable structure 15497

A 0.45m-wide stain of dark silt, possibly representing a structure, or else a more nebulous deposit of organic material, surrounded the head and shoulders of Burial 15496.

Barrow 16

Summary

Barrow 16 was situated immediately south-east of Barrow 15, on a slightly skewed alignment to it. It was rectangular in form, measuring 5.5m from east to west and 4.5m north to south internally (Figs 4.1 and 4.17). The ditch was excavated in seven segments (15314, 15526, 15498, 15500, 15502, 15516 and 15519) and had a variable U- or rounded-V profile, around 0.70m wide and 0.30m deep. There was generally a single gravelly sand fill.

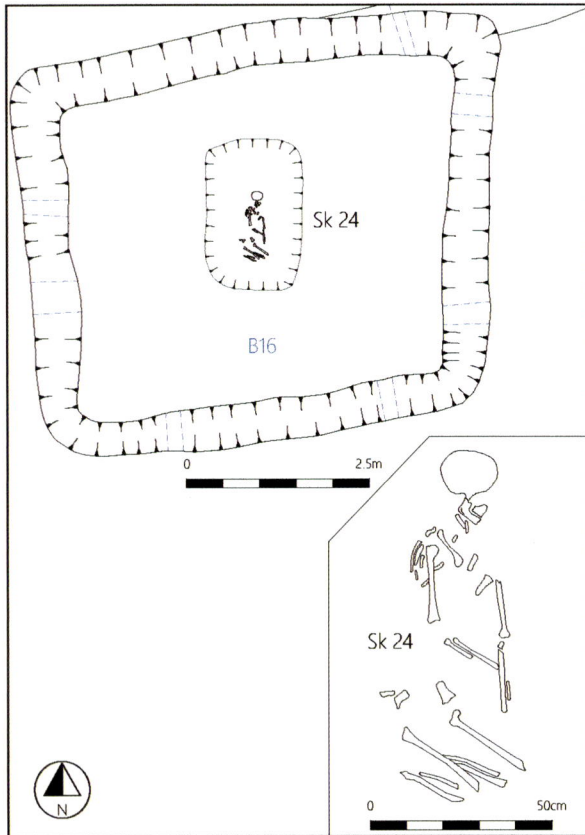

Figure 4.17 Plan of Barrow 16 and Skeleton 24 <15494>

Grave 15495

The grave (15495) was a relatively large and deep cut measuring 2.00m long, 1.30m wide and 0.35m deep, occupying the centre of the barrow.

Skeleton (15494 – Sk 24)

This was the poorly preserved and moderately fragmented skeleton of a possible male, 18–25 years old, lying in a flexed posture on the left side, with the head to the north and facing east. There was pronounced torsion of both femora.

Barrow 17

Summary

Barrow 17 was situated *c.* 4m south-west of Barrow 16, the two barrows having a common alignment. This barrow measured *c.* 5m across internally (Fig. 4.18). The relatively narrow and shallow ditch was excavated in eight segments (15566, 15569, 15572, 15583, 15580, 15575, 15578 and 15563). The ditch had a rounded profile and on average measured 0.50m wide and 0.15m deep. The primary fill consisted of a gravel-rich silty sand with darker silt above. There was an intrusive medieval sherd from the primary fill (15562) of the north-west corner. Stray cereal grains were recovered from 15577 and 15582 (the primary fills of the western and south-eastern ditches respectively).

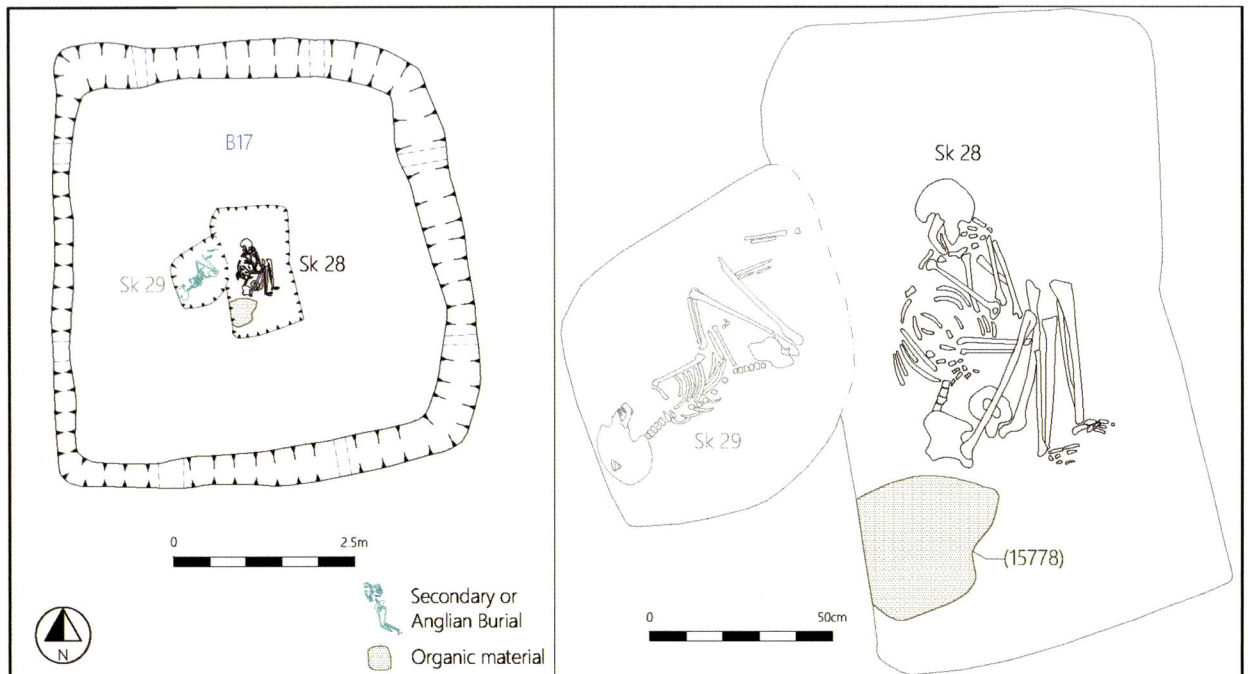

Figure 4.18 Plan of Barrow 17, Skeleton 28 <15630> and Anglian burial Sk 29 <15631>

Grave 15629

The centrally placed grave (15629) was sub-rectangular and measured 1.80m long, 0.95m wide and 0.20m deep. The western part of the grave was truncated by an Anglian burial (15631). An amorphous deposit of dark silt (15778) situated in the south-western part of the grave may represent the remains of organic material placed on the grave floor.

Skeleton (15630 – Sk 28)

The grave contained the poorly preserved and severely fragmented skeleton of an individual aged over 25 years, lying crouched on the left side with the head to the north, facing east. This individual had a DJC of the spine.

Barrow 18

Summary

Barrow 18 was a badly truncated square barrow situated south of Barrow 17 (Figs 4.1 and 4.19). As only the western and northern ditches were present, the overall dimensions are uncertain, but judging by the position of the grave it would appear to have been *c.* 4m across internally. The ditch was excavated in a single segment

(15682), showing it to be 0.28m wide and 0.05m deep, with a surviving fill (15682) of chalk gravel.

Grave 15623

The sub-rectangular grave (15623) measured 1.35m long, 0.75m wide and 0.24m deep.

Skeleton (15622 – Sk 27)

This was the moderately preserved and moderately fragmented skeleton of a male aged 36–45 years, lying in a flexed posture on the left side, facing east with the head to the north. One of the thoracic vertebrae was fractured. The spine had DJD and OA, and there was a DJC in the left hip socket. The skeleton was radiocarbon-dated to the period 380–170 cal BC (SUERC-83071).

Grave goods

A dark 'organic' deposit (15621) overlay the torso, and an iron Hull and Hawkes Type 2Cab involuted brooch of 3rd–2nd-century BC date (SF 24; Fig 11.1) was found near the chin.

Barrow 19

Summary

Barrow 19 was a slightly irregular square barrow lying *c.* 3m south-east of Barrow 18 (Figs 4.1 and 4.20). It pre-dated Barrow 20, which cut away Barrow 19's southern ditch. The internal dimensions were 4.8m east to west and 4.4m north

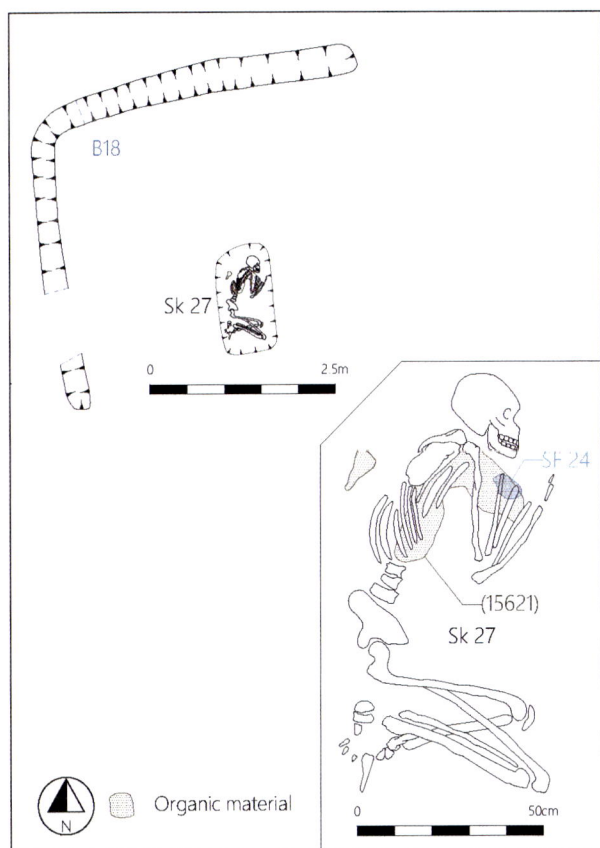

Figure 4.19 Plan of Barrow 18 and Skeleton 27 <15622>

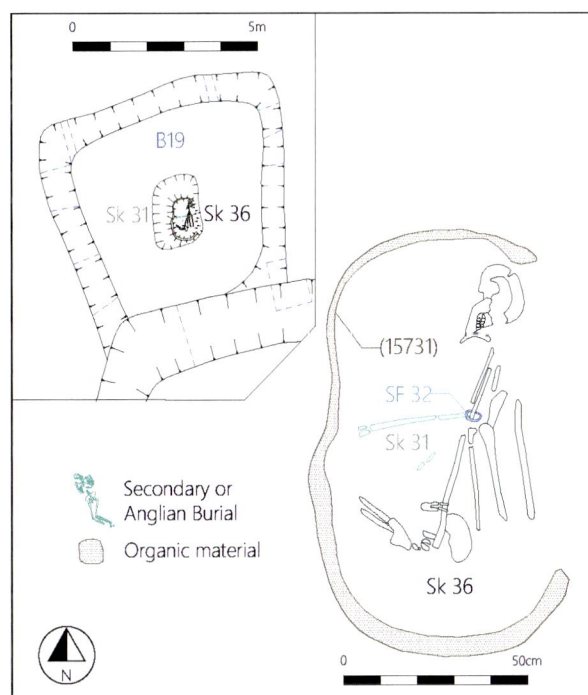

Figure 4.20 Plan of Barrow 19 and Skeletons 36 <15733> and 31 <15656>

to south. The ditch was excavated in seven segments (15644, 15647, 15650, 15653, 15635, 15638 and 15641), showing it to have a rounded profile, around 0.60m wide and 0.20m deep. The fills consisted of sandy gravel at the base, with darker silt at the top. The primary fill (15646) at the north-east corner contained an Iron Age sherd (see Chapter 12).

Primary grave 15732

The central sub-rectangular grave (15732) was relatively deep at 0.50m and was 1.30m long and 0.80m wide. The upper part of this grave was truncated by an Anglian secondary grave (15655).

Skeleton (15733 – Sk 36)

The crouched primary burial was that of a female aged 26–35 years, lying on the left side, with the head to the north, facing east. Her skeleton showed signs of CO.

Grave goods

An iron bracelet (SF 32) was found on the woman's right wrist.

Structure 15731

An oval ring of dark silt (15731), measuring 1.30m long, 0.80m wide and 0.47m deep appeared to be the remains of a decayed organic structure that surrounded the burial.

Barrow 20

Summary

As stated above, this barrow cut into the southern ditch of Barrow 19. Barrow 20 had an unusual trapezoidal shape and was 10m in length along its longest (north–south) axis. It varied in width east to west from 6m at the north to 9m at the south (Fig. 4.21). In keeping with the relatively large size of the barrow, its ditches were deep and wide. Eight ditch segments were excavated (15733, 15720, 15759, 15714, 15717, 15740, 15736 and 15747), showing that it was around 1.50m wide and between 0.50m and 0.60m deep, with a gravel fill at the base and dark silt towards the top. The primary fill (15719) at the north-east corner contained animal teeth, and a flint core-rejuvenation flake in 'fresh' condition was recovered from the upper fill (15751) of the east side. The primary fill of the east ditch (15758) contained bread wheat and barley grains.

No primary burial survived at the centre of this barrow; the inhumation found at the south-east corner was a secondary Anglian burial (15742).

Barrow 21

Summary

Barrow 21 lay to the west of Barrow 20; it was a square barrow, with rounded corners, measuring 4m across internally (Fig. 4.22). The ditch was excavated in eight

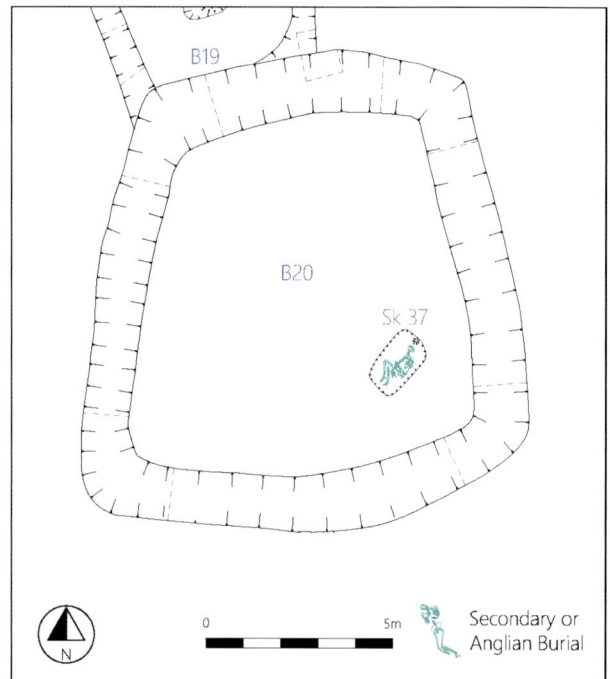

Figure 4.21 Plan of Barrow 20 and Skeleton 37 <15742>

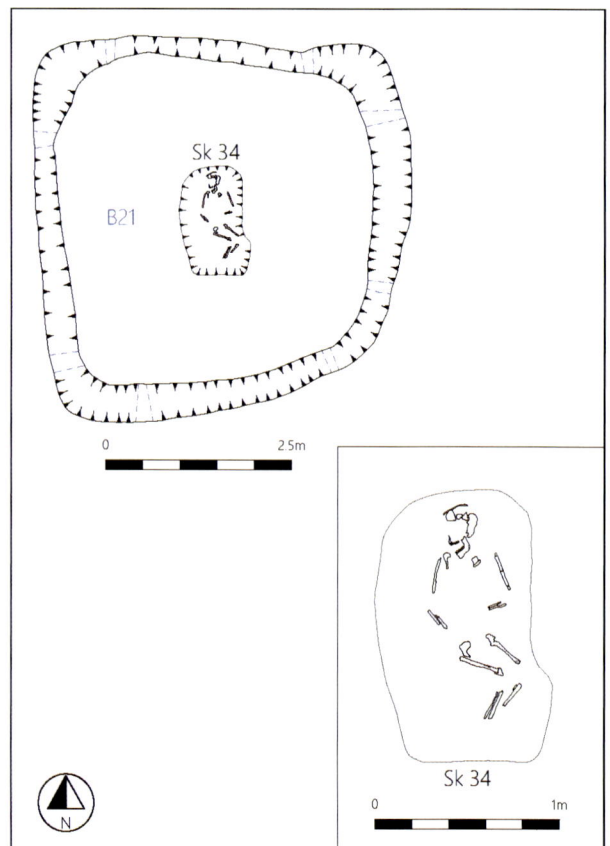

Figure 4.22 Plan of Barrow 21 and Skeleton 34 <15724>

segments (15673, 15671, 15669, 15667, 15681, 15679, 15677 and 15675) and had a U-shaped profile with a maximum width of 0.50m and depth of 0.15m. The single fill consisted of yellowish-brown sand with varying concentrations of chalk gravel.

Grave 15725

The shallow sub-rectangular central grave (15725) measured 1.52m in length, 0.84m in width and 0.15m in depth. An Iron Age sherd was recovered from the grave fill (15723).

Skeleton (15724 – Sk 34)

This was the very poorly preserved and severely fragmented skeleton of an unsexed individual aged 18–35 years, apparently prone and flexed, with the head to the north, facing west.

Barrow 22

Summary

Barrow 22, which slightly overlapped the southern ditch of Barrow 20, measured 3.0m from east to west and 3.5m from north to south internally (Fig. 4.23). Eight segments were excavated into the ditch (15703, 15705, 15708, 15691, 15695, 15697, 15699 and 15701), which proved to have a U-shaped profile with a maximum width of 0.45m and a depth of 0.15m. The ditch was filled with dark sandy silt with moderate chalk gravel.

Grave 15711

The moderately deep (0.36m) central rectangular grave (15711) measured 1.63m in length and 1.12m in width.

Skeleton (15710 – Sk 33)

An extremely poorly preserved and fragmented burial lay within a 'sub-cut' (15737) which indicated a structure had surrounded it. The skeleton was that of an adult of unknown sex, aged over 36 years; the head was to the south and what few bones survived suggested a crouched posture, possibly facing west.

Structure 15737

This structure was 1.30m long, 0.80m wide and 0.36m deep, with relatively straight sides but bowed ends. It was filled with gravel-rich silty sand (15709), and a darker silty sand with frequent gravel (15754) had been backfilled around it.

Barrow 23

Summary

Barrow 23 lay immediately south-east of Barrow 22 and was a putative square barrow (Fig. 4.24). Only the northern and western ditches survived, giving an internal measurement of at least 3m. The ditch was excavated in two segments (15798 and 15800) and was shown to have a variable shallow U or rounded-V profile that was 0.40m wide and 0.15m deep. A gravel primary fill was present at the north-west corner (15797), the remainder of the ditch fill consisting of darker, siltier material.

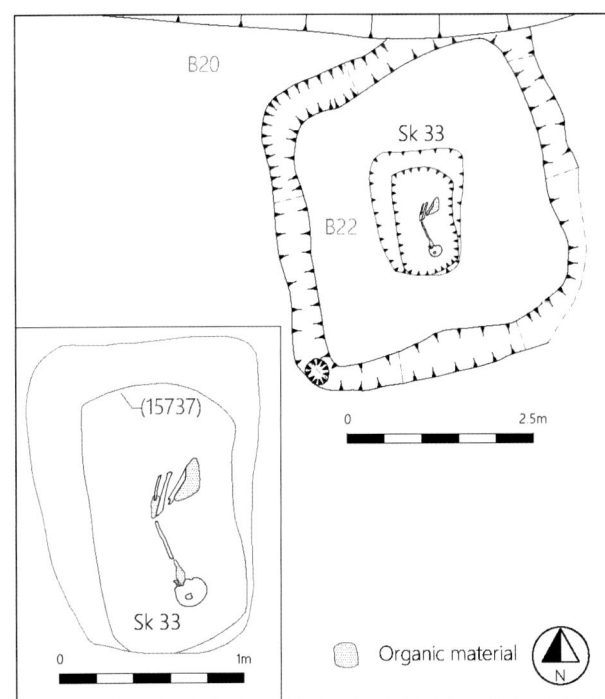

Figure 4.23 Plan of Barrow 22 and Skeleton 33 <15710>

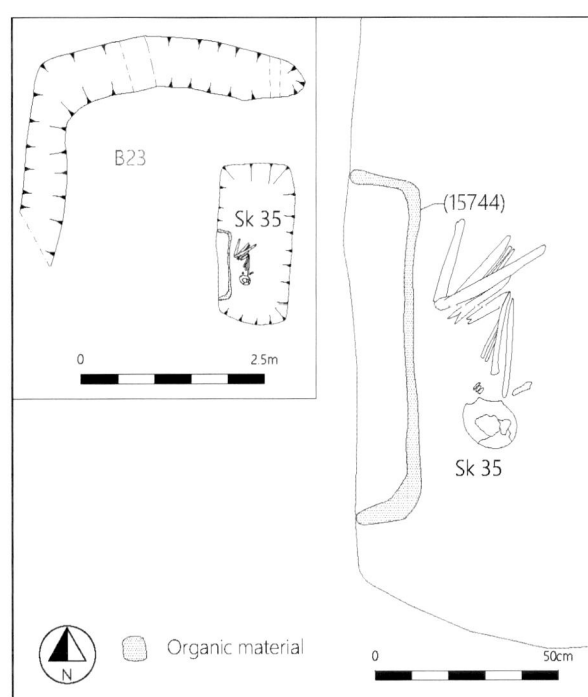

Figure 4.24 Plan of Barrow 23 and Skeleton 35 <15728>

Grave 15729

The rectangular central grave (15729) was relatively deep (0.50m) and was 2.10m long and 1.10m wide.

Skeleton (15728 – Sk 35)

The very poorly preserved and fragmented skeleton of an adult male, aged over 36 years, was laid on the left side, with the head to the south, facing west.

Structure 15744

A rectangular structure was identified along the western edge of the grave, showing as a distinct deposit of yellow-ish-brown gravel (15762) at the top of the grave, which extended downwards to the base where a C-shaped 'stain' of dark silt (15744) coincided with the base of 15762. This arrangement suggests the presence of a wooden box or compartment that was present for the full depth of the grave's western edge.

Barrow 24

Summary

This square barrow abutted the south-east corner of Barrow 20, but no physical relationship was recoverable. The barrow was rectangular and relatively small, measuring 3.4m from north to south and 2.6m from east to west internally (Fig. 4.25). The ditch was excavated

in four segments (15902, 15904, 15898 and 15900) and had a rounded-V profile, 0.70m wide and 0.17m deep. The ditch fill consisted of brown gravelly silt. A sherd of late Iron Age character was found in 15899 (fill of north-west corner ditch).

Grave 15847

The central grave (15847) was relatively large and deep, measuring 1.66m long, 1.04m wide and 0.60m deep.

Skeleton (15846 – Sk 43)

This was the very poorly preserved and extremely fragmented skeleton of an unsexed individual aged 26–35 years, lying in a crouched posture, on the left side, with the head to the south facing west. The skeleton was covered with an amorphous deposit of dark silt (15845) suggesting that organic material or an organic object had been placed over the body.

Barrow 25

Summary

This rectangular barrow was situated immediately east of Barrow 24 and measured internally 6m from east to west and 4m from north to south (Fig. 4.26). The ditch was excavated in six segments (15841, 15827, 15809, 15838, 15860 and 15865), and had a round-based V profile that varied along

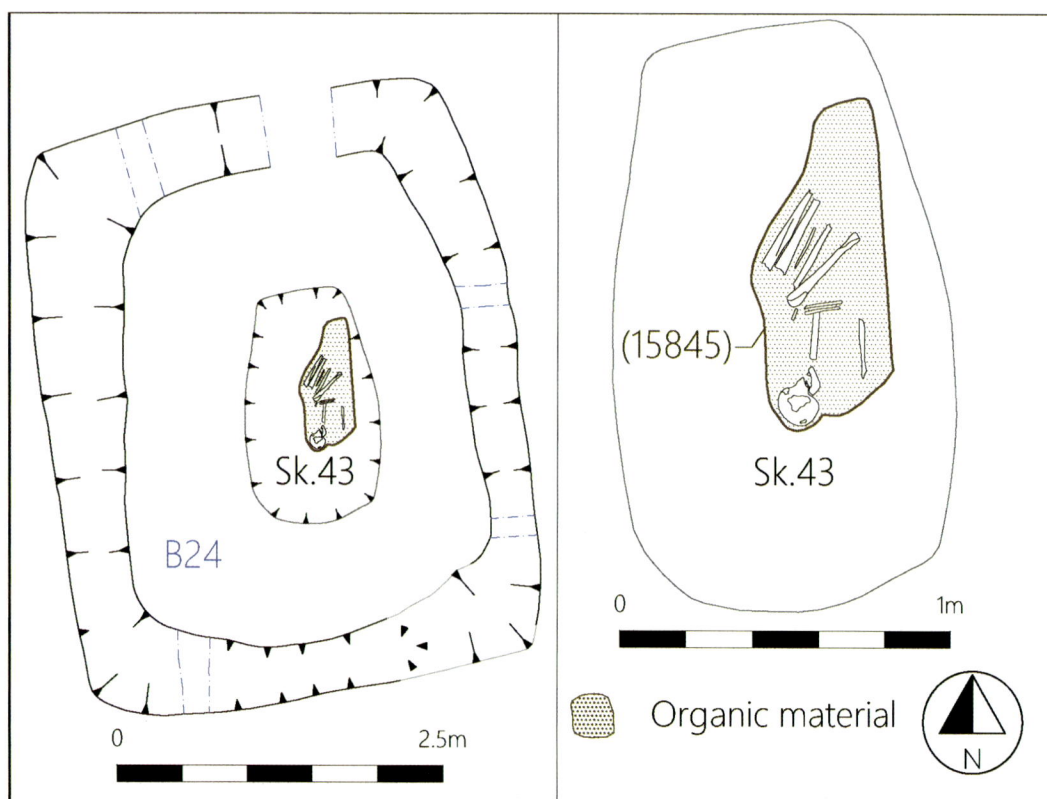

Figure 4.25 Plan of Barrow 24 and Skeleton 43 <15846>

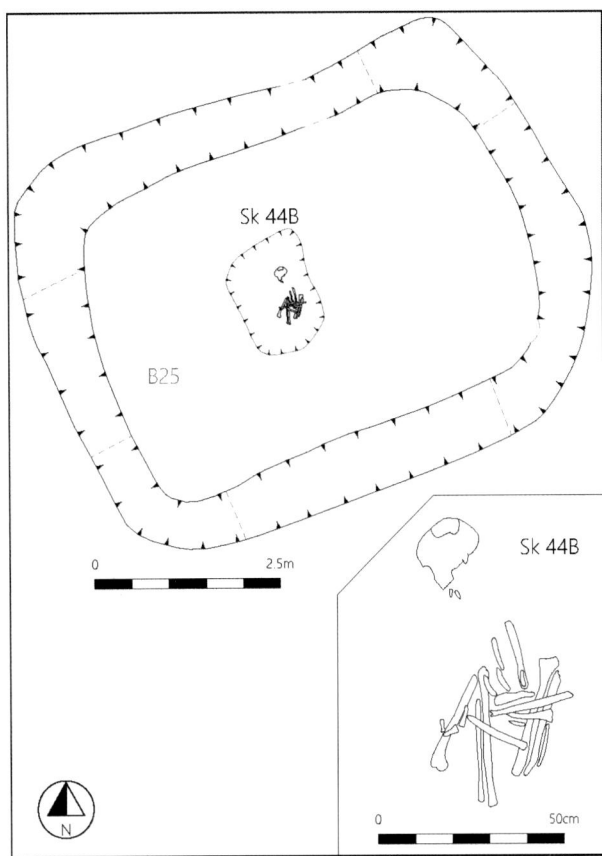

Figure 4.26 Plan of Barrow 25 and Skeleton 44B <15851>

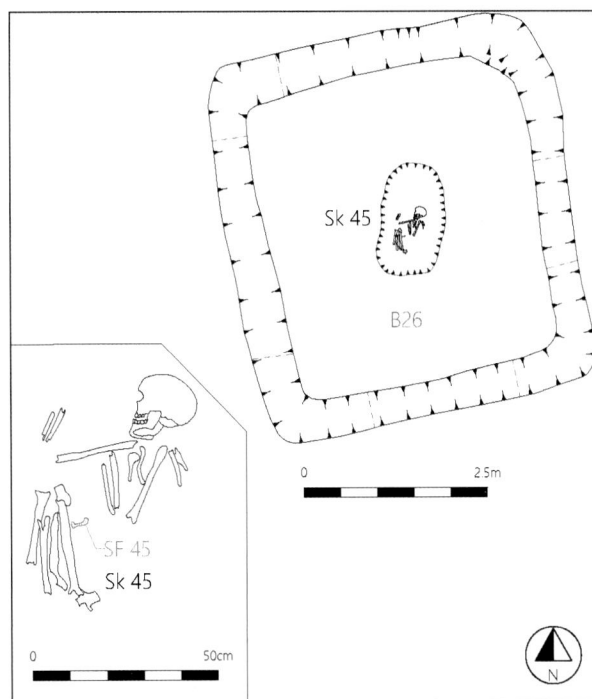

Figure 4.27 Plan of Barrow 26 and Skeleton 45 <15856>

its length; the maximum width was 0.95m, and depth 0.50m. It was filled with gravel at the base with brownish sandy silt towards the top. An Iron Age sherd was found in the top fill at the south-east corner (15807) and a Roman sherd was found near the top of the eastern ditch (15683).

Grave 15854

The central grave (15854) was an irregular rectangle in form, measuring 1.41m long and 1.12m wide, and 0.35m deep. The upper fill (15852) contained a late Neolithic/early Bronze Age 'fresh' flint flake.

Skeleton (15851 – Sk 44B)

This was the very poorly preserved and extremely fragmentary skeleton of a probable male aged over 36 years, crouched on the right side and with the head to the north, facing west. The partial remains of an adolescent *(Sk 44A)* were found at the top of the grave; this burial was dated to the Anglian period by the associated copper alloy buckle plate (SF 38).

Barrow 26

Summary

Barrow 26, which was situated close to the north-east corner of Barrow 20, was roughly square, measuring 4.1m from north to south and 3.7m from east to west

(Fig. 4.27). The ditch was excavated in eight segments (15872, 15882, 15880, 15878, 15876, 15872, 15869 and 15867) and had a U-shaped profile, approximately 0.50m wide and 0.15m deep. The homogeneous fill consisted of gravel-rich silty sand.

Grave 15857

The central grave (15857) was sub-rectangular and measured 1.48m in length, 0.89m in width and 0.29m in depth.

Skeleton (15856 – Sk 45)

The poorly preserved and severely fragmented skeleton of a probable male aged 18–25 years lay on the right side, with the head to the north, facing west. This individual suffered from maxillary sinusitis, CO and had slight pilasterism and bowing of the left humerus. The skeleton was radiocarbon-dated to the period 390–190 cal BC (SUERC-83076).

Grave goods

A Hull and Hawkes Type 2Ca iron involuted brooch decorated with small beads of red glass or stone (SF 45) was found in the midriff area and was of 3rd–2nd-century BC date.

Barrow 27

Summary

Barrow 27 was situated *c.* 10m south-east of Barrow 20. This was a relatively small rectangular barrow, 3.8m from to north to south, and 2.8m from east to

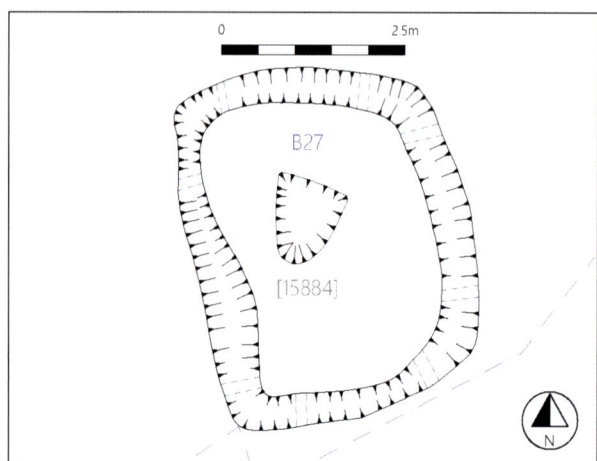

Figure 4.28 Plan of Barrow 27 and Grave 15884

west (Fig. 4.28). Eight segments (15890, 15934, 15937, 15940, 15943, 15946, 15949, and 15887) were excavated into the ditch. The ditch had a U-shaped profile that varied considerably along its course; the average width was around 0.50m and the depth was around 0.25m. There was a gravel-rich primary fill and a darker silt upper fill.

Possible grave 15884

The only possible indication of a grave was an irregular cut towards the north-west corner of the barrow; at only 1.05m long this was too small for an adult grave, and in any event no human remains were present within it.

Barrow 28

Summary

Barrow 28 was located immediately east of Barrow 27 and lay partly outside the excavated area. The barrow measured 6.0m from east to west and at least 3.2m from north to south (Fig. 4.29). The ditch was excavated in five segments (16047, 16050, 16053, 16041 and 16044), the profile varying from U-shaped to rounded-V, with a width of around 0.90m and a depth of between 0.35 and 0.45m. An Anglian grave (15862 – Sk 46) cut into the top of the central grave.

Grave 15910

The grave was steep-sided and rectangular, with a slightly bowed northern end; it measured 1.54m in length, 0.90m in width and 0.34m in depth.

Skeleton (15909 – Sk 48)

The very poorly preserved and extremely fragmented skeleton was that of an unsexed individual aged 18–25 years, lying in a crouched posture on the left side, with the head to the north, facing east.

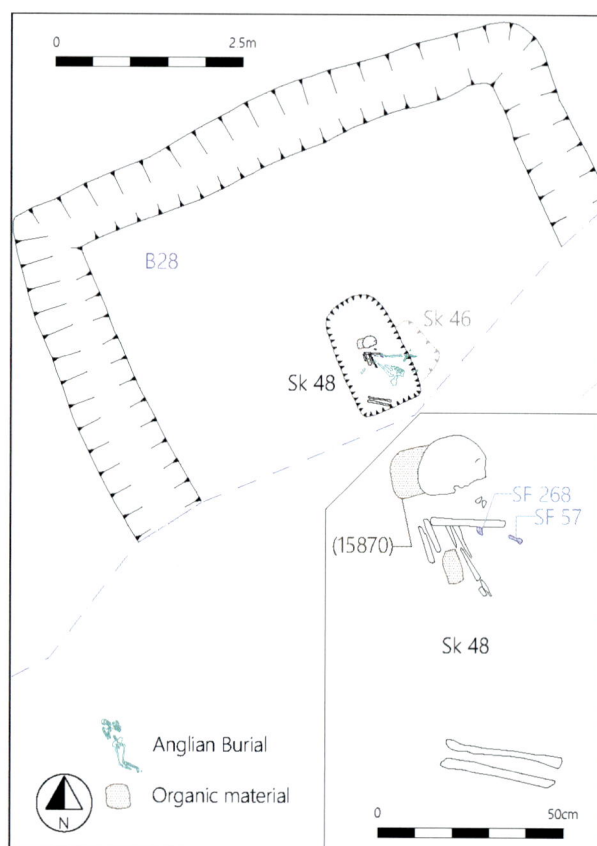

Figure 4.29 Plan of Barrow 28 and Skeleton 48 <15909>

Grave goods

A fragmentary iron bracelet (SFs 57 and 268) was found on the upper chest area.

Barrow 29

Summary

Barrow 29 was situated towards the north of the western barrow group between Barrows 8 and 16. This was a slightly irregular square barrow, 4.0m from north to south and 3.6m from east to west (Fig. 4.30). The ditch was excavated in eight segments (15916, 15918, 15920, 15922, 15924, 15926, 15912 and 15914), showing an irregular, generally U-shaped profile, around 0.70m wide and 0.30m deep. The single fill consisted of a gravel-rich brown silty sand. Medieval and post-medieval sherds were found in the fills of the western ditch (15911) and the north-west corner (15913).

Grave 15973

The central sub-rectangular grave measured 1.44m in length, 1.26m in width and 0.35m in depth.

Skeleton (15974 – Sk 54)

This was the moderately preserved but fragmented skeleton of a male aged 26–35 years, lying in a flexed and

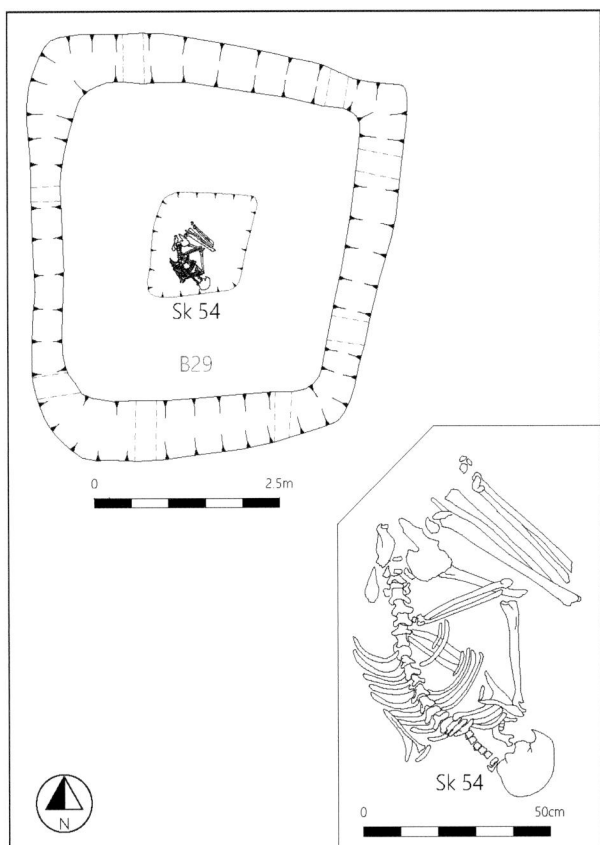

Figure 4.30 Plan of Barrow 29 and Skeleton 54 <15974>

prone posture, on the right side, with the head to the south, facing east. Endocranial and ectocranial porosities were present and both femora had marked pilasterism; the tibiae were both slightly bowed.

Barrow 30

Summary

This barrow and the following 14 barrows (Barrows 31–44) formed a discrete group at the central/northern part of the excavated area (Fig. 4.2). Barrow 30 had a sub-square form, measuring 5.0m from north to south and 5.5m east to west internally (Fig. 4.31). This barrow post-dated both Enclosure E and a sub-circular pit (16024, whose upper fill contained Iron Age sherds). The barrow ditch was excavated in eight segments (15981, 15984, 15987, 15990, 15993, 15996, 15999 and 15078) and had a rounded-V profile, between 0.60m and 1.10m wide, with an average depth of 0.35m. It had a primary fill of sandy gravel, with a darker silty sand above. The primary fill (15989) of the south-east corner contained two crumbs of Iron Age pottery. Eight Iron Age sherds, along with fragments of oak charcoal fuel waste, were found in the primary fill of the southern ditch (15992). The upper fill (15982) of the north-east corner contained alder charcoal.

Grave 16002

The central grave (16002) was rectangular, vertical-sided, flat-based, relatively deep (0.83m) and measured 1.96m

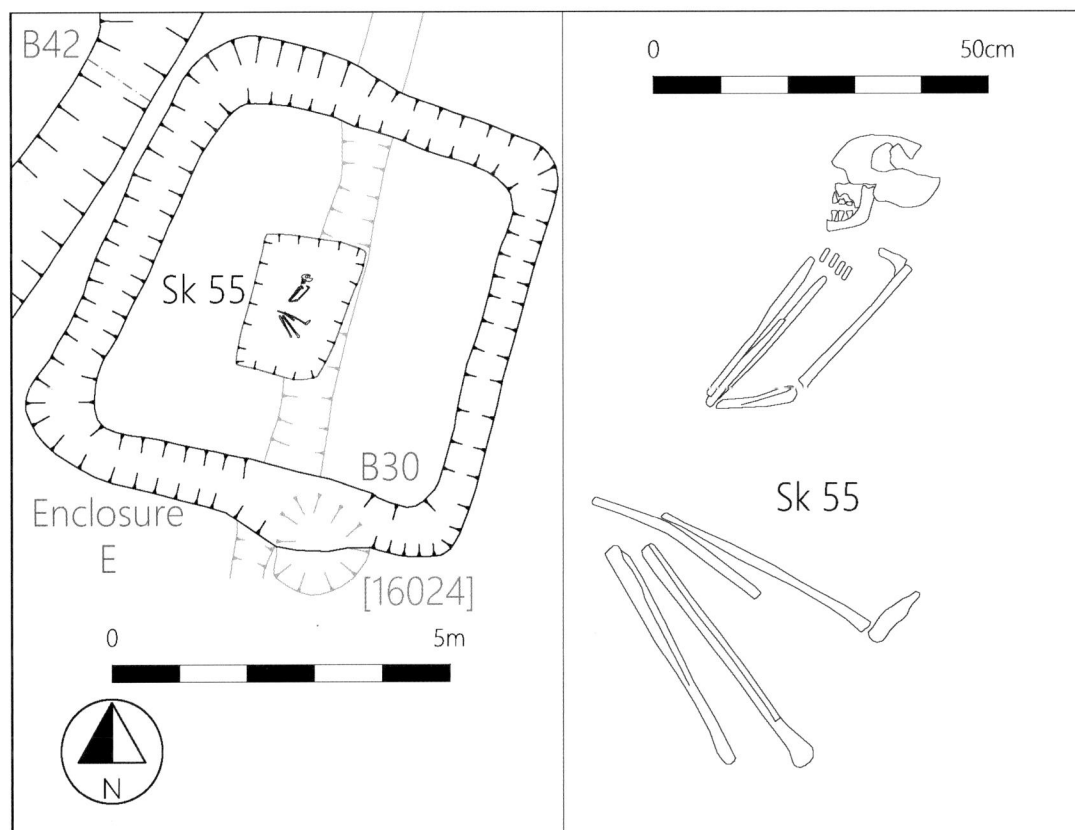

Figure 4.31 Plan of Barrow 30 and Skeleton 55 <16001>

by 1.70m in plan. The brown sandy silt fill (16000) contained 11 sherds from at least three different shapeless jars.

Skeleton (16001 – Sk 55)

The moderately preserved but severely fragmented skeleton was that of a female aged over 26 years, lying flexed on the right side, with the head to the north, facing west. CO and endocranial porosity were present.

Grave goods

A probable antler toggle (SF 74; Fig. 12.8) was found in the grave fill.

Organics

A keyhole-shaped deposit of dark silt (16114) covered the body apart from the head and neck, suggesting some form of organic covering; it contained four Iron Age sherds similar to those in the overall grave fill.

Barrow 31

Summary

Barrow 31 was situated *c.* 3m east of Barrow 30; it had a rounded-rectangular shape and was 4.0m in length from north to south and 3.1m in width from east to west (Fig. 4.32). The ditch was excavated in seven segments (16118, 16130, 16128, 16126, 16124, 16122 and 16120), showing it to have a broad-U profile *c.* 0.70m wide and 0.15m deep. The homogeneous single fill consisted of

brown silt and gravel. The fill of the western ditch (16121) contained a flint spall.

Grave 16034

The grave was slightly offset towards the north of the enclosed area, and was rectangular with steep sides, measuring 1.60m in length, 1.20m in width and 0.70m in depth.

Skeleton (16069 – Sk 58)

The skeleton was that of a female (sexed from DNA) adult aged over 36 years, lying in a crouched posture on the left side, with the head to the south and facing west. This individual had maxillary sinusitis. Two amorphous dark silt deposits (16032 and 16033) were recorded in the eastern side of the grave, partly overlying the body, and clearly represented decayed organic material. Fragmentary animal bone was recovered with the human skeleton.

Possible structure 16055

A regular line of dark silt (16053) at the northern end of the grave may have represented the remains of a structure.

Barrow 32

Summary

Barrow 32, which was situated *c.* 7m north-east of Barrow 31, was circular with an internal diameter of 4.4m (Fig. 4.33). The central grave cut an earlier, perhaps Beaker Period, pit (16164). The barrow ditch was

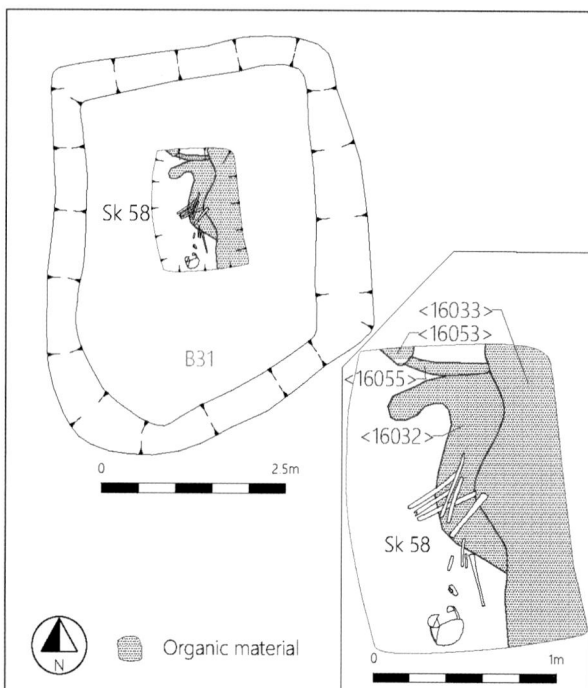

Figure 4.32 Plan of Barrow 31 and Skeleton 58 <16069>

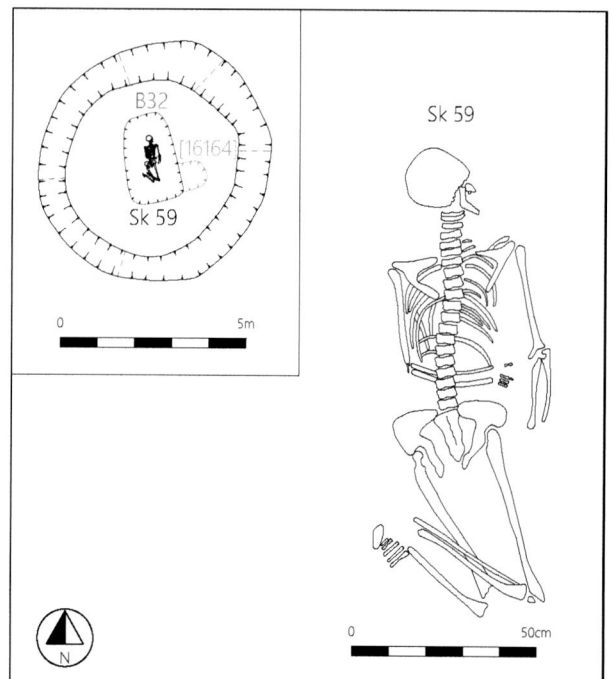

Figure 4.33 Plan of Barrow 32 and Skeleton 59 <16072>

excavated in four segments (16275, 16273, 16283 and 16281) and was cut away by a furrow on the southern side. The ditch had a variable broad-U profile, measuring from 0.80m to 1.25m in width, and between 0.25m and 0.30m in depth. Its fill consisted of an homogeneous gravel-rich soil, the fill at the south-west (16282) containing animal bone fragments.

Grave 16073

The central grave was rectangular and relatively large, measuring 2.18m from north to south, 1.38m from east to west and 0.64m deep. The dark grey 'organic' silt lower fill (16071) contained four small Iron Age sherds.

Skeleton (16072 – Sk 59)

The burial was that of a male aged 18–25 years, lying prone with the head to the north, facing east. The lower legs were bent backwards and upwards towards the pelvis and the left arm was folded under the torso. To describe this man as the victim of interpersonal violence hardly does justice to the pathology that he displayed. He had multiple peri-mortem trauma, consisting of blade injuries to the head, neck, left arm, lower right arm, right hand, spine, pelvis and left leg. The injuries to the head were delivered from above, possibly while the man was kneeling, while cuts to the left side and leg were delivered from below. The damage to the arms and hands represented defensive injuries, consistent with parrying blows from a bladed weapon. There was also massive blunt force

trauma to the left side of the face. On a more prosaic level, he had endocranial porosity and lamellar bone to the femora and left tibia.

Grave goods

A fragment of a curved iron-riveted strip (SF 75) was found near the feet of the burial. This object closely resembles the two strips forming the central spine of the shield in Barrow 37.

Barrow 33

Summary

Barrow 33 was located 13m to the west of Barrow 32 and was circular with an internal diameter of 4.2m (Figs 4.2 and 4.34). The ditch was excavated in four segments (16310, 16325, 16320 and 16317). The two western segments (16310 and 16317) had broad-V profiles that were around 1.00m wide and 0.35m deep. The two eastern segments (16325 and 16320) had variable flat-based V profiles of similar width to the other two but were generally deeper (up to 0.50m). The ditch had a gravel-rich primary fill with darker silt at the top. Iron Age sherds were found in the upper fills of the north-west and south-west ditches (16308 and 16315 respectively); 16308 also contained Roman pottery along with animal bone fragments and an undiagnostic slag fragment. Two graves were present within the area enclosed by the barrow ditch. The smaller of the two (16287 – Burial 16285, Sk 67) clearly pre-dated the presumed primary central grave (16019 – Burial 16018), and therefore appears to

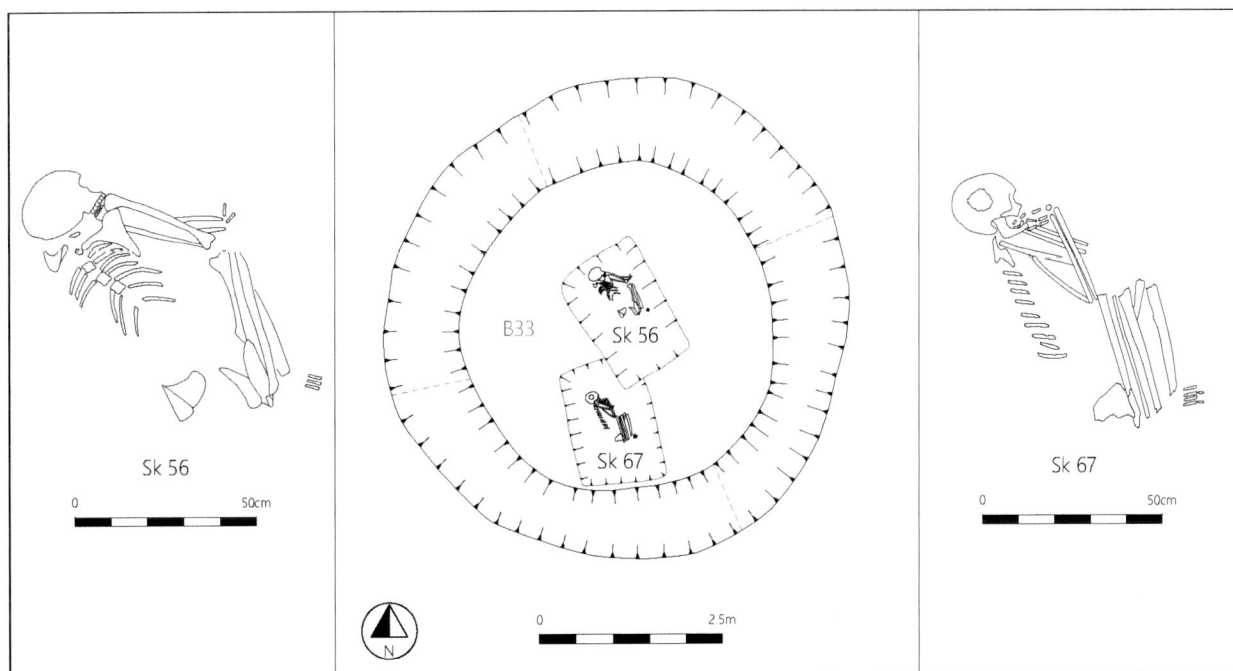

Figure 4.34 Plan of Barrow 33 and Skeletons 56 <16018> and 67 <16285>

have been an earlier flat grave (see section 4.2 below). The way in which the earlier grave sits between the barrow ditch and the central grave makes it possible that it was carefully incorporated into the area enclosed by the ditch with as little disturbance as possible.

Primary grave 16019

Grave 16019 was a relatively large rectangular cut, measuring 1.85m from north to south, 1.20m from east to west, and around 0.80m deep. The grave fill (16017) contained six Iron Age sherds and an iron involuted brooch (SF 66 – Hull and Hawkes Type 2AB) of middle Iron Age (probably 3rd century BC) date. The brooch was not directly associated with the burial but was found *c.* 0.40m above it.

Skeleton (16018 – Sk 56)

This was the moderately preserved but severely fragmented skeleton of a male aged 26–35 years, laid in a part crouched and part prone posture, face downwards, with the limbs tucked under the torso, and the head to the north facing slightly east. He had a fracture of the left clavicle and maxillary sinusitis and CO. A deposit of grey silt (16062) situated around the pelvis and lower back was probably associated with the decomposition of the body, or perhaps an indication that organic material was buried with it. This man was the 2nd- or 3rd-degree

relative of the man buried with a shield in B37 (Patterson *et al.* 2022).

Barrow 34

Summary

Barrow 34 was situated to the north-west of Barrow 33 and cut into Barrow 36 on the eastern side. The barrow was sub-circular, measuring 4.70m north to south and 4.20m east to west internally (Fig. 4.35). Four ditch segments were excavated (16136, 16132, 16144 and 16138), showing a U-shaped profile around 1.10m wide and 0.30m deep. The ditch fill consisted of a brown sandy silt which contained animal bone fragments on the north-west and south-west sides (16137 and 16143); 16143 also contained an Iron Age sherd and a late Neolithic/early Bronze Age flint scraper in 'fresh' condition.

A total of four isolated/secondary burials surrounded the barrow: (16165, Sk 64) was cut into the barrow's western ditch (see below) and three flat burials (16289, Sk 68; 16306, Sk 70; and 16334, Sk 71) were situated on the left side of the barrow (see below), perhaps in reverence to the primary burial.

Grave 16029

The rectangular central grave was 2.20m long, 1.40m wide and 0.50m deep.

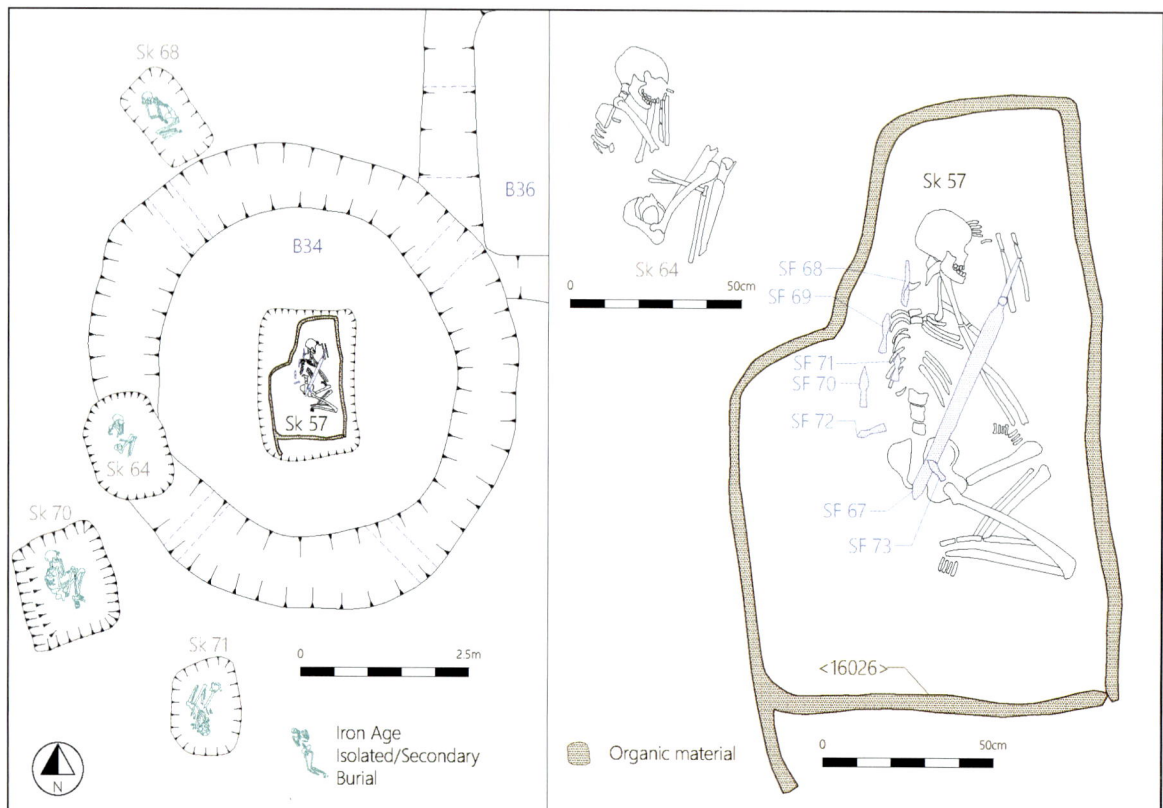

Figure 4.35 Plan of Barrow 34 and Skeletons 57 <16027> and 64 <16165>

Skeleton (16027 – Sk 57)

This was the poorly preserved and severely fragmentary skeleton of a male (from DNA) aged 18–25 years, laid on the left side, with the head to the north, facing east. There was lamellar bone on the right tibia. He was a 2nd- or 3rd-degree relative to the male primary burial (16109, Sk 61) of B35 and, on a different line, a 2nd- or 3rd-degree relative of an adult female (16166, Sk 65; see Fig. 4.96) buried in a flat grave on the east of the barrow group (Patterson *et al.* 2022).

Grave goods

The primary burial (16027) was accompanied by an exceptional suite of grave goods (Figs 4.35 and 4.36). An iron sword in a wooden scabbard and with horn grips (SF 67) lay across the torso, extending upwards over the left lower arm. A group of five iron spearheads were positioned along to the corpse's back; four (SFs 68–71) parallel to the spine and the other (SF 72) at the lower back, at right angles to it. Mineralised wood remains were found within the sockets of all the spears, with ash identified within spearhead SF 70. The presence of this wood implies that the spearheads were snapped off from the shafts as the grave would not have accommodated the full length of the spear shafts (see Chapter 19 for discussion of speared burials). An iron ferrule (SF 73), also with mineralised wood in the socket, lay on the tip of the sword, in the area of the pelvis.

Structure 16026

The primary grave contained the traces of a rectangular structure (16026) that had two transverse 'spars' (16035) extending part way across it. The pattern of the soil stain suggested that the north-west corner and southern side had collapsed. The structure measured 1.80m in length and 1.20m in width and was *c.* 0.20m high. The surrounding fill (16025) contained a residual flint flake.

Secondary burial

An oval secondary grave (16142), 1.55m long, 1.15m wide and *c.* 0.40m deep, was cut into the western ditch of Barrow 34. The very poorly preserved and severely fragmented skeleton *(16165 – Sk 64)* was of a probable female aged over 46 years, crouched and lying on the left side, with the head to the north and facing east. Her spine showed DDD, DJC and OA.

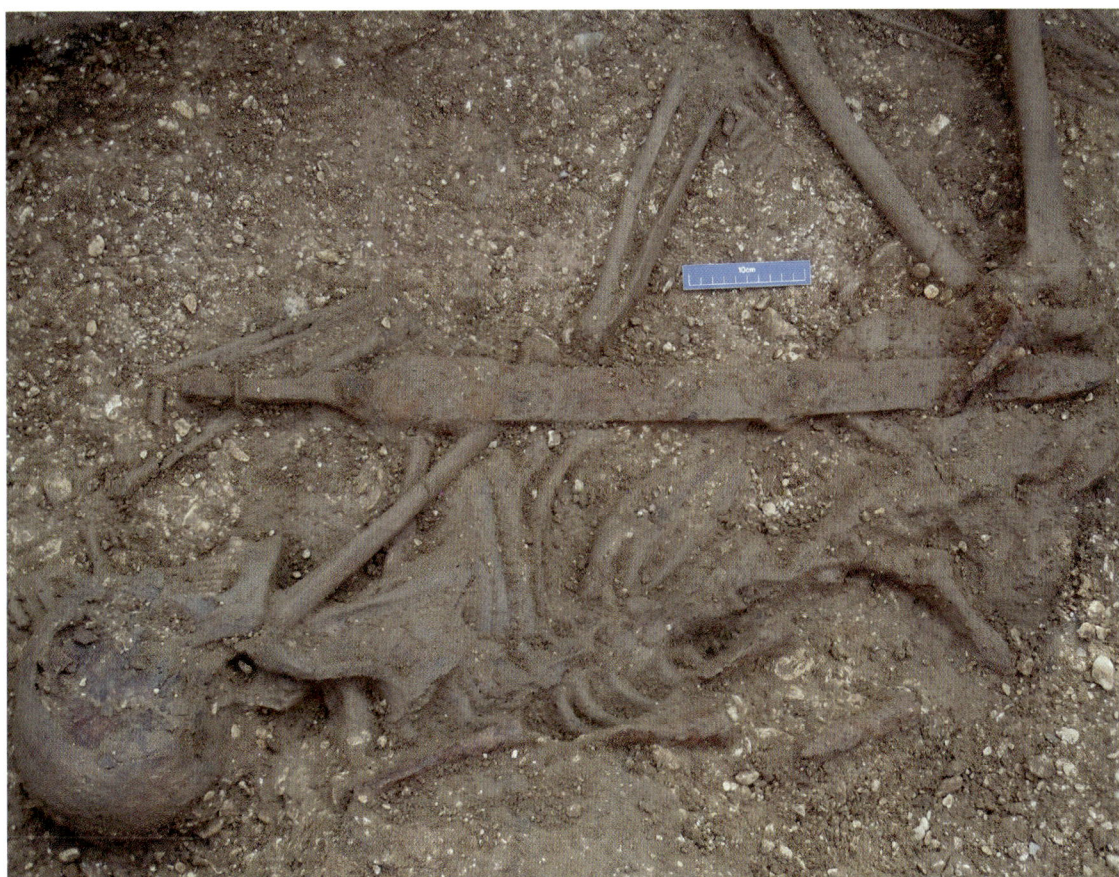

Figure 4.36 View of Skeleton 57 <16027> (facing east), showing SFs 67–73. 10cm scale

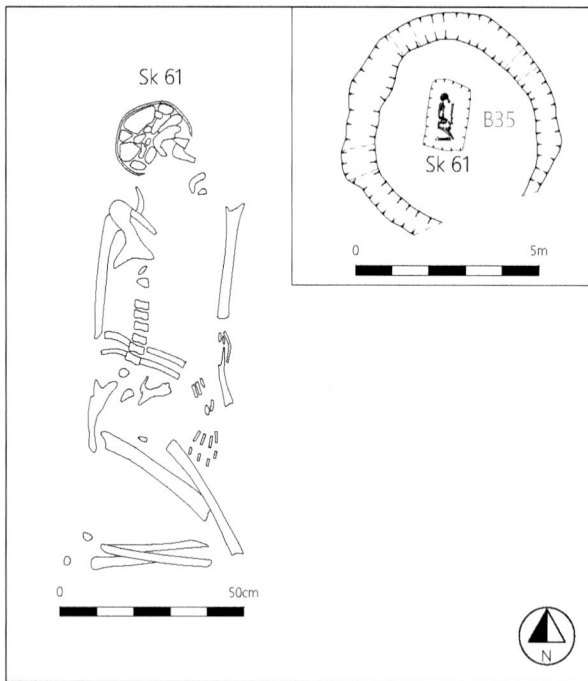

Figure 4.37 Plan of Barrow 35 and Skeleton 61 <16109>

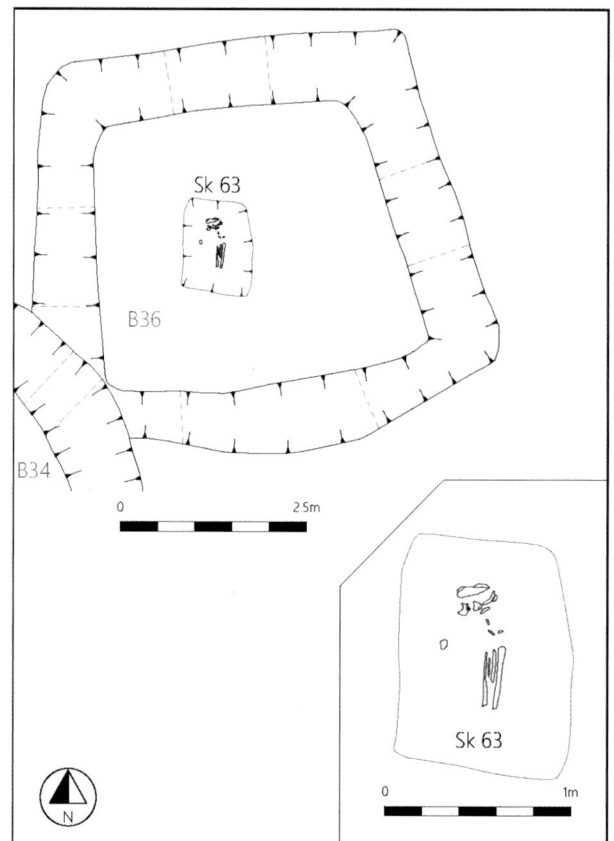

Figure 4.38 Plan of Barrow 36 and Skeleton 63 <16159>

Barrow 35

Summary

This was another circular barrow, located to the south of Barrow 32, with an internal diameter of 4.2m (Fig. 4.37). A later furrow (16016) truncated the southern part of the barrow. The ditch was excavated in three segments (16067, 16063 and 16065) and had a rounded-V profile, *c.* 0.80m wide and 0.20m deep. The fill consisted of homogeneous greyish-brown silty sand with gravel, the fill of the north-east quadrant (16068) containing an Iron Age sherd.

Grave 16110

The central grave was rectangular and measured 1.64m from north to south, 1.10m from east to west, and was around 0.35m deep.

Skeleton (16109 – Sk 61)

The poorly preserved and extremely fragmented skeleton was that of a male (from DNA), over 26 years of age, placed prone in a flexed posture, with the head to the north, facing east. There was pilasterism to both femora, along with lamellar bone on the left tibia. He was a 2nd- or 3rd-degree relative to the female primary burial of B38 and the male primary burial of B34 (Patterson *et al.* 2022).

Barrow 36

Summary

Barrow 36 was situated on the north-east side of Barrow 34 and was the earlier of the two. The barrow was slightly trapezoidal in plan and measured 3.7m from north to

south and 4.1m from east to west internally (Fig. 4.38). Eight segments were excavated (16075, 16089, 16087, 16085, 16083, 16081, 16079 and 16077). The ditch had a trough-shaped profile, *c.* 0.90m in width and 0.15m in depth, and was filled with gravel-rich silt. The fills of the north-west corner ditch (16076) and the southern ditch (16082) contained Iron Age sherds.

Grave 16160

The rectangular central grave was very shallow and accordingly, the skeleton (16159 – Sk 63) that it contained was in very poor condition. The grave was 1.25m long, 0.90m wide and 0.08m deep.

Skeleton (16159 – Sk 63)

This very poorly preserved and extremely fragmented skeleton was of a female (from DNA) over 18 years in age, laid with the head to the north, the rest of the posture being unclear. The skeleton was radiocarbon-dated to 180 cal BC–cal AD 10 (SUERC-78041).

Barrow 37

Summary

Barrow 37 was situated between Barrows 32 and 33 and was later than Enclosure E on the north-west side and a group of three pits on its south-east side (16542, 16544

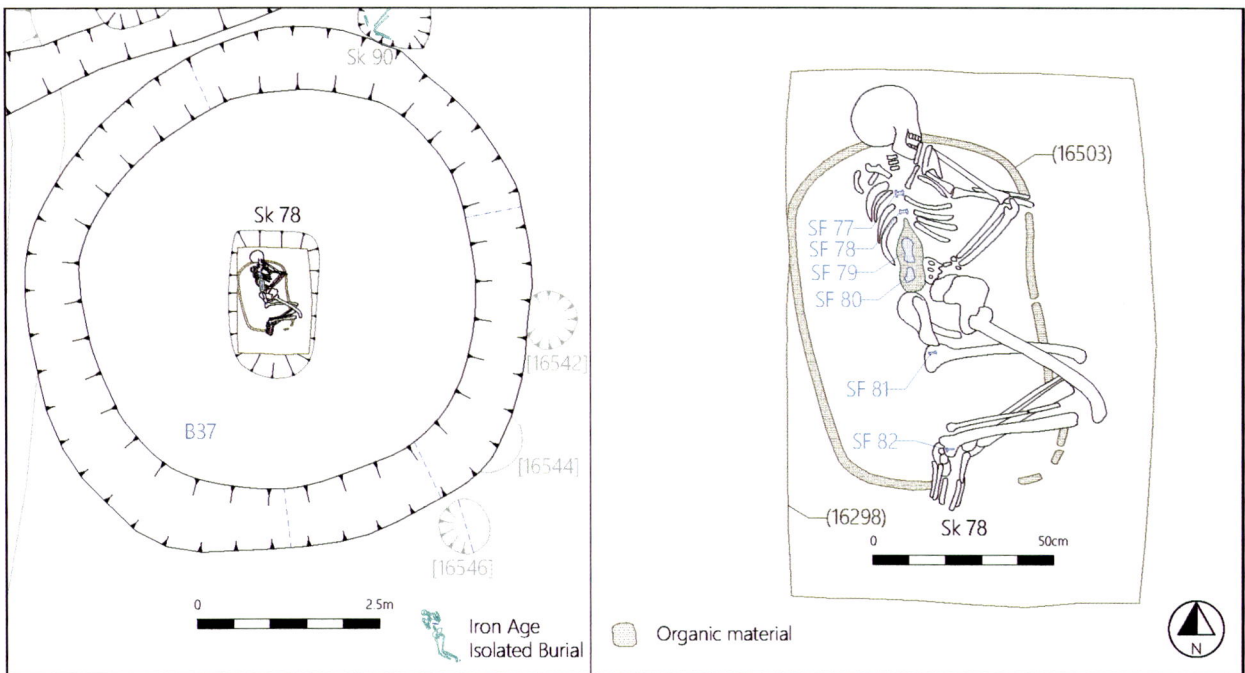

Figure 4.39 Plan of Barrow 37 and Skeleton 78 <16370>

and 16546 – the fill of 16542 [16541] containing Iron Age sherds) (Figs 3.1 and 4.2). The barrow was sub-circular in plan with an internal diameter of 5.2m (Fig. 4.39). Four segments were excavated (16478, 16481, 16484 and 16271), showing that the ditch had a rounded-V profile around 0.80m wide and 0.20m deep. There was a gravelly primary fill, with darker silt at the top. The upper fill on the south-west side (16482) contained animal bone fragments, while the primary fill (16485) contained four calcite-gritted sherds.

Grave 16300

The central grave, which was rectangular with a bowed southern side, measured 2.00m in length from north to south, 1.35m in width from east to west, and was *c.* 0.40m deep. The burial was covered with a deposit of dark silt (16563). Mixed gravel fills (16297–9) were present above the burial; 16297 contained two Iron Age sherds. Further mixed gravel deposits (16321, 16322 and 16497) surrounded the structure. This was another exceptional grave that contained evidence for a structure within it as well as having remarkable grave goods.

Skeleton (16370 – Sk 78)

This was the moderately preserved, severely frag-mented skeleton of an adult male, over 36 years of age, in a flexed posture, lying on the left side with the head to the north, facing east (Fig. 4.40). It appears the iron spine of a composite shield was placed over the body. He was a 2nd- or 3rd-degree relative of the male

primary burial of B33 (Patterson *et al.* 2022). There was evidence of CO.

Structure 16298

The structure was rectangular in form, *c.* 1.60m long and 1.20m wide. Thin bands of dark silt represented the sides of the structure; the eastern side was recorded as 16498, the southern as 16499, the western as 16500 and the northern as 16501. Another thin band of dark silt (16502) ran parallel and interior to the north side and demarcated a band of distinct gravel-rich pale silt (16322); this had a counterpart (16321) along the southern edge of the structure. Deposits 16321 and 16322 possibly represented bracing bars at the ends of the structure, or perhaps parts of a lid. Two Iron Age sherds were recovered from the overall fill of the structure.

Grave goods

The remains of a shield were found at the base of the grave and within the structure, consisting of a narrow band of dark silt (16503) forming a continuous rounded rectangle measuring *c.* 1.00m long and 0.70m wide. The metal elements of the shield (see Chapter 9) were represented by a line of metal objects that lay centrally through the area defined by the silt band 16503, from north to south: SF 77 (copper alloy rivet), SF 78 (copper alloy rivet), SFs 79–80 (parts of same 'spoon-shaped' iron object – the 'boss' and spine of the shield), SF 81 (copper alloy rivet) and SF 82 (copper alloy rivet).The soil stain (16503) represented the edge of the shield,

Figure 4.40 View of Skeleton 78 <16370> and shield, facing N. Scales: 1.5m and 1m

and since it ran *under* the upper legs of the skeleton, the shield must have been dismantled. The copper alloy rivets presumably originally attached the spine to the shield backing. An oval patch of dark silt (16563) lay under the metal parts of the shield 'boss', indicating that organic material had been attached to it.

Barrow 38

Summary

Barrow 38 was the latest in a sequence of three barrows situated in the northern part of the eastern barrow group (Fig. 4.2). A total of five secondary graves were associated with this barrow. Barrow 38 cut into the south-west corner of Barrow 39 and across the top of Enclosure E. It was a regular square barrow, with an internal width of 4.5m

(Fig. 4.41). The ditch was excavated in eight segments (16170, 16173, 16176, 16179, 16182, 16185, 16188 and 16191) and had a rounded-V profile, around 0.65m wide and 0.30m deep. The fills consisted of gravel at the base with darker silt at the top. The primary fill of the south-east corner (16178) contained five sherds from the same thin-walled vessel. A probably intrusive rye grain was found in the primary fill of the western ditch (16187), and a bread wheat grain in the primary fill of the south-east corner (16178).

Grave 16195

The primary grave was slightly off-centre in the southern half of the enclosed area and was a rectangular cut with vertical edges and a flat base, measuring 1.90m long,

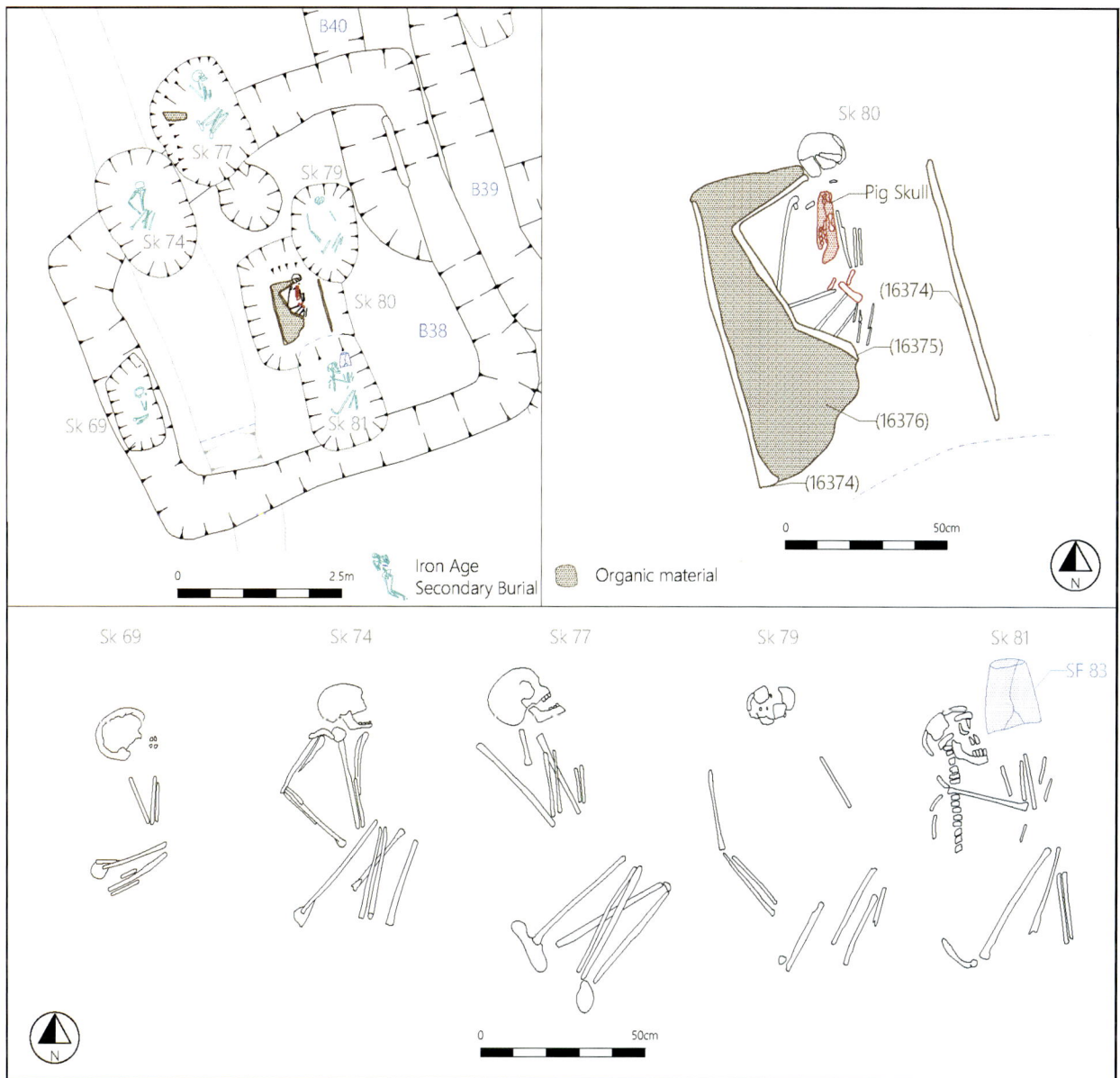

Figure 4.41 Plan of Barrow 38, Skeleton 80 <16373> and secondary burials

1.50m wide and 0.65m deep. The upper fill (16194) of the grave contained a late Mesolithic/early Neolithic edge-utilised bladelet.

Skeleton (16373 – Sk 80)

The poorly preserved and severely fragmented skeleton of an adult, probably female, aged over 18 years, was situated centrally within the structure described below, lying crouched on the left side with the head to the north, facing east. This woman showed evidence of CO and endocranial new bone, as well as DJC in the spine. Two small and distinct circular areas of dark silt (16377) were present at the rear of the skull, and an L-shaped band of dark similar material (16375) was traced on the left side of the burial. The area between the western edge of structure 16374 and deposit 16375 was occupied by a deposit of dark sandy silt (16376), perhaps indicating that organic material had been laid there.

Grave goods

The left forelimb and left side of the skull of a juvenile pig rested on the upper side of the burial's torso (see Chapter 14). This was the only clear instance of a 'food offering' of high-value meat within this Iron Age cemetery.

Structure 16374

The remains of a structure were recorded within the grave, consisting of two parallel lines of dark silt, perpendicular to the grave's longest sides (16374). The structure's north and south sides were unclear, but it was at least 0.90m long and 0.70m wide. The structure was covered by a deposit of dark 'organic' silt (16372).

Secondary graves in Barrow 38

Five secondary graves were associated with Barrow 38 (16193, 16197, 16295, 16327 and 16329) (Fig. 4.41).

Grave 16193 was rectangular and measured 1.65m in length, 1.25m in width and 0.84m in depth; it cut both the primary grave and the barrow's southern ditch. The north–south-aligned crouched burial *(16403 – Sk 81)* consisted of the moderately preserved but fragmented skeleton of a female aged 26–35 years, lying on the left side, with the head to the north, facing east. She had endocranial porosity and CO, along with lamellar bone on the right tibia. A complete, although crushed, wide-mouthed jar (SF 83, Fig. 12.1) lay in front of the skull in the north-east part of the grave. The skeleton was radiocarbon-dated to the period 360–110 cal BC (SUERC-78042).

Grave 16197, which cut into the north-eastern part of the primary grave, was sub-rectangular, measuring 1.26m in length and 0.94m in width, with a depth of 0.82m. The moderately preserved and fragmented burial *(16371 – Sk 79)* was an adult probable female aged over 26 years, aligned north to south in a crouched posture, lying on the left side, with the head to the north, facing east. This woman also had CO and endocranial porosity.

Grave 16295 cut the western barrow ditch and was a 1.42m long and 1.00m deep, relatively narrow (0.90m) feature containing the flexed skeleton *(16294 – Sk 69)* of a young juvenile aged 4–6 years, lying on the left side, with the head to the north, facing east.

Grave 16327 cut into the north ditch of the barrow and was an oval cut with a length of 2.00m, a width of 1.30m and a depth of 0.60m. The grave contained the north–south-aligned crouched skeleton *(16358 – Sk 74)* of a probable female, over 36 years old, lying on the left side, with the head to the north, facing east. She had CO.

Grave 16329 was immediately to the east of Grave 16327 and cut the barrow ditch; it measured 1.42m in length, 0.90m in width and 0.52m in depth. It contained the north–south-aligned crouched skeleton of a probable male over 36 years old *(16366 – Sk 77)*, lying on the left side, with the head to the north, facing east. This individual had DJC to the left temporo-mandibular joint and pilasterism of the femora. Two dark silt deposits were recorded at the base of the grave: 16368 was probably the stain left by the decay of the spine, but 16369 – a distinct rectangular patch in the north-western part of the grave – probably indicated the decay of an organic object.

Barrow 39

Summary

This barrow lay in the centre of the sequence of the three barrows, being earlier than Barrow 38, but later than Barrow 40. Barrow 39 lay immediately east of Barrow 38, but on a markedly different alignment. This was a regular square barrow, 6m across internally (Fig. 4.42). The ditch was excavated in eight segments (16200, 16203, 16206, 16209, 16212, 16215, 16218 and 16221), showing it to have a variable profile (from U-shaped to rounded-V), *c.* 1.00m wide and 0.30m deep. There was a gravelly basal fill with darker, siltier material towards the top. Finds were limited to a piece of possible smithing hearth bottom fragment (16201, the top fill of the north-east corner) and a piece of animal bone (16207 – the top fill of the south-east corner).

Grave/burial

No grave or burial survived.

Barrow 40

Summary

This was the earliest in the sequence of three barrows and was overlain by Barrows 38 and 39. It was roughly square in plan but with a bowed northern ditch, measuring 5.4m from north to south and 4.7m from east to west (Fig. 4.42). The ditch was excavated in eight segments (16224, 16227, 16230, 16233, 16236, 16239, 16242 and 16245) and its profile varied widely along its length, from rounded-V to broad-U. The width varied from 0.75m to 1.15m, and the depth from 0.27m to 0.40m. The fills of this barrow ditch were different from the norm, with most segments showing a predominant gravel fill and a relatively shallow dark silt fill at the top.

Grave 16247

The shallow, amorphous, primary grave was situated slightly to the north of the barrow's centre and was truncated on its north-west side by the north-west corner of Barrow 39. It measured 2.15m in length, 1.10m in width and 0.10m in depth. The fill (16246) contained an intrusive medieval sherd and part of an iron nail (SF 87), which was also presumably intrusive.

Skeleton 16493 – Sk 89

The very poorly preserved and severely fragmented skeleton was that of an adult female (from DNA), apparently crouched and with the head to the north. The skeleton was radiocarbon-dated to the period 720–390 cal BC (SUERC-78046).

Possible structure

Two thin lines of dark 'organic' silt (16494) immediately west and north of the burial may have been the remains of two sides of a structure.

Barrow 41

Summary

Barrow 41 was situated *c.* 8m north-east of Barrow 35. It consisted of a short stretch of a curving shallow ditch that partly enclosed a grave; this probably represented the remains of a circular barrow that had been truncated by a furrow (Fig. 4.43). The ditch was excavated in a single segment (cut 16292, fill 16291), showing a shallow-U profile filled with gravel-rich silty sand.

Grave 16279

The rounded-rectangular grave was relatively deep (0.50m) and measured 1.52m in length and 1.39m in width. The grave fill (16277) contained fragments of oak charcoal fuel waste.

Skeleton (16278 – Sk 66)

This was the poorly preserved and extremely fragmented skeleton of a female (from DNA), probably 26–35 years old, aligned east to west, lying on the left side with the head to the east, facing south. She had CO and lamellar bone to both legs.

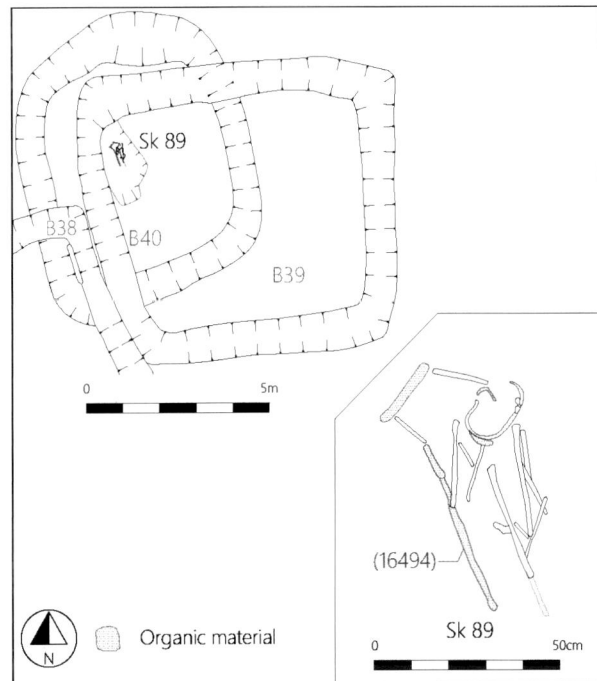

Figure 4.42 Plan of Barrows 39 and 40 and Skeleton 89 <16493>

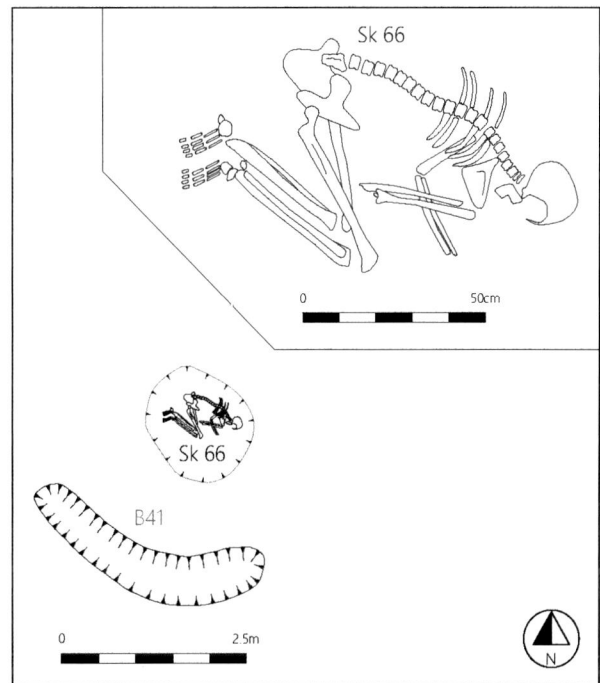

Figure 4.43 Plan of Barrow 41 and Skeleton 66 <16278>

Barrow 42

Summary

This was a large, regular square barrow that lay at the western edge of the eastern barrow group, measuring 7.5m across internally (Figs 4.2 and 4.44). The western ditch was affected by the insertion of a modern drain, so the ditch was dug in seven segments (16426, 16429, 16432, 16435, 16438, 16420 and 16423). The ditch was *c.* 1.30m wide and varied between 0.30m and 0.50m in depth, with a rounded-V profile. The primary fill was predominantly of gravel, with darker sandy silt towards the top. Primary fills 16422 (north-west corner), 16425 (north ditch), 16431 (east ditch) and 16437 (south ditch) all contained Iron Age sherds; 16431 additionally contained a fragment of possible smithing hearth bottom. Lithic finds consisted of two flint spalls from 16431, and another spall and two residual flint flakes from 16434 (the primary fill of the south-east corner). Context 16422 also contained a piece of undiagnostic burnt clay. Fragments of oak charcoal fuel waste were found in the primary fill of the southern ditch (16437), and a grain of bread wheat came from the primary fill of the north-east corner (16428).

Grave 16444

The central grave was almost square in plan, measuring *c.* 1.90m across; despite its large size it was relatively shallow (0.26m).

Skeleton (16443 – Sk 82)

This was the poorly preserved and severely fragmented crouched skeleton (16443 – Sk 82) of a possible female aged over 26 years, lying on the left side, with the head to the north, facing east. She had DJC in both temporo-mandibular joints, plus endocranial porosity and lamellar bone. This woman was the sister of the man buried centrally in B43 (Patterson *et al.* 2022). The skeleton was radiocarbon-dated to the period 350–50 cal BC (SUERC-83077).

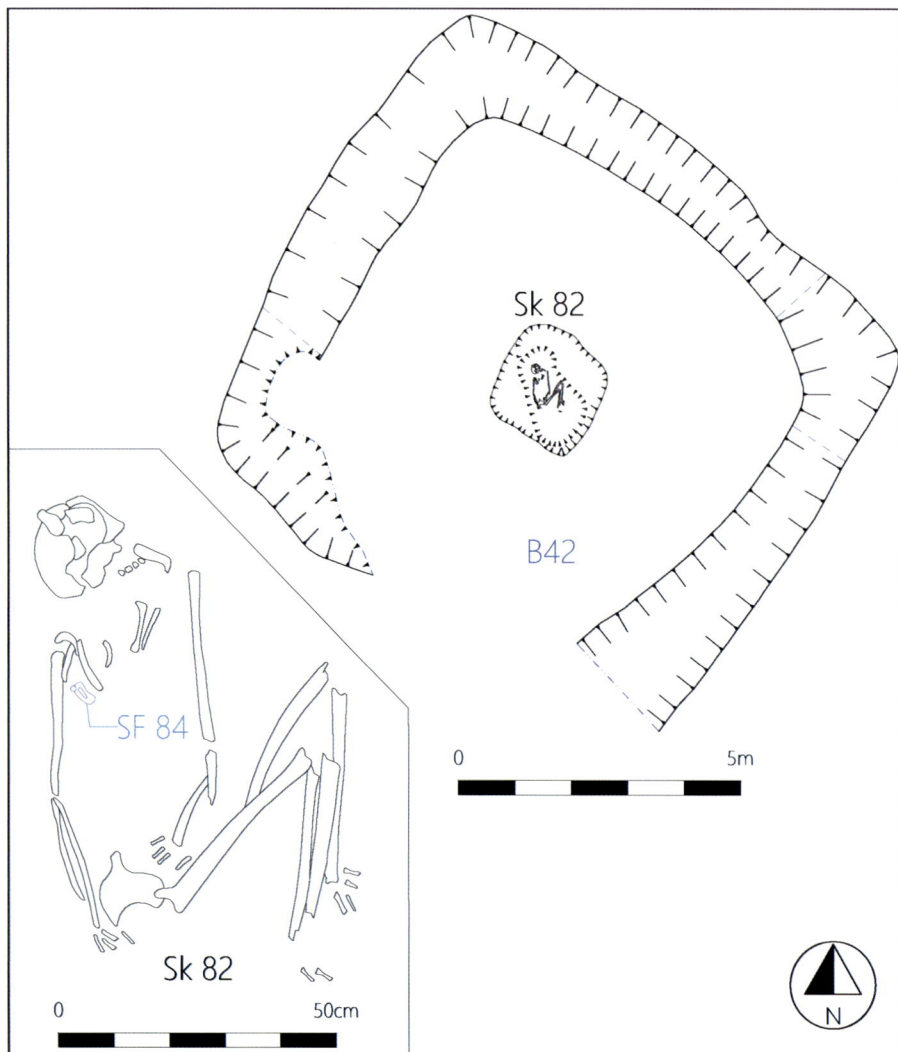

Sk 82

B42

Sk 82

0   50cm

0   5m

N

Figure 4.44 Plan of Barrow 42 and Skeleton 82 <16443>

Grave goods

A copper alloy bow brooch (SF 84, Fig. 11.5) of Hull and Hawkes Type 6, decorated with coral beads at the top and base, was found near the burial's right shoulder. It is probably of 1st-century BC date.

Possible structure

A sub-rectangular sub-cut (16455) lay diagonally across the grave, apparently representing the outline of a structure measuring 1.60m in length, 0.66–0.99m in width and 0.42m in depth. There were no soil stains to indicate organic remains. The fill of the structure (16452) contained four calcite-gritted Iron Age sherds and fragments of oak charcoal fuel waste.

Barrow 43

Summary

Barrow 43 was the latest of two square barrows that overlapped at the eastern edge of the eastern barrow group (the earlier barrow being Barrow 44) (Fig. 4.2). This was a relatively large barrow, measuring 6.3m from north to south and 6.7m from east to west (Fig. 4.45). Eight segments were excavated into the ditch (16383, 16386, 16389, 16392, 16395, 16398, 16401 and 16380), which averaged around 1.00m in width and 0.35m in depth, with a rounded-V profile. The fills were uniform throughout the ditch, with a sandy gravel primary fill and a darker silty sand above. Finds from the ditch were as follows: 16381 (top fill north side) an undated flint graver or burin in fresh condition; 16387 (top fill east side) animal bone fragments, a piece of smithing hearth bottom and an Iron Age pottery sherd; 16394 (primary fill south side) Iron Age pottery sherd; 16399 (top fill west side) animal bone fragment.

Graves

The ditch enclosed three graves (16468, 16474 and 16451).

Assumed primary grave 16468

Grave 16468 is assumed to be the primary grave as it was the largest of the three and lay roughly in the centre of the barrow. It had a rounded rectangular shape, 1.45m long, 1.15m wide and 0.51m deep. A 40mm-deep deposit of brown sandy silt (16467), which possibly represented decayed organic material, covered the base of the grave. The grave contained the moderately preserved but severely fragmented crouched skeleton of a male over 36 years old *(16466 – Sk 85)*, lying on the left side, with the head to the north, facing east. This man had DJC, OA and DDD of the spine, with further DJC of the temporo-mandibular joints, right radius, right knee and left calcaneus, as well as OA of the left ankle. He also had a fracture to the left clavicle, CO, endocranial porosity and lamellar bone. He was the brother of the woman buried at the centre of B42 (Patterson *et al.* 2022). The skeleton was radiocarbon-dated to the period 390–170 cal BC (SUERC-96433).

Grave 16474

Grave 16474 was situated immediately south of Grave 16468, and was a sub-oval shallow cut with steep sides, 1.01m long, 0.85m wide and 0.32m deep. The very poorly preserved and severely fragmented burial *(16473 – Sk 87)* was that of an adult male (from DNA) aged at least 36 years, lying on the left side in a crouched posture, with the head to the south facing west. He had new bone formation and pilasterism to

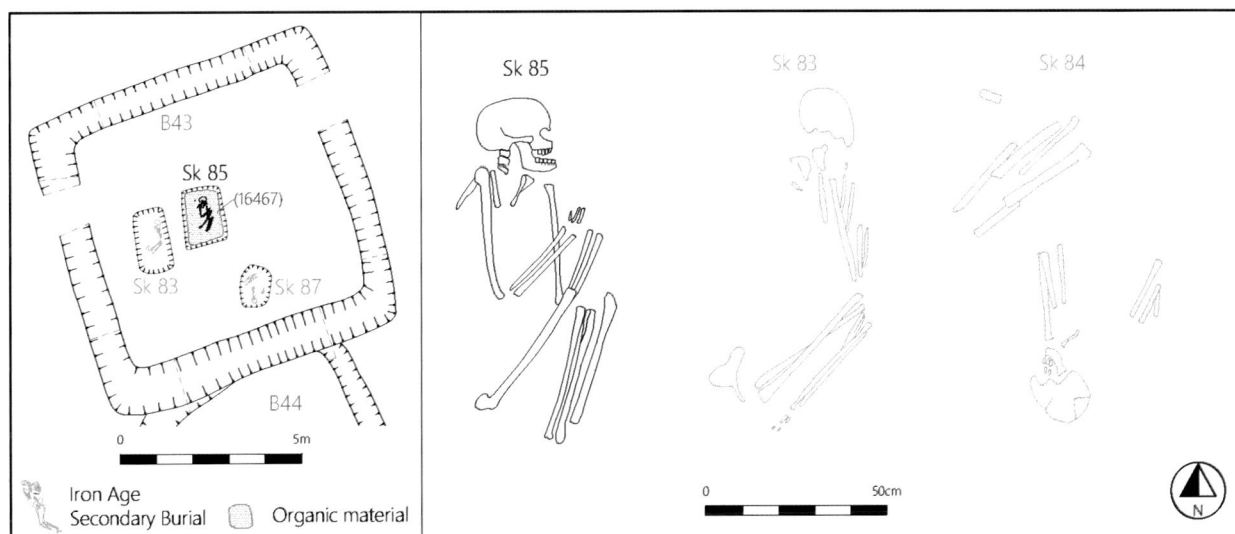

Figure 4.45 Plan of Barrow 43, Skeleton 85 <16466> and secondary burials Sk 83 <16450> and Sk 87 <16473>

both femora. An animal bone fragment was found up against the northern edge of the grave, above the level of the grave floor.

GRAVE 16451

Grave 16451 was located immediately west of the primary grave. This rectangular grave was relatively deep (0.85m) and was 1.75m long and 1.05m wide. The base of the grave was waterlogged. The moderately preserved and fragmented burial (*16450 – Sk 83*) was of an adolescent female aged 15–17 years, in a crouched posture, lying on the left side, with the head to the north, facing east. There was lamellar bone to both legs. The skeleton was radiocarbon-dated to the period 350–50 cal BC (SUERC-96429).

Barrow 44

Summary

Barrow 44 was situated on the southern side of Barrow 43, its northern ditch being cut away by the southern ditch of the latter. This was a regular square barrow measuring 5.2m across internally (Fig. 4.46). Seven ditch segments were excavated (16405, 16446, 16407, 16409, 16413, 16415 and 16461). The ditch had a rounded-V profile and was *c.* 0.70m wide and 0.15m deep. The fill was a homogeneous mix of dark sandy silt and gravel, the sole find being a late Mesolithic/early Neolithic flint bladelet in fresh condition from the top fill of the north-east corner (16410).

Grave 16471

The grave lay approximately in the centre of the barrow, and had a rounded rectangular shape, 1.55m long, 1.20m wide and 0.34m deep. Three animal teeth were found in the mixed grave fill (16469).

Skeleton (16470 – Sk 86)

Centrally within the grave was the very poorly preserved and severely fragmented flexed skeleton of a male (from DNA) aged over 36 years, lying on the left side with the head to the north, facing east. This individual had DJC of both temporo-mandibular joints and pilasterism of both femora.

Barrow 45

Summary

Barrow 45, which was situated *c.* 16m south-east of the eastern barrow group, was a square barrow that measured 5.8m across internally (Figs 4.2 and 4.47). A 2.2m wide 'causeway' crossed the western ditch of the barrow. The ditch was excavated in eight segments (16511, 16515, 16519, 16523, 16527, 16531, 16536 and 16540) and had a U-shaped profile. It was *c.* 0.70m wide and averaged 0.30m deep (0.40m deep at the two ditch terminals – 16536 and 16540), with three fills: gravel at the base, gravel and clay silt in the middle and dark clay silt at the top. The primary fill (16514) at the north-east corner contained an early Neolithic flint core, and another flint core of late Neolithic/early Bronze Age date was found in

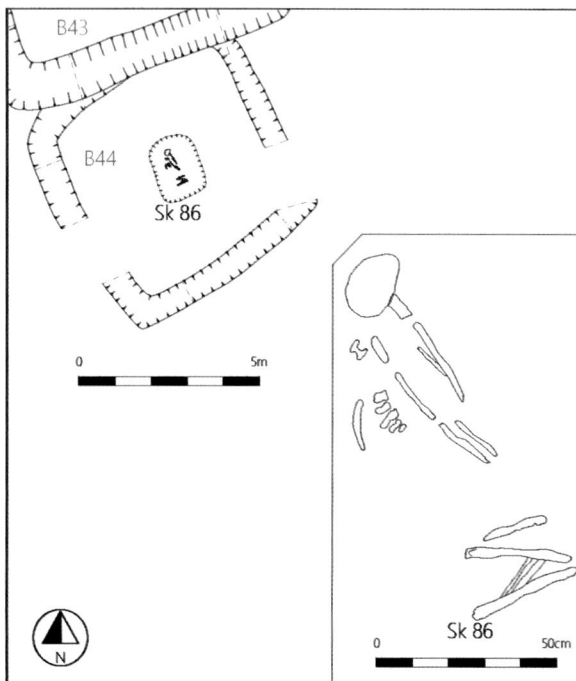

Figure 4.46 Plan of Barrow 44 and Skeleton 86 <16470>

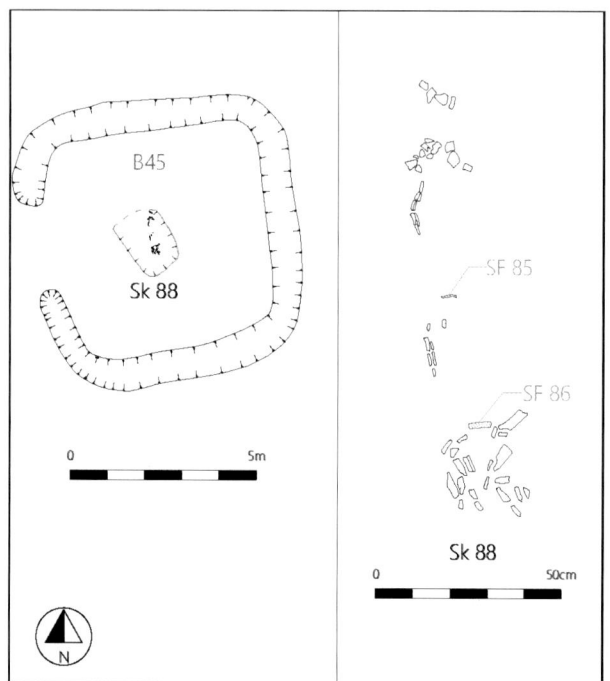

Figure 4.47 Plan of Barrow 45 and Skeleton 81 <16491>

the secondary fill of the north-west corner (16538); both were in fresh condition. The secondary fill of the north ditch (16509) contained over 80 sherds from the same Iron Age jar (SF 88, Fig. 12.1), and the primary fill (16510) contained a small Iron Age sherd and oak charcoal fuel waste. The secondary fill (16538) of the north-west corner contained nine small sherds from a single Iron Age vessel.

Grave 16492

The central grave had a rounded rectangular shape, measuring 1.73m long and 1.26m wide, but was very shallow (60mm).

Skeleton (16491 – Sk 88)

The shallowness of the grave no doubt contributed to the poor preservation and severe fragmentation of the skeleton; however, enough survived to show that an adult, aged over 36 years was represented, lying with the head to the north.

Grave goods

ANTLER TOGGLE

An antler toggle (SF 86, Fig. 12.9) was found at the burial's waist and so was perhaps related to dress fastening.

BROOCH PIN

A humped copper alloy pin (SF 85) from a penannular brooch was found in the grave fill but was not directly associated with the burial.

POSSIBLE MEAT OFFERING

A small number of undiagnostic animal bone fragments found with the skeleton may have been the remains of a meat offering.

Barrow 46

SUMMARY

With this barrow we return to the western barrow group, in which Barrow 46 was centrally placed (Fig. 4.1). Barrow 46 was a regular square barrow, *c.* 5.3m across internally (Fig. 4.48). Eight segments were excavated into the ditch (17080, 17194, 17183, 17197, 17032, 17188, 17177 and 17191), which had a variable profile and ranged from 0.55m to 1.05m in width, and between 0.27m and 0.35m in depth. There was a gravelly primary fill, with dark sandy silt at the top. The top fill on the north side (17182) contained medieval sherds and animal bone fragments. The primary fill (16412) contained a single grain of bread wheat.

Grave 17082

The central grave was rectangular with steep to vertical edges, measuring 2.00m long, 1.20m wide and 0.40m deep.

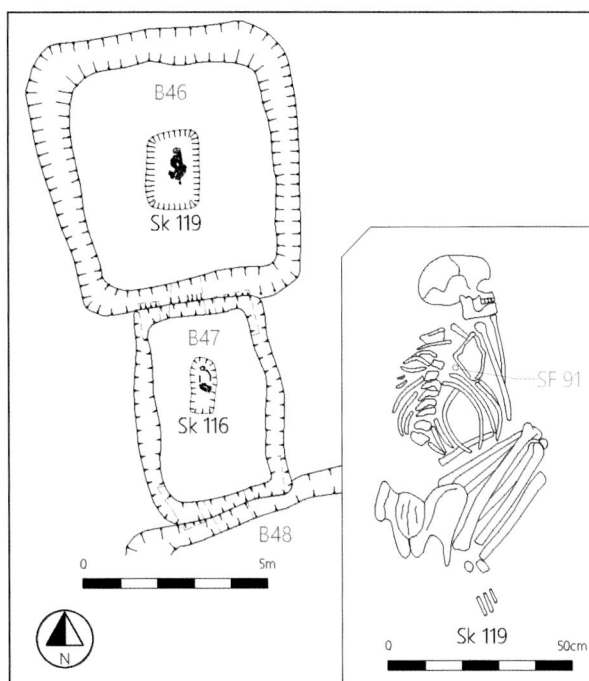

Figure 4.48 Plan of Barrow 46 and Skeleton 119 <17081>

Skeleton (17081 – Sk 119)

The grave contained the poorly preserved and moderately fragmented crouched skeleton of a female, aged over 46 years, lying on the left side, with the head to the north, facing east. This woman had DJC, DDD and OA of the spine, as well as CO. The skeleton was radiocarbon-dated to the period 360–120 cal BC (SUERC-83079).

Grave goods

A copper alloy Hull and Hawkes Type 2Cd involuted brooch with iron pin (SF 91), decorated with large bulbous beads of glass and a zoomorphic decoration of an apparent horse/duck hybrid that is unique in Britain (Fig. 11.2), was found near the right shoulder. The brooch has a mid-3rd to early 2nd-century BC date.

Barrow 47

Summary

Barrow 47 was inserted between Barrow 46 to the north and Barrow 48 to the south, clearly post-dating both barrows. This barrow was rectangular and relatively small, measuring 4.5m from north to south and 2.8m from east to west (Fig. 4.49). The ditch was excavated in eight segments (17026, 17006, 17008, 17011, 17014, 17017, 17020 and 17023). The ditch profile was a broad-U shape and varied between 0.30m and 0.70m in width and 0.14m and 0.20m in depth. There was a gravel-rich primary fill and a darker silty top fill.

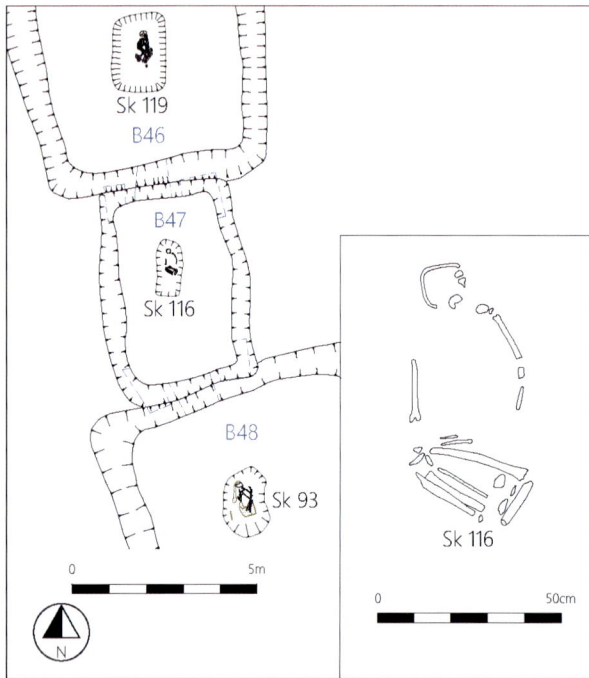

Figure 4.49 Plan of Barrow 47 and Skeleton 116 <17001>

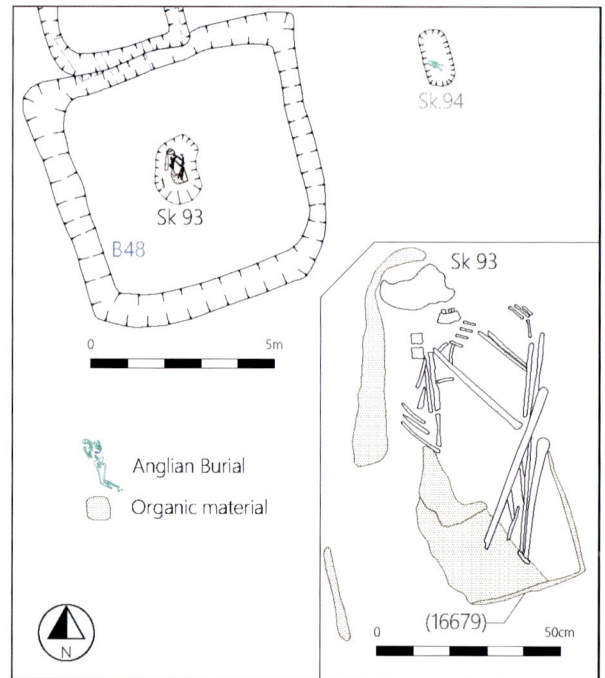

Figure 4.50 Plan of Barrow 48 and Skeleton 93 <16678>

Grave 17002

The sub-rectangular central grave was 1.45m long, 0.72m wide and 0.35m deep.

Skeleton (17001 – Sk 116)

This was the very poorly preserved and extremely fragmented flexed skeleton of an adolescent male (from DNA) aged 17–19 years, with the head to the north. He was the 2nd- or 3rd-degree relative of the female primary burial of B49 (Patterson *et al.* 2022).

Barrow 48

Summary

Barrow 48 lay immediately to south of Barrow 47, and pre-dated it. It formed a regular rectangle and measured 5.8m across internally (Fig. 4.50). The ditch was excavated in eight segments (16566, 16569, 16572, 16575, 16578, 16581, 16584 and 16587). The barrow ditch had a predominantly rounded-V profile, around 0.80m wide and 0.30m deep. There was a gravel-rich primary fill, with darker silty sand above. The primary fill at the south-east corner (16574) contained a grain of bread wheat.

Grave 16591

The central grave was an irregular oval in plan, measuring 1.85m long, 1.16m wide and 0.64m deep.

Skeleton (16678 – Sk 93)

The burial (16678 – Sk 93) consisted of the poorly preserved and extremely fragmented crouched skeleton of a mature adult, probable female, 36+ years in age, lying on the left side, with the head to the north, facing east. The spine had DDD and DJC, with further DJC of the jaw and right scapula. This woman was a 2nd- or 3rd-degree relative of the female primary burial of B2 (Patterson *et al.* 2022).

Structure 16679

Traces of a structure (16679) were shown by a straight, thin band of dark silt that delineated the southern end of the burial and extended part way up the west and east sides of the skeleton. The partial remains of the structure measured 0.70m wide and at least 0.35m long. The legs and arms partly overlay the eastern side of the structure. The more irregular line of silt behind the burial's spine, which also wrapped around the head, could point to the structure's collapse, or else the presence of further organics within the grave.

Barrow 49

Summary

Barrow 49, which was situated 10m to the north-east of Barrow 48, was a rectangular barrow measuring 5.4m from north to south and 4.2m from east to west (Fig. 4.51). The grave, burial and some parts of the ditches had been excavated during the August 2014 trial trenching. The barrow was excavated in seven segments (4006, 17056, 4004, 4019/17058, 17060, 4015 and 4010/17054). The ditch was *c.* 0.70m wide and 0.25m deep, with a U-shaped profile. The fill consisted of homogeneous brown gravel-rich silty sand (4018).

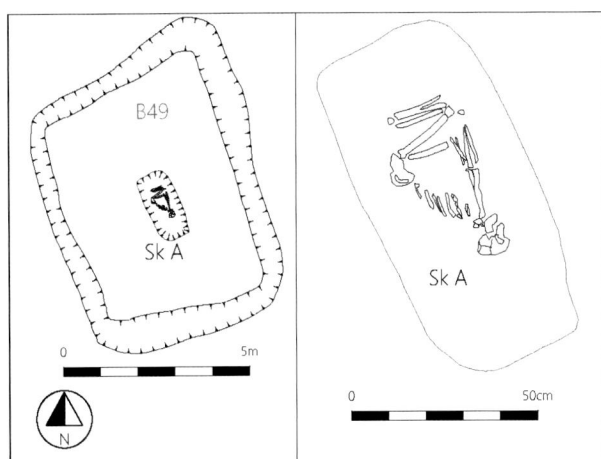

Figure 4.51 Plan of Barrow 49 and Skeleton A <4012> from Trial Trenching

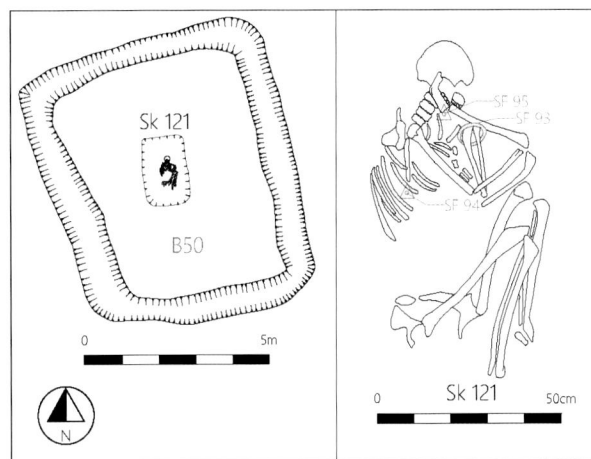

Figure 4.52 Plan of Barrow 50 and Skeleton 121 <17090>

Grave 4013

The central grave was sub-rectangular, measuring 1.9m long, 0.9m wide and 0.39m deep.

Skeleton (4012 – Sk A)

Grave 4013 contained the moderately preserved and fragmented crouched skeleton of a female aged 26–35 years, lying on the right side, with the head to the south, facing east. This woman had spondylolysis, a fracture to the lowermost lumbar vertebra, caused by trauma to a vertebra which had underlying developmental weakness, plus CO. She was a 2nd-degree relative to the adult woman buried centrally in B50, and a 2nd- or 3rd-degree relative of the male adult primary burials in B47 and B65 (Patterson *et al.* 2022).

Barrow 50

Summary

Barrow 50, situated 2m south of Barrow 49, was straight-sided and slightly rectangular, measuring 6.2m from north to south and 5.4m from east to west (Fig. 4.52). Eight segments were excavated into the ditch (16634, 16668, 16619, 16671, 16643, 16674, 16621 and 16677) which had a U-shaped profile and was *c.* 0.60m wide and 0.30m deep. The primary fill was predominantly of gravel, with a darker silty sand above. The primary fill (16620) of the western ditch contained hazel charcoal, a fragment of which was radiocarbon-dated to 420–380 cal BC (SUERC-78051; see Table 15.2).

Grave 17091

The grave in Barrow 50 was both off-centre and distinctly off-line from the alignment of the barrow's ditches. It was a relatively large rectangular cut with vertical sides that measured 1.7m long, 1.2m wide and 0.45m deep.

Skeleton (17090 – Sk 121)

The moderately preserved and fragmented skeleton was that of an adult female, over 26 years old, lying on the left side, with the head to the north, facing east. This woman's pathology included trauma (possibly a fracture) to the right clavicle, a right rib fracture, a developmental anomaly of the spine, possible gout, bowed legs and maxillary sinusitis. This woman was the 2nd- or 3rd-degree relative of the woman buried centrally in B49 (Patterson *et al.* 2022). The skeleton was radiocarbon-dated to the period 390–200 cal BC (SUERC-83080).

Grave goods

This woman had a copper alloy bracelet (SF 93, Fig. 11.8) on her right wrist, plus a fragmentary iron Hull and Hawkes Type 2Cb brooch (SF 94) and a small annular glass bead (SF 95, Fig. 12.6) on the upper torso/neck area. A small fragment of copper alloy tube was found during the cleaning of the skeleton.

Barrow 51

Summary

Barrow 51 was situated *c.* 10m north-east of Barrow 50 and was a regular square barrow, measuring *c.* 4.4m across internally (Fig. 4.53). Ditch D, the later boundary, cut across the north-east corner of this barrow. The barrow ditch was excavated in seven segments (17108, 17114, 17120, 17112, 17118, 17110 and 17116), showing a rounded-V profile that averaged 0.40m wide and 0.20m deep. The single fill consisted of dark sandy silt. Sherds of late Iron Age tradition pottery and burnt animal bone fragments were found in the fill of the eastern ditch (17113) and a medieval sherd and a possible iron slag fragment in the south-eastern corner (17119).

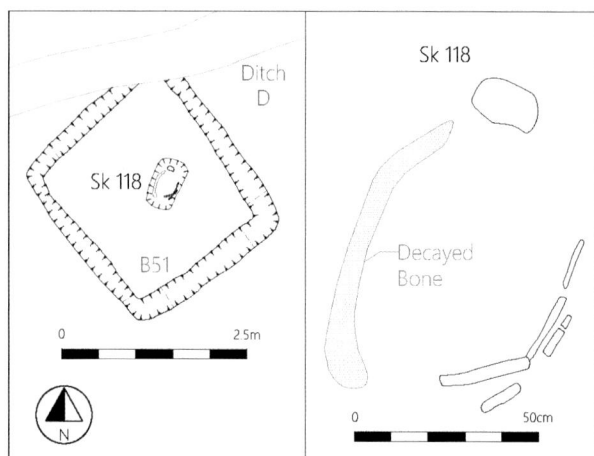

Figure 4.53 Plan of Barrow 51 and Skeleton 118 <17078>

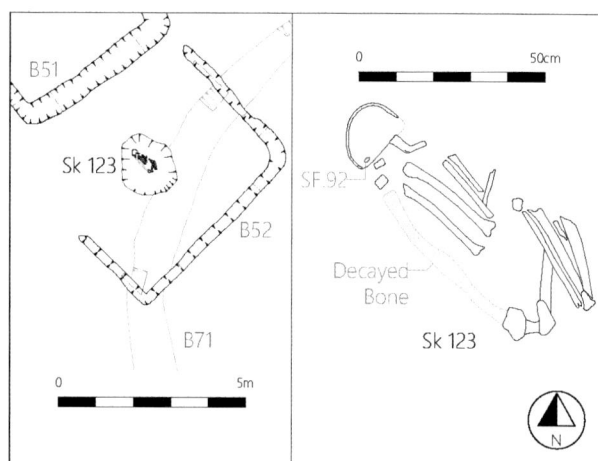

Figure 4.54 Plan of Barrow 52 and Skeleton 123 <17105>

Grave 17079

The alignment of the central grave differed markedly to the axis of the barrow. The sub-rectangular and vertically sided cut was 1.37m long, 0.82m wide and 0.36m deep.

Skeleton (17078 – Sk 118)

The extremely poorly preserved and severely fragmented crouched skeleton of an unsexed individual aged 18–35 years lay on the left side, with the head to the north, facing east. There was pilasterism of both femora.

Barrow 52

Summary

Barrow 52 was situated immediately south of Barrow 51 but was on a different alignment to it (Fig. 4.1). It cut into the northern side of the large round barrow (Barrow 71), and had been severely truncated, with only the south and east ditches surviving; four segments were excavated (17127, 17125, 17123 and 17121). The ditch was a shallow U in profile, *c.* 0.25m wide and 0.10m deep (Fig. 4.54). The fill consisted of dark silty sand with moderate gravel.

Grave 17104

The central grave formed a shallow oval cut measuring 1.60m long, 1.40m wide and 0.15m deep.

Skeleton (17105 – Sk 123)

The burial consisted of the poorly preserved and extremely fragmented crouched skeleton of an adult of unknown sex aged over 26 years, lying on the left side, with the head to the north, facing east. This individual had OA and DJC of the spine.

Grave goods

A complete copper alloy penannular brooch (SF 92) was found within the skull and was broadly dated to the 3rd–1st centuries BC (Fig 4.55).

Figure 4.55 Copper alloy penannular brooch (SF 92) from Skeleton 123 <17105>

Barrow 53

Summary

Situated *c.* 11m east of Barrow 52, Barrow 53 was severely truncated and cut into Barrow 71 to the south, and into the southern side of Barrow 55 to the north (Fig. 4.1). The surviving remains showed a barrow of irregular form, 3.5m wide from east to west and at least 4.5m long from north to south (Fig. 4.56). Three segments were excavated into the ditch (17142 – north, 17147 – west and 17149 – east). The barrow ditch was around 0.50 wide, but very shallow at less than 0.10m, and was filled with dark silty sand with a small proportion of gravel.

Grave 17133

The central grave was oval, measuring 1.70m long, 1.10m wide and 0.18m deep.

Skeleton (17135 – Sk 124)

The poorly preserved and severely fragmented crouched burial was of a possible male, aged over 26 years, lying on the right side, with the head to the south, facing east. There was pilasterism to both femora and lamellar bone on both tibiae.

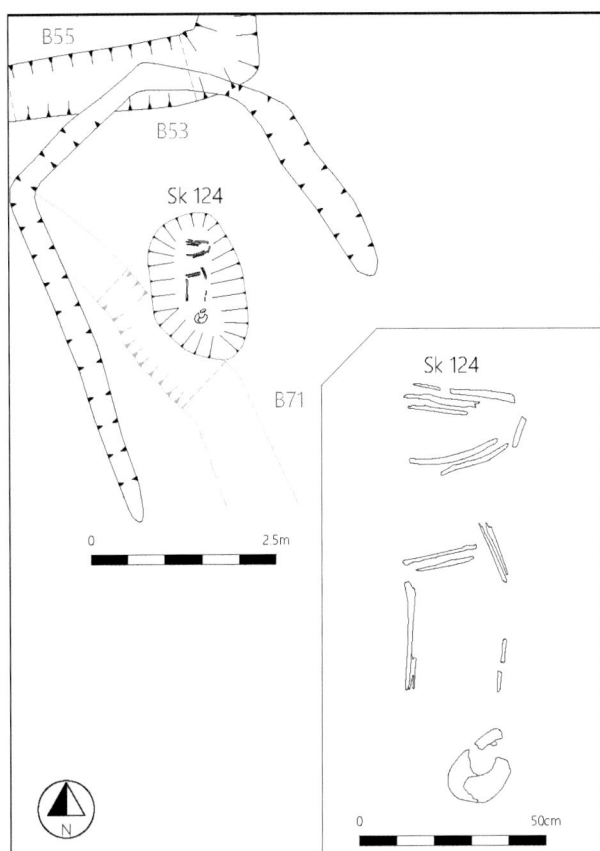

Figure 4.56 Plan of Barrow 53 and Skeleton 124 <17135>

Barrow 54

Summary

This was a regular square barrow that measured 4m across internally, situated between Barrows 51 and 55 (Figs 4.1 and 4.57). It cut the north-west quarter of Barrow 71. The ditch was excavated in eight segments (17153, 17151, 17165, 17163, 17161, 17159, 17157 and 17155) and had a U-shaped profile measuring around 0.60m wide and 0.15m deep. The fill consisted of brown silty sand with moderate gravel. A residual Neolithic edge-utilised flint blade was found in the fill of the eastern side (17166) and a medieval sherd in the north-west corner (17156). The fill at the south-west corner (17160) contained single grains of oat and barley.

Grave 17171

The central grave was severely truncated by furrow 17159, but survived as an irregular sub-circular cut, *c.* 1.00m across and 0.20m deep. The fill contained an intrusive post-medieval sherd.

Skeleton (17172 – Sk 125)

The truncation of the grave by furrow 17159 meant that only fragments of unidentified long bones survived, probably from an individual aged over 12 years. It was not possible to discern the posture and alignment of the burial.

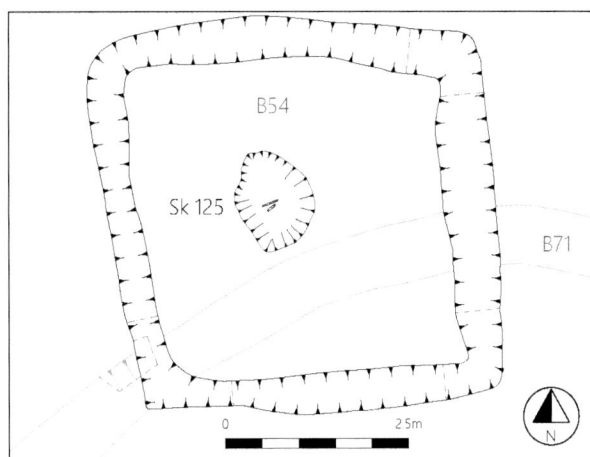

Figure 4.57 Plan of Barrow 54 and Skeleton 125 <17172>

Barrow 55

Summary

Barrow 55 cut into the northern side of Barrow 71 and formed a square enclosure that measured *c.* 4.7m across internally (Fig. 4.58). Eight ditch segments were excavated (17206, 17236, 17208, 17238, 17210, 17214, 17212 and 17234). The ditch profile varied from U-shaped to rounded-V and was around 0.50m across and 0.25m deep. The fill consisted of a dark sandy silt with moderate gravel.

Grave 17176

The rectangular central grave measured 1.55m in length, 1.06m in width and 0.22m in depth. The fill (17174) contained a possible iron slag fragment.

Skeleton (17175 – Sk 126)

This was the very poorly preserved and extremely fragmented skeleton of an adolescent of unknown sex, crouched on the left side, with the head to the south, facing west.

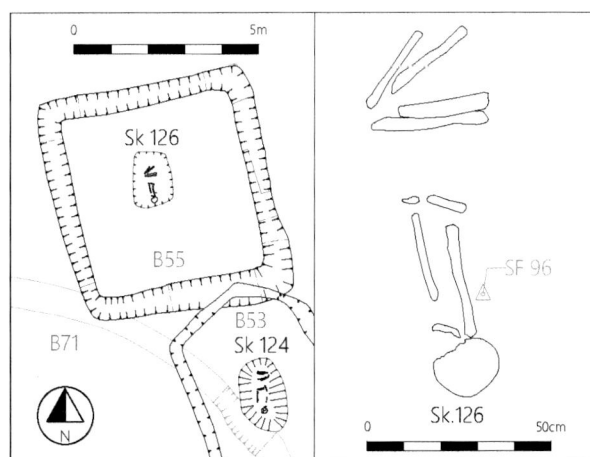

Figure 4.58 Plan of Barrow 55 and Skeleton 126 <17175>

Grave goods

An iron Hull and Hawkes Type 2Cb involuted bow brooch of mid-3rd to early 2nd-century BC date (SF 96) was found below the burial's right shoulder.

Barrow 56

Summary

Barrow 56 was situated immediately east of Barrow 25, towards the southern edge of the western group (Fig. 4.1). This was an irregular square barrow that measured 5.1m from north to south and 5.3m from east to west internally, the north-east corner of the barrow having a marked curvature (Fig. 4.59). A north–south furrow truncated the eastern part of the barrow. Eight segments were excavated into the barrow ditch (16854, 16875, 16872, 16869, 16866, 16863, 16960 and 16857), which had a rounded-V profile measuring around 0.38m wide and 0.15m deep. The primary fill consisted of sandy gravel, with darker silt above. The sole find was an Iron Age sherd from the primary fill (16859) of the western ditch.

Grave 16741

The oval central grave was at least 1.30m long, 1.30m wide and 0.20m deep. An Anglian secondary burial (Sk 98, grave cut 16739) cut into the top of this grave.

Skeleton (16745 – Sk 99)

This poorly preserved and extremely fragmented skeleton was of an adult of indeterminate sex, aged over 36 years, lying tightly crouched on the left side, with the head to

the north, facing east. This person had DJC of both temporo-mandibular joints.

Structure 16825

A curvilinear line of dark silt (16825) surrounded the burial, forming an arrangement that was 1.10m long and 0.60m wide. This represented either the remains of a structure or traces of organic material around the body.

Barrow 57

Summary

Barrow 57 cut into the south-west part of Barrow 71 and was truncated in turn by a furrow that removed its southern ditch. This slightly trapezoidal barrow measured 5.5m from east to west and a maximum of 4.45m from north to south, internally. The barrow ditch was excavated in six segments (16767, 16773, 16759, 16756, 16772 and 16770), illustrating a U-shaped or rounded-V profile, 0.50m wide and 0.15m deep (Fig. 4.60). The fill consisted of dark silt and moderate gravel, with the addition of a gravel primary fill at the north-west and south-east corners and along the eastern side. The primary fill at the north-west corner (16769) contained animal bone fragments.

Grave 16785

The grave was situated in an off-centre position in the southern part of the enclosed area. It was sub-rectangular in shape and measured 1.20m in length, 0.65m in width and 0.15m in depth.

Skeleton (16783 – Sk 102)

This was the poorly preserved and moderately fragmented skeleton (16783 – Sk 102) of a young juvenile aged around 2 or 3 years old, in a flexed posture and lying on the left side, with the head to the north,

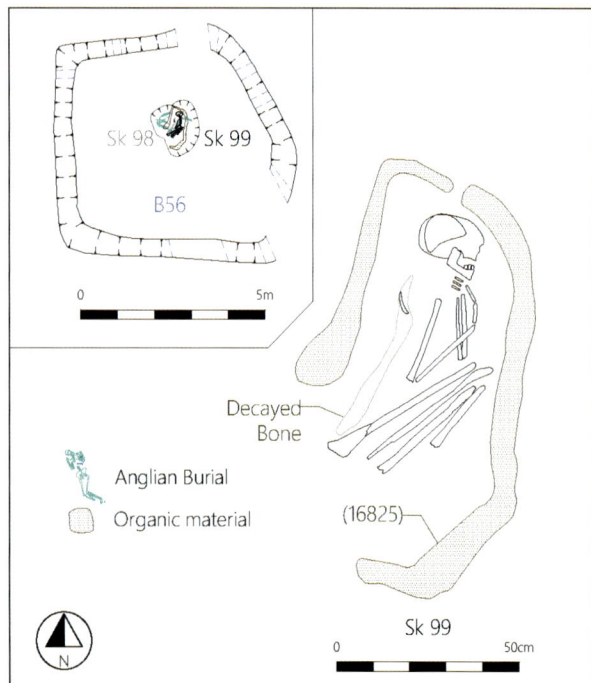

Figure 4.59 Plan of Barrow 56 and Skeleton 99 <16745>

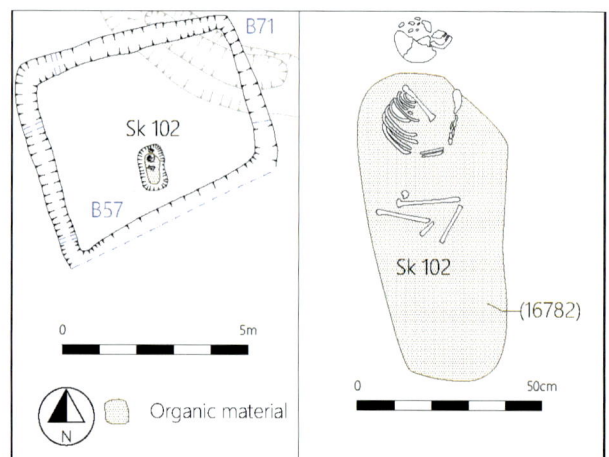

Figure 4.60 Plan of Barrow 57 and Skeleton 102 <16783>

facing east. There was evidence of CO and new bone. A 20mm-deep, sub-rectangular deposit of dark silt (16782) overlay the entire body, apart from the head, suggesting that the body had been deliberately covered with organic material.

Barrow 58

Summary

Barrow 58 was situated south-west of Barrow 57, with its northern ditch partly truncated by the same furrow that truncated the latter's southern ditch. This was a small barrow, roughly square in plan, that measured 3.5m from north to south and 3.1m from east to west internally (Fig. 4.61). The full complement of eight segments was excavated into the ditch (16715, 16717, 16719, 16721, 16725, 16703, 16707 and 16711), which had a U-shaped profile and was *c.* 0.40m wide and 0.25m deep. The ditch had a gravel-rich primary fill along the western side and south-eastern corner; the top of the ditch (and the remainder of the segments) was filled with darker silt.

Grave 16727

The central grave was rectangular with rounded corners and measured 1.40m long, 1.00m wide and 0.52m deep.

Skeleton (16728 – Sk 95)

The burial was placed along the eastern edge of the grave in a distinctly off-centre position. This was the poorly preserved and severely fragmented crouched skeleton of a female aged 18–35 years, lying on the left side, with the head to the north, facing east. The woman had a potential ossified haematoma on her left femur; this is a condition resulting from a forceful blunt trauma (such as being kicked by a horse) causing deep bruising and bleeding. She was the 2nd- or 3rd-degree relative of the woman buried centrally in B2 (Patterson *et al.* 2022).

Barrow 59

Summary

Barrow 59 was located immediately south-west of Barrow 58 and was badly truncated by furrows on the western and southern sides. It was at least 3.5m across internally, with a rounded-rectangular shape (Fig. 4.62). Four segments (16840, 16843, 16846 and 16849) were excavated into the ditch, showing it to have a trough-shaped profile measuring 0.50m in width and 0.15m in depth. The ditch fills consisted of a gravel-rich primary deposit, with darker silty sand above.

Grave 16781

The grave had a distinctly ovoid shape and was 1.45m long, 0.95m wide and 0.60m deep, with vertical edges. The lower part of the grave was filled with dark silt (16779 – probably from the decay of organic material) with a more mixed fill (16778) above. A residual early Neolithic denticulate blade was found in fill 16779.

Skeleton (16780 – Sk 101)

The very poorly preserved skeleton was of unknown sex, probably aged 18–25 years, lying on the left side in a crouched posture, with the head to the north, facing east. This individual had CO.

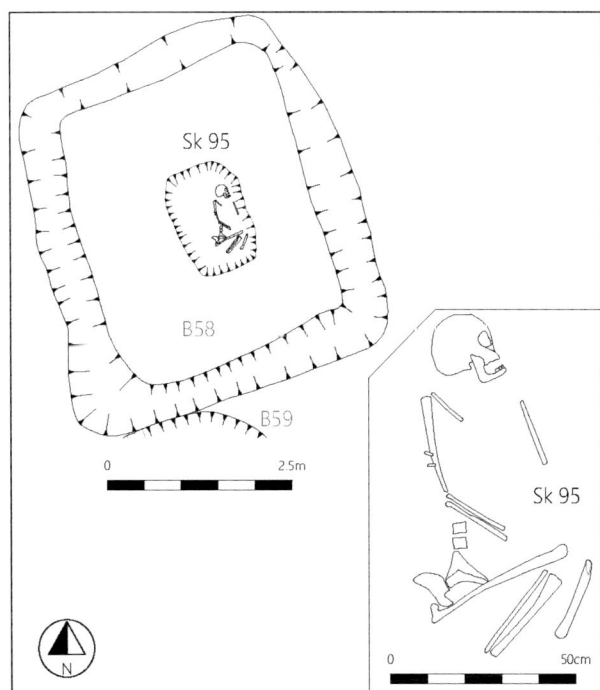

Figure 4.61 Plan of Barrow 58 and Skeleton 95 <16728>

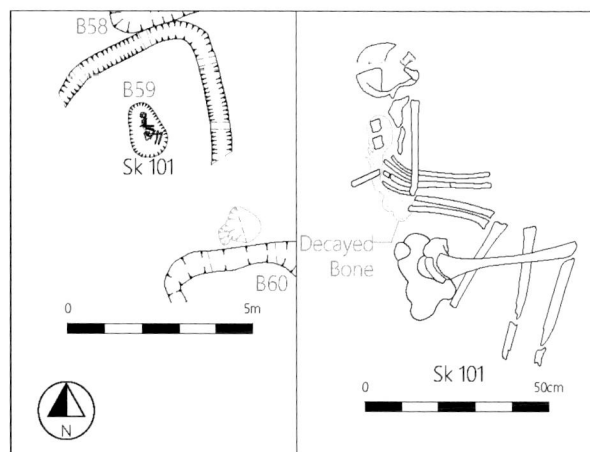

Figure 4.62 Plan of Barrow 59 and Skeleton 101 <16780>

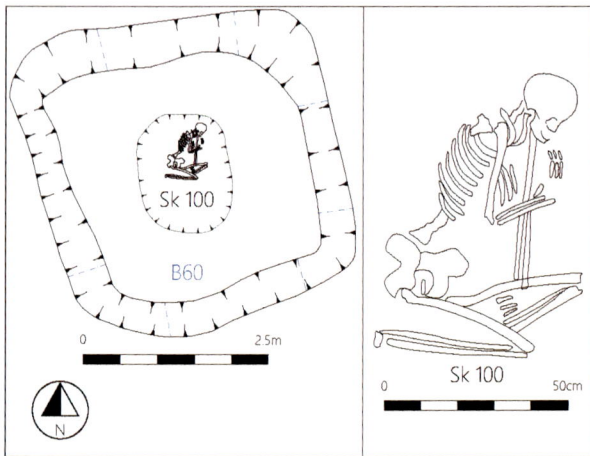

Figure 4.63 Plan of Barrow 60 and Skeleton 100 <16747>

Barrow 60

Summary

Barrow 60, situated immediately south of Barrow 59, was a small square barrow with rounded corners, measuring 3.1m across internally (Fig. 4.63). The ditch was excavated in eight segments (16797, 16800, 16803, 16806, 16809, 16811, 16791 and 16794). The profile of the barrow ditch varied from U-shaped to rounded-V and averaged 0.35m wide and 0.17m deep. The primary fill contained frequent gravel, with a darker sandy silt above.

Grave 16748

The central grave had a rounded rectangular shape, measuring 1.60m long, 1.22m wide and 0.56m deep.

Skeleton (16747 – Sk 100)

This was the poorly preserved skeleton of an adult female, probably 26–35 years old, lying in a crouched posture on the left side, with the head to the north, facing east. The burial was situated in an off-centre position in the northern part of the grave. The skull showed evidence of lamellar endocranial new bone.

Barrow 61

Summary

Barrow 61 was situated north-east of Barrow 60 and was the latest in a sequence of four barrows (the others being Barrows 65–67). It was a regular square in shape, measuring 3.8m across internally (Fig. 4.64). Eight segments were excavated (16812, 16814, 16820, 16817, 16818, 16819, 16916 and 16815). The barrow ditch, which had a U-shaped profile and was *c.* 0.45m wide and 0.15m deep, was filled with a dark silty sand with frequent chalk gravel. The fill of the southern and eastern ditches (16818 and 16820 respectively) contained small pieces of undiagnostic burnt clay.

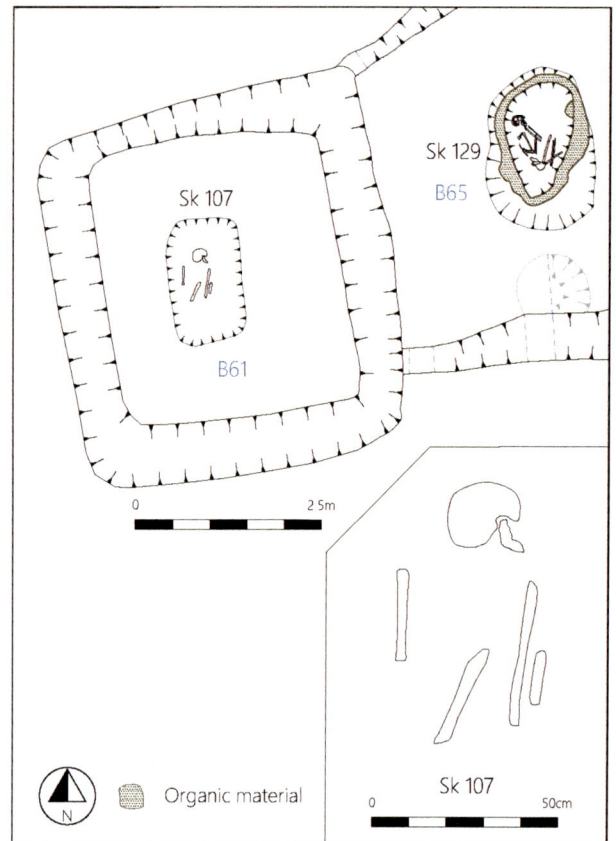

Figure 4.64 Plan of Barrow 61 and Skeleton 107 <16883>

Grave 16851

The barrow's grave was situated centrally to the enclosed area and had a rounded rectangular form that was 1.50m long, 1.00m wide and 0.38m deep. (An Anglian secondary burial [16829] was cut into the top of the primary grave.)

Skeleton (16883 – Sk 107)

The skeleton was poorly preserved and extremely fragmented, but enough survived to suggest that it was crouched, with the head to the north, facing east. A possible female aged over 36 years was represented, with soft tissue trauma to the right femur and evidence of further trauma to the right tibia, in the form of a small, ossified haematoma. She also had DJC of the right temporo-mandibular joint.

Barrow 62

Summary

Barrow 62 was situated immediately east of Barrow 60 and was a square barrow measuring 4.1m from north to south and 3.8m from east to west (Fig. 4.65). Eight segments were excavated into the barrow ditch (16931, 16933, 16935, 16938, 16923, 16925, 16927 and 16929). The ditch had a broad-U profile, measured around 0.30m wide and 0.10m deep, and was filled with a homogeneous deposit of dark sandy silt with moderate gravel. The fill of the western ditch (16928) contained a stray grain of bread wheat. The grave of an Anglian secondary burial (16881, Sk 106) cut into the top of the central grave.

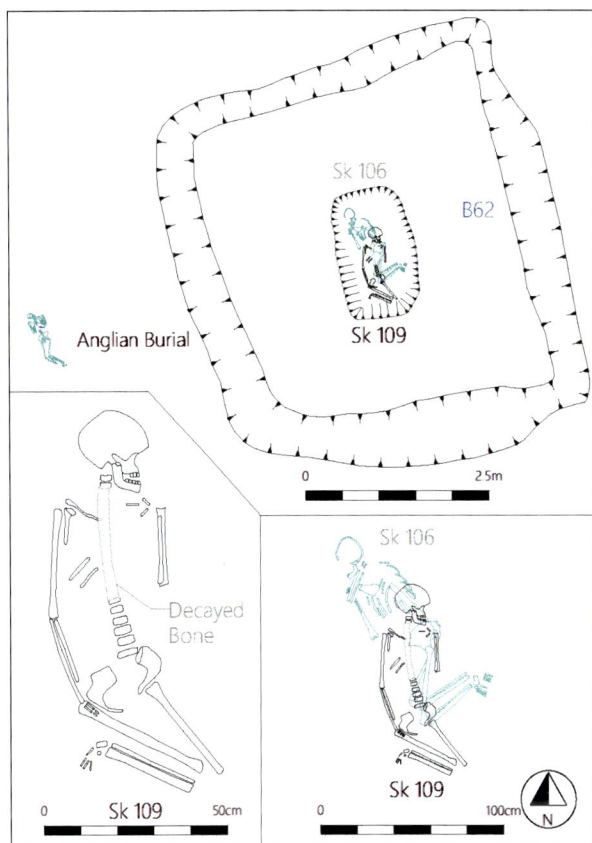

Figure 4.65 Plan of Barrow 62 and Skeletons 109 <16896> and 106 <16881>

Grave 16880

The central primary grave had a regular rectangular form and was 1.70m long, 1.05m wide and 0.60m deep, with vertical edges. The fill (16895) contained two undiagnostic slag fragments.

Skeleton (16896 – Sk 109)

The burial was placed in an off-centre position in the southern part of the grave. The poorly preserved and extremely fragmented skeleton was that of a probable female aged 18–25 years, lying on the right side in a flexed posture, with the head to the north, facing east. CO was present.

Barrow 63

Summary

This was a large square barrow, situated in the southern part of the excavated area, to the south of Barrow 60 (Fig. 4.1). It was slightly rectangular in shape, measuring 6.2m from north to south and 5.4m from east to west (Fig. 4.66). Later linear features truncated the south-west and north-west corners of the barrow, and part of the south-east ditch was beyond the area of excavation. The barrow ditch was excavated in six segments (16904, 16907, 16910, 16913, 16916 and 16919). The ditch was at its most extensive on the eastern side, where it was *c*. 1.00m wide and 0.50m deep, with a U-shaped profile. There was a primary fill of gravel, with darker silty sand in the remainder of the ditch.

Grave 18176

The central primary grave was a regular rectangle in shape and was slightly askew to the alignment of the barrow ditches. It measured 1.60m in length, 0.95m in width and

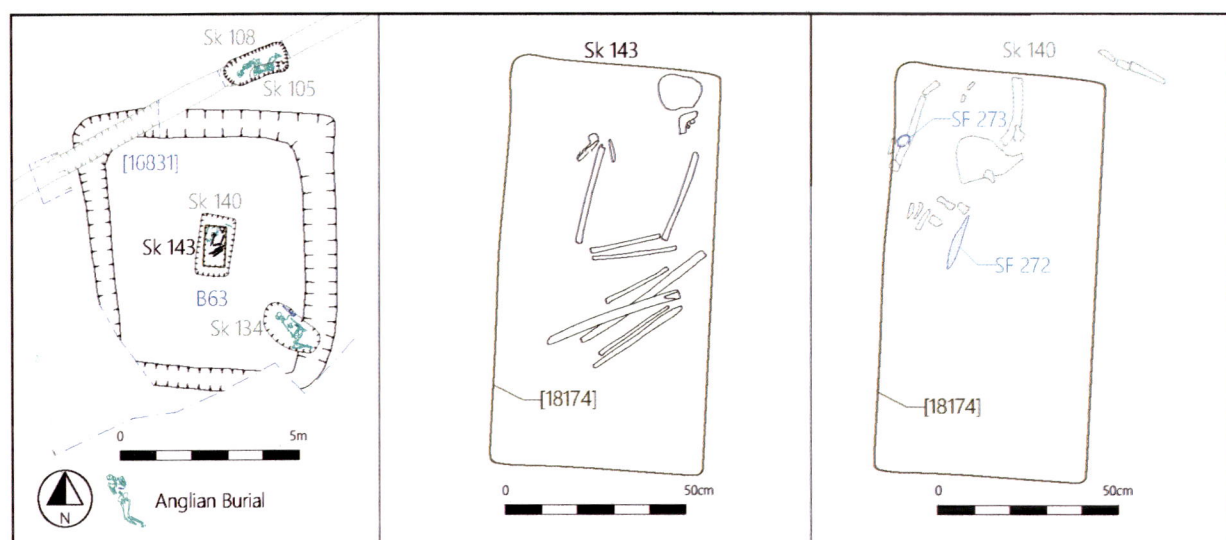

Figure 4.66 Plan of Barrow 63 and Skeletons 143 <18173> & 140 <18135>

0.22m in depth. The upper part of the grave was filled by deposit 18171 (yellowish-brown sandy silt), and deposit 18175 (yellowish-brown sandy silt) surrounded grave structure 18172.

Skeleton (18173 – Sk 143)

This was the very poorly preserved and severely fragmented skeleton of an individual of unknown sex, aged between 26 and 35 years, laid in a crouched posture, with the head to the north, facing east. Three disarticulated bone fragments (skull, leg and clavicle) from another individual, possibly secondary burial 18135, were included with this skeleton.

Structure 18174

A distinct rectangular block of fill (18172) represented a structure within the grave; this was slightly askew to the grave's edges (Fig. 4.67). The structure was 1.10m long, 0.60m wide and 0.25m deep.

Anglian secondary burials

These consisted of a severely truncated secondary burial (18135, Sk 140) that was inserted into the top of the primary grave, and another secondary burial (18085, Sk 134) dug into the south-east corner of the barrow.

Barrow 64

Summary

Barrow 64 was situated immediately east of Barrow 63; much of the centre of this barrow and its southern ditch were truncated by a later furrow (16978). Barrow 64 was slightly rectangular in form and measured 4.2m from north to south and 3.4m from east to west internally (Fig. 4.68). The barrow ditch was excavated in seven segments (18046, 18049, 18052, 18055, 18058, 18062 and 18065). The ditch had a rounded-V profile and was around 0.50m wide and 0.24m deep. The primary fill consisted mainly of gravel, with dark sandy silt above.

Grave 16991

The rounded rectangular central primary grave was 1.25m long, 0.94m wide and 0.48m deep.

Skeleton (16990 – Sk 113)

This poorly preserved skeleton was of a male aged 26–35 years who suffered from stress fractures (spondylolysis) of the lower back. He lay in a crouched posture in the eastern half of the grave, on his left side, with the head to the north, facing east. The skeleton was radiocarbon-dated to the period 400–200 cal BC (SUERC-96434).

Figure 4.67 View of Barrow 63, Skeleton 143 <18173>, facing north. Scale: 0.5m

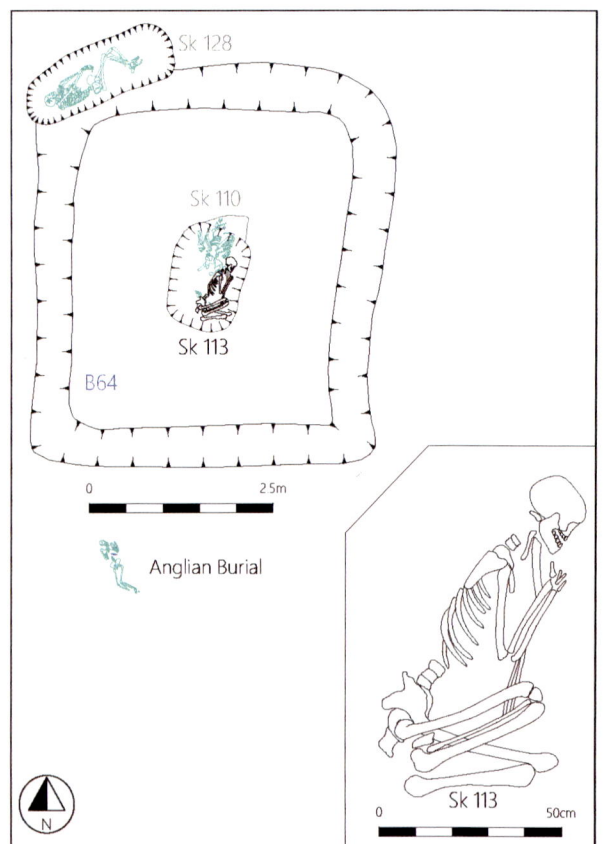

Figure 4.68 Plan of Barrow 64 and Skeleton 113 <16990>

Secondary burials

An assumed Anglian secondary burial (16968, Sk 110) overlay the primary burial with a further Anglian burial (18006, Sk 128) cutting into the ditch at the north-west corner of the barrow.

Barrow 65

Summary

Barrow 65 was situated immediately east of, and was cut by, Barrow 61. This was a square barrow, but with a curiously rounded north-east corner, measuring *c.* 4.5m across internally (Fig. 4.69). Eight ditch segments were excavated (16966, 16963, 16960, 16957, 16954, 16777, 16986 and 16984). The ditch had a rounded-V profile and was *c.* 0.60m wide and 0.34m deep. There was a gravel-rich primary fill, with darker sandy silt above. The primary fill of the north-east corner of the ditch contained undiagnostic slag.

Grave 18012

The relatively large central grave was 2.20m long and 1.20m wide, with a maximum depth of 0.40m. A ring of dark silt (18014), which measured 1.60m in length, 1.15m in width and around 0.20m in height, surrounded the burial, and its presence suggests that the base of the

grave may have been lined with organic material. The primary grave was cut by an Anglian burial (16994, Sk 114).

Skeleton (18013 – Sk 129)

The poorly preserved and severely fragmented primary burial was of a male (from DNA) aged over 46 years, lying in a crouched posture on the left side, with the head to the north, facing east. This man had indications of soft tissue trauma to the right femur and right tibia, along with DJC, DDD and OA of the spine, and further DJC of the right shoulder and left hip socket, plus CO, maxillary sinusitis and pilasterism of both femora. A piece of ossified cartilage was found in the torso area. He was a 2nd- or 3rd-degree relative of the female primary burial in B49 (Patterson *et al.* 2022).

Barrow 66

Summary

Barrow 66 lay on the eastern side of Barrow 65, which cut into its western ditch, but was later than Barrow 67 to the south. This barrow was sub-rectangular in form, measuring 4.5m from north to south, and 5.5m from east to west (Fig. 4.70). The ditch was excavated in seven segments (18139, 18142, 18145, 18148, 18151, 18154

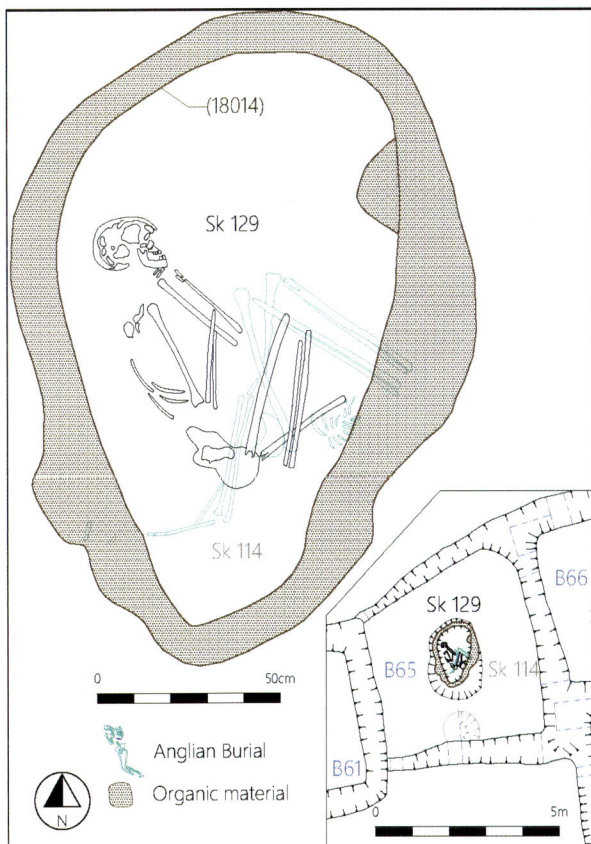

Figure 4.69 Plan of Barrow 65 and Skeletons 129 <18013> and 114 <16994>

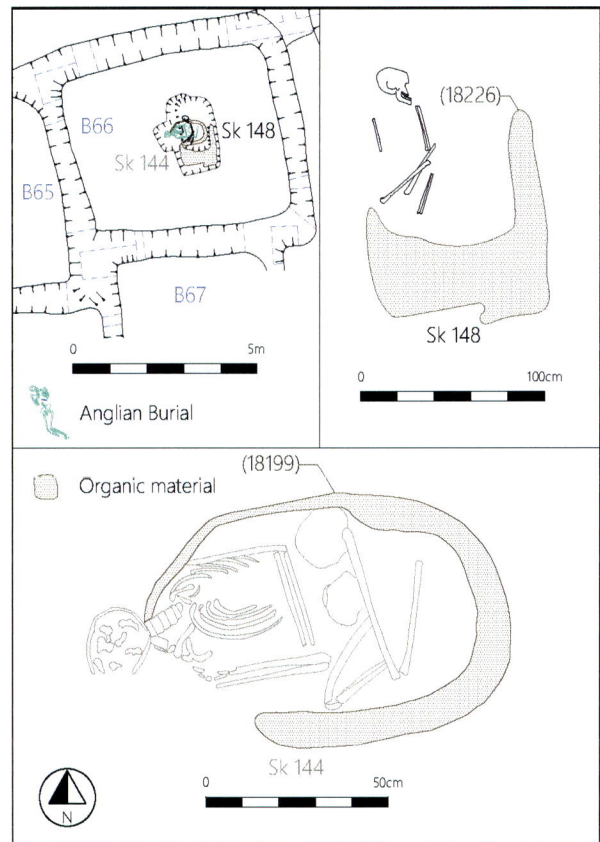

Figure 4.70 Plan of Barrow 66 and Skeletons 148 <18224> and 144 <18198>

and 18157) and had a rounded-V profile, with a width of 0.85m and a depth of 0.30m. There was a shallow primary fill of gravel, with darker sandy silt above. An Anglian secondary burial (18198, Sk 144) cut into the top of the primary grave.

Grave 18201

The primary grave lay slightly off-centre to the east of the enclosed area and was a relatively large and deep cut measuring 2.20m long, 1.20m wide and 0.88m deep.

Skeleton (18224 – Sk 148)

The burial lay in the western part of the structure described below and was represented by the very poorly preserved and severely fragmented skeleton of an individual of unknown sex, aged between 18 and 35 years, in a crouched posture and lying on the left side, with the head to the north, facing east. There was evidence of endocranial new bone.

Structure 18226

The presence of a structure was indicated by a band of dark silt (18226) that lay parallel to the eastern edge of the grave and a straight sheer-line in the fills immediately west and south-west of the skeleton. The structure measured approximately 1.70m in length and 0.70m in width.

A secondary burial located within the grave dated to the Anglian period (18198, Sk 144) was also surrounded by organic material.

Barrow 67

Summary

Barrow 67 was situated immediately south of Barrow 66, which truncated its northern ditch. It was slightly rectangular in form, measuring 4.3m from north to south and 3.8m from east to west (Fig. 4.71). Six ditch segments were excavated (18193, 18190, 18187, 18184, 18181 and 18178). The ditch had a variable U-shape to rounded-V profile and was around 0.45m wide and 0.23m deep. The primary fill was predominantly of gravel, with darker silt above.

Grave 18161

The central primary grave was rectangular with rounded corners and had steep sides. It measured 1.80m in length, 1.20m in width and 0.40m in depth.

Skeleton (18164 – Sk 142)

This was the very poorly preserved and extremely fragmented skeleton of a possible male aged over 36 years, lying in a flexed posture on the left side, with the head to the north, facing east. This individual had DJC of the spine. A piece of disarticulated human bone was included with this skeleton.

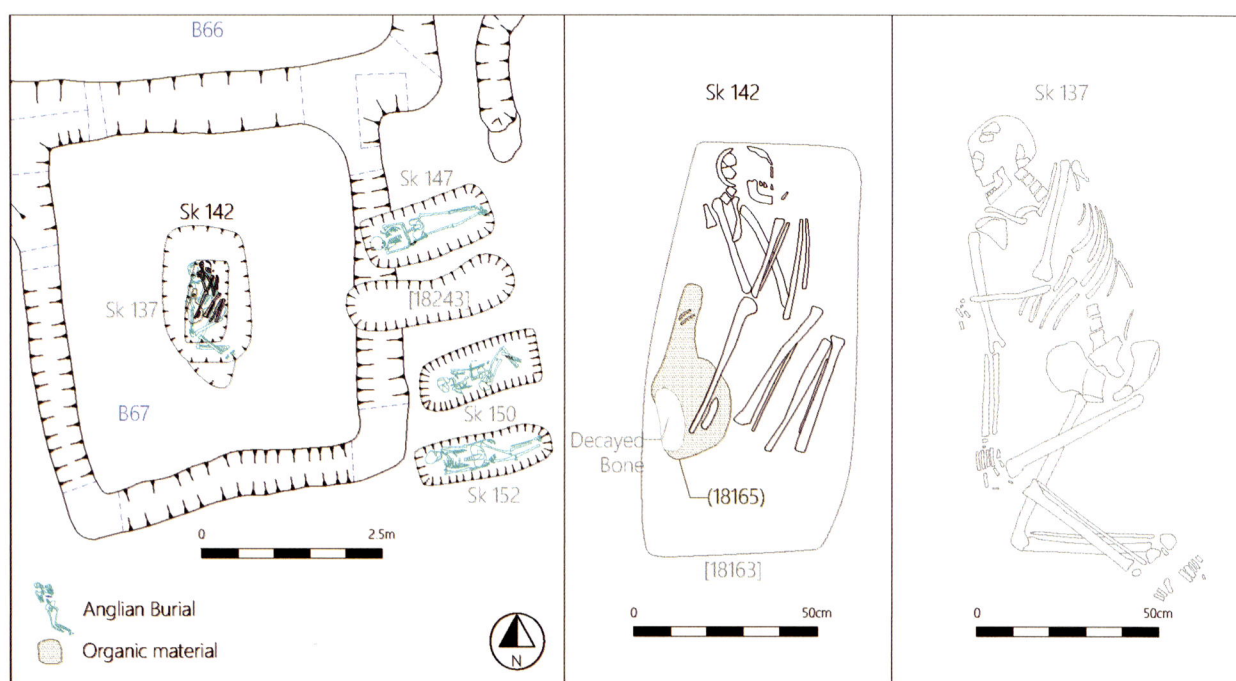

Figure 4.71 Plan of Barrow 67 and Skeletons 142 <18164> and 137 <18126>

Structure 18163

The burial was tightly positioned within the remains of a rectangular structure (18163) that was identified by the sharp division between the overall grave fill (18162) and a sub-rectangular deposit (18165 – in effect the fill of the structure). It measured 1.10m in length, 0.50m in width and 0.36m in depth. The structure had straight edges along the north, west and south sides, but the slightly bowed eastern edge suggested its partial collapse.

Anglian secondary burials

An Anglian burial (18126, Sk 137) cut into the central grave, with three further Anglian burials (18222, Sk 147; 18269, Sk 150; 18293, Sk 152) cutting into the barrow's eastern ditch, plus a possible grave (18243), with no skeleton present.

Barrow 68

Summary

This was an irregularly shaped square barrow situated to the north of Barrow 65; it cut into the southern part of Barrow 71 and its southern ditch was truncated by a later furrow (Fig. 4.1). It was 3.8m across internally from east to west (Fig. 4.72). The barrow ditch was excavated in four segments (18092, 18090, 18098 and 18094), showing it to have a rounded-V profile, with a width of *c.* 0.30m and a depth of 0.15m. The ditch was filled with yellowish-brown silty sand.

Grave 18273

The central grave had an unusual sub-circular shape, with a diameter of *c.* 1.3m, a depth of 0.28m, and a bowl-shaped profile.

Skeleton (18272 – Sk 151)

This poorly preserved and extremely fragmented skeleton was that of an unsexed individual aged 36–45 years, lying in a crouched posture on the left side, with the head to the north, facing east. This individual had DJC of the spine, as well as CO. (The sample from the fill around this skeleton contained an amber bead [SF 573], which was probably intrusive from an Anglian secondary burial (18130, Sk 138), and a small piece of iron sheet and disarticulated human bone fragments presumably came from the same source.)

Anglian secondary burials

Two Anglian secondary burials (18208, Sk 145 and 18130, Sk 138) cut into the central grave.

Barrow 69

Summary

Barrow 69 lay at the south-eastern extremity of the western barrow group (Fig. 4.1). It extended beyond the limit of excavation, but it was 9m across from east to west internally (Fig. 4.73). A later ditch (16831) cut the northern side of the barrow. The ditch was excavated in five segments (18037, 18018, 1699, 18008 and 18101), showing a relatively large feature measuring 1.40m wide and 0.60m deep, filled with gravel at the base and a darker sandy silt at the top. Animal bone fragments were found in the upper fills of both the northern ditch (18040) and north-eastern corner (18022). The primary fill of the western corner (18010) contained a Neolithic flint bladelet (SF 564) in 'very fresh' condition, and a late Neolithic/early Bronze Age flake (SF 583), also 'very fresh', was found in the fill above (18009).

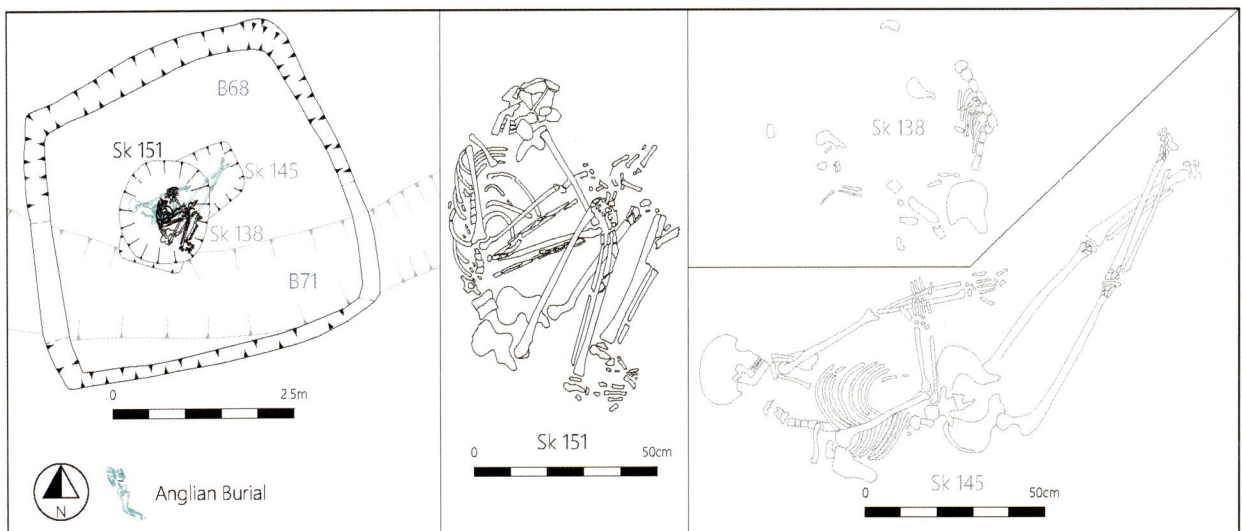

Figure 4.72 Plan of Barrow 68 and Skeletons 151 <18272>, 138 <18130> and 145 <18208>

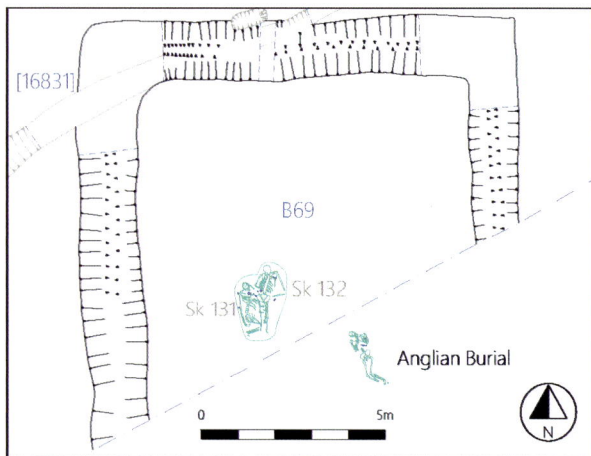

Figure 4.73 Plan of Barrow 69

Grave/burials

No Iron Age primary burial was present, but two Anglian secondary burials (18071, Sk 131 and 18073, Sk 132) cut into the area enclosed by the barrow's ditches.

Barrows 70 and 71 are assigned to the Bronze Age and discussed in Chapter 3.

Barrow 72

Summary

Barrow 72 was anomalous feature consisting of a large, slightly trapezoidal enclosure with a relative wide and deep ditch. It lay to the north-east of Barrow 66 and cut into the ditch of Barrow 71 at its north-west corner; it was badly truncated through the centre by a later furrow (Fig. 4.1). The internal measurements were 11m from north to south and 7m from east to west (Fig. 4.74). The ditch was excavated in seven segments (18128, 18297, 18206, 18229, 18298, 18119 and 18104) and had a broad-V profile measuring 1.35m wide and 0.60m deep. The ditch was filled with gravel at the base and dark sandy silt at the top. The primary fill in the eastern ditch (18205) contained animal bone fragments, and the primary fill of the north-west corner yielded an Iron Age sherd. The upper fills of the north-west corner (18105), the southern ditch (18069) and the south-west ditch (18262) contained medieval sherds, with the addition of animal bone fragments and a piece of CBM from the latter. Flint finds from the barrow ditch consisted of a broken late Mesolithic/early Neolithic flint blade in 'fresh' condition (from 18069, the upper fill of the southern ditch), and a broken middle Neolithic leaf-shaped arrowhead in 'very fresh' condition (SF 581 – from 18267, the primary fill of the north-west corner). Carbonised plant remains associated with this barrow consisted of single grains of bread wheat, spelt wheat and barley (in the primary fill of the north-east corner – 16428) and a trace of alder charcoal (in the primary fill of the northern ditch – 18129).

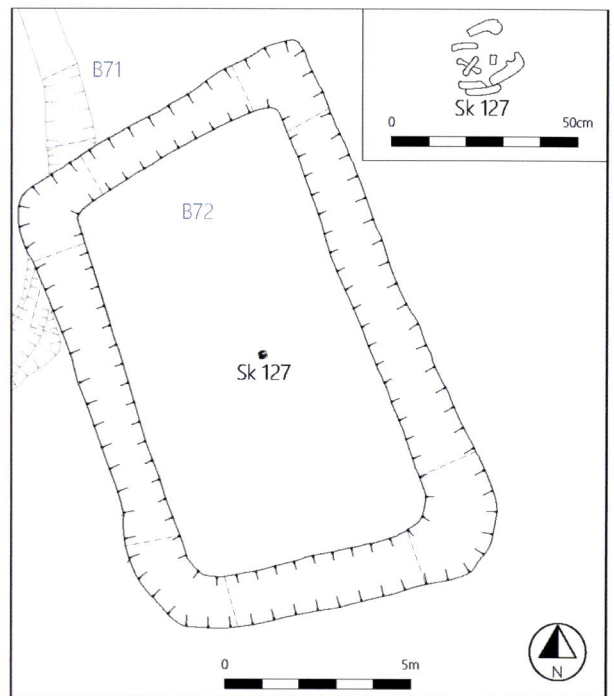

Figure 4.74 Plan of Barrow 72 and Skeleton 127 <18004>

Skeleton (18004 – Sk 127)

A small group of human bones was recovered from the base of the furrow that cut through the centre of the area enclosed by the barrow's ditches; these were possibly the surviving remains of a truncated central burial. The bones consisted of the partial hands and left arm of an individual aged over 16 years.

Barrow 73

Summary

Barrow 73 was a regular square barrow situated southeast of Barrow 72. This was a relatively large, slightly rectangular barrow that was 5.2m from north to south and 6.0m from east to west (Fig. 4.75). The barrow ditch was excavated in eight segments (18247, 18260, 18231, 18257, 18238, 18252, 18249 and 18255). The ditch was *c.* 0.65m wide and 0.30m deep, with a rounded-V profile. The fill generally consisted of dark sandy silt with plentiful gravel at the top, and a paler sandy silt in places towards the base.

Primary grave 18301

The primary grave had a rounded-rectangular plan and was 1.75m long, 0.90m wide and *c.* 0.35m deep.

Skeleton (18303 – Sk 153)

The poorly preserved and severely fragmented skeleton was of a possible male aged 18–35 years, lying on the left side, with the head to the south, facing west. This man suffered from a DJC in his temporo-mandibular joint and had CO and pilasterism of the femora.

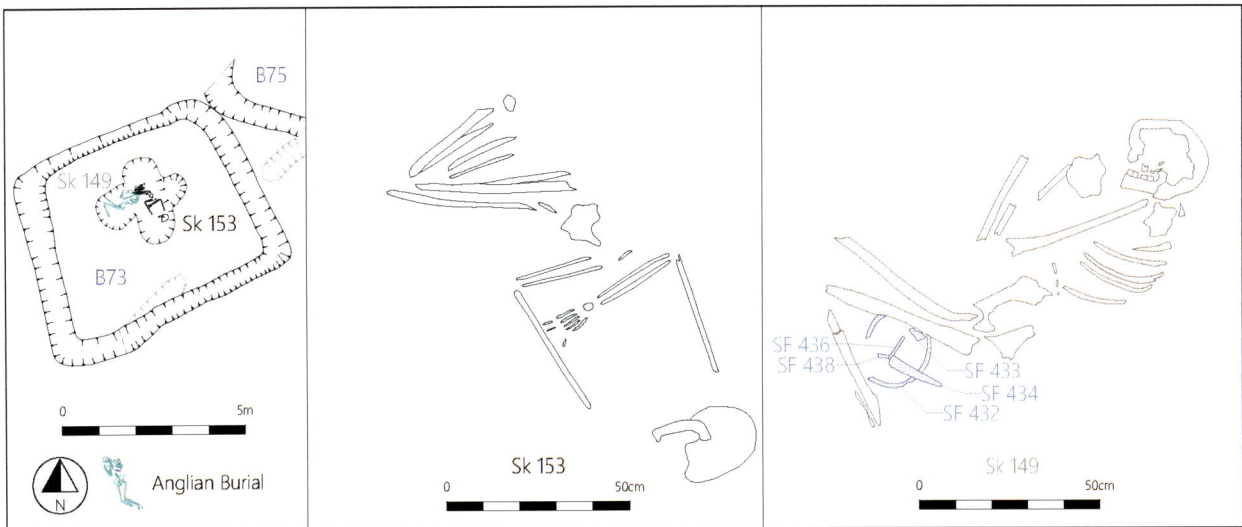

Figure 4.75 Plan of Barrow 73 and Skeletons 153 <18303> and 149 <18264>

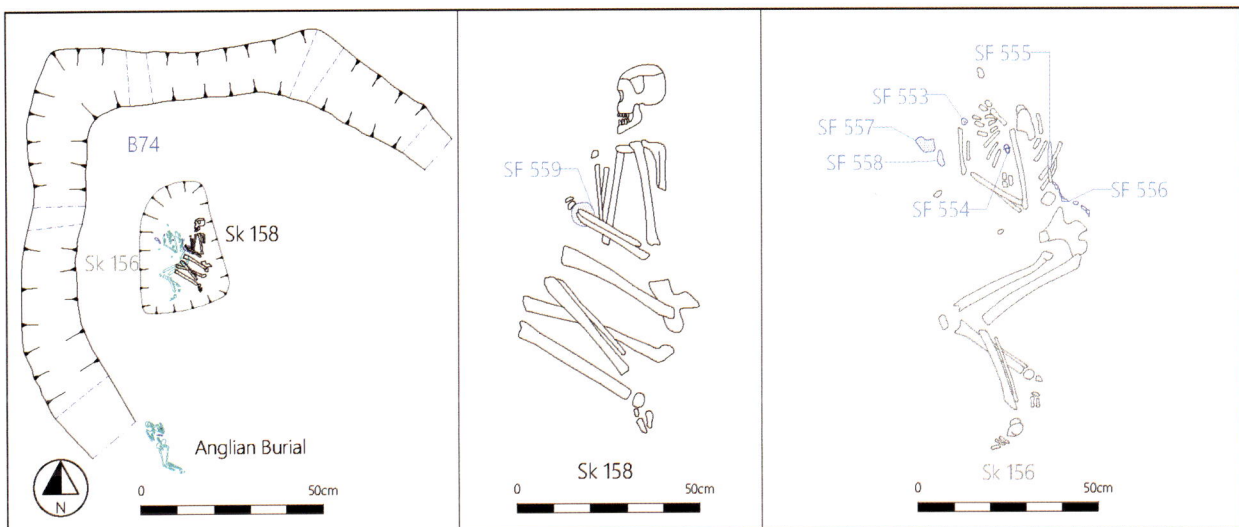

Figure 4.76 Plan of Barrow 74 and Skeletons 158 <18348> and 156 <18342>

Anglian secondary burial

The primary grave was truncated by an east–west-aligned Anglian burial (18264, Sk 149).

Barrow 74

Summary

Barrow 74 was situated at the eastern limit of the western barrow group. Its eastern side was not available for excavation as it lay under the site access road, but the full internal dimensions of this square barrow were established as 4.5m from north to south and 4.0m from east to west (Fig. 4.76). The southern part of the barrow was destroyed by a furrow. The barrow ditch was excavated in four segments (18276, 18279, 18282 and 18285). The ditch was 0.60m wide and 0.25m deep, with a broad-U profile, filled with gravel at the base and darker silty sand above. A late Neolithic/early Bronze Age flint scraper (SF 279) in moderate condition was recovered from the primary fill (18275) of the north-west corner.

Grave 18349

The central grave was sub-rectangular with a bowed northern end; it had a length of 1.7m, a width of 1.2m and a depth of 0.3m.

Skeleton (18348 – Sk 158)

The burial was placed in the south-east corner of the grave: the poorly preserved and extremely fragmented skeleton was probably female and aged 18–25 years, lying in a crouched posture on the right side, with the head to the north, facing west.

Grave goods

A plain iron bracelet (SF 559) was found on the left wrist of the burial. The bracelet was in seven pieces, but the breaks were old.

Anglian secondary burial

An Anglian burial (18342, Sk 156) cut into the top of the primary grave.

Barrow 75

Summary

Barrow 75 was situated immediately south of Barrow 74. The northern ditch was completely truncated by a furrow, and a ditch (16831) cut through the south-east corner. This barrow appeared to be square and *c.* 4m across internally (Fig. 4.77). The ditch was excavated in four segments (18312, 18315, 18318 and 18321) and had a variable U-shaped to rounded-V profile, with a maximum width of 0.70m and a depth of 0.24m. There was a gravel-rich primary fill, with darker silty sand above.

Grave 18330

The central primary grave was oval and measured 1.30m long, 0.95m wide and 0.49m deep, with a trough-shaped

profile. The grave fill (18328) contained a late Neolithic/ early Bronze Age scraper, and a worked stone disc (SF 562; see Chapter 12), which was not directly associated with the burial and may have been intrusive.

Skeleton (18329 – Sk 155)

The burial was placed centrally within the grave and comprised the poorly preserved and severely fragmented skeleton of a woman aged 26–35 years, lying on the left side, with the head to the south, facing west. She had a DJC in her right mandible, CO and maxillary sinusitis. The primary burial was truncated by an east–west Anglian secondary burial (18326, Sk 154).

Barrow 76

Summary

Barrow 76 was situated a few metres north-east of Barrow 72 (Fig. 4.1). As the eastern ditch lay under the site access road, its form was uncertain, but it appears to have been square in plan, measuring 3.5m from north to south internally (Fig. 4.78). Four ditch segments were excavated (18324, 18333, 18377 and 18340), displaying a broad-U profile 0.70m wide and 0.19m deep. The fills consisted of sandy gravel at the base with darker sandy silt above.

Grave 18344

The primary grave was an oval cut in the centre of the barrow, measuring 1.60m long, 0.90m wide and 0.45m deep.

Skeleton (18346 – Sk 157)

The burial was tightly crouched in the northern part of the grave, leaving the southern part apparently empty. The poorly preserved and extremely fragmented skeleton was an individual of unknown sex, aged at least 26 years, lying with the upper part of the body supine, but with the legs tightly folded to the east; the head was to the north.

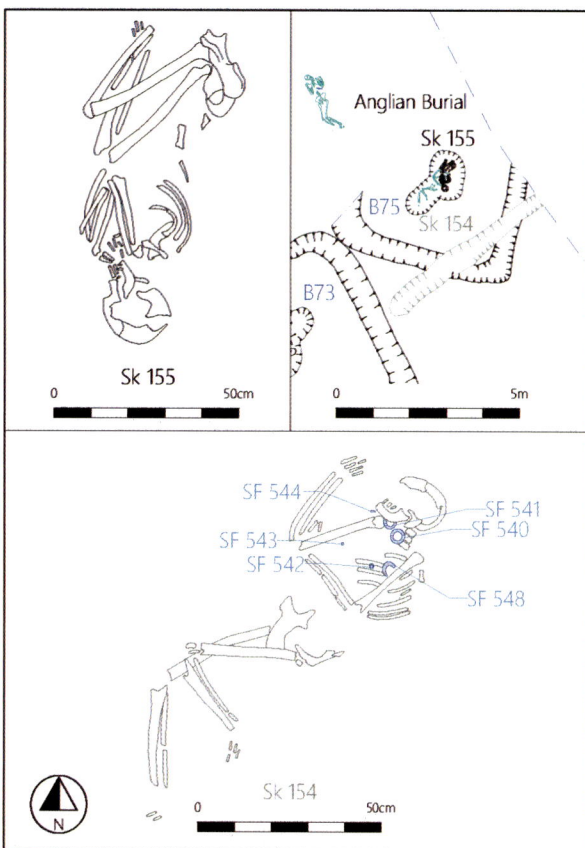

Figure 4.77 Plan of Barrow 75 and Skeletons 155 <18329> and 154 <18326>

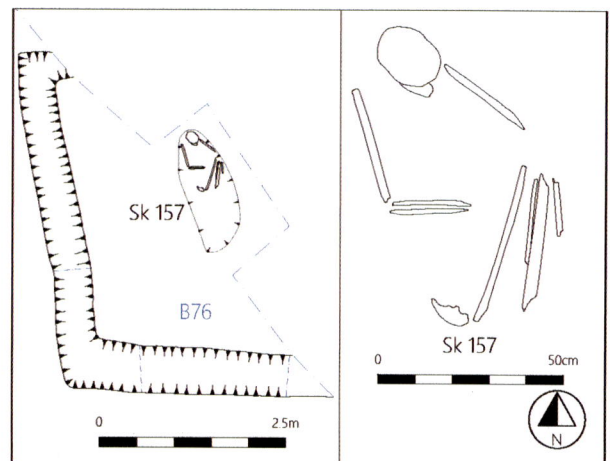

Figure 4.78 Plan of Barrow 76 and Skeleton 157 <18346>

Barrow 77

Summary

Barrow 77 was an outlying 'square' barrow situated adjacent to Barrow 45 in the eastern part of the excavated area (Fig. 4.2). The northern part of the barrow was truncated during the unsupervised removal of a large spoil-heap that had been dumped in this area. The barrow's shape was slightly trapezoidal, with measurements of between 5.1m and 3.8m from east to west and *c.* 5.2m from north to south internally (Fig. 4.79). The ditch was excavated in eight segments (18421, 18427, 18430, 18445, 18439, 18436, 18433 and 18421). There was wide variation in the ditch's profile, from dished to broad-U, with the width varying from 0.55m to 1.00m, and the depth from 0.10m to 0.44m. The primary fill consisted of sandy gravel, with darker silty sand above.

Grave 18442

The truncated central grave was sub-rectangular in shape, 1.20m long, 0.70m wide and 0.12m deep.

Skeleton (18441 – Sk 159)

The skeleton was very poorly preserved and extremely fragmented with only a few fragmentary, probably adult, leg bones remaining. From the position of the leg bones within the grave it is likely that the head lay to the south; otherwise no information about the posture or orientation remained.

Barrow 78

Summary

This barrow was situated *c.* 10m south-west of Barrow 6, in the north-west corner of the southern field (Fig. 4.3). It was badly truncated by ploughing on its western side while to the north it extended into the unexcavated strip between the two fields. The barrow appeared to be square, measuring approximately 4m across internally (Fig. 4.80). Three ditch segments were excavated (307, 305 and 286), showing it to have a U-shaped profile, 0.70m wide and 0.17m deep, filled with dark sandy silt. The fills of segments 305 and 307 (304 and 306 respectively) contained rye grains.

Grave 017

The large, oval primary grave measured 1.70m long, 1.25m wide and 0.57m deep, and was slightly askew to the axis of the barrow.

Skeleton (016 – Sk 161)

This was the poorly preserved and moderately fragmented skeleton of an adult male, aged 36–45 years, in a crouched posture, lying on the left side, with the head to the north, facing east. This individual suffered from DJC to the spine and bowing to the humeri and femora.

Barrow 79 is assigned to the Bronze Age and discussed in Chapter 3.

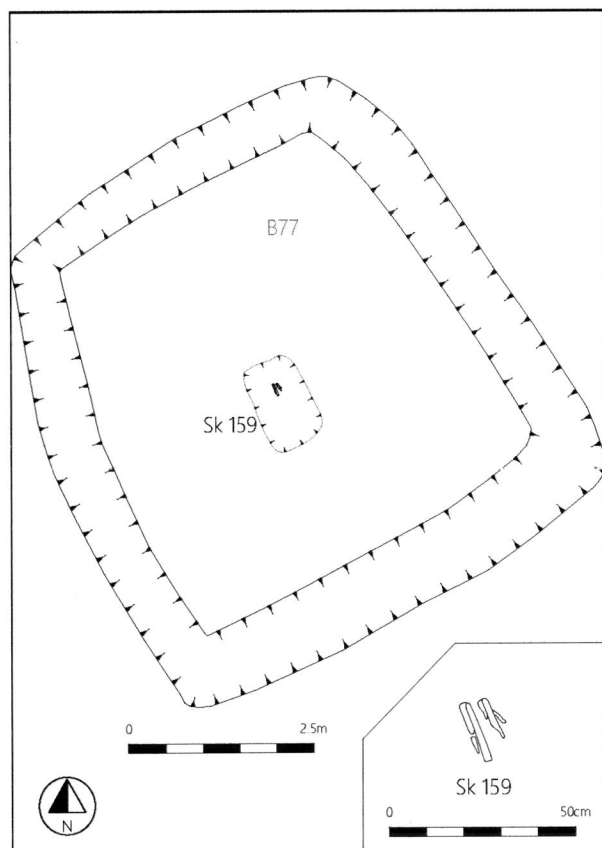

Figure 4.79 Plan of Barrow 77 and Skeleton 159 <18441>

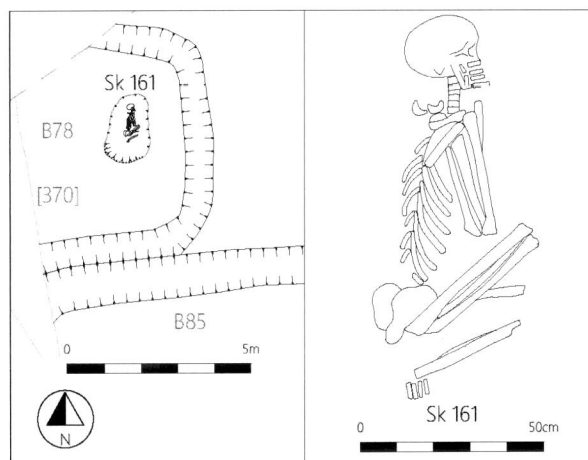

Figure 4.80 Plan of Barrow 78 and Skeleton 161 <016>

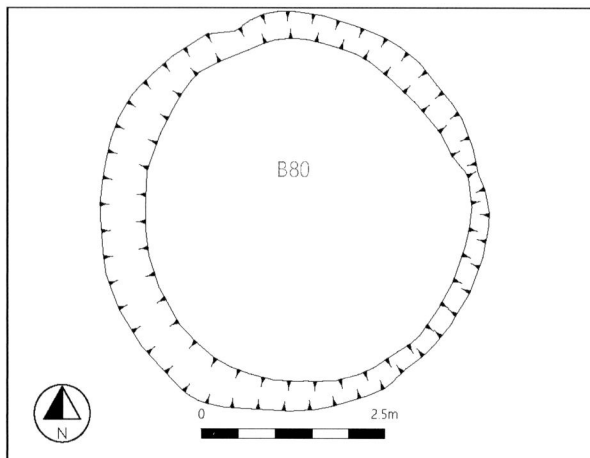

Figure 4.81 Plan of Barrow 80

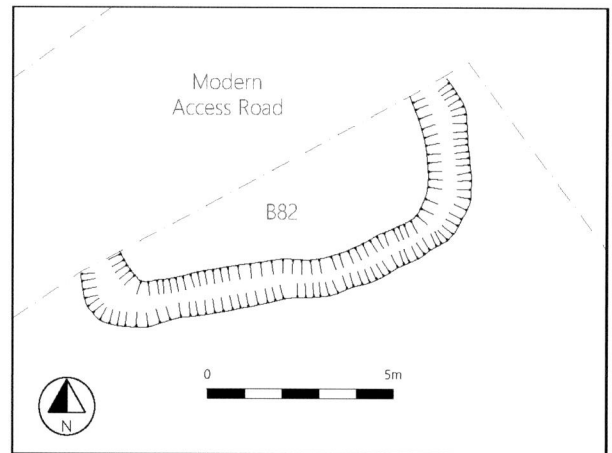

Figure 4.82 Plan of Barrow 82

Barrow 80

Summary

This was a round barrow, with an internal diameter of *c.* 4.1m, that was situated in the south-western part of the excavated area (Figs 4.3 and 4.81). The centre of the enclosed area and much of the northern and southern circuit of the ditch were badly truncated by a north–south-aligned furrow. The ditch was excavated in four quadrants (93, 96, 98 and 100), showing a U-shaped profile with a maximum width of 0.60m and depth of 0.17m. The primary fill consisted of gravel, with a covering deposit of dark silty sand surviving in the western part of the ditch. Fills 91, 95 and 99 all produced moderate amounts of presumably intrusive rye and other indeterminate grains.

Grave

There was no surviving grave for this barrow, but any putative grave or burial is likely to have been removed by later ploughing.

Barrow 81

Summary

Barrow 81 was situated 10m north-east of Barrow 78. It extended northwards into the unexcavated zone between the two fields and probably formed the south-eastern corner of Barrow 6, excavated in the field to the north (Figs 4.2 and 4.3). The barrow measured at least 3.5m from east to west internally. Three ditch segments were excavated (110, 112 and 114), showing a rounded-V profile, around 1.00m wide and 0.25m deep. The fill consisted of dark sandy silt with moderate gravel, and all three segments (fills 109, 111 and 113) contained large amounts of rye grain, with 111 also containing bread wheat, and 113, oat grains.

Grave

If this barrow was distinct from Barrow 6, any associated grave did not fall within the excavated area.

Barrow 82

Summary

This barrow was situated *c.* 80m east-north-east of Barrow 81 and similarly extended into the unexcavated zone separating the two fields (Fig. 4.2). Only the southern ditch was present within the excavated area, along with part of the eastern ditch (Fig. 4.82). The barrow was *c.* 7.5m wide from east to west. Four segments were excavated (120, 124, 128 and 132), showing the ditch to have a U-shaped profile that varied between 0.75 and 1.10m wide, and 0.28m and 0.40m deep. The primary fill consisted mainly of gravel with darker silty sand above and contained a late Neolithic/early Bronze Age core rejuvenation flake in moderate condition.

Grave

No features were present within the excavated part of the barrow's interior.

Barrow 83

Summary

Barrow 83 was a large barrow, slightly rectangular in form, that was situated in the south-west corner of the excavated area (Fig. 4.3). This barrow cut into the earlier circular Barrow 86 to the south and measured 12.5m from north to south and 11.0m from east to west (Fig. 4.83). Eight ditch segments were excavated (249, 242, 236, 230, 221, 438, 384, 376=384=373 and 388) showing a rounded-V profile, which was 1.65m wide and 0.65m deep. The ditch generally had a gravel-rich primary fill, with bands of sandy silt and gravel above. A whetstone was recovered from the top fill of the east ditch (231). The upper fill of the south-west corner segment (381) contained 14 sherds plus crumbs from an Iron Age shapeless jar. Rye grains were found in the top fill (237) of segment 242.

Grave

No traces of a surviving grave were present within the area enclosed by the barrow's ditches.

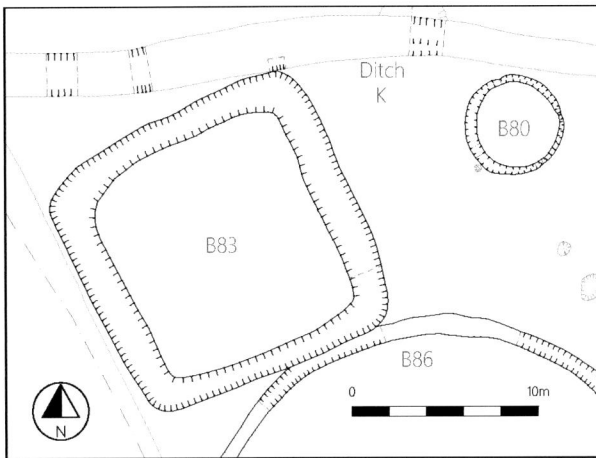

Figure 4.83 Plan of Barrow 83

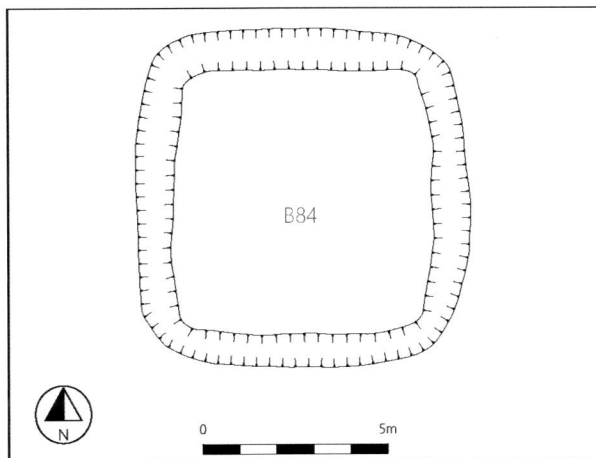

Figure 4.84 Plan of Barrow 84

Barrow 84

Summary

Barrow 84 was an extreme outlier to the barrow cemetery that was situated 30m to the south-east of Barrow 79 (Fig. 3.3). This was an intact square barrow measuring *c.* 6.8m across internally (Fig. 4.84). The barrow's ditch, which was truncated by a furrow (163), was excavated in eight segments (172, 169, 166, 187, 184, 181, 178 and 175) giving a rounded-V profile that averaged 0.95m wide and 0.30m deep. The fills consisted of the customary gravel deposit at the base with darker silty sand above.

Grave

There were no indications of a grave within the area enclosed by Barrow 84's ditches.

Barrow 85

Summary

Barrow 85 was situated immediately south of Barrow 78 and partly within the verge on Burnby Lane's eastern

side (Fig. 4.3). The north-west corner of this barrow was truncated by a later ditch (370), and subsequently the entire western side was truncated by the roadside ditch (471) that flanked the eastern side of Burnby Lane. Additionally, the remainder of the barrow, apart from the eastern ditch, had been truncated by a furrow (400) as well as later truncation. The interior of the barrow measured 7.1m across from north to south and at least 7.1m from east to west (Fig. 4.85). The barrow ditch was excavated in seven segments (running from the north-west corner: 372, 457=307, 281, 278, 463, 466 and 469), and had a broad-U profile, around 1.00m wide and 0.25m deep. There was a gravel-rich primary fill, with darker silty sand above.

Chariot burial

As with the excavators of the Ferry Fryston vehicle (Brown *et al.* 2007, 122), the term 'chariot' is preferred in this report to 'cart', which seems too dismissive a description for a vehicle that appears to have been more than prosaic. While acknowledging that the term 'chariot' brings certain assumptions, it is surely right to emphasise its status.

GRAVE 401

Even in its truncated form the central grave (401) was of exceptional size, measuring 3.6m from north to south and 2.6m from east to west, although only surviving to a maximum depth of 0.30m. A human and two ponies were buried with the chariot (Fig. 4.86).

HUMAN BURIAL (394 – SK 165)

The moderately preserved but severely fragmented and truncated remains of the burial overlay the southern end of the chariot pole (Fig 4.87). Only the left side of the skull, part of the left arm and the upper left torso, partial left femur and left patella, and miscellaneous hand and foot bones remained. These lay on the left side, with the head to the north, facing east, and enough bone was present to show that this was an adult (over 25 years) and possibly male. This individual had calcified pleura, which are associated with pulmonary diseases, including tuberculosis, and showed signs of CO.

The burial lay directly on top of an amorphous deposit of dark silt (402), which suggests that the body may have been wrapped or placed on some form of bedding.

THE CHARIOT

The principal remains of the chariot consisted of: the circular iron tyre (SF 4) and lower nave-hoop (SF 16) of a wheel in the south-eastern part of the grave; a further nave-hoop (SF 8) in the south-western part of the grave (all of which lay horizontally); and the soil stain of the pole (406) (Fig. 4.85).

The iron tyre (SF 4) was approximately 0.83m in diameter and enclosed soil marks (397) representing the

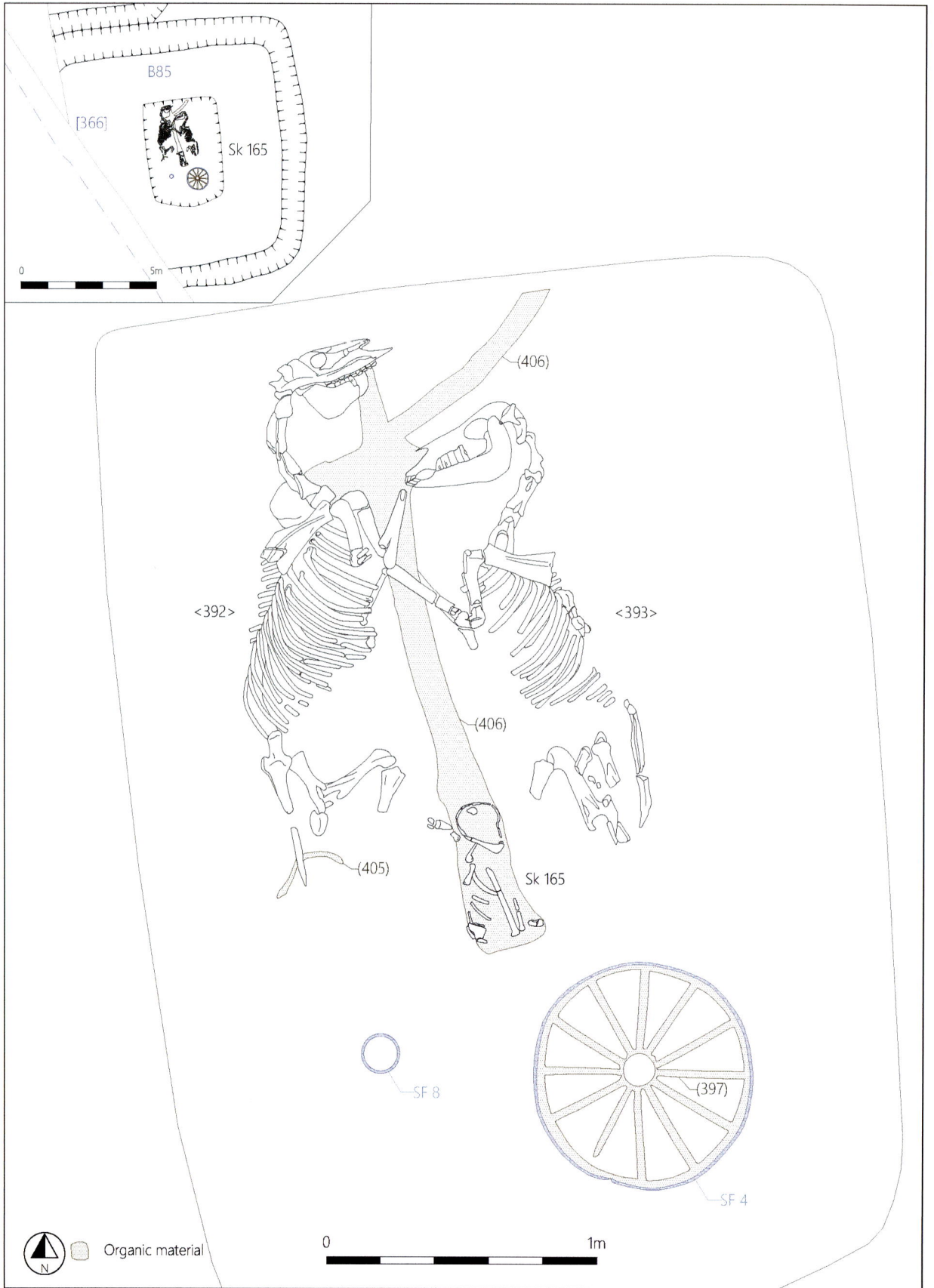

B85

[366]

Sk 165

0   5m

(406)

<392>   <393>

(406)

(405)   Sk 165

SF 8

(397)

SF 4

N

Organic material

0   1m

Figure 4.85 Plan of Barrow 85 and chariot burial

Figure 4.86 View of ponies and eastern wheel, facing north. Scales: 2 × 1m

Figure 4.88 View of eastern wheel as excavated, facing east. Scale: 0.4m

Figure 4.87 View of ponies and human burial (at far right), facing east. Scale: 2 × 1m

wooden wheel rim, 12 spokes (spokes a–l) and the nave (Fig. 4.88). There was a deposit of mixed gravel (398) between the soil stains. Five samples from minerally preserved wood attached to the iron tyre showed that the wheel rim was made from one or more pieces of ash. A

small piece of iron sheet (SF 14) was found between two of the spokes. The chariot fittings are described in more detail in Chapter 10.

The lower iron nave-hoop (SF 16) for the east wheel was found approximately 80mm below the remaining upper part of the hub and was *c.* 0.13m in diameter, with a D-shaped cross-section. The interior surface had the mineralised remains of leather/skin with visible hair fibres. As the leather was only present on the interior of the hoop, it does not appear to have represented binding or reinforcement; perhaps it was a washer to ensure a tight fit with the nave. A small piece of iron corrosion (SF 11) lay adjacent to the hub of the eastern wheel, and a small amorphous patch of dark silt (408) lying below the wheel could represent the remains of an organic element associated with it. The wheel itself lay on a deposit of mixed gravel (403) whose limits approximately conformed to those of the iron tyre.

The corresponding lower iron nave-hoop (SF 8) for the western wheel was located 1m to the west of the centre of the east wheel. This nave-hoop was also *c.* 0.13m in diameter and had a D-shaped cross-section. It too had mineralised leather or skin with attached hair on the interior surface.

An iron horse bit directly underlay the eastern wheel and consisted of a pair of iron rings (SFs 9 and 13) with a curved, folded iron snaffle bar (SF 12) between. Both the rings had traces of non-ferrous plating, and one of the rings had a knop close to one of the terminals. A small L-shaped fragment of iron sheet (SF 14), lying a short way to the south of the bit, may have been associated with it (Chapter 10).

The pole was represented by a 0.10m wide linear soil stain (406) that extended for 2.30m along the axis of the grave; the southern end was shown by a shallow linear void in the top of deposit 404. The pole appeared to be square in section, but this may be due to the remains being compacted by the covering deposits rather than a true representation of its form. A sub-circular deposit of distinct dark silt (409) lay at the northern end of the pole; whilst this deposit obviously represented the decay of an organic object, it is not immediately clear what it may have been. A further dark silt deposit aligned south-west to north-east near the northern end of the pole could speculatively represent the remains of a yoke, although it is offset from the pole and not at right-angles to it.

Both the pole and the western nave-hoop overlay a distinct rectangular deposit of clean gravel (404) in the south-west corner of the grave. The edges of this deposit were not marked by dark soil stains suggestive of decayed organic material, but even so its straight-edged form suggests that it may have filled a void, such as the interior of a box or other structure. Alternatively, it may represent differential backfilling of the grave.

Ponies 392 and 393

The human burial was 'framed' between the lower legs of two adult ponies that lay facing each other in the northern part of the grave (392 to the west and 393 to the east; see Chapter 14). Both ponies were lying with their heads to the north, 392 facing east and 393 facing west.

The right foreleg of the western pony (392) was bent northwards towards the muzzle of the eastern pony, but the foot was missing. The dentition of this pony shows that it was fully adult. The absence of the front of the skull and canine teeth means the sex of this pony is unknown. The right hind leg of 392 was also missing, but the left hind leg was bent (or arranged) to the south. The right sides of the pelvis and skull were truncated. The tail appeared to be bent back along the spine, possibly represented by a soil stain (405). The ribs partly overlay the left foreleg of the eastern pony. The eastern pony (393) was laid on its right side, facing west towards the other pony. This pony was better preserved than its western counterpart, although the hind legs were truncated. The right foreleg lay beneath the soil stain of the pole, but the left foreleg lay above it, extending westwards beneath the ribs of the western pony. The form of the canine teeth of this pony showed that it was a male and lipping to his right femur indicated age and/or his employment as a traction animal (to be expected for an animal that had probably pulled a chariot!). The wear on this pony's teeth suggested an age of between five and seven years and the exposure of dentine suggests damage by a bit. Pony 393 was 1.29m (12.7 hands) tall at the withers.

Unfortunately, the highly fragmented condition of the ponies' crania means that it was not possible to determine if they were killed by pole-axing, although this may have been the preferred way of despatching them as it would have solved the problem of moving heavy carcases about if carried out in the grave.

Grave fills

The mixed deposit (391) overlying the ponies contained a series of very small copper alloy fragments (SF 15), one of which was possibly part of a ring. Due to the truncation of the grave, these fragments could be intrusive and therefore perhaps not associated with the chariot.

A straight, vertical sheer-line (413) within the grave's fill appeared to retain a mixed gravel deposit (396) in the north-east corner of the grave. This could indicate a structure within the grave or equally have been created by the backfilling of different soils.

Two amorphous dark silt deposits (411) underlying the western pony and the pole were further evidence of organic material within the grave, but whether from the decay of the pony or from structural/other elements of the chariot is unclear.

A small number of rye grains were recovered from deposit 395 (the material uppermost within the iron tyre) and material (405) around the pelvis of the western horse; this grain could potentially be of great significance, but the quantities recovered were not sufficient for radiocarbon dating. However, elsewhere on site, late or post-medieval radiocarbon dates were obtained for larger groups of rye grains, so it is likely that the rye associated with the chariot grave was also intrusive, presumably through bioturbation.

The mixed lower fill of the grave (410) contained a tiny fragment of copper alloy (SF 17), perhaps from a pin.

Radiocarbon date

A radiocarbon date of 205–51 cal BC [number not available] was obtained from one of the ponies. This gives the mid-2nd century BC as the central date for the chariot burial, sitting towards the later end of the results obtained by the project dating eight other Yorkshire chariot burials (Jay *et al.* 2012, 181)

Barrow 87

Summary

Barrow 87 was situated between Barrow 5 and Barrow 20 in the western barrow group; it was only classified as a barrow during the post-excavation phase (Fig. 4.1). It consisted of a C-shaped ditch that wrapped around grave 15771 and was at least 3.6m from north to south and 3.0m from east to west (Fig. 4.89); the western ditch and south-western corner were not present, but the barrow was probably square in form. The northern ditch and north-east corner were excavated as segment 15687, the remainder of the ditch as segment 15685. The ditch had a variable, rounded profile, ranging from 0.50m to 0.80m wide, with

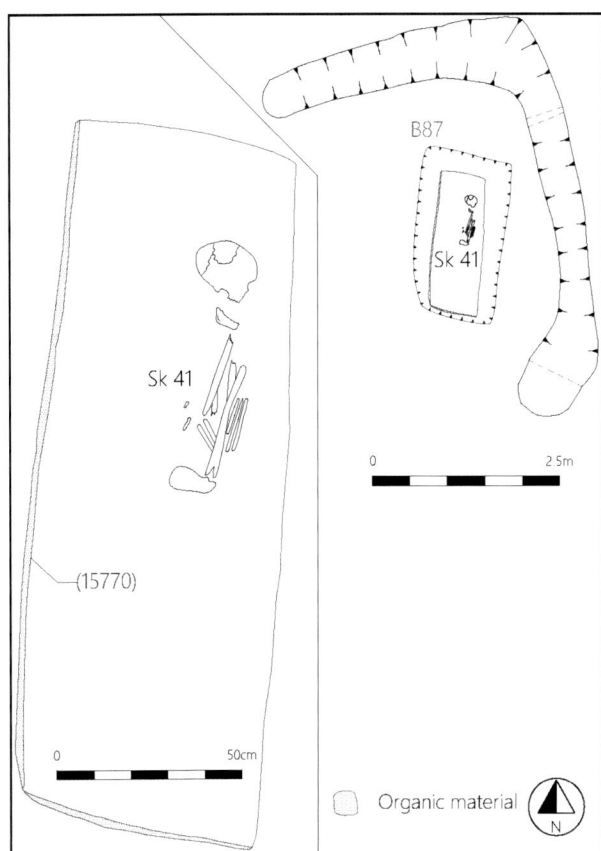

Figure 4.89 Plan of Barrow 87 and Skeleton 41 <15782>

an average depth of 0.20m, and was filled with an homogeneous brown sandy silt mixed with moderate gravel.

Grave 15771

This relatively large, sub-rectangular grave was 2.15m long, 1.20m wide and *c.* 0.35m deep. It was off-centre to the barrow ditches.

Skeleton (15782 – Sk 41)

A structure contained the very poorly preserved and extremely fragmented skeleton of an individual of unknown sex, aged over 35 years, lying in a contracted posture on the left side with the head to the north, facing east. Four small pieces of ossified soft tissue were recovered from the torso area, perhaps indicating a chronic lung infection or disease. The burial was placed in the northeast part of the structure, leaving most of the structure apparently empty.

Structure 15770

The grave contained a distinct rectangular deposit of dark silt (15768), which was bounded on the south and east sides by a narrow dark soil stain (15770) representing the traces of a rectangular structure measuring 1.82m long, 0.65m wide and 0.25m deep.

Flat graves with structures

Some 39 graves (plus 15515 described above with Barrow 13 and three possible graves) did not have surrounding ditches; these are described in this report as 'flat graves'. The fact that there were only slight traces of the ditches of some barrows (notably Barrows 13, 18, 23, 70 and 87) makes it possible that some of the flat graves had been enclosed by ditches that were destroyed by later ploughing. The following burials are, at the time of writing, believed to be Iron Age in date, largely because of their north–south alignments, and in some cases through associated grave goods. However, given the fact that the Anglian burial repertoire includes both north–south alignment and crouched or flexed postures, it is possible that some of the following burials are from periods other than the Iron Age.

Five flat graves (007, 15275, 15427, 16104 and 16463) contained the remains of rectangular structures (Fig. 4.90).

Grave 007 – burial 035

Summary

Grave 007 was situated immediately east of Barrow 85 and was a large, slightly trapezoidal cut that was 3.00m long, 2.00m wide and 0.84m deep (Figs 4.3 and 4.91).

Skeleton (035 – Sk 163)

The structure contained the poorly preserved and severely fragmented skeleton of a female of 36–45 years, crouched on the left side, with the head to the north, facing east. She had DJC of the left temporo-mandibular joint, as well as maxillary sinusitis and CO.

Structure

A distinct rectangular block of brown sandy gravel (004) indicated the presence of a structure centrally within the grave. The structure measured 1.25m in length, 0.82m in width and 0.40m in height. The 'interface' between deposit 004 and the surrounding grave fill (006), representing the edges of the structure, was recorded as context 036. Deposit 004 filled the structure, with paler sandy gravel (006) surrounding it, and with an area of darker soil (005) at the structure's north-west corner. The upper part of the grave was filled with mixed sand and gravel (003).

Grave 15275 – burial 15274

Summary

Grave 15275 was situated in the south-western part of the western barrow group, forming a rectangular cut 1.95m long, 1.50m wide and 1.03m deep (Figs 4.90, 4.92 and 4.93). The fills of this grave were noticeably moist, which made for challenging excavation conditions, but contributed to the preservation of the soil stain of a 'box' structure (15262).

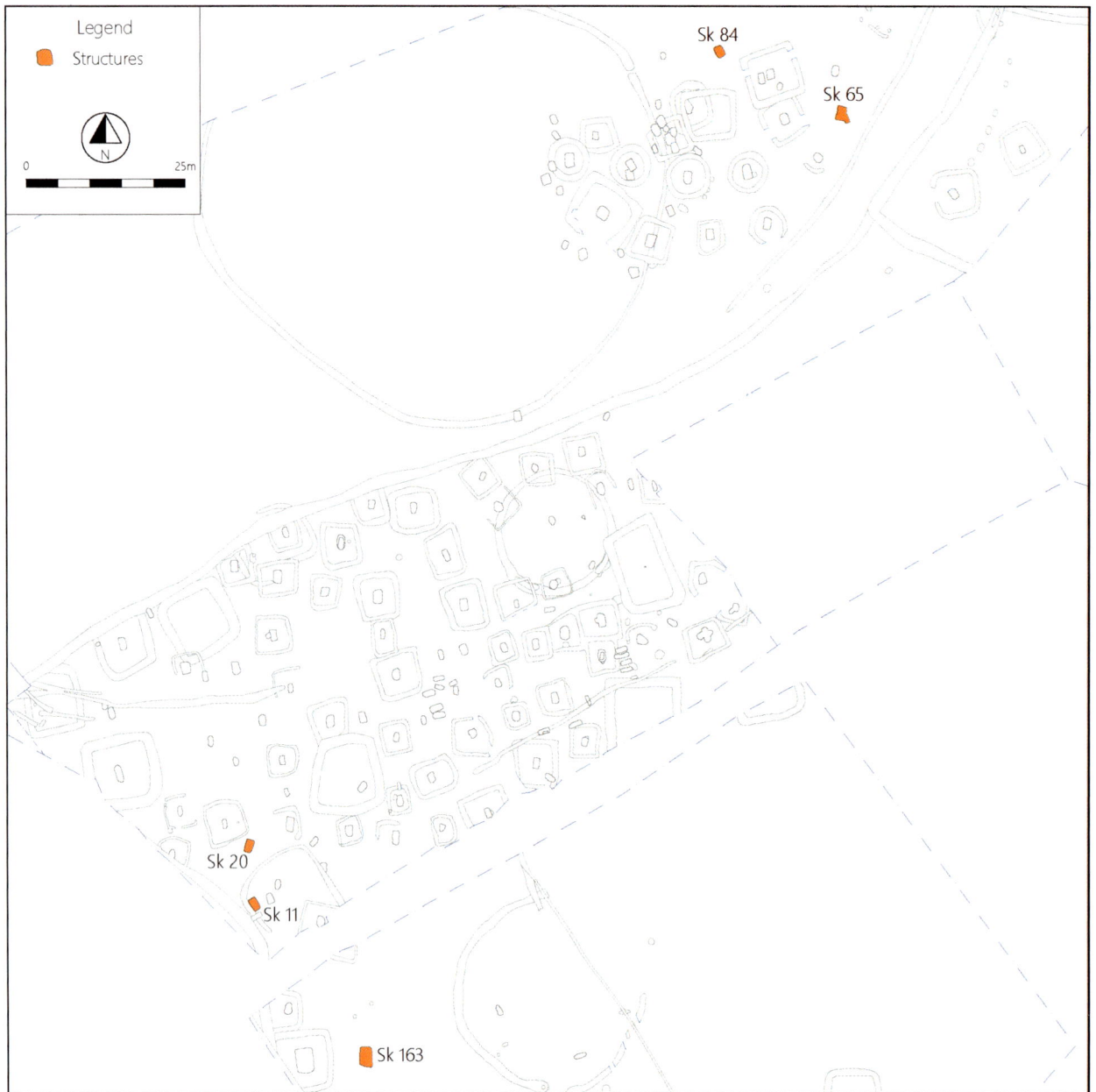

Figure 4.90 Distribution of flat burials with structures

Skeleton (15274 – Sk 11)

Centrally within the structure was the poorly preserved and severely fragmented skeleton of a probable female who was probably aged 26–35 years, lying in a flexed posture, and with the torso apparently supine, with the head to the south, facing west. This individual had CO and pilasterism of both femora.

Structure

The structure was shown by a 10mm-wide band of dark grey silt (15262) that delineated a rectangle 1.22m long, 0.62 wide and 0.27m high. Two separate elongated rectangular deposits of dark grey silt (15271 and 15288), which dipped downwards within the box fill, were interpreted as the remains of timbers that had separated from the structure. Deposits 15271 and 15288 were not extensive enough to represent conclusively the remains of a lid but may be evidence of the partial collapse of the structure, which is also suggested by the separation of the southern and eastern sides at the south-east corner. There was no evidence for a base. The structure was filled with two separate deposits of yellowish-brown gravel (15261 and 15273), with a slightly darker gravel fill (15263) surrounding it.

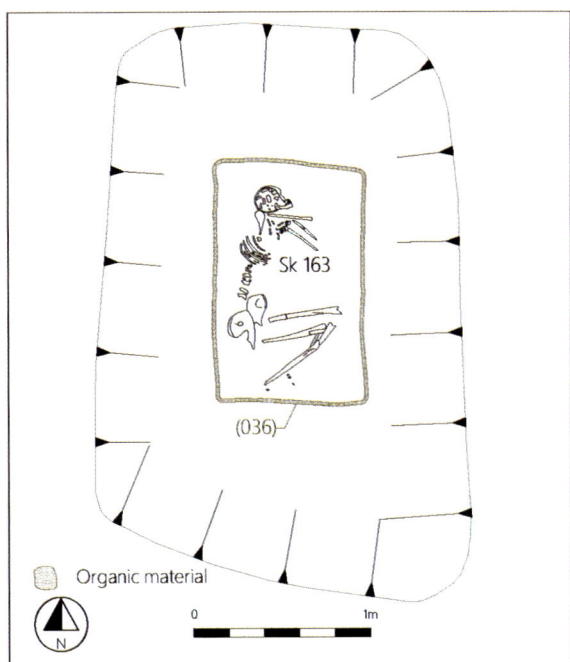

Figure 4.91 Plan of Skeleton 163 <035> in Grave 007

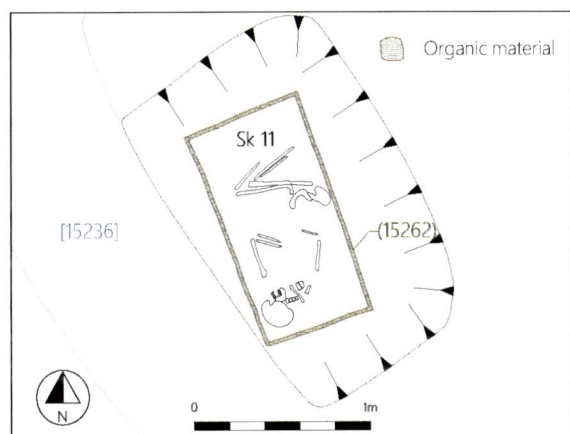

Figure 4.92 Plan of Skeleton 11 <15274>

Figure 4.93 View of Skeleton 11 in flat grave 15275, facing west. Scales: 1m and 0.5m

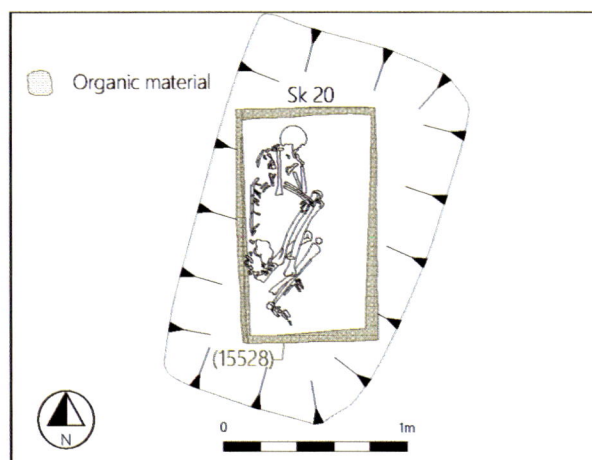

Figure 4.94 Plan of Skeleton 20 <15428> in Grave 15427

Figure 4.95 View of Structure 15480 in Grave 15427, facing east, showing stepped construction. Scale: 1m

Grave 15427 – burial 15428

Summary

Grave 15427 was situated *c.* 5m north of Grave 15275. This was a large rectangular cut, its maximum extent being 2.20m long, 1.50m wide and 0.50m deep (Figs 4.94 and 4.95). The grave had an unusual, stepped profile indicating that it was constructed in three stages.

Skeleton (15428 – Sk 20)

This was the poorly preserved and moderately fragmented skeleton of a probable male, who was probably between 36 and 45 years old. He lay along the left side of the structure, in a crouched posture on his left side, with head to the north, facing east. He had pilasterism of both femora. Part of a disarticulated maxilla from another individual was found with the skeleton. The skeleton was radiocarbon-dated to the period 370–160 cal BC (SUERC-81073).

First stage – structure 15528

The earliest stage was a rectangular cut (15528) in the base of the grave, measuring 1.14m long, 0.77m wide and 0.15m deep, which represented a gravel-filled structure (15549).

Second stage – structure 15480

The second-stage structure (15480) consisted of a shallow 'shelf' (15649), measuring 1.20m long, 0.65m wide and 0.15m high. A deposit of gravel filled this structure (15484) and there was a further deposit of gravel 'packing' surrounding it (15429).

Third stage

The third stage consisted of another rectangular cut (15427) at the top of the grave; this was on a markedly different alignment to the two previous stages and was also filled with mixed gravel (15550).

Grave 16104 – burial 16166

Summary

Grave 16104 was located on the eastern edge of the eastern barrow group and cut into an earlier grave (16263 – see below). This was a large rectangular cut, 2.25m long, 1.55m wide and 0.60m deep (Fig. 4.96). As with Grave 15275, the grave was wet and there was remarkable preservation of a rectangular structure within it. The upper grave fill (16102) contained four joining sherds from a

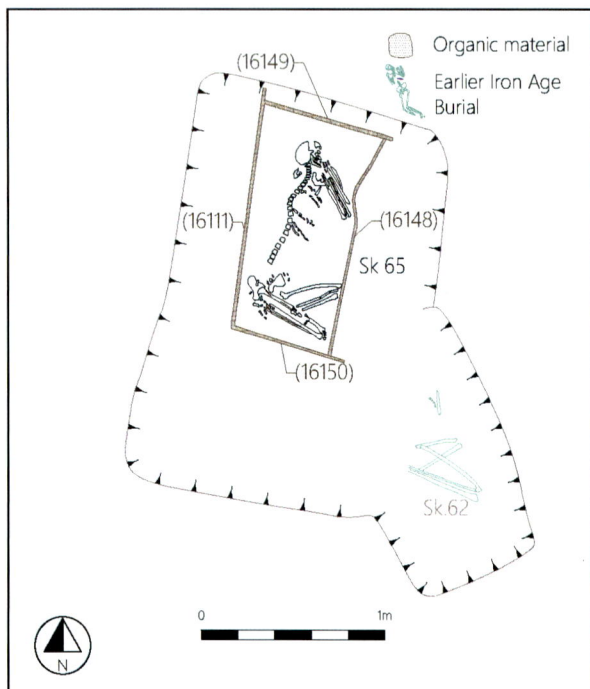

Figure 4.96 Plan of Skeletons 65 <16166> and 62 <16116> in Grave 16104

thin-walled cylindrical jar, along with eight undiagnostic pieces of slag and three possible smithing hearth fragments. Context 16102 also contained two flint cores and three flakes of broadly Neolithic or early Bronze Age date. Fill 16115 (a dark deposit beneath the skull) contained a piece of undiagnostic slag.

Skeleton (16166 – Sk 65)

This moderately preserved and extremely fragmented skeleton was of a female aged over 26 years, lying on the left side, with the head to the north and facing east. This woman had OA and DJC of the spine, further DJC of the left mandibular joint and HFI.

Structure

The form of the structure was shown by rectangular bands of dark grey silt, suggesting it was 1.25m long, 0.65m wide and 0.25m high. The north side was recorded as 16149, the east side 16148, the south side 16150, and the west side 16111. The eastern and northern edges were off-set from the adjoining edges, suggesting the partial collapse of the structure, which was filled with silty sand (16176), overlying the burial. Two horizontal planes of dark silt (16145 and 16146) directly overlay the structure, possibly representing the remains of a lid. A very dark silt deposit (16101), presumably the remains of organic material, covered the 'lid'. Two successive deposits of gravel (16102 and 16103) filled the remainder of the grave, the latter containing a late Neolithic/early Bronze Age edge-utilised flint flake. A piece of undiagnostic slag was found within context 16149.

Grave 16463 – burial 16464

Summary

This was a large grave situated north of Barrow 39 on the northern fringe of the eastern barrow group (Fig. 4.90). It was a regular rectangular cut with vertical sides, measuring 1.80m in length, 1.35m in width and 0.65m in depth (Fig. 4.97). The primary fill (16462) contained nine sherds of Iron Age pottery.

Skeleton (16464 – Sk 84)

The skeleton, positioned centrally within the structure, was of a probable male aged over 36 years, lying in a crouched posture on the left side, with the head to the north, facing east. This individual had DJC of the spine and both hip joints. He had a fracture of the left radius, possibly caused by a blow to the left forearm. There was also lamellar bone on both lower legs. A group of three amorphous deposits of dark silt (16456) on the eastern side of the grave might be traces of organic material (or objects?) that had been deposited there.

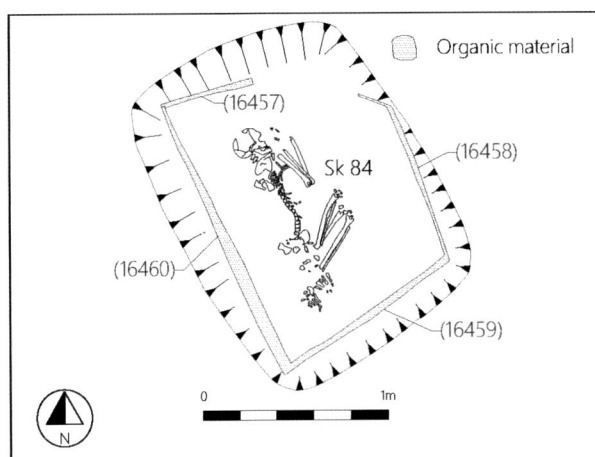

Figure 4.97 Plan of Skeleton 84 <16464> in Grave 16463

Structure

The structure within the grave was represented by thin bands of organic silt along each of its edges: 16457 at the northern edge, 16460 along the west, 16459 along the south and 16458 along the east. The north-east corner of the structure had apparently collapsed (or was at least missing), but it was possible to ascertain the length at 1.56m, the width at 1.05m and the height at a minimum of 0.15m. Another thin band of dark silt (16461) at the north-west corner may have been the remains of a separate 'compartment'.

Flat graves without structures

The following 34 (plus two possible) graves had no indications of structures within them. They are assumed to be Iron Age because of their north–south alignments, crouched posture and, in three cases, associated finds (SF 589 – an iron bow brooch with Burial 15773; an iron short involuted brooch with Burial 16997 (SF 155); and an iron bow brooch with Burial 18133 (SF 300)).

Grave 15084 – burial 15092

Summary

Grave 15084 was situated in the north-western part of the western barrow group, between B2 and B12 (Fig. 4.98). It was cut through by a later gully (15082), which had badly disturbed the burial. The grave was a relatively shallow oval cut, measuring 1.4m long, 0.70m wide and 0.22m deep. The grave fill (15083) contained re-worked indeterminate grain.

Skeleton (15092 – Sk 1)

The extremely poorly preserved and severely fragmented skeleton was of an adult of unknown sex and appeared to be crouched with the head to the north.

Grave 15191 – burial 15192

Summary

Grave 15191 lay immediately south of Grave 15084, between B2 and B12 (Fig. 4.98). The grave was a relatively deep, rounded rectangular cut, 1.50m long, 1.05m wide and 0.62m deep, with two separate mixed gravel fills (15190 at the base and 15189 at the top). Fill 15189 contained an Iron Age sherd, and a disarticulated human clavicle from another individual was also present.

Skeleton (15192 – Sk 4)

The poorly preserved and severely fragmented skeleton was that of a possible female aged 17–35 years who was placed in the northern part of the grave. The body appeared to be supine with the legs drawn up into a crouched position and the head to the north.

Grave 15234 – burial 15233

Summary

This relatively deep, rectangular grave was situated immediately east of Grave 15275 and a modern engineering test pit (15229) clipped its north-west edge (Fig. 4.98). The grave, which was sub-rectangular with steep edges and a flat base, was 1.65m long, 1.16m wide and 0.43m deep.

Skeleton (15233 – Sk 8)

The very poorly preserved and severely fragmented skeleton was tightly crouched in a prone posture, with the head to the north, facing downwards. This was a female aged 26–35 years who had stenosis to the neck (which may have caused pain, weakness or numbness), a possible well-healed fracture to the right tibia, plus CO. The skeleton was radiocarbon-dated to the period 380–170 cal BC (SUERC-96408).

Grave 15256 – burial 15255

Summary

This burial was situated between Barrow 6 and Barrow 20 (Fig. 4.98). The grave was a shallow amorphous cut, 1.40m long, 1.00m wide and *c.* 0.10m deep. The grave fill (15254) contained a 'very fresh' and unsnapped flint bladelet of early Bronze Age date.

Skeleton (15255 – Sk 9)

The very poorly preserved and severely fragmented skeleton was of a possible female, aged 17–19 years, lying apparently prone in a crouched posture, with the head to the north, facing east. Both femora were slightly bowed.

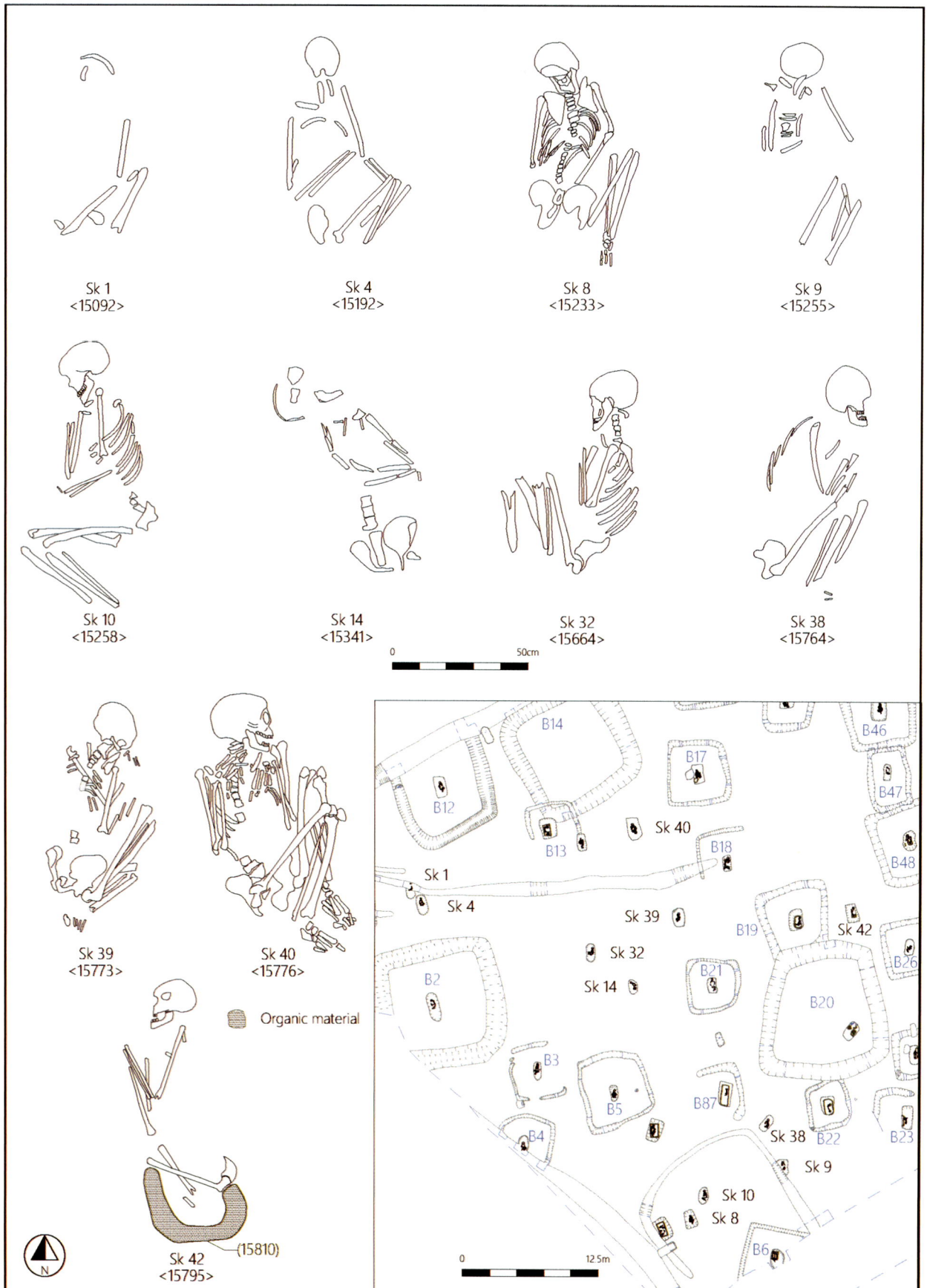

Figure 4.98 Plan of flat grave Skeletons 1 <15092> to 42 <15795>

Grave 15259 – burial 15258

Summary

Grave 15259 was situated north-east of Grave 15234 (Fig. 4.98). The grave was a relatively shallow, oval cut, 1.55m long, 0.55m wide and 0.25m deep.

Skeleton (15258 – Sk 10)

The poorly preserved and severely fragmented skeleton was of a probable female aged 18–25 years, lying flexed against the eastern edge of the grave, on the right side, with the head to the north, facing west. This woman had lamellar bone on both tibiae and some of her ribs. The skeleton was radiocarbon-dated to the period 410–230 cal BC (SUERC-78038).

Grave 15342 – burial 15341

Summary

This grave was situated north-east of Barrow 5 and was badly truncated by ploughing (Fig. 4.98). The grave was a shallow, oval cut 1.12m long, 0.85m wide and 0.12m deep.

Skeleton (15341 – Sk 14)

The poorly preserved skeleton, which was missing its legs, was of a probable female, aged 18–35 years, lying on the left side, with the head to the north, facing east.

Grave 15665 – burial 15664

Summary

Grave 15665 was situated *c.* 8m east of Barrow 2 (Fig. 4.98). The grave was a rounded rectangular cut, 1.60m long, 0.80m wide and 0.28m deep.

Skeleton (15664 – Sk 32)

The very poorly preserved burial was probably of a male aged over 46 years old, lying in a crouched posture on the right side, with the head to the north, facing west. This individual had DDD and DJC of the spine, plus soft tissue trauma and a possible greenstick fracture to the right leg above the knee.

Grave 15765 – burial 15764

Summary

Grave 15765 lay between Barrow 22 and Barrow 87 (Fig. 4.98). This grave was rectangular in form with rounded ends and was aligned roughly north–south. It measured 1.55m in length, 0.78m in width and 0.36m in depth. The upper fill of the grave (15632) contained a late Neolithic/early Bronze Age flint flake in 'fresh' condition, and the burial itself was surrounded by brown silt (15763).

Skeleton (15764 – Sk 38)

The very poorly preserved and moderately fragmented skeleton was of a possible female, aged 18–25 years,

aligned south-west to north-east and lying on the left side in a tightly crouched posture, with the head to the north, facing south-east. The distinct brown silt (15763) surrounding the skeleton, along with its tightly crouched posture, suggest this burial may have been wrapped.

Grave 15774 – burial 15773

Summary

This grave lay in between Barrow 18 and Barrow 21 and was a relatively large and deep sub-rectangular cut, measuring 1.67m in length, 1.15m in width and 0.32m in depth (Fig. 4.98).

Skeleton (15773 – Sk 39)

The very poorly preserved and severely fragmented skeleton was of a female probably aged 36–45 years. The body was in a crouched as well as prone posture, with the head to the north, tilted to the east. A fragmentary iron bow brooch (SF 589) was found with this burial. The skeleton was radiocarbon-dated to the period 390–190 cal BC (SUERC-83075).

Grave 15777 – burial 15776

Summary

Grave 15777 was situated east of Barrow 13. It was rectangular in plan, with a rounded southern end, and was 1.95m long, 1.2m wide and 0.10 deep (Fig. 4.98).

Skeleton (15776 – Sk 40)

The poorly preserved and moderately fragmented skeleton was female, probably aged from 36–45 years old, lying in a crouched posture on the left side, with the head to the north, facing east. This woman had maxillary sinusitis. The skeleton was radiocarbon-dated to the period 370–160 cal BC (SUERC-96413).

Grave 15793 – burial 15795

Summary

Grave 15793, which was situated immediately north of Barrow 20, was a slightly trapezoidal cut, with a length of 1.70m, a width of 1.10m and a depth of 0.33m. A C-shaped deposit of dark silt (15810) which enclosed the area of the burial's lower legs was presumably the remains of organic material, perhaps a lining to the grave (Fig. 4.98). Above this, a separate and distinct rectangular deposit of dark silt (15794) covered the entire body apart from the head, suggesting that organic material was placed over the burial.

Skeleton (15795 – Sk 42)

The poorly preserved and severely fragmented skeleton was of indeterminate sex, aged over 36 years, lying in a crouched posture, on the right side, with the head to the north, facing west. Endocranial new bone was present.

Grave 15958 – burial 15957

Summary

This burial and the following ten burials were situated adjacent to, or within, the eastern barrow group (Fig. 4.99). Grave 15958 lay in between Barrow 30 and Barrow 42, and was an oval cut, 1.35m long, 0.95m wide and 0.40m deep.

Skeleton (15957 – Sk 50)

The very poorly preserved and severely fragmented skeleton was of a 10½–12½ year-old, in a crouched posture, lying on the right side, with the head to the north, facing west.

Grave 15961 – burial 15960

Summary

Grave 15961 was situated between Barrow 30 and Barrow 37. It measured 1.60m long and 1.02m wide and was relatively deep at 0.65m (Fig. 4.99).

Skeleton (15960 – Sk 51)

The moderately preserved and moderately fragmented skeleton was of a female, aged 26–35 years, in a supine posture, with the head to the north, facing east; the lower legs were bent at the knee and tucked back up under the right upper leg and the arms were bent at the elbow back up against the torso. This woman had DJC of the spine, a cyst that had caused joint change at the right hip, and CO.

Grave 15964 – burial 15963

Summary

This grave was situated immediately south of Barrow 30 (Fig. 4.99). It was a relatively deep and irregular cut that measured 1.85m in length, 1.50m in width and 0.67m in depth. The grave fill (15962) contained an Iron Age sherd.

Skeleton (15963 – Sk 52)

The moderately preserved and severely fragmented skeleton was of a probable male aged 18–25 years, lying in a crouched posture on the left side, with the head to the north, facing east. There was lamellar bone on the left tibia.

Grave 15967 – burial 15966

Summary

This grave, which was situated north of Barrow 34, was relatively large with a sub-rectangular plan that measured 1.51m in length, 0.96m in width and 0.62m in depth (Fig. 4.99).

Skeleton (15966 – Sk 53)

The poorly preserved and severely fragmented burial was of an individual aged 10–12 years, in a contracted posture, lying on the left side, with the head to the north, facing east.

Grave 16093 – burial 16092

Summary

Grave 16093 was situated to the east of Barrow 43 on the eastern edge of the barrow group (Fig. 4.99). This was another relatively large and deep feature of sub-rectangular form, measuring 1.70m long, 1.15m wide and 0.55m deep. The primary fill (16091) contained ten Iron Age pottery sherds (from four separate vessels) and burnt animal bone fragments, plus a piece of possible smithing hearth bottom, three pieces of undiagnostic slag and oak charcoal fuel waste.

Skeleton (16092 – Sk 60)

The poorly preserved and severely fragmented skeleton was a female aged 26–35 years, lying in a crouched posture on the left side, with her head to the north, facing east. There was endocranial new bone.

Grave 16263 - burial 16116

Summary

The north-eastern part of Grave 16263 was cut away by Grave 16104, both graves being situated on the eastern margin of the barrow group (Fig. 4.99). Grave 16263 had a regular rectangular form, measuring 1.38m long, 0.76m wide and 0.40m deep.

Skeleton (16116 – Sk 62)

Much of this poorly preserved and extremely fragmented skeleton was missing due to truncation, but it appeared to be either crouched or flexed and lying on the left side, with the (missing) head to the north, presumably facing east. An individual of unknown sex, aged over 18 years, was represented. The extra cranium found at the south end of Grave 16104, which truncated this burial, apparently belonged to this skeleton.

Grave 16287 – burial 16285

Summary

Grave 16287 lay within the circuit of Barrow 33 and pre-dated the barrow's central burial (16018, grave 16019; see Fig. 4.34). Grave 16287 was rectangular, with vertical edges to a depth of 0.95m; it measured 1.40m in length and 1.28m in width (Fig. 4.99). The upper grave fill (16284) contained pieces of oak charcoal fuel waste and a late Neolithic/early Bronze Age knife or scraper. The base of the grave was covered with dark grey silt (16286), which contained five Iron Age calcite-gritted sherds, plus

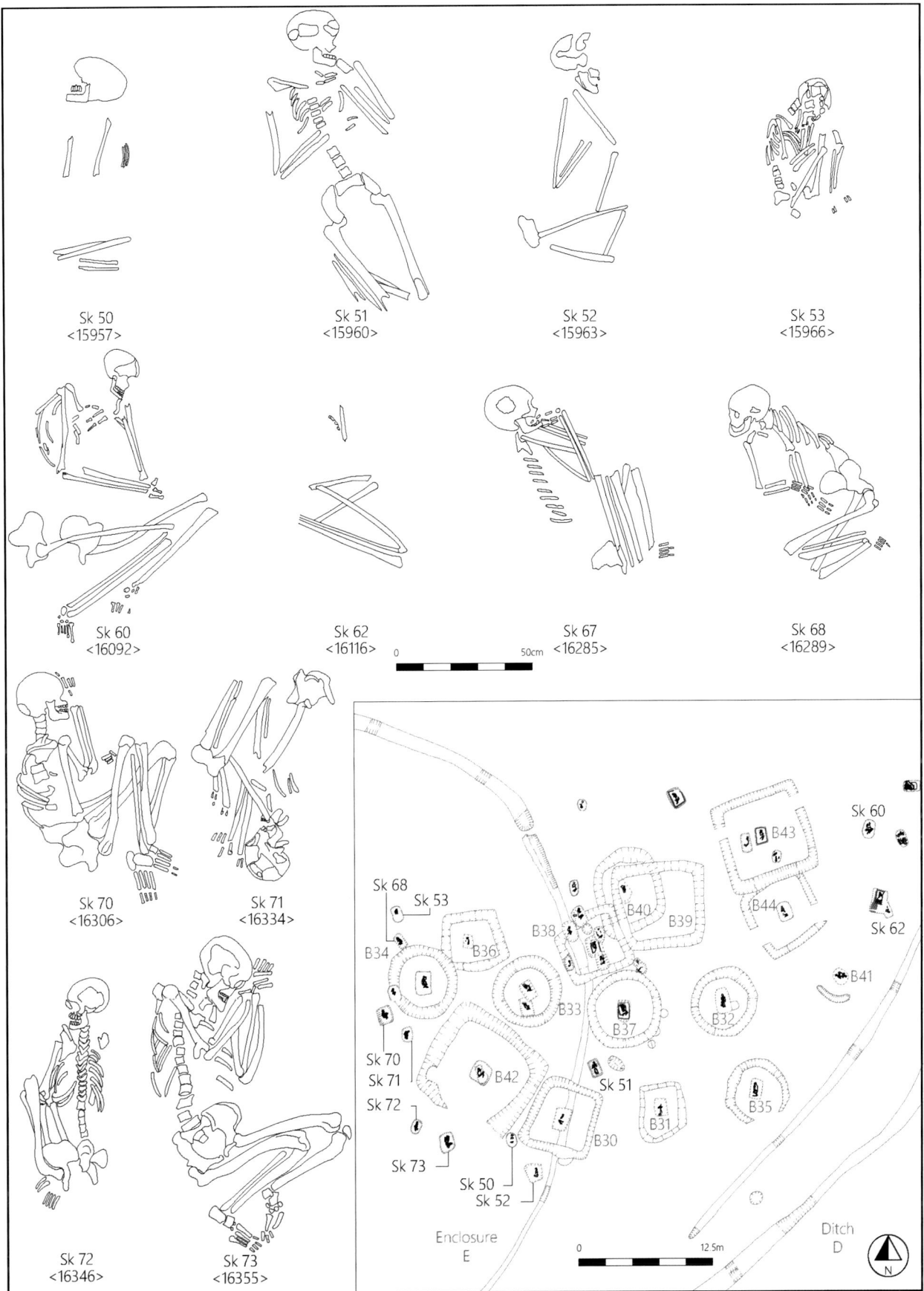

Figure 4.99 Plan of flat grave Skeletons 50 <15957> to 73 <16355>

animal bone fragments. The surface of deposit 16286 had an uneven wave-like appearance, which makes it possible that it was composed of individual turves that had lined the base of the grave.

Skeleton (16285 – Sk 67)

This moderately preserved but severely fragmented skeleton was of a male aged 18–35 years, lying in a crouched posture on the left side, with the head to the north, facing east, and rested directly on deposit 16286. Severe pathological lesions on the left side of the face and mandible, the base of the cranium and the cervical vertebrae were infectious in nature; these were possibly caused by tuberculosis or another lung infection. There was also evidence of CO. The skeleton was radiocarbon-dated to the period 350–40 cal BC (SUERC-79417).

Grave 16290 – burial 16289

Summary

This grave was situated immediately north of Barrow 34 (Fig. 4.99). It was another example of a relatively large and deep sub-rectangular grave, measuring 1.42m in length, 0.91m in width and 0.64m in depth.

Skeleton (16289 – Sk 68)

The flexed burial of a female aged over 46 years lay centrally within the grave, on the right side, with the head to the north, facing west. The skeleton was poorly preserved and severely fragmented. This woman had DDD and DJC of the spine, with further DJC of the right hip; there was also endocranial new bone and lamellar bone on both tibiae.

Grave 16307 – burial 16306

Summary

Grave 16307 was situated immediately south-west of Barrow 34 (see Fig. 4.35). This grave (16307) was large and sub-rectangular, measuring 1.3m long, 1.18m wide and 0.52m deep (Fig. 4.99). The burial (apart from the knees) and the western half of the grave's base was covered by a rectangular deposit of dark silt (16304), making it possible that it was deliberately covered by organic material. The fact that the knees protruded from the organic deposit probably indicates that it was not the base of a structure. The overall grave fill (16305) contained an undiagnostic slag fragment.

Skeleton (16306 – Sk 70)

The poorly preserved and moderately fragmented skeleton was of a male aged over 46 years, lying in a crouched posture on the left side, with the head to the north, facing east. This man suffered from OA, DJC and DDD of the spine, along with OA on the right clavicle,

the latter matching with a DJC on the right acromion. There was further DJC at the right hip. Three probable gallstones were found in the torso area, and a twig-like ossified structure found with the skull was probably an ossified part of the stylohyoid ligament and associated with Eagle's syndrome.

Grave 16335 – burial 16334

Summary

This grave was situated south-east of Grave 16307, and was of similar form and size, but with the axis skewed slightly to the north-east (Fig. 4.99). It measured 1.37m in length, 1.13m in width and 0.67m in depth. A distinct deposit of charcoal-rich dark brown sandy silt (16333) filled the base of the grave, possibly representing organic material that was laid over the burial.

Skeleton (16334 – Sk 71)

The poorly preserved and severely fragmented skeleton was possibly male, aged over 36 years, lying in a tightly crouched posture on the left side, with the head to the south, facing west. This man had DJC in the right hip and spine, OA in the left hip, maxillary sinusitis, potential stress fractures to the necks of both femurs, CO, potential osteopenia (reduced mineral content) in the long bones and pilasterism of the femora.

Grave 16347 – burial 16346

Summary

This rectangular grave lay immediately south-west of Barrow 42 and measured 1.32m in length, 0.89m in width and 0.49m in depth (Fig. 4.99).

Skeleton (16346 – Sk 72)

The moderately preserved and fragmented skeleton was of a female aged 26–35 years, lying contracted in a prone posture, with the legs and arms drawn up under the torso, and with the head to the north, facing west. At 149.7cm tall she was well below average height for Iron Age women of the period (161cm) and had CO.

Grave 16356 – burial 16355

Summary

Grave 16356 was immediately south of Barrow 42, and was another large, deep, sub-rectangular example. It measured 1.71m in length, 1.39m in width and 0.98m in depth (Fig. 4.99). The north-western part of the grave's base was covered by a deposit of dark-brown sandy silt (16354) that overlapped the western part of the burial, pointing to the presence of organic material in the grave. The overall grave fill (16353) contained two Iron Age sherds, animal bone fragments and a residual Neolithic flint blade.

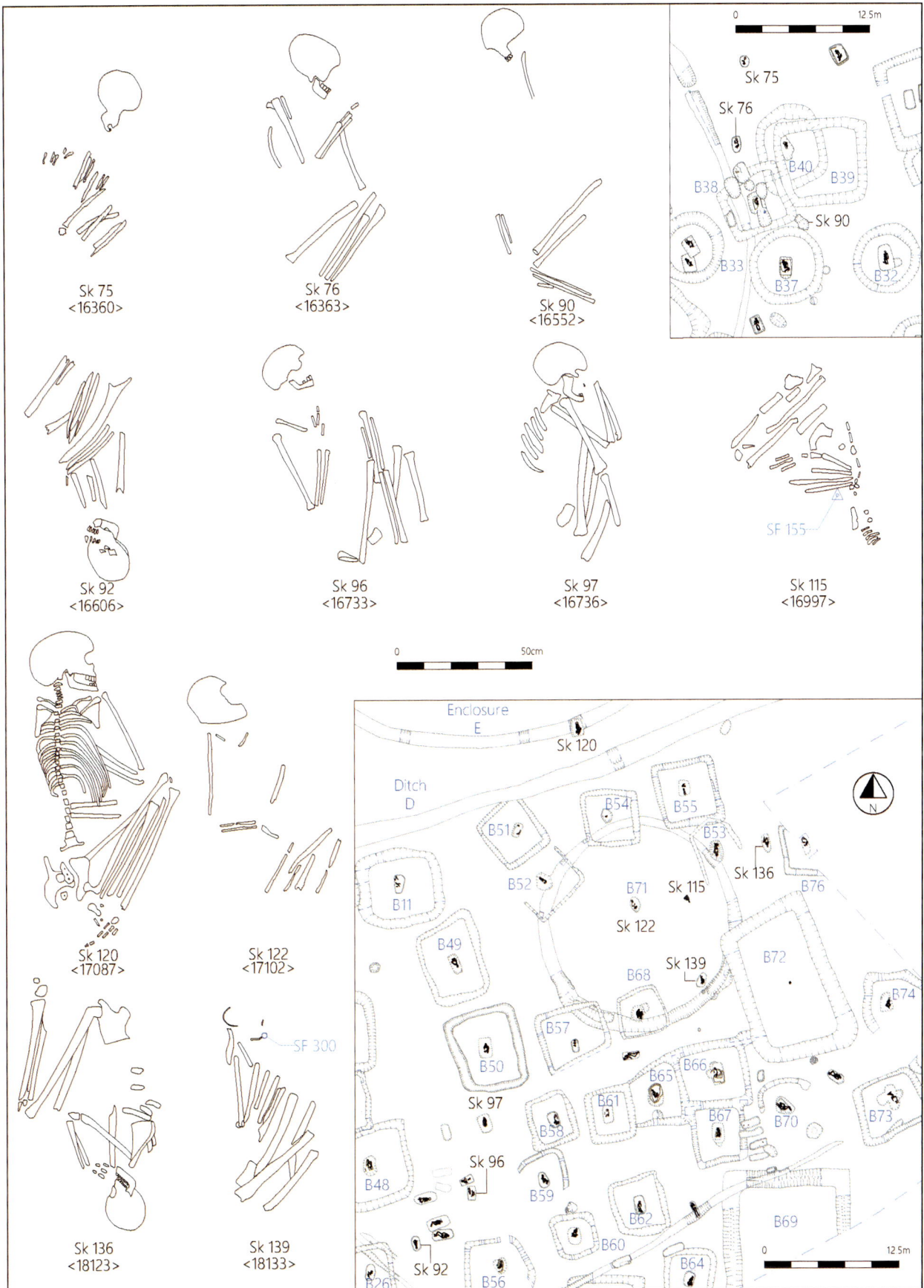

Figure 4.100 Plan of flat grave Skeletons 75 <16360> to 139 <18133>

Skeleton (16355 – Sk 73)

The preservation of the moderately fragmented skeleton was good. This was a male, probably aged between 36 and 45 years, laid with the torso supine and the legs flexed, with the head to the north, facing east. His spine had DJC and OA, DJC to the temporo-mandibular joint, and CO. The skeleton was radiocarbon-dated to the period 180 cal BC– cal AD 10 (SUERC-96415).

Grave 16361 – burial 16360

Summary

Grave 16361 lay a few metres north of Barrow 40 and was *c.* 1.00m in diameter and 0.36m in depth, with a distinct bowl-shaped profile (Fig. 4.100).

Skeleton (16360 – Sk 75)

The very poorly preserved and severely fragmented skeleton was of a juvenile aged from 8 to 10 years, lying in a crouched posture on the left side, with the head to the north, facing east. There was endocranial new bone.

Grave 16364 – burial 16363

Summary

Grave 16364 was immediately north of Barrow 38. This was a rounded-rectangular, relatively deep cut (at 1.12m) and was 1.40m long and 0.40m wide (Fig. 4.100). The mixed sandy grave fill (16362) contained a Neolithic edge-retouched blade in moderate condition, plus an Iron Age sherd.

Skeleton (16363 – Sk 76)

This was the poorly preserved and severely fragmented skeleton of a probable male over 36 years of age, in a crouched posture, lying on the left side, with the head to the north, facing east. This individual had pilasterism of the femora, plus lamellar bone on the left tibia.

Grave 16559 – burial 16552

Summary

Grave 16559 lay between Barrows 37 and 38 and was a sub-rectangular cut, around 0.35m deep, which was badly truncated by a later pit (16551) (Fig. 4.100).

Skeleton (16552 – Sk 90)

This burial consisted of the poorly preserved and severely fragmented skeleton of an individual of unknown sex, aged over 36 years, who was laid on their right side with the head to the north, facing west. This individual had CO, endocranial new bone and HFI.

Grave 16607 – burial 16606

Summary

This sub-rectangular grave was 1.37m long, 0.84m wide and 0.23m deep and was filled with dark grey sandy silt (16605). It was situated in the western barrow group, to the east of Barrow 26 (Figs 4.1 and 4.100).

Skeleton (16606 – Sk 92)

Burial 16606 was the very poorly preserved and severely fragmented skeleton of an individual of unknown sex, over 46 years old, in a crouched posture, with the legs tightly drawn up over the chest and the head to the south, facing west. There was pilasterism to both femora.

Grave 16734 – burial 16733

Summary

Grave 16734 was situated between Barrow 48 and Barrow 59 in the centre of the western barrow group; it was truncated by a later furrow (16731), particularly on the northern side. (The fill of the furrow (16730) contained four fragments of disarticulated human leg bones, which were presumably disturbed from the truncated burial.) The grave was a regular rectangular cut, 1.30m long, 0.80m wide and 0.25m deep, and contained an Iron Age sherd (Fig. 4.100).

Skeleton (16733 – Sk 96)

The skeleton was of a male aged over 26 years, lying on the left side in a tightly crouched posture, with the head to the north, facing east. This man had DJC in the atlas (uppermost cervical) vertebra. A loose lower canine tooth was included with this burial.

Grave 16737 – burial 16736

Summary

Grave 16737, which lay to the south of Barrow 50, was sub-rectangular and relatively large in plan, measuring 1.65m in length and 1.20m in width, but quite shallow (0.20m) (Fig. 4.100).

Skeleton (16736 – Sk 97)

The poorly preserved and severely fragmented skeleton was probably female, aged over 36 years, lying contracted on the left side, with the head to the north, facing east. This woman had a long list of pathological conditions: there was DJC, DDD and OA to the spine, further DJC to the temporo-mandibular joints, maxillary sinusitis and potential osteopenia in the long bones.

Grave 16998 – burial 16997

Summary

This grave lay within the eastern part of the area enclosed by the ditch of Bronze Age Barrow 71; its shallowness suggests that it may have been cut through the barrow mound (Fig. 4.100). The form and dimensions of the grave could not be accurately recovered due to its truncation. An early Bronze Age flint blade in moderate condition was found in the fill (16996).

Skeleton (16997 – Sk 115)

The moderately preserved but extremely fragmented skeleton was of an adult of unknown sex, lying in a crouched posture on the left side, with the (missing) head to the south, presumably facing west. The skeleton was radiocarbon-dated to the period 390–200 cal BC (SUERC-83078).

Grave goods

An iron short involuted brooch (SF 155) of Hull and Hawkes Type 2Cb and of mid-3rd- to early 2nd-century BC date was found in the area of the upper torso.

Grave 17088 – burial 17087

Summary

Grave 17088 was situated at the extreme north-eastern tip of the western barrow group and truncated the late Neolithic/early Bronze Age Enclosure E (see Fig. 3.1). The grave was an exceptionally deep, vertically sided regular rectangular cut, measuring 1.55m in length, 1.20m in width and 1.05m in depth (Fig. 4.100). The upper fill (17085) contained an undiagnostic slag fragment and a residual and abraded decorated Beaker sherd.

Skeleton (17087 – Sk 120)

The poorly preserved and severely fragmented skeleton was of a probable male, aged between 26 and 45 years, lying with the torso prone in a crouched posture, with the head to the north, facing east. This man had un-united fractures in the left forearm, with necrosis (dead tissue) around the break in the ulna. Additionally, there was endocranial lamellar bone, lamellar bone to the right leg and slight pilasterism to the femora.

Grave 17101 – burial 17102

Summary

Grave 17101 was situated approximately in the centre of Period 2 (Bronze Age) Barrow 71 (Fig. 4.100). The oval grave was 1.20m long and 0.90m wide, with a depth of 0.29m.

Skeleton (17102 – Sk 122)

This was the moderately preserved and extremely fragmented remains of an older juvenile between 9½ and 11 years old, with the skull to the north and lying on the left side facing east. There was extensive endocranial lamellar bone, and further lamellar bone on the left femur. The skeleton was radiocarbon-dated to the period 400–200 cal BC (SUERC-79418).

Grave 18124 – burial 18123

Summary

Grave 18124 was situated immediately west of Barrow 76 on the eastern edge of the western barrow group and was aligned with the western ditch of the barrow. This grave was sub-rectangular with a curved southern end, and measured 1.70m long, 0.78m wide and 0.25m deep (Fig. 4.100).

Skeleton (18123 – Sk 136)

The poorly preserved and extremely fragmented skeleton was of an individual of unknown sex, probably aged between 18 and 25 years, lying in a crouched posture on the left side, with the head to the south, facing west. This individual had inflammation in the left temporo-mandibular joint, CO and lamellar bone to the right leg.

Grave 18132 – burial 18133

Summary

Grave 18132 was situated in the southern part of the area enclosed by the ditch of Barrow 71, and partly cut into the inside edge of the barrow ditch (Fig. 4.100). The grave had a sub-oval shape and measured 1.20m in length, 0.80m in width and 0.40m in depth, the axis being markedly south-west to north-east. The position of the burial was anomalous as it lay diagonally across the centre of the grave in a north–south alignment rather than conforming to that of the grave cut.

Skeleton (18133 – Sk 139)

The skeleton was of an adult of unknown sex, aged over 26 years, lying on the left side, with the head to the north-east, facing south-east. This individual had DJC in both temporo-mandibular joints. The skeleton was radiocarbon-dated to the period 470–390 cal BC (SUERC-83081).

Grave goods

An iron bow brooch (SF 300 – Hull and Hawkes Type 2Ab) was found under the skull; this brooch dated to the middle Iron Age, with a more precise date possibly in the 3rd century BC.

Possible graves

Probable grave 042

Grave 042 lay 5m to the east of the south-west entrance of Barrow 79 (Fig. 4.101). Its rounded rectangular shape and the nature of the fills identified it as a likely grave and human bone fragments from the main fill (039) seem to confirm that assumption. The grave's alignment was north to south, and it was 1.78m long, 1.25m wide and 0.58m deep. A deposit of dark organic silt around the edge of the grave (041) contained a significant number of carbonised rye grains, which were probably intrusive.

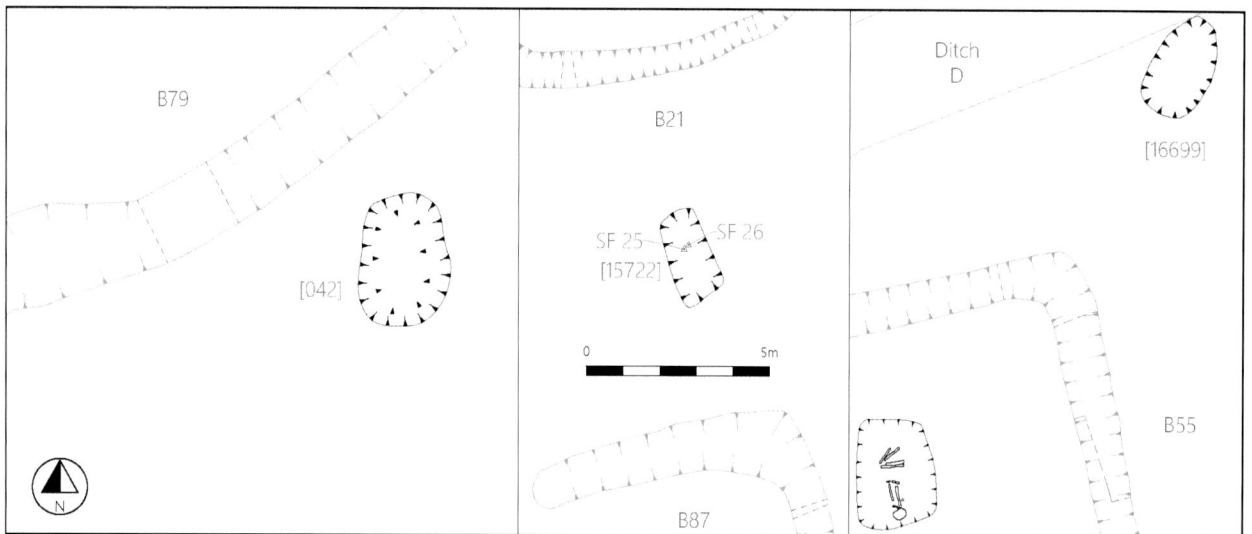

Figure 4.101 Plan of possible graves: 042, 15722, 16699 and 18081

Possible grave 15722

This feature was located between Barrow 21 and Barrow 87 and was a north–south-aligned rectangular cut, measuring 1.30m long, 0.58m wide and 0.38m deep (Fig. 4.101). Two spherical clear glass beads were found at the base of the feature (SF 25 plain, SF 26 with pale yellow glass inlaid in a spiral pattern – Foulds Class C; Figs 12.2 and 12.3)). Although no human remains were recovered from this feature, its rectangular form, north–south alignment and the presence of beads at the base make it highly probable that this was a grave. It is likely that the bone was completely dissolved by the acidic soil, as was the case with grave 042 and the large-scale erosion of the skeleton of the central burial of B9. Such erosion would be more likely to be seen with an infant or juvenile skeleton, and the relatively small size of the 'grave' would be more suited to a child than an adult.

Possible grave 16699

This feature lay to the north-east of Barrow 55 (Fig. 4.101), and as with Probable Grave 042, its function as a grave was suggested by its distinctive form and north-east to south-west alignment, and also supported by the presence of seven human bone fragments within its yellowish-brown sandy silt fill (16698). The cut formed a straight-sided rounded rectangle, 0.88m wide, 1.40m long and 1.06m deep.

Possible grave 18081

Cut 18081 (between Barrow 70 and Barrow 72) contained disarticulated human lower leg and foot bone fragments (*Sk 133* – fill 18080); while the circular shape and dished profile make it possible that this was a pit, it is equally likely that this was a severely truncated grave (4.101).

Other Iron Age features and the post-Iron Age landscape

Mark Stephens

Cow burials

Two poorly preserved cow burials were situated on the eastern fringe of the eastern barrow group (Fig. 5.1; see Chapter 14).

Cow burial 16349

This burial pre-dated a post-medieval east–west ditch or furrow (16312) and lay within a sub-rectangular cut (16314) measuring 1.60m in length, 0.95m in width and 0.67m in depth. The tail end lay to the north, but the head had been removed and placed on the hind-quarters. The lower leg and foot bones were also disarticulated and were placed along the area of the spine. The lower fill (16348) around the skeleton consisted of yellowish-brown clay, with yellowish silty sand (16313) above; neither fill contained any finds. This animal was classed as 'senile'.

Cow burial 16627

This cow burial was contained within another deep, vertically sided rectangular cut (16628), *c.* 3m north of the other burial. The 'grave' measured 1.57m in length, 1.05m in width and 0.70m in depth. The cow was placed tightly in the western end of the grave, lying on its left side with the head to the west, facing east. The head lay at a higher level than the body, and the neck was bent so that the skull faced towards the hindquarters. The legs were folded up against the northern and eastern edges. The lower part of the tail was missing but survived as a dark 'organic' stain (16694), pointing north-eastwards. The lowest fill around the skeleton consisted of a dark silt (16626) which contained two Iron Age sherds and a small number of bones (apparently unrelated to the skeleton). The two remaining fills (16625 and 16624) became progressively sandier in character towards the top of the grave. This animal was 3 to 4 years old or younger at death. Radiocarbon dating failed due to insufficient carbon.

Oval ring gully A

An oval ring gully was situated between the eastern barrow group and Enclosure H to the east (Figs 4.2 and 5.2). It consisted of three arcs of curvilinear ditch (16336/16638/16649, 16948/16946/16942 and 16685) enclosing an area *c.* 12m long (south-west to north-east) and 7.5m wide. There were 'entrances' to the south-west and north-east sides, and a wider interval along the southern side, all of which may have been accentuated by later ploughing and truncation by furrows. The ditch itself had a variable width and depth, averaging 0.80m and 0.30m respectively. The gully terminal 16944 had a posthole cut into it (16942). Animal bone fragments were recovered from fills 16635 (NW quadrant), 16941 and 16945 (SE quadrant), with two Iron Age sherds also from 1694, and five Iron Age sherds and two undiagnostic slag fragments from 16683 (SE quadrant). Carbonised plant remains associated with the oval ring gully consisted of oak charcoal from deposit 16630 (the middle fill of 16632) and 16947 (the fill of 16948, the east terminal), and trace amounts of cereal grain from 16650 and 16651 (respectively the post pipe and outer fill of posthole 16652). A possible pit or large posthole (16697) lay centrally to the ring gully and had a sandy primary fill (16696) with more silty material above (16695).

Enclosure H

Enclosure H occupied much of the excavated area east of the oval ring gully and north of Barrow 77 (Figs 4.2 and 5.3). Period 4 Boundary Ditch D crossed the enclosure ditch at its south-west corner. The enclosure ditch ran into the excavated area from the north, before taking a right-angled turn at a point 15m north of Barrow 77 and continuing for a further 55m to the south-east. Five segments were excavated into the enclosure's ditch (18358, 18362, 18368, 18376 and 18395), showing it to be over 1.00m wide and between 0.21m and 0.53m deep, with

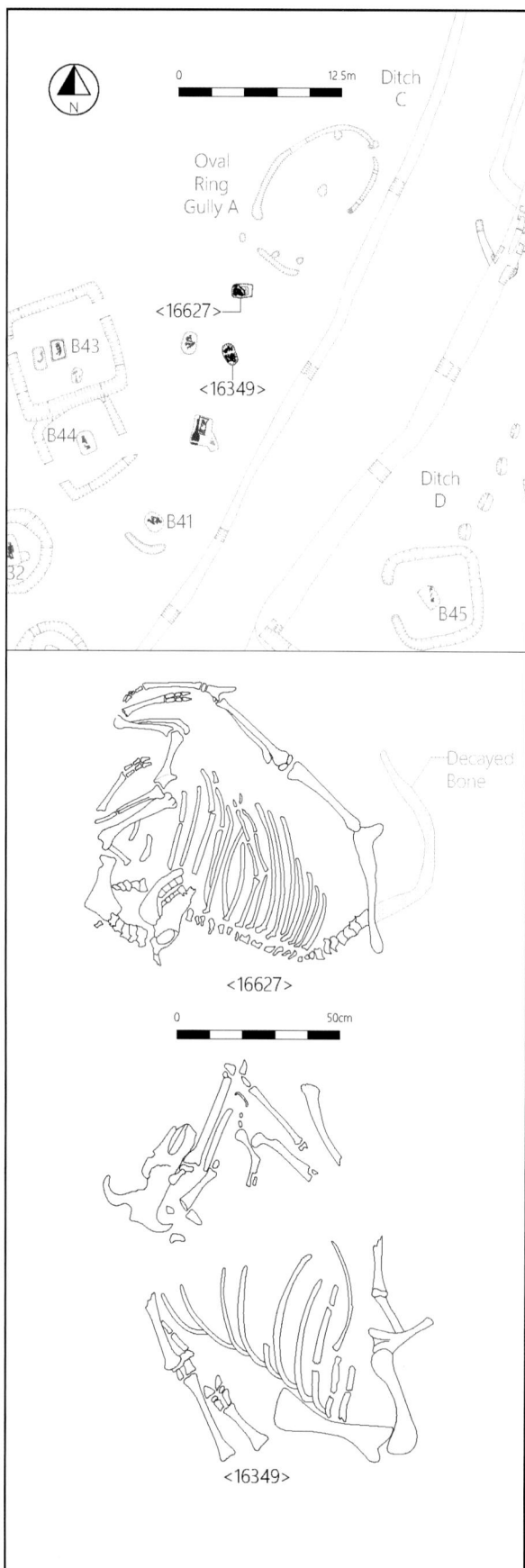

Figure 5.1 Plan of cow burials <16627> and <16349>

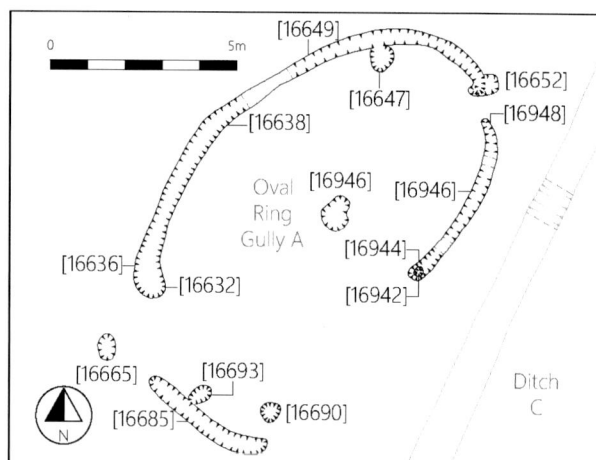

Figure 5.2 Plan of Oval Ring Gully A

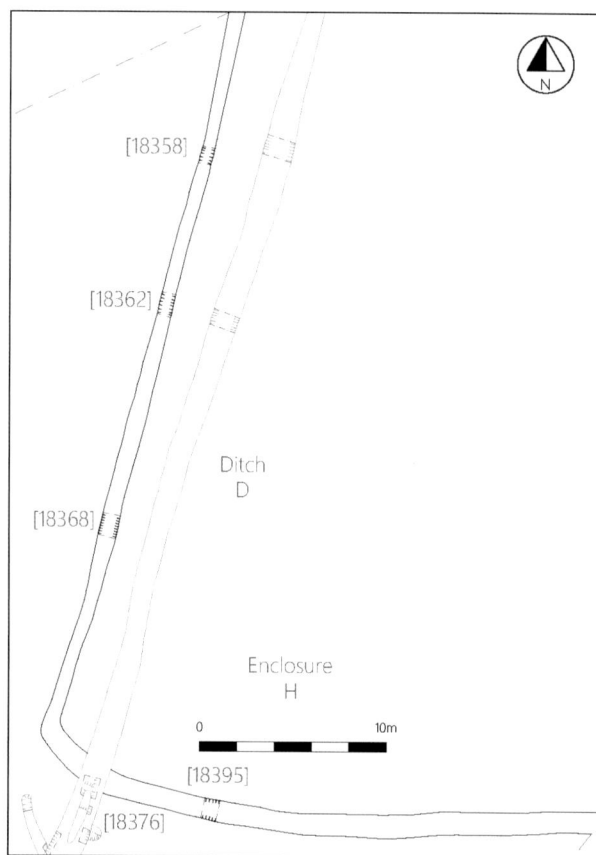

Figure 5.3 Enclosure H

a profile that varied between rounded-V and broad-U. The fills consisted of yellowish sandy silt with gravel at the south-west corner, changing markedly to pale brown clay as the ditch carried on to the south-east, reflecting the change in natural from sandy gravel to silty clay with gravel. The only finds were fragments of horse jaw and teeth from 18367 (the fill of segment 18368). The primary fill (18394) of segment 18395 contained poorly preserved barley grains. No features were identified within

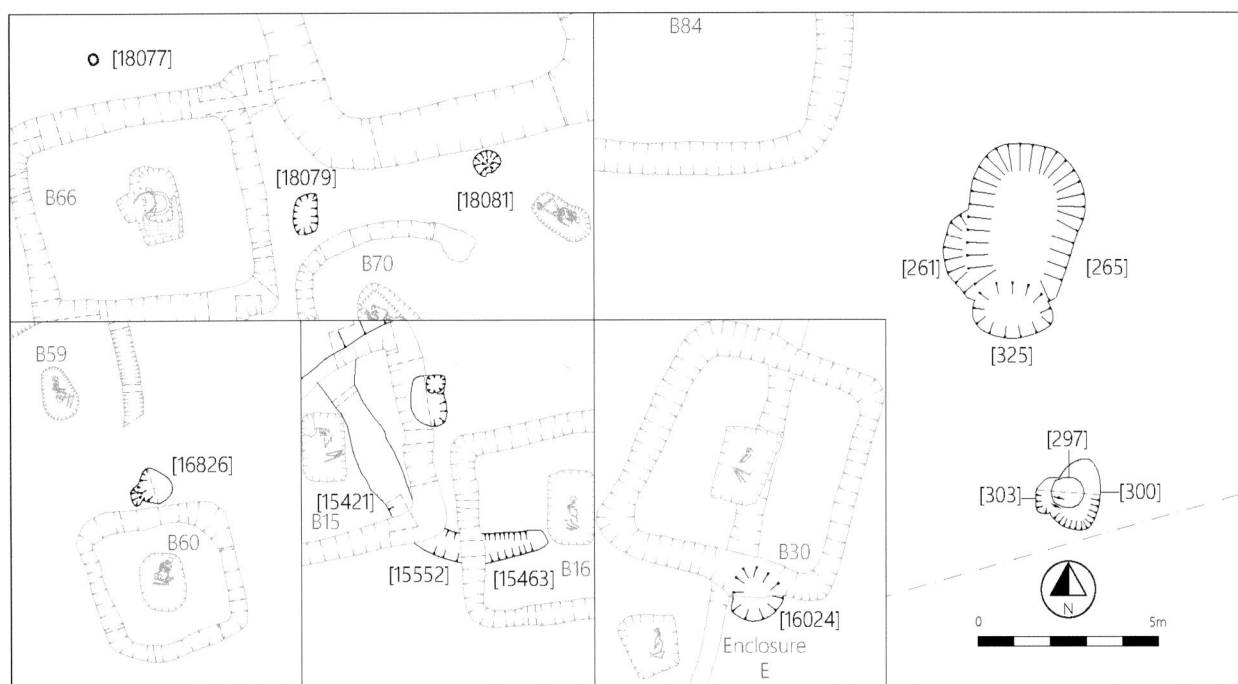

Figure 5.4 Iron Age pits and gully

Enclosure H, and no entrances through the ditch were present within the excavated area.

Iron Age pits and gullies

There was a scattering of pits and gullies across the excavated area, some of which contained Iron Age pottery, others pre-dating individual barrows but still apparently belonging to the Iron Age phase (Figs 4.1 and 5.4).

Within the western barrow group, Pit 16826 was situated between Barrows 59 and 60. Pit 18079 (situated between Barrows 66 and 70) contained animal bone fragments (fill 18078). A possible posthole (18077) was excavated adjacent to the northern ditch of Barrow 66.

Gully 15421 pre-dated Barrows 15 and 16 in the western barrow group and ran roughly north to south across the interior of Barrow 15. It was truncated at the northern end by both the barrow ditch and Ditch D. The gully curved to the east (as 15552) and continued through the western part of Barrow 16 (as 15463).

Pit 16024 pre-dated Barrow 30 within the eastern barrow group and was *c*. 1.00m in diameter and 0.30m in depth. The brown sandy silt upper fill (16022) contained four Iron Age sherds.

Two groups of inter-cutting features, each comprising three pits (297, 300 and 303; 261, 265 and 325) were recorded in the area immediately south-east of Barrow 84.

Pit 303 was sub-rectangular in form and measured over 1.20m long, 0.90m wide, and 0.66m deep. It had a sandy primary fill (302) with sandy gravel above (301), the latter containing animal bone fragments. Pit 300 cut

into the eastern side of 303, and was slightly larger, with a length of 1.80m. Again, there was a sandy primary fill (299) with darker gravel above (298); neither contained any finds. Pit 297, which cut across the top of the earlier two pits, was sub-circular, with a diameter of 0.85m. The dark silty fill (296) contained animal bone fragments.

The other sequence of three pits began with Pit 265, a large sub-rectangular cut that measured 4.40m in length, 3.05m in width and 0.85m in depth. The grey mixed silty gravel fill (264) contained animal bone fragments and the base of a pot (SF 3), which possibly had been deliberately placed at the bottom of the north-east corner of the pit. Pit 325 cut through the southern end of Pit 265, which formed a regular rectangle, 1.85m long, 1.25m wide and 0.99m deep; the fill (324) contained many animal bone fragments. Finally, a more amorphous feature, Pit 261, cut in the top of the two preceding pits, measuring 2.40m long, 1.85m wide and 0.25m deep. The dark silty fill (260) also contained a large amount of animal bone, plus pieces of industrial residue, and some barley grains.

Post-Iron Age landscape

Following the abandonment of the square barrow cemetery there was a period of land reorganisation that involved the cutting of substantial boundary ditches across the site. In the northern field the boundaries consisted of Ditch D, which was flanked by Ditch C for the eastern part of its course. Associated dating evidence was scarce, but as Ditch D cut into the northern edges of square barrows 1, 7, 9, 10, 12, 14, 15 and 51, this phase obviously post-dated the Iron Age. The presence of Roman sherds within the ditch fills, coupled with the fact that an Anglian burial cut into Ditch D, indicates a Romano-British date. The associated pottery suggests that Ditch D was dug in the late 1st century AD and continued in use until the 2nd or early 3rd century. In the southern field, Ditches J and K ran parallel to each other on a sinuous west-northwest to east-southeast alignment (Fig. 4.3), associated finds suggesting that they were contemporary to Ditch D. This period will be described in greater detail in a forthcoming volume, along with the early prehistoric, Anglian, medieval and post-medieval periods.

There were 44 inhumations of presumed Anglian date, based on their alignment, stratigraphic position and/ or associated grave goods. A single barrow (B70) was radiocarbon-dated to the Anglian period. In addition to the inhumations, there was a single, truncated, Anglian cremation in a pottery vessel.

6

Iron Age barrows at The Mile

Mark Stephens

Two Iron Age barrows, one square and one circular, were identified during the excavation of an Anglian settlement at The Mile, on the northern edge of Pocklington, East Yorkshire (centred at SE 806498) (Fig. 6.1). The square barrow had a central grave containing the inhumation of a mature adult male placed upon an inverted shield inside a largely intact chariot, with two attendant upright ponies. The ditches of the circular barrow enclosed a central grave containing an adult male inhumation accompanied by a group of iron and bone spears, and a dismantled composite shield. An adult female was an apparent 'satellite' burial to the circular barrow. The excavated site had a total area of *c.* 3.5ha, and the barrows were located at the north-west fringe of the Anglian settlement (to the extent that the square barrow may have formed a marker for one of the Anglian boundaries) (Fig. 6.2).

The site has an elevation of around 40m AOD and is part of a flat gravel expanse on the west side of Pocklington Beck, on the northern outskirts of Pocklington.

The excavation was funded by Persimmon Homes (Yorkshire) Ltd and was carried out between May and September 2018. ASWYAS had previously established the archaeological potential of the Anglian settlement site by geophysical survey and trial trenching, with additional trial trenching by MAP. Thanks are due to Paola Ponce and Malin Holst of York Osteoarchaeology Ltd for their analysis of the three human skeletons described below, Jane Richardson for examining the pony and pig bones, and Maggs Felter (YA) for advice on the treatment and lifting of metal objects from the chariot burial and the conservation of the metal objects from the graves. The chariot burial was excavated by Martyn King, Sergio Quintero-Cabello and Mark Stephens, and the circular barrow by Angela Fawcett, Kelly Hunter and John English.

The two Iron Age barrows at The Mile were situated *c.* 2km north of Burnby Lane, forming part of a landscape to either side of Pocklington Beck that contains groups and looser concentrations of square barrows (plus other multi-period features) (Fig. 1.4). This landscape extends from the point where Pocklington Beck and Millington Beck converge (*c.* 2km north of The Mile site) to Burnby Lane and the surrounding archaeological landscape previously described. Further square barrows are known as cropmarks in the area to the north of The Mile and include the barrows excavated by ASWYAS at the Pocklington Flood Alleviation Scheme (POCFAS) *c.* 300m north of the site.

Square barrow and chariot burial
Barrow ditches
The ditches of the barrow enclosed an area approximately 6.5m across (Fig. 6.3). As at Burnby Lane, the ditches were excavated in eight segments (the four corners plus the four sides – clockwise from the north-west corner segments 2598, 2595, 2592, 2589, 2586, 2580, 2483 and 2577), and were up to 1.20m wide and 0.35m deep. The ditches appeared to have filled up from the interior of the barrow, a gravel deposit along the inside edge and at the base (contexts 2597, 2593, 1591, 2588, 2585, 2579, 2582 and 2576 respectively) suggesting that the barrow mound had slumped or eroded into the ditch. The top of the ditch was filled by slowly deposited reddish-brown sandy silt.

Grave 3613
The grave was placed centrally within the area enclosed by the ditches and measured 4.40m from north to south and 2.40m from west to east. It was over 1.00m deep, with vertical sides and a flat base, its large size indicating the exceptional burial contained within it. Careful excavation revealed the grave contained an intact chariot burial, with both the chariot and the two ponies placed upright in the grave pit (Figs 6.4–6.6).

The earliest fill was a layer of dark silt (2568), around 10mm thick, in the south-western corner of the grave, which had apparently been deposited from the south. The western iron tyre of the chariot rested directly on top of

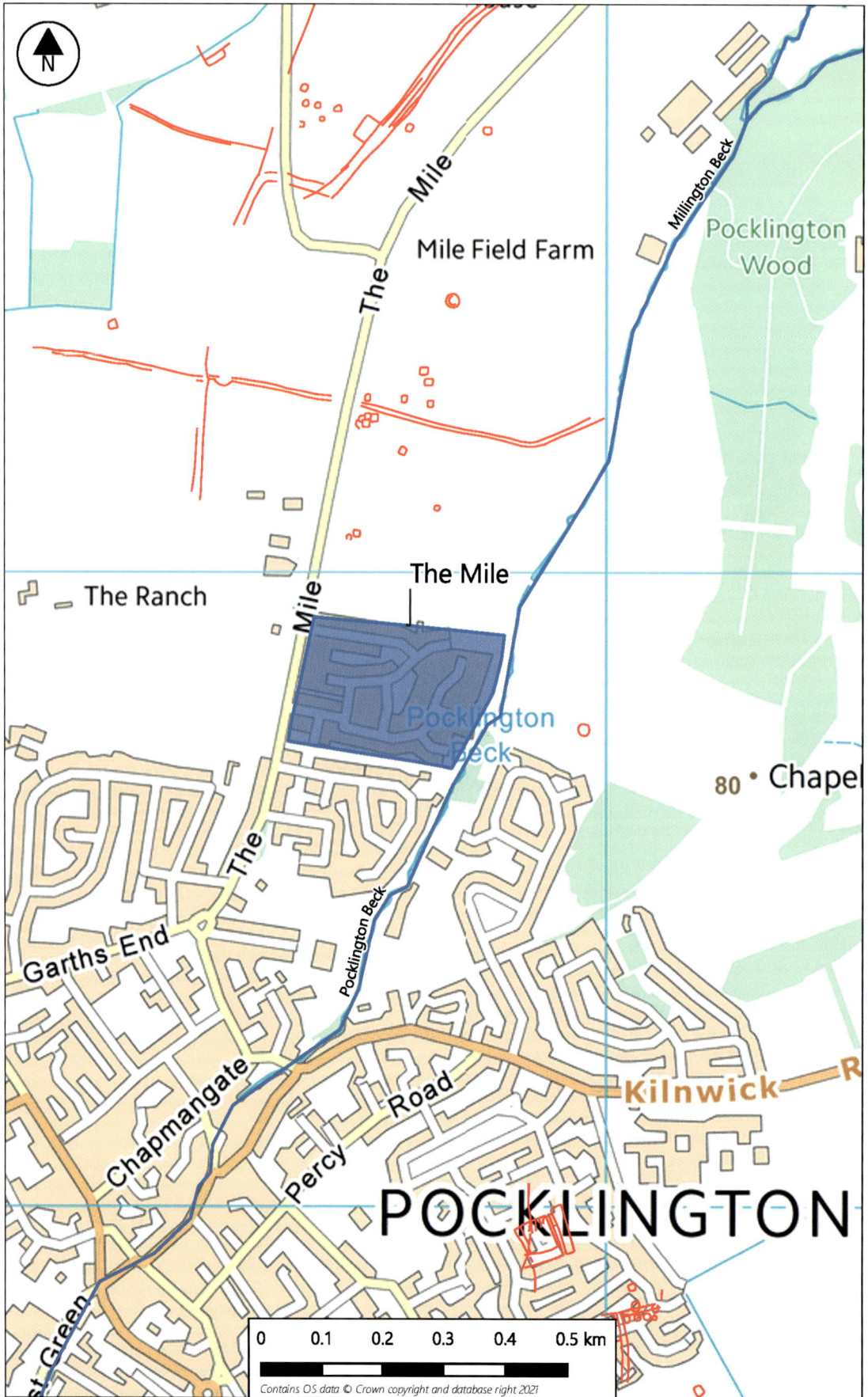

Figure 6.1 The Mile: site location with cropmarks

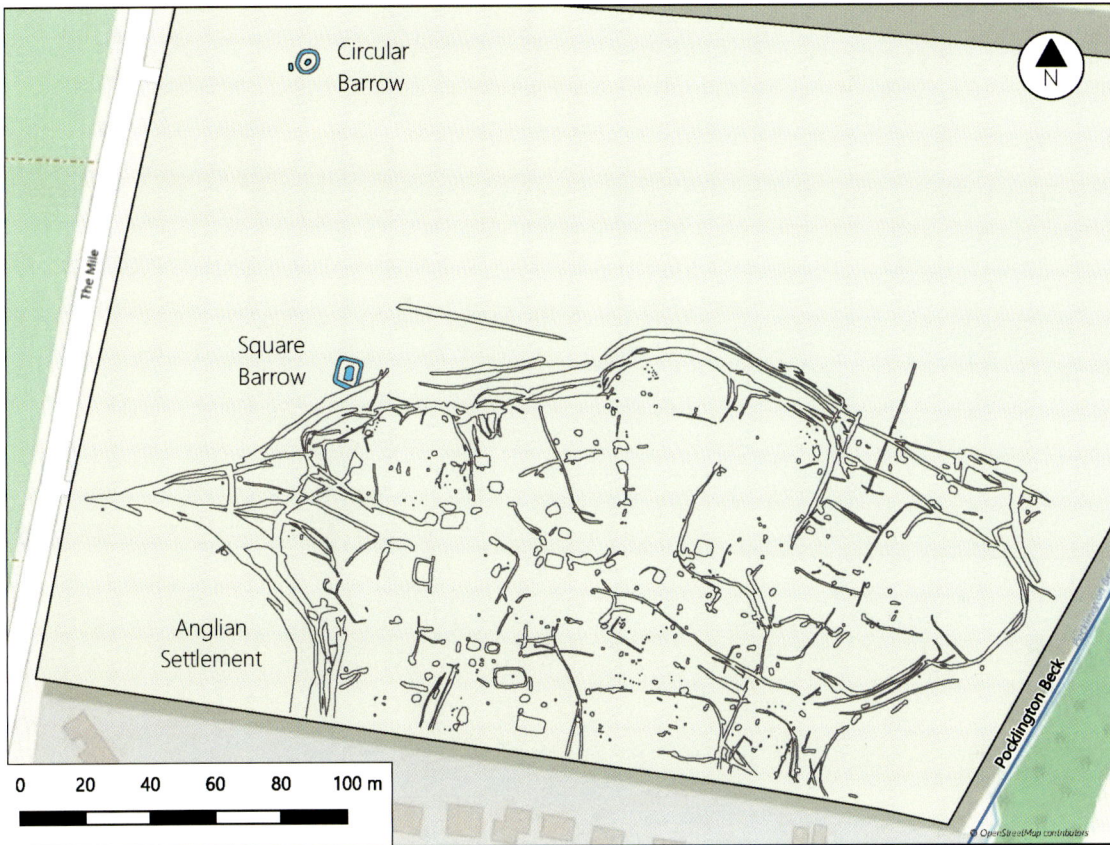

Figure 6.2 The Mile: site plan

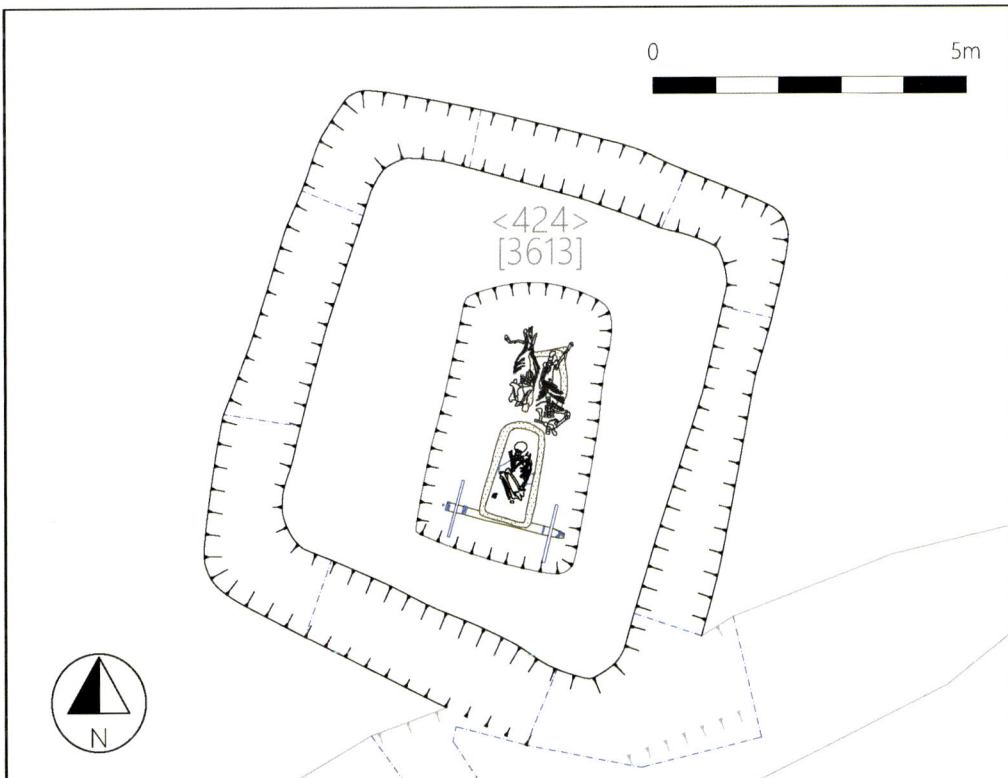

Figure 6.3 The Mile: square barrow and chariot plan

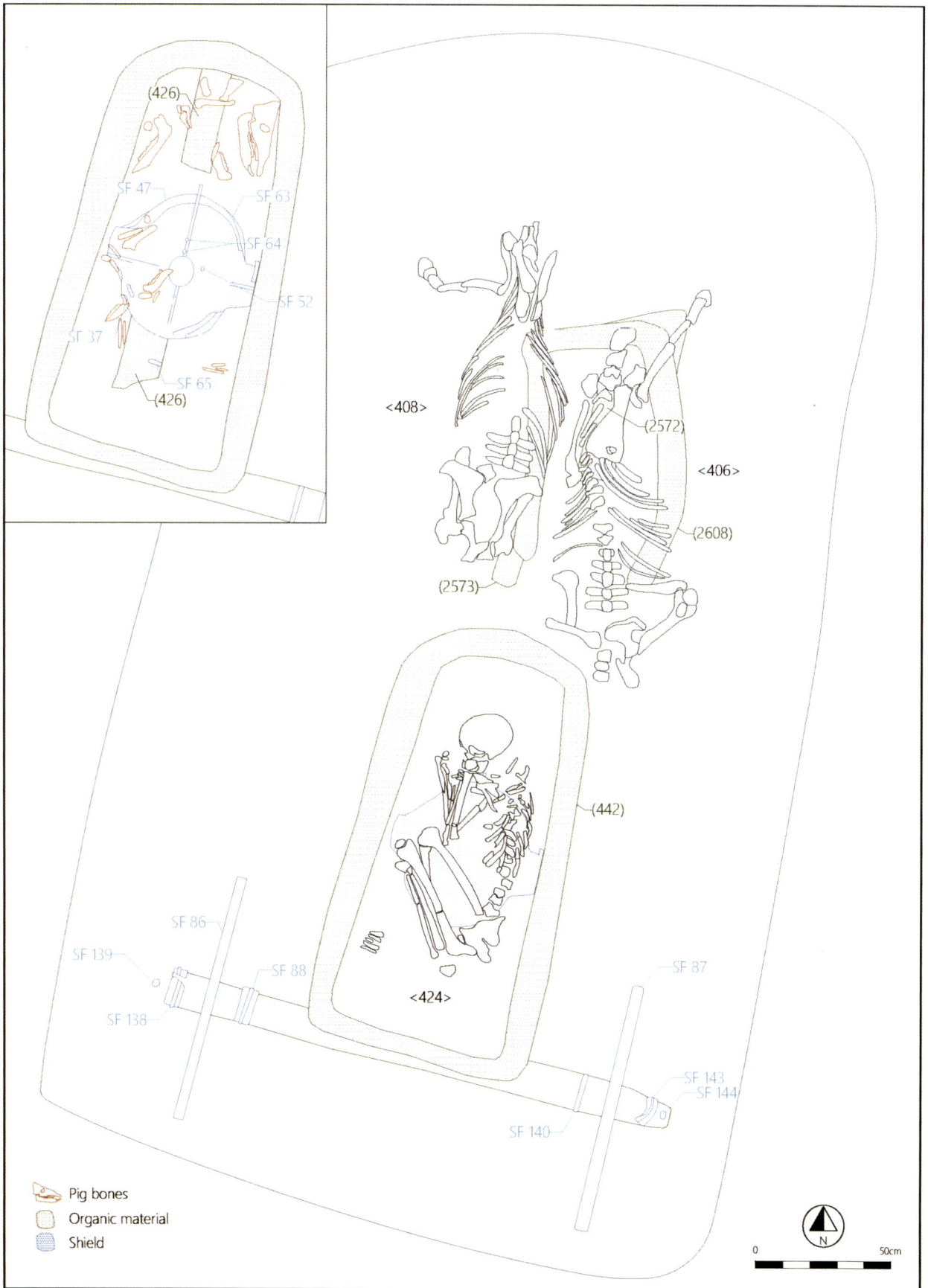

(426)

SF 47   SF 63

SF 64

SF 52

SF 37

SF 65
(426)

<408>

(2572)

<406>

(2608)

(2573)

(442)

<424>

SF 86

SF 139

SF 88   SF 87

SF 138

SF 143
SF 144

SF 140

Pig bones

Organic material

Shield

0   50cm

N

Figure 6.4 The Mile: chariot and inhumation plan

Figure 6.5 View of ponies, chariot and inhumation, looking north. Scale: 1m

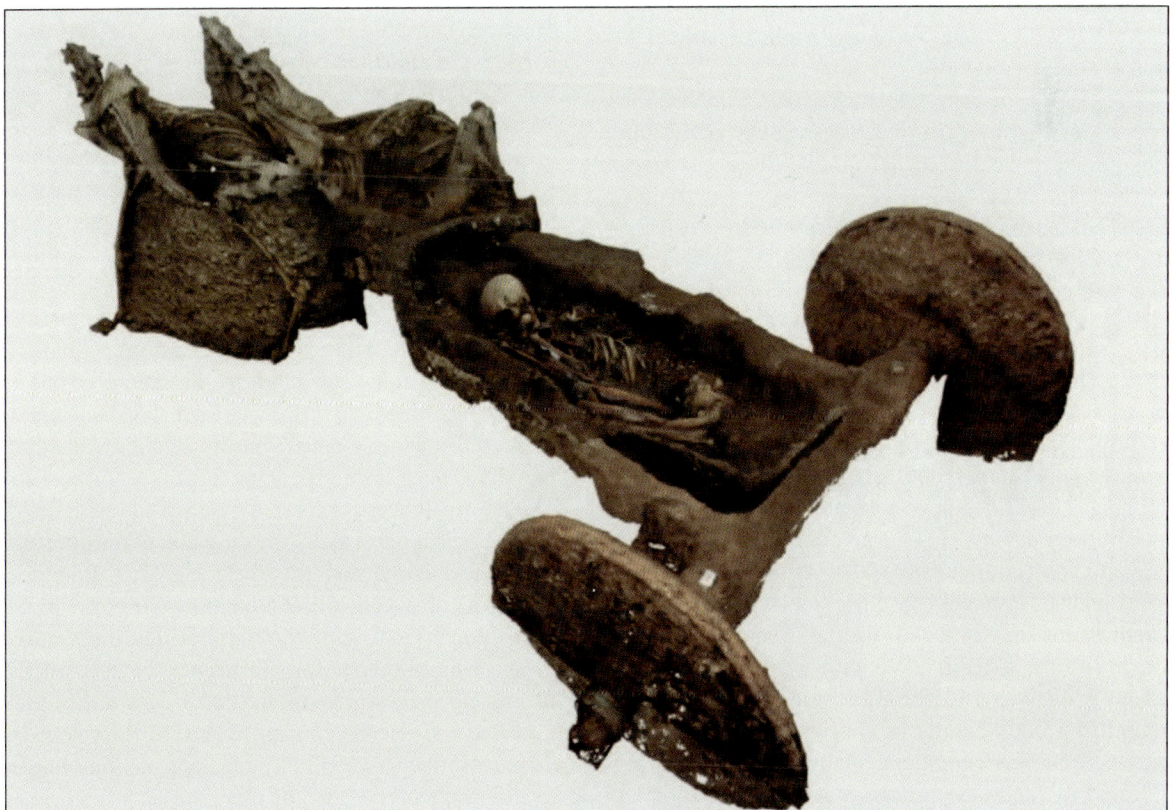

Figure 6.6 3-D model of the chariot

this layer of silt, indicating that it was deposited before the chariot was placed in the grave. It could be that the silt accumulated in a single event, such as a sharp rainstorm (like that which occurred during the excavation, causing flooding at one end of the grave and leaving a thin accumulation of silt). It is also possible that deposit 2568 represented organic material deliberately laid in the grave.

The remainder of the grave was largely filled with an amorphous dump of mixed sandy gravel (arbitrarily divided into deposit 400 at the top and deposit 429 below the level of the chariot box, with other divisions in specific sectors around the chariot). There were darker patches or stains within this gravel, but it is felt that these were largely the result of topsoil becoming mixed with the overall gravel backfill; any of these deposits that are understood to have more potential significance will be described below.

Burial Sk 424

The burial was placed within the chariot box (described below). This was a mature adult male over 46 years of age who was arranged in a crouched posture, on the right side with the head to the north, facing west (Fig. 6.4). The legs were tightly drawn up against the abdomen and chest, leaving the feet near the pelvis. The hands were placed together in front of the face. The skeleton dipped downwards to the south-east, probably due to the collapse of the box floor. He was 173.9cm tall, significantly taller than the mean height of 168cm for Iron Age males nationally.

The skeleton of this man had evidence of trauma, shown by a fractured rib that was healing at the time of death, and muscle damage to the left thigh. Bilateral spondylolysis in the spine may also have the result of trauma. His advancing age was illustrated by osteoporosis, DJCs to the pelvis, left clavicle, shoulders, wrists, knees and toes, and long-standing poor oral health resulting in some tooth loss, diseased gums and a dental abscess. The isotope analysis (see below) suggests that he spent his childhood on chalk, presumably the Yorkshire Wolds.

The skeleton in burial 424 provided a radiocarbon date of 370–150 cal BC (SUERC-81686).

Grave goods

COPPER ALLOY BOW BROOCH (SF 52)

A copper alloy bow brooch (Figs 6.4 & 11.4) was found pin-side upwards after the skeleton was lifted, suggesting that it was displayed on the right side of the body. The brooch had a body mainly of copper alloy, with a coral or paste glass roundel on the dorsal side and an iron pin; the decoration and design suggest a dragonfly complete with tail.

SHIELD (SF 37)

The inhumation was placed directly on top of a wood/copper alloy composite shield, which was laid face downwards, and like the inhumation, dipped down to the southeast (Fig. 6.7). The copper alloy elements of the shield consisted of a two-part central spine, a central boss, two plaques, tabs attached to the plaques, an openwork cut-out frieze and a series of clips along the top and left edges (Fig. 6.4). The shield is described and discussed fully in Chapter 7; what follows is a summary only.

The spine consisted of two ribs that were both attached to a central ovoid boss by two rivets. The ribs contained a long piece of ash wood, possibly for strength in the same way as the spine of the shield from Rudston burial R148 (Stead 1991a, 62–3). The ash wood spine appears to have been a halved conversion forming a natural half-round cross-section laid with its flat side on the outer surface of the shield and fastened to it by copper alloy pins. The wooden spine tapered towards the ends but thickened as it passed through the void made by the boss to form a handgrip.

The boss slightly overlapped two crescent-shaped plaques, each with similar repoussé decoration (Fig. 7.1). Both plaques had a copper alloy tab extending outwards to the edge of the shield but these were not the same size. They were also decorated in repoussé work, but with different motifs. An openwork frieze consisting of 20 individual small cut-out plates of copper alloy strip was riveted to the backing to surround the central plaques. The bottom and left side of the front of the shield were indicated by six copper alloy binding clips – SFs 72, 90, 119 and 120 along the left edge, and 65 and 76 along the base (Fig. 7.2). The binding clips consisted of copper alloy strips bent into a semi-circle lengthways with rivets to attach to the shield backing. In addition, the exterior end of the left-hand tab was bent over to act as a binding clip.

Binding clips were not present along the top or right sides, but the position of the *in situ* clips indicated that the shield board was rectangular, measuring 690mm long and 540mm wide. The interior dimensions of the clips suggest that the shield board was 7mm thick and minerally preserved organic material on the shield's inner surface may have been leather padding.

The shield board consisted of ash wood with the grain at 90° to the longest axis. The direction of the grain would make the shield board less likely to shatter or splinter as the result of a vertical, overhand sword blow; as Steve Allen points out, while this implies that the shield was constructed allowing for the proper needs of defence, it does not necessarily imply that it was either used or intended for use in combat. There is, however, blade damage in the shape of a 25mm-long slanting linear cut to the lower part of one of the plaques, which could be use damage or symbolic of the act of burial.

Figure 6.7 Shield (SF 37) during excavation. Scale: 0.4m

It is not known how many pieces of wood were used to construct the shield board, but the arrangement of the pins holding the spine to it – two on either side of the grip and one at each end of the spine – could indicate there were three pieces laid horizontally edge to edge. This configuration would be easier to make rather than using one larger piece.

Pig bones

Deposit 423, which overlay and surrounded the inhumation (Figs 6.4 and 6.8), contained a large quantity of bone from at least five sub-adult pigs, along with many bones that were probably from the same younger animal who was under a year old (see Chapter 14). Only bones from the head and forelimb (mostly left but some right) were present, with some paired examples suggesting articulation and deliberate selection. There were 11 male and 1 female tusks, so predominantly males were selected. The bones were butchered at the shoulder and elbow joints, again suggesting the careful choice as well as preparation of specific cuts of meat.

One of the groups of ribs had an iron object (SF 27; Fig. 6.9) with wood remains on the inside attached firmly to it; this was originally interpreted as a meat hook because of its close association with the group of ribs. While it remains possible that this interpretation was correct, the conservation and cleaning of the object showed it to be a narrow iron strip with three round-sectioned bars running out at right-angles from it, two of which terminated in rounded projections. There was minerally preserved wood on the inside of the bar, but not on the projections. Alternative interpretations are therefore possible, but the object's precise function remains unclear.

Beads

A decorated copper alloy bead (SF 22) with a diameter of 19mm was found in context 404, which overlay the chariot box. It was decorated with three raised lines along the circumference (Fig. 12.7).

A tiny hexagonal dark blue glass bead (SF 17) came from the top fill of the grave (context 400). With no other Iron Age parallels, the location of the bead near the top of the grave increases the likelihood that it was intrusive.

Figure 6.8 Chariot inhumation with pig bones. Scale: 1m

Figure 6.9 Unidentified iron object (SF 27)

The chariot

The remains of the chariot were largely complete, apart from the yoke, and appeared to be still assembled, with the wheels upright and attached via the naves to the axle (Figs 6.4 and 6.10). Much of the form of the axle and chariot body were recovered by the recognition of soil stains and cleave lines within the grave fill. The metal fittings are described in more detail in Chapter 10.

Axle

The axle was approximately 2m in length, the exact figure being uncertain because of the poor preservation of its western end, shown by the western lynchpin being out of position. The eastern tip of the axle (3611) is also likely to have suffered post-depositional damage, as the 30mm interval between its tip and the lynchpin is less than the amount apparently needed to avoid structural damage (100mm was quoted in Brown *et al.* 2007, 142). In any event, the axle was a large piece of timber *c.* 140mm thick. The profile of the axle was broader at the base than the top, suggesting that it was deliberately dressed to that shape.

The lynchpins (SF 139 for the western wheel, SF 144 for the eastern) were of the rod type and each was paired with a small iron ring at the top end for attachment to the axle. The pins were aesthetically well-formed with a knop at the top end and a further, less-pronounced swelling at the bottom end, plausibly echoing the form of a horse's fetlock and hoof. The heads of the pins were embellished with a circle of white enamel on their tops, in keeping with the motif on the two surviving copper alloy terrets.

Naves

Both naves appeared to be roughly flush with the axle, and judging by the position of the nave hoops, were *c.* 300mm long. Preserved wood on the interior of the inner nave hoop of the west wheel showed that it was made of ash. Of the four copper alloy nave hoops, three (SFs 88, 138 and 143) were superficially similar in form:

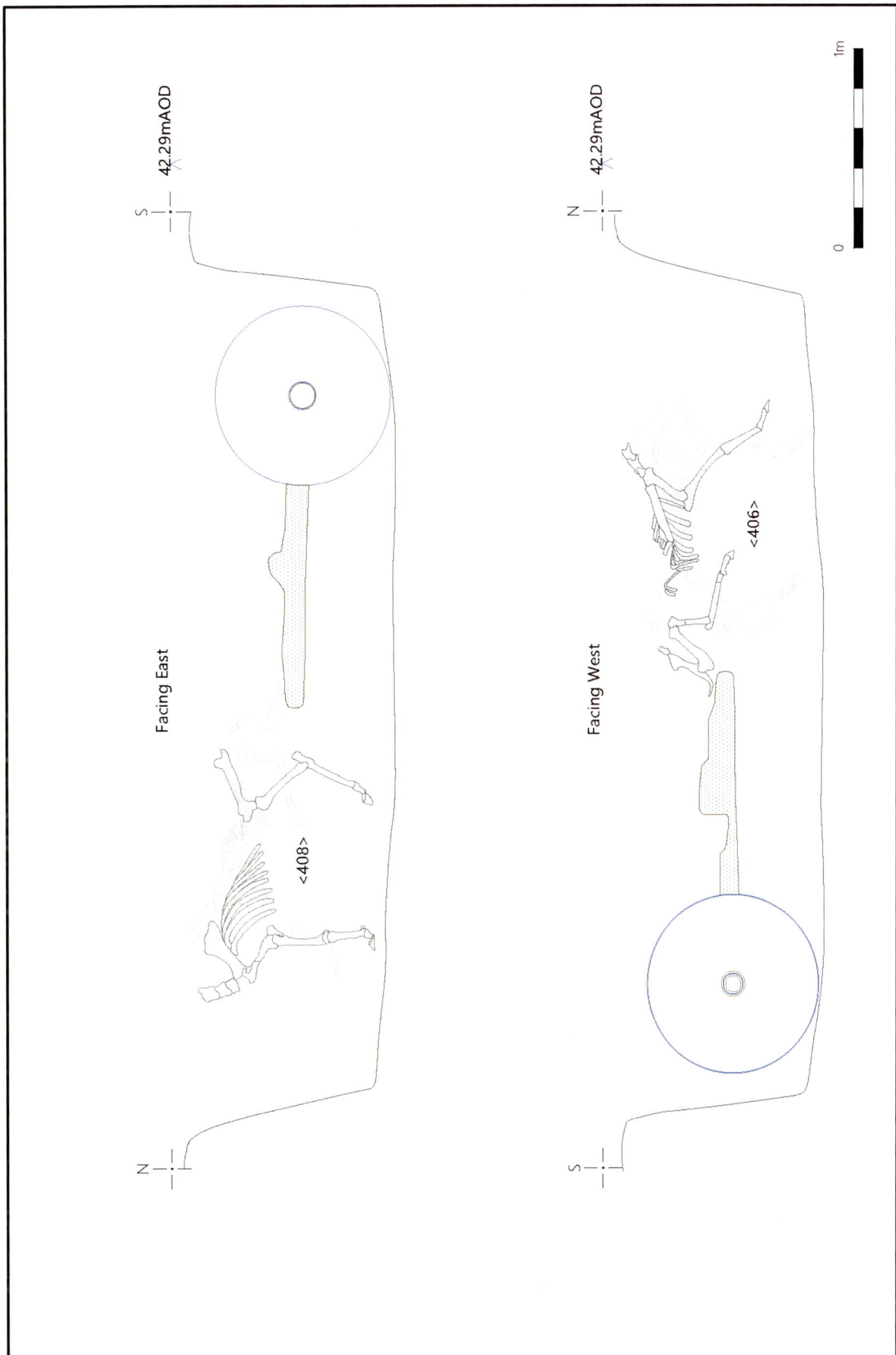

Facing East

42.29mAOD

S

N

<408>

Facing West

42.29mAOD

N

S

<406>

1m

0

Figure 6.10 Chariot profiles

c. 50mm wide and with medial raised bands that no doubt provided both decoration and strengthening. However, SF 88 (west wheel inner) was different in that the raised band contained a strip of iron and the terminals failed to meet but were united by an iron strap that probably represented a repair. The other nave hoop (SF 140 – east wheel inner) was a much narrower, plain ring consisting of a copper alloy sleeve over an iron core, measuring *c.* 25mm wide and with a D-shaped cross-section. It could be deliberate that the two outer nave bands were a matched pair intended to present a more coherent display than the anomalous inner hoops.

Wheels

Using the distance between the outside of the upright iron tyres as a guide, the chariot had a gauge of *c.* 1.58m. Both iron tyres survived, SF 86 for the western wheel, SF 87 for the eastern (Figs 6.11 and 6.12).

Possibly because the wheels were buried in an upright position, there was limited evidence of spokes. Six spokes were indicated by organic soil stains for the western wheel and the position of four more was suggested by the

Figure 6.11 Eastern wheel (SF 87), facing south. Scale: 0.3m

Figure 6.12 Western wheel (SF 86), facing west. Scales: 1m and 0.3m

distribution of gravel within the infill of the tyre. These remains showed that the wheel originally had 12 spokes, in common with other excavated examples in East Yorkshire (*e.g.* Burnby Lane (this volume), Humber/Wolds/Melton (Stephens and Ware 2019, 29), Garton Station and Kirkburn (Stead 1991a, 40–4) as well as further afield (Ferry Fryston – Brown *et al.* 2007, 144). The wooden rim was shown by a *c.* 30mm-wide band of organic staining on the inside of the iron tyre, and darker and looser material (2566) from 7 o'clock to 9 o'clock on the wheel. For the western wheel, only one spoke (3612) was recognised, at 7 o'clock, but there were indications of the entire wooden wheel rim (3609).

Bodywork

The body of the chariot was shown by a dark soil stain (442), which was relatively narrow and shallow, with a tapered front end. It had a length of 1.45m internally, with a width of 0.65m at the south (rear) end, dropping to *c.* 0.25m at the north (front) end. The chariot body was recognised to a height of *c.* 0.25m, and its make-up changed slightly from the top half (422) to the bottom half (442); whether this is because its actual fabric changed, perhaps representing two horizontally laid timbers, is by no means certain. There were indications of another structural element on the exterior rearward half of the main superstructure, evidenced by a deposit of loose yellowish-brown silty sand (441), conjecturally representing a more permeable material such as wicker work. On the eastern side, the elements of the superstructure rested on top of the axle, whereas on the western side the superstructure appeared only partly to overlap the axle – perhaps it had collapsed within the grave at this point. There were no indications of how the superstructure and axle were joined, but this could have been done by either carpentry (pegs or tenons) or hide lashings.

There were no clear signs of the base of the 'box', but it appears to have collapsed, causing the downward tipping of the inhumation and the shield referred to above. It is likely that the difficulty of consolidating the grave backfill beneath the chariot box caused the collapse of the base. A surviving patch of dark silt (3614) adjoining the axle, and level with the axle's base, could have been part of the base of the box. The fact that the base did not leave any other clear traces implies that it was not substantial, which supports the suggestion made by the excavators of the Ferry Fryston chariot that it was composed of hide – either as a single sheet or a network of interlaced strips (Brown *et al.* 2007, 144).

The pole

The pole was represented by an intermittent soil stain (426) that dipped down from the front of the chariot between the ponies towards the chariot box; it was not traced further to the north, perhaps because any remains in that area were disrupted by the decay of the ponies. Its northern end was probably truncated by the same process that removed the ponies' heads, and presumably the yoke. The soil stain suggested that the pole was 0.15m wide and at least 1.35m long.

Copper alloy harness fittings

Three out-of-position terrets (SFs 3, 4 and 5 – Figs 10.12–10.14) were recovered from the disturbed horizon at the top of the grave. All three terrets were of different form, two being of studded D-ring type, made from copper alloy with iron suspension bars, the other was a plain ring type, made from iron plated with possible tin. It is possible that the damage on SF 3 was caused after its deposition, given its location in the disturbed zone at the top of the grave.

The ponies

The ponies at the chariot's front end were buried in an upright position in keeping with the intact nature of the chariot (Figs 6.5 and 6.9). Unfortunately, neither head survived, making it difficult to sex the animals conclusively and shed light on their selection (see Chapter 14). However, the pelvis of pony 406 suggested that it was a mare, and the same characteristic on the pelvis of 408 was not so well-developed as to be conclusively male, so this pony may have been a gelding. Their bones were all fused, showing that they were not juvenile animals, and the mineralisation of some of the soft tissue of the west pony (408) suggests that this was a mature specimen. Slight lipping to the scapulae of 406 and possible early onset of spavin to 408 also suggest that these were mature animals. Interestingly, pony 406 had a healing wound in the form of squared hole 13mm across to the left scapula, showing that it had survived a significant penetrating injury, perhaps even a battle wound. This pony also had a likely infection to the same shoulder.

The two ponies were a well-matched pair, with 406 being between 11.8 and 12.4 hands (1.20–1.26m) at the withers and 408 between 11.9 and 12.3 hands (1.21–1.25m).

The remarkable aspect to the burial of the two ponies was that they were in an upright position – not simply standing but posed as if they were still pulling the chariot (Fig. 6.5).

During the excavation and recording of the ponies there was speculation that they had been posed in their standing position by packing soil around them during the backfilling of the grave. However, when the lifting of the skeletons was underway soil stains were revealed which may well have represented structures that held the ponies upright (Fig. 6.4). These structures were represented by rectangular stains beneath and between the ponies, 2572 dipping to the south and 2573 dipping to the north, and a box-shaped structure (2608) that was open-ended to the south and could have been used in conjunction with straps and dumps of soil.

Circular barrow

The circular barrow was situated *c.* 90m north-north-west of the chariot grave. This barrow was not strictly circular, but oval, the ditches enclosing an area 4.8m east to west and 5.8m north to south (Figs 6.2 and 6.13). The distinct, sub-rectangular central grave was situated at the centre of the enclosed area.

Barrow ditch

The ditch was *c.* 1.0m wide and 0.5m deep, and was excavated in four segments (453, 454, 461 and 464). The basal fill consisted of brown gravel-rich silt (454, 457, 461 and 464 respectively), with less stony material above (452, 456, 460 and 463 respectively); an uppermost, largely stone-free fill was also noted in places (451 in 454, 455 in 458).

Central grave 243

The grave was a sub-rectangular cut, aligned roughly north-east to south-west and measuring 1.84m long, 1.18m wide and 0.72m deep. The sides were steep and the base flat.

Burial SK 303

The central grave contained the well-preserved skeleton of a young adult male, 18–25 years old, laid in a crouched posture on his left side, with the head to the north, facing east and orientated slightly east of north to south (Fig. 6.13). The arms were bent at the elbows and both hands were drawn up in front of the face.

This man had ante-mortem fractures to both his nasal bones and evidence for healed blunt force trauma to the frontal bone; these injuries could have been caused at the same time. He also had bilateral maxillary sinusitis, which can result from upper respiratory tract infections, pollution, smoke, dust, or allergies. His teeth had evidence of dental enamel hypoplasia, an indicator of early childhood stress. He was 168.2cm tall, very close to the mean height (168cm) for Iron Age males. Isotope analysis (see Chapter 17) suggests that he lived his early life on the margin of land between the chalk and Pocklington, perhaps regularly moving between the two areas, before returning to Pocklington in his final years.

Two radiocarbon dates are available from this skeleton (SUERC-83085 and -93580; 2136 ±24 BP and 2127 ±32 BP, respectively); these combine to form mean Sk 303 (2133 ±20 BP), which calibrates to 350–50 cal BC (SUERC-83085).

Grave goods

SHIELD FITTING

Four elements of the copper alloy central spine and boss of a shield were present (Fig. 6.13; see Chapter 9). From north to south these consisted of part of the spine

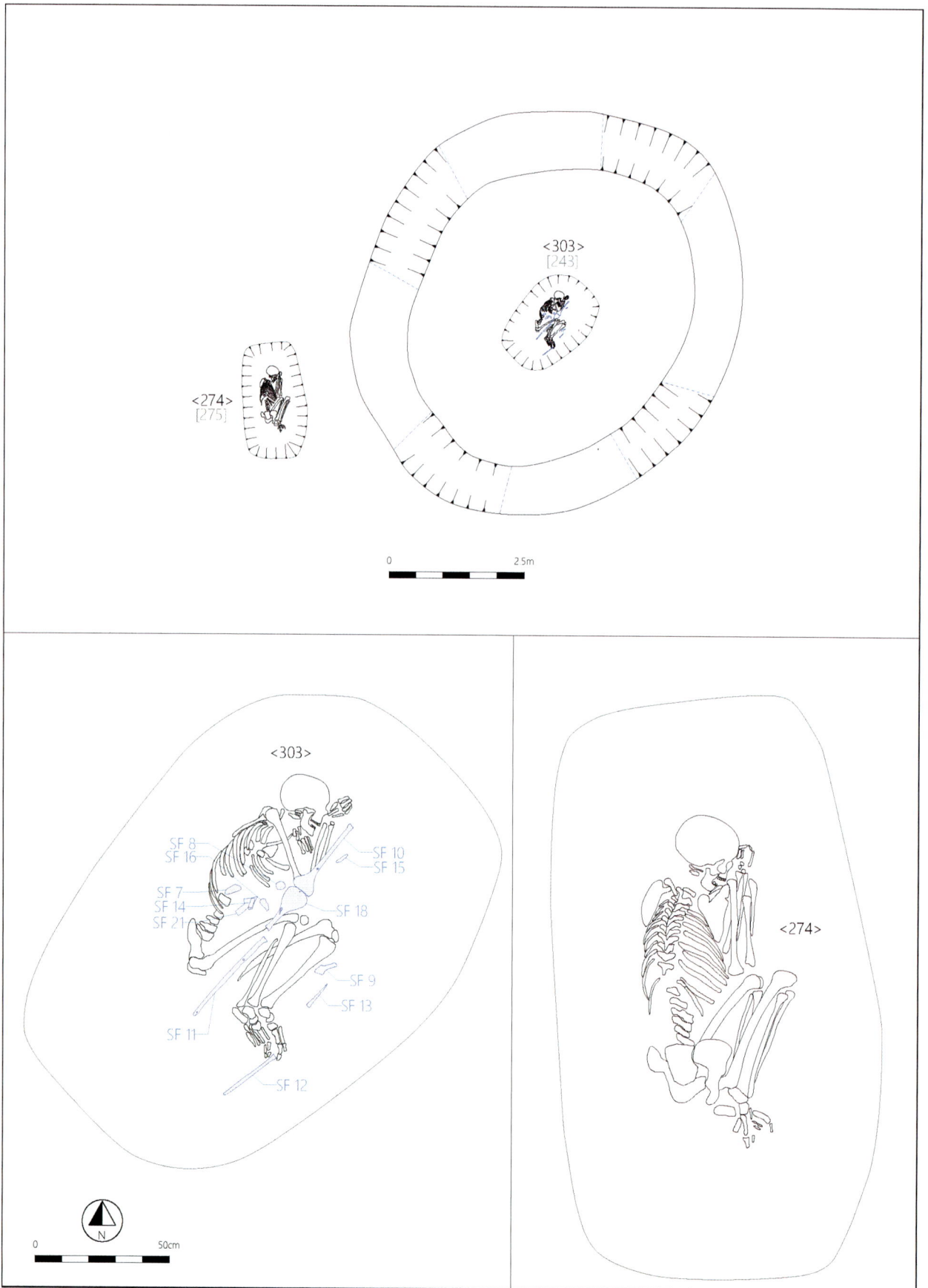

Figure 6.13 The Mile: circular barrow plan and skeletons

and the northern part of the boss (SF 10), which was joined to the southern part of the boss and an attached shorter length of spine (SF 18); a length of spine (SF 11), slightly out of position but roughly in line with SF 18; and another length of spine (SF 12) detached and placed in the south-east corner of the grave; this was the detached northern extension of SF 10. Two copper alloy rivets were also present: one at the top (north) end of SF 10, and the other at the bottom (south) end of SF 18, showing how the spine was attached to the shield backing.

The shield fittings had been forcibly removed from the shield backing, the evidence for this being the distorted and burred ends of spine fragments SF 10, 11 plus the completely detached position of SF 12 in the corner of the grave. If the shield backing had been placed on top of the skeleton it would have obscured most if not all the eight spearheads that also accompanied the burial; it certainly would have ruled out the 'spearing' of the corpse. There were no obvious traces of the shield backing within the grave, although the minerally preserved wood (probably ash) on some of the iron spearheads, with the grain at right-angles to the axis of the spearheads, shows the presence of one or more pieces of wood in the grave which may be the remains of the backing. Curiously, the shield boss and the central part of the spine were aligned in approximate order over the skeleton as if still attached to the backing.

Spearheads

The body was also associated with five iron throwing spearheads and three bone points (Figs 9.6–9.10 and 9.11–9.13), which formed a loose group in the central part of the grave. The iron spearheads were as follows: SF 7 at a 45° angle at the lower right ribs; SF 8 in a vertical position between the torso and the right arm; SF 9 pointing slightly downwards near to the right knee; SF 16 close to the horizontal between the right knee and the torso; and SF 21 positioned similarly to SF 16 and horizontal beneath bone spearhead SF 14. Of the bone points, SF 13 was horizontal between the lower left leg and the grave's eastern edge, SF 14 was at a 45° angle in front of the abdomen, and SF 15 was at a 60° angle east of the right arm (and recorded as having 'no impact'). Perhaps coincidentally, the bone points were more peripheral to the group, with only one (SF 14) placed towards the centre.

SF 13 had two opposed small holes at the end of the socket, presumably for rivets to attach the shaft (the rivets were not present). SF 14 was cracked along its length and this was probably old damage. Mineralised wood within the sockets of two of the iron spearheads (SF 9 and SF 21) was a ring-porous hardwood, probably ash.

'Satellite' burial' 274

Grave 275

This deep rectangular grave, which was located *c.* 1m to the south-west of the circular barrow, measured 1.90m in length, 1.15m in width and 0.98m in depth. The grave was filled with reddish-brown fine silt (273) around the skeleton, and a brown gravel-rich silt (272) above.

Burial Sk 274

This was the inhumation of a young adult woman aged 18–25 years, in a crouched posture, with her legs bent and her torso partly supine, and the hands positioned in front of the face (Fig. 6.13). Her head was to the north, facing east. She had a height of 155.6cm, below the average height (162cm) for Iron Age women. Like the man buried in the adjacent barrow, analysis of the skeleton identified dental enamel hypoplasia, plus cribra orbitalia and ossicles, all of which indicate that she had suffered early childhood stress. She also had spina bifida occulta, so-called 'hidden' spina bifida. Interestingly, the sternal ends of some of the central ribs of this woman were abnormally bent inwards. The abnormalities appear to have been acquired or developed rather than congenital and resulted from the constriction of the chest as if by a corset. There is no other evidence for the wearing of corsets in the Iron Age and the abnormalities themselves are highly unusual for the period, so the origins of this condition remain uncertain. The skeleton in Burial Sk 274 was radiocarbon-dated to the period 340 cal BC – cal AD 10 (SUERC-93579).

Discussion

The three burials at The Mile relate more to the dispersed arrangement of square barrows seen at and in the vicinity of the Pocklington Flood Alleviation Scheme (POCFAS) site than to a nucleated cemetery as such. What is apparent is the high quality of the primary burials of the barrows at The Mile, with both central burials containing rich grave assemblages.

The relatively isolated position of the square barrow suggests that the burial of the man within it did not refer to other individuals nearby and presumably was linked in some other way to the surrounding landscape.

The man buried centrally within the circular barrow and the woman buried in the adjacent grave have overlapping radiocarbon dates, which most likely makes them contemporaries and hints at a connection between them. Furthermore, the date for the central burial suggests that circular barrows were constructed within the later stages, or perhaps at the end, of the currency of the classic Arras-style square barrow rite.

The shield from The Mile chariot burial

Melanie Giles and Matthew Hitchcock

with contributions by Steven Allen (shield board interpretation and line drawings), Mags Felter (shield conservation and SEM analysis), Dominic Powlesland (photogrammetric recording and 3D-modelling), Marcus Abbott (shield imaging); additional illustrations by Rowan May (ArcHeritage)

Shield form and materials

Overview and terminology

The wood and copper-alloy composite shield found in the chariot burial from The Mile is a unique example of robust *repoussé* insular Celtic art. It shows the legacy of continental-influenced vegetal and plastic styles finding expression in the relief or embossed tradition of middle Iron Age British insular art (Stead 1996; Harding 2007). It is a thus new example of prestige metalwork characteristic of the mature phase of 'innovation and experimentation' known as the Torrs-Witham-Wandsworth style, emerging around 300 BC (Harding 2007, 143). The piece shows specific design affinities with two Celtic art icons: the Torrs 'pony-cap' from Scotland and the Loughnashade horn-end from Ireland, embodying motifs and decorative elements from Stead's Insular Celtic art Stages IV–V (1996) now generally recognised as chronologically overlapping in time, sometimes on the same objects (Macdonald 2007; Garrow *et al.* 2008). Yet the form of the decorative plaques links it closely to examples from Grimthorpe (Mortimer 1905a) and Hunmanby (Sheppard 1907), suggesting a distinctive regional shield style.

In order to describe its components, we have employed the following terminology (Fig. 7.1): shield boards, shield plaques, spines, boss, tabs and clips, with the term 'rivet' used to describe larger penetrative attachments, and 'pin' reserved for smaller ones, with 'tacks' reserved for the smallest elements used on the scalloped sheet edging. We will discuss each of these components in turn before evoking the overall appearance and impact of what we will class here as a defensive *and* offensive weapon, briefly situating it in within the canon of Celtic insular art and British Iron Age shield design. From observation in the field and interpretation of the appearance of its decorative scheme, we suggest that the shield was simply turned over and laid 'face down' in the chariot box, since the slightly shorter length of Spine 1 (found to the north end of the burial) gives us to believe this is the 'upper' register of the shield as it was meant to be held, wielded and seen (analogous to the shorter upper register of the Witham shield, Harding 2007, 149, fig. 7.3).

Shield shape, shield boards and organic 'padding'

The overall length of the Pocklington shield was no less than 690mm and its width 540mm, with shield boards ranging from 7mm to 11mm thick (based on the U-shaped clamps or 'shield clips' running along one side and edge), producing a shield that looks strangely squat and wide (Fig. 7.2). (From the 3D-photogrammetry undertaken by Powlesland, it is clear that as at Ferry Fryston, this shield only just fitted within the width of the chariot box). This makes The Mile shield similar in overall length to the Battersea shield but much shorter than the elongate form found in Garton Slack burial 4 (1.12m, analogous to the Witham shield, Stead 1991a, 63). Interestingly, this ratio of width:length, as well its sub-rectangular form, matches the soil stain of the largely organic shield from Burnby Lane cemetery Barrow 37, as well as a miniature shield from the East Riding reported to the Portable Antiquities Scheme (YORYMB1781: 'with oval boss ... single vertical groove running along its length ... almost

Shield Part Terminology

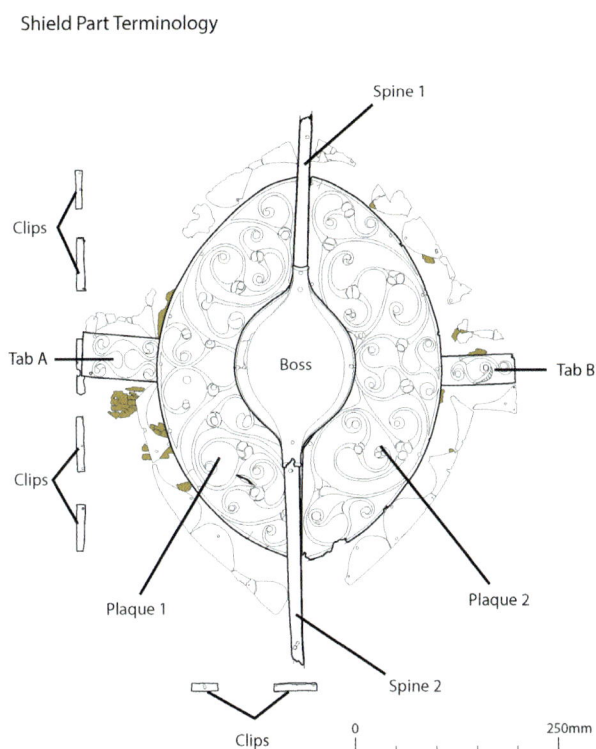

Figure 7.1 The Mile shield: terminology and components (drawing by S.J. Allen, YAT)

rectangular with slight curved edges'). This shape is paralleled elsewhere in the Witham (Lincolnshire, UK) and Clonoura shields (Co. Tipperary, ROI) yet this form was something of a surprise given the initial impression generated by its ovate copper alloy elements. It contrasts with both the 'waisted' Battersea shield form (which may be a metal skeuomorph of the contraction seen in bark shields, demonstrated experimentally as part of the Enderby shield project, see Kipling and Beamish 2018) as well as the oval design suggested for the Great Wold Valley shields (Stead 1991a, 62) based on the copper alloy Chertsey shield, the chalk model shield from Garton Slack and the miniature bronze shields from Lady's Spring, Malton (see Stead 1991b) or the 'hide-shape' shield of Mill Hill, Deal (Parfitt 1995).

It is not known whether the shield board was made from a single piece of wood: if so, this would have been at least 700mm wide by 7mm thick. Alternatively, several pieces may have been laid edge to edge. Nor can the conversion of the board(s) be identified but six attachment pins (one either side of the boss, two above and below it, and two at the terminal ends of the spines, Fig. 7.3) show how wood and copper alloy elements were held together. Soil marks clearly show that the wood grain ran across the width or waist of the shield, rather than along its length (Fig. 7.4). While construction would perhaps have been easier had this orientation been longitudinal, it does mean that an overhead sword blow would not cut

into the 'end grain' of the wood, thus strengthening the shield board's resistance to splitting. This does suggest that despite its decorative elements, The Mile example was not a mere 'parade' shield: it was knowingly designed to withstand combat impact. Wood species identification was carried out following Schweingruber (1982), based on an examination of Scanning Electron Microscope (SEM) images taken by Mags Felter of YAT Conservation for the boards, and sampling of the remains of the spine for direct microscopic observation. All of the samples (from the board and from the spine) proved to be ash, *Fraxinus excelsior L.* Ash is a ring-porous hardwood, native to the British Isles and North-west Europe. The tree has a widespread distribution but seems to thrive on damper, base-rich soils relative to other tree species. It is valued for its shock resistant and elastic nature. It tends not to split or shatter and has been used in the past for tool handles, wheels, furniture and similar applications where these properties would be useful. However, this contrasts with the wood species identified on shields from the Great Wold Valley, where boards made of maple, cherry or lime, willow or poplar, birch and alder were identified (Stead 1991a, 61–4). It is possible that the choice of these woods was influenced not merely by material affordances but their colours, creating shields that were visually distinct in both form and appearance, within and between the East Yorkshire districts (Giles 2012, 163–4).

Dark organic staining can also be seen in the photogrammetric record of the shield's excavation, *overlying* the wood impressions (i.e. on the reverse of the shield, D. Powlesland pers. comm.), and this was also noted in conservation and tentatively identified as hide products (M. Felter pers. comm.). Where the stratigraphy of this could be observed, it looked as if the leather-like substance was perhaps designed to give some cushioning to the shield-bearer, softening blunt-force impact and minimising bruising during training or combat (a modification also made by some re-enactment groups, S. Burrows, pers.comm.).

Shield clips (edge-bindings)

The six rectangular copper alloy shield clips (SFs 119, 120, 72, 90, 76 and 65, running in sequence parallel to Tab A and round its lower edge, below Spine 2; Fig. 7.2) are U-shaped in section, range from 35mm to 66mm in length and 10mm to 17mm in width, averaging a height (and thus board 'grip') of 7–11mm, widest along the basal edge of the shield. The Mile chariot shield board(s) sit between the fine 5–6mm shield boards from the Great Wold Valley, and the thickest examples from those same cemeteries, which could reach up to 15mm in places (Stead 1991a, 64). Variation in shield-board thickness was also noted in the U-shape fittings from the Ferry Fryston chariot burial, averaging *c.* 8mm but with one clip of 10mm height, this time gripping boards made of alder (Boyle *et al.* 2007, 145). With such hand-worked wood, some variation in

Overall View of Shield

Outer Face

Inner face

Obscured by soil and debris

Decayed wood traces

Shield boss plate

Shield board plate

Outer face

Cu Alloy Loop attached to inner face

SF 119

SF 120

SF 72

SF 90

SF 76

SF 65

0

250mm

A

B

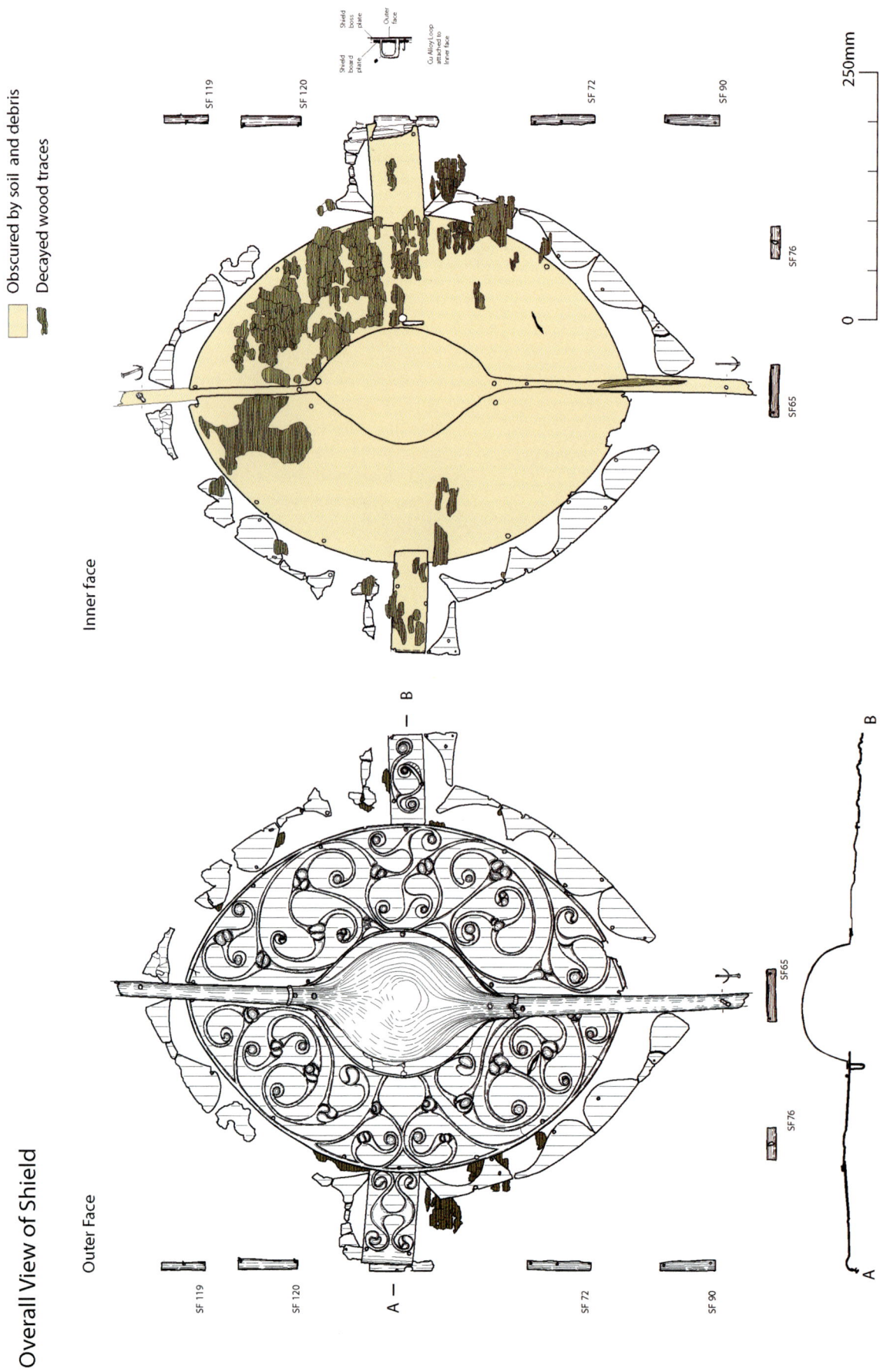

Figure 7.2 The Mile shield: inner and outer faces (drawing by S.J. Allen, YAT)

Outer face, metal fittings except
clips omitted

Wooden Elements of Shield:
Suggested reconstruction

Visible positions of pins/rivets passing through metal attachments.
NB not all of these necessarily pass through the wooden board

Wooden spine c.12.5mm w, 9mm th at extreme ends
Broadens to at least 18mm w, 14mm th at edge of handgrip

Board c. 7mm th

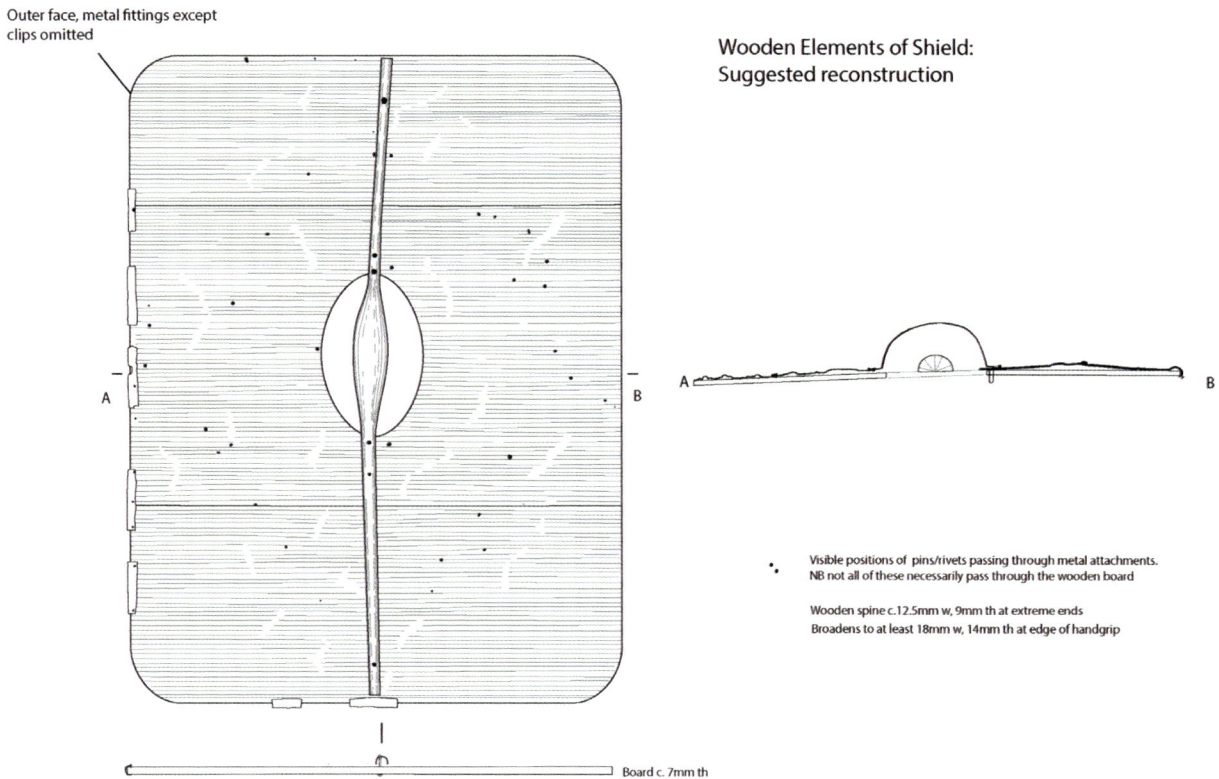

Figure 7.3 Reconstruction of wooden elements on inner face (drawing by S.J. Allen, YAT)

Figure 7.4 The inner face of the shield. Height: 690mm; width: 540mm (photogrammetric image by M. Abbott)

backing-board thickness should be expected across a single object but The Mile shield sits at the more robust end of this scale.

The Mile clips are straight in form with no curvature and no decoration. Simple copper alloy rivets or pins with flat heads of 1.5–3.5mm diameter and sharp-ended shank lengths of 7–11mm were used to 'tack' the clips in place: most had two rivets at either end, but one (clip SF 72) had three. Some of these were 'bent over' at right angles *in situ*, presumably where they failed to match up with and penetrate the opposite rivet hole and were bent flat against the internal edge of the clip. They were spaced apart in an uneven sequence, focused along the side bearing the larger tab A and around its adjoining shorter edge (interpreted here as the basal edge). Unless the shield had lost many such clips during its lifetime, they may indicate remedial repairs of the 'leading edge' of the implement, reinforcing splitting boards that had seen greater impact damage against a foe or from resting on the ground (see Chittock 2021 for a wider discussion of Iron Age repairs). Yet they would also have created a wooden rim set with copper alloy elements: a 'serrated' materials effect, each clip capable of tearing open an opponent's flesh. Anything that 'opened' a wound was capable of leading to long-term infection (P. Ellinger pers. comm.) – surely one of the 'deferred' but no less fatal causes of death in these later prehistoric communities. As reinforcements that also acted as 'skin splitters', they served a dual purpose, reminding us that the shield was not merely a defensive but also an offensive weapon. The crushing, pinning and tearing properties of even highly decorated Iron Age shields like The Mile have thus been under-appreciated.

Shield grip

Nothing remains of the (presumably organic) shield grip situated inside the protective raised dome of the boss. Where examples of the grip have been found, they tend to run parallel to the 'width' or waist of the shield (not its long axis) as seen on the Chertsey shield (British Museum 1986, 0901.1) as well as miniature versions (e.g. Netherhampton, British Museum 1998, 0401.5 from the 'Salisbury hoard'). Both of these examples have a very slight upwards slant, suggesting they were designed to be held comfortably in the left fist by a right-handed individual wielding spear or sword, with the long axis of the shield slightly tipped to protect both arm and torso. We can therefore make sense of the small copper alloy 'loop' or staple-shaped fitting on the reverse of the board (Figs 7.2 and 7.3) as related to this grip and its attachment to the shield board. Its projecting nature means that it would have sat just outside of the closed fist clasping the grip and it may also have served as a tie-off for an organic thong, looped around the wrist. Should the shield be 'knocked' from the hand, it would not be dropped but dangle, allowing the defender to hitch and reclasp their mode of defence.

Wooden spine and copper alloy spine-covers/fittings

The decayed remains of a wooden spine running along the long axis of the shield are present and show that this was a piece of ash, tapering towards each end from 18mm wide and 14mm thick in the centre (at the edge of the handgrip) to 12.5mm wide and 9mm thick at the terminal ends. The piece has a probable halved conversion forming a natural half-round cross-section. The flat side of this rod was placed against the outer face of the shield board and fastened in place by copper alloy rivets passing though the metal facing, through the wood, and riveted at each end. Where the spine passes across the void behind the boss it would be logical for the spine to have been expanded out to form the handgrip, although there is no surviving evidence for the shape or dimensions of this grip.

This roundwood core was covered by longitudinal, U-profile-shaped copper alloy spine-covers (Fig. 7.5). Spine 1 (interpreted here as the upper fitting) is 194mm long and 20mm wide (at the centre where it conjoins to and sits slightly under the boss), narrowing to 15mm wide at its terminal end, which is broken and ragged. A single pin at the terminal end had a shank of 23mm long

Figure 7.5 The outer face of the shield. Height: 690mm; width: 540mm (photogrammetric image by M. Abbott)

with a slightly domed head of 5mm diameter (the foot of this rivet was not observable), penetrating copper alloy cover, wooden spine and back board. Spine 2 is slightly longer at 243mm in length (leading to our interpretation that this is the lower part of the shield, based on comparative examples from the Great Wold Valley shields, Stead 1991a). It is, however, identical in width to Spine 1, and also tapers to the basal edge of the shield where the terminal is once again slightly broken in a jagged manner. The single rivet *in situ* at this point is slightly bent into a curve with a shank of 23mm length (excluding terminals) and a pin head of 5mm diameter on the front of the shield and a larger rivet foot of 8mm on the rear. This makes The Mile spines shorter than Grimthorpe's 280mm-long (upper) and 290m (lower) spine, though its rivets are longer than the 17mm-long Grimthorpe examples (Stead 1979, 55) reinforcing the impression of a squatter and thicker design.

It is likely that these copper alloy spines once had sub-rounded terminals, as seen in the iron spine-covers from Ferry Fryston (Boyle *et al.* 2007, fig. 103 no. 23), Grimthorpe, North Grimston and Eastburn (Stead 1979, 57), as well as the adjacent shield burial just to the north of The Mile chariot. The 'ragged' damage observed on these spine terminals from the chariot burial suggest the top and bottom of the shield had seen significant impact and wear. Given the propensity for the ritual damaging of shields in the funerary performance (Stead 1991a; Giles 2015 – and particularly seen in The Mile shield burial to the north), we should consider if this was deliberate tearing or fragmentation at the point of deposition. Yet the presence of clip SF 65 fixed directly *below* the broken end of Spine 2 (Fig. 7.2) suggests an ancient repair at a known point of damage and vulnerability. In addition, no trace of rounded terminal ends was observed in the assemblage of small copper alloy fragments recovered with the shield from the chariot burial (*cf* North Grimston, Stead 1979, fig. 19.8).

Boss

The large ovate boss is approximately 251mm long and 157mm wide and comprises a single piece of thick copper alloy sheet, hammered into a raised elongate dome which protrudes *c.* 45mm above the shield boards (Figs 7.2 and 7.5). Despite its polished and rounded appearance, it would have been useful in pinning or crushing an opponent, with blunt, bruising power. The dome is not exactly symmetrical: the slight protuberance or swelling out towards the right-hand upper quadrant is mirrored by oppositional swelling towards the lower left-hand quadrant. Its effect (echoed in other elements of the shield's decoration, discussed below) is to draw the eye clockwise round the shield boss, and back up towards the apex of the spine. Flattened flanges flank the dome to allow it to be fixed to the shield boards, *c.* 16mm wide at the maximum 'waist' of the boss. This component sits over Plaques 1 and 2, pinned right at the edge of the flange, left and right, with a single large rivet with domed head. On the left-hand side, the rivet has torn through the thinner flange sheet, causing subsidiary cracking and damage (though the rivet is still present underneath). It is uncertain whether this is the result of pre-burial damage or post-depositional crushing from the weight of the body placed on top. The boss tapers to the north and south, pinching into a U-shape profile, terminating neatly at both ends in a robust, raised cordon edge. These terminals sit *over* the spines, riveted to them with four large domed rivets whose heads are *c.* 4mm in diameter: two on the northern boss/spine junction and two on the southern boss/spine junction. The northern rivets are intact and *in situ* but the upper southern rivet is missing, whilst the lower one (although still visible) has apparently 'torn through' the terminal end of the boss, leaving a series of two or three serrated circular impressions. This may have been caused by a series of percussive blows, causing this rivet head to 'pull through' the sheet of the boss at this junction with the spine, which now sits strangely elevated above the spine itself – damage which will be discussed further below.

Shield plaques

Plaques 1 and 2 (Figs 7.1, 7.2 and 7.5) consist of arch-shaped beaten sheets designed to sit either side of (and underneath) the flanges of the central ovate boss, with two straight-edges apiece that flank and underlie the shield spines.

Plaque 1 has a raised cordoned edge on the exterior arch and near-perfect mirror symmetry around its horizontal axis, making it the most complex and accomplished of the *repoussé* work on this shield. The middle of the design comprises a complex lyre loop with sub-peltate 'head' that terminates in opposed tendrils with 'ornithomorphic intent' (as Raftery might describe it, 1983, 40): resembling a stylised bird-head with eye and rounded, up-turned beak. These motifs closely resemble the birds' heads on the rear of the Torrs cap (Fig. 7.6), interpreted by Fox as reminiscent of the 'shoveler duck' species (1958, 24). An alternative zoomorphic interpretation would be to see the complete lyre/peltate motif as more bovine in design with horns, eyes and rounded muzzle. Side tendrils run symmetrically off the small triskele-shaped junctions to merge into the cordoned edge of the boss. Flanking this central motif are triskele wave tendrils with three stems similar to Fox's 'trumpet spirals' (1958, fig. 82 no. 30): one end curling round to terminate in a domed boss, another running off to the interior edge of the plaque and the final spiral springing off, to pivot around a further triskele-shaped junction (with central boss). Here it bifurcates; again, one of these tendrils ends in a domed boss, whilst the second springs to another triskele boss junction. These springing wave tendrils have the appearance of spindly strands of vegetation – bracken perhaps, with its coiled tips about to unfurl. Yet the complete effect (when the shield is turned slightly on is its side) can also be interpreted as three semi-abstract 'nested and crested' bird's-head designs facing the main lyre-loop: the lowest (close to the boss and spines) with an up-turned beak, the upper two with down-turned beaks. Bird's head begets bird's head. Very slight differences in the positioning of these heads (the lower register is brought closer to the centre of the shield) helps create movement but detracts from strict symmetry. A wave bifurcation at the final junction ends in small, curled domed bosses at the northern and southern edges of the plaque.

Plaque 2 also has a raised, cordon edge on the exterior arch. In contrast to Plaque 1, it is nearly but not quite symmetrical around its horizontal axis, due to the transposition of elements in the lower quadrant of the plaque. This gives this side of the shield a strong sense of clockwise rotational movement. Its central motif mimics the empty lyre-loop of Plaque 1, but it is larger and is not a closed form. Here it is filled with a triskele wave tendril, two lines of which spiral to terminate in small bosses, whilst the third springs off to a domed boss junction, from which further waves emerge to develop the lower right-hand quadrant

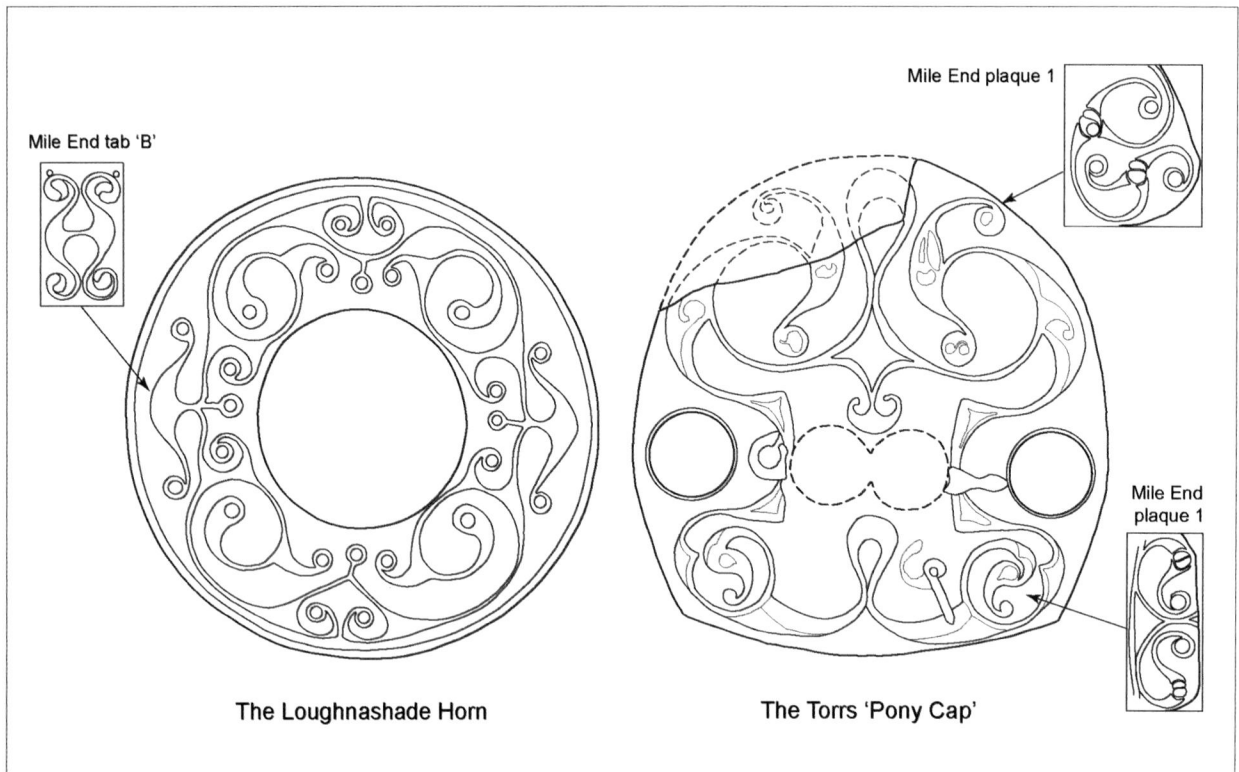

Figure 7.6 Celtic art motif comparisons with the Loughnashade horn end (after Raftery 1983) and the Torrs 'pony cap' (after Fox 1958; redrawn and annotated by R. May, ArcHeritage)

of the shield. These components create the impression of an 'S-scroll' motif, mimicked by a second 'S-scroll' to its right. In both lower and upper quadrants, tendrils run back over the 'S' form to create the arch of the 'lyre', whilst another springs off to merge with the outer cordoned rim of the plaque. That latter line arcs back into the upper and lower quadrants towards the spines, where the line bifurcates at a bossed junction. The resulting voids are filled by further springing wave tendrils with two large 'triskele' bossed junctions creating the impressions of birds' heads with impressive feathered, bifurcating plumes and convex beaks – this time facing away from the central motif. These two designs almost look like a mirrored pair but in the upper quadrant the plume repeats the 'S' shape of the central motif whilst the lower one is a reverse 'S', drawing the eye down and around to the spine. At the far ends, a final triskele junction bifurcates into two boss spiral ends, the looseness of the upper one drawing the eye to the right and down, the lower one drawing the eye round towards Plaque 1. The overall effect of Plaque 2 is of movement: the oppositional rotation of the two largest spirals drawing the viewer's attention, with tighter spirals closing in and swirling more forcibly in the lower half. The bottom half of Plaque 2 has some slight damage on its outer edge, with the loss of some raised cordon edging.

Plaque 1 is further distinguished by a single, sharp-edged puncture wound in the lower half of the register.

It has come from the front of the shield and measures 22mm long by *c.* 3mm wide (Fig. 7.7), suggesting the lenticular profile of the tip of a fine, sharp-bladed weapon such a short sword or dagger. This profile matches the blade width of Group E middle–late Iron Age swords from East Yorkshire (Stead 2006, 13); for example, the Grimthorpe sword tip narrows to 26mm before its sharpened tip (Stead 1979, 61). This could be the result of a deflected puncturing thrust towards the lower half of the defender's body but there is no sign of attempted repair. Either it was left as a mark of fighting renown (having successfully defended its wielder) or this was a deliberate stab 'wound' to the shield at the time of burial, in keeping with other dramatic moments of martial performance involving the 'ritual killing' of weaponry (see examples in Stead 1991a): appropriately noisy spectacles analogous to the modern 'gun salute' (Giles 2012, 242; Inall 2015). It was the force of this blow which probably caused the minor damage seen across fixtures and fittings in that quadrant: the torn flange around the rivet on the left-hand side of the boss and subsequent slight displacing of the boss itself towards Tab A, slightly obscuring the design on that sheet and revealing rivets on Plaque 2 which were probably meant to be 'hidden' under the boss flange; the torn end of the southern boss terminal away from the lower spine and back board; and finally, the 'warping' or deforming curvature of one of Spine 2's rivets.

Figure 7.7 Puncture mark on the exterior of Plaque 1 (length: 22mm)

Shield tabs

On either side of the Plaques are two Tabs, made from small rectangular copper alloy sheets. As with the Plaques these are not a matching pair: Tab A (like Plaque 1) has mirror-symmetry along its horizontal axis whereas Tab B (adjoining Plaque 2) is non-symmetrical. The positioning of these has the effect of drawing the eye clockwise, around the slighter asymmetrical design towards the dominant symmetry of Tab A, reinforcing the movement achieved in the Plaques.

Tab A has a rolled rim that clamps the shield back board (although it has broken along this edge, following deposition). The other end of the Tab sits under Plaque 1 where they join. It is decorated with a palmette-derived motif, composed of a triskele wave tendril with two symmetrical arms rising to form back-turned ends, from which spring snail-shell-like spiral bosses, with yin-yang design. The third tendril flows into the arm of its mirror-image companion, such that this upper design is repeated identically on the bottom register of the plaque. Conjoined, they create the impression of mirror-image lyre-loops. (Fascinatingly, a close parallel can be seen on the Loughnashade horn end, where they are split either side of the central void (Raftery 1983); Fig. 7.6.) The junction of the three stems shows some skilful shaping or

beating, creating the sense of a slight spine either side of the junction of the back-to-back motifs. Tab A once had four rivets symmetrically placed: two located close to the shield edge and two mid-way along the Tab edge, though one is now lost. It measures 84mm long by 48mm wide and is noticeably wider than Tab B (though not as long).

Tab B is a cleanly cut piece of copper alloy sheet with no evidence for a raised or rolled rim. Like Tab A, it sits under Plaque 2 where they meet. This Tab is decorated with a non-symmetrical design of a simple triskele wave-spiral, where two arms form a design *almost* identical to that of Tab A, but one of the terminals turns in the opposite direction from the other, ending again in a snail-shell boss – these bosses end in simple comma-stops, not the yin-yang design of Tab A (and thus, they mimic some of the bosses on Plaque 1 not Plaque 2). The middle tendril curls under and back on itself to mimic the direction of the outermost tendril. Together this design has the effect of a fancy capital 'T'. Once again, the body of this design is moulded into three-dimensional relief, creating a sense of a ridge and slight slopes to the raised design. Uniquely, the lowermost wave tendril appears to have small incised parallel 'laddering' on the back of the tendril. It has a more random location of rivets: one at the far edge of the shield has broken and been lost, whereas the other two sit above and below the raised motif, around the mid-point of the Tab. This component measures 87mm long by 35mm wide: slightly longer but much slimmer than Tab A.

Repoussé elements of The Mile shield

Although the tabs are of different shapes and designs, the beaten copper alloy plaques are identical in size and shape and despite their different design schemas, all four components were feasibly made as a pair in the same 'workshop', if not by the same hand. It might be argued that the lack of either *strict* fold-over symmetry (as in the Torrs cap) or rotational symmetry (seen in the Witham and Wandsworth shields), mark The Mile shield as inferior in craft skill to analogous *repoussé* artworks of the period. Yet what is fascinating is the attempt to achieve both in Plaques 1 and 2 respectively. This creates the impression of an artistic 'conversation' between the plaques. They echo and complement each other, and whilst employing abstract design elements that conjure tangled vegetation or swirling pools and eddies (as Jope suggests for this phase of insular Celtic art, 2000) the key motif that emerges is (to our eyes) avian: flaring, feathered heads and snaking beaks, positioned skilfully to create movement between the two pieces.

This is interesting as both Raftery (1983, 240) and the Megaws (1989, 196) read some of the motifs on the Torrs pony cap and the Loughnashade horn as birds' heads (see Fig. 7.6). For example, the Torrs pony cap features large, mirrored open-looped pelta motifs on each side that end in boss-ended trumpet spirals, and these motifs appear multiple times, in a more 'spindly' form than our 'nested' birds' heads on both plaques. Similar motifs also appear on the bronze horn end from Loughnashade (Raftery 1983, no. 781) except these trumpet spirals both curve inwards on themselves, and the entire scheme is more slender and finely tooled. The decision to ornament a shield with avian imagery may initially strike us as odd but both the Wandsworth boss (with its hooked-beak birds' heads, abstract wings and webbed feet) and the red-eyed crested heads at the centre of the Witham shield suggest this was part of a wider zoomorphic tradition of shield ornamentation. Real-world and fantastical beasts were used to enhance symbolic meaning, visual effect and even apotropaic power of these martial objects (Aldhouse Green 1996, 94; Fitzpatrick 2007; Giles 2008). For some Celtic art analysts, the key bird being evoked here was the swan (Jope 2000): dazzling in strength, plumage and aggressive behaviour. In the Witham shield we might note a closer link with species like the crested grebe (Megaw and Megaw 1989), renowned for its colourful head crest and ruff which inflate to exaggerate performance during courting, territorial display and fighting. In the case of The Mile, as with Torrs and Loughnashade, it is the sinuous beaks of wetland birds which seems to be evoked: the avocet (elegant birds renowned for posturing displays designed to deter or intimidate rivals) or the curlew perhaps (territorial yet gregarious, often combining to defend communally the wider group).

Domed bosses, seen on both the Loughnashade horn and Torrs cap, are also a distinguishing feature of The Mile shield. These are variously formed into two or three lobes, forming the classic 'yin-yang' and 'tricorne' designs identified by Fox (1958, fig. 83 F52 and F54). On Plaque 2, more major triskele junctions have tricorn bosses whereas the spiral-end terminal bosses are more likely to be divided two-fold, into a simpler yin-yang design. On Plaque 1, the spiral-end terminals sometimes form a simple, undivided boss, but both tricorn boss triskele junctions and yin-yang terminal tendril ends can also be seen. They are reminiscent of the carved domed stone beads on the brooch from Danes Graves (burial no. 57, YORYM 1948.930.2). Whilst these motifs employ the 'usefully ambiguous' forms so cleverly deployed in Celtic art (see Garrow and Gosden 2012), they may mimic the dome of snail shells (Giles 2012, 139): aesthetically pleasing, miniaturised embodiments of protection, perhaps considered apt apotropaic devices for such a defensive object. Whether these interpretations of The Mile shield symbolism are accepted or not, we can note the general affect of this complex tendril-wave art to captivate, intimidate and impress, its decoration becoming part of its martial power over an enemy (Giles 2008). As Megaw and Megaw put it, art which stood as 'a symbol of rank and achievement' also had 'the apotropaic intention of warding off harm' (1990, 72).

Many authors have linked the Torrs cap and Loughnashade horn together stylistically (Megaw and Megaw 1989, 196) and Fox even goes so far as to suggest the Torrs cap might have been made in north-eastern Britain (1958, 25). Harding, however, suggests a northern Irish-Scottish axis is more feasible (2007, 143). A link between the incised 'scabbard' art of East Yorkshire and north-east Ireland has long been posited (Raftery 1994, 482) whilst the nearest parallels for the bronze box or canister from Wetwang Slack chariot burial 2 and the miniature glass beads from Wetwang Village chariot burial are to be found in Ballydavis and other Irish cremations (Giles 2012, 228). The Mile shield thus strengthens this sense of privileged craft connections between East Yorkshire, north-east Ireland and south-west Scotland, seen in objects which embody 'exquisite' qualities of crafting prowess and shared designs which, although idiosyncratically produced, bound distant places together (see Fontijn 2019).

Scalloped edging

The shield is finally decorated with delicate but coarsely cut copper alloy scalloped edging (Figs 7.2 and 7.4–5). This has suffered considerable damage and fragmentation in the grave, represented in the many pieces of fine sheet no longer *in situ* but recovered during excavation. The form and position of this scalloped edging mimics and exaggerates the ovate design of the Plaques rather than the sub-rectangular shield boards. This scheme is symmetrical both horizontally and vertically, so that all four quadrants contain a near-identical wave of sub-peltate designs, comprising a major pair of rounded whale-back-like designs, which meet at a sharp point (visually referencing the apex of a pelta motif). The 'wave' of this scalloping alternates from convex to concave, creating the visual effect of S-shapes/reverse-S shapes, meeting end to end. At the waist of the shield, each quadrant scroll terminates in small arcs, mimicked either side of the tabs. This is the area on the shield where the other famous element of insular Celtic art design is seen: a play between negative and positive, light and dark, fill and void (Jope 2000; Joy 2010), embodied in the contrast between copper alloy plates and ash shield board.

Looking more closely, the scalloped edging is not continuous but cut in sections from remarkably thin beaten sheet, less than 1mm thick. It is notable for the coarseness of its preparation: on some edges, a quite ragged and unfinished line is visible – crudely cut, with some faint provisional incisions or marking lines visible. The design elements are riveted in place with the finest of tacks: their heads a mere 2–3mm in diameter and their shanks *c.* 1mm in diameter. These tacks are quite randomly distributed around the edges of the scrollwork, around 2–3 rivets per section, possibly reflecting an improvised response to where the fine sheet need fastening down. The thinness of sheet and finesse of rivets might explain some of the difficulty in achieving a neat finish but overall, it has the appearance of a rather coarse exaggeration of the main shield designs, arguably undertaken by a different hand. It may be a later addition although stratigraphically they appear to underlie the Plaques and Tabs: there is nothing to suggest the scalloped edging was not integral to the original shield design despite disparities in craft skill. Whilst exuding a kind of 'halo' effect, the ephemeral nature of this scalloped edging visually 'fades' into the background, overshadowed by the more massive *repoussé* boss, spines and plaques.

Such a scalloped border around the plates is an unusual decorative device, but it is not entirely without parallel. The handle cover found with the Battersea shield (Stead 1985, 21–2) employs a similar scheme of decorative cut-out forms that frame its large oval hand-hole. Here, the design appears almost as a negative of that from The Mile shield, with mirrored pairs of diagonal lentoid cut-out holes forming a semi-circle on the outer edge and a triangle with curved sides on the inner. Interestingly, the Wandsworth boss has an incised running wave around its central umbo, whereas the Witham shield has an incised running frill around both boss and spine, which may (in miniature) evoke the kind of art-effect achieved here through cut-out sheetwork. Incised running waves or 'bordering bands' are also seen on many contemporaneous East Yorkshire scabbards, such as one from Wetwang Slack, and Irish scabbards such as Lisnacrogher (Stead 1996, 32, fig. 30).

Discussion: the Celtic art context of The Mile chariot shield

In terms of its regional context, the two arch-shaped plaques flanking the boss and spine covers are most obviously reminiscent of those from the Grimthorpe shield burial (Mortimer 1905a; Stead 1968; Fig. 7.8). The ponies drawing The Mile chariot were positioned as if 'galloping' north, up towards the rising chalk of the Wolds where Grimthorpe is located, although this north–south orientation for the burial is also very much in keeping with the dominant crouched inhumation orientation for all of the Iron Age Arras cemeteries (Giles 2012, 69). Discovered in a chalk pit in the south-western section of this hillfort, located less than a mile to the north-west of The Mile, the fittings of the shield in this burial appear to have been configured in a similar way, tentatively alluding to a localised design tradition. Decorated with an incised stepped geometric motif around their edges, the Grimthorpe plaques had cracked with wear and been detached and re-attached to shield-board backings multiple times (Chittock 2021). This history of re-setting and repair, combined with the contrast in decoration between the plaque borders, the cross-quartered circle with hatching incised on the boss cover and the swirling La Tène design on the small circular plaque, suggest that they may be older than the

other less-worn *repoussé* metallic fittings thought also to relate to the shield (Chittock 2021; Giles 2012, 164). As argued above, there is nothing to suggest that the fittings of The Mile shield were not all made and fitted as one piece (apart from the edge-binding Clips). A lack of engraved ornament (apart from the slight 'ribbing' on Tab B) is notable.

The slim, semi-tubular spine covers are more characteristic of longer shields from East Yorkshire which seem to emphasise the vertical axis, in contrast to the later, oval and hide-shaped shields of the South. Similar examples from Rudston (R148 and R163) and Garton Station (GS4) are fashioned from iron (Stead 1991b), whilst the 'speared' burial just to the north-west of The Mile chariot is made from bronze. However, all of these either have, or likely had, a pair of linked convex discs (a 'figure of 8' design resembling the overlapping bowls of spoons) that may once have covered a wooden boss and were made as integral components of spine covers, whereas the chariot burial shield discussed here had separate boss and spine components. Meanwhile, the shield clips or edge-bindings are most reminiscent of the Ferry Fryston chariot burial, which also had a bow-fronted chariot box of very similar dimensions to The Mile: a burial which closely parallels this funerary rite in many ways, involving an older man laid on his shield in a chariot box, where the vehicle had been wheeled 'assembled' into the grave pit (Boyle *et al.* 2007). Yet if the Hunmanby chariot burial shield had survived its collapse into a gravel quarry, it may well have been the closest parallel for The Mile – Sheppard's description is worth quoting in detail:

> lying on the bottom of the grave was a large shield of wood, ornamented on the upper surface with exceedingly thin plates of bronze, and with a border of more substantial material … hammered over into a U-section, into which the edge of the wood shield had clearly been fitted … fastened by means of bronze rivets … The portion of the shield remaining was nearly two feet [=0.61m] long, almost straight-sided, except towards the ends, where the edges curved round … the whole of the shield had not been covered with bronze, but was ornamented with thin plates, riveted on to the wood. Where the bronze has not entirely disappeared it was seen to be ornamented with the scroll-work in repoussé, so characteristic of the late Celtic period … Across one end of the shield were the remains of a flattened tube of thin bronze, of which little more than the cast remained … the chariot … had been buried in a normal standing position. (Sheppard 1907, 483–4)

Hunmanby's upright chariot burial rite, its shield length and shape, the *repoussé* work plates, thin copper alloy sheeting, U-shape spine fittings and shield board edging or clips match The Mile shield in almost every detail. Yet such shields need not be dismissed as mere idiosyncratic

Objects found with a Skeleton on Grimthorpe Wold, near Pocklington.   (Page 150).

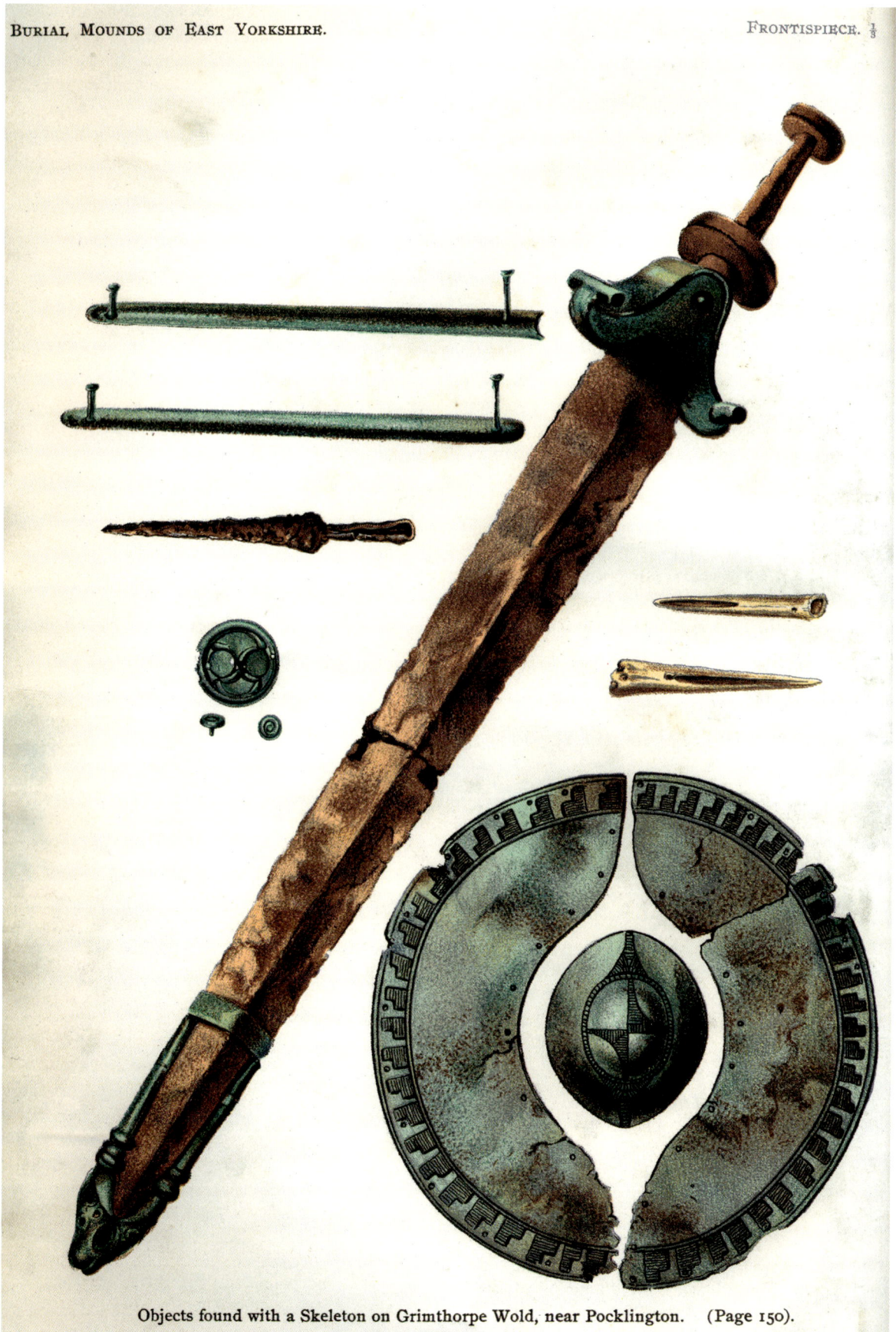

Figure 7.8 The Grimthorpe shield and grave goods (frontispiece, Mortimer 1905)

products of East Yorkshire smiths or shield-makers. We have already discussed its affinities with the Torrs-Witham-Wandsworth style: objects that speak of links from London to Lincolnshire, and from Dumfries and Galloway in Scotland to the iconic site of Loughnashade in Co. Armagh – a small bog pool below the 'royal site' of Navan (Emain Macha). The raised artwork bears the more 'rounded technique and higher relief masses of Torrs and Witham' compared with the crisper line of Wandsworth (Harding 2007, 150). Arch-shaped plaques with raised cordon edging are known from the River Thames at High Bridge (British Museum WG.1514 and WG.1517), suggesting this combination of boss-and-plaques was not exclusive to East Yorkshire. Firm evidence for this comes from the peltate copper alloy sheet 'plaques' of Tal-y-llyn (held at St Fagan's: Amgueddfa Cymru/National Museum of Wales 63.419/5 and 6) with their engraved triskele and basket-work ornament which once flanked a *repoussé* boss. Interestingly, these plaques have engraved chequered geometric and zig-zag running waves, slightly reminiscent of the effect of The Mile scalloped edging. Another pair of copper alloy peltate plaques was found with a solid copper alloy spine and boss (and iron 'swords') under the rubble of the inner rampart at Moel Hiraddug hillfort (Denbighshire, Amgueddfa Cymru/National Museum of Wales 32.175/2 – fortunately pre-served as electrotypes following the theft of the originals). Finally, although the miniature shield from Tydden Mawr Farm (Gwynedd) is oval in shape with a fine ovate boss, two areas of design either side of this boss might be meant to evoke such plaques: created through alternating incised, rocked tracer crescent or lunate motifs, infilling a defined peltate form (Amgueddfa Cymru/National Museum of Wales 2001.35H). Two incised roundels sit north and south of the boss itself (reminiscent of the Witham and Battersea shields) but more pertinent for The Mile form, two lines run from the peltate 'plaques' west and east, flaring out into curved triangle or trum-pet-shapes. They are the nearest evocation of side 'tabs' running between plaque and shield edge known, although another fragment of miniature shield reported to the Portable Antiquities Scheme from Lincolnshire may also allude to side 'tabs' represented here as two parallel raised cordons running from the side of the boss to the shield edge (LIN-ADA9D0).

Conclusion

From the above discussion, we propose that The Mile shield was not merely a defensive object but one with offensive potential, enhanced not just by its projecting copper alloy elements and reinforced leading edges but the visual complexity and symbolism of its Celtic art, which combine to create a powerful affect upon viewer

or opponent. It was worn and damaged by the time of its interment, seen in the fragmented ends of the spines. The single 'puncturing' sword blow to the lower left quadrant of Plaque 1 could be further damage sustained during its use-life but is more plausibly seen as a rupturing act of symbolic damage carried out as part of the funeral performance, which warped fixtures and fittings in this area of the shield.

We have noted its Celtic art affinities which place it within the Torrs-Witham-Wandsworth school of *repoussé* work dating to the 4th to 3rd century BC, linking it to craft pieces in Ireland and Scotland, whilst its form is charac-teristic of both East Yorkshire shield shapes and principles of shield décor from Wales to the Thames region. From the slight disparity in spine length, the rotational Celtic art scheme and visual 'weight' of design, we have suggested that it was made to be held in the left-hand by a right-handed sword or spear-wielder, and simply turned over to be laid face-down in the chariot box. This mortuary 'rite of reversal' has been noted with both the chainmail shirt from the Kirkburn chariot burial (K5, Stead 1991a, 54) and the shields in Wetwang Slack chariot burials (Dent 1985) and is interpreted ethnographically as either a way of 'confusing' the deceased and encouraging departure into the next world or consigning objects to the funerary realm (Norbeck 1971). Certainly the body was framed, contained and 'shielded' behind this object in death, as in other Yorkshire burials, the closest parallels being the male chariot burials from Wetwang Slack and Ferry Fryston, as well as Hunmanby. Such a robust base for the corpse helped preserve the integrity of the body, perched *in situ* above the chariot frame as can be seen in the photogram-metric recording during excavation (Fig. 6.6), whilst other elements of the box-structure have notably decayed and slumped around the robust 'T' join of axle and pole shaft (D. Powlesland pers. comm.).

Shield-burial is a phenomenon recorded ethnograph-ically amongst other chiefdom societies as a mark of respect and renown, as amongst the 'spear masters' of the Dinka (Lienhardt 1961, 302). In Hoplite warfare, the shield was valued above other martial objects due to its role in protecting not only one's own body but comrades-in-arms (Plutarch *Moralia* 1961, vol. 3, 220.2). Indeed, Spartan mothers sent their sons out to battle with the warning that they should return with their shield or upon on it (Plutarch *Moralia* 1961, vol. 3, 241)! Whilst single or small-group combat seems to characterise forms of conflict in these late Iron Age Yorkshire communities (King 2010), the shield may still have been an appropriate symbol of charismatic leadership. Quite apart from its rarity, illustrious appearance and history, the use of the shield as a 'bier' for a renowned defender of the people may thus explain the rich symbolism behind this part of The Mile chariot burial funerary rite.

An Iron Age weapon burial from Burnby Lane

Yvonne Inall

The assemblage of weapons recovered from the Burnby Lane Iron Age cemetery at Pocklington presents perhaps the most significant find of weapons in East Yorkshire for a generation. One Iron Age burial (16027, a man aged between 18 and 25 years buried centrally within Barrow 34) included offensive weaponry consisting of five iron spearheads, an iron ferrule and an iron sword (Figs 4.35 and 4.36). This assemblage contributes substantially to our understanding of weaponry during the Iron Age. The burial adds to the small number of 'speared-corpse' ritual burials recorded for Iron Age Britain and offers new insights into this practice. A further speared burial was located at The Mile, Pocklington and is discussed in Chapter 9.

Spearheads

16030, SF 68 small throwing iron spearhead

A small, diamond-bladed spearhead which can be allocated to Inall (2015) Type 1.1.b.1 (Fig. 8.1). The total length of the spearhead is 124mm. The blade is small, with an elongated, diamond-shaped profile measuring 57mm long and 25mm wide. The very tip of the blade is missing, likely the result of use wear. The blade has a slightly lenticular section. The blade measures 3.8mm at its thickest, around the mid-blade, with a fine blade edge of 1.3mm. The blade to socket transition is smooth and the blade edges and shoulders appear symmetrical. The socket has a visible weld-seam, which can be observed up to 31mm from the base of the socket. The remainder of the weld seam is obscured by corrosion product. Wood and corrosion product fill the socket so that it is not possible to determine the depth of the socket void, or the degree of overlap in the weld-seam. Similarly, it is not possible to identify any rivet hole in the socket and none is visible on the x-ray. Wood samples taken from the socket were analysed by Steven Allen, who was able to confirm it was hardwood but it was not possible to identify the wood species (Felter and Wilkinson 2015). Traces of organic material remain adhering to the spearhead, on the blade and along the socket.

Figure 8.1 Iron spearhead SF 68

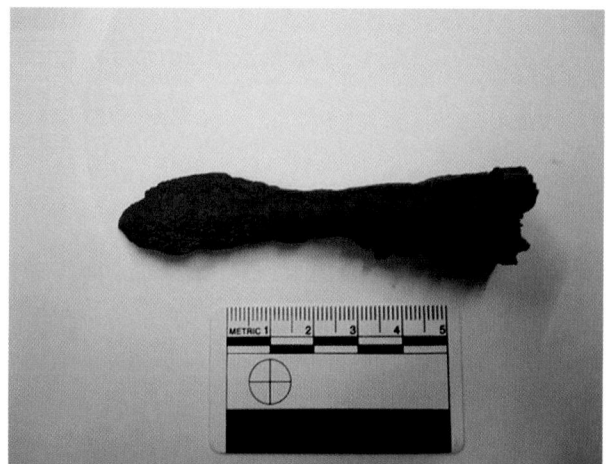

Figure 8.2 Iron spearhead SF 69

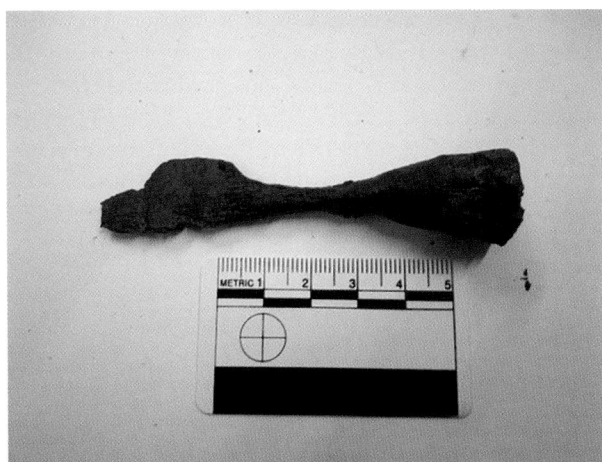

Figure 8.3 Iron spearhead SF 70

Figure 8.4 Iron spearhead SF 71

16030, SF 69 small throwing iron spearhead

A small-bladed spearhead which can be tentatively allo-cated to Inall Type 1.1.a.2 (Fig. 8.2). The total length of the spearhead is 93mm, with a blade 37mm long. The blade has a maximum width of 20mm at the mid-blade. The blade is very thin with a flat section 2mm thick. The blade is bent slightly, possibly as a result of use-wear. The transition from blade to socket is smooth, with a minimum diameter of 10mm at the neck. The socket is well made with a weld that remains closed, although corrosion product around the seam highlights its position. The socket base has an external diameter of 19mm, and an internal diameter of 16mm. No rivet holes are observable.

Organic material remains preserved in the base of the socket. Samples taken were analysed by Steven Allen, who was able to confirm it was hardwood, although it was not possible to identify the wood species (Felter and Wilkinson 2015).

16030, SF 70 small throwing iron spearhead

A small-bladed spearhead which can be tentatively allo-cated to Inall Type 1.1.a.2 (Fig. 8.3). The total length of the spearhead is 88mm. The blade is incomplete with damage to both sides of the blade, and the tip is missing. The extant length of the blade is 34mm, preserved to a maximum width of 18mm. The form is consistent with other members of Inall Type 1.1 and the original blade dimensions were likely similar to SF 68. The blade is very thin, less than 1mm at blade edge, with a near-flat section that thickens slightly along the centre of the blade. The transition from socket to blade is very thin, with a minimum diameter of 5mm. The socket is rounded and the weld seam is open. The external diameter of the socket is 19mm, with an inner diameter of 16mm. Two small rivet holes are preserved in the lateral sides of the socket, each approximately 2mm in diameter. The

rivet holes are not aligned and were clearly drilled or punched separately.

Traces of organic material are preserved in the base of the socket. Samples taken from the socket and analysed by Steven Allen revealed the wood to be ash (*Fraxinus excelsior L. sp.*) (Felter and Wilkinson 2015).

16030, SF 71 small throwing iron spearhead

A small spearhead which can be allocated to Inall Type 1.1.b.1 (Fig. 8.4). The total length of the spearhead is 112mm with an elongated, diamond-shaped blade meas-uring 58mm long and 21mm at widest point, close to the mid-blade. There is some slight corrosion damage to the blade edges but the tip is well-preserved. The blade has a lenticular section with a thickness of 4mm at the mid-blade and 1mm at the blade edge. The socket, at 54mm long, has a similar length to the blade. There is a smooth transition from socket to blade with a diameter of 10mm at the neck. The socket has an external diameter of 18mm and an internal diameter of 16mm. The weld seam has cracked but was originally well-closed. Pitting in the corrosion product at the base of the socket may indicate the presence of rivet holes, although these cannot be con-firmed with the naked eye. Voids in the x-ray also suggest the possible presence of small rivet holes.

There is some organic material preserved in the socket interior, but there was not enough to take a sample for analysis (Felter and Wilkinson 2015).

16030, SF 72 small throwing iron spearhead

A small spearhead which can be allocated to Inall Type 1.1.a.2 (Fig. 8.5). The total length of the spearhead is 98mm, with a small diamond-shaped blade measuring 36mm long and 20mm wide at the mid-blade. The blade edges and the transition to socket are smooth, with a slight shoulder. There is some damage to one of the blade edges (possibly the result of corrosion) but the tip of the spearhead remains intact. The base of the socket is not entirely closed and is open for a length of approximately 32mm from the base of the socket. There are traces of wood in the socket, although there was insufficient quantity for further analysis (Felter and Wilkinson 2015). There are two large rivet holes on the lateral sides of the socket base. The rivet holes align very well and both have a diameter of approximately 4mm, suggesting they may have been created simultaneously. The blade is very thin, with an almost flat section, measuring approximately 2mm at its thickest.

Discussion

All of the spearheads from burial 16030 can be identified as throwing spearhead forms. Each is a member of the small, diamond-bladed Inall Type 1.1, defined as 'small, socketed iron spearheads featuring a small blade, widest around the mid-blade, giving the form a distinctive diamond-shaped profile' (Inall 2015, 58). The examples can be allocated to two distinct sub-types: SFs 68, 69 and 70 can all be allocated to the sub-type 1.1.a.2, exemplified by the presence

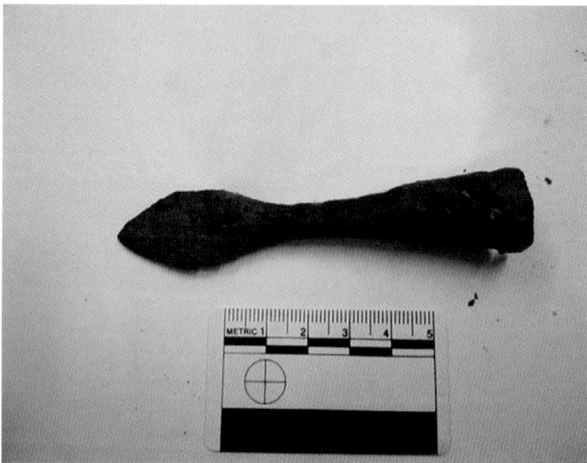

Figure 8.5 Iron spearhead SF 72

Figure 8.6 Iron ferrule SF 73

of a blade approximately as wide as it is long, with a socket measuring approximately twice the length of the blade. By contrast, SFs 71 and 72 feature elongated blades typical of Type 1.1.b.1. Type 1.1.b.1 is defined as having a 'similar diamond-shaped blade profile to Type 1.1.a, however, the blade is elongated to approximately twice the width of the blade. The socket of these spearheads is approximate to the length of the blade' (Inall 2015, 58).

Ferrule
16030, SF 73 Iron ferrule

The ferrule measures 101mm in total length (Fig. 8.6). The socket has a round section with an external diameter of 19mm (16mm internal) and is hollow to a depth of 35mm. Approximately 37mm from the base of the socket, the section of the ferrule transitions from circular to a pyramidal wedge with a rectangular section. The wedge is wider on the side which features the weld seam: 12mm wide where the weld seam ends, tapering to 4.3mm at the tip. The wedge of the lateral sides is narrower, measuring 9.7mm wide at the end of the weld seam and 2.5mm towards the tip. The very tip of the wedge is at an oblique angle, tapering to a sharp edge. The weld seam measures 45mm total length, with a visible overlap of approximately 6mm.

The lateral sides of the socket feature two long, distinct rectangular rivet slots measuring 11.9mm by 1.8mm and 10.4mm by 2.3mm. They appear to have been cut or punched into the sides of the socket. This was likely performed before the socket was rolled, while the iron was still a flat sheet.

Discussion

Ferrules are comparatively rare for the British Iron Age, although examples are known. The closest example, geographically, comes from Garton Station, excavated by Ian Stead (Stead 1991a). Currently held in the British Museum (1985, 0305.55), the ferrule was recovered from GS10, a crouched burial where it was associated with 14 iron spearheads and a shield. The tip of the GS10 ferrule appears to have been flattened to form a blade and may have been repurposed as a spearhead, although a continued function as a counterpoint cannot be excluded in light of such a minor modification (Inall 2015).

Also in Yorkshire, an early Iron Age unurned cremation burial at Birdsall (Barrow 108) was reported to have yielded a bronze ferrule, although it was poorly preserved and had apparently been subjected to the funeral pyre (Mortimer 1905a; Hill 1995). A bronze ferrule was also noted by John Dent (1984) as one of the grave goods from Wetwang burial 244, a male aged 25–35 years. This ferrule measured 31mm total length with a socket diameter of 17.5mm and a conical section. Brewster (1980) also reported two bronze ferrules from a chariot burial at Garton Slack; these were interpreted as possibly associated with a 'whip'. They were described as formed from sheet bronze, tapered cylindrical in form, riveted at the base end with bronze rivets. The dimensions were described as each measuring 25mm long, the first having a socket diameter of 13mm and a diameter at the narrower end of 11mm. The second had a base diameter of 12mm and a tip diameter of 10mm. Brewster's (1980) interpretation of a whip, or perhaps a goad associated with horse equipment, seems most likely.

Outside of Yorkshire, an iron ferrule was reported amongst the finds from the Durotrigian cemetery at Jordan Hill, Dorset, although the dimensions and precise context were not recorded (Whimster 1979). The Owslebury Warrior burial, Hampshire, also included an iron ferrule in addition to a spearhead, sword and shield (Collis 1968). Similarly, the Kelvedon Warrior burial, Kent included a conical iron ferrule in association with a spearhead, shield, sword and dagger (Sealy 2007). Three horn ferrules were recorded amongst the martial objects recovered from

Figure 8.7 Iron sword SF 67 (Overall length: 760mm; blade length: 610mm)

the late Iron Age deposit at the south-western gateway complex at South Cadbury Castle (Barrett *et al.* 2000).

The rectangular section presented by the Pocklington ferrule appears to be unique in Britain. Ferrules with rectangular sections are, however, known from the Continent, where they formed a minor tradition (Brunaux and Rapin 1988). The majority of Continental ferrules also presented a conical section, and tanged examples predominated over socketed ones.

Sword

SF 67 iron sword

A medium-length iron sword with an organic hilt, which fits within Stead's (2006) Group E classification of earlier swords in the north of Britain. The sword has a total length of 760mm, with a blade length of 610mm (Fig. 8.7). The overall length of 760mm makes it one of the longer Iron Age swords in the north of Britain (Fig. 8.8): only the North Grimston longsword (Stead 2006, no. 79), perhaps originally as long as 831mm; Grimthorpe (Stead 2006, no. 177), at 720mm; and the sword from Rudston burial R146 (Stead 2006, no. 185), measuring 778mm, are longer.

The hilt is of tripartite construction with two washers, one close to the hilt guard, which has a maximum diameter

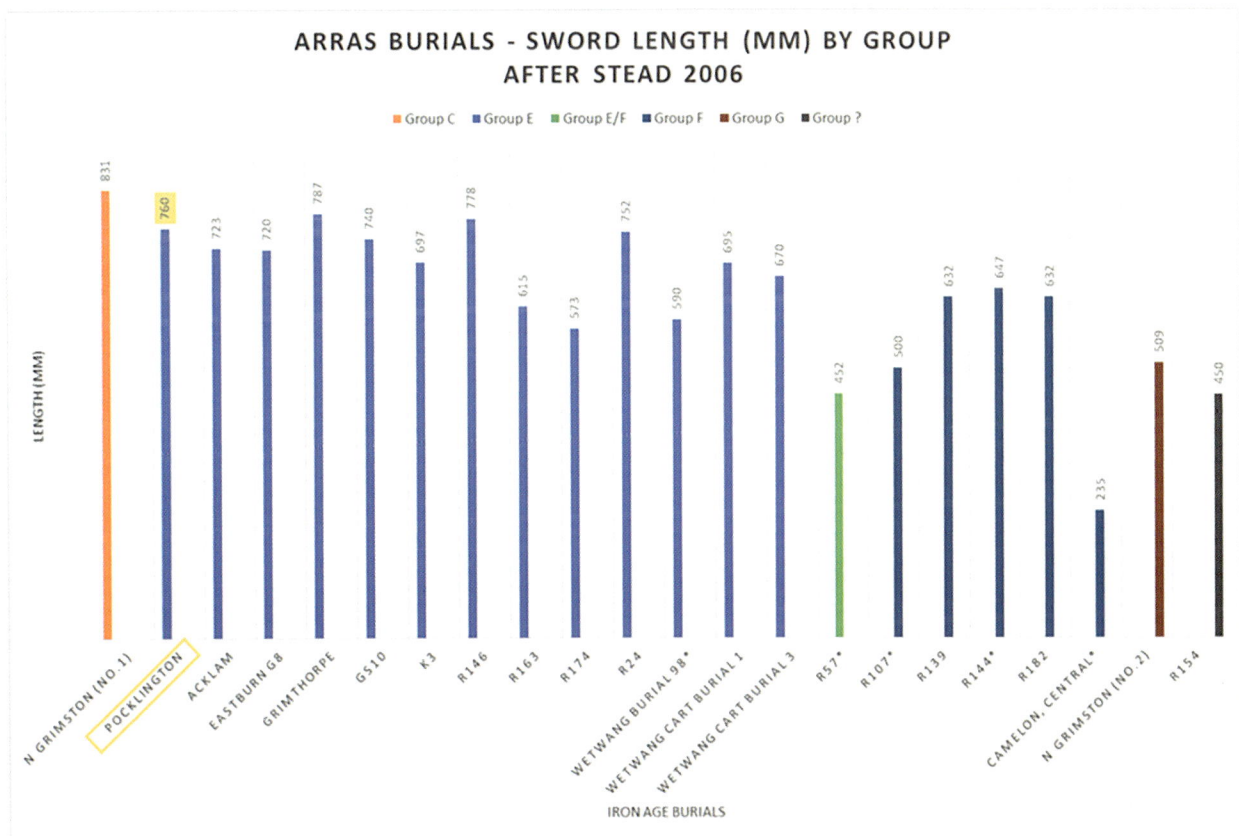

Figure 8.8 Length of swords recorded from Arras Culture burials by Stead Type Group (after Stead 2006)

of 31mm. The second washer is positioned close to the pommel, with a maximum diameter of 26mm (Fig. 8.9). The washers have a slightly ovoid profile, suggesting the hilt grip also had an ovoid section. The conservation report reveals that the grip was constructed of horn. The organic pommel is not well-preserved but suggests a rounded form.

Swords with tripartite hilts were identified by Stead (1991a) at Rudston from burials R24, R154 and R174 (R24 and R174 are identified in Stead 2006 as nos 184 and 186 respectively. R154 is not included in Stead's 2006 volume). Like the Burnby Lane sword, the main organic component in each of these examples was horn (Stead 1991a).

The form of the hilt guard is consistent with Stead's (2006) Type vi: swords with campanulate hilt end from northern Britain. Stead identifies the form as one of the earlier types in the north, which he associates with La Tène I to La Tène III. Campanulate hilt ends appear in both northern and southern sword forms in Britain. The feature is identified in the south of Britain by Stead (2006), with examples nos 17, 77 and 86 (all from the Thames), and no. 56 (Orton Meadows, Orton Longueville, Peterborough, Cambridgeshire). Nos 17 and 77 were medium-length swords and no. 86 was a longsword.

There is some observable variation within the campanulate forms. Stead's (2006) no. 17 (from the Thames at Hammersmith, London) has a similar campanulate profile to the Burnby Lane sword, and the hilt grip suggests a similar composite construction technique with a tang and an iron washer, which secured a copper alloy ovoid cylinder (Stead 2006, 157). Stead's no. 77 (Thames, London) features a similar campanulate hilt end, extending slightly further beyond the blade edges than the Burnby Lane example. Unfortunately, while the tang is preserved, no other parts of the hilt remain to inform our understanding of its construction.

Stead's (2006) no. 86 (Thames at Little Wittenham, Oxfordshire), is distinct from the Pocklington sword and the other examples from the Thames in that the campanulate hilt end is cast copper alloy, featuring decoration in the form of raised dots. Little of the tang survives and none of the organic components of the hilt was preserved.

While the example from Orton Meadows, Cambridgeshire (no. 56) does feature an iron campanulate hilt end, the profile differs from the other southern examples and from the present example, having a much lower arc.

The northern examples also show some variation in hilt form. The two examples from Wetwang Slack (Stead 2006, nos 173 and 174), from Cart burials 1 and 3 respectively, feature low campanulate iron hilt ends with a profile similar to the Orton Meadows example. The hilts of the Wetwang swords are also heavily decorated with metal roundels featuring enamel inlay, in the same tradition as the Kirkburn sword (Stead 1991a; 2006).

Stead's (2006) nos 184, 185, 186, 187, from Rudston (burials R24, R146, R174 and R163 respectively), and the sword from burial R154, all feature iron campanulate hilt ends very similar to that of the Burnby Lane sword (Stead 1991a). The associated campanulate scabbard forms from these burials were all dated by Stead to the 3rd century BC.

Stead's (2006) no. 188, from Garton Station (burial GS10), features an iron campanulate hilt end, with horn organic construction, similar to Burnby Lane. However, the construction method employed is different, with bipartite rather than tripartite construction. The organic components of Stead's (2006) no. 189, from the Acklam Wold warrior burial, are not preserved, but this sword also had a similar campanulate hilt end; Stead has argued that traces of wood adhering to the blade indicate it has been sheathed in a wooden scabbard, as the Burnby Lane sword appears to have been.

The North Grimston longsword (no. 79) features a campanulate hilt-end with a much higher arc than the Burnby Lane sword, and Stead (1991a) assigned this sword a La Tène II or La Tène III date. The sword was found with traces of an iron scabbard.

A small, circular copper-alloy stud or roundel at the base of the Burnby Lane hilt is preserved as a decorative element (Fig. 8.10). The roundel has a diameter of 14mm and a maximum height of approximately 6mm. The stud

Figure 8.9 The hilt of the Pocklington sword

Figure 8.10 Detail of the campanulate hilt end and decorative copper alloy stud (diameter of stud: 14mm)

has a rimmed edge, 2.5mm wide, indicating that its construction was likely similar to those on the Kirkburn sword (Stead 2006, no. 172 and fig. 87), which have similar dimensions to this example. The technique consists of pinning a small domed piece into a flat, rimmed washer. The pin is clearly visible in the difference in coloration at the centre of the stud. However, the example here appears to have been constructed solely of copper alloy components, rather than the copper alloy and iron composition observed at Kirkburn. The two examples from Wetwang Slack mentioned above were also heavily decorated with metal roundels, again featuring enamel inlay, in the same tradition as the Kirkburn sword (Stead 1991a; 2006). The sword from Rudston burial R24 also preserved three studs at the base of the hilt, fixed with iron pins as in the Kirkburn construction. However, there were no traces of enamelled decoration recorded for either the Rudston or Burnby Lane swords.

The 610mm blade tapers slightly with a maximum width of 45mm. At 50mm from the tip, the blade begins to round to a point. Stead (2006, 58) identified swords with similar, slightly tapered blade profiles from Rudston (nos 184, 185 and 186 from burials R24, R146 and R174 respectively). These examples also feature similarly rounded tips and campanulate hilt ends. The blade lengths of the swords from R24 and R146 are also similar,

measuring 598mm and 620mm respectively. The swords thus appear to belong to a single tradition.

The blade has a shallow but easily discernible midrib running the entire length of the blade. Stead (2006) does not note midribs for any of the comparable swords in his catalogue, although his descriptions rarely offer this level of detail regarding blade form.

The scabbard was made of wood, and traces of timber were preserved in the corrosion product, although it was not possible to identify species (Felter and Wilkinson 2015). The scabbard form is not identifiable and no metal chape was found *in situ*. This is consistent with other organic scabbards identified in the Arras tradition (Stead 2006). Stead allocates organic scabbards to his Type Za, with clear examples from Rudston and Stanwick and possible examples from Garton Station and Acklam. Three organic scabbards recorded from Rudston demonstrate that different construction techniques could be used in the construction of organic scabbards and that they could be constructed wholly of wood, or wood with a leather overlay or cover. Wood species observed at Rudston burial R24 were willow (*Salix* sp.) or poplar (*Populus* sp.), while R146 was encased in a scabbard of ash (*Fraxinus* sp.). An organic scabbard from Rudston burial R163 had wood tentatively identified as possibly maple (*Acer* sp.), cherry (*Prunus* sp.) or lime (*Tilia* sp.).

Other Iron Age weaponry from Burnby Lane and The Mile

Mark Stephens

Central grave of Barrow 37, Burnby Lane

At the base of the grave and within the structure identified in Barrow 37 at Burnby Lane (Figs 4.39 and 4.40), a rectangular soil stain was recorded consisting of a narrow band of dark silt (16503) which formed a continuous rounded rectangle measuring 1.00m in length and 0.70m in width. A line of metal objects lay along the centre of the area delineated by 16503 and on top of burial 16370 (Sk 78). From north to south the objects were: SF 77 (copper alloy rivet), SF 78 (copper alloy rivet), SFs 79 and 80 (parts of same 'spoon-shaped' iron object forming the 'boss' and spine of the shield with soil concretion), SF 81 (copper alloy rivet) and SF 82 (another copper alloy rivet) (Figs 4.39 and 9.1). The soil stain (16503) represented the edge of the shield, and the copper alloy rivets attached the spine to the shield backing. An oval patch of dark silt (16563) lay under the metal parts of the shield 'boss' and represented organic material that had been attached to it – perhaps the remains of the grip.

Copper alloy rivets

SF 77. Double-headed rivet. One end is flat and circular with end of rivet protruding for *c.* 1mm. Diameter: 7mm. Other head is also circular and completely flat. Diameter: 4.5mm. Shank has circular cross-section. Diameter: 2.5mm. Overall Length: 29mm.

SF 78. Double-headed rivet, shank slightly curved. One head is flat and circular, with end of rivet protruding through. Diameter: 7mm. Opposing head is circular and completely flat. Diameter: 4mm. Shank has circular cross-section. Diameter: 3mm. Overall length: 35mm. Traces of mineralised wood running perpendicularly along the shank.

SF 81. Single-headed rivet (although other end has broken away, but not recently), with patches of mineralised organic material. Circular, flat head. Diameter: 4mm. Shank has circular cross-section. Diameter: 2mm. Overall length: 29mm.

SF 82. Double-headed rivet with curved shank. One head is circular, with end of rivet protruding through slightly. Diameter: 7.5mm. Opposing head is circular and flat. Diameter: 4mm. Overall Length: 20mm. Patches of mineralised organics along shank.

Iron strip

SFs 79 and 80. Two pieces of curved and riveted iron strip that were found together in a spoon-shaped mass of iron corrosion, suggesting that they were part of the same object. Both objects have rivet holes with parts of iron rivets surviving within them.

SF 79, L: 95mm, W: 28mm. SF 80, L: 57mm, W: 18mm.

Discussion

The curved iron strips echo the arrangement of the iron boss and spine cover on the shield that accompanied Rudston Burial 148 (Stead 1991a, 61–2). The rectangular soil stain 16503 forming the edge of the B37 shield recalls the wooden reinforcing to the edge of the Enderby bark shield (Leicester University 2019). The copper alloy rivets presumably attached a leather shield covering to the central spine, which could have been of wood or other organic material. Although the position of the spine fittings along the burial's torso suggests that the shield covered the body, this cannot have been the case because the edge-stain of the shield extended *under* the body's upper legs. It therefore appears that the spine was removed from the main part

Figure 9.1 Copper alloy rivets SFs 77–78, 81–82 and iron fittings SFs 79–80

Figure 9.2 Iron strip SF 75

Figure 9.3 Copper alloy shield fittings SFs 10 and 12

of the shield, the burial placed on top of the shield backing, and the complete but detached spine arranged on top of the body. The shield burial from the circular barrow at The Mile (see Chapter 6) had pieces of the fragmentary copper alloy shield spine and boss laid alongside the body, but the damaged ends of these elements, and their physical separation (one being in the corner of the grave) showed that this shield must also have been dismembered. The shield fittings in grave R148 at Rudston were also out of position and perhaps dismembered (Stead 1991a, 61), and it is likely that the shield from a late Iron Age burial at Mill Hill, Deal, was also deliberately damaged before burial (Parfitt 1995, 64).

Central grave of Barrow 32, Burnby Lane

A fragment of iron strip was found in the fill (context 16070) of the central grave of circular barrow B32.

Iron strip fragment

SF 75 Curved fragment of iron strip with a rivet hole containing the stump of a possible rivet (Fig. 9.2). Mineralised wood was present on the under-surface, but not enough to allow further study. L: 60mm, W: 18mm.

Discussion

This object is very close in form to SFs 79 and 80 that formed the spine of the shield in Barrow 37 and is paralleled by shield remains from grave R148 at Rudston (Stead 1991a, fig. 49, 6).

Shield remains from the central grave of The Mile circular barrow

Six copper alloy components (Figs 9.3 9.5) of a composite shield were present within the central grave of the circular barrow at The Mile, consisting of two boss fragments (SFs 10 and 18), each with integral lengths of spine; two detached spine fragments (SFs 11 and 12); and two detached rivets (SFs 19 and 20).

Boss/spine fragment (SF 10)

Copper alloy object with 'spoon-shaped' head at one end, the other end broken (Fig. 9.3). Rivet hole at merger of head and spine. Overall length: 326mm; head diameter: 89mm; spine diameter: 19mm.

Spine fragment (SF 12)

Rivet hole at undamaged, rounded end and another at the opposite end, which is broken and splayed (Fig. 9.3). Length: 261mm, width: 19mm.

Boss/spine fragment (SF 18)

Identical in form to SF 10 above, but with shorter length of spine remaining (Fig. 9.4). Damaged and split rivet hole at end of 'spoon' head and bent rivet present at junction of head and spine; head of rivet has circular incised decoration. Overall length: 190mm; head diameter: 90mm: spine diameter: 19mm.

Spine fragment (SF 11)

One end is broken/burred over (where it would have joined with SF 18), other end rounded (Fig. 9.4). Rivet holes at both ends, and another 98mm from the damaged end. Length: 415mm, width: 19mm.

Rivet (SF 19)

Complete rivet with incised ring design on head (Fig. 9.5); the other end is narrower but also decorated with a ring. Length: 32mm; diameter of larger head: 10mm; diameter of smaller head: 6.5mm.

Rivet (SF 20)

Complete rivet (Fig. 9.5), shank tapering from a circular head that is decorated with an incised ring. Shank bent into L-shape away from head end. Length: 23mm; head diameter: 6mm; shank diameter: 2mm.

Discussion

Boss/spine element SF 10 joins with spine fragment SF 12, and boss/spine fragment SF 18 joins with spine fragment SF 11, making a copper alloy version of the arrangement seen on the Burnby Lane and Rudston R148 shields. The combined length of the fittings suggest that the shield was 1190mm in length along its axis. The

damage to the shield fittings and the position of SF 12, which was detached and placed in a corner of the grave, show that the shield was dismembered before being put in the grave, recalling the way in which R148's shield was placed.

Spearheads from the circular barrow at The Mile

Eight spearheads were found alongside the adult male buried centrally within the circular barrow at The Mile (Fig. 6.13) and were associated with the shield remains described above. These were the heads from throwing spears, five of iron and three of bone. The description of the iron spearheads follows Inall's typology (Inall 2015) and can be defined as Type 1.1: 'small, socketed iron spearheads featuring a small blade, widest around mid-blade, giving form a distinctive diamond-shaped profile'; damage to the blades hampers further typological refinement.

The iron and bone spearheads are paralleled at other East Yorkshire cemeteries and the inclusion of both iron and bone spearheads with the same burial is seen at Garton Slack (GS5) and Rudston (R146 and R174) (Stead 1991a, 33). Damage to some of the spearheads could have arisen during practice or ceremonial use, as much as being the result of combat. A discussion of the

Figure 9.4 Copper alloy shield fittings SFs 11 and 18

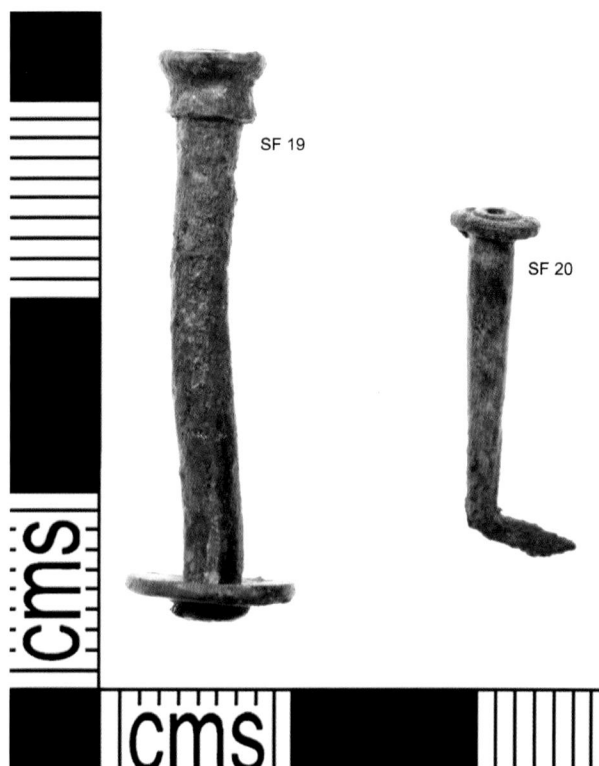

Figure 9.5 Copper alloy rivets SFs 19 and 20

circumstances of the placement of the spearheads can be found in Chapter 19.

Iron spearhead (SF 7)

Diamond-shaped blade with a length of 31mm and a width of 16mm, partly broken with old damage (Fig. 9.6). The tapering socket has a length of 64mm and a width of 16mm. Total length: 95mm. Possibly Inall Type 1.1.b.1. Wood remains present at the join between the blade and socket, with further remains inside.

Iron spearhead (SF 8)

Largely complete small iron spearhead with a total length of 100mm (Fig. 9.7). Diamond-shaped blade with narrow central rib, length: 40mm, width: 22mm. Tapering socket, length: 60mm, max. width: 17mm. Probably Inall Type 1.1.b.1.

Iron spearhead (SF 9)

Largely complete small iron spearhead, some old damage to socket (Fig. 9.8). Blade of diamond form, length: 44mm, width 28mm. Socket length: 48mm, max. width: 22mm. Rivet hole at end of socket but opposite area is damaged, so not possible to confirm presence of opposing rivet hole. Ring-porous hard wood remains on blade at right-angles to axis of spearhead and inside the socket. Possibly Inall Type 1.1.b.1.

Iron spearhead (SF 16)

Small iron spearhead, largely complete, but blade is missing tip (Fig. 9.9). Diamond-shaped blade, length: 29mm, width: 16mm. Socket length: 32mm, width: 20mm. Two opposed

Figure 9.6 Iron spearhead SF 7

Figure 9.7 Iron spearhead SF 8

Figure 9.8 Iron spearhead SF 9

rivet holes are present at the end of the socket. Wood remains (ash) on blade at right-angles to spear axis. Possibly Inall Type 1.1.b.1.

Iron spearhead (SF 21)

Largely complete iron spearhead (Fig. 9.10). Blade length: 40mm, width: 17mm. Gently tapering socket, length: 38mm, max. width: 22mm. Rivet hole at far end of socket, opposite a V-shaped notch that possibly represents wear

or old damage. Wood remains (probably ash) present on surface, again at right-angles to blade axis.

Bone spearhead (SF 13)

Bone spearhead composed of hollowed animal bone, whittled to a point and with lateral working facets; side partly cut away and distinct splay at socket end (Fig. 9.11). There are two opposed small circular peg or rivet holes near the end of the socket. Length: 108mm, diameter: 10mm.

Bone spearhead (SF 14)

Form as SF 13 above but broken at socket end (Fig. 9.12). Length: 56mm, diameter: 11mm.

Bone spearhead (SF 15)

Similar to SFs 13 and 14, end of socket damaged (Fig. 9.13). Length: 101mm, diameter: 10mm.

Figure 9.9 Iron spearhead SF 16

Figure 9.10 Iron spearhead SF 21

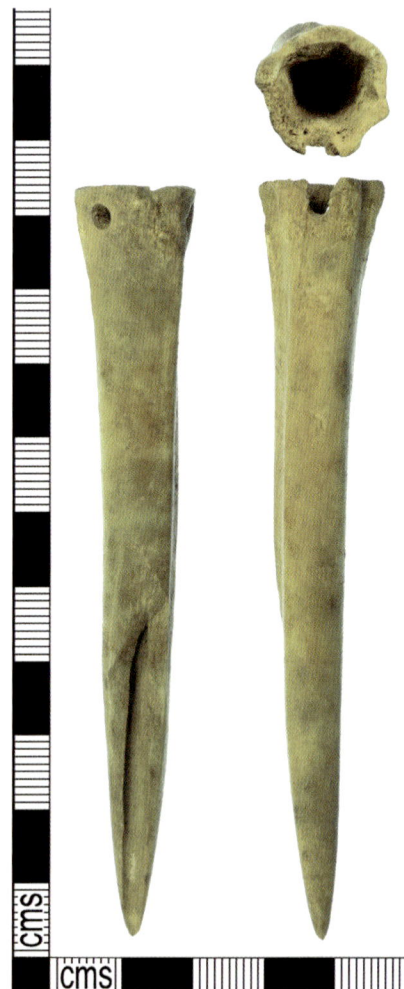

Figure 9.11 Bone spearhead SF 13

Figure 9.12 Bone spearhead SF 14

Figure 9.13 Bone spearhead SF 15

10

The chariot fittings from Burnby Lane and The Mile

Mark Stephens

Both the Burnby Lane and The Mile chariot burials had been truncated by ploughing. At Burnby Lane one wheel survived along with two iron nave hoops, and there was an iron snaffle bit below the wheel. At The Mile, only the upper part of the chariot burial had been plough-damaged, which meant that the iron tyres of both wheels survived fully assembled to the axle and naves, as did the four copper alloy nave hoops and two iron lynchpins. Three terrets (one of iron and two of copper alloy) were found within the disturbed zone at the top of the grave.

Chariot fittings from Barrow 85, Burnby Lane
Iron tyre (SF 4)
(Context 401) Complete iron tyre with mineralised preserved organic (MPO) material representing one or more

felloes of ash on the interior (see Fig. 4.88). Diameter: 830mm; width: 38mm; thickness: 4mm.

Nave hoops
(SF 8 – context 404)
Plain iron ring with D-shaped cross-section (Fig. 10.1). MPO of leather or hide on the interior presumably represents the remains of a washer. Diameter: 142mm; width: 8mm; thickness: 5mm.

(SF 16 – context 397)
Plain iron ring with D-shaped cross –section (Fig. 10.2), distorted into an oval shape; MPO as SF 8. Length: 132mm, width: 124mm; thickness: 5mm.

Figure 10.1 Burnby Lane: iron nave hoop SF 8

Figure 10.2 Burnby Lane: iron nave hoop SF 16

Snaffle bit

(Context 398)

Composed of four elements: two free-running iron rings (SFs 9 and 13) or rein-rings (one detached) and two linked bars (SF 12) forming the snaffle bit. The bit consists of iron bars linked together in the centre by loops, with the other ends thickened and bent round to form apertures for the relevant rein-ring. Rein-ring SF 9 had traces of non-ferrous plating running around the outside and a knop or stop close to one terminal, which may have been designed to keep the snaffle bar away from the join in the rein-ring. Alternatively, Stead (1965, 36) suggests that stops on the Pexton Moor rein-rings protected the bronze casing from excessive wear by the side-link at the end of the snaffle bar.

Snaffle bars – Length: 75mm; width: 18mm down to 6mm at loop end.

Rein-rings – Diameter: 74mm; thickness: 6mm.

SF 14 – a small L-shaped piece of iron sheet was found close to the snaffle bit. Length: 14mm; width 14mm.

Chariot fittings from The Mile

Iron lynch-pins: SFs 139 and 144

A pair of near identical 'vase-headed' rod-type iron lynch-pins, SF 139 (Fig. 10.3) for the west wheel, SF 144 (Fig. 10.4) for the east. The tops have flattened and rounded knops, narrowing to the necks, then expanding to a circular swelling with a central perforation, separated from the necks and shanks by incised lines. The shanks have a square cross-section that tapers downwards to an elongated and rounded knop with a circular foot at the base – these last two elements seemingly echoing the form of a horse's fetlock and hoof. The heads of each lynch-pin are decorated with a roundel of enamel, which appears pinkish-white in colour. Length: 99mm; head diameter: 19mm; shank width:10– 13mm; foot diameter: 10mm. Both lynch-pins were accompanied by iron annular attachment rings with circular cross-sections and diameters of 22mm.

Nave hoops

Inner hoop of the west nave – SF 88

Complete nave hoop (Fig. 10.5) made from a copper alloy strip that has a rounded band along the centre, raised

Figure 10.4 The Mile: iron linchpin SF 144

Figure 10.3 The Mile: iron linchpin SF 139

Figure 10.5 The Mile: copper alloy and iron inner hoop (SF 88) of the western nave

c. 3.5mm from the outer surface and which contains an iron strip on the inside. The terminals of the band do not meet but are joined by a piece of copper alloy strip, backed by the internal iron band and joined at the terminals by two rivets on each side. Diameter: 132mm; width: 38mm; thickness: *c.* 0.75mm.

Outer hoop of the west nave – SF 138

Copper alloy nave hoop (Fig. 10.6), complete, but ends broken and in a fragile condition. This hoop has a similar raised band to SF 88 but lacks the internal iron element. The raised band was formed by hammering from the inside. The terminals are fragile and broken, but one

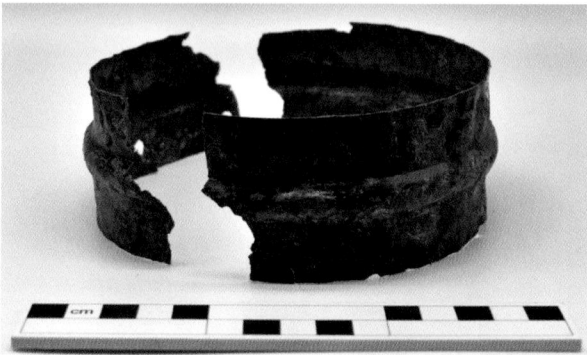

Figure 10.6 The Mile: copper alloy outer hoop (SF 138) of the western nave

Figure 10.7 The Mile: copper alloy and iron inner hoop (SF 140) of the eastern nave

rivet hole survives. Diameter: *c.* 132mm; width: 50mm; thickness: 0.5mm.

Inner hoop of the east nave – SF 140

Largely complete plain nave hoop (Fig. 10.7), but there is a gap between the terminals. D-shaped cross-section, copper alloy sleeve with iron core, with a narrow horizontal gap running along the inside of the copper alloy sleeve. The iron core probably originally joined the terminals together but is now corroded away. Diameter: 135mm; width: 13.5mm; thickness 6.5mm.

Outer hoop of the west nave – SF 143

Largely complete nave hoop (Fig. 10.8), but one end detached and fragile overall condition. Made from thin copper alloy sheet with a raised central band, which has no iron internal strip, like the corresponding outer hoop from the west wheel. The terminals are asymmetric, one being straight/perpendicular and the other having two protrusions and traces of an iron rivet, presumably to join the two terminals together. The outer edges have some loss of the original surfaces, which is old damage because the corrosion products extend over the edges; this damage possibly represents wear from use. Diameter: 132mm; width: 49mm; thickness: *c.* 0.5mm.

Discussion

Three of the nave hoops from The Mile are of Stead's 'cordonned' style, examples existing elsewhere either with or without an internal iron rod. Nave hoops with the internal iron rod were found in the Lady's Barrow at Arras (Stead 1965, fig. 14.1), parallels entirely of copper alloy being present at Cawthorn Camps and Nanterre (*ibid.*

Figure 10.8 The Mile: copper alloy outer nave hoop (SF 143) of the eastern nave

fig. 14, nos 2 and 10 respectively), with other examples from K5 at Kirkburn (Stead 1991a, 42–3) and WS 454 at Wetwang Slack (Dent 1985, 88). It is worth noting that at The Mile, the mismatched nave hoops with iron cores were both on the inner side of the naves, and those without an iron core were on the outside.

Iron tyres

Tyre of western wheel – SF 86

The iron tyre (SF 86 – Fig. 10.9) survived intact and had a sub-rectangular cross-section and a variable width, perhaps due to post-depositional corrosion or damage. One edge has areas of lipping towards the inside of the wheel. Interior is covered with minerally preserved wood, which is ash. Diameter: 890mm; width: 38mm; thickness: 4mm.

Tyre of eastern wheel – SF 87

A complete iron tyre (SF 87 – Fig. 10.10) with a sub-rectangular cross-section. Interior is covered with minerally preserved ring-porous hard wood remains, probably ash. Diameter: variable, *c.* 885mm; width: 38mm; thickness: 4mm.

Terrets

D-shaped terret – SF 3

Studded copper alloy and iron oval ring with a flattened top (Fig. 10.11). The ends of a largely corroded iron attachment bar are inserted into the terminals of the copper alloy ring. At the top two struts sweep upwards from the ring to support a moulded copper alloy cup (12.5mm diameter) to which a stud of white organic material, probably coral, is attached by a flat-headed copper alloy pin. There is incised line decoration at the top and base of the cup. Two smaller (8mm diameter) cups are mounted at the junctions between the struts and the oval ring, one of which also has a white coral stud attached by another flat-headed copper alloy pin. These cups are both decorated by an inverted triangle which is formed by incised lines on the cup with the surviving stud and by punched dots on the other cup. There are settings for two opposed cups on the lower part of the ring, one of which survives (diameter: 9mm) and is disc shaped and decorated with a horizontal incised ring. The other cup is missing but its setting shows as

Figure 10.9 The Mile: iron tyre (SF 86) of the western wheel

Figure 10.10 The Mile: iron tyre (SF 87) of the eastern wheel

Figure 10.11 The Mile: copper alloy terret (SF 3)

an oval perforation with a slight raised ridge around the top. The ring swells slightly towards the terminals, which are decorated by two concentric lines. The white coral studs on this terret and SF 4 described below, are an apparent reference to the berries recalled by 'fused knobs' and 'clustered knobs' described by Lewis on later D-shaped terrets (2020, 113). At the risk of stretching the allusion too far, and assuming that the original colour of the coral was indeed white, there may be reference to the white berries of mistletoe, which is poisonous as well as having associations with fertility.

Oval ring length: 56mm; height (excluding upper cup support): 46mm; diameter: 6mm.

D-shaped terret – SF 4

Studded oval copper alloy ring with square-sectioned flat iron attachment bar (Fig. 10.12). One moulded cup at the top of the ring, slightly off-centre, with triangular incised decoration like that on one of the cups of the terret described above (SF 3). This cup contains a hemispherical

stud of white organic material, probably coral, which is attached to the ring by a copper alloy pin. On either side of the cup, the upper sides of the ring are decorated with incised sprigs, picked out with minute punched dots, which run down to the swollen terminals. The terminals are decorated with a triangle with concave sides, perhaps in allusion to horses' hooves, an impression that is reinforced by the thickened terminals. The triangular panels are filled with minute punched dots. One side of the stud is flattened, perhaps evidence of wear or post-depositional damage; there are no other indications of wear on this terret.

Length: 36mm; height (excluding cup and stud): 29mm; thickness: 3.5mm increasing to 7.5mm at the terminals.

Plain ring terret – SF 5

Complete round-sectioned iron ring (Fig. 10.13) covered with silver-coloured non-ferrous plating, possibly tin. The terminals of the ring are thickened with non-ferrous metal, possibly showing where they were soldered together. The plating is pulled outwards into a slight lip at one point, perhaps suggesting damage or wear incurred during use.

Diameter: 40mm; thickness: 8mm.

Figure 10.12 The Mile: copper alloy terret (SF 4)

Figure 10.13 The Mile: iron terret (SF 5)

11

Iron Age brooches and bracelets from Burnby Lane and The Mile

Sophia Adams

Bow and penannular brooches

Thirteen Iron Age bow brooches were recovered from the Pocklington excavations (12 from Burnby Lane and one from The Mile), both copper alloy and iron examples. The iron brooches are relatively well preserved to the extent that decoration is visible on one (SF 10 Burnby Lane). All the Burnby Lane copper alloy bow brooches were found with adult women or remains most likely to be those of a woman. The single copper alloy brooch from The Mile was found with the man buried with a complete chariot and two ponies. Iron brooches were found in both male and female burials. Only three penannular copper alloy brooches (or parts thereof) were found in the excavations: two from unsexed adult graves and one from an infant burial. The latter is probably early medieval, while the former are difficult to date by the objects alone.

The majority of bow brooches are middle Iron Age types typologically dated to the 3rd and 2nd centuries BC. The radiocarbon date range achieved through Bayesian modelling gives a potentially broader period of deposition from the 4th to 2nd century BC for the burials with brooches (see Chapter 16). The penannulars are even less-precisely dated types and range from possibly the 3rd century BC into the 1st century AD. The bow brooches have been dated on typological grounds by comparison to other Iron Age brooches in Britain, in particular those from the cemetery at Wetwang, East Yorkshire whose chronology is supported by Bayesian analysis of radiocarbon dates from several of the burials (Jay *et al.* 2012). Bow brooches are typically described as having a head, bow and foot, the head being the torsion end formed either as a spring or hinge. The foot is the opposite end of the brooch including, but also extending beyond, the catchplate that holds the pin in place. The bow joins the two ends having a hip near the foot end and shoulders near the head end. Over time the shape and style of these features alters and it is these changes which have been identified as chronological markers (e.g. Hull and Hawkes 1987; Adams 2014).

The brooch assemblage from Pocklington is important both in terms of the quality of preservation of the artefacts and their association with specific graves and skeletal remains. The iron brooches are in a far less-corroded condition than other local examples and the presence of intact coral decoration is a rare feature. The assemblage also includes types that have not previously been recovered from stratified archaeological contexts (e.g. SF 5 Burnby Lane). This evidence is thus invaluable to wider research on Iron Age chronology and artefact dating.

The majority of the bow brooches are familiar in a Yorkshire Wolds Iron Age cemetery context conforming to Hull and Hawkes 1987 typology of brooches from England, Wales and Scotland and to the regional typologies of John Dent and Ian Stead for the Yorkshire Wolds (Dent 1982; Hull and Hawkes 1987; Stead 1991a). The assemblage includes straight bowed, involuted and decorated types. There are two straight bowed brooches of Type 2Ab (Hull and Hawkes 1987, 139–42) equivalent to John Dent's flat bow brooches (1982, 44) and Ian Stead's long flat bow brooches Type C (1991a, 81–3). The majority (8 out of 13) are involuted brooches where the bow and pin are concave rather than convex. These are Hull and Hawkes Type 2C including longer, shallower and shorter, more deeply concave sub-types 2Ca–2Cd (Hull and Hawkes 1987, 156–67); equivalent to Dent's long and short involuted brooches (1982, 44) and Stead's longer and shorter involuted brooches types D–J (Stead 1991a, 83–9). Comparable brooches have been excavated from the cemeteries of Wetwang (Dent 1982), Burton Fleming and Rudston (Argam Lane, Opposite Argam Lane, Bell Slack and Makeshift) (Stead 1991a) and in the chariot burials of Ferry Fryston (Brown *et al.* 2007, 147) and Wetwang Village.[1] The same types have also been recovered from eastern and southern England and Wales, although they are less common in graves in these locations (Adams 2014, 59–63, 262, map 6.17).

The three remaining bow brooches may be loosely placed within Hull and Hawkes typology but are relatively rare forms: Types 2B (SF 5 Burnby Lane and SF 52 The Mile) and 6 (SF 84 Burnby Lane). The latter, previously unknown in Yorkshire, resides at the end of the typological development of middle Iron Age bow brooches, potentially in the mid- to late 2nd century BC, at the cusp of the transition to the more ubiquitous forms of the late Iron Age such as Nauheims and Colchester brooches (Mackreth 2011). Type 6 brooches tend to be found in south-west England but occasional examples have been identified in Norfolk and the East Midlands (Adams 2014, 310–11). Hull and Hawkes grouped a number of brooches under their middle Iron Age decorative Type 2B forms. Types in this mixed group have individual characteristics but connected designs and applied decorative details. None was found at Stead's sites and only two, plate-like versions were found at Wetwang, which Dent described as inlaid bow brooches (Dent 1982, 442, fig. 4; Hull and Hawkes 1987, 154 no. 7902, pl. 43). As a single type they do not sit within the main typological sequence but examination of individual features allows them to be placed alongside this chronology. The type potentially has a long period of use but increasing numbers of discoveries allow sub-types to be anchored more precisely to chronological phases. The Burnby Lane 2B brooch (SF 5) is now part of a group of very similar inlaid brooches mostly found through metal-detecting activity but with two examples previously unrecognised from Wheeler's Maiden Castle excavations (Wheeler 1943, 270–1, fig. 88.1, 2). Fair comparisons to the Type 6 brooch (SF 84) have also been found at Maiden Castle. The H-framed form leads me to describe this decorated brooch as Type 2BH. They have double-lugged hinges and hooked catchplates, similar to those found on plate brooches of possible 3rd- to 2nd-century date (Adams 2014, 112–13).

The brooch from The Mile (SF 52) is a unique item that may loosely be classified within Hull and Hawkes Type 2Bc: anomalous forms of generally low-arched bow brooches with moulded and inlaid decoration and all with the foot cast in one with the bow (Hull and Hawkes 1987, 152–3, pl. 43). This foot form places it towards the end of the middle Iron Age brooch development. Two other brooches from Pocklington also exhibit this solid cast foot form: the already mentioned Type 6 (SF 84) and the highly decorated involuted brooch (SF 91), both from Burnby Lane. Other local comparisons with the foot cast solid with the bow are two brooches from

Danes Graves (Greenwell 1906, 266–7, figs 13 and 14; Hull and Hawkes 1987, 159, pl. 44, nos 2243 and 2245) and one from Makeshift grave R32 (Stead 1991a, 87 R32 G1). The Bayesian-modelled radiocarbon dates described in this volume (Chapter 16) indicate that these stylistically and technologically late foot forms are also from burials that have a range starting and ending slightly later than the others with brooches, supporting their probable chronological position.

Decoration is generally minimal on all the Pocklington brooches but a small selection are embellished with applied materials: some opaque glass, others coral. The former is often described as sealing-wax glass owing to its opaque red colouring. The coral is now white but may originally have been a pinkish-red 'coral' colour. Where the coral on other local brooches has been analysed by Raman Spectroscopy it has proven to be Corallium, most probably *Corallium rubrum* (Adams 2014, 157–9, 313–19), which originates in the Mediterranean and has a reddish colour. Coral with a more local source is known, derived from the North Sea, but this cold-water form is in fact a different species (*Lophelia pertusa*) and has not yet been positively identified on any Iron Age objects. The material used on the Pocklington brooches has been identified visually with comparison to other scientifically identified examples; no material science methods had been applied at the time of writing. At least 70 middle Iron Age brooches appear to have once been decorated with non-metallic materials, although very few retain the actual material through to recovery by excavation or other means. Coral decoration is associated with middle Iron Age objects in England and has been found on 24 other brooches, of which 14 were discovered in burials (Adams 2014, 158), perhaps the most famous being that from 'Queen's Barrow', Arras (Greenwell 1906, 296, fig. 43; Stead 1965, 48, fig. 25; 1979, 65; Hull and Hawkes 1987, 144, no. 3693, pl. 42; Adams 2014, 156, fig. 5.8, no. 10620). Brooches SF 5 and SF 84 are distinguished by the preservation of applied coral decoration. Two brooches from Burnby Lane (SF 45 and SF 91) and the single brooch from The Mile (SF 52) have beads of red glass attached as decoration comparable to those found on fewer than ten brooches from middle Iron Age graves in East Yorkshire (Henderson 1991; Adams 2014, 160, 229). They are even more rare in non-burial contexts. The use of glass as inlay on other metal objects, particularly items of horse tack, is familiar in the middle and late Iron Age, although in the later period and beyond it is gradually usurped by enamel, including on brooches from the first centuries AD.

The red glass-embellished brooch SF 91 further develops the connection between these materials and horses through the form of its catchplate and foot bearing a zoomorphic shape – an intentionally ambiguous combination of a horse and a duck's head being grappled by an animal with paws (see brooch description below for more details). This intriguing brooch has comparisons (albeit all slightly different) in other Yorkshire Wold cemeteries: Makeshift, Danes Graves and Bell Slack (Stead 1979, figs 26.4 and 26.5; 1991a, 191, R32.2 and 217, fig. 63). The Makeshift and Danes Graves examples are so similar as to suggest they were made by the same hand or under the influence of the same craftsperson. The beautifully formed and decorated brooch SF 91 was the only inorganic item adorning the burial of an older adult woman (46+ years old) buried within barrow B46. The coral-decorated brooch SF 5 was also found in an older woman's grave in barrow B2. She was also buried wearing a copper alloy bracelet on each arm. The unique brooch from The Mile (SF 52) was found in the burial of an older adult, the aforementioned man with ponies and chariot. As he lay on top of a copper alloy shield, the tiny brooch could have been lost in the impressive display of this grave. All the other brooches were found with adults who appear to have been younger than 46 years at death. While all these brooches would have contributed to the overall visual appearance of the deceased during burial, the quality of the production and the complexity of the designs could only be fully appreciated in close proximity to the individual wearers. The brooches are summarised in Table 11.1.

Catalogue: bow brooches

Straight bowed Type 2Ab

SF 66, BARROW 33, BURNBY LANE

Iron, long, straight bowed brooch in two fragments with a hinge formed as a mock spring, Hull and Hawkes Type 2Ab and Stead Type C (Hull and Hawkes 1987, 139–42; Stead 1991a, 81–3). This straight bowed brooch has a very slightly concave bow profile. It has an Adams Type A Developed Mock Spring Hinge 'DMS' (Adams 2014, 82, fig. 3.12). This consists of a two-coil bilateral mock spring: the bow head is inserted between the two coils of the spring and held in place with a central rivet (Stead 1991a, 80, fig. 59). Only a stub of the pin survives at the end of the spring on the right side of the brooch. The bow extends direct from the top of the spring coils. At the opposite end the curvature of the hip of the bow indicates the now-missing foot was once reverted and would have rested on the bow at this point, probably with the end attached to the bow by means of a separate collar.

The brooch has a dark brown patina with a fractured surface. It was found in circular barrow B33 in the grave of an adult male aged 26–35 years old although the exact association with this individual was not clear as it was located in the grave fill some 0.4m above the skeleton.

Wt: 3.8g; L: 53.48mm; Max. W: 9.07mm

Context: 16017. Burial 16018. Sk 56. Circular barrow B33.

Comparable examples: at least 67 definite examples of 2Ab brooches are known from England and Wales, over 83% of which are made from iron; the remainder are of copper alloy. Their distribution is focused in north-east and south-west England and south Wales (Adams 2014, 261, map 6.15); they are particularly common in the cemeteries of the Yorkshire Wolds and western hillforts.

- Garton Slack, North Humberside, East Yorkshire, straight bowed iron 2Ab brooch found in 1969 in the burial of a male, Grave 1, Barrow 1, Site IX (Hull Museum KINCM:2006.11303.828; Hull and Hawkes 1987, 126, pl. 37 no. 1554; Adams 2014, 293 and 309, no. 10921).
- Wetwang Slack, East Yorkshire, burial 117, Site VI (Hull Museum KINCM:2010.7.93; Dent 1982; Adams 2014, 292 and 308, no. 10888).
- Grandcourt Farm, Middleton, Norfolk [10647] copper alloy with real spring but the bow profile is very similar (Adams *et al.* 2012; Adams 2014, 78, fig. 3.10 no. 10647).
- Argam Lane cemetery, Rudston, East Yorkshire, iron brooch from grave BF6 with a similar bow shape and possible hinge mechanism. (BM 1978,1202.8; Stead 1991a, fig. 116 BF6.2; Adams 2014, no. 10185).
- Argam Lane cemetery, Rudston, East Yorkshire, BF10 in copper alloy decorated with a haematite and calcium carbonate substance, possibly coloured quartz, red limestone or marble. This has a very similar bow profile and the Type A Developed Mock Spring Hinge (BM 1978,1202.14; Stead 1991a, fig. 117. BF10.1; Hull and Hawkes 1987, 140, pl. 40 no. 4377bis; Adams 2014, 56, 157, fig. 3.3 no. 10175).

SF 300, GRAVE 18132, BURNBY LANE

Iron, almost complete, long, straight bowed brooch in two pieces, Hull and Hawkes Type 2Ab, Stead Type C. One part consists of the bow, catchplate and foot of the brooch (62.17mm long), the other the head and pin (66.03mm long). This straight bowed brooch has a Developed Mock Spring Hinge Type B (Adams 2014, 82, fig. 3.12 no. 10201) giving the appearance of a two-coil bilateral spring. The hinge consists of the pin head bent round to sit either side of the bow head. This pivots on a rod passed through the coils and head end of the bow. The foot is bent back towards the bow (reverted) and its toe rests on the sub-angular hip of the bow. It has a lozenge-shaped flat disc that narrows to a collar-like snout wrapped around the bow.

Dark-brown iron brooch with a fractured surface and small patches of corrosion on the head, pin and foot. Hints of fibres are preserved in the corrosion deposits on the bow and broken pin end. The brooch was found

Table 11.1 Brooches from Burnby Lane and SF52, from The Mile

SF No.	X-Ray	Bow or penannular	Brooch type	Ctxt no	Burial ctxt	Cem phase	Skeleton	Main material	2ndary material	Applied material
5	X8461	Bow: decorated, inlaid	2BH	15176	15176	Iron Age	Sk 2	Copper alloy	n	Coral
10	X8510	bow: involuted	2Cb	15326	15327	Iron Age	Sk 13	Iron	n	glass?
24	X8552	bow: involuted	2Cab	15620	15622	Iron Age	Sk 27	Iron	n	n
45	X8552	bow: involuted	2Ca	15850	15856	Iron Age	Sk 45	Iron	n	glass or stone?
66		bow: straight	2Ab	16017	16018	Iron Age	Sk 56	Iron	n	n
84	X8572	bow: sloped	6	16443	16443	Iron Age	Sk 82	Copper alloy	n	coral
91	X8572	bow: involuted	2Cd	17081	17081	Iron Age	Sk 119	Copper alloy	Iron pin	glass
94	X8572	bow: involuted	2Cb	17090	17090	Iron Age	Sk 121	Iron	n	n
96	X8572	bow: involuted (tiny)	2Cc	17174	17175	Iron Age	Sk 126	Iron	n	n
155	X8588	bow: involuted	2Cb	16996	16997	Iron Age	Sk 115	Iron	n	n
300	X8626	bow: straight	2Ab	18133	18133	Iron Age	Sk 139	Iron	n	n
589	X8647	bow: involuted	2Cb	15773	15773	Iron Age	Sk 39	Iron	n	n
52		bow: decorated, inlaid	2Bc	–	–	Iron Age	Sk 424	Copper alloy	Iron pin	glass
85	X8587	penannular	?(pin only)	16490	16491	Unknown	Sk 88	Copper alloy	n	n
92	X8572	penannular	Booth Type Aa2	17105	17105	Post Iron Age?	Sk 123	Copper alloy	n	n

(Continued)

underneath the front of the right side of the face of an adult aged 25+ of unknown sex. The burial was an unenclosed flat grave.

Wt: 12.8g; L: 88.02mm; Max. W: 10.39mm

Burial 18133. Sk 139.

X-ray: X8626

This brooch is a more complete example of SF 66 and hence comparable examples are the same plus:

- Danes Graves, Kilham, East Yorkshire, iron straight bowed 2Ab brooch from burial 94; the profile of the bow and foot is a particularly good match for SF 300

(Hull and Hawkes 1987, 121, pl. 35, no. 3102; Adams 2014, 282 and 302, no. 10524).

Shallow involuted Type 2Ca
SF 45, BARROW 26, BURNBY LANE

Iron, long, shallow involuted brooch, Hull and Hawkes Type 2Ca and Stead Type D (Hull and Hawkes 1987, 157–63, pls 45–47; Stead 1991a, 85), decorated with small beads of what appears to be degraded red glass or red stone, one either side of the head of the brooch and one on top of the foot. These are attached with small iron rivets. The brooch has a Developed Mock Spring Hinge Type C (Adams 2014, 82, fig. 3.12) which retains only the slightest hint of the spring form from which

Table 11.1 (Continued)

SF No.	Weight (g)	Length (mm)	Width (mm)	Grave	Other grave goods	Sex	Burial Info
5	25.1	51.83	31.59	B2 square barrow	Bracelets × 2	F? 46+	Adult female, mature
10	6.5	48.73	12.6	B9 Square Barrow		F 36–45	adult female (based on DNA analysis)
24	4.7	47.26	10.48	B18 Square Barrow		M 36–45	adult male, crouched
45	2.8	44.82	9.26	B26 small square barrow		M 18–25	young adult male? Crouched
66	3.8	53.48	9.07	B33 circular poss residual in this burial		M 26–35	did not appear to be directly associated with adult male burial
84	9.6	40.17	19.8	B42 large square barrow		F 25+	near right shoulder of primary burial. Female. Sister to SK85
91	18.6	47.91	17.71	B46 square barrow		F? 46+	adjacent to right shoulder in primary burial
94	4.33	38.5	8.1	B50 square barrow	Bracelet and bead	F 25+	adult female 26+ on right side facing east. Also SF 93 bracelet at wrist & glass bead SF 95 by neck
96	1.63	24.4	4.1 max	B55 square barrow		Un 15–17	15–17 yr old unsex. Lying on left side facing west, brooch half way along right upper arm
155	4.7	35.64	14.57	Truncated, unenclosed flat grave		Un 18+	found in neck area, head missing – heavily truncated grave
300	12.8	88.02	10.39	Unenclosed flat grave		Un 25+	adult, crouched, brooch underneath front of right side of face
589	2.09	Overall min 29.9	6.4	Flat grave		F 36–45	36–45? Yr old female, lain on left side facing east. Brooch was found adhering to lower part of skull when it was about to be washed
52	9.87	35.88	12.4	Chariot burial with ponies	Shield, Chariot, rack of ribs	M 46+	adult male, laid on shield on chariot complete with two ponies
85	0.4	23.62	Th of pin 2.23	B45 large square barrow	Bone or antler toggle	Un	shallow central grave – disturbed by ploughing
92	4.1	Diam of ring 23.45	Th of ring 2.97	B52 square barrow		Un	adult, crouched in shallow central grave

it is derived. The flat head of the bow and the pin are placed side by side, a glass bead is placed next to these on either side and a rivet is passed through one bead, then the bow head, then the pin head and out through the other bead where the end is flattened to secure it in place. The rivet for the decorative beads also acts as the pivot bar of the hinge. It is unclear from this fragile piece exactly how the reverted foot was attached to the bow though it was probably in the same manner as the other examples found here where the split toe is wrapped around the bow.

This thin, fragile brooch has a dark greyish-brown patina with large areas of corrosion on both the pin and the foot end of the bow. The applied decorative material is much degraded. A cast of fibres, possibly the mineralised remains of textiles, has been preserved within the corrosion deposits on the pin and bow. The glass beads are heavily degraded to the extent that the one surmounting the foot has lost all the shiny exterior surface.

This brooch was found in the area of the midriff of an adult male aged 18–25 years buried at the centre of a small square barrow (B26).

Wt: 2.8g; L: 44.82mm; Max. W: 9.26mm.

Context: 15850. Burial 15856. Sk 45. Square barrow B26.

X-ray: X8552

Comparable examples:

- Wetwang Slack cemetery, East Yorkshire, burial 250, excavated 1977. This is a very similar brooch with decorative beads of red stone applied to either side of the head of the brooch and to the top of the foot (Dent 1982, 442, fig. 4, 250; Hull and Hawkes 1987, 162, no. 4387, pl. 47; Adams 2014, 292 and 308, no. 10893).
- Makeshift Cemetery, Rudston, East Yorkshire, burial R27, iron 2Ca involuted brooch E2, with a foot originally decorated with an applied bead of glass or stone. This was found just beside the head and in front of the face in the jaw area of a female aged 17–25 years old. The bow is slightly longer and shallower than SF 45 (BM 1975,0401.29, Stead 1991a, 85, fig. 104, E2; Adams 2014, 277 and 298, no. 10226).
- Wetwang Slack, Wetwang, East Yorkshire, burial 192 Site VII, iron 2Ca involuted brooch with a similar profile, although this does not have the small head of the SF 45 brooch (Hull Museum KINCM:2010.7.79; Dent 1982, 442, fig. 4 192; Hull and Hawkes 1987, 162, pl. 47 no. 1095: Adams 2014, 208 and 292, no. 10907).
- Bell Slack, Burton Fleming, East Yorkshire, burial BF41, iron 2Cb brooch with glass bead attached to the foot albeit it on a shorter, more tightly concave involute (BM 1978,1203.7; Stead 1991a, 86–7, fig. 63, E8; Adams 2014, 153–61 and 319, figs 5.7 and 5.8, no. 10193).

SF 24, BARROW 18, BURNBY LANE

Iron, Hull and Hawkes involuted Type 2C brooch (Fig. 11.1). The form is part way between the shallow curved 2Ca brooches and the shorter, deeply curved 2Cb brooches and therefore may be described as a 2Cab brooch. The brooch is missing most of the pin and the catchplate. It has a Developed Mock Spring Hinge Type C (Adams 2014, 82, fig. 3.12 no. 10664) and a reverted foot. The latter is attached to the bow by means of wrapping the toe around the bow (this is damaged on one side, so it is not clear if it wrapped around one or both sides of the bow). The thin foot disc is slightly convex and bears no sign of having been decorated with applied material; there is no sign of a rivet or other means of attaching decoration to this disc. The head end of the brooch is covered in corrosion deposits which appear to preserve the impressions of fabric fibres.

The brooch has a dark-brown patina. It is in a solid but fractured conditioned with friable corrosion deposits over the hinge and head of the brooch. It was found buried with an adult male aged 36–45 within square barrow B18.

Wt: 4.7g; L: 47.26mm; Max. W: 10.48mm

Context: 15620. Burial 15622. Sk 27. Square barrow B18.

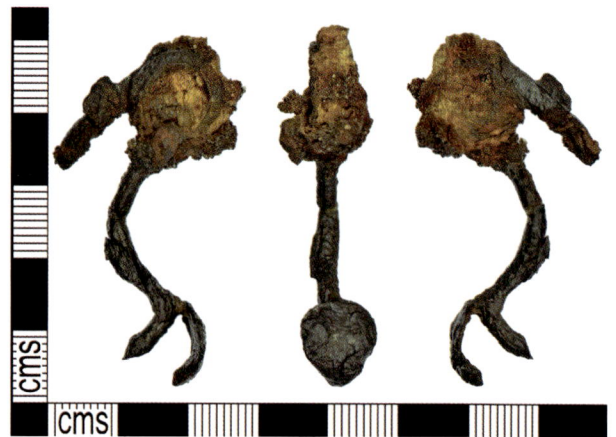

Figure 11.1 Iron bow brooch SF 24, Barrow 18, Burnby Lane

X-ray: X8552

Comparable examples:

- Bell Slack, Burton Fleming, East Yorkshire, iron 2Cb involuted brooch from burial BF31; similar-sized foot disc albeit less curved than SF 24 (BM 1978,1203.5; Stead 1991a, 87, fig. 64, F11; Adams 2014, 285, 304, no. 10192).
- Makeshift cemetery, Rudston, East Yorkshire, iron 2Cb brooch from burial R35, similar curvature to the foot and catchplate. The foot disc a bit larger but otherwise similar (BM 1975,0401.44; Adams 2014, 277 and 298, no. 10229).
- Grandcourt Farm, Middleton, Norfolk, copper alloy 2Cb short involuted brooch FN70 with a similar overall shape except the foot disc on the copper alloy brooch is wider and decorated with a moulded design (Adams *et al.* 2012, FN70; Adams 2014, 194–5, 230, no. 10651).

Short, deep involuted Type 2Cb

SF 10, BARROW 9, BURNBY LANE

Iron, short involuted brooch, Hull and Hawkes Type 2Cb and Stead Type E (Hull and Hawkes 1987 163–7, pls 47–49; Stead 1991a, 85–7) in two pieces, possibly once decorated with applied material such as glass. This involuted brooch has a short concave bow and pin. The foot is reverted and attached to the bow at the top of the hip by means of wrapping the toe end around the bow. The brooch is opened and closed by means of a Developed Mock Spring Hinge (Adams 2014, 82, fig. 3.12). The hinge has an unusually complex design for an iron brooch: the head of the bow is formed into a hoop; the head of the pin is inserted through a hole in the base of the bow hoop. The pin head appears to be pierced or looped and pivots on a small bar passed through this hole in the hoop, although this is only faintly visible in the X-ray. The pivot bar appears to have been secured in place with a stirrup of iron bent through and round the exterior of the bow head and over the pin junction. This hinge is similar to Stead's Type G 'Involuted brooches with hinged pins mounted within the head' (Stead 1991a, 87–8, G1–G5, fig. 65).

The foot has a circular flat disc terminal. Such features were typically decorated with applied decorative beads in glass, stone or coral. The presence of a small rivet hole in the centre of the disc indicates this was once likewise decorated. A small, corroded lump on the top of the disc may be the remnants of that decorative material. Just below the foot disc, as the foot bends towards the (now missing) catchplate, is a further small, flattened circular area with a tiny, corroded fragment of reddish material still attached to it. It is possible that both parts were once decorated with opaque red glass beads attached to the brooch. Unusually, the brooch has an indented design on the upper surface of the concave bow with a series of parallel diagonal lines creating a pattern of small, raised squares giving a negative lattice impression reminiscent of a diamond-twill fabric, a type familiar in an Iron Age Yorkshire context (see *e.g.* Crowfoot 1991, 119–22).

The brooch has a dark-brown patina, minimal corrosion and is in a solid condition but with a fractured surface. It was found with the burial of an adult woman aged 36–45 which was the central grave in a small square barrow B9.

Wt: 6.5g (+ corrosion fragment 0.1g); L: 48.73mm; Max. W: 12.60mm

Context: 15326. Burial 15327. Sk 13. Square barrow B9.

X-ray: X8510

Comparable examples:

• Bell Slack, Burton Fleming, East Yorkshire, iron 2Cb involuted brooch from burial BF31, similar angle of foot disc so that it is flat with top of bow (BM 1978,1203.5; Stead 1991a, 87, fig. 64, F11; Adams 2014, 276 and 298, no. 10192).
• Makeshift cemetery, Rudston, East Yorkshire, iron 2Cb brooch from burial R35 with a similar overall shape and large foot disc although the foot disc is more curved than SF 10 (BM 1975,0401.44; Adams 2014, 277 and 298, no. 10229).
• Makeshift cemetery, Rudston, East Yorkshire, copper alloy involuted 2Ca brooch with similar hinge form from the burial of an adult aged 35–45 years old (burial R32) (BM 1975,0401.36; Hull and Hawkes 1987, 159, no. 4376, pl. 44; Stead 1991a, 87 R32 G1; Adams 2014, 82, no. 10227).
• Cold Kitchen Hill, Brixton Deverill, Wiltshire, iron 2Cb brooch, slightly tighter concave bow but similar general shape with a flattened foot disc (Devizes Museum 1003; Hull and Hawkes 1987, 165, pl. 48 no. 5476; Adams 2014, 239, no. 10551).

• Grandcourt Farm, Middleton, Norfolk, copper alloy 2Cb short involuted brooch FN140 with a similar bow shape but no decoration on the foot (Adams *et al.* 2012 FN140; Adams 2014, 194–5, 285 and 304, no. 10654).

SF 94, Barrow 50, Burnby Lane

Small iron, short involuted Hull and Hawkes Type 2Cb and Stead Type E brooch; incomplete and in two fragments. The remainder of the reverted foot where it attached to the concave bow is finished in a simple thin, curved disc with no evidence for applied decoration. The brooch has a dark-brown patina with small fracture seams in the iron and a patch of corrosion on the side of the head against the bow and where the pin would have been. It is not clear from the remains (nor the X-rays) how the brooch was hinged but the circular open ring of the head shows it to have been one of the Developed Mock Spring Hinges typical of the East Yorkshire assemblages, either Type B, C or D (Adams 2014, 82, fig. 3.12). Hints of textile fibres can be seen in the corrosion deposit around the head of the brooch pin.

This small brooch was found in the grave of an adult female, aged 25 years or older, who was laid on her left side facing east. She also wore bracelet SF 93 on her wrist and a round bead, SF 95, was found by her neck. She was buried in the central grave of square barrow B50.

Wt. 1.63g; L. 24.4mm; W. 4.1mm.

Grave 17090. Sk 121. Square barrow B50.

X-ray: X8572

Comparable example:

• Iron 2Cb brooch from Makeshift cemetery, Rudston, grave R134 (BM1975, 0503.27; Stead 1991a, 88, fig. 64 F9 & 202; Adams 2014, 277 no. 10246), probable female burial, aged 35–45, found near right elbow.

SF 96, Barrow 55, Burnby Lane

Very small, tightly curved, iron Hull and Hawkes Type 2Cb/2Cc short, deep involuted brooch; complete but in several fragments. This is shorter than the others in the assemblage, with a narrower and deeply concave bow that sits closer in shape to Stead's Type J brooches but without the applied decoration on the foot (Stead 1991, 88–9). Hull and Hawkes saved their Type 2Cc for those with such a short bow that it had become almost straight, but I would be inclined to open this category to these very short and deeply concave examples similar to SF 96 (Hull and Hawkes 1987, 167, pl. 50). The reverted foot appears to be attached to the bow by means of bending either side of the end around the hip of the bow creating the effect of a collar. The thin, damaged foot once formed a plain disc on the top side. No added decorative features are visible. The hinged head now has the appearance of being entirely encased in metal with no central hole but it seems to have been formed like a Type B Developed Mock Spring Hinge with the outer sides attached to the pin and the inner hoop being formed from the head of the bow, a cylinder or bar providing the joining component and pivot. The presence of traces of non-ferrous metal identified during conservation may be the remnants of a copper alloy cylinder or rod pivot. A very faint hint of a small protrusion on the outside of the head is reminiscent of the stopper on the Developed Mock Spring Hinges that reference the external chord of the springs from which they are descended. Unfortunately, the condition of the piece makes it impossible to verify the exact structure of the hinge. The brooch is dark brown with patches of iron corrosion on the pin, bow and foot.

This brooch was found in square barrow B55 with an individual aged 15 to 17 years old (the sex could not be identified from the remains). The deceased was found laid on their left side facing west with the brooch beneath the right shoulder.

Wt. 4.33g; L. 24.5mm; W. 8.1mm.

Context: 17174. Burial 17175. Sk 126. Square barrow B55.

X-ray: X8572

Comparable example:

- Iron 2Cb brooch from Argam Lane, Rudston, grave R194 (BM 1994,1001.23; Stead 1991a, 88, fig. 64. F3 & 221; Adams 2014, 278 and 299, no. 10253), probable female aged 17–25, found on neck.

SF 155, Grave 16998, Burnby Lane

Iron, short involuted Hull and Hawkes Type 2Cb brooch in two pieces: one piece consists of the bow, catchplate, foot and part of the head of the brooch, the other a fragment of the pin only. This has a short, deeply concave bow and reverted foot attached to the bow on the top of the hip. The brooch is damaged at the end of the foot, so it is not clear if the foot was held to the bow by means of a separate iron collar or by wrapping the toe around the bow. The foot has a large flat foot disc with no sign of decoration. Only part of the head of the brooch survives but it appears to have once formed a complete open hoop and the pivoting pin would have been attached to this possibly by means of a copper alloy cylinder securing the two parts together and acting as the pin pivot. The corroded end of the pin survives in the catchplate, indicating the brooch was closed when buried and the remainder of the pin crumbled away while it lay in the ground.

The brooch has a dark brown patina with small fracture seams in the iron. It was found in the neck area of an adult (aged 18+) buried in an unenclosed flat grave [16997].

The deceased's head was missing owing to truncation of the grave through later activity on the site.

Wt: 4.7g; L: 35.64mm; Max. W: 14.57mm

Grave 16998. Sk 115.

X-ray: X8588

Comparable examples:

- Makeshift cemetery, Rudston, East Yorkshire, two iron short involuted 2Cb brooches, one from burial R35 and the other from R194. The depth of the curvature of the SF 155 bow is partway between these two brooches (BM 1975,0401.44; Stead 1991a, 87–8, fig. 64 F1 and F3; Adams 2014, 277–8 and 298–9, nos 10229 and 10253).
- Beckley, Oxon, copper alloy although this has a slightly deeper bow curve than SF 155 (Ashmolean, AN 1886.1141; Hull and Hawkes 1987, 163, pl. 47, no. 2244; Adams 2014, 61, fig. 3.4 no. 10546).

SF 589, Grave 15774, Burnby Lane

Small, fragmented, iron Hull and Hawkes Type 2Cb short involuted brooch. The pin is still attached to the base of the open, circular head, which once formed a Developed Mock Spring Hinge of Type B, C or D. Unfortunately, this piece is too poorly preserved for more precise identification. The brown crumbling fragments of the brooch show no visible signs of having been decorated in any way.

This incomplete brooch was found during post-excavation work adhering to the lower part of the skull of an adult female aged between 36 and 45 years.

Wt. 2.09g; L. 20.4mm; W. 6.4mm.

Context: 15774. Flat grave. Burial 15773. Sk 39.

X-ray: X8647

Comparable example:

- Iron 2Cb brooch from Rudston grave R194. (BM 1994,1001.23; Stead 1991a, 88, fig. 64 F3 & 221; Adams 2014, 278 and 299, no. 10253).

Short involuted with foot cast in one with bow 2Cd
SF 91, Barrow 46, Burnby Lane

Copper alloy, short involuted brooch with iron pin and large, bulbous beads of glass added as decoration to the head and foot (Fig. 11.2); affectionately nicknamed the 'Ducky-Horse' brooch. The foot is cast as one with the bow which is shorter and less dramatically concave than the pin. Hull and Hawkes classified examples of this type within their 2Cb brooches but the gradual increase in examples suggests they warrant a separate sub-type: a development of the Hull and Hawkes short

Figure 11.2 Copper alloy bow brooch SF 91, Barrow 46, Burnby Lane

involuted examples with such a short bow that it is almost straight (Hull and Hawkes 1987, 158–9 and 167, pl. 44 nos 2243, 2245 and 4376). These I will call Type 2Cd. Stead included his only example of this form within his Type G on the basis of the hinged pin mounted within the head of the example from Makeshift cemetery grave R32 (Stead 1991, 87). The part of the foot that extends from the catchplate up to the disc is cast with moulded decoration. When the brooch is turned with the pin uppermost and the bow below, the decoration has the appearance of an animal's head, having both an anatine and an equine quality with a long horse-like head with bulbous eyes and a beak-like snout resting on a horse hoof shape, and a rippled mane over a long goose-like neck. The back of the animal is formed from the bow. The neck and ripples at the top of the head also have the appearance of the forelimb and grasping paw of an animal. Although this decoration is unique for a brooch of this period in Britain, three very similar examples are known with moulded decoration, all from burials in East Yorkshire, although none is as explicitly zoomorphic as SF 91 (see list of comparanda below). The copper alloy rivet that secures the two large bun-shaped beads to either side of the head of the brooch is round at one end but the other is a delicately rendered, segmented bulbous cruciform shape. This is a shape known in a larger form on middle Iron Age plate brooches and pin heads (e.g. brooches: PAS BERK-4EffC6; Batheaston brooch BM 1989,0601.200; Adams 2014, 88 and 91, figs 3.15 and 3.17; pins: Allen and Webley 2007, 94, figs 3.17 and 3.18; Adams 2014, 68, fig. 3.7). The foot bead rivet has a similarly decorated end: a segmented bulbous cruciform shape.

The bow and pin are covered in thick corrosion deposits but the visible parts indicate a particularly thick bow, possibly a necessity owing to the dimensions of the applied glass beads. The x-ray shows thinning of the metal in the centre of the bow but it is not clear whether this is a result of corrosion or an intentional design but the former is more probable. The glass bead at the foot end of the brooch is now separated from the brooch and only a few fragments survive but the height of the central rivet (10.55mm) and the diameter of the footplate on which it rested (14.70mm) indicate this was of exceptional proportions, larger than those on the head of the brooch and similar to that on the short involuted iron brooch from burial R199, Makeshift (Rudston, East Yorkshire; Stead 1991, 87 fig. 63, E7). Although neither reaches the size of the 30mm wide and 20mm high glass bead on the foot of the Ferry Fryston involuted brooch from the burial of an adult male with a chariot, who died somewhere between 355–155 cal BC (Brown *et al.* 2007, 1478; Adams 2014, 92 and 114, no. 10009).

The head of the brooch is a large circular hoop, wider on the underside than on the top. It is not entirely clear how the hinge is formed. On the basis of the visible parts and the x-ray, the hinge appears to have a been similar design to the Adams Type E Developed Mock Spring Hinge as seen on the 2Ca from burial R32 at the Makeshift cemetery, Rudston (BM 1975,0401.36; Hull and Hawkes 1987, 159 no. 4376, pl. 44; Adams 2014, 82, fig. 3.12, no. 10227). The iron pin would therefore be inserted into the base of the head of the copper alloy bow and hooked around a pivot bar (as discussed above in relation to brooch SF 10). The glass beads are then secured to the sides of the head in a manner similar to that found on the Danes Graves brooch which has a fixed disc in the centre of the ring-shaped head pierced by the rivet that holds the beads on either side of the head (Yorkshire Museum 930.2.48; Greenwell 1906, 266–7, fig. 13; Hull and Hawkes 1987, 159, no. 2243, pl. 44; Adams 201, 134, no.10555). In the case of the Danes Graves brooch, the beads appear to be made out of carved, red-coloured stone.

The brooch has a pale bluish-green patina on the visible copper alloy parts, but much of the brooch is obscured by a thick iron corrosion deposit over all of the pin and much of the bow. On the left side this deposit contains visible casts of woven textile. It was found in the grave of an adult over 46 years, probably female. It is notable that, like SF 5, this distinctive brooch is associated with one of the oldest women to be buried in this cemetery – one of the individuals who lived the longest. Her grave was the central burial in square barrow B46.

Wt: 18.6g (+glass bead fragments separated from brooch: 0.7g; *+bone fragments: 0.2g);* L: 47.91mm; Max. W: 17.71mm

Ctxt: 17081. Sk 119. Square barrow 46.

X-ray: X8572

Comparable examples:

- Copper alloy 2Cb involute brooch from burial R32, Makeshift cemetery, Rudston, East Yorkshire (BM 1975,0401.36; Hull and Hawkes 1987, 159 no. 4376, pl. 44; Stead 1991, 87 R32 G1; Adams 2014, 82, fig. 3.12, no. 10227). This is the best comparison, with a thick bow and moulded decoration between the foot and the catchplate. The decoration is of a very similar composition to SF 91 with equine-like head and duck-like shape although it is even more abstracted than the Burnby Lane brooch. The similar shape is dictated in part by the shape of the catchplate which is wider and deeper at the open end than the closed end. The foot is surmounted by a bead of glass attached by a rivet. This brooch was just beyond the top of the skull in a crouched inhumation.
- Copper alloy 2Cb involute brooch from burial 1, round barrow 48 at Danes Graves, Kilham, East Yorkshire. The catchplate and foot are decorated with moulded decoration. Although this decoration is less overtly zoomorphic than SF 91 it does follow a very similar shape and composition with an horse-like head and duck-like shape (BM 1918,0710.1; Hull and Hawkes 1987, 159, no. 2245, pl. 44; Stead 1979, fig.26.4; Adams 2014, 82, fig. 3.12, no. 10201).
- An involuted brooch with similar foot and catchplate moulding was found during Ian Stead's excavations at Bell Slack, Burton Fleming from Burial BF41, albeit in less well-preserved condition. The BF41 brooch was also covered with corrosion deposits containing fabric impressions. The foot was surmounted by a bead of red glass with an off-centre rivet. Below this is the zoomorphic moulding of horse/duck form but in the Burton Fleming example the top of the head is directly below the footplate and the nose or bill is next to the catchplate; the head is the other way up on the Burnby Lane example. The head of the BF41 brooch also has a different form to the SF 91 example, being a hinge with open centre rather than covered by the two side glass beads. The bow is also of a slimmer form on BF41 brooch (BM 1978,1203.7; Stead 1991, 86–7 E8 & 217; Adams 2014, no. 10193). The brooch was located in front of the face of an adult male (aged 25–35 years).

Decorated and inlaid Type 2B

SF 5, Barrow 2, Burnby Lane

Copper alloy, low arched brooch with coral inlay in an H-shaped frame, Adams Type 2BH (Fig. 11.3). A new sub-category of Hull and Hawkes Type 2B 'Decorative forms, peculiar to Britain' (Hull and Hawkes 1987, 143–55; Adams 2014, 64–6). The central bar of the H forms the low arch of the bow with a wavy rod of coral inserted into the central groove of the frame. The coral is

Figure 11.3 Copper alloy bow brooch SF 5, Barrow 2, Burnby Lane

held in place at either end by a small copper alloy rivet that passes all the way through the bow. The head end of the brooch has a slightly curved rod of coral inlaid into the central groove and held in place with a single copper alloy rivet towards the centre. The coral itself does not show any sign of having been carved or otherwise shaped. Such evidence may have been lost in the degradation of the surface of the coral but it clearly has not been carved into elaborate designs *contra* to examples found on the Continent (e.g. two brooches from Pleurs in the Morel Collection, Stead and Rigby 1999, 58–60, ML.1631 and ML.1632). The brooch is slightly thicker at the foot end where it is also decorated with an inlaid rod of coral held in place by a single central rivet. On either side of the head and foot of the brooch the copper alloy frame narrows to a small, rounded collar. On the back of the head of the brooch are cast the double lugs of the hinge. The catchplate at the opposite end consists of a solid hook cast on the back of the foot end. The length of the bow is comparable to other known examples of this type. The pin survives intact and still pivots on a copper alloy rod fixed between the double lugs at the head end of the brooch. This curved pin protrudes beyond the end of the bow. The presence of the inlaid coral, double lug hinge and hooked catchplate place this brooch in the middle Iron Age.

Further finds of this specific, narrow H-frame brooch form with a central channel for inlay have come to light since the typology was last revised (Adams 2014), although it is rare for the inlaid material to survive intact. It is now possible to separate this from other coral-inlaid brooches of 2Ba1 Type and place them in a distinct sub-type group 2BH (Adams 2014, 62–8, fig. 3.5). This is the first example of the narrower H-frame 2BH sub-type to be found in a secure archaeological context. The form has previously been referred to as Bunwell type after the incomplete example recorded by Richard Hattatt from Bunwell, Norfolk (Hattatt 1982, no. 722; Adams 2014, 65 and 289, no. 10806). Two incomplete examples were also found at Maiden Castle but were not recognised as brooches by Mortimer Wheeler (Wheeler 1943, 270–1, fig. 88.1, 2). The only independently dated comparable example is the flatter, wider H-framed plate brooch from the burial of an adult woman, grave 155 at Wetwang Slack, decorated with a mosaic of several small pieces of coral attached to the upper surface of the brooch (East Riding Museum KINCM 2010.7.237; Dent 1982, 442, fig. 4 no. 155; Hull and Hawkes 1987, 154, pl. 43, no. 7902). Two radiocarbon samples from the human bone in grave 155 were modelled, as part of an examination of chariot burials, to a mean date of 400–200 cal BC (HAR-1665; 2110±80 BP and OxA-14077; 2269±29 BP) (Jay *et al.* 2012, 170, table 1).

The original casting has a small flaw at the foot: a little droplet-shaped hole through the side of the copper alloy body. The brooch is in a good, solid condition with a mid- to bright green patina and whitened coral slightly tarnished in places by small deposits of green corrosion deposits from the copper alloy.

This brooch (SF 5) was found in the grave of one of the older people in the cemetery (aged 46+), probably the remains of a woman. She was also buried wearing two bracelets (the only burial to have more than one bracelet), one on each arm. One of the bracelets (SF 4; Fig. 11.7) was decorated with pink-coloured shell or possibly thin slivers of coral. The other had a simple copper alloy band and open central circle feature (SF 3; Fig. 11.6). The brooch was found near her shoulder. Perhaps the quantity of personal ornaments and their distinct form is connected to her age. She was buried in the central grave of the large square barrow B2.

Wt. 25.1g; Total length: 51.83mm; Length of bow: 37.97mm; max. width: 31.59mm

Context: 15171. Burial 15176. Sk 2. Square barrow B2.

X-ray: X8461

Comparable examples are derived from across England. All are copper alloy:

- Yapham, East Yorkshire, PAS: YORYM-ACFE1D. Very similar form with shaped ends of the cross bar at the head and foot but the coral is missing and there is no evidence for rivets that could have attached the missing inlay.
- Norfolk BM 1990,1005.1. Complete except for the inlay which is missing. This example has a slightly higher arched bow than SF 5 (Adams 2014, 83, fig. 3.13 no. 10318).
- Maiden Castle. Two incomplete examples, both with the inlay missing. Both are missing the hinge attachment and the hooked catchplate only survives on the smaller of the two (Wheeler 1943, 270–1, fig. 88.1, 2).
- Congham, Norfolk (PAS: NMS-39885) and South Walsham, Norfolk (PAS: NMS-85BED1). Both are metal detected finds, the former in a better condition than the latter but both are missing the inlay material.

- Stockton, Wiltshire, well preserved example but missing the pin and inlay (PAS: WILT-5664E9).

SF 52, CHARIOT BURIAL, THE MILE

Copper alloy, cast, well-preserved, unusual, moulded bow brooch with an iron pin (now mostly absent). The bow is inlaid with a single, opaque, pinkish-red glass bead (Fig. 11.4). Hull and Hawkes Type 2Bc: anomalous forms with foot cast in one with the bow, generally low arched with moulded and inlaid decoration (Hull and Hawkes 1987, 152–3, pl. 43; Adams 2014, 62–8, figs 3.5 and 3.6). This is a unique find though it employs features found on other contemporary middle Iron Age brooches from the Yorkshire Wolds and beyond. The head has the skeuomorphic form of a long spring, but is instead a horizontal, ridged barrel with a small gap in the middle containing a narrow rod around which the head end of the pin would have been bent and pivoted. This spring cover is reminiscent of that found on the coral-decorated brooch from 'Queen's Barrow', Arras (Greenwell 1906, 296, fig. 43; Stead 1965, 48, fig. 25; 1979, 65; Hull and Hawkes 1987, 144, no. 3693, pl. 42; Adams 2014, 156, fig. 5.8 no. 10620). The stub of the iron pin is visible in a patch of iron corrosion at the back of the head of the brooch. Remnants of iron corrosion in the catchplate show the pin was in place when burial occurred disintegrated either before or during excavation owing to its heavily corroded state.

Viewed from above, the broad head is attached to a central, roughly circular shallow cup that forms the bow and cup for the inlaid, domed, glass bead. The glass bead is 11.5mm in diameter and rises to 7mm above the side of cup in which it is held. Below this

Figure 11.4 Copper alloy bow brooch SF 52, Chariot burial, The Mile

bulbous bow is a tapering foot bisected by parallel rounded ridges. The overall appearance from above is reminiscent of an insect. During excavation, Mark Stephens noticed this brooch has a form reminiscent of a dragonfly, the skeuomorphic spring head being the head of the insect with large eyes to the side, the bulbous red glass forming the abdomen and the ribbed foot forming the tail. A possible variety of dragonfly represented is the Common Darter which has a red body and is found across England, Wales and Ireland (information courtesy of the British Dragonfly Society), although the overall form of the object is more bulbous than this elegant, winged insect.

Side on, the dragonfly form is not visible but the solid cast head, bow and foot, including the catchplate, are decorated with moulded forms. On either side of the head, at the end of the barrel-like skeuomorphic spring, is found a concave-sided triangle. On the sides of the bow and catchplate the concave-sided inverted triangle is between two spread petals or lenticular leaf-shapes. The bow has a flat, smooth underside. It is probable the pin was concave to allow it space to curve from the pivot in the head to the sloped catchplate. The central glass bead appears to be plano-convex, though it is not possible to confirm the shape of the underside as it is still held secure in the cup of the bow by a rivet pin which passes all the way through the bead and bow, being just visible on the underside of the bow. The top of the rivet is cruciform, with four splayed arms that appear to have been distorted by hammering the surface. Comparing with SF 91 from Burnby Lane (Fig. 11.2), it is suggested this rivet head was once a bulbous cruciform in shape like that holding the red glass beads to the foot and head of SF 91. This form is also found on pin heads and Type 2Bb2 plate brooches from this period, more recently referred to as Vale brooches owing to their dominance near the Vale of White Horse on the Oxfordshire/Berkshire border (Adams 2014, 63–8, fig. 3.6; Byard 2019). The rivet head may have been hammered to prevent the glass bead from falling out of its socket. This is suggested owing to the crack that is visible across the bead from head end to foot end of the brooch. This crack contains a dark substance which could be evidence for a prehistoric adhesive repair similar to the birch-bark tar that is known to have been used to secure glass on contemporary chariot fittings in the Yorkshire Wolds (Stacey 2004). The hammering of the rivet head would have helped hold this repaired bead in place.

The brooch was found on the body of an adult male (46+ years) in an elaborate burial assemblage including complete chariot, upright ponies, decorated shield and other remains. The copper alloy components of the brooch have a deep brownish-green patina and the bead is a faded reddish-pink colour.

Wt: 9.87g; L: 35.8mm; Max. W: 12.4mm.

Grave 3613, Sk 424, Chariot Burial, The Mile.

Comparable examples: no direct parallels are known for this brooch, but individual features are found on other examples:

- Bulbous, round red opaque glass beads set in shallow cups with central copper alloy rivets to secure them have been found on several brooches in the Yorkshire Wolds including SF 91 from Burnby Lane (Fig. 11.2) as well as brooches from grave BF41 Bell Slack, Burton Fleming brooch (BM 1978,1203.7; Stead 1991, 86–7 E8 & 217; Adams 2014, no. 10193), grave R32, Makeshift cemetery, Rudston (BM 1975,0401.36; Hull and Hawkes 1987, 159 no. 4376, pl. 44; Stead 1991, 87 R32 G1; Adams 2014, 82, fig. 3.12, no. 10227) and burial BF10 from the cemetery opposite Argam Lane, Rudston (BM 1978,1202.14; Stead 1991, 214, fig. 117.1).
- The moulded leaf-shaped design can be found on the solid cast copper alloy bracelet SF 93 from Burnby Lane (Fig. 11.8) and as part of the moulded design on the copper alloy Type 2Ab brooch from burial BF10 from the cemetery opposite Argam Lane, Rudston (BM 1978,1202.14; Stead 1991, 214, fig. 117.1).
- The cruciform rivet pin head is also seen on SF 91 Burnby Lane and the shape is known from heads of pins found at Fairfield Park, Bedfordshire and Ludford Lincolnshire (Allen and Webley 2007, 94, figs 3.17 and 3.18).
- The form of the hinged pin is approximate to that of the Queen's Barrow brooch from Arras (Greenwell 1906, 296, fig. 43; Stead 1965, 48, fig. 25; 1979, 65; Hull and Hawkes 1987, 144, no. 3693, pl. 42; Adams 2014, 156, fig. 5.8 no. 10620).

Arched bow, solid cast Type 6
SF 84, BARROW 42, BURNBY LANE

Copper alloy Hull and Hawkes Type 6 brooch (Hull and Hawkes 1987, 193–6; Adams 2014, 74–5, fig. 3.9) decorated with two coral beads attached to the bow by copper alloy rivets: one at the top of the bow, the other at the end of the foot (Fig. 11.5). It has a high arched bow, plano-convex in cross-section that broadens and flattens towards the V-shaped catchplate. The pin still rests in the catchplate which curves around the end of the pin, almost enclosing it. The foot has the appearance of a reverted foot bent up and back to the bow, but it has been cast as complete with the bow. The coral bead at the junction of the foot and bow is heavily degraded, the other less so. Both are a pale pinkish-white colour and the materials has only been identified through visual, macroscopic examination. The brooch has an eight-coil spring that was made separate from the bow and attached to it by means of a central rivet. The external chord is now missing but the pin is intact and has small patches of corrosion deposits that appear

Figure 11.5 Copper alloy bow brooch SF 84, Barrow 42, Burnby Lane

to be remnants of mineralised textile from the fabric to which is was attached. The top of the foot up to the coral bead is decorated with eight small circular low-relief dots within the frame of a shallow groove. A very faint V-shape decorates the head of the brooch where it is inserted into the middle of the separate spring. The beads of coral are set within shallow cups and secured with central rivets similar to those on the plate brooch from the 'Warrior Grave' at Mill Hill Deal (BM 1990,0102.25; Parfitt 1995, 87, fig. 32 no. 4; Stead 1995, 86–7, brooch 2, grave 112; Adams 2014, 67, 91–2, 157–9, figs 3.17 and 5.8, no. 10002) and the highly decorated copper alloy brooch from a burial at Newnham Croft, Cambridgeshire (Cambridge MAA 1903.211; Hull and Hawkes 1987, 147, pl. 42, no. 4283; Adams 2014, 91–2, 157–9, fig. 3.17 no. 10575). The former burial has been radiocarbon-dated to *c.* 355–57 cal BC (OxA-17506; 2158±28 BP; at 95% probability, calibrated using OxCal4.4 IntCal 20) (Garrow *et al.* 2010, 87 and 103; Adams 2014, 99 and 112).

Brooch SF 84 is in a solid condition with minimal corrosion, mostly confined to the end of the catchplate and the collar around the coral bead on top of the bow. It has a dark, greenish-brown patina. Textile fibre impressions are just visible in the corrosion around the spring.

This brooch belongs to the little-studied Hull and Hawkes Type 6 which have long mock springs. The bow and foot are cast as a single piece, but the form references the earlier reverted and attached foot style. No comparable examples are known with applied coral decoration. Type 6 brooches are typically found in settlements and hillforts in southern England and occasionally as unstratified finds in Norfolk (a region producing similar brooches to the middle to late Iron Age examples from Yorkshire). At present associated radiocarbon dates are lacking for this specific type and the majority are unstratified finds.

This is one of only two brooches decorated with coral in this assemblage and like the other (SF 5) it was buried with an adult woman (aged over 25). This grave was located in large square barrow B42. Her brother was also buried in a barrow in the Burnby Lane cemetery (Barrow 43, SK 85), as indicated by DNA analysis.

Wt: 9.6g; L: 40.17mm; Max. W: 19.80mm

Context: 16443. Sk 82. Square barrow B42.

X-ray: X8572

Comparable examples:

- Portsea Island, Hampshire, copper alloy, unstratified brooch find. This is the closest comparison although the reverted foot is held in place with a rivet rather than cast as a solid piece (Ashmolean Museum AN 1992.0062; Hull and Hawkes 1987, 176, S1, no. 3418). This brooch was ascribed to Type 3 which is closely associated with the Type 6 brooches but the foot is reverted and attached to the bow rather than it being cast solid with it.
- Hod Hill, Stourpaine, Dorset unstratified copper alloy brooch Type 6 from the hillfort, similar to SF 84 but with a thicker bow and higher, rounded arch. The reverted foot is cast as one with the bow and both parts are simply decorated with moulded curvilinear lines (BM 1892,0901. Ex Durden Collection; Hull and Hawkes 1987, 196, pl. S5, no. 5645; Adams 2014, 311, no. 10974).
- Spetisbury Rings ('Crawford Castle'), Spetisbury, Dorset estimated to have been excavated from a burial pit (Gresham 1939, 128–31). Copper alloy brooch with iron pivot rod for the mock spring. The reverted foot is cast as one with the bow like the Hod Hill example. The long spring on this example is real rather than mock, with an iron central supporting bar. The slope of the foot from the catchplate up to the bow is much sharper on the Spetisbury brooch than on SF 84 (BM 1862,0627.2; Hull and Hawkes 1987, 195, pl. S5, no. 3505; Adams 2014, 311 no. 10971).
- Maiden Castle, Dorset, copper alloy undecorated brooch from the upper fill of a pit with Durotrigian ceramics (Sharples 1991, fig. 130.2; Adams 2014, 311 no. 10957).
- Glastonbury Lake Village, Somerset, several incomplete copper alloy Type 6 brooches including the closest parallel E22, excavated in 1892 from the area of Mound 6 (Bulleid and Gray 1911, 198, pl. XI E22; Hull and Hawkes 1987, 194, 0877; Adams 2014, 311 nos 10961 and 10962).
- Narborough, Norfolk metal-detected copper alloy brooch, the mock spring missing (PAS: NMS-ECCC53; Adams 2014, 310 no. 10727).
- Congham, Norfolk, also a metal-detected find but a less-complete example (PAS: NMS-E74824; Adams 2014, 310 no. 10726).

Catalogue: penannular brooches

Of the three penannular brooches recovered from the site, one is complete (SF 92), one consists only of the humped pin (SF 85), and the third (from context 15485) has a pin lost to corrosion and is early medieval in date. The Iron Age types are not unknown in north-eastern England but they are not particularly common to the area. They are all poorly dated types ranging from potentially mid-3rd century BC to 1st century AD or even later (Booth 2015).

SF 85, BARROW 45, BURNBY LANE

Copper alloy humped pin from a penannular brooch. Fine, curved pin fragment broken at both ends. The pin has a round cross-section that is thinner towards the head end where it would have looped around the ring of the brooch. The brooch has a mid-greenish-brown patina with an uneven surface.

Humped pins for penannular brooches are more frequently associated with north-east England in the Iron Age and early Roman period although they have a relatively wide distribution in Britain (Booth 2015, 119) and continue in use during the Roman period. The brooch was recovered from the burial of an adult aged 36+ of unknown sex, in the shallow central grave of a large square barrow B45. The grave had been disturbed by ploughing.

Wt: 0.4g; L: 23.62mm; Diameter of pin: 2.23mm.

Context: 16490. Burial 16491. Sk 88. Square barrow B45.

X-ray: X8587

SF 92, BARROW 52, BURNBY LANE

Complete copper alloy penannular brooch with simple terminals defined by a groove and everted rims and flat ends (Fig. 4.55). This is an atypical terminal form best compared to Booth's Type Aa2 penannular brooches with plain terminals defined by the groove between the terminal and the rest of the hoop (A. Booth pers. comm.). These are not well dated, but the earliest seem to be of 3rd- to 2nd-century BC date (Booth 2015, 117–19, fig. 4.2). They continue in use into the 1st century AD in Scotland where uptake of the small penannular brooch is a later phenomenon than further south.

A total of 70 Type Aa2 brooches have been recorded by Booth (2015). While they are more common in south-west England and Wales, their distribution does include eastern and northern England (Booth 2015, 118–19 and 335). Aa2 brooches are less common in mortuary contexts than the undecorated Aa1 and grooved hoops of the Aa3. They typically have humped pins. The simple fixing of the pin by means of bending the end over the hoop of the brooch is more commonly associated with the Iron Age

penannulars than later types. One of the earliest examples was found at Maiden Castle associated with 4th-century BC pottery, while another from the same site came from a 3rd-century context. Few of the Aa brooches are dated by non-stylistic, independent means so this find from a burial context is important to our understanding of the chronology of this type. This example was found in an adult grave of unknown sex, aged 25+, in the shallow central grave of barrow B52.

Wt: 4.1g. Max. Diameter of ring: 23.45mm; Ring thickness: 2.97mm; Pin L: 35.65mm; Pin thickness: 2.05mm

Context: 17105. Sk 123. Square barrow B52.

X-ray: X8572

Bracelets

Six Iron Age bracelets were found in the Burnby Lane cemetery, of which two (SF 3 and SF 4) derived from the same grave (Grave 15427; burial 15428; SK 2) and one is so incomplete as to render its identification uncertain (fragments SF 57 and SF 268). Three are cast copper alloy objects and three are forged in iron Table 11.2). All were found with adult women, with the exception of the two fragments which were derived from an unsexed adult grave (B28). For the most part these may be classified as bangles owing to their rigid form. It would have been necessary for the wearer to pass their hand through the bangle in order to slip it onto the wrist. There appears to be no preference as to which arm the bangle was worn on (they are found on both the right and left arms). The design of SF 4 with a shallow mortice and tenon joint allows for a slight expansion making it slightly easier to remove from the wrist than those with complete, solid bands. The tiny narrow gap in the otherwise solid cast SF 93 would also have provided a little give to enable the bangle to be pushed over the hand. The latter bangle shows the most visible signs of wear. All the bangles appear to be unique items but with strong similarities to other bracelets found in the middle Iron Age Yorkshire Wolds cemeteries and decoration similar to that found on local brooches. The local connections in the designs may be further evidence for regionality in the period (Haselgrove *et al.* 2001). Present evidence suggests a potential 3rd-century BC date for these finds. No direct parallels for the bracelets are known from continental Europe where the contemporary examples tend to be more elaborately decorated. Affinities in the shape and use of decorative features, such as inlaid coral and open circles, suggest some connectivity with France during or prior to the period of deposition, as indicated by the 4th-century BC cast bracelets from the Paris Basin (Baray 2016, 366, pls 167 and 413).

Table 11.2 Bracelets

SF No.	Description	Material	Context	Burial Ctx	Sk	Grave	Burial (F = female)	Period	Weight (g)	Diam (mm)	Thickness horizontal (mm)	Thickness vertical (mm)
3	Cast bangle with decorative open circular feature	Copper alloy	15171	15176	Sk 2	B2 square barrow	Same as brooch SF 5	Iron Age	27	66.5	4.5	4.1
4	Cast, inlaid with coral or shell ornament, with shallow mortice & tenon joint	Copper alloy	15171	15176	Sk 2	B2 square barrow	Same as brooch SF 5	Iron Age	12.2 decoration: 13.1	63.4	3.9	2.2
32	Forged bangle adorned with single, domed, opaque red glass bead	Iron	15733	15733	Sk 36	B19	F: 26–35 yrs r wrist	Iron Age	6.4	est 57.2	4.2	
93	Cast with moulded decoration along band. Simple abutting joint	Copper alloy	17090	17090	Sk 121	B50 square barrow	r wrist with involuted brooch SF 94	Iron Age	47.8	68	4.8	7.2
559	Thin, plain forged bangle (in 7 pieces)	Iron	18347	18348	Sk 158	B74	?F 18–25 yrs l wrist	Iron Age?	2.4 (bag 1.3)	62.3		3.3
57	Thin, curved tapered band; part of small bracelet incorporating SF 268	Iron	15908	15909	Sk 48	B28 square barrow	18–25 yr old unsexed; primary burial in square barrow	?	2.3	L=34.1. potential diam 76	7.1	4.4
268	Thin, curved tapered band; part of small bracelet incorporating SF 57	Iron	15908	15909	Sk 48	B28 square barrow		?	1.04	L=37.1 potential diam 70 so slightly tighter curve than 57 but not unfeasible are part of same object		

Catalogue: copper alloy bracelets

SF 3, BARROW 2, BURNBY LANE

Copper alloy cast bangle with central open circular decorative feature (Fig. 11.6). This simple, smooth cast bracelet has a plano-convex band 4.5mm by 4.1mm. The band is plain with two raised collar terminals, one on either side of the open circle that forms the centre piece of the bangle. This circle was intentionally open in the centre so it would have been possible to see the wearer's skin through the middle. A well-preserved object with thin patches of corroded mid-bluish-green, pitted surface and patches of more solid, brownish-green polished surface.

Wt. 27g; Diameter: 66.5mm; Band W: 4.5mm; Band Th: 4.1mm.

Ctxt: 15171. Burial 15176. Sk 2. B2

X-ray: X8461

Comparable examples:

- Wetwang Slack grave 236 with single central circular opening and a raised collar on either side. Unlike SF 3, this has a twisted band and a mortice and tenon joint with one of the collars (Dent 1982, 444, fig. 6.236).
- Wetwang Slack grave 160. A more elaborate version with twisted band, two open opposing circles and coral inlaid bosses on either side of the circle. Despite these differences the solid form of the bangle and the

plano-convex open circles are very similar to SF 3. The inlaid cupules and twist of the band also bear some relation to SF 4 from the same grave, albeit with a more exaggerated twisted cord effect than on SF 4 (Hull and East Riding Museum; Dent 1982, 444, fig. 6.160).

SF 4, BARROW 2, BURNBY LANE

Cast copper alloy bangle inlaid with shell or polished coral decoration in a low relief decorative boss (Fig. 11.7). A well-preserved object with thin patches of corroded mid-bluish-green pitted surface and patches of more solid, brownish-green polished surface. Five out of the original seven pieces of inlay survive. The band has a plano-convex profile and faint traces of indented parallel grooves on either edge, giving a shallow ribbed effect to the sides This moulding is heavily worn and only visible in some areas where the original surface is still intact, but not in all such areas. The alignment of the surviving ridges and grooves would have allowed for the decoration to curve over the top of the outside of the band creating a twisted cord effect. Alternatively, the cord effect was only ever located on the sides; either way it shows that the bracelet was well worn before the deceased was buried.

The central round boss is inlaid in the centre with a slightly domed, solid, circular piece with a swirling pink, white and cream pattern formed from curving and

Figure 11.6 Copper alloy bracelet SF 3, Barrow 2, Burnby Lane

Figure 11.7 Copper alloy bracelet SF 4, Barrow 2, Burnby Lane

bending thin, coloured striations. The surface has a sheen and occasional pitting. The inlaid material is estimated to be coral given the nature of the colouring, the structure and the pitting in the surface of the pieces. Surrounding the dome in the middle of the central boss are four inlaid segments forming curved oblongs dividing the disc into unequal quadrants. The pieces are not the same length, ranging from only 5.5mm up to 7.7mm. These also have a pinkish-white hue but the striations follow the length of each piece suggest these are pieces of shell which have been careful selected and shaped to follow the curvature of the disc. On either side of the central boss lie two smaller bosses with central cupules which originally held inlaid material (probably coral or shell), one now partially filled with corrosion. The central boss has a small hole on the back which may have accommodated a small pin to hold the inlay in place. The two outer cupules have a smaller, deeper central indentation, perhaps to aid the fixing of the inlay in place. Organic remnants in the bottom of the empty sockets for the inlay show they were further secured with a form of natural resin (plant-based rather than animal-based). This may be similar to the birch-bark resin previously identified on Iron Age brooches from East Yorkshire (Stacey 2004). The use of coral and pink shell inlay is also found on a brooch from Grave 95, Danes Graves, Driffield (Hawkes 1946; Giles 2012, 139): the bow is decorated with round domed discs of inlaid in cupules and elongated cells containing longer strips of inlay.

This single band bracelet is carefully shaped to join on one side, just beyond the end of one cupule: the concave terminal at the band end simply rests in the convex terminal of the boss end forming a mortice and tenon joint; although more shallow than other such joints on known examples including two bracelets from Arras, Argam Lane (Stead 1991, 90 & 215 fig. 118.2). Although the bracelet is now in two pieces, if re-joined at the break it appears that the terminals did not rest in the intended location, rather the terminal next to the decorative boss lay over the top of the other end of the band. Either it was worn slightly wrapped over, so as to create a smaller bracelet circumference than was cast, or its alignment was distorted during burial.

Only two items of personal adornment at Burnby Lane were decorated with coral: both brooches (SF 5 and SF 84). One was found in this grave (SF 5) along with the bracelets.. This burial of an older adult, aged 46+, probably female, was placed in the central grave in a square barrow. As mentioned in the brooch description (see above), it is possible the quantity and quality of her ornaments are connected with her longevity. The grave assemblage may be compared with that of the so-called Queen's Barrow from Arras, grave A.4 (Greenwell 1906, 295–300, figs 42, 43, 46–51), who was buried with an unusual Type 2Ba brooch that had coral inlay with a

flower-like foot feature of petals or rays of coral emanating from a central domed boss. She was buried with two bracelets: one twisted copper alloy with a central inlaid boss and mortice and tenon joint, and the other with a plain band and bead-like setting with possibly coral inlay. She also had a coral-decorated pendant, toilet instruments (one on a ring), a small, thick bronze ring, a penannular 'bronze armlet', 'about one hundred' blue and white glass beads and, according to the excavator, a gold ring but this never made its way into the museum collection and has been lost (Greenwell 1906, 299). Although no record was made of the biological sexing of the skeleton, the assumption that the grave belonged to a female is supported by the association of the blue and white beads and bracelets with contemporary female burials in the Yorkshire Wolds (Giles 2012, 147). The design of the Queen's Barrow pendant is also reminiscent of the central boss on this bracelet, with concentric rings of narrow strips of shell or coral around a central dome, although the pendant's dome is made from sandstone (Giles 2012, 152). Coral-decorated objects are found buried with both women and men. They are included in some of the more elaborately furnished graves, such as the Wetwang Chariot burial (see reference above) and Grave 112 at Mill Hill, Deal, the male 'warrior' (Parfitt 1995, 86–7), but they also occasionally occur in more simply furnished graves and in non-burial contexts (Adams 2017, 64).

Wt. 13.1g; D. 63.4mm; Band W. 3.9mm; Band Th. 2.2mm. W. of decorative boss: 13.6mm.

Context: 15171. Burial 15176. Sk 2. B2

X-ray: X8461

Comparable examples:

- Copper alloy bracelet with a mortice and tenon fastening found on the right arm of an adult female in grave BF11 at the cemetery opposite Argam Lane, Burton Fleming (Stead 1979, 73, v, fig. 29.2; Stead 1991, 90 & 215 fig. 118.2). It is loosely reminiscent of SF 4 but instead has two pairs of circular cupules in which coral beads were affixed, each with central copper alloy rivets.
- Arras grave W.24., East Yorkshire. Two bracelets: one with a central boss consisting of a single cupule inlaid with a reddish stone. This bracelet has a collared terminal on either side of the boss, which forms the mortice part of the mortice and tenon joint on one side (Stead 1979, 72–3, fig. 27.2). The other bracelet has two bosses, one on either side of the bangle, each with a wide, shallow cupule now missing the inlaid material (Stead 1979., fig. 27.3). It has a mortice and tenon joint on one side next to the boss, and the band has faint traces of a twisted cord pattern

on the edges, once thought to have encompassed the outside of the band but now worn, like the Burnby Lane bracelet SF 4.
- Wetwang Slack grave 160 (see SF 3 above).
- Wetwang Slack grave 210 plain bracelet with plano-convex band and shallow mortice and tenon joint (Dent 1982, 444, fig. 6.210).

SF 93, BARROW 50, BURNBY LANE

Solid cast copper alloy bangle with moulded decoration (Fig. 11.8). A heavy, thick band with a smooth interior, rounded plano-convex cross-section and repeated moulding round the exterior of the band. It has a mid-greenish-brown polished patina, with small rough patches of bluish-green corrosion. A neat hairline gap across the band (<1mm wide), all the way through the object appears to be part of the original construction of the bracelet allowing for a small expansion to slide the bangle over the hand. The moulded decoration consists of pairs of thin elongated leaves that join either side of a bisected oval (or seed/ berry), reminiscent of the sinuous leaf ornament observed on items decorated with 'Celtic Art' (Jacobsthal 1944, 83). The possible representation here of natural forms follows a pattern already observed by Melanie Giles, who has noted the connection between the natural world such as 'berries and leaves' and decorative designs on personal ornaments in the Yorkshire Wolds burials (Giles 2012, 139). The closest parallel for this design is found on the top

of the straight bow of a Type 2Ab brooch from burial BF10 in the cemetery opposite Argam Lane, Rudston (BM 1978,1202.14; Stead 1991, 214, fig. 117.1), although in that example it is surrounded with parallel grooves that highlight the leaf and berry pattern. The BF10 brooch is from the same grave as the closest bracelet parallels (see below) and further raises the possibility of local connections in the decorative designs. The decoration on bangle SF 93 is repeated six times, giving the effect of a continuous, sinuous design. It is heavily worn in two areas and more visible between these. If the band is imagined as an analogue clock face with the gap at 6 the most worn area is between 2 and 3 o'clock and at 7 o'clock, while the least worn is between 10 and 11 o'clock. The circumference of the bracelet is also distorted from a complete circle, being slightly flattened and wider across the wrist than from the top to underside of the wrist. Given that the bracelet was found on the right wrist of the deceased adult woman and taking into consideration the worn areas and the shape of the bracelet, it is probable that the it was worn with the 11–1 area uppermost on the wrist so that area 2–3 was on the inside of the right wrist, where it would have become worn by the friction of the clothing on the body, and area 7 on the outside of the wrist where it would be exposed to wear through daily activity (or vice-versa with 7 on the inside and 2–3 on the outside). The damage to the decoration implies long-term wearing of the bracelet on the right wrist by this woman, as opposed to a freshly made object placed on the deceased before burial. It could have been an item acquired as she reached adulthood or at some point in her life, at least a few years prior to death. A short involuted (Type 2Cb) iron brooch (SF 94) was also found in the grave and a glass bead by the neck of the deceased (SF 95). This grave was the primary burial in square barrow B50. The 25+ year old woman was lain on her left side facing east.

Wt. 47.8g; D. 68mm; Band W. 4.8mm; Band Th. 7.2 mm.

Context: 17090. Sk 121. B50

X-ray: X8572

Comparable examples:

- Opposite Argam Lane, Burton Fleming, East Yorkshire. Two copper alloy bracelets with overlapping terminals, not an exact pair. Length of low-relief ornament with trumpet motif and then a lobe on BM1978,1202.15 and elongated trumpet motif on BM1978,1202.16. These were found in burial BF10 along with a copper alloy 2Ab brooch with moulded decoration on bow and hinge and adorned with glass beads either side of head (and probably originally on top of the footplate)

Figure 11.8 Copper alloy bracelet SF 93, Barrow 50, Burnby Lane

(BM1978,1202.14; Stead 1979, 74–5, xv, fig. 28.4-5; Stead 1991, 214, fig. 117.1; Adams 2014, 158, fig. 5.8, no. 10175). These bracelets have been bent so that the terminals overlap side by side rather than finishing end to end like the Burnby Lane example. The diameters of these overlapped bracelets are 59mm and 57mm respectively, i.e. approximately 10mm narrower than SF 93, in theory allowing for expansion to that larger size. It is of note in this instance that burial BF10 was also of a woman but only aged about 17–20 years old. BM 1978.1202.15 was found on her left wrist (Stead 1991, 214 fig. 117.2) and BM 1978.1202.16 on her right (Stead 1991, fig. 117.3).

- Simple, solid, cast copper alloy bangles with abutting ends and simple low relief decoration are known from the continent, for example from tomb no. 48 at Saint Suplice, Vaud, Switzerland; this item is now held in the Lausanne Musée Cantonal d'Archéologie et d'Historie (Kaenel and Müller 1991, 252). These have been dated to the second half of the 5th century BC, potentially 150 years or more earlier than the anticipated date for the Burnby Lane finds. Perhaps these finds are unconnected, or this shows evidence for long-term use of forms; the St Suplice bangles have a more geometric form of decoration so perhaps the latter is true.

Catalogue: iron bracelets

Iron bracelets are a rarity in Iron Age burials in Britain, including those in the cemeteries of the Yorkshire Wolds. Where they have been found, they are rarely illustrated and tend to be plain, thin wire bangles (Stead 1979, 75). The designs of those found here are very simple and the only decorated example is perhaps best paralleled in contemporary brooches; where simple iron forms are embellished, the attached beads of material are typically of a reddish colour (Stead 1991; Giles 2012; Adams 2014).

SF 32, Barrow 19, Burnby Lane

Thin iron bangle with applied decoration. A fine, thin iron band with a small, now russet-coloured striated bead attached as decoration by means of an iron rivet. The bead is possibly extremely decayed glass. It is not clear if the current oblong shape of the bead is its original form. The central iron rivet covers almost 70% of the upper surface, suggesting the bead may now be much diminished. The remnants of the platform on which the bead rested would allow for a larger attachment. The dark greyish-brown band is split and corroded and very fragile, such that is now broken in several places, but the original shape appears to have been roughly circular with a round cross-section, and possibly an unbroken band. This would have been suited to a slender wrist (and a small hand if the bracelet was ever to be removed during life).

It was found on the right wrist of a woman aged 26–35, who was lain on her left side facing east in the central burial of square barrow B19.

Wt. 6.4g; D: 57.2mm; Th. 4.2mm.

Context: 15733. Sk 36. B19

X-ray: X8552

SF 559, Barrow 74, Burnby Lane

Thin iron bangle in seven fragments. A very fine, thin, rounded iron band, roughly oval shaped, with no evidence for decorative features. The band has a dark greyish-brown patina with several large patches of yellowish-brown corrosion. This fragile band would have only fitted over a small hand and wrist, making it suitable for a person with narrow wrists and hands. Bracelets could have been put on at a young age and left on the wrist as the person grew, so it could have been worn by someone whose hands were eventually too large to extract through the bangle. This bracelet was found on the left wrist of an adult aged 18–25 years, possibly a woman. The deceased had been lain on their right side facing west.

Wt. 2.4g; D. 62.3mm; Th. 3.3mm.

Context: 18347. Burial 18348. Sk 158. B74

X-ray: X8647

Comparable examples:

- Danes Graves 46 & 56 (Greenwell 1906, 271 & 305; Stead 1979, 75, xxiii & xxiv). Greenwell mentions two thin iron wire bracelets which Stead notes are now missing. One of these was apparently found on the wrist of a child.

SF 57 and SF 268, Barrow 28, Burnby Lane

Two fragments of a curved, thin iron band tapering towards one end. The wider end is fragment SF 57 and the thinner is fragment SF 268. These were found in the same context in the same grave. They both have a dark greyish-brown patina with several large patches of yellowish-brown corrosion. Comparison of the size and curvature to the other iron bracelets suggest these are parts of a similar object that perhaps had a thicker central area which may have been decorated, but since both parts are snapped at either end it is not possible to confirm the identification. These fragments were found in the primary burial of barrow B28, a young adult aged 18–25 years (sex unknown). This grave was cut by the later burial 15861 (Sk 467): an adult also of unknown sex, aged 18+.

Wt.3.34g; L. of each piece 34.1mm and 37.1mm; Potential diameter 70–76mm; Th. max. 7.1mm; Th. min. 4.4mm.

Context: 15908. Burial 15909. Sk 48. Square barrow B28.

X-ray: X8572

Abbreviations used in the text

PAS: Portable Antiquities Scheme database reference ID
BM: British Museum catalogue number

SF: Small Find Number
Sk: Skeleton number
Wt: weight, L: length, W: width

Note

1   https://www.britishmuseum.org/collection/object/H_2001-0401-21

12

Other Iron Age finds

Summary of Iron Age pottery from Burnby Lane

Mark Stephens

Some 346 sherds of Iron Age pottery were recovered from the Burnby Lane excavation. The assemblage came from 73 separate contexts, predominantly the fills of barrow ditches and graves, but with a significant group from the Oval Ring Gully.

The date of the material is predominantly Middle Iron Age (*c.* 400–100 BC), but there were also two sherds of late Bronze Age/early Iron Age date (*c.* 850–600 BC). The assemblage is described in Table 12.1.

Condition and quantification

The size of the sherds ranged from below 1cm ('crumb') to 12cm, and the weight from <1g to 82g. The assemblage weighed 3460g and had an average sherd weight of 10g. Seven vessels were represented by more than four sherds. A minimum of 120 vessels was represented.

Fabric descriptions follow Rigby's typology (Rigby 2004). Five different fabrics were present: calcite tempered (CTW – 332 sherds), erratic tempered (ETW – 7), flint tempered (FTW – 4), vesicular (VSW – 2), and shelly (STW – 1), the assemblage being dominated by CTW material.

Discussion

This is a moderately sized group of Middle Iron Age pottery, which is associated with both the Iron Age cemetery and possible peripheral domestic activity (Oval Ring Gully). Approximately 120 separate vessels are represented.

The greater part of the assemblage is in CTW, but with a presence of ETW, FTW, VES and STW. The two vesicular sherds may be the result of the calcite temper dissolving out, rather than indicating the former presence of organic material. The dominance of calcite tempering is interesting, given that the site is peripheral to the Wolds (the source of calcite) and in an area where the local gravel deposits might yield tempering from glacial erratics.

As activity at Burnby Lane in the Iron Age was largely concerned with the cemetery, it follows that most of the contexts containing Iron Age material were either barrow ditch or grave fills. The remaining contexts that yielded Iron Age pottery were probable domestic contexts associated with the Oval Ring Gully and two other pits, plus residual sherds from Ditch D and an Anglian grave.

One largely complete wide-mouthed straight-sided jar (SF 83, Fig. 12.1) was a deliberate grave offering associated with the burial of an adult female within a secondary grave in B38. There was also a large group of sherds from another wide-mouthed jar with everted rim and splayed base (SF 88, Fig. 12.1) from the northern ditch of B45, perhaps an instance of 'placed deposition', and 14 sherds plus crumbs from a similar vessel recovered found in the south-west corner of Barrow 83.

The predominant form at Burnby Lane is the wide-mouthed jar with either chamfered or pinched rim, readily comparable to pottery from the Iron Age cemeteries at Rudston and Burton Fleming (Rigby 1991). The exceptions are a jar with a rounded shoulder (16509) from Barrow 45 and sherds from three large late Bronze Age/early Iron Age jars with decorated rims, one from context 16240 (Barrow 41) and the other two from context 16422 (Barrow 42), comparable with examples from Devil's Hill (Stephens 1986, figs 6, 4 and 13). Apart from the three sherds from contexts 16240 and 16422, the pottery is Middle Iron Age in date (*c.* 400–100 BC).

Table 12.1 Catalogue of Iron Age pottery from Burnby Lane

Context no.	No. sherds	Fabric Code	Description
8003	2	CTW	Small body sherds
8008	1	CTW	Abraded body sherd
9018	1	CTW	Abraded body sherd
10003	5	CTW	Body sherds (L-shaped ditch)
12005	13	CTW	10 body sherds & 3 crumbs from same vessel
15004	1	CTW	Body sherd from a thick-walled jar (Ditch D)
15014	1	CTW	Body sherd with oxidised exterior (Ditch D)
15034	1	VES	Body sherd, oxidised outer surface, some voids (B1 E ditch)
15050	1	CTW	Body sherd (Ditch D)
15085	2	CTW	2 body sherds from different vessels (B2 NE)
15118	2	ETW	2 joining body sherds (fresh break) (B2 SE)
15124	1	CTW	Body sherd (Ditch D)
15189	1	CTW	Body sherd (Grave 15191)
15226	1	ETW	Abraded body sherd with grey erratic & flint tempering (1–2mm) (B7 SE)
15304	2	CTW	2 joining base sherds from a jar with a splayed base (Ditch D)
15383	2	FTW	2 body sherds from same vessel, sparse flint temper (1–2mm) (B8 SE)
15386	1	CTW	Body sherd (B8 E ditch)
15388	3	CTW	Rim sherd, pinched-rim jar (diam. 13cm) + 2 body sherds (B8 central grave)
15405	1	CTW	Abraded body sherd (B15 E ditch)
15433	2	CTW	2 joining rim sherds, wide-mouthed jar, pinched rim (diam. 22cm) (B15 NW)
15556	1	CTW	Body sherd (B14 NW)
15607	1	CTW	Thick-walled, abraded body sherd (Ditch D)
15645	1	ETW	Body sherd from a thick-walled jar; flint, grey igneous, grog & sand tempering. Exterior with smoothing lines & sooting (B19 NE)
15723	1	CTW	Body sherd (B21 central grave)
15807	1	CTW	Abraded body sherd (B25 SE)
15962	1	CTW	Body sherd with sparse tempering (<2mm) (B30 S ditch)
15989	2	CTW	Small body sherds (B30 SE)
15992	8	CTW	Small body sherds (B30 S ditch)
16000	11	CTW	Rim sherd from a wide-mouthed, pinched-rim jar (diam. 21cm) + 2 body sherds; 2 finely tempered rim sherds from same vessel; 6 body sherds, probably from different vessels (B30 central grave)
16008	1	CTW	Base sherd, slightly splayed (diam. 11cm) (Ditch D)
16017	1	FTW	Rim sherd, chamfered-rim jar (diam. 20cm); temper 2–6mm (B33 grave)
16022	4	CTW	3 body sherds, same vessel with oxidised exterior; frequent calcite (<4mm); body sherd, partly vesicular, oxidised exterior, + rare quartz (Pit 16024)
16068	1	CTW	Body sherd, abraded and partly vesicular (B35 NE)
16071	4	CTW	Body sherds from the same vessel (B32 central grave)
16076	1	CTW	Crumb-sized (B36 NW)
16082	6	CTW	Splayed base sherd from a wide-mouthed jar, external pinching (diam. 14cm); 2 body sherds from same vessel, fine fabric, sparse tempering; 3 body sherds from different vessels (B36 S ditch)
16091	13	CTW	1 splayed base & 12 body sherds from 4 separate vessels (Grave 16093)
16102	4	CTW	4 joining sherds from the rim &and shoulder of a cylindrical jar with a pinched rim. Unevenly distributed calcite (<3mm); (diam. 16cm) (Grave 16104)

(Continued)

Table 12.1 (Continued)

Context no.	No. sherds	Fabric Code	Description
16114	4	CTW	3 small bodysherds from same vessel + another (B30 central grave)
16143	1	CTW	Body sherd (B34 SW)
16178	5	CTW	Body sherds from same thin-walled vessel (B38 SE)
16193	34	CTW	Largely complete, but crushed, wide-mouthed jar with slightly squared, everted ('chamfered') rim. Fine calcite tempering + some flint (<13mm). Rim diam. 16cm, base diam. 12cm. SF 83. (Fig. 12.1) (B38 secondary grave 16138)
16240	1	CTW	Rim sherd from a large thick-walled jar; top has finger-tip impressions (diam. 28cm). (B40 W ditch)
16286	4	CTW	4 body sherds, probably from separate vessels (Grave 16287)
16297	2	CTW	Body sherds from a thick-walled vessel, with frequent calcite tempering & less-frequent & & grey igneous rock (<3mm) (B37 central grave)
16309	1	ETW	Body sherd, frequent sub-angular grey igneous rock (<1mm), infrequent ironstone (<1mm) & frequent voids (B33 NW)
16315	5	CTW	Body sherds, probably from separate vessels
	1	STW	Body sherd, frequent shell + some calcite tempering (B33 SE)
16353	2	CTW	2 body sherds from same vessel with external smoothing lines (Grave 16356)
16362	1	FTW	Abraded body sherd with sparse, evenly distributed flint tempering (1–2mm) with additional rare ironstone & quartz (Grave 16364)
16387	1	CTW	Sherd with splayed base (B43 E ditch)
16394	1	CTW	Body sherd with some voids (B43 S ditch)
16422	3	CTW	Jar with 'pie frill' decoration on rim, calcite with rare flint & chalk tempering (<9mm) (diam. 22cm); rim sherd from thin-walled jar, top of which is decorated with diagonal notches (diam. 22cm); body sherd (B42 NW)
	1	ETW	Body sherd with grey igneous rock, flint & quartz tempering (1–4mm)
16425	11	CTW	2 joining rim & body sherds from shapeless jar, chamfered rim, slight external lip or bead. Diam. 18.5cm. (B42 N ditch)
16431	1	CTW	Body sherd (B42 E ditch)
16437	4	CTW	Small & abraded body sherds (B42 S ditch)
16452	4	CTW	Rim sherd from a chamfered-rim jar; 3 body sherds from separate vessels (B42 central grave)
16462	9	CTW	9 body sherds, probably from same vessel (Grave 16463)
16485	4	CTW	Body sherds, probably from 3 separate vessels (B37 SW)
16509	80+	CTW	SF 88 (Fig. 12.1) 1 rim, 5 base, plus body sherds from a jar with an out-turned rim, slightly curved shoulder & splayed base. Rim diam. 17cm, base diam. 10cm. (B45 N ditch)
16510	1	CTW	Small body sherd (B45 N ditch)
16538	9	CTW	Small body sherds, probably from same vessel (B45 NW)
16683	5	CTW	Body sherds from thick-walled jar (Oval Ring Gully)
16732	1	CTW	Body sherd (Grave 16734)
16859	1	ETW	Body sherd, oxidised surfaces; grey rock tempering (<1mm), rare flint & quartz (1–2mm) (Primary fill B55 W ditch)
16882	1	VSW	Body sherd, angular voids (from calcite?) (B62 Anglian secondary grave)
16941	1	CTW	Rim sherd from shapeless jar with a chamfered rim, diam. 19cm (Oval Ring Gully terminal)
17046	5	CTW	Body sherds from 2 separate vessels (B11 E ditch)
17052	2	CTW	Thick-walled body sherd, fully oxidised; thin-walled body sherd, oxidised exterior (Ditch D)
18110	1	ETW	Body sherd, oxidised throughout, frequent quartz tempering, with rarer biotite & grey rock (*c.* 1mm) (B70 central grave)

(Continued)

Table 12.1 Catalogue of Iron Age pottery from Burnby Lane (Continued)

Context no.	No. sherds	Fabric Code	Description
18159	4	CTW	Body sherd with oxidised exterior; 3 body sherds from same thin-walled vessel (Grave 18160)
18270	1	CTW	Body sherd with oxidised surfaces (Anglian grave 16268)
18296	1	CTW	Small body sherd (B72 NE ditch)
18402	1	CTW	Body sherd (Ditch D)
05-19-15			
264	15+	CTW	15 sherds + crumbs from base of the same jar (SF 3). Unevenly mixed flint and exterior voids (10–15mm; chaff or chopped straw?) (Pit 265)
381	14	CTW	Sherds from a jar with a pinched rim and relatively thin (6mm) wall, diam. 19cm (B83 SW)

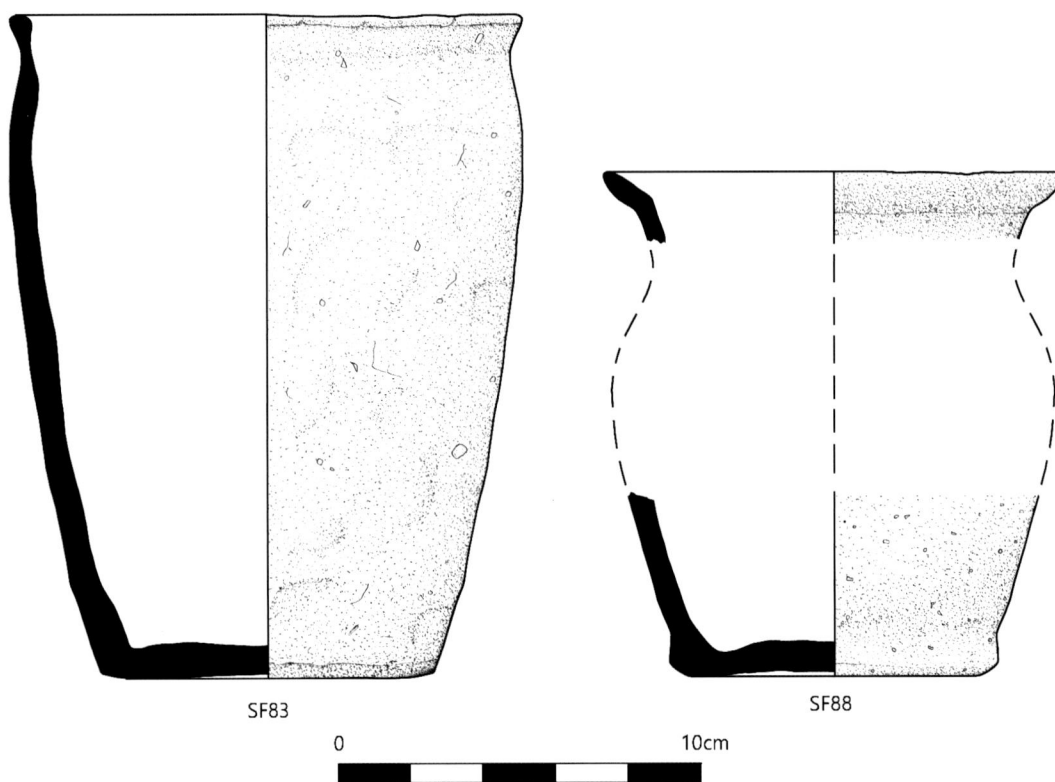

Figure 12.1 Pottery vessels SF 83 and SF 88, Burnby Lane

Iron Age beads from Burnby Lane and The Mile

Mark Stephens

Eight Iron Age beads, seven of glass and one of copper alloy, plus an undated glass example from an Iron Age context, were recovered from graves at Burnby Lane and the chariot burial at The Mile. The beads from Burnby Lane were found in a possible Iron Age 'empty grave' (15722), the central burial of B50 and two Anglian graves (15907 and 15391). Two beads were associated with the chariot burial at The Mile.

Context 15721 (Burnby Lane)

(Fill of 'empty grave' 15722)

Foulds Class 6

SF 25: barrel bead in translucent pale green glass, with traces of swirled blue glass on the surface (Fig. 12.2).

Figure 12.2 Glass bead SF 25, Grave 15722, Burnby Lane

Figure 12.3 Glass bead SF 26, Grave 15722, Burnby Lane

Figure 12.4 Glass bead SF 269, Context 15905, Burnby Lane

Weathered, 'residual' condition. Height: 10mm; diameter: 14mm.

SF 26: barrel bead in translucent pale green glass, decorated with a single row of three surface spirals of yellow glass (Fig. 12.3). Surfaces are weathered/abraded. Height: 10mm; diameter: 14.5mm.

Context 15905 (Burnby Lane)

(Fill of Anglian E–W grave 15907)

Foulds Class 4A

SF 269: polychrome 'eye' bead (Fig. 12.4). Opaque blue glass body, with three evenly spaced white glass circles with reddish-brown blobs in the centre. One end of the perforation is oval (7mm by 5mm), the other slot-shaped (5mm by 1.5mm). The surface is pitted and weathered; residual condition. Height: 13mm; diameter: 15.4mm. There is a similar bead from Gussage Down, Dorset (Foulds 2014, appendix F, DB no. 3999).

Context 15928 (Burnby Lane)

(Upper fill of E–W Anglian grave 15931)

Foulds Class 4A

SF 58: simple polychrome 'eye' bead that is badly distorted through burning. Decoration is similar in colour and style to SF 269 (above), with white eyes with reddish-brown centres, but arrangement of eyes appears to be in a 2-1-2 pattern. Dimensions unclear.

Context 15929 (Burnby Lane)

(Deposit below skull of burial 15930, E–W Anglian grave 15931)

Foulds Class 6

SF 62: barrel bead in pale green glass with a single row of three yellow spirals on the surface (Fig. 12.5). The central perforation has a gold cylinder running through it, the ends of which are flattened into a collar decorated with fine incised lines. Height: 14mm; diameter: 14mm.

SF 64: barrel bead with similar/identical decoration to SF 62, but without the gold cylinder. Height: 11mm;

Figure 12.5 Glass bead SF 62, Context 15929, Burnby Lane

diameter: 13.5mm. There are similar 'Meare Spiral' beads from Meare Lake Village and Garton Slack (Dent 1984, fig. 2.18b). These two beads accompanied the burial of an Anglo-Saxon woman, <15930>.

Context 17090 (Burnby Lane)

(Central grave, B50)

Foulds Class 1

SF 95: a small, plain, annular bead in milky white glass with a granular surface found at the neck of the adult woman buried in the central grave of B50 (Fig. 12.6). Height: 4mm; diameter: 9.5mm.

Context 400 (The Mile)

(Chariot grave)

SF 17: very small blue dark blue glass bead from top fill of the chariot burial grave (context 400). Approx. 2.5mm in width and hexagonal in shape. Very small blue circular glass beads were found in a Wetwang Slack chariot burial (Foulds 264–5), but the hexagonal form of The Mile bead does not appear to be represented in the Iron Age, and its position near the top of the grave increases the likelihood that it was intrusive.

Context 404 (The Mile)

(Chariot grave)

SF 22: copper alloy bead decorated with three raised lines along the circumference (Fig. 12.7) found in context

Figure 12.6 Glass bead SF 95, Barrow 50, Burnby Lane

404 (deposit overlying the chariot box). The bead was manufactured from two separate strips of metal, bent into semi-circles and then riveted together. Height: 5mm; diameter: 19mm. A bead of similar construction, though larger, was found with the K6 burial at Kirkburn (Stead 1991a, fig. 69.3).

Discussion

The glass beads, apart from the example from The Mile, are of types familiar from other East Yorkshire cemeteries as well as domestic contexts in southern England.

At Burnby Lane, only two glass beads (SFs 25 and 26) were found in a probable Iron Age funerary context – the 'empty' grave (15722) on the western fringe of the western barrow group. All the other glass beads that were recovered came from secondary contexts, that is Anglian graves. Bead SF 62 with the gold cylinder is an example of the adaptation of Iron Age beads into Anglo-Saxon jewellery, with other examples being known from Cow Low, Derbyshire and Street House in Cleveland (Foulds 2017, 170). Whether the other glass beads are instances of Anglian curation is uncertain, since although present in Anglian graves, they were not directly associated with the burials concerned. The plain glass bead (SF 95) found with the woman buried centrally in Barrow 50 made a stark contrast to the rich brooch and bracelet (SFs 93

Figure 12.7 Copper alloy bead SF 22, chariot burial, The Mile

Figure 12.8 Antler toggle SF 74, Barrow 30, Burnby Lane

and 94) that also accompanied her. This bead is unusual in being a plain bead in white, rather than blue glass – at Wetwang, the only colour used for beads of single hue was blue (Dent 1984, 62).

The copper alloy bead from The Mile chariot burial is paralleled at the K6 central burial from a square barrow at Kirkburn (Stead 1991a, 93–4).

Objects of antler

Mark Stephens

Antler toggles were found with the central burials of two square barrows (B30 and B45).

SF 74: (B30 central grave, Burnby Lane)

A probable antler toggle consisting of part of a tine with neatly trimmed ends and smoothed lateral surfaces (Fig. 12.8). Length: 56mm; width: 26mm; thickness: 23mm.

SF 86: (B45 central grave, Burnby Lane)

A toggle consisting of part of an antler beam, neatly trimmed at the ends and with the lateral surfaces largely smoothed (Fig. 12.9). It was found at the burial's waist so

Figure 12.9 Antler toggle SF 86, Barrow 45, Burnby Lane

Table 12.2 Catalogue of slag-like residues

Context	SF no.	Undiagnostic slag		Iron smithing residues		Other		Description
		No.	Wt. (g)	No.	Wt. (g)	No.	Wt. (g)	
15375		6	129					Possibly relates to iron production, but undiagnostic of specific process
		1	5					Possibly metallurgical but undiagnostic of specific production process
15393		1	40					Possibly relates to iron production, but undiagnostic of specific process
15467						1	95	Possible fragment of partially forged off-cut of iron object
15568						1	95	Probable natural stone
15590		3	35					Possibly relates to iron production, but undiagnostic of specific process
15863						1	50	Probable iron-rich stone
16030						1	5	Probable iron-rich stone
16091				1	170			Possible smithing hearth bottom
		1	50					Undiagnostic slag
	293	2	5					Possibly relates to iron production, but undiagnostic of specific process
16102		8	305					Possibly relates to iron production, but undiagnostic of specific process
				2	340			Fragments of possible smithing hearth bottom
				1	405			Possible smithing hearth bottom
16115		1	115					Possibly relates to iron production, but undiagnostic of specific process
16149	423	1	10					Undiagnostic slag
16201				1	60			Possible smithing hearth bottom
16305		1	60					Undiagnostic slag
16308		1	190					Undiagnostic slag
16387				2	350			Possible smithing hearth bottom
16431				1	115			Fragment of possible smithing hearth bottom
16683		1	55					Possibly relates to iron production, but undiagnostic of specific process
		1	10					Undiagnostic slag
16895		2	10					Undiagnostic slag
16962	672	1	<5					Undiagnostic slag
17085		1	65					Possibly relates to iron production, but undiagnostic of specific process
17119		1	90					Possibly relates to iron production, but undiagnostic of specific process
17174		1	50					Possibly relates to iron production, but undiagnostic of specific process

could be a dress fastening. Length: 47mm; width: 25mm; thickness: 16.5mm.

Discussion

Both objects were from the central graves of square barrows. The toggle from B45, found *in situ* at the burial's waist, was apparently deliberately placed, but the example from B30 was found near the top of the grave and might either have been deliberately cast in to the grave or included accidentally. Antler objects are rarely found in East Yorkshire funerary contexts, but an antler tine from Rudston barrow R141 was possibly a tool handle or burnisher (Stead 1991a, 202).

Stone object

Mark Stephens

SF 562 (fill of primary grave B75, Burnby Lane)

A shaped, sub-circular stone disc; both top and bottom surfaces are concave, probably an abandoned attempt at perforation. Edges are roughly trimmed, with some straight facets. Possibly a partly manufactured spindle whorl, but if so, it is of probable Roman type (and so intrusive to the grave). Diameter: 34.5mm; thickness: 11mm.

Assessment of slag-like residues from Burnby Lane, Pocklington, East Yorkshire

Rod Mackenzie

An archaeometallurgical assessment was carried out of possible metalliferous slag recovered from Iron Age contexts during archaeological fieldwork at Burnby Lane, Pocklington. The aim of the assessment was to identify the slag-like material and determine whether further analysis could provide additional information about the site or specific processes carried out there. Slag and residues have been visually examined and material from each context has been quantified by type and catalogued in Table 12.2; a summary of the results of the assessment are described below.

Results

The assemblage appears to consist predominantly of slag residues that relate to the production of iron. As well as typical amounts of undiagnostic metallurgical slag, there are a number of 'smithing hearth bottoms'. The assemblage also contains a fragment of what may be an off-cut of a partially manufactured iron object or billet/bar of iron (context 15467 – the upper fill of B15 NE).

Initial interpretation of the assemblage

The pieces of smithing hearth bottom slag are diagnostic of pre-industrial iron smithing. The presence of a significant amount of smithing slag in the assemblage suggests the former presence of a smith's forge in the vicinity during the Iron Age.

The potential off-cut of iron from the upper fill of B 15's NE corner (context 15467) may be of relatively early date; an x-ray would show what lies beneath the surface corrosion to allow a decision on its future curation and/or analysis and the intention is to publish the results of this in a future volume presenting the additional scientific analysis of aspects of the Pocklington sites.

Osteological analysis, Burnby Lane and The Mile

Burnby Lane: Anwen Caffell and Malin Holst
The Mile: Paola Ponce and Malin Holst

This chapter briefly sets out some of the results of the osteological analysis of the human remains from the Burnby Lane and The Mile excavations. The detailed reports have been uploaded to the Archaeological Data Service (ADS) and can be viewed in their entirety at: https://doi.org/10.5284/1095747. The main discussion in this chapter deals with the Iron Age population; the Anglian burials included in some of the tables will be reported on in detail in a future publication on Anglian Pocklington.

A total of 121 Iron Age skeletons were excavated at Burnby Lane, as well as 211 disarticulated bones, the latter of which could not be dated and were likely of mixed date. A minimum of 128 individuals was calculated based on the disarticulated and articulated bones from both the Iron Age and Anglian phases combined (Table 13.1). The MNI is calculated by counting all long bone ends, as well as other larger skeletal elements recovered; the largest number of these is then taken as the MNI. The MNI is likely to be lower than the actual number of skeletons which would have been interred on the site but represents the minimum number of individuals which can be scientifically proven to be present. This included 108 adults and 20 non-adults (a foetus/perinate, 3 younger juveniles, 8 older juveniles, 8 adolescents) (Tables 13.2 and 13.3; Figs 13.1 and 13.2).

The preservation of skeletons was poor, which had a negative impact on completeness and caused the likely loss of some pathological changes.

At The Mile, three burials were located which included one burial (Sk 274) in a plain grave, another (Sk 424) formed an element of a 'chariot burial' accompanied by two ponies, a composite shield, an elaborate brooch and a large number of pig bones and a third (SK 303) was interred at the centre of a round barrow, together with eight spear heads and a dismantled shield. Skeletons 274 and 303 displayed minimal degrees of fragmentation, while Sk 424 had undergone severe fragmentation. Likewise, surface preservation ranged from very good to poor (Table 13.4).

The completeness of the three skeletons ranged from 90–95%. Comparative analysis is vital in order to place the results of the osteological analysis into a regional context and as such, living height and prevalence rates for disease and trauma will be compared with the national period averages, as calculated by Roberts and Cox (2003).

The Iron Age skeletal assemblage will also be compared with several others from the local area, including two cemeteries from Melton, East Riding of Yorkshire, which contained 20 (Melton A63; Caffell and Holst 2011) and 44 inhumations (Melton Business Park; Ponce and Holst 2020) respectively. Additionally, 12 Iron Age burials from Low Street, Sherburn-in-Elmet, North Yorkshire (Newman and Holst 2016) and 18 Iron Age burials excavated at Wattle Syke in West Yorkshire (Caffell and Holst 2013) will be used for comparison.

Pathological analysis

Pathological conditions (disease) can manifest themselves on the skeleton, especially when these are chronic conditions or the result of trauma to the bone. The bone elements to which muscles attach can also provide information on muscle trauma and excessive use of muscles. All bones were examined macroscopically for evidence of pathological changes. Fuller descriptions of the pathological lesions observed can be found in the full report.

Table 13.1 Summary of osteological and palaeopathological data for the articulated skeletons from Burnby Lane

Sk no.	Context	SP	F	%	Age	Age group	Sex	Stature	Dental pathology	Skeletal pathology
						Iron Age (123* Skeletons)				
1	15092	5+	Sev	20–30	18+	a	U	–	Calculus	–
2	15176	4	Sev	40–50	46+	ma	F?	–	AMTL; calculus; caries; hypercementosis	Osteoporosis; DDD, OA & DJC of spine (?Erosive lesions); possible subluxation C2–4; DJC of left shoulder & right hip; OA & possible erosive lesions in left wrist (ambiguous); cavities on sides C4–6 (bilateral carotid aneurysm?)
3	15187	5	Mod	70–80	26–35?	yma?	M?	–	Calculus; DEH	DJC of spine; cribra orbitalia; femoral torsion; porosity on endocranial occipital; soft tissue trauma to left gastrocnemius
4	15192	4	Sev	60–70	17–35	ya/yma	F??	–	Calculus; DEH; additional root on LM^3; fracture RM^2	Pilasterism & torsion of femora
5	15219	5	Sev	40–50	36+	oma/ma	F?	–	Calculus; caries; AMTL; fracture of tooth	–
6	15223	5	Sev	50–60	18–35	ya/yma	M?	–	Calculus; crowding; possible fracture of LP^2; additional root on RM^3	–
7	15331	5	Sev	20–30	6½–8½	oj	–	–	Calculus; single buccal pits on deciduous canines	–
8	15233	3	Sli	90+	26–35	yma	F	167.3	Calculus; caries; DEH; crowding; rotation; slight PD; enamel chips	Cribra orbitalia; porosity on external frontal; border shift (slightly lumbarisation S1): stenosis of right transverse foramen of C7; very thin underdeveloped ischiopubic rami; groove on distal joint of right tibia (possible trauma); lytic lesions on both calcanei (probably developmental); developmental anomaly of right navicular
9	15255	5	Sev	30–40	17–19	ad	(F??)	–	Calculus	Torsion & bowing of both femora
10	15258	4	Sev	60–70	18–25	ya	F?	–	Calculus; enamel pearls	Rib lesions; lamellar bone on right tibia
11	15274	4	Sev	40–50	26–35?	yma?	F?	–	Calculus; DEH; unusual wear LI^1	Cribra orbitalia; pilasterism
12	15300	4	Sev	40–50	18–35	ya/yma	U	–	Calculus; enamel chips; additional roots on lower 2nd molars; small upper third molars; fracture RP^2; enamel chips	Pilasterism

(Continued)

Table 13.1 Summary of osteological and palaeopathological data for the articulated skeletons from Burnby Lane (Continued)

Sk no.	Context	SP	F	%	Age	Age group	Sex	Stature	Dental pathology	Skeletal pathology
13	15327	5	Sev	20–30	36–45	oma	U	–	Calculus; additional root on LM$_1$	Pilasterism; flattened tibiae
14	15341	4	Mod	30–40	18–35	ya/yma	F?	–	Calculus; additional root on RM$_3$	–
16	15394	4	Mod	90+	17–20	ya	F	–	Calculus; DEH; peg tooth (LM^3?)	Spondylolysis; Schmorl's node; sacroiliitis left sacroiliac joint; abnormal right sacroiliac joint (partially fused?); endocranial porosity on occipital
17	15394	4	Sev	20–30	32–40wiu	f/p	–	–	–	–
18 (=19?)	15399	5+	Ext	<5	18+?	a?	U	–	–	–
19 (=18?)	15400	5+	Ext	<10	18+?	a?	U	–	–	–
20	15428	4	Mod	60–70	36–45?	oma?	M?	–	Calculus; caries; DEH; probable abscesses (or considerable PD); enamel chips; possible fracture LP^2	Pilasterism
21	15476	4	Sev	40–50	14½–16½	ad	–	–	Calculus; enamel extensions	Endocranial bone; lamellar bone on legs
24	15494	5+	Mod	40–50	18–25	ya	M?	–	Calculus; enamel chips; enamel pearl	Torsion of both femora
25	15496	5	Sev	30–40	36–45?	oma?	M	–	Calculus; DEH; PD; fracture RM^1 & RM$_1$; enamel chips	Cribra orbitalia; pilasterism
26	15514	4	Sev	50–60	36–45	oma	M	–	Calculus; fractures LP^1, LP^2, RP^1; enamel chips	OA of spine & right wrist; DJC of both TMJs; endocranial bone; pilasterism of both femora; osteochondritis dissecans; maxillary sinusitis
27	15622	3	Mod	90+	36–45	oma	M	177.3	Calculus; DEH; enamel chips; PD	DDD; OA of spine (& bodies C3–4, T10–11); Schmorl's nodes; partial cleft neural arch of C7; border shift (thoraco–lumbar border); slight developmental anomaly of C4–5; odd vertebral bodies T8–L4, including probable fracture of posterior body of T12; bowed left humerus & both ulnae
28	15630	4	Sev	60–70	25+	a	I (F??)	–	Calculus; caries; DEH; enamel chips	DJC of spine; slight pilasterism of femora
32	15664	5	Sev	50–60	46+?	ma?	M?	–	AMTL; calculus; caries; abscesses; enamel chips	DJC spine; extensive soft tissue trauma to vastus medialis, coupled with possible well–healed fracture (greenstick?)
33	15710	5+	Ext	<10	36+	oma/ma	U	–	Calculus; caries	–
34	15724	5	Sev	30–40	18–35	ya/yma	U	–	Calculus; peg tooth (LM^3?)	–

(Continued)

Table 13.1 (Continued)

Sk no.	Context	SP	F	%	Age	Age group	Sex	Stature	Dental pathology	Skeletal pathology
35	15728	5	Ext	20–30	36+	oma/ma	M?	–	Calculus	Thick cranial vault – probably normal
36	15733	4	Sev	50–60	26–35	yma	F	–	Calculus; 2x peg teeth (RM³? & LM³?); RM$_3$ NP/U; AMTL	Cribra orbitalia; possible early HFI
38	15764	5	Mod	50–60	18–25	ya	F??	–	Calculus; caries; additional root on LM³	–
39	15773	5	Sev	60–70	36–45?	oma?	F	–	AMTL; calculus; caries; PD; enamel chips	Bowed tibiae; pilasterism of femora
40	15776	4	Mod	80–90	36–45?	oma?	F	168.2	Calculus; caries; abscess; crowding; rotation; enamel chips	Border shift – possible sacralisation L5; maxillary sinusitis; long bones slender relative to length & 'flattened' rib necks and heads (developmental)
41	15782	5	Ext	20–30	36+	oma/ma	U	–	Calculus; caries	Calcified structures
42	15795	4	Sev	30–40	36+	oma/ma	I	–	Calculus; caries; enamel chips; fracture LM$_2$	Endocranial bone
43	15846	5	Ext	20–30	26–35?	yma?	U	–	Calculus; small RM³	Slight pilasterism of both femora
44B	15851	5	Sev	20–30	36+	oma/ma	M?	–	Calculus	–
45	15856	4	Sev	40–50	18–25	ya	M?	–	Calculus; caries; PD	Bowed left humerus; pilasterism; slightly bowed tibiae; cribra orbitalia; maxillary sinusitis
48	15909	5	Ext	10–20	18–25	ya	U	–	Calculus; caries; hollows in occlusal surfaces of 1st molars (developmental)	–
50	15957	5	Sev	20–30	10½–12½	oj	–	–	Calculus; DEH; discoloured enamel on upper first molars (developmental)	–
51	15960	3	Mod	80–90	26–35	yma	F	–	Calculus; DEH; abscess; enamel chips	DJC spine; cribra orbitalia; endocranial bone & nodule on frontal; cyst – R acetabulum; lamellar bone – both tibiae & fibulae
52	15963	3	Sev	20–30	18–25	ya	M?	–	Calculus; fracture RM$_1$; enamel chips; LI² with double root	Lamellar bone on left tibia
53	15966	4	Sev	60–70	10–12	oj	–	–	Calculus; DEH; enamel chips; diastema; LC$_1$ with bifid root	–
54	15974	3	Mod	90+	26–35	yma	M	–	Calculus; PD; unusual wear; enamel chips; fracture RP²; crowding of mandible	Endocranial & ectocranial porosity; slight asymmetry L4 & L5 and auricular surfaces (developmental); pilasterism of femora & slight bowing of tibiae

(Continued)

Table 13.1 Summary of osteological and palaeopathological data for the articulated skeletons from Burnby Lane (Continued)

Sk no.	Context	SP	F	%	Age	Age group	Sex	Stature	Dental pathology	Skeletal pathology
55	16001	3	Sev	30–40	26+ (36+?)	a (oma/ma?)	F	–	Calculus; caries; PD; LM_3 NP/U; possible fracture RM_1; DEH	Cribra orbitalia; HFI; endocranial porosity & lamellar bone; elongated depression on L tibia anterior crest (possibly developmental/ potential taphonomy)
56	16018	3	Sev	70–80	26–35	yma	M	–	Calculus; PD; peri-apical lesion; enamel chips	Cribra orbitalia; maxillary sinusitis; ectocranial porosity; healed fracture of L clavicle; slight bowing of humeri and tibiae
57	16027	4	Sev	70–80	18–25?	ya?	M?	–	Calculus; caries; additional cusp(s) on RM_3	Lamellar bone on R tibia
58	16069	3	Sev	40–50	36+?	oma/ma?	M?	–	Calculus; caries; DEH; PD; ?abscess; enamel chips	Sinusitis; ?early HFI; oval lytic lesion in left orbit
59	16072	3	Sev	90+	18–25	ya	M	–	Calculus; DEH; enamel chips; peri-mortem fracture LM_3; AM/ peri-mortem fracture LM_2	Lytic lesions on bodies T7 & T9; asymmetry of lumbar vertebrae; endocranial porosity on occipital; lamellar bone on both femora & left tibia; ?fracture/ calcaneus secundarius both calcanei; congenital absence R transverse foramen of C4; multiple peri-mortem injuries to skull, both arms, both hands, pelvis, left leg
60	16092	4	Sev	60–70	26–35	yma	F	–	Calculus; caries; DEH; enamel chips	Endocranial bone; slight bowing of both tibiae
61	16109	4	Ext	40–50	26+	a	M??	–	Calculus; caries; retained deciduous lower 2nd molars; enamel chips	Pilasterism; lamellar bone on L tibia
62	16116	4	Ext	10–20	18+	a	U	–	Calculus; DEH; enamel chip	–
63	16159	5	Ext	10–20	18+	a	U	–	AMTL; abscess	–
64	16165	5	Sev	70–80	46+	ma	F?	–	Calculus; caries; abscess; PD; peg tooth; enamel chips	OA & DJC of spine
65	16166	3	Ext	60–70	26+	a	F	–	Calculus; abscess; PD; caries; enamel chips	DJC & OA of spine; DJC of TMJs; asymmetrical occipital; HFI; porosity on endocranial occipital
66	16278	4	Ext	60–70	26–35?	yma?	M	–	AMTL; calculus; DEH; short roots – RM^3 & LM^3	Depressions in R & L parietals (normal variation); lamellar bone on both femora & tibiae; cribra orbitalia
67	16285	3	Sev	70–80	18–35?	ya/ yma?	M	–	Calculus; caries; DEH; retained deciduous molar; vertical cleft in LI^2; small LM^3; LM_3 probably not present; no socket for LM_2 but is still present	Cribra orbitalia; Schmorl's nodes; severe pathology targeting left side of face and mandible, left cranium, base of cranium, possibly also cervical vertebrae – most likely related to infection
68	16289	4	Sev	70–80	46+	ma	F	–	AMTL; calculus; caries	Schmorl's node; DJC – spine & L hip; endocranial bone; lamellar bone on tibiae

(Continued)

Table 13.1 (Continued)

Sk no.	Context	SP	F	%	Age	Age group	Sex	Stature	Dental pathology	Skeletal pathology
69	16294	4	Sev	20–30	4–6	yj	–	–	DEH	
70	16306	4	Mod	90+	46+	ma	M	–	Calculus; DEH; abscess; PD; fractures of RP_2 & LM_1; enamel chips	OA & DJC of spine; OA – medial R clavicle; DJC – R acromion & L hip; ?ununited fracture of styloid process of R temporal; L foramen ovale & foramen spinosum filled in with bone sheet; 3 calcified structures (probable gallstones)
71	16334	4	Sev	50–60	36+ (probably 46+)	oma/ ma	M??	–	AMTL; calculus; DEH; caries; fractures $?LM^3$, LM_3, LC^1 & LP^2; unusual wear	DJC – spine & R hip; OA – L hip; cribra orbitalia; sinusitis; possible bilateral partial hip fractures – osteoporosis?; pilasterism
72	16346	3	Mod	80–90	26–35?	yma?	F	149.7	Calculus; caries; DEH; abscess; LM_1 & RM_1 with three roots (upper molar pattern); PD; unusual wear; enamel chips	Cribra orbitalia; small plaque of lamellar bone on internal frontal; porosity on internal occipital; border shift at thoraco–lumbar border
73	16355	2	Mod	90+	36–45?	oma?	M	–	Calculus; crowding; LM^3 not present & super-eruption LM_3; fractures of RM^1, LM^1, RM_2; enamel chip	DJC & OA of spine; DJC of R TMJ; Schmorl's nodes; cribra orbitalia; slight developmental anomaly L3–5; porosity of internal occipital; cysts on margin R acetabulum
74	16358	4	Sev	40–50	36+	oma/ma	F?	–	Calculus; caries; PD; unusual wear; enamel chip	Cribra orbitalia
75	16360	5	Sev	30–40	8–10	oj	–	–	Calculus; DEH; unusual wear	Endocranial bone
76	16363	4	Sev	40–50	36+?	oma/ ma?	M?	–	Calculus; caries; PD; fracture/ odd wear LM_2	Endocranial porosity; pilasterism; ?bowing of tibiae; lamellar bone on left tibia
77	16366	4	Sev	30–40	36+	oma/ma	M?	–	Calculus; caries; PD; fracture RM^2; enamel chips	DJC – L TMJ, spine; endocranial porosity; pilasterism; ?osteopenia
78	16370	3	Sev	90+	36–45?	oma?	M?	–	Calculus; caries; fractures; enamel chip; crowding of mandible; rotation RC_1	Cribra orbitalia; endocranial porosity; lamellar bone on tibiae
79	16371	3	Mod	20–30	25+	a	F?	–	Calculus	Cribra orbitalia; endocranial bone
80	16373	4	Sev	20–30	18+	a	F?	–	Calculus; caries; RM_2 with three roots	DJC – spine; cribra orbitalia; HFI; endocranial bone; possible osteopenia
81	16403	3	Mod	40–50	26–35?	yma?	F	–	Calculus; caries; PD; RM_3 not present/ unerupted	Cribra orbitalia; endocranial porosity; lamellar bone on R tibia; Schmorl's nodes
82	16443	4	Sev	40–50	25+	a	F??	–	AMTL; calculus; caries; abscess	DJC – both TMJs; endocranial bone & porosity
83	16450	3	Mod	60–70	15–17	ad	(F)	–	Calculus; rotation LP^2	Lamellar bone on femora and tibiae

(Continued)

Table 13.1 Summary of osteological and palaeopathological data for the articulated skeletons from Burnby Lane (Continued)

Sk no.	Context	SP	F	%	Age	Age group	Sex	Stature	Dental pathology	Skeletal pathology
84	16464	3	Ext	60–70	36+	oma/ma	M?	–	Calculus; DEH; abscess; PD; enamel chips; unusual wear	DJC – spine & hips; healed fracture of right radius & well–healed infection; lamellar bone on both tibiae & 6 metatarsals
85	16466	3	Sev	60–70	36+	oma/ma	M	–	AMTL; calculus; PD; enamel chips	DJC & OA – spine; DJC – both TMJs, R elbow, R knee; OA – L ankle (probable trauma); cribra orbitalia; fracture of L clavicle; lamellar bone on both tibiae & R fibula; lytic area on internal occipital & endocranial lamellar bone
86	16470	5	Sev	40–50	36+	oma/ma	M?	–	Calculus; DEH; unusual wear; odd root patterns in third molars; enamel chip	DJC – both TMJs; slight pilasterism both femora
87	16473	5	Sev	30–40	36+	oma/ma	M??	–	Calculus; fractures LI^1, possible fractures of RI^1 & RI^2; and possible fracture; enamel chips	Pilasterism of both femora; slight bowing of both tibiae; endocranial bone
88	16491	4	Ext	0–20	36+	oma/ma	U	–	–	–
89	16493	5	Sev	20–30	18+	a	U	–	–	–
90	16552	4	Sev	20–30	36+	oma/ma	U	–	Calculus; DEH; enamel chips	Cribra orbitalia; endocranial bone; possible early HFI
92	16606	5	Sev	10–20	46+	ma	U	–	Calculus; caries; DEH	Pilasterism of both femora
93	16678	4	Sev	50–60	36+	oma/ma	F?	–	AMTL; calculus; DEH; PD; LM_3 not present/ unerupted; diastema; rotation; enamel chips	DJC – spine, R shoulder, L TMJ; DDD – cervical spine; possible osteopenia
94	16701	4	Ext	10–20	36+	oma/ma	U	–	AMTL; calculus; PD; fracture RP_2; enamel chips	Osteopenia
95	16728	4	Sev	30–40	18–35	ya/yma	F	–	Calculus; caries; PD; enamel chips; rotation RP_2; short roots	Small possible haematoma on L femur
96	16733	3	Sev	50–60	25+	a	M	–	Calculus; caries; DEH; PD; enamel chips; enamel pearl	DJC – spine
97	16736	4	Sev	60–70	36+	oma/ma	F?	–	Calculus; caries; DEH; abscess; PD; fractures; enamel chips; LM_2 with 3 roots	OA & DJC – spine; DJC – both TMJs, R acromion; maxillary sinusitis; HFI; osteopenia
99	16745	4	Ext	30–40	36+	oma/ma	I	–	Calculus; PD; DEH; enamel chip; small third molar; RM_3 unerupted/ not present	DJC of both TMJs

(Continued)

Table 13.1 (Continued)

Sk no.	Context	SP	F	%	Age	Age group	Sex	Stature	Dental pathology	Skeletal pathology
100	16747	4	Ext	50–60	26–35?	yma?	F	–	Calculus	Endocranial bone; possible early HFI
101	16780	5	Sev	40–50	18–25?	ya?	U	–	Calculus; RM$_3$ with double mesial root	Cribra orbitalia
102	16783	4	Mod	30–40	2–3	yj	–	–	–	Cribra orbitalia; endocranial bone
107	16883	4	Ext	20–30	35+	oma/ma	F??	–	Calculus; caries; fracture RM$_1$; enamel chip	DJC – R TMJ; soft tissue trauma of R femur; ossified haematoma on R tibia
109	16896	4	Ext	40–50	18–25	ya	F?	–	Calculus; enamel extensions	Cribra orbitalia
113	16990	4	Ext	60–70	26–35	yma	M	–	Calculus; DEH; enamel chips	Slight bowing of femora: spondylolysis of L5
115	16997	3	Ext	10–20	18+	a	U	–	–	–
116	17001	5	Ext	10–20	17–19	ad/ya	–	–	Calculus; DEH; unusual wear; buccal root of RP^1 & LP^1 both partly divided into two (3 root pattern)	–
117	17004	5	Sev	30–40	18+	a	U	–	Calculus; hypoplastic 3rd molar – almost peg tooth	–
118	17078	5+	Sev	~10	18–35	ya/yma	U	–	Calculus	Pilasterism of femora
119	17081	4	Mod	80–90	46+	ma	F?	161.1	Calculus; caries; PD; fractures & enamel chips	OA & DJC of spine; Schmorl's nodes; DDD of spine; cribra orbitalia; torsion & pilasterism of femora; slight border shift at TL border
120	17087	4	Sev	70–80	26–45	yma/ oma	M?	–	Calculus; caries; PD; enamel chips	Endocranial bone; ununited fractures of left radius & ulna, bone slightly necrotic; lamellar bone on R femur & tibia
121	17090	3	Mod	80–90	25+	a	F	–	Calculus; PD; both lower 2nd premolars unerupted/ absent; enamel chips	Sinusitis; possible fracture to R clavicle (or ossified haematomas); large lytic areas in left wrist – possible joint disease or cysts; bowed femora & pilasterism; fracture of R rib
122	17102	3	Ext	30–40	9½–11	oj	–	–	Calculus	Endocranial bone; lamellar bone on L femur
123	17105	4	Ext	30–40	25+	a	U	–	Calculus; DEH; enamel chip	DJC & OA of spine; lamellar bone on R tibia
124	17135	4	Sev	20–30	25+	a	M??	–	Calculus; caries; enamel chips; LM^2 almost has 4 roots	Slight pilasterism; lamellar bone on both tibiae
125	17172	5+	Ext	<5	12+	ad/a	U	–	–	–
126	17175	5	Ext	10–20	15–17	ad	–	–	Calculus; fracture RI^1	–
127	18004	4	Mod	<5	16+	a?	–	–	–	–

(Continued)

Table 13.1 Summary of osteological and palaeopathological data for the articulated skeletons from Burnby Lane (Continued)

Sk no.	Context	SP	F	%	Age	Age group	Sex	Stature	Dental pathology	Skeletal pathology
129	18013	4	Sev	40–50	46+?	ma?	M?	–	Calculus; caries; DEH; abscess; PD; abnormally shaped LM^3 with 4–5 roots; RC$_1$ with two roots; crowding & rotation; enamel chips, fracture RP^2	DDD, DJC & OA of spine; DJC of R shoulder, L hip; cribra orbitalia; sinusitis; pilasterism & bowing of femora; soft tissue trauma of R femur; small haematoma on R tibia; calcified structures
136	18123	4	Ext	20–30	18–25?	ya?	U	–	Calculus; caries; retained deciduous canine; small R 3rd molars (esp RM^3); enamel chips	Cribra orbitalia; lamellar bone & porosity around LM$_1$ (associated with caries); inflammation of L TMJ; lamellar bone on R femur & both tibiae
139	18133	4	Sev	30–40	25+	a	U	–	Calculus; caries; fracture	DJC of both TMJs
142	18164	5	Ext	30–40	36+	oma/ma	M??	–	Calculus; fractures; enamel chips; RM$_2$ with 3 roots	DJC of spine
143	18173	5	Sev	20–30	26–35?	yma?	U	–	Calculus; caries; retained deciduous molar; RM^3 with 4 roots; enamel chip	–
148	18224	5	Ext	10–20	18–35	ya/yma	U	–	Calculus; caries; enamel chips; RM$_3$ with bifid mesial root	Endocranial bone
151	18272	4	Ext	40–50	36–45?	oma?	U	–	Calculus; caries; DEH; enamel chips	DJC of spine; cribra orbitalia
153	18303	4	Sev	60–70	18–35	ya/ yma	M??	–	Calculus; unusual wear; enamel chips	DJC – L TMJ; cribra orbitalia; endocranial porosity; slight pilasterism; flattening of tibiae
155	18329	4	Sev	80–90	26–35	yma	F	–	Calculus; caries; DEH; LM$_3$ NP/U; unusual wear; LP$_1$ slightly rotated; PD	Cribra orbitalia; sinusitis; endocranial porosity; DJC – R TMJ
157	18346	4	Ext	30–40	25+	a	U	–	Calculus; enamel chips	–
158	18348	4	Ext	30–40	18–25?	ya?	F?	–	Calculus; DEH; enamel chips; enamel pearl	–
159	18441	4	Ext	<10	12+	ad/a	U	–	–	–
160	009	4	Ext	<5	5–6	yj	–	–	DEH	–
161	016	4	Mod	60–70	36–45	oma	M	–	Calculus; caries; PD; LM$_3$ with slightly bifid mesial root; LM^3 with four roots	DJC – spine; slight bowing of humeri and femora; pilasterism; lamellar bone on tibiae
163	035	4	Sev	80–90	36–45	oma	F	–	Calculus; DEH; PD	DJC – L TMJ; cribra orbitalia; maxillary sinusitis; possible border shift at TL border

(Continued)

Table 13.1 (Continued)

Sk no.	Context	SP	F	%	Age	Age group	Sex	Stature	Dental pathology	Skeletal pathology
165	394	3	Sev	20–30	25+	a	M??	–	Calculus; PD	Cribra orbitalia; HFI?; endocranial lamellar bone; calcified pleura
A	4012	3	Mod	70–80	26–35	yma	F	–	Calculus; DEH; enamel chips; PD; enamel extensions; crowding	Cribra orbitalia; spondylolysis of L5, possible spondylolysis of a second lumbar vertebra
Anglian (41 Skeletons)										
15	15391	5	Mod	70–80	25+	a	F	–	Calculus; caries; abscess; PD	Cribra orbitalia; HFI; deep right sigmoid sulcus
22	15479	4	Sli	90+	36–45	oma	F	163.0	Calculus; PD; enamel chips; crowding	DJC C7–T1, left TMJ; maxillary sinusitis; cribra orbitalia; endocranial bone; border shift (vestigial right 12th rib); healed fracture of right rib 11; torsion of right femur; lamellar bone on right tibia
23A**	15486	-	-	–	~1½–4	yj	–	–	Dental calculus	Cribra orbitalia; endocranial porosity
23B**	15486	-	-	–	~1½–4	yj	–	–	–	–
29	15631	4	Sev	50–60	6½–8½	oj	–	–	Calculus; enamel chip	New bone formation (woven/ transitional) – right humerus, left radius & ulna, right femur
31	15656	5	Sev	<5	18+	a	U	–	–	–
37	15742	5	Sev	80–90	36–45?	oma?	M	–	Calculus; caries; PD; LP$_2$ & RP$_2$, LM$_3$ & RM$_3$ all NP/U	Cribra orbitalia; DJC of right hip; lamellar bone of left ulna
44A	15851	4	Ext	10–20	10–16y	oj/ad	–	–	Calculus	–
46	15861	5	Sev	20–30	18+	a	U	–	–	–
47	15906	4	Mod	80–90	15–16	ad	(M??)	–	Calculus; enamel chip	Lamellar bone on femora and tibiae; soft tissue trauma to metatarsal (possibly LM4); possible trauma to acetabula (or developmental anomaly)
49	15930	4	Sev	90+	46+	ma	F	–	Calculus; caries; PD; enamel chips	DDD; OA & DJC of spine; DJC R TMJ
91	16603	5	Sev	80–90	26–35?	yma?	M	–	Calculus; enamel chips; enamel pearls; LM^3 with 4 roots	DJC – spine; possible fracture of vertebral body; craniosynostosis/ sutural agenesis of R occipito–mastoid suture; pilasterism & bowing of both femora
98	16744	4	Sev	50–60	14½–16½	ad	(F??)	–	Calculus; PD	Spongy cortical bone – possible metabolic condition
103	16787	3	Sev	40–50	36+	oma/ma	M?	–	Calculus; PD; crowding; unusual wear	DDD; OA – spine; DJC – spine, both TMJs, both shoulders, hip; fusion L2–3 (trauma?); cribra orbitalia; lesion in R orbit; lamellar bone – ulnae, R radius, L femur, ?tibia, R fibula; rib lesions; possible border shift; deviations in sagittal suture

(Continued)

Table 13.1 Summary of osteological and palaeopathological data for the articulated skeletons from Burnby Lane (Continued)

Sk no.	Context	SP	F	%	Age	Age group	Sex	Stature	Dental pathology	Skeletal pathology
104	16829	3	Mod	40–50	26–35	yma	M	–	–	Schmorl's nodes; DJC – spine; OA – hand; border shift; possible rib fracture; osteochondritis dissecans of left femur head; cyst in R acetabulum; possible non–osseous coalition in R MC3 (or avulsion fracture?)
105	16836	4	Mod	30–40	6–7½	oj	–	–	Calculus; DEH; odd enamel defects; additional small cusp on Rdm^1	–
106	16881	4	Ext	60–70	46+	ma	F?	–	AMTL; calculus; caries; PD	DJC & OA of spine; sinusitis
108	16885	3	Mod	80–90	46+	ma	F	–	Calculus; PD; abscess perforating nasal floor; absence both lower 2nd premolars & all 3rd molars; RC^1 tilted; diastemata between all canines & 1st premolars; fracture of LI^1	OA of spine (including dens & posterior body of sacrum), both elbows; DJC of spine, L acromion, both elbows, both hips, L TMJ; fusion of C2–3; cribra orbitalia; sinusitis; possible early HFI; osteoma on L temporal; small nodule on R rib; osteopenia; slight pilasterism & bowed humeri; osteitis of L tibia; calcified structures
110	16968	4	Ext	20–30	18+	a	U	–	Calculus; enamel chip	DJC & OA of spine; DJC of hip (unsided)
111	16981	4	Sev	70–80	36–45	oma	F?	–	Calculus; caries; PD; enamel chips; displacement RP^1	Cribra orbitalia; sinusitis; endocranial porosity; probable trauma to L mandible (fracture with haematoma); lamellar bone on tibiae
112	16988	4	Sev	70–80	36–45	oma	M	–	Calculus; caries; PD; multiple diastemata; rotation RC_1; enamel chips	Endocranial bone; spondylolysis – probably L5 & possibly unilateral; lamellar bone on both tibiae & R fibula; slight pilasterism
114	16694	3	Sev	30–40	18+	a	U	–	–	OA of L wrist & at least one hand; DJC of left wrist, L hip, & at least one hand; possible erosive lesions at distal IP joints of hands; well-healed fractures of L ulna & radius (2 fractures in radius); possible small ossified haematoma on R tibia
128	18006	3	Mod	90+	18–25	ya	M	174.9	AMTL; calculus; caries; PD; possible fracture RP^2; enamel chips; rotation	Sinusitis; cribra orbitalia; endocranial bone; lytic lesions on sphenoid; lamellar bone on L ulna, both femora, both tibiae, LMT5; border shift at TL border
131	18071	3	Mod	70–80	46+	ma	F	171.3	AMTL; unusual wear	DDD, DJC & OA of spine; DJC of hands, hips, knees; lamellar bone on endocranial surface (possible early HFI?), rib, R tibia, both fibulae
132	18073	3	Mod	80–90	26–35	yma	F	160.5	Calculus; caries; abscess; PD; enamel chips; hybrid RI_2 and RC_1 present; crowding	Schmorl's nodes; sinusitis; cribra orbitalia; woven bone on mandible; lamellar bone on fibulae; endocranial lamellar bone & possible early HFI; developmental anomaly of manubrium; rib lesions; fractures of both sacral alae; border shift at TL border; partly bifid head on R 5th proximal phalanx

(Continued)

Table 13.1 (Continued)

Sk no.	Context	SP	F	%	Age	Age group	Sex	Stature	Dental pathology	Skeletal pathology
134	18085	3	Mod	70–80	46+?	ma?	M	–	Calculus; DEH; PD; unusual wear; parastyle	Sinusitis; lamellar bone on endocranial occipital & both tibiae; healed fracture of L clavicle; possible bowing of humeri and tibiae; thickened intermediate hand phalanx (trauma or developmental); fused intermediate and distal foot phalanx
135	18111	4	Sev	70–80	46+?	ma?	M	–	Calculus; caries; enamel chips; PD	DJC of spine, both TMJs; thick U–shaped projection on superior body wall of lumbar vertebra, with lytic lesions on inferior annular ring of another lumbar vertebra and large osteophyte on the body of S1; ossified structure
137	18126	4	Sev	80–90	46+	ma	M	–	Calculus; caries; abscess; DEH; PD; fracture LP²; enamel chips; crowding & rotation	DDD & DJC of spine; DJC of L TMJ, L medial clavicle, R shoulder, both hips, both knees; cribra orbitalia; sinusitis; possible HFI; endocranial bone on occipital; fractures in R clavicle and L fibula; pilasterism of both femora; bowing of both tibiae
138	18130	3	Ext	10–20	18+	a	U	–	–	OA of L wrist; DJC of sacrum; endocranial porosity; possible depressed fracture in R parietal, small depression in L parietal (developmental)
140	18135	4	Sev	10–20	36+45?	oma?	U	–	–	Cyst in L acetabulum
141	18159	4	Sev	70–80	46+	ma	I	–	AMTL; calculus; caries	OA, DJC & DDD of spine; DJC of L TMJ & R hip; OA of both wrists, L hip, & one hand; cribra orbitalia; frontal sinusitis; lamellar bone on two metatarsals, one possibly fractured
144	18198	4	Ext	40–50	36–45	oma	F	–	Calculus	Endocranial bone on occipital; developmental anomaly of L mandibular condyle & neck; rib lesions; new bone (remodelling woven, & lamellar) on both tibiae & fibulae
145	18208	4	Sev	80–90	46+	ma	F	–	AMTL; calculus; caries; abscesses; PD; crowding; enamel chips; parastyle	DDD of spine; OA of cervical bodies, lumbar spine, hand; DJC of spine, both shoulders, L hip, R knee, hand; lump on internal frontal; osteopenia
146	18220	4	Sev	10–20	11–12	oj	–	–	Calculus	Endocranial bone & porosity; lamellar bone on L mandible

(Continued)

Anwen Caffell, Malin Holst and Paola Ponce

Table 13.1 Summary of osteological and palaeopathological data for the articulated skeletons from Burnby Lane (Continued)

Sk no.	Context	SP	F	%	Age	Age group	Sex	Stature	Dental pathology	Skeletal pathology
147	18222	4	Mod	90+	26–35	yma	M?	177.7	Calculus; DEH; enamel chips	Schmorl's nodes; small R hypoglossal canal (developmental); lamellar bone on external cranium, esp L side & on tympanic sections of temporal bones; endocranial bone; lamellar bone on L humerus, both femora, both tibiae (most pronounced on R with possible overlying soft tissue injury and ossified haematoma), R fibula, feet; bowing of both humeri
149	18264	4	Sev	40–50	13–14½	ad	–	–	Calculus; DEH; LM_1 with slightly bifid mesial root	Cribra orbitalia; endocranial bone; lamellar bone on both femora
150	18269	4	Sev	50–60	10½–12	oj	–	–	Calculus; DEH	Cribra orbitalia; endocranial bone; lamellar bone on femora & tibiae; torsion & pilasterism of femora, possible bowing
152	18293	3	Mod	70–80	46+	ma	M	–	Calculus; caries; PD; lower molars NP/U; rotation; enamel chips; possible fracture lower incisor	DDD, DJC & OA of spine; DJC of both shoulders, hips, knees, 1 finger; possible ossified haematoma on frontal bone; endocranial bone; cyst or developmental anomaly in occipital; cribra orbitalia; sinusitis; ununited clay shoveler's fracture T1; asymmetric vertebral facets (developmental); lamellar bone on both tibiae; bowing of both tibiae & pilasterism of femora
154	18326	4	Sev	40–50	46+	ma	F	–	Calculus; caries; PD; ?abscess/cyst	DJC – spine; lamellar bone – both tibiae
156	18342	4	Ext	40–50	6–12	oj	–	–	–	–
162	030	5	Mod	50–60	25+	a	F?	–	AMTL; calculus; caries; DEH; PD; enamel chip	Cribra orbitalia; HFI?; endocranial capillary impressions; healed fracture to left clavicle
164	066	3	Sev	20–30	25+	a	M?	–	Calculus; rotation RP_2; RP_1 possibly small	DJC & OA – spine; Schmorl's node; DJC – L acetabulum, intermediate hand phalanx

Key: SP = Surface preservation: grades 0 (excellent), 1 (very good), 2 (good), 3 (moderate), 4 (poor), 5 (very poor), 5+ (extremely poor) after McKinley (2004a); C = Completeness; F = Fragmentation: min (minimal), sli (slight), mod (moderate), sev (severe), ext (extreme)

Non-adult age categories: f (foetus, <38weeks *in utero*). p (perinate, ~birth), n (neonate, 0–1 months), i (infant, 1–12 months), yj (young juvenile, 1–5 years), oj (older juvenile, 6–11 years), j (juvenile, 1–12y), ad (adolescent 12–17y)

Adult age categories: ya (young adult, 18–25 years), yma (young middle adult, 26–35 years), oma (old middle adult, 36–45 years), ma (mature adult, 46+ years), a (adult, 18+ years)

Dental pathology: DEH (dental enamel hypoplasia), AMTL (ante-mortem tooth loss), PD (periodontal disease)

Skeletal pathology: OA (osteoarthritis), DDD (degenerative disc disease), TB (tuberculosis), HFI (hyperostosis frontalis interna); TMJ (tempero-mandibular joint), MC (metacarpal), MT (metatarsal), C (cervical vertebra), T (thoracic vertebra), L (lumbar vertebra), S (sacral vertebra)

* 123 skeletons in total if Skeleton 18 and Skeleton 19 are accepted to be the same individual

** Two young juveniles, bones co-mingled and not possible to distinguish which belonged to which individual. Both similar in size and probably similar in age. See Appendix C for full catalogue of bones present

Table 13.2 Iron Age non-adult age distribution (articulated skeletons) from Burnby Lane

Age group	n	%
f/p	1	7.1
i	0	0.0
yj	3	21.4
oj	5	35.7
ad	5	35.7
Total	14	

Key: Age group: i = infant; yj = young juvenile; oj = older juvenile; ad = adolescent; n = number

Congenital conditions

Heredity and environment can influence the embryological development of an individual, leading to the formation of a congenital defect or anomaly (Barnes 1994). The most severe defects are often lethal and if the baby is not miscarried or stillborn, it will usually die shortly after birth. Such severe defects are rarely seen in archaeological populations, but the less-severe expressions often are and in many of these cases the individual affected will have been unaware of their condition. Moreover, the frequency with which these minor anomalies occur may provide information on the occurrence of the severe expressions of these defects in

Table 13.3 Iron Age adult age distribution: all age categories (articulated skeletons) from Burnby Lane

Age group	Males		Females		Unsexed/Indet.		Total adults	
	n	%	n	%	n	%	n	%
ya	5	12.8	5	13.5	3	9.1	13	11.9
ya/yma	3	7.7	3	8.1	4	12.1	10	9.2
yma	5	12.8	10	27.0	2	6.1	17	15.6
yma/oma	1	2.6	0	0.0	0	0.0	1	0.9
oma	7	17.9	3	8.1	2	6.1	12	11.0
oma/ma	11	28.2	5	13.5	7	21.2	23	21.1
ma	3	7.7	5	13.5	1	3.0	9	8.3
a	4	10.3	6	16.2	10	30.3	20	18.3
a?	0	0.0	0	0.0	4	12.1	4	3.7
Total	39		37		33		109	

Key: Age group: ya = young adult (18–25); yma = young middle adult (26–35); oma = old middle adult (36–45); ma = mature adult (46+); a = adult (18+); n = number

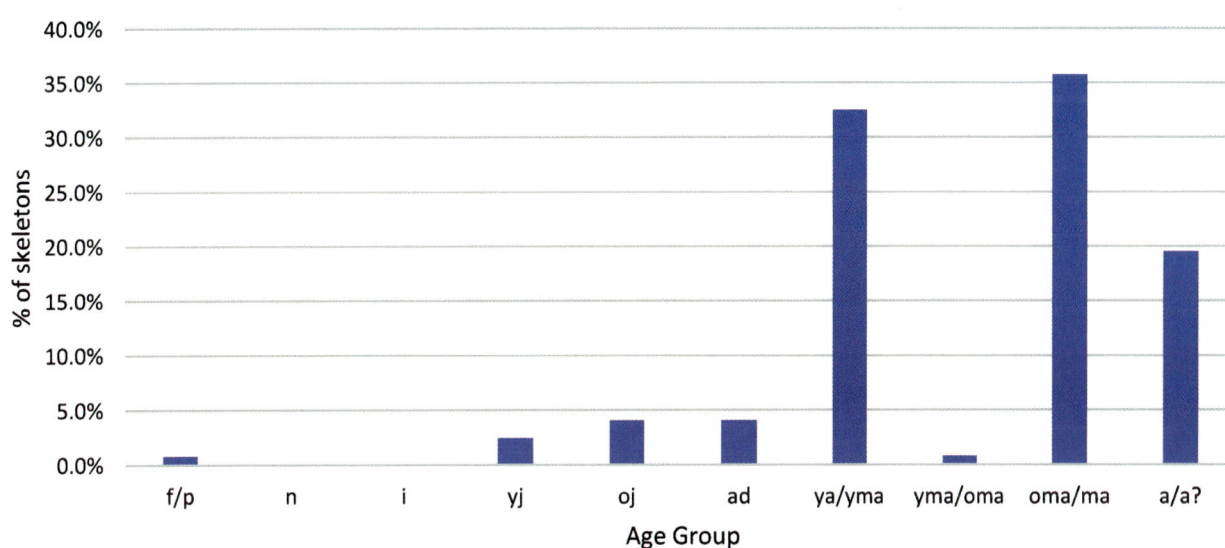

Figure 13.1 Iron Age: age distribution (broad adult age categories) at Burnby Lane

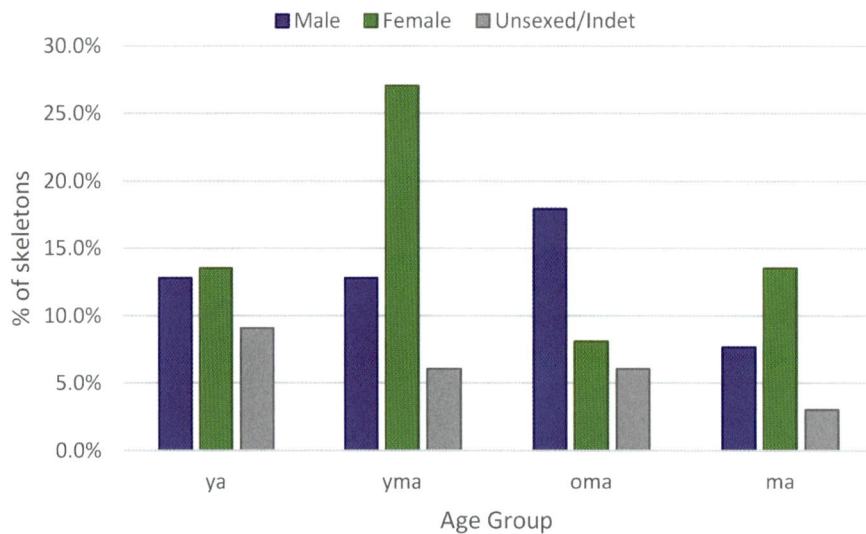

Figure 13.2 Iron Age: adult age and sex distribution (precise age groups) at Burnby Lane

Table 13.4 Summary of articulated skeletons from The Mile

Sk no	Burial type	Position	Orientation	Artefacts	Notes
274	Plain	Crouched, lying on left side	N–S	–	Buried facing down with both hands underneath the left side of the face
303	Plain central inhumation in round barrow	Crouched, lying on left side	NNE–SSW	Cu Al shield components ×4, Fe spear heads ×5, bone spear heads ×3	Buried with both hands close to the face
424	Square barrow	Crouched, lying on right side	N–S	2 horses, bronze/Cu Al objects, including an Arras type brooch, pig bones	Chariot burial with both hands close to the face

the population involved (ibid) and may provide information on maternal health (Sture 2001).

Variation in number of vertebral segments

The usual number of segments in the spine is 33, including 7 cervical (neck) vertebrae, 12 thoracic vertebrae (bearing the ribs), 5 lumbar vertebrae (lower back), 5 fused segments in the sacrum (back of the pelvis) and 4 segments in the coccyx (tailbone). Occasionally the overall number of segments may vary. It is more common for an individual to have an additional vertebra than to have a reduction in the number of vertebrae (Barnes 1994, 78). When additional vertebrae occur, they often appear at the borders between the thoracic and lumbar spine, or between the lumbar vertebrae and sacrum. They may appear as a fully fledged thoracic or lumbar vertebra, but frequently they will take on a mixture of the characteristics of the vertebrae on either side of the border, so appearing to be part-thoracic/ part-lumbar, or part-lumbar/part-sacrum (Barnes 1994, 78). When this occurs, they are described as 'transitional vertebrae'.

Scoliosis

Scoliosis is a term used to describe lateral (sideways) curvature of the spine, rather than being a specific disease (Salter 1999). It can result from congenital vertebral anomalies, neurological problems and disease or trauma (Barnes 1994; Salter 1999; Resnick 2002; Skyrme *et al.* 2005) and it can be associated with complex congenital syndromes (Resnick 2002). However, 80–85% of modern people with scoliosis develop idiopathic scoliosis, where the cause is unknown (Aufderheide and Rodríguez-Martín 1998; Salter 1999). Most modern individuals with idiopathic scoliosis first develop their condition during adolescence and girls are far more commonly affected than boys; Skyrme *et al.* (2005) report a ratio of between 4:1 and 10:1.

Cribra orbitalia

Cribra orbitalia is a term used to describe fine pitting in the orbital roof, which develops during childhood and often recedes during adolescence or early adulthood. Until recently, iron deficiency anaemia was the accepted cause

Figure 13.3 Slight antero-posterior bowing of the right tibia of Iron Age Skeleton 56, medial view

of these lesions (Stuart-Macadam 1992), but a strong case has been made by Walker *et al.* (2009) for different types of anaemia as the causative factor. These include megalo-blastic anaemia in the New World, suggesting a diet deficient in vitamin B_{12} (i.e. plant-based and lacking in animal products) and/or folic acid. Such dietary deficiency could have been exacerbated through poor sanitation leading to infection and infestation with gut parasites. In malarious areas of the Old World, haemolytic anaemia (e.g. sickle cell anaemia and thalassemia) may be important in the development of cribra orbitalia. However, for areas such as northern Europe they have proposed that cribra orbitalia may be more likely related to conditions such as scurvy (vitamin C deficiency) or chronic infections. Cribra orbitalia is often used as an indicator of general stress (Lewis 2000; Roberts and Manchester 2005) and is often found associated with agricultural economies (Roberts and Cox 2003).

Bowed long bones

Several skeletons had slight bowing of their long bones, although it was difficult to determine whether these changes represented residual childhood rickets, another pathological condition, or were simply due to normal variation. Rickets (in children) and osteomalacia (in adults) develop as a result of a lack of vitamin D (Lewis 2007, 119). The poorly mineralised bone resulting from vitamin D deficiency is incapable of supporting normal loads and as a result, it bends under weight-bearing (Fig. 13.3). As children are growing, the long bones are affected; in adults the bones of the torso are more commonly involved (Ortner 2003, 393–401; Brickley and Ives 2008, 75–150). Although vitamin D can be obtained from food sources (primarily eggs and oily fish), most vitamin D is synthesised by the body during exposure to sunlight (Brickley and Ives 2008, 82–4). Therefore, the development of rickets and osteomalacia is usually associated with post-medieval urban populations (Lewis 2007, 121; Ortner 2003, 393). However, cultural practices can also have an impact on diet and the amount of sunlight exposure. These include infant and child feeding practices, the type of clothing worn, amount of time spent outdoors, housing styles and work environments and all can vary according to age, sex and social status (Brickley *et al.* 2014). The impact of such cultural practices could be greater in more northern latitudes, where longer, darker

winters would already limit the amount of sunlight exposure during half the year. A diet deficient in calcium can also lead to the development of rickets.

Hyperostosis frontalis interna

Hyperostosis frontalis interna (HFI) appears as irregular nodules of bone on the internal surface of the frontal bone, believed to be the result of changes in the hormones secreted by the pituitary gland. HFI is almost always seen in females over the age of thirty and has been associated with pregnancy and acromegaly (Aufderheide and Rodríguez-Martín 1998, 419; Roberts and Manchester 2005, 249).

Osteoporosis

Osteoporosis develops when bone mass is lost, making the bones less dense and more fragile. Bone mass is lost with increasing age in both sexes, but the change is more rapid in post-menopausal women. Bone mass can also be lost in response to pathological conditions, including endocrine disorders, malnutrition and as a result of reduced mobility (Aufderheide and Rodríguez-Martín 1998; Ortner 2003). Osteoporotic bone is more prone to fractures, as the bone is no longer capable of withstanding normal biomechanical forces and certain sites are characteristic fracture locations. These include the distal radius (wrist), neck of the femur (hip) and vertebral bodies (spine) (Ortner 2003; Roberts and Manchester 2005).

Trauma

The evidence for trauma in archaeological populations is restricted to that visible in the skeletal remains, unless soft tissue is preserved (Roberts and Manchester 2005, 85–6). Therefore, most of the soft-tissue injuries sustained by archaeological populations will be invisible, although occasionally soft tissue injuries can be inferred through ossification of the tissues at the site of damage, known as myositis ossificans. Much of the evidence for trauma in archaeological populations focuses on fractures to the bones (Roberts and Manchester 2005, 84–5), although long-standing well-healed fractures may be hard to detect (Jurmain 1999, 186).

Ante-mortem injuries occurred during life and show evidence for healing, whereas peri-mortem injuries occurred around the time of death and consequently no evidence for healing will be seen. Peri-mortem injuries did not necessarily occur at the instant of death. It takes time for evidence of healing to be visible in the bone following an injury and also for bone to lose the physical characteristics it had in life following death. Therefore 'peri-mortem' really refers to a three-week window either side of death (Roberts and Manchester 2005, 114). Distinguishing between peri-mortem trauma and post-mortem

Figure 13.4 Potential posterior ring apophysis fracture/posterior limbus vertebra of the inferior body of T12 of Iron Age Skeleton 27

Figure 13.5 Soft tissue trauma to the vastus medialis muscle on the right femur of Iron Age Skeleton 32, postero-medial view

damage can be difficult. Generally, post-mortem breaks will have a paler surface than the surrounding bone and broken edges will usually be perpendicular to the bone (Lovell 1997, 145; Sauer 1998; Roberts and Manchester 2005, 114–16). Recent post-mortem breaks are usually easily distinguished but breaks that occurred while the skeleton was in the burial environment and long before the skeleton was excavated may be much harder to identify as such. This proved to be a particular problem at Burnby Lane, due to the unusual ceramic-like quality of some of the bones that had apparently resulted in post-mortem breaks that mimicked peri-mortem trauma (Fig. 13.4).

Ante-mortem fractures

Eight adults had ante-mortem fractures (7.3%, 8/109), including six males and two females. The proportion of males with ante-mortem fractures (15.4%, 6/39) was three times higher than the proportion of females (5.4%, 2/37). At Melton A63, two females suffered from ante-mortem trauma (22.2% of adults, 33.3% of females; Caffell and Holst 2011) and the prevalence was considerably higher than the average proportion of Iron Age individuals suffering fractures (4.7%, Roberts and Cox 2003).

Eight adults, most of whom were male, had suffered fractures during life which were well-healed; these

mostly affected the collar bones, legs and forearms. Clavicle fractures are an injury typically sustained during a fall (Dandy and Edwards 2003, 181–3). Fractures to the radius and ulna together are usually the result of considerable direct force (de Buren 1962). Complications during healing are common and can include malunion (which had occurred in an unsexed adult) and failure of the fracture to unite (which had occurred in a middle-aged male) (Dandy and Edwards 2003, 200–2). The prevalence rate of fractures was, however, much lower than in the comparative populations. Notably, spondylolysis, where part of the vertebral arch becomes detached from the rest of the vertebra was observed in 15.0% of adults and was much more common than in comparative populations. These fractures have been associated with stress placed on the lower spine during sporting activities, although a congenital weakness in the spine has also been implicated (Roberts and Manchester 2005, 106). Osteochondritis dissecans, a form of trauma where a fragment of joint detaches and sometimes re-attaches was observed in one individual. Three females showed evidence for ossified haematomas, indicative of blood clots due to direct trauma or muscle tears; two on the legs and one on the collar bone.

Soft tissue trauma

Injury to the soft tissues can sometimes lead to ossification at the points where the tendons and ligaments attach to the bone (myositis ossificans traumatica) (Fig. 13.5).

Peri-mortem injuries

Multiple peri-mortem injuries were observed in Skeleton 59 (young adult male), including sharp-force (blade) injuries, penetrating injuries and blunt-force injuries. The identification of these injuries to the bones, particularly the blunt force injuries, was complicated by the unusual preservation at Burnby Lane that resulted in post-mortem breaks mimicking peri-mortem trauma.

Skeleton 59 had a linear blade injury at least 60mm long across the top of the cranium, predominantly on the left parietal but extending across the sagittal suture onto the right parietal (Fig. 13.6). The cut had been delivered from above and to the left and angled into the bone slightly from behind. It had penetrated most of the way through the cranial vault and the internal part of the vault had fractured. There was a peri-mortem fracture line radiating anteriorly from the right end of the cut and there was a potential area of blunt-force trauma to the left parietal, but since this coincided with the end of the peri-mortem cut it was not possible to distinguish whether some of the radiating fracture lines radiated from the end of the cut or from a separate blunt-force injury. Probable blunt-force trauma to the left side of the face had shattered part of the mandible, fractured two teeth and fractured the left maxilla (upper jaw), zygoma (cheekbone) and temporal bone (which supports the ear and articulates with the mandible). There were further potential peri-mortem fractures to the base of the cranium (in the basilar process of the occipital bone) and to the area above the left orbit (eye socket), but these may have been unusual post-mortem breaks.

Figure 13.6 Peri-mortem blade injury (a) to the left and right parietal bones of Iron Age Skeleton 59, with radiating fracture at the right end of the cut (b) and a penetrating injury (c) with associated radiating peri-mortem fractures (d)

The blunt-force injuries to the left side of his head and face would be consistent with face-to-face combat with a right-handed assailant (Novak 2000). However, other injuries had been delivered from different directions, including the penetrating injuries to his cranium. The blade injury to the top of his head must have been delivered from above, so either the attacker was positioned higher or the victim was already crouching or kneeling on the ground. The injuries to the hands and forearms could have been defence injuries (Fig. 13.7). Analysis of the remains of soldiers who fought and died at the Battle of Towton in AD 1461 found that defence injuries were more frequently observed in the right arm (Novak 2000). It was suggested that the right arm would have been vulnerable to counter-attack when delivering blows and likely to be injured if using a weapon to parry a blow (Novak 2000, 93). It is possible that the relatively shallow injuries to the right arm and hand of Skeleton 59 were sustained in such a manner. The injuries to his left elbow would have been fairly disabling, with the cut to the humerus injuring his brachialis, brachioradialis and triceps brachii muscles. Triceps brachii acts to extend the elbow, while both brachialis and brachioradialis act to flex the elbow. Brachioradialis also contributes to pronation and supination of the forearm (turning the hand palm up or palm down). The crushing injury to his left elbow would have impacted on movement and also damaged the common extensor muscles that act to extend

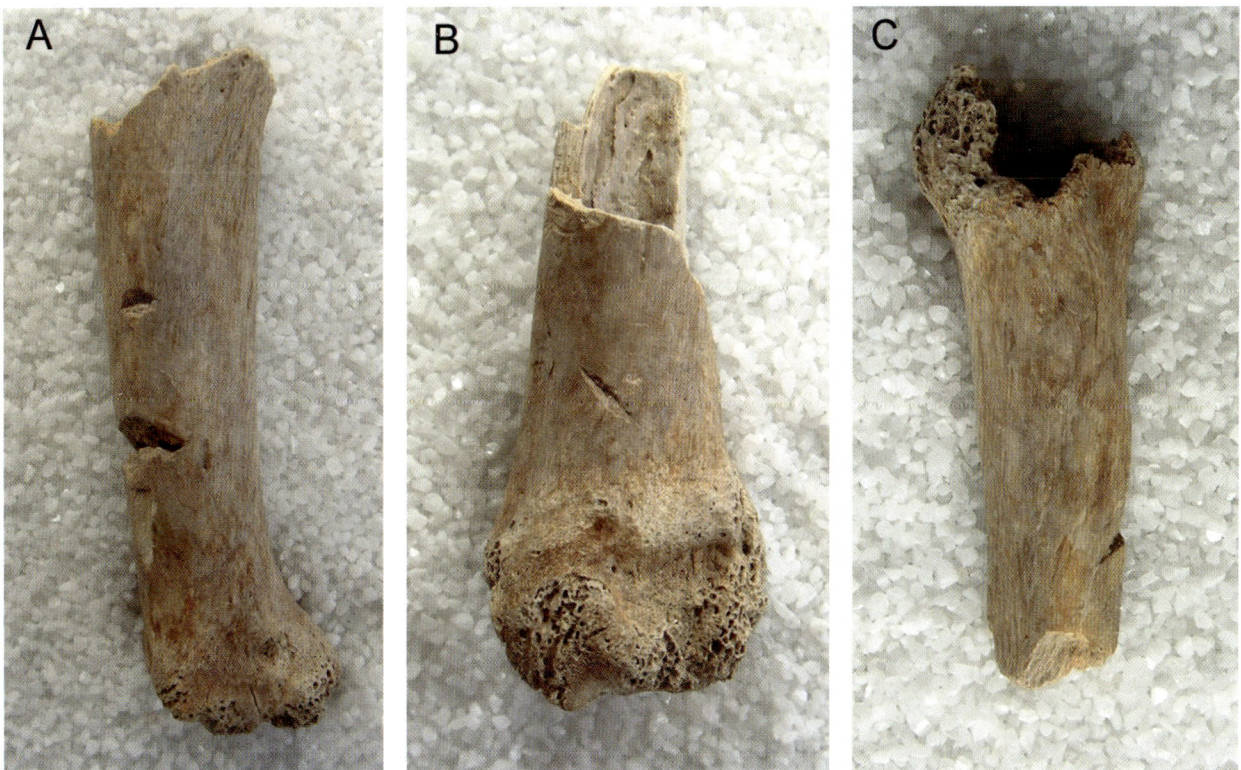

Figure 13.7 Peri-mortem cuts to the right metacarpals of Iron Age Skeleton 59; A) two cuts to the dorsal shaft of right? MC3; B) Shallow cut to the dorsal surface of right MC2; C) cut to the dorsal surface of right MC4/5

the wrist. At Towton, fewer injuries were observed in the lower body, possibly as a result of protective armour (Novak 2000, 93). From the injuries, it is not known whether Skeleton 59 was wearing any protective armour or carrying a shield.

The crude prevalence rate for weapon trauma in the Iron Age was 2.3% (Roberts and Cox 2003, 98), but was much lower for the East Riding of Yorkshire according to Stead (1991a; 1.2%). At Wetwang Slack, weapon-related trauma was recorded in 11 individuals (2.5%). This included mostly sharp force injuries, healed penetrating injuries caused by a bladed weapon such as a spear, sword, dagger or axe as well as depression fractures (Jay *et al.* 2013). Unlike the injuries observed at Burnby Lane and Melton Business Park, most injuries on skeletons from the Wolds were healed, suggesting that these individuals survived conflict (Giles 2012, 104–8). While both sexes could be affected by weapon trauma, this was mostly seen in young adults, as at Burnby Lane and Melton Business Park (Ponce and Holst 2020).

Infectious disease

Infectious disease can involve the skeleton, but since bone cannot respond quickly only evidence for chronic, longstanding infections can be observed in archaeological skeletal remains (Roberts and Manchester 2005, 167). Acute conditions, where the patient either recovers or dies within a short space of time will not be seen. Initial bone formation in response to infection is disorganised (woven bone), but with time, as healing takes place, woven bone is remodelled and transformed into lamellar bone. Consequently, woven bone presence indicates an infection that was active at the time the person died, whilst lamellar bone indicates an infection that had healed; a combination of both suggests a recurring or longstanding infection. Although specific diseases may cause new bone to be deposited on the skeleton, it is almost always impossible to diagnose these from the bones alone. Hence, evidence for infection is discussed as 'non-specific' infection.

It is likely that evidence for inflammation among the skeletons from Burnby Lane will have been lost as a result of the poor surface preservation. The heavy erosion of the surfaces seen in many of the skeletons would have removed traces of new bone formation, particularly fragile deposits. It is suspected that woven bone may have been particularly vulnerable since it would not have been firmly attached to the bone.

Maxillary sinusitis

Infection of the maxillary sinuses can result from upper respiratory tract infections, pollution, smoke, dust, allergies, or a dental abscess that has penetrated the floor of the sinus cavity (Roberts and Manchester 2005, 174–6). Chronic sinusitis was observed in approximately a third of adults, which is an unusually high prevalence rate for the Iron Age, suggesting exposure to air polluted with

smoke, dust, or other allergens such as pollen. Notably, sinusitis was more common among females, which may hint at different environmental exposure between the sexes (Fig. 13.8).

Rib lesions

The presence of new bone formation on the pleural surfaces of the ribs has been associated with lung infections, including tuberculosis (Santos and Roberts 2001; 2006; Mays *et al.* 2002; Roberts and Manchester 2005, 190; Matos and Santos 2006). However, because other lung infections (such as chronic bronchitis and pneumonia, Roberts and Cox 2003) can also cause these lesions, tuberculosis cannot be diagnosed purely on the presence of rib lesions alone (Fig. 13.9). Exposure to polluted atmospheres and the inhalation of fungal spores may also precipitate the development of rib lesions.

Figure 13.8 Sinusitis in the right maxilla of Iron Age Skeleton 163

Figure 13.9 Rib lesions in the ribs of Iron Age Skeleton 67: cross section of a right rib showing multiple layers of new bone formation

Endocranial new bone formation

Bone formation on the internal surfaces of the cranium is more commonly seen in infants and young children than in adults. It has been associated with inflammation or haemorrhage of the meningeal blood vessels, but the potential causes of these lesions are not clear at present. In children, possible causes identified include chronic meningitis, trauma, anaemia, neoplastic disease, metabolic diseases (scurvy and rickets), venous drainage disorders and tuberculosis (Lewis 2004; 2007). Less information is available concerning the aetiology of these lesions in adults.

Osteitis and osteomyelitis

Infection of the cortex of the bone is known as 'osteitis', while involvement of the medullary cavity in the centre of the bone is known as 'osteomyelitis' (Roberts and Manchester 2005, 168). In the latter, enlargement of the bone shaft is observed as a result of new bone formation, which eventually may surround the original surface completely. Destruction of the internal structures of the bone occurs with pus formation and a fistula may form allowing the pus to drain into the surrounding tissues. Death of the original bone shaft may occur (Roberts and Manchester 2005, 168–9).

Sacroiliitis

The sacroiliac joints are the joints between the sacrum (at the base of the spine and the back of the pelvis) and the blades of the pelvis and the joint surfaces are called the auricular surfaces. Inflammation of these joints is called sacroiliitis and this can be caused by infection. Infection of the sacroiliac joints is typically seen in children and young adults and when it occurs in adults it is usually associated with intravenous drug use and infections of the skin, respiratory tract, or urinary tract that have spread haematogenously (Vyskocil *et al.* 1991; Bindal and Krabak 2007). Tuberculosis can also lead to the development of sacroiliitis (Gao *et al.* 2011). Other possible causes include infection of the spine or pelvis, or injury to the joint and it has also been reported as a rare complication of pregnancy (Vyskocil *et al.* 1991; Almoujahed *et al.* 2003; Bindal and Krabak 2007). Symptoms include fever and pain in the lower back and buttocks which worsens during walking or weight bearing and movement can be impaired as a result (Almoujahed *et al.* 2003; Bindal and Krabak 2007). In most patients the onset of the condition is sudden, but around a quarter will experience gradual onset with less pain and minimal fever (Bindal and Krabak 2007). Individuals with sacroiliitis will have widening of the sacroiliac joint, destruction of the joint surface and without treatment may develop abscess formation and septicaemia, with spread of the infection elsewhere in the body (ibid) (Fig. 13.10). Modern patients are treated with antibiotics and surgery, but prior to the development of antibiotics death was common (Vyskocil *et al.* 1991).

Orofacial infection – possible tuberculosis

A male skeleton (Sk 67) under the age of 35 had layered new bone formation on his ribs, including active and remodelling bone deposits, indicating he had suffered a longstanding or recurring infection. This may have been associated with a severe infection in the left side of his face and cranium that had largely destroyed the posterior half of the left side of his lower jaw (Fig. 13.11). Further

Figure 13.10 Complete destruction of the left sacral auricular surface of Iron Age Skeleton 16, with potential abscess formation, probably as a result of sacroiliitis

Figure 13.11 Irregular rough deposits of lamellar bone on the inner surface of the basilar process of Iron Age Skeleton 67 and in and around the left hypoglossal canal

Figure 13.12 Degenerative joint change in the right temporo-mandibular joint of Iron Age Skeleton 65 (adult female)

lesions were present in the base of his cranium and upper spine. He may have suffered from a tuberculous infection of the skin on his face called *lupus vulgaris.*

These factors would certainly be consistent with the spread of the infection via the temporalis muscle. While Ortner (2003, 250) indicates that targeting of these areas is typical in young children, *lupus vulgaris* is a chronic condition that can progress over decades: Yaldiz *et al.* (2015) reports a woman who developed *lupus vulgaris* as a four-year-old child who sought treatment in her mid-forties. Therefore, it is possible that Skeleton 67 had sustained the infection as a child. Ortner (2003, 249–51) also describes rare infection of the upper neck vertebrae associated with tuberculosis, with superficial erosion of the anterior parts of the vertebrae and involvement of the base of the cranium around the foramen magnum. Again, the character and pattern of the lesions in the base of the cranium and neck vertebrae of Skeleton 67 are consistent with this.

Skeleton 67 has been dated to the Iron Age. Santos and Roberts (2001) state that the earliest identification of tuberculosis in Britain dates to the 4th century AD. However, this has been revised by Taylor *et al.* (2005), who suggest that the earliest instance of tuberculosis dates to the Iron Age. Skeletal evidence for tuberculosis in Britain dating to the Roman period has been found in Dorset, Hampshire, Gloucestershire and Lincolnshire (Roberts and Cox 2003, 119). They suggest that increased trade with the continent and movement of people may have been responsible for an increase in tuberculosis.

Degenerative joint changes

Degenerative joint changes (DJC) were recorded when synovial joints displayed a combination of porosity and osteophytes (bone growth) on or around the joint surface (Fig. 13.12). Note that this combination of changes is sometimes defined as osteoarthritis (e.g. Rogers 2000; Roberts and Manchester 2005, 135–6).

Iron Age population discussion

Only *c.* 11% of the Iron Age population at Burnby Lane was made up of non-adults, in particular older juveniles and adolescents, as well as two foetuses/perinates. Adult age was difficult to estimate due to the poor preservation, with one quarter of adults having to be assigned to the generic adult age group. The remainder were largely aged 36 years or older, followed by the 18–35 year group, with a tendency of males outliving females – perhaps due to dangers associated with childbirth. The proportion of females to males was similar. Female living height compared well with the average for the period, while the stature of the only male whose height could be calculated was considerably taller than the male mean Iron Age height.

Several individuals had evidence for congenital anomalies, which were mostly in the spine. The most severe developmental changes were two blocked holes in the base of a man's skull, though they did not appear to have had an adverse effect on him. A very rare anomaly was observed in a young adult female, whose pelvis was extremely thin at the front.

While childhood stress lesions were more widespread in the Burnby Lane population than those at the two Iron Age Melton cemeteries, these combined with low childhood mortality. This may suggest that the Burnby Lane population was better at surviving stress during childhood compared to the Melton group, but that those who had experienced childhood stress tended to die younger in adulthood, especially females. It is possible that some childhood stress was related to the large prevalence of residual rickets observed in this population, which may have been associated with cultural practices or keeping sickly children indoors. Males were affected more than females, but mostly appear to have been able to survive episodes of vitamin D deficiency.

Nodules on the internal surface of the cranium, associated with hormones and pregnancy, were observed in nine skeletons. Seven individuals showed evidence of possible osteoporosis. Healed fractures were seen in only a small proportion of individuals and affected mostly males, particularly in the collar bones, legs and forearms, indicative of both accidental and defensive injuries. However, spondylolysis, a fracture related to stress in the lower spine was common. A number of individuals suffered from potential haematomas, caused by direct trauma or muscle tears.

Notably, one young adult had sustained numerous unhealed weapon injuries, including several bladed and blunt force injuries to his head, shallower cuts to his left hand and forearms, which may have been defensive injuries and further cuts to his left leg and hip. He had

Figure 13.13 Potential general aggressive periodontal disease (GAP) around the lower right and second and third molars of Iron Age Skeleton 20

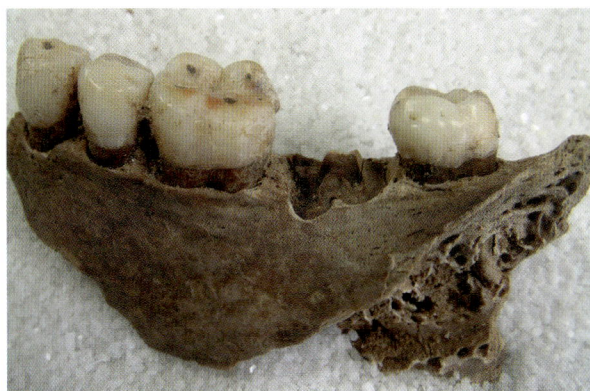

Figure 13.14 Fracture of the lower left second molar of Iron Age Skeleton 59

also fractured at least one of his teeth in the assault. It is clear that this individual had not survived this attack.

Bone inflammation was extremely prevalent at Burnby Lane. Chronic sinusitis was seen in a third of adults, which is an unusually high prevalence for the period, with females more commonly affected than males. A third of the population suffered from inflammation on the internal surface of the skull, which was unusually common and may have been associated with chronic meningitis, trauma, anaemia, rickets, scurvy and tuberculosis. Further inflammation was recorded in 22 individuals, particularly in the shins and in males, though the majority of these inflammatory lesions were healing at the time of death. Rib lesions indicative of lung infection were recorded in two individuals. Notably, one adult male suffered from tuberculosis, with a severe infection of the left side of his face and skull, which destroyed the posterior part of his lower jaw, as well as milder lesions in his ribs and spine. A likely pregnant female young adult female had an inflammation in the joints in the back of her hips called sacroiliitis, which has been reported as a rare complication of pregnancy. It is probable that she suffered from fever, pain in her lower back and buttocks that worsened during walking or weight-bearing and her movement may have been impaired. The condition can cause septicaemia and it seems likely that it contributed to her death and the death of her unborn baby.

A third of the population at Burnby Lane had spinal stress lesions (Schmorl's nodes), which were much less common than in local contemporary populations. Degenerative changes in the spine affected a quarter of adults and were mostly observed in the neck area, which also tended to be the area most affected by osteoarthritis. Males tended to have more prevalent and a wider distribution of degenerative changes and osteoarthritis in extra-spinal joints compared with females, possibly because they lived longer. Two individuals had erosive joint diseases, perhaps rheumatoid arthritis, psoriatic arthritis or gout.

Other age-related conditions observed included gallstones and calcified soft tissue.

The dental health of the Iron Age population was similar to the contemporary local populations, with mineralised plaque, cavities and dental abscesses being slightly less common than the local norm, while periodontitis was widespread, as was dental trauma, particularly in males (Fig. 13.13). The presence of notches in the teeth suggested that they were used as tools, which may have contributed to the high prevalence of dental trauma (Fig. 13.14).

The Mile

The three skeletons from The Mile, Pocklington, displayed similarity in the degree of fragmentation as all three out the five skeletons were minimally fragmented. Completeness was in the range 90–95%. The Mile assemblage consisted of three adults. Skeleton 274 was a young adult female aged 18–25 years old, Skeleton 303 was a young adult male aged 18–25 years old, and Skeleton 424 a mature adult male aged 46+ years old. The skeletons belong to the Arras culture due to the similarities in burial practices found in East Yorkshire and continental France.

Stature could be estimated for the three skeletons, all of whom were shorter than the mean for the nearby Burnby Lane cemetery population. The female was also shorter than national Iron Age mean, while the males were taller than the Iron Age male mean stature. A small number of cranial and post-cranial non-metric traits were observed, with the traits in the ankles (lateral and medial squatting facets) of Skeletons 274 and 303 suggesting that these individuals engaged in habitual squatting. The dentitions at The Mile, Pocklington were well preserved for analysis, with 96 tooth positions and 71 teeth. A total of 25 teeth had been lost ante-mortem and not a single tooth was recorded as not present/unerupted. All the teeth lost ante-mortem came from mature adult male Skeleton 424.

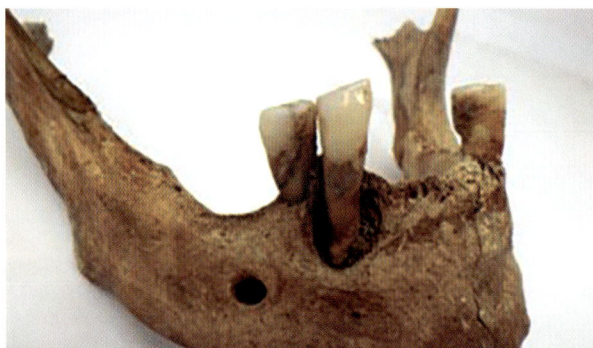

Figure 13.15 Dental abscess on the right mandibular canine of Skelton 424

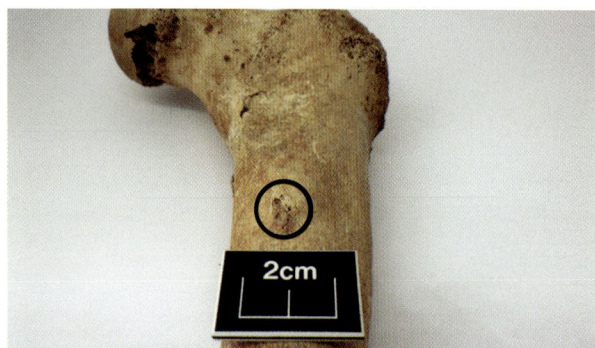

Figure 13.16 Ossification of vastus medialis of Skelton 424, known as myositis ossificans

All three of the skeletons suffered from some form of dental disease (Fig. 13.15). Dental plaque concretions (calculus) were the most common dental condition observed on the dentitions of all individuals analysed. Periodontal disease was present in two individuals. Two dental anomalies were seen in two third molars – impaction and an extra cusp. Dental enamel hypoplasia was seen in two skeletons and was represented as linear and pitting defects, suggesting possible periods of severe stress, such as episodes of malnutrition or disease, during the first seven years their childhood.

The individual buried in the chariot (Sk 424) was a male aged 46 years+ and was of average height for the period. As indicated by his advanced spinal joint disease in many spinal and some extraspinal joints, as well as the number of teeth lost ante-mortem, this individual represented the oldest individual. During life he sustained a number of traumatic lesions such as spondylolysis (fracture) of the fifth lumbar vertebra. This suggested that he was physically active and that he possibly engaged in repeated anterior-posterior bending and lifting of the lower back. He also suffered from trauma to the soft tissues of his thigh, as represented by myositis ossificans traumatica on his left femur and a broken rib that was healing at the time of death (Fig. 13.16). He suffered from possible osteoporosis, as demonstrated by the reduction of weight in bones relative to other bones of the same size. Indeed, rib fractures in older men with osteoporosis account for 24% (126/522) of all incident non-spine fractures in a clinical study conducted by Barrett-Connor *et al.* (2010), thus suggesting a possible

link between the systemic pathology and the traumatic lesion in this individual.

Skeleton 303 was a young adult male of average Iron Age height who showed evidence for early childhood stress in the form of dental enamel hypoplasia. He also suffered from chronic sinusitis at the time of death. He had sustained several traumatic lesions which were represented by two ante-mortem nasal fractures and healed blunt force trauma on the frontal bone (Fig. 13.17). Nasal fractures are relatively common in the face due to their prominent position and their thinness (Brickley and Smith 2006). They are often interpreted as resulting from interpersonal violence, although they may just represent accidents such as falling. In Skeleton 303, the presence of the nasal fractures in combination with a possible blunt force trauma on the frontal bone may suggest less mundane circumstances of trauma and possibly the use of a weapon, although no evidence for specific weapon-related lesions could be identified. Whether these injuries resulted from activities such as being a warrior cannot be confirmed.

Skeleton 274 was a young adult female of below average height. She had suffered from early childhood stress, observed in the form of cribra orbitalia in her orbits and dental enamel hypoplasia in her teeth. She had a congenital anomaly called spina bifida occulta, which meant that the back of her tail bone was open, though the nerves would have been covered in soft tissue (Fig. 13.18).

The osteological analysis has given further insight into the East Yorkshire Iron Age population enabling our narrative regarding the many conditions that affected life to be expanded.

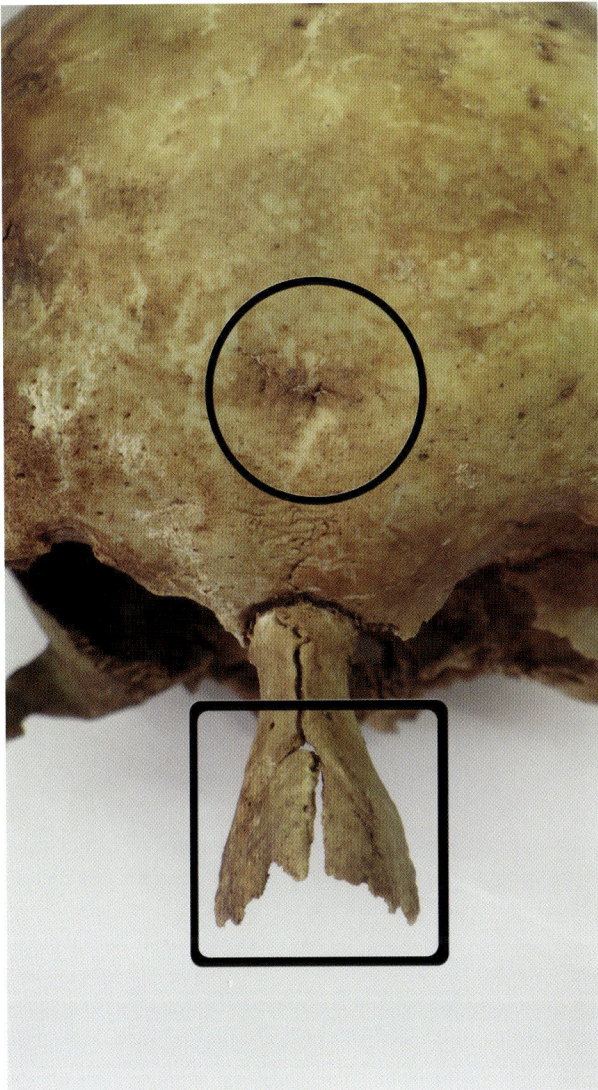

Figure 13.17 Fractured nasal bones (squared) and possible blunt force trauma in the frontal bone (circled) of Skeleton 303

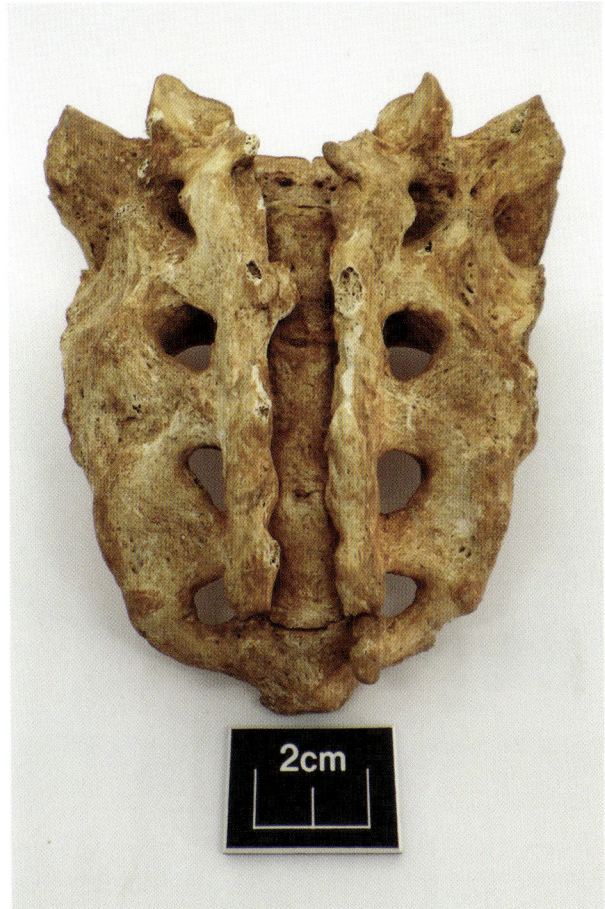

Figure 13.18 Spina bifida occulta in the sacrum of Skeleton 274

14

The animal bone from Burnby Lane and The Mile

Jane Richardson

Burnby Lane

Approximately 1194 bone fragments and one oyster shell were recovered from hand-excavated features and subsequent soil sampling. Non-repeatable diagnostic bone zones were recorded for partial skeletons, with the remaining disarticulated assemblage recorded in its entirety. All records are held in an SQL database. Unstratified bones, and tiny fragments of bone recovered from sample retents, were scanned but otherwise not recorded. Bone zones were identified to taxa wherever possible, although lower-order categories (e.g. cattle-size) were also used.

Only 314 bone fragments were recognised as diagnostic bone zones (*c.* 26% of the assemblage) and these are tabulated below by phase (Table 14.1). The majority represents domestic animals (cattle, horse, sheep/goat, pig and chicken) but red deer, roe deer and an unidentified small mammal are also represented. Further taxa represented only by non-diagnostic zones are dog and an unidentified bird. Marine resources are poorly represented with only one oyster shell. No fish bones were noted.

Table 14.1 Diagnostic bone zones by phase

Taxon/Phase	3	4	5	6	Not phased
Cattle	109/95	2	1	–	21
Horse	110/108	2	–	1	–
Sheep/goat	5	–	–	2	32/31
Pig	10/5	–	–	–	–
Red deer	1	–	–	–	–
Roe deer	–	–	–	1	–
Cattle-size	6	–	–	1	1
Small mammal	1	–	–	–	–
Chicken	–	–	8/8	–	–
Total	273	4	9	5	23

Figures in *italics* refer to zones from partial skeletons

The majority of deposits containing animal have been assigned to one of four phases: 3, Iron Age; 4, Roman; 5, Anglian; and 6, medieval. The bones that remain unphased are not considered further, with the exception of a partial skeleton.

Condition and treatment

The assemblage is fragmented, with the disarticulated bone typically eroded and often porous in condition. The skeletons recovered are usually better preserved but generally burial conditions were not optimal for bone survival. The degraded and porous nature of bone surfaces may explain the absence of any observed cut marks and the very low proportion of gnawed bones (0.4%). Burnt bones were more common (2%) but still rare, although the frequency of cremated bones (burnt white) was noticeably higher from the retents than from hand-excavated deposits, presumably due to improved visibility within processed retents.

Disarticulated assemblage

Once the partial skeletons are excluded, the remaining disarticulated bones are too few to warrant further study (67 zones from disarticulated bones compared to 247 zones from the skeletons – see Table 14.1). Certainly, no interpretations relating to animal husbandry or diet are possible given the size of the assemblage and the broad timeframe represented. Instead, only the articulated remains are considered below.

Animal burials

Seven partial skeletons were recovered during the excavations at Burnby Lane, five animals from Iron Age contexts, one from an Anglian grave, and one currently unphased (Table 14.2).

Perhaps of greatest significance were the two horse skeletons (392 and 393) buried in Barrow 85. The animals were laid on opposing sides (393 on its right side, 392 on its left), so that they faced each other, with their legs bent (Fig. 4.85). Horse 393 was a male based on the presence of canine teeth (typically reduced or absent in females) but unfortunately horse 392 was missing the front of its mandible and skull so its sex was not determined. For both animals, the heads were lifted as a block and have not been dismantled. This has precluded the detailed analysis of age based on dental wear although both individuals had fully erupted adult dentition and all the bones are osteologically mature. No evidence for any bit wear was apparent on the anterior side of the first cheek teeth (second premolar). It is clear from the range of bones represented that the animals were entire when placed in the ground, but as both crania were heavily fragmented, death by pole-axing was not determined.

The male (393) had bony changes to his right distal femur with lipping above the epiphyseal line both distally and medially. One of the Kirkburn cart burial horses also showed bony changes (Legge 1991, 144) that might indicate age and/or its use as a traction animal. Certainly, it is safe to assume that the two Pocklington animals represent the draught animals used to pull the cart. The chariot found relatively recently in West Yorkshire was also intended to be pulled by two animals, although in this case, no horses were interred with the vehicle (Boyle *et al.* 2007, 126–9).

Measurable bones (a radius and metacarpal) were only recovered from the male (393). These indicate an animal of approximately 1.29m at the withers (just under 13 hands) using Kiesewalter's factors (1888 in von den Driesch and Boessneck 1974). This compares to mean values of 1.34m and 1.42m for the two horses from the cart burial at Kirkburn. Single specimens of a metacarpal and metatarsal from the Iron Age 'King's Barrow' at Arras indicate a smaller horse (or horses), at 1.32m for the former and 1.30m for the latter (Stead

1991a, 59). Based on their heights, all these horses were in fact ponies.

The other Iron Age animal burials include two poorly preserved cattle skeletons (16627 and 16349) from features presumed to have been dug with the intention of their burial. The former represents a young adult animal based on fusion and dental wear data, while the latter was 'senile' (after Halstead 1985) based on its dental wear. They may represent deposition of animals imbued with symbolic meaning or alternatively the hygienic disposal of unwanted carcasses.

A partial pig skeleton (16372) was recovered from the primary burial [16195] of Barrow 38 and is likely to represent a food offering to accompany the departed (here an adult female). It represents the only recovered example of such an offering from this Iron Age cemetery (Stephens and Ware 2019, 24–5). The use of a juvenile animal (distal humerus and proximal radius only just fusing) may be significant as it is likely to represent high-value meat. Also significant is the choice of left forelimb bones and only bones from the left side of the skull. The same choices (left forelimb and skull) have been commonly noted from barrows at Rudston, with further examples from Burton Fleming (Legge 1991, 140–1, 142), Wetwang (Dent 1984, 27) and Pocklington (Moore 2018), and two more from recently excavated barrows near Melton (Richardson 2019).

Chicken bones (16967) were found in association with an adult inhumation (SK 110 – a later insertion into Barrow 64) that is presumed to be Anglian in date (but could be Roman). This deposit is also assumed to be food offering. Such a phenomenon has been noted elsewhere for the Iron Age (Morris 2008, 87) and Roman period graves (Richardson 2013, 236).

The final animal, a probable sheep, was recovered from pit [449] belonging to the Roman phase, and cut into

Table 14.2 Partial skeletons

Phase	Context	Feature	Taxa	Description
3	392	Barrow 85	Horse	Adult pony. Sex unknown as front of jaw absent. 54 non-repeatable zones present
3	393	Barrow 85	Horse	Adult pony. Male based on presence of canines. 54 non-repeatable zones present; height *c.* 1.29m
3	16349	Pit 16348	Cattle	Senile cattle skeleton (after Halstead 1985); 28 non-repeatable zones present
3	16627	Pit 16628	Cattle	Young adult cattle skeleton (after Halstead 1985), while unfused distal radii suggest an animal 3½–4 years or younger (after Silver 1969); 67 non-repeatable zones present
3	16372	Barrow 38	Pig	Elements of juvenile pig skeleton, largely left forelimb but also skull/tooth fragments; 5 non-repeatable zones present
5	16967	Grave in Barrow 64	Chicken	Incomplete chicken skeleton (part of right wing and left and right leg and vertebrae); 8 non-repeatable zones present
0	447/448	Pit 449	Sheep	Sheep/goat, most likely sheep based on metatarsal characteristics; 31 non-repeatable zones present; Age *c.* 3–4 years after Payne (1973)

Boundary Ditch K. The feature is likely to have been cut for the purpose of burying this animal and a ritual purpose cannot be discounted.

Conclusions

The animal bone assemblage from this site is significant due to the high proportion of animal skeletons recovered, particularly when compared to the background 'noise' of disarticulated bone fragments. Two ponies (one clearly male) were buried with their cart and owner, presumably slaughtered specifically to complete this significant and highly structured deposit. The cattle and sheep skeletons are harder to interpret as they may represent the prosaic disposal of diseased animals or unwanted carcasses but they may equally reflect the ritualised disposal of valuable assets within this extensive funerary landscape. Certainly the pig and chicken bones were interred as part of the burial rituals and are likely to be the food used by the deceased as they travelled into the afterlife.

The Mile

The pair of horses (406 and 408) from The Mile are noteworthy due to the position they had been placed in, upright as if ready to pull the chariot and their male companion forwards on his next journey. How this might have been achieved is unclear, but pole-axing the animals *in situ* is certainly one option that would have avoided the manhandling of heavy carcasses. Unfortunately, neither horse head survived to confirm this means of slaughter; they had most likely been removed by the plough. It was also impossible to identify whether male or female animals were chosen based on the presence (likely male) or absence (likely female) of canine teeth. In contrast, the characteristics of the *tuberculum pubicum* for horse 406 suggest a female, while the less complete pelvis for horse 408 appears less 'female' than 406 although the *tuberculum pubicum* is not so well developed as to be definitively male (a stallion); a gelding is possible.

Apart from their heads, the two horse skeletons from the barrow are entire, with all limb bones in excellent condition apart from some bone loss on the extremities of the hooves. This allowed a number of bones to be measured for each animal, providing height ranges between 1.20–1.26m for horse 406 and 1.21–1.25m for horse 408 using Kiesewalter's factors (1888 in von den Driesch and Boessneck 1974). These measurements suggest a well-matched pair, both in the region of 12 hands.

Horse 408 displays very slight dense osteophytes around the proximal articular surface of a metatarsal that might indicate the early signs of spavin, while horse 406 reveals some slight lipping to both scapula joints, likely infection (pitted, porous bone growth) to the neck of the left scapula and a possible penetrating injury to the proximal end of the right scapula. A 'squared' hole, 13mm across, is evident, surrounded by pitted new bone indicative of some healing. While a prosaic explanation for this damage could be given, it is tempting, given its burial context, to at least raise the possibility of a battle injury.

The pigs

The chariot burial from The Mile also contained a large collection of pig bones. Clear selection is indicated in favouring forelimbs (all forelimb bones are represented) and excluding any hindlimbs. There is some apparent preference towards left elements but right elements are also present. The presence of some paired pig bones suggests further choices were made. For nearly all elements, a younger animal is represented and, based on condition and size, these are probably all from the same animal. If correct, this individual was just under a year (based on fusion of the second phalange and only the partial eruption of the second molar). The other pigs represented are likely to have been between one and two years old at death (the proximal radii are fused, while the metacarpals are not – after Silver 1969). Of the 12 tusks (many of them loose), 11 are male and one female, suggesting predominantly male animals were chosen. Butchery marks to a number of scapulae and humerii indicate dismembering of shoulder and elbow joints. Similar deposits (left and right forelimbs and skull bones) have also been noted from barrow deposits at Garton Station, Kirkburn (Legge 1991, 142) and Arras (Giles *et al.* 2019, 53–5).

Summary of carbonised plant macrofossils and charcoal from Iron Age contexts at Burnby Lane

Diane Alldritt

A total of 770 environmental samples ('GBA' *sensu* Dobney *et al.* 1992), taken from two phases of excavation at Burnby Lane (MAP site codes: 5.19.15 and 5.37.12, the southern and northern fields respectively), were fully analysed for carbonised plant microfossils and charcoal. The samples dated from all periods of activity represented at the site.

Previous archaeobotanical research on the Arras culture is scarce, with many of the square barrow sites unfortunately excavated at a time before environmental archaeology was widely practised. Burnt plant remains from Iron Age deposits at Wetwang Slack have previously been reported on (Brewster 1980; Dent 1984).

The excavations at Pocklington have enabled a modern systematic programme of environmental sampling to be carried out, and as such have provided a unique opportunity to examine a plant assemblage associated with the Arras culture. Feasting events and other activity accompanying burial practices may be detectable from analysis of the cereal grain and other plant remains.

Methods

Bulk environmental samples were processed by MAP using a Siraf-style water flotation system (French 1971). Sample volumes ranged from 10 to 40 litres according to the nature of the sampled deposits. The resultant 'flot' from each sample was dried before examination under a low-powered binocular microscope typically at ×10–×20 magnifications. All identified plant remains including charcoal were removed and bagged separately by type.

Wood charcoal was examined using a high-powered Vickers M10 metallurgical microscope at magnifications up to ×200. The reference photographs of Schweingruber (1990) were consulted for charcoal identification. Plant nomenclature utilised in the text follows Stace (1997) for all vascular plants apart from cereals, which follow Zohary

and Hopf (2000). The term 'seed' is used in the broadest sense in the text to include achenes, nutlets and so forth.

Results

The environmental samples produced a mixed sample of carbonised plant material consisting of charcoal, cereal grain, weed seeds and occasional hazel nutshell, with the samples from the second phase of excavation (5.19.15) proving the most consistently abundant, with from <2.5ml up to 25ml of carbonised remains present (Table 15.1). The samples from the 5.37.12 phase, in contrast, produced consistently low amounts, with many sterile samples recorded. However, Pit 15456 in the ditch on the eastern side of Barrow 15 proved a notable exception to this with recovery of 250ml of charcoal, mostly found to be oak, suggesting a fire pit in this location. Preservation of both charcoal and cereal grain was generally very good from 5.19.15, with some very well-preserved cereal grain recorded in the pit, barrow and grave features, whilst the grain from 5.37.12 tended to be more degraded with a higher amount of indeterminate material found, suggesting perhaps mixed/residual remains or trampled material from nearby burning activity. Charcoal fragments from both phases of work consisted of pieces 1.0cm to 3.0cm in size amongst crushed detritus.

Modern material was fairly scarce with from 2.5ml up to 15ml of root detritus, and occasional modern seeds and earthworm egg capsules found, indicating that a degree of bioturbation was possible. However, almost all of the samples from both phases produced highly crushed fragments of coal and clinker, as well as often quite large amounts of snail shell, both burrowing and non-burrowing types, suggesting that there was possibility of biological movement through some of the deposits, and possibly accounting for the presence of some of the more degraded cereal grain found in trace amounts in earlier features.

Table 15.1 Summary of carbonised plant remains from Burnby Lane

Context	15115	15186	15226	15301	15333	15340	15418	15474	15456	15592	15613	15643	15758	15813	15928	15992
Site code 5-37-12: samples	54	59	62	69	78	87	115	119	116	148	150	168	202	213	255	269
Barrow & grave features	B1 ditch	B3 grave	ditch	B7 ditch	enc ditch	isol burial	B15 NE ditch	B13 grave	pit B15 E ditch	B14 W	B14 N ditch	B19 N ditch	B20 E ditch	pit	deposit	B30 ditch
Total sample vol (l)	20	40	20	20	20	20	20	20	20	20	20	20	20	20	20	20
Carbonised cereal grain																
Bread wheat	3	1	–	–	1	1	4	–	–	–	1	–	1	1	–	–
Barley: indet.	2	2	2	1	1	–	1	–	–	1	–	3	1	–	–	–
Indet. grain	–	–	–	2	–	–	–	1	–	3	–	–	1	–	–	–
Total grain	5	3	2	3	2	1	5	1	–	4	1	–	3	–	–	–
Other cultivars: peas, beans	–	–	–	–	–	1 (1sp.)	–	1 (1sp.)	1 (1sp.)	–	1 (1sp.)	–	–	–	–	–
Charcoal																
Oak	–	–	–	–	–	–	–	–	60 (9.27g)	–	–	–	1 (0.05g)	–	–	5 (0.21g)
Alder	–	–	–	–	–	–	–	–	–	–	–	–	–	–	1 (0.23g)	–
Carbonised wild resources																
Hazel nutshell	–	–	–	–	–	–	–	–	–	–	–	–	–	3 (0.09g)	–	–
Cultivated/disturbed ground	–	–	–	–	–	–	–	–	–	–	2 (1sp.)	–	–	–	–	–

Context	16011	16091	16162	16178	16187	16201	16274	16277	16284	16286	16410
Site code 5-37-12: samples	262	293294	322	339	342	405	333	334,335	360	361	441
Barrow & grave features	pit	grave	B32 grave	ditch	B38 ditch	B ditch	B ditch	grave	grave	B33 org	B ditch
Total sample vol (l)	10	40	20	20	20	20	20	30	20	40	20
Carbonised cereal grain											
Oat	–	–	1	–	–	–	–	–	–	–	–
Bread wheat	–	–	–	1	–	–	1	–	–	–	1
Rye	–	–	–	–	1	–	–	–	–	–	–
Barley: hulled	–	–	–	–	–	1	–	–	–	–	–

(Continued)

Table 15.1 (Continued)

Context	16011	16091	16162	16178	16187	16201	16274	16277	16284	16286	16410
Site code: 5-37-12: samples	262	293294	322	339	342	405	333	334,335	360	361	441
Barrow & grave features	pit	grave	B32 grave	ditch	B38 ditch	B ditch	B ditch	grave	grave	B33 org	B ditch
Total sample vol (l)	10	40	20	20	20	20	20	30	20	40	20
Barley: indet.	–	1	1	–	–	–	–	–	–	–	–
Indet. grain	–	–	–	–	–	–	–	–	–	–	2
Total grain	–	**1**	**2**	**1**	**1**	**1**	**1**	–	–	–	**3**
Charcoal											
Oak	10 (6.86g)	10 (0.76g)	1 (0.20g)	–	–	–	–	7 (0.56g)	3 (0.45g)	10 (0.27g)	–

Context	16419	16437	16452	16510	16550	16574	16620	16630	16651	16716
Site code: 5-37-12: samples	423	427	412	464	450	505	538	596	600	609
Barrow & grave features	B ditch	B42 S	B42 grave	B45 N	pit B37	B48 SE	B50 E ditch	pit	PH	ditch
Total sample vol (l)	20	30	30	20	20	5	20	10	10	20
Carbonised cereal grain										
Bread wheat	–	–	–	–	–	1	–	–	–	–
Barley: hulled	–	–	–	–	1	–	–	–	–	–
Indet. grain	–	–	–	–	–	–	–	–	2	2
Total grain	–	–	–	–	**1**	–	–	–	**2**	**2**
Charcoal										
Oak	7 (1.31g)	10 (0.83g)	10 (0.94g)	5 (0.10g)	–	–	–	2 (0.02g)	–	–
Hazel	–	–	–	–	–	–	1 (0.03g)	–	–	–

(Continued)

Table 15.1 Summary of carbonised plant remains from Burnby Lane (Continued)

Context	16729	16928	16947	17162	17213	18072	18107	18110	18113	18117	18172	18129	18230	18365	18394	18409	18420
Sitecode: 5-37-12: samples	614	665	662	544	579	707	708	789,790	788	710	809	717	821	879	883	884	888
Barrow & grave features	grave	B ditch	gully	B54	B55	grave	B ditch	B70 grave	grave silt	ditch	box	ditch	ditch	ditch seg	ditch H	pit	ditch
Total sample vol (l)	20	20	10	12	10	10	20	30	20	10	20	20	20	10	10	10	10
Carbonised cereal grain																	
Bread wheat	–	–	–	1	1	–	–	–	–	–	3	–	1	–	–	–	–
Spelt wheat	–	1	–	–	–	–	1	–	–	–	–	–	1	–	–	–	–
Barley: hulled	1	–	–	1	–	–	1	–	–	–	–	–	–	–	–	–	–
Barley: indet.	–	–	–	–	–	–	–	–	–	1	–	–	1	–	1	–	–
Indet. grain	–	–	–	–	–	–	–	–	–	–	–	–	–	–	–	1	3
Total grain	**1**	**1**	–	**2**	**1**	–	**2**	–	–	**1**	**3**	–	**3**	–	**1**	**1**	**3**
Charcoal																	
Oak	–	–	1 (0.15g)	–	1 (0.02g)	–	–	9 (0.19g)	10 (1.34g)	–	–	–	–	1 (0.09g)	–	–	–
Alder	–	–	–	–	–	–	–	–	–	–	–	1 (0.15g)	–	–	–	–	–
Birch	–	–	–	–	–	2 (0.35g)	–	–	–	–	–	–	–	–	–	–	–

Context	8	11	14	21	29	33	37	26	46	48	54	59	65	109,111,113	150	154
site code: 5-19-15: samples	1	3	2	4	15	28	11	5	12	13	14	30	18	25,26,27	34	32
Pit & posthole features	grave	ditch	grave	postpipe	grave	B81 ringd	B79 ditch	PH	pit	pit	pit upper	B79 slot	grave [067]	B81 ditch	curvilinear	E-W linear
Total sample volume (l)	20	20	20	10	20	20	20	10	20	10	10	20	10	60	20	20
Carbonised cereal grain																
Oat	–	–	–	–	–	–	–	–	–	–	–	1	–	2	9	–
Bread wheat	4	–	–	2	–	–	–	–	4	–	–	1	1	5	–	–
Rye	22	11	33	16	31	7	20	17	8	4	18	16	28	53	30	20
Barley: Indet.	–	–	–	–	–	–	–	–	–	3	2	–	1	–	–	–
Indet. Grain	3	2	29	8	11	5	–	12	–	1	2	10	18	16	15	9
Total grain	29	13	62	26	42	12	20	29	12	8	22	28	48	76	54	29

(Continued)

Table 15.1 (Continued)

Context	8	11	14	21	29	33	37	26	46	48	54	59	65	109,111,113	150	154
site code: 5-19-15: samples	1	3	2	4	15	28	11	5	12	13	14	30	18	25,26,27	34	32
Pit & posthole features	grave	ditch	grave	postpipe	grave	B81 ringd	B79 ditch	PH	pit	pit	pit upper	B79 slot	grave [067]	B81 ditch	curvilinear	E-W linear
Total sample volume (l)	20	20	20	10	20	20	20	10	20	10	10	20	10	60	20	20
Other cultivars: peas, beans	–	–	–	–	–	–	–	–	–	–	–	–	–	1 (1sp.)	–	–
Charcoal																
Oak	–	–	1 (0.05g)	–	–	–	–	–	–	–	–	–	–	–	–	–
Alder	–	–	–	–	–	–	1 (0.04g)	1 (0.04g)	–	–	–	–	–	–	–	–
Conifer	–	–	1 (0.04g)	–	–	–	–	–	–	–	–	–	–	–	–	–
Carbonised weeds																
Cultivated/disturbed ground	–	–	1 (1sp.)	1 (1sp.)	–	–	–	–	–	–	–	–	–	–	–	–
Grassland	–	–	–	–	–	–	–	–	–	–	–	1 (1sp.)	–	–	–	–
Woods and hedgerows	–	–	2 (2sp.)	–	1 (1sp.)	–	–	–	–	–	–	–	–	–	–	–

Context	189	200	202	260	304,306	313	391	395	451
site code: 5-19-15: samples	36	41	42	83	68,69	71	125,126,127,128,129	107,122	101
Pit & posthole features	small pit	pit	pit	pit	B78 N	N-SE ditch	W horse	wheel	fire pit
Total sample volume (l)	10	10	10	20	40	20	150	45	30
Carbonised cereal grain									
Oat	–	1	3	–	–	4	2	–	–
Bread wheat	–	1	–	–	–	–	–	–	–
Rye	12	2	–	–	16	5	–	3	2
Barley: Indet.	–	–	–	1	–	3	–	–	–
Indet. Grain	12	–	6	–	7	7	16	3	3
Total grain	**24**	**4**	**9**	**1**	**23**	**19**	**18**	**6**	**5**
Charcoal									
Oak	–	–	–	7 (1.24g)	–	–	–	–	–
Hazel	–	–	–	–	–	–	–	–	7 (2.40g)

Burnby Lane north field: Site 5.37.12

Pit and posthole features

Two of the Iron Age pits and one posthole produced carbonised remains, consisting of negligible cereal grain content with the majority of burnt material found to be charcoal.

Pit 15456 from the eastern ditch of Barrow 15 contained the largest concentration of charcoal across the site as a whole, with an abundant quantity of *Quercus* (oak) charcoal in fragment sizes 2.0–3.0cm in amongst crushed charred detritus. This would have represented a significant fire pit during its use, and is interesting in terms of location, as it may have been associated with the burial ceremony in B15 or could represent later activity. Pit fill 16630 (associated with the Oval Ring Gully) contained oak charcoal but in much smaller amounts.

Trace amounts of indeterminate cereal grain were found in the two fills (16650 and 11651) of Posthole 16652, which was associated with the Oval Ring Gully; these were probably swept in from nearby burning or are otherwise intrusive.

Barrow and grave features

Thirty-five of the contexts associated with barrow and grave deposits produced carbonised plant material, mainly found to be small amounts of charcoal and cereal grain.

The cereal grain recovered from the barrow and grave deposits was mainly found to be *Triticum aestivum* (bread wheat), with small amounts of *T. spelta* (spelt wheat) and *Hordeum vulgare* var. *vulgare* (six-row hulled barley), together with rare *Avena* sp. (oat) grains. Whilst a few stray grains were found in various grave features, for instance 15186 (B3), 15474 (B13) and 16162 (B32), and probably intrusive from nearby burning activity, the presence of charred grain in some of the barrow ditch features does suggest a degree of cooking or cereal-drying activity occurring in the vicinity, albeit some of this material may be residual. The samples from 15301 (primary fill, south-west corner of B7), 15613 (primary fill of northern ditch of B14) and 15758 (primary fill of eastern ditch of B20), contained traces of bread wheat cereal along with poorly preserved indeterminate material that was probably intrusive. Stray grains of bread wheat were also recovered from 15577 and 15582 (primary fills of B17 western ditch and south-west corner respectively), 15616 (primary fill of east ditch of B14), 16178 (primary fill of B38 south-east corner), 16412 (fill of B44 south-west corner), 16428 (primary fill of B42 north-east corner), 16574 (primary fill of south-east corner of B48) and 17160 (fill of south-west corner of B54). Context 18230 (the fill of the eastern ditch of B72), contained single grains of bread wheat, spelt wheat and degraded barley.

The primary fill (15418) of the north-eastern corner ditch of B15 produced slightly better-preserved grain, with bread wheat and barley present, but again only in small amounts, whilst context 15434 (the primary fill of B15's north-west corner) produced stray degraded and vesicular grains which could not be identified. An indeterminate grain was found in the fill (15083) of flat grave 15084. These remains have probably all found their way into the barrow ditch from burning occurring nearby, perhaps wind-blown or trampled, or deposited in the ditches as part of cooking waste.

Two *Pisum sativum* (garden pea) found in the upper fill (15474) of the central grave of B13 and the primary fill (15613) of the northern ditch of B14 could also be waste from cooking events. Single specimens of degraded and rubbed *Secale cereale* (rye) from the primary fill (16187) of B38's western ditch and the fill (16408) of B11's southern ditch were probably intrusive from later activity. Interestingly, a small amount of spelt wheat was found in the fill (16928) suggesting the presence of this type of cereal as well as bread wheat.

Charcoal formed a larger component of the barrow and grave samples and is most likely to be fuel waste, with the majority consisting of *Quercus* (oak) fragments. These were found in two contexts from B30 (15982 – north-east corner and 15992 – primary fill of the western ditch), the primary fills (16437) of B42's southern ditch (16437), B45's northern ditch (16510) and the primary fill of B72's northern ditch (18129), plus the fills of the central graves of B41, B42 and B70 (16277, 16452 and 18110 respectively) and flat graves 16093 and 16287 (16091 and 16284 respectively). A single poorly preserved fragment of hazel charcoal was recovered from the primary fill (16620) of B50's western ditch. The charcoal assemblage from the barrows probably represents fuel waste from nearby fires or hearths, sometimes but not always found in association with carbonised cereal grain, suggesting oak being used for cooking and heating, and possibly associated with burial rituals such as feasting.

DITCHES

A single context from a ditch – 16947, the fill of the south-eastern terminal of the Oval Ring Gully – yielded a small amount of oak charcoal, suggesting it was on the periphery of any burning activity, or kept clean of burnt waste so that only a trace amount found its way into the feature.

Burnby Lane south field: Site 5.19.15

Pit 261

The fill of Pit 261 (260) contained an indeterminate barley grain, perhaps from an episode of cooking.

Barrow and grave features

Fourteen samples from barrow, grave and associated features produced large quantities of well-preserved cereal grain together with small amounts of charcoal. Lesser trace quantities of charred material were found in 11 others, mainly consisting of degraded cereal grain plus rye.

Rye was the main type of cereal grain recorded from these features with large amounts found in the ditch fills of B80 (091, 095 and 099), B81 (109, 111 and 113) and lesser quantities in B83 ditch fill 237, and B78 ditch fills 304 and 306. Rye was also found in the deposit (395) surrounding wheel SF 4, around pony 392 and in the fill (041) of probable grave 042. Oat cereal grain was found in B81 ditch fill 115 and around pony 392 and around the wheel spokes (398), whilst bread wheat was found in B81 ditch fill 111. The rye, bread wheat and oat are potentially of great significance, but may represent intrusive material. (Rye and bread wheat grains, respectively from an Anglian grave (fill 029) and a posthole (fill 021), gave 19th-century radiocarbon dates of 154±26 BP (SUERC-77973, GU46869) and 134±23 BP (SUERC-77969, GRU 46868) respectively.

Conclusion

The environmental samples from the two phases of excavation at Burnby Lane, Pocklington contained concentrations of carbonised plant remains consisting of cereal grain, charcoal, weed seeds and other material, producing strong signatures for burning activity in certain key features. There was a marked contrast between the types and volumes of carbonised remains recovered from the two phases, with the first phase being largely sterile apart from some notable exceptions, whilst the second phase consistently produced greater amounts and some quite different cereal grain.

The identification of the cereal grain highlighted the possibility for a temporal difference in the types being cultivated and consumed, with bread wheat and barley from pit and barrow features, and larger amounts of rye (some of late date) from the second excavation phase.

Charcoal recovery from the site was quite low overall apart from the concentration of oak charcoal in a pit that cut the primary fill of the eastern ditch of B15. This concentration could represent a single large event, perhaps related to cooking or feasting. Pocklington has the potential to be of national and international importance to the understanding of the Arras culture but the Anglian phase may also prove to be of significance.

Chronological framework: the radiometric and typological dating evidence from Burnby Lane and The Mile

Derek Hamilton and Sophia Adams

Of the 159 inhumation burials excavated at Burnby Lane, Pocklington, 119 were phased to the Iron Age period and the other 40 to the early medieval period. Of these total burials, samples from 25 Iron Age burials at Burnby Lane and two from The Mile were submitted for radiocarbon dating by accelerator mass spectrometry (AMS). The sampling was carried out for two reasons. The primary aim was to produce a framework in calibrated years for the chronology of the cemeteries. The secondary aim was to inform wider research on material culture of the cemeteries of the Yorkshire Wolds, and beyond, by citing typologically discrete artefacts within a chronometric framework based on the date at which these objects were buried. The results of this study place the burials of Burnby Lane and The Mile within a specific time period in the Iron Age between the 5th and 1st centuries BC. The data also raise questions about the relative dating of characteristic features and finds (particularly brooches) in this Yorkshire Wolds setting in comparison to evidence from continental Europe.

Radiocarbon procedure

All 27 samples consisted of single entities (Ashmore 1999) of human bone or tooth dentine. The samples were submitted to the Scottish Universities Environmental Research Centre (SUERC), East Kilbride where they were pre-treated and measured as described by Dunbar *et al.* (2016). The SUERC lab maintains rigorous internal quality assurance procedures, and participation in international inter-comparisons (Scott 2003; Scott *et al.* 2010) indicate no laboratory offsets; thus validating the measurement precision quoted for the radiocarbon ages. The results are

presented (Table 16.1) as conventional radiocarbon ages (Stuiver and Polach 1977). The probabilities are shown in Figures 16.1, 16.2 and 16.4 and have been calibrated using the internationally agreed terrestrial calibration curve (IntCal20) of Reimer *et al.* (2020) and the OxCal v4.4 computer program (Bronk Ramsey 2009). Simple calibrated results are presented at 95% confidence intervals (unless otherwise noted) in plain text and rounded outward to 10 years. The *italicised* dates presented in the text below are posterior density estimates derived from mathematical modelling of archaeological problems and have been rounded outward to 5 years. These dates can change with the addition of new data or when the modelling choices are varied.

Methodological approach

A Bayesian approach (Buck *et al.* 1996) has been applied to the interpretation of the chronology of the Iron Age burials at Burnby Lane. Although simple calibrated dates are accurate estimates of the radiocarbon age of samples, this is not, usually, what archaeologists really wish to know. It is the dates of the archaeological events represented by those samples that are of interest. For example, the start and end of burial activity is of interest. Additionally, a small number of the burials also contained artefacts whose typology is likely to be chronologically distinct (i.e. brooches). All of these burials were radiocarbon-dated and included in recent work on the chronology of British Iron Age brooches, funded by The Leverhulme Trust. In these cases, the date of the individual is also important as it relates directly to when the associated brooch was removed from circulation.

Table 16.1 Radiocarbon dates on Iron Age burials at Burnby Lane and The Mile

Lab ID	Sk no.	Material dated	δ¹³C (‰)	δ¹⁵N (‰)	C:N	Radiocarbon age (BP)	Calibrated date (95% confidence) cal BC	Modelled date (95% probability) cal BC
			The Mile (5.32.16)					
SUERC-81686	424	Rib; n.s.	−20.6	11.3	3.2	2181±28	370–150	
SUERC-83085	303	Rib; left	−20.5	11.0	3.3	2136±24		
SUERC-93580		Rib; left	−20.6	10.6	3.2	2127±32		
mean Sk 303	T'=0.1; df=1; T'(5%)=3.8 (Ward and Wilson 1978)					2133 ±20	350–50	
SUERC-93579	274	Rib; right	−20.8	11.4	3.2	2096±32	340 cal BC– cal AD 10	
			Burnby Lane (5.37.12)					
SUERC-83069	2	Humerus; right head	−20.8	12.1	3.3	2242±25	390–200	*390–345 (27%) or 315–200 (68%)*
SUERC-96408	8	Femur; right shaft	−19.7	10.3	3.3	2203±29	380–170	*370–170*
SUERC-78038	10	Rib; left	−20.8	11.5	3.3	2295±29	410–230	*405–350 (67%) or 285–205 (28%)*
SUERC-83070	13	Femur; left shaft	−20.8	11.7	3.3	2226±25	390–190	*385–340 (20%) or 320–200 (75%)*
SUERC-81073	20	Humerus; right shaft	−20.7	11.7	3.3	2190±27	370–160	*360–165*
SUERC-79413	21	Femur; right shaft	−20.7	11.4	3.3	2177±37		
SUERC-78039		Rib; n.s.	−20.9	11.5	3.3	2279±29		
mean Sk 21	T'=4.7; df=1; T'(5%)=3.8 (Ward and Wilson 1978)					2241±23	390–200	*390–345 (26%) or 315–200 (69%)*
SUERC-78040	26	Rib; right	−20.5	11.7	3.3	2302±29	410–230	*410–350 (74%) or 285–225 (22%)*
SUERC-83071	27	Rib; n.s.	−20.6	11.9	3.3	2205±25	380–170	*370–175*
SUERC-83075	39	Rib; n.s.	−20.6	11.5	3.2	2226±25	390–190	*385–340 (20%) or 320–200 (75%)*
SUERC-96413	40	Femur; right shaft	−20.6	11.2	3.3	2190±29	370–160	*365–165*
SUERC-83076	45	Femur; left shaft	−20.8	11.9	3.2	2227±25	390–190	*385–340 (20%) or 320–200 (75%)*
SUERC-78041	63	Femur; left shaft	−21.1	11.6	3.5	2082±29	180 cal BC– cal AD 10	*340–320 (4%) or 200–85 (91%)*
SUERC 79417	67	Tibia; left shaft	−20.8	11.3	3.4	2126±37	350–40	*355–285 (24%) or 230–90 (71%)*
SUERC-96415	73	Femur; left shaft	−20.7	11.0	3.2	2076±29	180 cal BC– cal AD 10	*340–325 (3%) or 200–80 (92%)*
SUERC-78042	81	Left leg shaft	−20.3	10.0	3.4	2173±29	360–110	*360–145*
SUERC-83077	82	Rib; n.s.	−20.9	11.6	3.3	2136±25	350–50	*345–310 (11%) or 210–110 (84%)*
SUERC-96429	83	1ˢᵗ molar; lower right	−20.5	12.8	3.4	2136±29	350–50	*350–290 (24%) or 210–95 (71%)*

(Continued)

Table 16.1 Radiocarbon dates on Iron Age burials at Burnby Lane and The Mile (Continued)

Lab ID	Sk no.	Material dated	$\delta^{13}C$ (‰)	$\delta^{15}N$ (‰)	C:N	Radiocarbon age (BP)	Calibrated date (95% confidence) cal BC	Modelled date (95% probability) cal BC
SUERC-96433	85	1st molar; lower left	−20.2	13.0	3.5	2208±29	390–170	*375–335 (11%) or 300–170 (51%)*
SUERC-78046	89	Lower left leg shaft	−21.2	11.1	3.3	2385±29	720–390	*445–390*
SUERC-96434	113	1st/2nd molar	−20.5	12.1	3.2	2239±29	400–200	*390–340 (26%) or 320–200 (69%)*
SUERC-83078	115	Femur; left shaft	−20.6	11.7	3.2	2233±25	390–200	*385–340 (22%) or 320–200 (73%)*
SUERC-83079	119	Rib; n.s.	−20.6	10.6	3.3	2171±25	360–120	*360–275 (50%) or 260–145 (45%)*
SUERC-83080	121	Rib; n.s.	−20.8	11.0	3.3	2243±24	390–200	*390–345 (27%) or 315–205 (68%)*
SUERC-79418	122	?Humerus; right shaft	−20.5	9.5	3.3	2255±37	400–200	*395–340 (32%) or 320–200 (63%)*
SUERC-83081	139	Femur; left shaft	−21.5	10.3	3.2	2362±25	470–390	*445–385*

The methodology used here allows the combination of these different types of information explicitly, to produce realistic estimates of the dates of archaeological interest. The posterior density estimates produced by this modelling are not absolute, rather they are interpretative estimates, which can and will change as further data become available and as other researchers choose to model the existing data from different perspectives. The technique used is a form of Markov Chain Monte Carlo sampling and has been applied using the program OxCal v4.4 (http://c14.arch.ox.ac.uk/). Details of the algorithms employed by this program are available in Bronk Ramsey (1995; 1998; 2001; 2009) or from the online manual. The algorithm used in the models can be derived from the OxCal keywords and bracket structure shown in Figure 16.2.

Samples and models

The extensive nature of the Burnby Lane cemetery provided very few instances where dated Iron Age graves intercut, or even where barrow ditches with existing central burials intercut, and so no observable stratigraphy was incorporated into the chronological model. As such the model for the cemetery is relatively simple and follows a slightly modified version of the bounded phase form presented in detail in Hamilton and Kenney (2015). In Figure 16.2, the burials are presented in two groups – those that are the central grave of a barrow and those that are either off-centre in a barrow or not within an existing ditch.

While the preferred sample for dating the death and burial of an individual was the rib (see Chapter 17 for a discussion on the relationship between skeletal elements and bone collagen turnover rates), this element was most likely to fail to produce high-quality collagen during extraction. Therefore, the radiocarbon dating and modelling for Burnby Lane consists of dates on 15 long bones (e.g. femur, humerus and tibia samples), eight rib samples, and three molars. While the radiocarbon date from a rib sample can be expected to reflect accurately the ¹⁴C atmospheric concentration at the time of death, the long bone samples will reflect the ¹⁴C over a longer period of time, perhaps anywhere from 5 to 20 years, with the turnover period correlating with age (i.e. slower turnover as a person ages). The teeth samples will only reflect the ¹⁴C in the atmosphere during their period of formation, and since the three teeth are molars (1st molars in two cases and a 1st/2nd molar in the third), the date is actually a reflection of the time when the individual was around 7–10 years old, since it is an average of all the extracted collagen in the dentine. This only creates a significant offset for Sk 85 and Sk 113, who were aged 36+ years and 26–35 years at death, respectively. Therefore, the dates of these two individuals should not be considered their date of death, and this is highlighted in Figure 16.1. It is worth noting, however, that neither of these individuals has a radiocarbon date that is near the beginning or end of the dated burial activity at Burnby Lane, and so there is no concern that including them without modification for the few decades of offset between the date and the actual death of the individual will have an adverse effect on the modelled results.

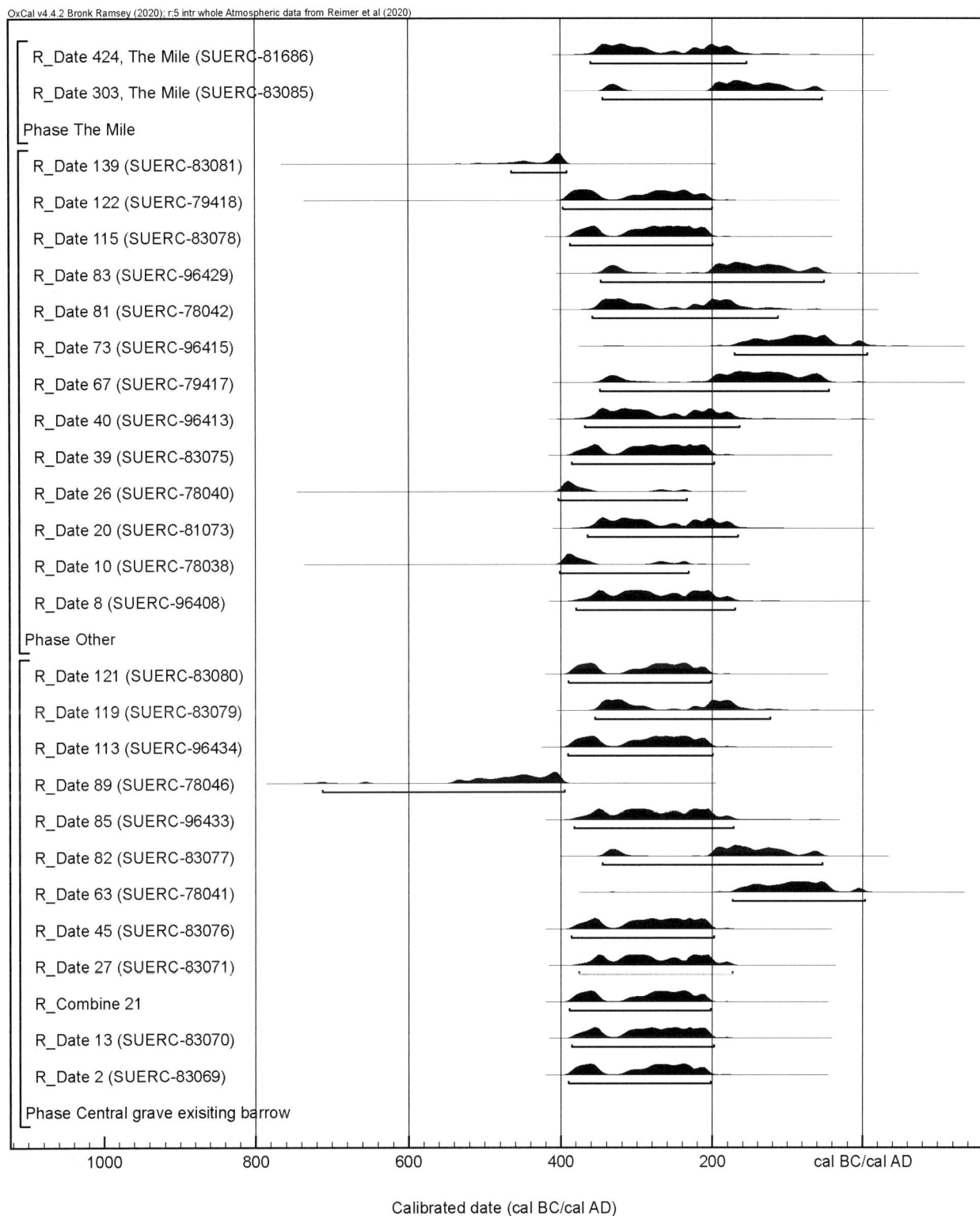

Figure 16.1 Calibrated dates from Burnby Lane and The Mile

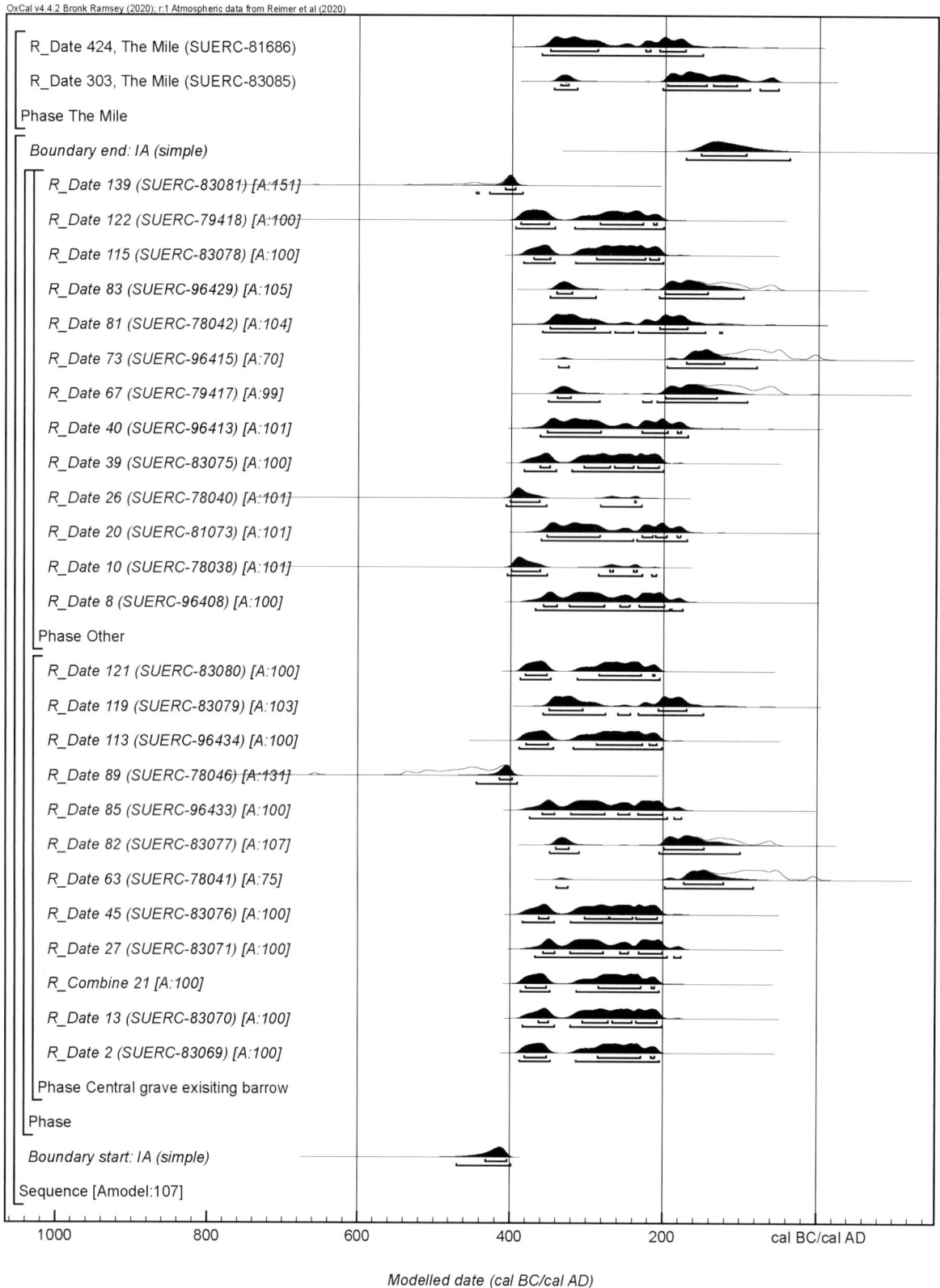

Figure 16.2 Simple chronological model for burial activity at Burnby Lane and the two calibrated dates from The Mile. Each distribution represents the relative probability that an event occurred at some particular time. For each of the radiocarbon measurements two distributions have been plotted, one in outline, which is the result of simple radiocarbon calibration, and a solid one, which is based on the chronological model use. The other distributions correspond to aspects if the model. For example, 'start: IA (simple)' is the estimated date that Iron Age burial began at the site, based on the radiocarbon-dating results. The large square 'brackets' along with the OxCal keywords define the overall model exactly

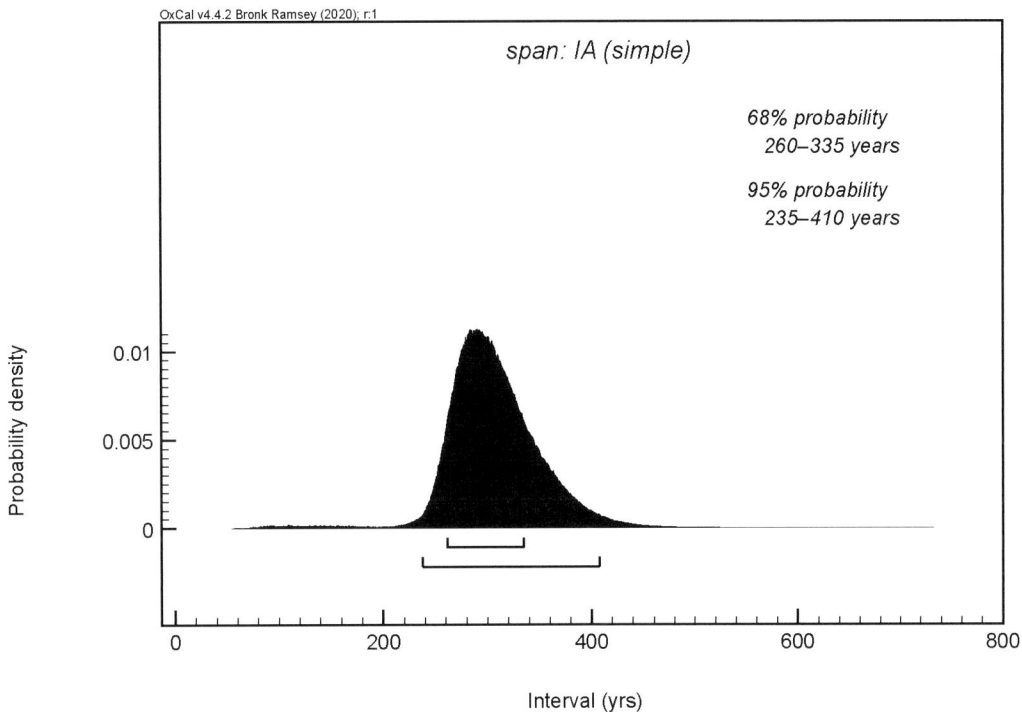

Figure 16.3 Span of the burial activity modelled at Burnby Lane. The span is derived from the modelling shown in Figure 16.2

This initial simple bounded phase model has good agreement (Amodel=107) and estimates burial began in *470–395 cal BC (95% probability*; Fig. 16.2; *start: IA (simple)*), and probably in *435–400 cal BC (68% probability)*. Iron Age burial ended in *175–35 cal BC (95% probability*; Fig. 16.2; *end: IA (simple)*), and probably in *155–95 cal BC (68% probability)*. The overall span of the dated burials is *235–410 years (95% probability*; Fig. 16.3; *span: IA (simple)*), and probably *260–335 years (68% probability)*.

Alternative model

A modification to the simple bounded phase has been made based on DNA data indicating that Sk 82 and Sk 85 are a sister-brother pair (Patterson *et al.* 2022). Both siblings lived to their adult years – the female (Sk 82) was aged to 25+ years and the male (Sk 85) to 36+ years – but Sk 82 was dated from her rib (date near death) and Sk 85 from his 1st molar (date from childhood). Given the age of the sister, she would need to have been born nearly 25 years before her full-brother and died very shortly thereafter for the date from her rib to contain radiocarbon representative of the time before his tooth was forming – since collagen in rib bone turns over at a relatively fast rate the radiocarbon is always reflecting the final few years of a person's life. Therefore, the radiocarbon date for the brother (Sk 85) has been placed earlier than his sister's (Sk 82) radiocarbon date. Furthermore, a conservative uniform prior value of 0–100 years was applied to these two dates to indicate the possible range of time which the

radiocarbon dates from these two skeletal elements will reflect. This range would be the equivalent of the brother being approximately 25 when his sister was born and her living to around 75 years of age.

This alternative model also has good agreement between the radiocarbon dates and the modelled assumption (Amodel=107). This model estimates burial began in *470–395 cal BC (95% probability*; Fig. 16.4; *start: IA (alternative)*), and probably in *435–400 cal BC (68% probability)*. Iron Age burial ended in *175–45 cal BC (95% probability*; Fig. 16.4; *end: IA (alternative)*), and probably in *155–100 cal BC (68% probability)*. The overall span of the dated burials is *235–395 years (95% probability*; Fig. 16.5; *span: IA (alternative)*), and probably *260–330 years (68% probability)*.

The probabilities given for the simple model above are within 10 years of the updated probabilities, and just as likely to be the result of randomness in the modelling process. Therefore, the overall model is not sensitive to the inclusion of the aDNA, skeletal element, and age information. However, this information does have a direct effect on the modelled date for Sk 82 and Sk 85, and so this alternative model is the preferred model choice as it best reflects not only the archaeological information about the cemetery but also the individuals buried within.

Discussion

The radiocarbon dating provides a robust chronological framework within which we might consider some of the

Derek Hamilton and Sophia Adams

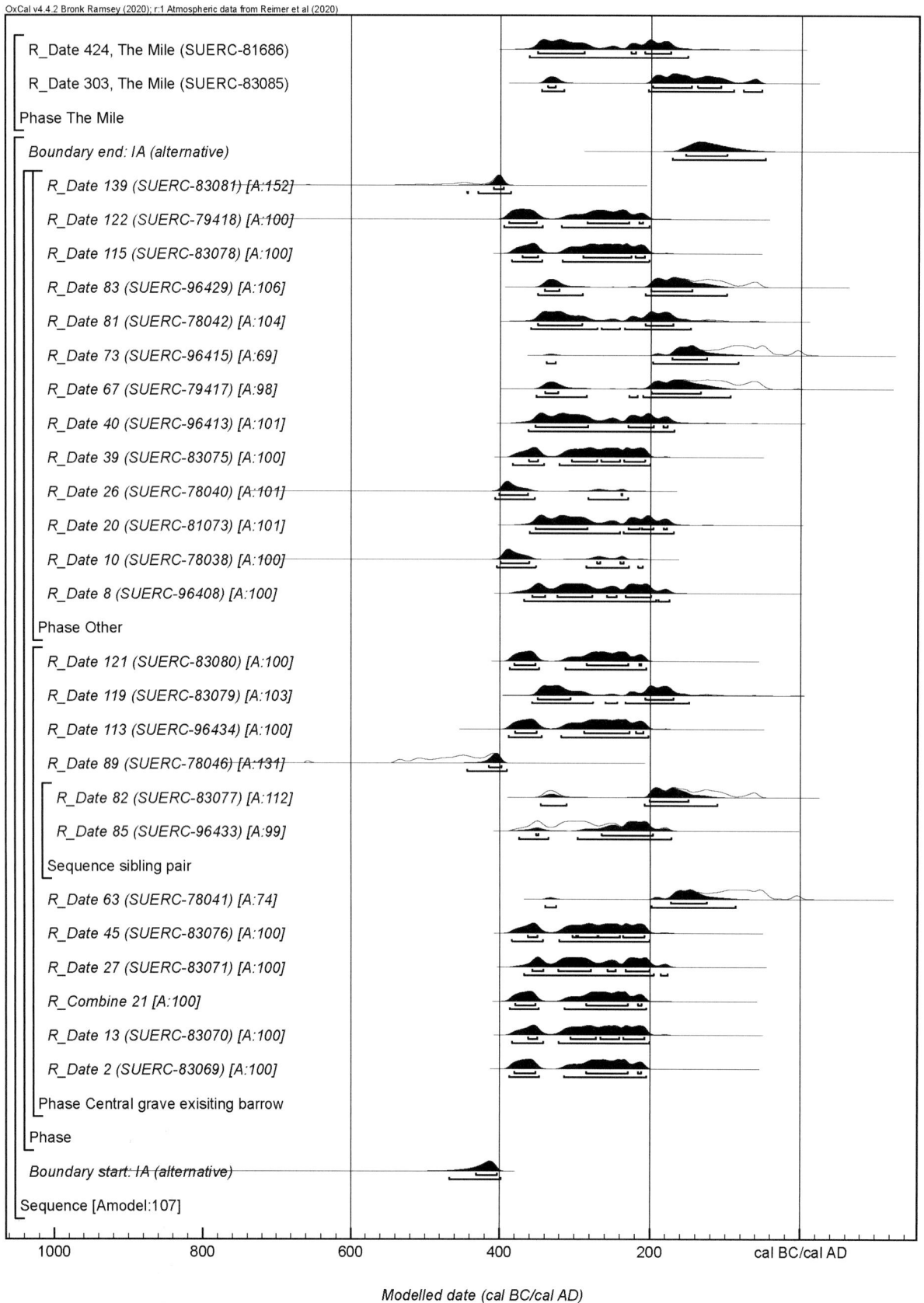

Figure 16.4 Alternative chronological model for burial activity at Burnby Lane and the two calibrated dates from The Mile. The model includes the data from the aDNA analysis, as well as the inferred temporal relationship between the date on the tooth from Sk 85 and the rib of Sk 82. The model structure is as described in Fig. 16.2

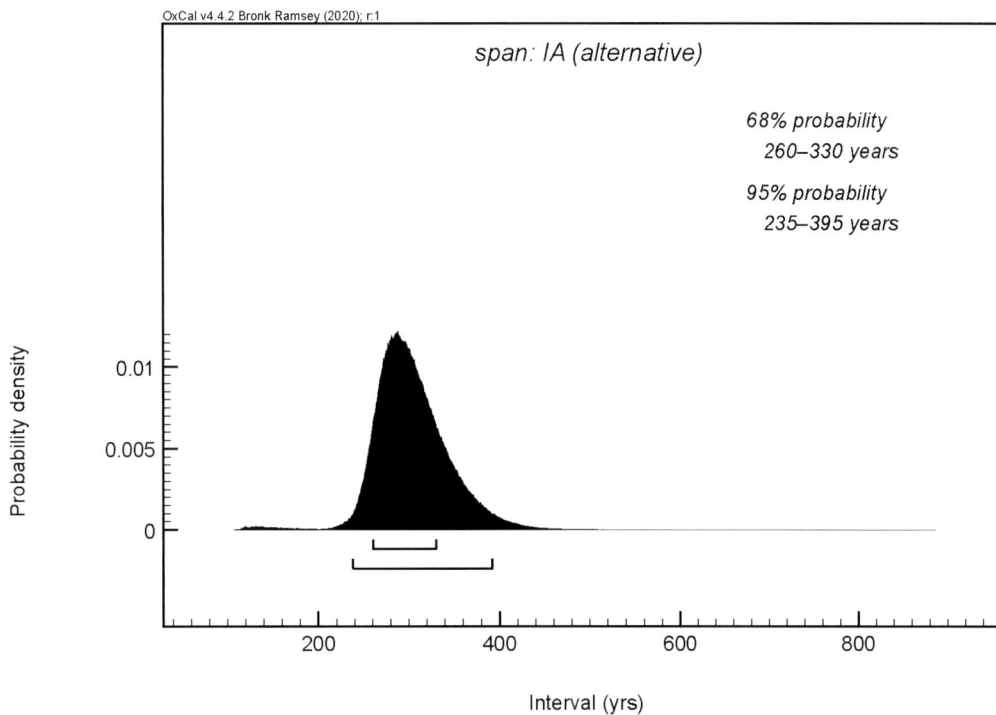

Figure 16.5 Span of the burial activity modelled at Burnby Lane. The span is derived from the modelling shown in Fig. 16.4

artefactual remains and reflect on their use to provide dates for burials. To provide a calendrical date to a burial, these 'relative' dating techniques rely on connections drawn between new finds and previous discoveries. One of the most thoroughly researched areas of typological dating is the study of brooches, both locally and internationally (e.g. Stead 1991a; Marion *et al.* 2008; Adams 2014; Baray 2016). The individual brooches from graves at Burnby Lane (*n* = 12) and the single brooch find from The Mile are described in detail in Chapter 11. On the basis of the typology of these artefacts the main focus of the burials at the Pocklington sites would appear to span the 3rd and into the 2nd century BC (i.e. 300–150 BC). Radiocarbon dating of these and other burials from the site generally supports this interpretation but also adds further clarity and complexity to the chronology of the cemetery (Fig. 16.4). These results have also been incorporated into a larger-scale study of Iron Age brooch chronology in England, Scotland and northern France. The following discussion expands upon these results and their implication for the dating of the Pocklington burials.

The preferred Bayesian model (the alternative model) for the site shows the first burials at Burnby Lane occurred at the end of the 5th century cal BC (*435–400 cal BC at 68% probability*), a little over a century earlier than originally anticipated. The modelled results from two burials have a particular impact on this start date: one with a brooch (Sk 139, SUERC-83081) and one without (Sk 89, SUERC-78046). Both push the results ahead of the known wiggle that spans the period approximately 400–200 cal BC. Of interest here is the fact that these include the earliest type of brooch from the site: a straight bowed brooch of Mark Hull and Christopher Hawkes' Type 2Ab (1987, 139–42) equivalent to John Dent's Flat bow brooches (1982, 44) and Ian Stead's long flat bow brooches Type C (1991a, 81–3) (Adams 2014, 58, 110–11). These brooches develop the form of the early La Tène style brooches with an arched bow and reverted foot (sometimes referred to as Marzabotto brooches or Type 1A). In the 2Ab brooches the bow is now flattened and the reverted foot rests all the way back onto the hip of the bow where it is attached to the bow by wrapping the snout-like end around it. Two such brooches were found at the site but only one of the graves had good enough contextual data and bone preservation for radiocarbon dating: this was an unenclosed flat grave containing an adult in a crouched position (Sk 139).

Dating of the transition from the early arched forms to these flat brooches has been reliant on a comparison with transitions in brooch foot design (the part at the end of the catchplate) in north-west continental Europe, in particular the large-scale cemeteries in France which have vast enough datasets for seriation. In France this marks a change from the La Tène B2 reverted foot resting on the bow to La Tène C1 (La Tène II) where the reverted foot is attached to the bow (e.g. Marion 2004, 59–60; Baray 2016, 138–9, 156–9), thus placing the development of the foot form in the 3rd century BC (Marion *et al.* 2008, 37, fig. 16; Baray 2016, 413–15). However, the long straight, flat bow of the 2Ab brooches in southern Britain with the foot attached so close to the hip is not found in the cemeteries in France. In the latter, the reverted foot is attached further up the bow and the bow still retains a more convex, arched profile. To examine whether we are potentially making an incorrect assumption in the comparison with the continental evidence we can turn to the results of our Bayesian models of brooch types which places the majority of the examples of this type within a broad early 4th- to late 3rd-century cal BC range sitting across the entire period of the wiggle in the calibration curve. The Burnby Lane result stands out against all others, being focused at the start of this period, suggesting either this is the earliest known example of such a brooch type being buried or it may be a statistical outlier. Further research on the *Setting Artefacts Free* project will add clarity to this issue. Therefore, we cannot rule out the possibility that these brooches are contemporary with La Tène C1 in France (*c.* 250–200 BC) but there is also the possibility they are indeed earlier.

The majority of the Pocklington brooches are of involuted type, which have concave bows varying from a shallow wide downward curve in the bow and pin to a short, very deep downward curve. These are Hull and Hawkes Type 2C brooches with sub-types based on the length and depth of the curve (Hull and Hawkes 1987, 156–67; Adams 2014, 59–63, 113–14); Dent's long and short involuted brooches (1982, 44) and Stead's longer and shorter involuted brooches types D–J (Stead 1991a, 83–9). Seven of the radiocarbon-dated burials contained involuted brooches (Sk 13, SUERC-83070; Sk 27, SUERC-83071; Sk 39, SUERC-83075; Sk 45, SUERC-83076; Sk 115, SUERC-83078; Sk 119, SUERC-83079; Sk 121, SUERC-83080). The modelled dates for these graves lie comfortably with the 400 to 200 cal BC range with the exception of Sk 119, an older adult, probably female (46+ years old), who was potentially buried during the 4th–3rd century BC but possibly in the earlier part of the 2nd century BC. Her brooch is a spectacular find of cast copper alloy with a forged iron pin and a foot shaped like a combination of a horse head and a duck (SF 91). The brooch was adorned at the foot and head ends with opaque red glass beads attached by means of tiny pins ending in a bulbous cruciform shape. The application of rounded glass beads to brooches is common during the Middle Iron Age, particularly in Yorkshire, and three other brooches with forms resembling a variation of this brooch have been found in contemporary burials at Danes Graves, Makeshift cemetery and Bell Slack (see Chapter 11; Hull and Hawkes 1987; Stead 1991a). The single brooch from The Mile was found in the grave of a man (Sk 424) buried atop a complete chariot with ponies at the yoke. It is also decorated with a red glass bead, located in the centre of this tiny, moulded cast copper alloy brooch. Again, the bead is held in place with a tiny cruciform-ended rivet which appears to have been hammered at some point to secure the bead further, possibly after it cracked (a crack can be seen across the top of the bead). The Mile burial straddles the 4th, 3rd and 2nd centuries BC. He may have

lived and died around the same time as the woman in Burnby Lane (Sk 119).

There are two brooches from Burnby Lane that were decorated with coral. One, an H-framed brooch inlaid with three small stems of coral (SF 5, Sk 2, Barrow B2, SUERC-83069), is a form found elsewhere in England but with the coral inlay missing (Type 2BH brooches, as described in Chapter 11). This is the only known example from an independently dated archaeological context and has been found to occupy the same time frame as the involuted brooches *c.* 400–200 BC. SK 2 was the burial of an older adult, probably a woman (46+ years), who was also wearing two cast, copper alloy bangles; one on each arm and one decorated with pieces of shell or polished coral. The use of coral as inlay on brooches, bangles and occasionally other copper alloy and iron objects is a phenomenon seen across Europe during the Iron Age. The fashion falls into decline in the 2nd century BC.

The final brooch is considered to be slightly later in style, a Type 6 brooch (SF 84, Sk 82, large square barrow B42, SUERC-83077). This is deemed later based on the way that the foot is now cast as one piece with the bow but retains the open shape of the earlier reverted attached forms. It also has a long mock spring at the head of the brooch similar to other examples from south-west England (see Chapter 11). These are rare and no previous examples have been found decorated with tiny beads of coral. The brooch was located near the right shoulder of the adult woman buried here (aged 25+ years). As mentioned above, the preferred model incorporates information about the aDNA, skeletal element sampled, and age of her and her brother (Sk 85, SUERC-96433), which has led to a refined date for this woman's death and burial (*210–110 cal BC; 84% probability* – Fig. 16.1), though a small amount of the overall probability lies in the latter half of the 4th century cal BC. The Type 6 brooch is conventionally thought to sit at the cusp of the Middle and Late Iron Age periods in England (Adams 2014, 120), which accords well with the modelled 84% probability range, and supports the notion of this being one of the more recent graves from Burnby Lane to be buried with a brooch.

In conclusion, the radiocarbon dates from Pocklington generally support dating via other means, in particular the typological dating of brooches, but they also high-light some issues over the precise date at which these individuals died. We may be looking at the burial of a chariot and later Middle Iron Age-style brooches with attached reverted feet earlier than previously thought for this region. Or these same burials may be more recent in the anticipated date range placing them slightly younger than expected. The results highlight the need to keep inter-rogating the dating and our assumptions and to sample as much material as possible: the more radiocarbon dates we have, the better we can refine the chronology of the cemeteries and associated material culture.

Diet and mobility: stable isotope analyses of the Iron Age population at Burnby Lane and The Mile

Derek Hamilton, Thomas G.B. Fox, Sophia Adams, Michelle Alexander, Kerry L. Sayle and Katharine Steinke

Skeletal remains offer archaeologists insights into how past people and animals lived their lives. At the visual level, they can be used to reconstruct population demographics, while at the molecular level isotopic analyses have the ability to unlock information related directly to diet, and by extension residence and mobility. Stable carbon (δ^{13}C) and nitrogen (δ^{15}N) isotope analyses are the standard tools for reconstructing the diet of past people and animals (Müldner 2013). However, palaeodietary studies are not limited to carbon and nitrogen isotope analysis. Richards *et al.* (2001) were the first to use sulphur isotope studies (δ^{34}S) from ancient bone collagen to investigate human palaeodiet and population residence/ mobility, and the technique has seen a slow, but steady, uptick in archaeological applications (Craig *et al.* 2006; Privat *et al.* 2007; Nehlich *et al.* 2010; 2011; Lamb *et al.* 2012; Sayle *et al.* 2013; 2014; 2016a; 2016b). More recently, Hamilton *et al.* (2019) used δ^{34}S to investigate animal mobility in Iron Age Wessex, while Jay *et al.* (2013) applied this isotope to study 'Arras culture' burials from Wetwang Slack. This chapter presents the results of two isotopic studies that were undertaken on the human remains from the Burnby Lane and The Mile sites, near Pocklington, with a particular focus on the individuals inhumed at the site in the Iron Age.

Stable isotopes: diet and mobility

The proverbial phrase 'You are what you eat' takes on a renewed and slightly more literal meaning when considering the isotopes within the tissues of plants and animals. When a living creature eats another animal or plant, an isotopic trace of that food source is incorporated into the various tissues of the consumer species (Sealy 2001). The stable isotope ratios of carbon (^{13}C/^{12}C, expressed as δ^{13}C), nitrogen (^{15}N/^{14}N, expressed as δ^{15}N), and sulphur (^{34}S/^{32}S, expressed as δ^{34}S) in the tissues of the consumer can be used to determine broadly whether it had consumed terrestrial-, marine-, or freshwater-based resources, or a combination of all three (DeNiro and Epstein 1978; 1981; Richards *et al.* 2001). As molecules undergo phase transitions (*i.e.* a change from solid to liquid or to gas) the isotopes of the constituent elements are prone to what is known as *isotopic fractionation*, whereby either heavier or lighter isotopes of an element are preferentially taken up. For biological processes, this generally takes the form of kinetic isotopic fractionation, which results in the lighter isotopic species (*e.g.* ^{12}C rather than ^{13}C or ^{14}N rather than ^{15}N) being preferred. Due to this isotopic fractionation, herbivores have δ^{13}C bone collagen values enriched by about 5‰ relative to their diet (van der Merwe and Vogel 1978). If we consider that terrestrial C$_3$ plants exhibit δ^{13}C values of about −26.5‰ (Smith and Epstein 1971), an individual that has consumed a wholly terrestrial C$_3$ plant diet would have a bone collagen δ^{13}C value of about −21.5‰. However, when comparing the δ^{13}C value of bone collagen in a consumer relative to the source of their dietary protein, there is an increase only of about +1‰ in this value (DeNiro and Epstein 1978). Therefore, carnivores that consume solely terrestrial protein would display bone collagen δ^{13}C values of about −20.5‰, while individuals that consume an exclusively marine-based diet would have bone collagen δ^{13}C values of about −12‰ (Schoeninger *et al.* 1983).

In general, terrestrial nitrogen-fixing plants (*i.e.* legumes such as the Celtic bean (*Vicia faba* L.)), have

$\delta^{15}N$ values that range between $-2‰$ and $2‰$ (Peterson and Fry 1987). However, plants can also take up nitrogen in the form of ^{15}N-depleted ammonia from decomposing organic matter, and their $\delta^{15}N$ values can be as low as $-8‰$ (Nadelhoffer and Fry 1994). Unlike carbon, nitrogen isotopes can increase significantly between the ratios in the diet and those in the tissues of consumers. Schoeninger and DeNiro (1984) estimated this trophic-level shift to be approximately $+3‰$ to $+5‰$ in the marine and terrestrial food chains. More recently, Fernandes (2015) estimated the $\delta^{15}N$ offset between dietary protein and human bone collagen to be $+5.5 \pm 0.5‰$. Therefore, taking an average trophic shift value of $+4.5‰$, we might expect herbivores and carnivores to have $\delta^{15}N$ values of approximately $2.5‰$ to $6.5‰$ and $7‰$ to $11‰$, respectively, in a simple terrestrial food web. Within the marine environment, baseline oceanic nitrate $\delta^{15}N$ values are approximately $5.0‰$, and as a consequence of marine food webs being considerably longer and more complex than in the terrestrial biosphere, $\delta^{15}N$ values of the apex predators can range between about $15‰$ and $20‰$ (DeNiro and Epstein 1981; Schoeninger *et al.* 1983; Schoeninger and DeNiro 1984).

The $\delta^{34}S$ values for terrestrial and freshwater vegetation can vary between $-22‰$ and $+22‰$, with the variation largely driven by differences in the local bedrock that physically and chemically weathers to form the soil (Peterson and Fry 1987). This wide variation is in sharp contrast to plants and algae at the base of the marine food web, where the $\delta^{34}S$ values usually vary between $17‰$ and $21‰$. Most of the earth's sulphur supply originates from either the lithosphere or hydrosphere, with sulphides in shale and sulfates in evaporites exhibiting $\delta^{34}S$ values between $-40‰$ and $+30‰$ (Claypool *et al.* 1980; Strauss 1997) and marine waters currently providing a very isotopically uniform reservoir of $+21‰$ (Rees *et al.* 1978). Terrestrial plants primarily assimilate sulphur in the form of sulfate via their root systems. This process occurs with little fractionation, such that sulphur isotopes can provide additional information about the geographical origin of a plant as its $\delta^{34}S$ value will be similar to its surrounding environment (Trust and Fry 1992). Some plants, such as mosses and lichens, are capable of absorbing atmospheric SO_2 with little or no fractionation (Krouse 1977), while the wet deposition of SO_2 in the form of acid rain (H_2SO_4) can provide soils with an additional source of sulphur. However, isotopic fractionation in this instance can be large during the oxidation process (Harris *et al.* 2012). Similarly, in areas closer to the coast, soil $\delta^{34}S$ values will generally increase to approach values comparable to seawater due to sulphur-containing particles being blown inland; this is known as the sea-spray effect (Wadleigh *et al.* 1994). Similar to carbon, an increase of about $1‰$ is observed in bone collagen $\delta^{34}S$ values compared with the source of dietary protein (Peterson and Howarth 1987).

By analysing the stable isotope ratios of carbon, nitrogen, and sulphur in the bone collagen of human remains, it is not only possible to determine broadly the diet of an individual, but the isotopes can also be used to provide meaningful information on the residence and mobility of an individual. The use of strontium ($^{87}Sr/^{86}Sr$) and oxygen ($\delta^{18}O$) isotopes to investigate the latter is more commonly known to archaeologists and relies on measuring these isotopes in the enamel of an individual's tooth, which form at various points in childhood and trap the isotopic signature of the diet at that point in life. The results can then be compared to the local bioavailable isotope values, either through empirical analysis of local flora and fauna or to maps of the distribution of these isotopes across a region. This enables inferences to be made as to (1) whether the individual was raised in the area where they were buried, and (2) from where the person came if they have a non-local origin.

By using the isotopes in the bone collagen, it is possible to trace the residence of an individual across multiple points in their lifetime, rather than simply identifying if they were buried in a geologic area different from their childhood. This ability relies on the fact that bone collagen in most skeletal elements is continually replenished throughout life, but that turnover rates vary with age and between different bone types. In general, bone collagen has a faster turnover in adolescents compared to adults (Hedges *et al.* 2007), and collagen is replenished more slowly for harder (*i.e.* cortical) bone than for softer, spongy (*i.e.* trabecular) bone (Ubelaker *et al.* 2006). When combined with stable isotope measurements on primary tooth dentine, which is fixed in youth (Cook *et al.* 2006), this allows us to look at variations in diet and residence across most of a person's lifespan. Relatively speaking, the tooth dentine provides a glimpse at the early years, the cortical bone (*e.g.* long bone shaft, such as femur) the middle years, and the trabecular bone (*e.g.* rib) the later years. This differential approach to isotopic sampling and measurement should not be confused with incremental/sequential sampling of tooth dentine, which has been used to look at dietary and residence changes at fine temporal resolutions during an individual's first 15–20 years of life (Lamb *et al.* 2014; Beaumont *et al.* 2013).

Finally, for producing a robust interpretation of a consumer's isotope ratio values successfully, it is necessary to establish a baseline for the expected values. Baselines are often derived from direct empirical study of samples that can be spatially and temporally related to the consumers. The most robust baseline would come from archaeological material from the same site as the consumers being studied, but often when looking at human remains from cemetery contexts it is necessary to target nearby settlements for that material and make new measurements as part of the isotope programme or collate isotope data that were created as part of other projects. When considering human diets, the data often include stable isotope measurements on associated terrestrial herbivores (*e.g.* sheep/goat and cattle), omnivores (*e.g.* pig), and marine or freshwater fish, where recovered. The goal is to better understand the isotopic values associated with the food-stuffs that provided protein for the replenishment of the bone collagen. When looking at sulphur isotopes, in addition to determining the expected value for the consumer from a given faunal assemblage, by considering the total variability of the isotope within the population, it is also preferable to use the data to determine a baseline 'local' value for the geology of the site. Following the assumption that the majority of animals from a prehistoric site will have been reared locally, this can be accomplished through applying statistical methods that cluster isotope groups and then following the 'criterion of abundance' (Bishop *et al.* 1982), setting the isotope range of the largest group as the 'local' range. This method was used by Hamilton *et al.* (2019) and is being researched further. Where it is not possible to determine the baselines from relevant, similarly aged material, more generic expected values are usually substituted, often either temporally different but spatially similar material, or even through the use of modern analogues, though the latter is not desirable due to anthropogenic impacts on the environment.

Methods

Samples from burials at Burnby Lane and The Mile were taken and analysed as part of two distinct research projects. The first was an MSc research project investigating the diet of Iron Age and early medieval individuals. This work was carried out within the BioArCh group at the University of York. A total of 80 burials was sampled, with 64 burials producing collagen that was of sufficiently high quality for analysis. Of the 64 burials that were able to be analysed further, 40 are presented here as they are phased with the Iron Age burials (or as Iron Age/early medieval). The second research project, undertaken at SUERC, aimed to use stable isotopes to investigate mobility of Iron Age and early medieval people. This research ran concurrent with the radiocarbon-dating programme from the site and was designed to be complementary to similar research being undertaken at SUERC on Iron Age sites of a similar date in Wessex and as an extension in East Yorkshire to the previous work by Jay *et al.* (2013) from Wetwang Slack. The 31 Iron Age burials from Burnby Lane and two burials from The Mile are presented here.

The methods used in York and SUERC vary, especially with regard to the instrumentation used and isotopes measured. The York measurements for dietary stable isotopes only include $\delta^{13}C$ and $\delta^{15}N$, while at SUERC, measurements were made for $\delta^{13}C$, $\delta^{15}N$, and $\delta^{34}S$. Where

the same element on a burial was sampled and analysed from both facilities, the measurements were combined for further statistical analysis. The same element might not always be the same actual bone, such that two different ribs might have been sampled or both femurs were sampled. Since there is the possibility for differences in isotope values due to the variable rate of collagen turn-over, there are instances where the two values are less similar than one might expect if the two laboratories were working with aliquots of the same sample. Nevertheless, it was felt the averaging of these measurements was the best approach to handling the large and complex dataset. Furthermore, all measurements are provided in Table 17.1, with the standard quality-assurance values (e.g. %N/C/S and the molar ratios) so that future researchers are able to 'decompile' our analyses.

Overall sampling methodology

Selection of individuals was guided by the osteological report for the site (Caffel and Holst 2017) and through conversations with MAP Ltd. Further contextual information on burials at the site consisting of site mapping, photographs, and skeleton sheets was also provided. Although the sampling was undertaken using the provisional phasing of burials, many of the burials were subsequently radiocarbon-dated (*n* = 44), and the results presented here rely on both forms of dating.

With regard to the physical remains, upon examination, surface preservation appeared poor in many of the inhumations, so this was the first criterion used in sample selection. The idea here is that better surface preservation is indicative of better collagen preservation. In addition, at this early stage, individuals were selected from which both bone and tooth samples had been recovered, as the mobility study aimed to incorporate a differential approach to the sampling. In addition, for the dietary study undertaken at the University of York, individuals without skeletal sex identification or deemed unidentifiable were discounted, apart from juveniles where sex identification is impossible.

During preparation at both York and SUERC, 10–15% of the bone samples selected failed to yield sufficient, if any, collagen for study. Samples were re-prepared, as described below, and still failed to yield sufficient collagen to be weighed out. While the York dietary study had the opportunity to resample, the SUERC mobility study was able to request some new material be posted, but otherwise needed to abandon a few samples after multiple attempts. The result of the preservation problems has been that in a few instances, a long bone, such as the femur, has been used in place of a rib bone. Since the rib bone is thought to reflect the last 2–5 years of a person's life (Cox and Sealy 1997) and long bone, such as the femur, a far longer period (Hedges *et al.* 2007), it raises the possibility that dietary changes in an individual's lifetime – not just the types of food consumed but from where it was obtained – might increase the overall variability in the final dataset. This is unavoidable given the nature of samples on hand and the assumption is made here, for the purposes of the dietary analysis, that there was generally low mobility in the Iron Age period such that little change is expected in diet over a person's lifetime. If variance by age (skeletal tissue element) is observed, then this might be teased out by a comparison between the isotope ratios of the rib and femur bones.

For the mobility study at SUERC, fragments of rib, femur, and a tooth were sampled from the selected individuals. Wherever possible the femur was sampled at a distance approximately 25–30% from the end of the bone, with the proximal end preferred when available. The 1st molar was removed where available, with selection moving to the next available tooth (*e.g.* 2nd molar, pre-molar). The 1st molar was preferred since it forms between the moment of birth and 13 years of age (Beaumont and Montgomery 2015). In the laboratory, the tooth was sub-sampled with a 'corner' sliced out longitudinally from the root to the crown, generally exiting at or very near where the occlusal surface meets one of the sides. This produces a bulk sample that incorporates collagen from the entire period of tooth formation but is weighted against the pre-weaning period as very little dentine is included from beneath the crown. This method also enabled preservation of a substantial amount of material for potential isotopic work of incremental samples of the dentine. This could be especially useful for identifying the age at which a person moved if there was a significant difference between the isotopes in the tooth and other skeletal tissues.

Isotope methodology – BioArCh

For the dietary stable isotope research undertaken at the University of York, bone samples initially had the outer layers removed using a scalpel. This step primarily removes adhering soil and highly degraded bone. The ~0.5g fragment was then placed into a clean glass tube. To the tube was added 8ml of 0.6M HCl [pH 0.222] and the tube was stored at 4°C for demineralisation. After the bone fragments fully demineralised, leaving 'spongy' pseudomorphs, the fragments were rinsed three times in distilled water.

After rinsing, the tube was filled with 8ml of 0.001M HCl [pH 3] and placed in a heat block at 80°C to gelatinise the pseudomorphs. The process usually takes 48 hours. Once gelatinisation was complete, the gel was transferred to a test tube and filtered using a 60–90μm spore screen Ezee-Filter™ to remove the insoluble fraction. The resultant filtrate was placed in a freezer at −10°C for 48 hours before being transferred to a freeze drier and lyophilised for 48 hours.

Stable carbon and nitrogen isotopic compositions were determined using a Sercon 20–22 continuous flow isotope ratio mass spectrometer coupled to a Sercon GSL elemental analyser. Accuracy was determined by measurements of international standard reference materials within each analytical run. These were IAEA 600 ($\delta^{13}C_{raw}$ = −27.73±0.120‰; $\delta^{13}C_{true}$ = −27.77±0.043‰; $\delta^{15}N_{raw}$ = +1.16±0.4‰; $\delta^{15}N_{true}$ = +1.0±0.2‰), IAEA N2 ($\delta^{15}N_{raw}$ = +20.3±0.18‰, $\delta^{15}N_{true}$ = +20.3±0.2‰), and IA Cane ($\delta^{13}C_{raw}$ = −11.67±0.11‰; $\delta^{13}C_{true}$ = −11.64±0.03‰). The overall uncertainties on the measurements of each sample were calculated based on the method of Kragten (1994) by combining uncertainties in the values of the international reference materials and those determined from repeated measurements of samples and reference materials. These are expressed as one standard deviation. The maximum uncertainty for all samples across all runs was <0.17‰ for $\delta^{13}C$ and <0.25‰ for $\delta^{15}N$.

In addition, a homogenised bovine bone was extracted and analysed within the same batch as the samples; it produced the following average values: $\delta^{13}C$ = −22.85±0.13‰ and $\delta^{15}N$ = +7.01±0.26‰. This was within the overall mean value from 50 separate extracts of this bone sample, which produced values of $\delta^{13}C$ = −23.04±0.66‰ and $\delta^{15}N$ = +6.66±0.43‰.

Isotope methodology – SUERC

Samples from both Burnby Lane and The Mile were processed at SUERC for research into past mobility of people. The research used stable isotope analysis of bone collagen, with $\delta^{34}S$ providing the key isotopic fingerprint relating to geographic residence, as it relates to geology. As described above, the overall strategy aimed to use a differential approach to sampling, which has resulted in multiple samples being removed from many of the individuals. In total, 56 individuals were sampled, 33 of which were dated to the Iron Age. While every effort was made to take three samples per individual, not only was this not always possible, but the higher-than-normal number of samples with poor-quality collagen resulted in some individuals only having one or two suitable samples for analysis. Therefore, 76 samples had collagen of sufficiently high quality to produce 90 results. Two individuals sampled produced no results (Sk 59 <16072> and Sk 126 <17175>), while three individuals only have $\delta^{13}C$ and $\delta^{15}N$ values (Sk 10 <15258>, Sk 45 <15856>, and Sk 63 <16159>). Additionally, 29 animal teeth (cattle = 12; horse = 9; sheep/goat = 5; pig = 2; deer = 1) were pre-treated in the same manner as the human teeth and bone to provide a baseline dataset for interpreting the stable isotopes, and especially the $\delta^{34}S$ values as currently there is very little understanding of the spatial distribution of $\delta^{34}S$ values across prehistoric Britain.

Bone and teeth samples were processed for collagen extraction following the standard methods of the SUERC radiocarbon laboratory (Dunbar *et al.* 2016). Bone samples were initially cleaned using a precision high-speed drill fitted with a diamond-coated sanding tip. Bulk sampling for tooth dentine was undertaking by slicing the selected tooth longitudinally from the cusp to the root tip with the high-speed drill fitted with a diamond-coated cutting disc. These samples were immersed in 100mL of 1M HCl at room temperature for approximately 24 hours to begin demineralisation and remove the bulk of the humic substances. The acid was then decanted, the sample rinsed well with ultrapure MilliQ® water, and immersed in a fresh 100mL of 1M HCl for 48 hours to demineralise the sample fully.

The acidic solution was decanted, and the gelatinous-like material was rinsed with ultrapure water to remove any remaining dissociated carbonates, acid-soluble contaminants, and solubilised inorganic components. The material was immersed in ultrapure water and heated gently to ~80°C for ~5 hours to fully denature and solubilise the collagen. After briefly cooling, the solution was filtered, reduced to ~5mL, and frozen prior to freeze-drying over a period of 48–72 hours.

A number of samples failed to produce high-quality collagen in the first instance. These almost always were rib bones but did include samples from femurs as well. When this occurred, the sample was pre-treated for a second time following a protocol whereby the demineralisation step was slowed down, taking place at 4ºC rather than room temperature. Furthermore, extra care was taken in handling the samples to avoid sample losses while decanting the HCl and rinsing, with that step utilising a centrifuge and pipetting.

The freeze-dried collagen samples were measured following the methods of Sayle *et al.* (2019). In brief, the samples were combusted in a Thermo Scientific™ EA IsoLink™, with the resulting N_2, CO_2, and SO_2 gases produced in the reactor separated using a temperature-variable GC column, and then transferred to a Thermo Scientific™ DELTA V™ Advantage IRMS via the ConFlo Universal Interface. Results are reported as per mil (‰) deviations, relative to the internationally accepted standards V-PDB, AIR, and V-CDT for $\delta^{13}C$, $\delta^{15}N$ and $\delta^{34}S$, respectively. The 1σ precisions given in Table 17.1 are based on the precision derived from the DHB19 internal bone collagen standard.

Results

Results: dietary stable isotopes

A total of 54 individuals dating to the Iron Age that were buried at Burnby Lane, Pocklington were analysed using the traditional suite of dietary stable isotopes ($\delta^{13}C$ and $\delta^{15}N$). The data used in these analyses are provided in Table 17.1. While most of the elements analysed and reported here were rib bones, there are instances where the rib bone failed collagen extraction and the result comes from a long bone (*e.g.* femur, tibia, etc). While the burials were phased to either the Iron Age or early medieval period, 25 individuals were radiometrically dated to the Iron Age (see Chapter 16). Two individuals could have been buried in either period but are discussed here within the aggregate and plotted separately.

Dietary baseline

The collagen extracted from the dentine of 29 animal teeth had their stable isotopes measured at SUERC, and the $\delta^{13}C$ and $\delta^{15}N$ values are presented here as a dietary baseline. While these teeth have come from the burial contexts, given the non-domestic nature of the archaeology, it is impossible to say if the frequencies represented at the cemetery are similar to what might be found in an associated domestic context. As such, the isotopes are used here only in aggregate for a broad discussion of diet. Furthermore, the $\delta^{13}C$ and $\delta^{15}N$ values for terrestrial herbivores are usually separated out from omnivores, such as dog or pig. Given there are only two pig samples in the group for this study, they have been excluded to produce a terrestrial herbivore baseline (*POCK Herb*; Fig. 17.1). It is assumed the animal remains recovered from the Burnby Lane burials represent a catchment area of perhaps 5–10 km around the site (cf. Chisholm 1962; Higgs and Vita-Finzi 1972), and that the individuals buried at the cemetery were living in a similar area. This data is complemented by a much larger dataset from Jay and Richards (2006) that used the animal remains from Wetwang Slack for developing a robust 'local' baseline for analysing the dietary stable isotopes of the population there. Their dataset includes measurements of 48 samples from terrestrial herbivores typically found on Iron Age sites (e.g. cattle, horse, deer, and sheep/goat; E YORKS Herb; Fig. 17.1) and 18 samples from omnivorous mammals (e.g. pig, dog, and fox; E YORKS Omni; Fig. 17.1). The mean values and 95% confidence ranges are plotted in Figure 17.1 alongside a green box that signifies the generally expected area for these isotopes from terrestrial animals in the UK, based on Mays (1998, fig. 9).

Animal isotopes: Pocklington vs Wetwang Slack

The results of unpaired Students *t*-tests show the $\delta^{13}C$ values for POCK Herb and E YORKS Herb are significantly different (*p* value = 0.0023), while the $\delta^{15}N$ values are extremely significantly different (*p* value < 0.00001).

Table 17.1 Summary of isotopic data discussed in Chapter 17

Sample ID	Lab ID	Sampled Element	$\delta^{15}N$ (‰)	$\delta^{13}C$ (‰)	%N	%C	%S	$\delta^{34}S$ (‰)	C:N	C:S	N:S	Other Lab ID
				The Mile								
	GUsi7487	femur; right shaft	10.0±0.2	−20.4±0.1	14.7	43.8	0.19	11.6±0.3	3.5	614	176	
Shield Sk 303	GU49423 A	rib; left	11.0±0.1	−20.7±0.1	14.8	41.5	0.19	9.9±0.3	3.3	586	178	SUERC-83085
	GU49423 B		11.0±0.1	−20.6±0.1	14.9	41.6	0.18	10.3±0.3	3.3	608	186	
	GUsi7747	UL M1	10.4±0.2	−20.7±0.1	15.5	44.8	0.21	12.2±0.3	3.4	571	169	
Chariot Sk 424	GU48906	rib	11.3±0.2	−20.4±0.1	15.1	41.3	0.20	6.9±0.4	3.2	555	174	SUERC-81686
	GU48907	tooth	10.6±0.2	−19.9±0.1	13.3	35.9	0.16	14.0±0.4	3.1	603	192	
				Burnby Lane								
A (4012)	TGBF SK4012	rib	8.6	−20.7	14.7	39.9			3.2			
	GU49411 A	humerus; right head	12.1±0.1	−21.0±0.1	14.1	40.3	0.18	9.9±0.3	3.3	605	182	SUERC-83069
	GU49411 B		12.1±0.1	−21.0±0.1	14.3	40.3	0.18	10.0±0.3	3.3	613	187	
Sk 2	GUsi7428	leg bone fragment	12.6±0.1	−20.8±0.1	14.3	41.2	0.20	10.2±0.4	3.4	556	166	
	GUsi7748	M	11.9±0.2	−20.6±0.1	15.2	44.7	0.19	11.3±0.3	3.4	638	186	
	TGBF SK2	rib	11.7	−20.9	15.6	42.0			3.2			
Sk 3	TGBF SK3	rib	8.6	−20.5	14.0	37.4			3.1			
Sk 6	TGBF SK6	rib	10.1	−20.6	14.6	39.5			3.2			
	GUsi7429	femur; right shaft	10.3±0.1	−19.9±0.1	14.4	41.1	0.21	13.0±0.4	3.3	518	156	SUERC-96408
	GUsi7749	M1	8.9±0.2	−19.6±0.1	15.1	44.0	0.20	15.9±0.3	3.4	596	175	
Sk 8	TGBF SK8	rib	10.5	−20.3	15.1	41.1			3.2			
	GUsi7272	rib; right	11.1±0.1	−20.2±0.1	15.3	42.2	0.18	12.6±0.2	3.2	640	199	
Sk 10	TGBF SK10	rib	11.3	−21.0	14.8	40.6			3.2			
	GU46851	rib; left	11.5±0.3	−20.9±0.2	15.5	43.8			3.3			SUERC-78038
Sk 11	TGBF SK11	tibia	11.3	−20.3	14.5	39.5			3.2			
Sk 12	TGBF SK12	fibula	11.3	−21.1	13.2	36.7			3.2			
	GU49412	femur; left	11.7±0.1	−21.2±0.1	10.2	28.9	0.15	4.2±0.3	3.3	520	157	SUERC-83070
Sk 13	GUsi7430	femur; left shaft	11.9±0.1	−20.6±0.1	13.9	39.2	0.23	4.4±0.4	3.3	454	138	
	TGBF SK13	fibula	11.1	−21.0	13.0	36.3			3.3			

(Continued)

Table 17.1 (Continued)

Sample ID	Lab ID	Sampled Element	δ15N (‰)	δ13C (‰)	δ34S (‰)	%N	%C	%S	C:N	C:S	N:S	Other Lab ID
Sk 14	TGBF SK14	long bone (arm)	11.0	-21.2		15.2	42.5		3.3			
	GUsi7431 A	femur; left shaft	10.8±0.1	-20.6±0.1	9.1±0.4	15.0	39.4	0.20	3.1	533	174	
	GUsi7431 B		10.7±0.1	-20.6±0.1	9.1±0.4	14.3	40.1	0.20	3.3	544	166	
Sk 16	GUsi7750	LL M1	10.8±0.2	-20.3±0.1	9.0±0.3	14.3	41.4	0.17	3.4	645	190	
	TGBF SK16	rib	10.5	-20.9		14.4	39.9		3.2			
	GUsi7273	rib; right	11.3±0.1	-20.7±0.1	9.9±0.2	14.3	40.0	0.18	3.3	593	181	
Sk 20	GU48384	humerus; right	11.7±0.3	-20.6±0.2	9.7±0.1	10.0	28.2	0.14	3.3	547	165	SUERC-81073
	TGBF SK20	ulna	10.7	-20.6		16.0	43.5		3.2			
Sk 21	GU47481	femur; right	11.4±0.3	-20.7±0.2	6.4±0.1	15.1	42.4	0.18	3.3	622	190	SUERC-79413
	GU46852	rib	11.5±0.3	-20.9±0.2		13.7	39.0		3.3			SUERC-78039
Sk 24	TGBF SK24	femur	10.6	-20.6		15.5	42.5		3.2			
Sk 26	TGBF SK26	rib	11.1	-20.6		14.9	40.4		3.2			
	GU46853	rib; right	11.7±0.3	-20.6±0.2		13.7	39.0		3.3			SUERC-78040
Sk 27	GUsi7752	M	11.8±0.2	-20.5±0.1	7.9±0.3	13.9	39.9	0.20	3.4	520	155	
	GUsi7433	occipital	12.1±0.1	-20.7±0.1	8.5±0.4	14.1	40.1	0.20	3.3	538	162	
	TGBF SK27	rib	11.7	-20.7		14.8	40.6		3.2			
	GU49413	rib	11.9±0.1	-20.6±0.1	8.0±0.3	10.7	30.0	0.12	3.3	659	202	SUERC-83071
Sk 29	TGBF SK29	rib	10.3	-20.8		12.6	33.8		3.1			
Sk 32	TGBF SK32	rib	9.9	-20.8		14.0	37.8		3.2			
Sk 34	TGBF SK34	humerus	11.0	-20.7		10.2	29.0		3.3			
Sk 36	TGBF SK36	long bone (leg)	8.8	-20.5		8.2	23.4		3.3			
Sk 37	TGBF SK37	rib	10.6	-20.7		12.9	34.4		3.1			
Sk 38	TGBF SK38	rib	10.2	-20.2		13.1	36.5		3.2			
Sk 39	GUsi7434	femur; right shaft	11.4±0.1	-20.6±0.1	8.9±0.4	14.1	38.5	0.20	3.2	508	159	
	GUsi7434	M1	11.7±0.2	-20.5±0.1	10.5±0.3	15.1	44.0	0.20	3.4	586	173	
	GU49414	rib	11.5±0.1	-20.7±0.1	7.4±0.3	12.3	34.0	0.14	3.2	648	201	SUERC-83075
	GUsi7435	femur; right shaft	11.2±0.1	-20.6±0.1	10.7±0.4	14.7	41.5	0.19	3.3	576	175	
	GUsi7754	LL M1	11.6±0.2	-20.7±0.1	9.7±0.3	15.0	43.8	0.21	3.4	561	165	SUERC-96413
Sk 40	TGBF SK40	rib	11.1	-20.8		15.1	41.4		3.2			
	GUsi7275 A		11.8±0.1	-20.8±0.1	10.0±0.2	14.9	40.8	0.16	3.2	673	211	
	GUsi7275 B	rib	11.7±0.1	-20.8±0.1	10.4±0.2	14.8	40.8	0.16	3.2	669	209	

(Continued)

Table 17.1 Summary of isotopic data discussed in Chapter 17 (Continued)

Sample ID	Lab ID	Sampled Element	$\delta^{15}N$ (‰)	$\delta^{13}C$ (‰)	$\delta^{34}S$ (‰)	%N	%C	%S	C:N	C:S	N:S	Other Lab ID
Sk 42	TGBF SK42	long bone (leg)	10.4	−20.8		12.9	36.2		3.3			
Sk 44B	TGBF SK44B	long bone (arm)	11.5	−20.6		15.0	40.7		3.2			
Sk 45	GU49415	femur; left	11.9±0.1	−20.9±0.1	8.5±0.3	10.6	29.2	0.11	3.2	726	226	SUERC-83076
	GUsi7437 A	femur; right shaft	12.5±0.1	−20.8±0.1	9.8±0.4	14.2	39.4	0.20	3.2	532	164	
	GUsi7437 B		12.4±0.1	−20.8±0.1	9.7±0.4	14.0	38.9	0.20	3.2	526	162	
Sk 51	GUsi7756 A	M	12.3±0.2	−20.6±0.1	10.1±0.3	15.4	45.1	0.23	3.4	527	154	
	GUsi7756 B		12.3±0.2	−20.6±0.1	10.3±0.3	15.5	45.4	0.23	3.4	534	157	
Sk 52	GUsi7438	femur; left shaft	10.3±0.1	−20.2±0.1	9.0±0.4	11.4	32.5	0.19	3.3	454	136	
	GUsi7757	LR M1	10.9±0.2	−20.2±0.1	14.1±0.3	14.6	41.9	0.21	3.3	536	160	
Sk 53	TGBF SK53	rib	11.3	−20.6		13.7	37.8		3.2			
	GUsi7439 A	femur; left shaft	10.2±0.1	−20.5±0.1	7.7±0.4	14.5	40.0	0.19	3.2	572	178	
	GUsi7439 B		10.2±0.1	−20.4±0.1	7.6±0.4	14.5	39.4	0.18	3.2	578	182	
Sk 54	GUsi7758	LR M1	10.6±0.2	−20.3±0.1	7.1±0.3	14.6	42.6	0.19	3.4	586	173	
	TGBF SK54	rib	9.5	−20.8		13.9	38.7		3.2			
	GUsi7279	rib; right	10.5±0.1	−20.5±0.1	7.7±0.2	13.1	35.5	0.18	3.2	538	170	
Sk 56	GUsi7440	femur; right shaft	11.8±0.1	−20.8±0.1	8.9±0.4	14.7	40.6	0.19	3.2	566	176	
	GUsi7759	M	11.7±0.2	−20.4±0.1	9.4±0.3	14.4	41.1	0.19	3.3	572	172	
	TGBF SK56	rib	9.8	−20.7		13.5	36.9		3.2			
Sk 57	TGBF SK57	rib	9.0	−19.9		14.1	38.4		3.2			
Sk 58	GUsi7760	LL M2	12.1±0.2	−20.3±0.1	8.0±0.3	15.5	45.0	0.23	3.4	521	154	
Sk 63	GU46854	femur; left	11.6±0.3	−21.1±0.2		9.0	26.9		3.5			SUERC-78041
Sk 64	TGBF SK64	rib	11.7	−21.0		13.6	37.4		3.2			
	GUsi7442	femur; left shaft	11.2±0.1	−20.7±0.1	3.4±0.4	14.7	39.4	0.21	3.1	509	163	
Sk 67	GUsi7761	LR M1	12.2±0.2	−20.7±0.1	9.5±0.3	14.7	43.1	0.21	3.4	549	160	
	TGBF SK67	rib	10.9	−20.8		15.1	41.6		3.2			
	GU47482	tibia; left	11.3±0.3	−20.9±0.2	6.7±0.1	8.3	24.4	0.13	3.4	514	149	SUERC-79417

(Continued)

Table 17.1 (Continued)

Sample ID	Lab ID	Sampled Element	$\delta^{15}N$ (‰)	$\delta^{13}C$ (‰)	$\delta^{34}S$ (‰)	%N	%C	%S	C:N	C:S	N:S	Other Lab ID
Sk 68	TGBF SK68	rib	9.5	−20.9		14.5	40.7		3.3			
Sk 72	TGBF SK72	rib	9.9	−20.8		13.9	38.3		3.2			SUERC-96415
	GUsi7443	femur; left shaft	11.3±0.1	−20.6±0.1	9.0±0.4	14.4	39.6	0.16	3.2	672	210	
	GUsi7762 A	LL M1	10.2±0.2	−20.1±0.1	11.3±0.3	15.2	44.2	0.23	3.4	524	154	
	GUsi7762 B		10.2±0.2	−20.1±0.1	11.3±0.3	15.1	44.0	0.22	3.4	530	156	
Sk 73	TGBF SK73	rib	10.4	−20.9		13.9	38.2		3.2			
	GUsi7283 A	rib; right	11.1±0.1	−20.6±0.1	8.3±0.2	14.6	40.5	0.19	3.2	574	178	
	GUsi7283 B		11.1±0.1	−20.7±0.1	8.9±0.2	14.8	41.4	0.18	3.3	630	193	
Sk 74	TGBF SK74	rib	11.7	−21.2		14.6	41.4		3.3			
	GUsi7444 A	femur; right shaft	10.5±0.1	−20.5±0.1	7.1±0.4	15.5	42.5	0.18	3.2	631	197	
	GUsi7444 B		10.5±0.1	−20.5±0.1	6.9±0.4	15.4	42.2	0.18	3.2	624	195	
Sk 81	GU46857	leg; left	10.3±0.3	−20.5±0.2		11.9	34.4		3.4			SUERC-78042
	GUsi7763	LL M1	9.5±0.2	−20.0±0.1	8.3±0.3	15.5	45.2	0.22	3.4	540	158	
Sk 82	GUsi7445	femur; right shaft	11.3±0.1	−20.8±0.1	8.1±0.4	14.4	40.4	0.17	3.3	651	199	
	GU49417	rib	11.5±0.1	−21.6±0.1	9.3±0.3	12.7	35.5	0.13	3.3	722	222	SUERC-83077
Sk 83	GUsi7764	LR M1	12.3±0.2	−20.5±0.1	4.7±0.3	15.4	44.3	0.22	3.4	532	159	SUERC-96429
Sk 85	GUsi7447	femur; right shaft	12.1±0.1	−21.1±0.1	0.9±0.4	9.8	27.0	0.14	3.2	517	160	
	GUsi7765	LL M1	13.0±0.2	−20.8±0.1	8.9±0.3	15.1	44.8	0.23	3.5	529	153	SUERC-96433
Sk 89	GU46858	lower leg; left	11.1±0.3	−21.4±0.2	8.1±0.1	8.9	24.9	0.14	3.3	489	150	SUERC-78046
Sk 93	TGBF SK93	rib	11.1	−20.8		15.2	42.0		3.2			
Sk 94	TGBF SK94	tibia	10.5	−20.8		14.5	39.9		3.2			
Sk 97	TGBF SK97	rib	11.0	−21.0		15.6	42.6		3.2			
Sk 102	TGBF SK102	rib	11.3	−21.2		15.3	42.0		3.2			
Sk 113	GUsi7452	femur; right shaft	11.5±0.1	−20.7±0.1	6.0±0.4	13.0	35.8	0.15	3.2	646	201	
	GUsi7770	M1/M2	12.1±0.2	−20.6±0.1	3.2±0.3	15.4	44.0	0.22	3.3	545	163	SUERC-96434
Sk 115	GU49418	femur; left	11.7±0.1	−20.7±0.1	8.6±0.3	11.2	30.9	0.15	3.2	564	176	SUERC-83078
	GUsi7453	femur; left shaft	11.3±0.1	−20.6±0.1	9.0±0.4	14.4	39.8	0.17	3.2	620	193	

(Continued)

Table 17.1 Summary of isotopic data discussed in Chapter 17 (Continued)

Sample ID	Lab ID	Sampled Element	$\delta^{15}N$ (‰)	$\delta^{13}C$ (‰)	$\delta^{34}S$ (‰)	%N	%C	%S	C:N	C:S	N:S	Other Lab ID
	GUsi7454	femur; right shaft	10.2±0.1	−20.7±0.1	9.3±0.4	14.1	37.9	0.16	3.1	623	199	
	GUsi7771	M	9.8±0.2	−20.9±0.1	8.8±0.3	12.7	35.8	0.21	3.3	461	141	
Sk 119	TGBF SK119	rib	9.8	−20.7		11.9	32.4		3.2			SUERC-83079
	GU49419 A	rib	10.6±0.1	−20.8±0.1	9.7±0.3	11.7	32.9	0.11	3.3	766	234	
	GU49419 B	rib	10.6±0.1	−20.8±0.1	9.2±0.3	11.3	31.6	0.12	3.3	689	211	
Sk 120	GUsi7455	femur; right shaft	11.9±0.1	−20.8±0.1	5.6±0.4	11.4	30.8	0.12	3.1	707	225	
	GUsi7772	M1/M2	12.2±0.2	−20.4±0.1	5.8±0.3	14.5	41.1	0.21	3.3	535	162	
	GUsi7456 A	femur; left shaft	11.0±0.1	−20.7±0.1	4.2±0.4	14.5	39.1	0.15	3.1	678	216	
	GUsi7456 B		11.0±0.1	−20.7±0.1	4.4±0.4	14.4	39.0	0.15	3.2	678	214	
Sk 121	GUsi7773 A	M	11.4±0.2	−20.4±0.1	1.7±0.3	15.6	45.7	0.22	3.4	546	159	
	GUsi7773 B	M	11.3±0.2	−20.6±0.1	1.7±0.3	15.5	44.5	0.22	3.3	534	159	
Sk 121	TGBF SK121	rib	10.6	−20.7		14.2	39.0		3.2			
	GU49420	rib	11.0±0.1	−20.9±0.1	4.9±0.3	12.5	35.0	0.13	3.3	723	221	SUERC-83080
Sk 122	GU47484	arm; right (?humerus)	9.5±0.3	−20.5±0.2	11.2±0.1	11.2	31.8	0.15	3.3	563	169	SUERC-79418
	GUsi7458	femur; right shaft	11.1±0.1	−21.1±0.1	9.1±0.4	14.8	41.1	0.16	3.2	692	214	
Sk 129	GUsi7775	M1/M2	11.0±0.2	−20.7±0.1	10.1±0.3	15.7	44.6	0.20	3.3	585	176	
	GUsi7294	rib	11.1±0.1	−20.8±0.1	9.1±0.2	14.4	41.5	0.21	3.4	517	154	
	GU49422 A	femur; left	10.3±0.1	−21.4±0.1	−6.6±0.3	4.1	11.4	0.09	3.2	332	104	
Sk 139	GU49422 B		10.4±0.1	−21.5±0.1	−6.4±0.3	4.7	12.8	0.12	3.2	280	89	SUERC-83081
	GUsi7779	pM	10.5±0.2	−20.3±0.1	8.8±0.3	15.5	45.1	0.20	3.4	611	180	
Sk 155	GUsi7784	LL M1	9.2±0.2	−19.9±0.1	7.0±0.3	15.4	43.4	0.19	3.3	610	186	
Sk 158	GUsi7785	M1/M2	11.4±0.2	−20.3±0.1	10.6±0.3	15.5	44.1	0.18	3.3	646	195	

The standard deviations for the samples from the University of York (TGBF) are <0.17‰ for $\delta^{13}C$ and <0.25‰ for $\delta^{15}N$. The $\delta^{13}C$ values for the SUERC samples (GUsi and GU) all come from a continuous flow isotope ratio mass spectrometer (CF-IRMS). These may vary slightly from the $\delta^{13}C$ values associated with the same sample as reported in Chapter 16, as the $\delta^{13}C$ value associated with the SUERC ^{14}C measurement was made on a dual inlet system using an aliquot of the CO_2 gas from the sample combustion during graphitisation

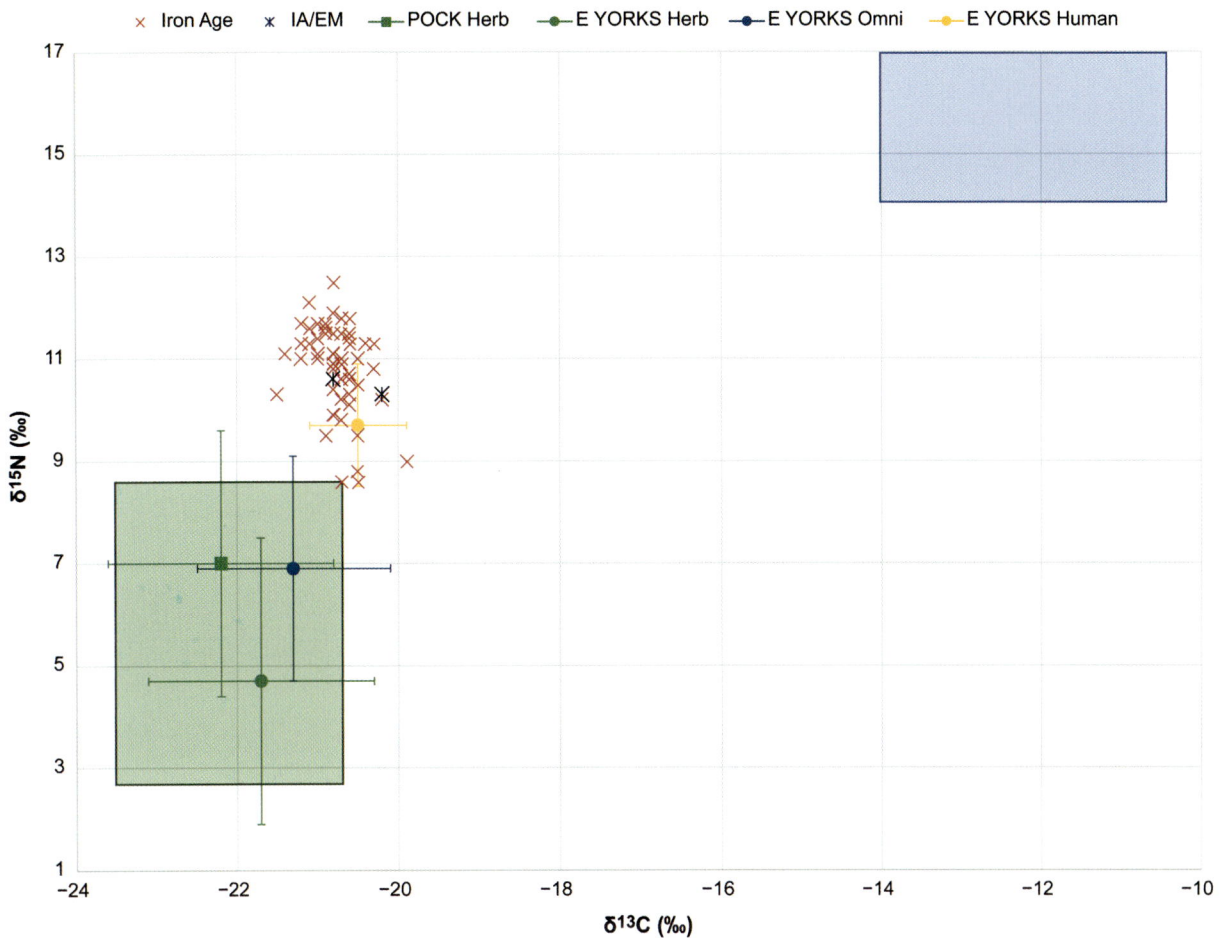

Figure 17.1 Plot of the δ¹³C and δ¹⁵N values for the Iron Age and Iron Age/early medieval burials from Burnby Lane. The green square in the lower-left and blue square in the upper-right corners, respectively, designate the generally expected range for these values in terrestrial herbivores (green) and marine fish and mammals (blue) (after Mays 1998, fig. 9). The POCK Herb *data are from this study (shown in Fig. 17.2), with the* E YORKS *data derived from Jay et al. (2013)*

On average, $\delta^{15}N_{POCK\ Herb}$ is enriched by 2.7‰ over $\delta^{15}N_{E\ YORKS\ Herb}$, with $\delta^{13}C_{POCK\ Herb}$ depleted by 0.6‰ in relation to $\delta^{13}C_{E\ YORKS\ Herb}$. There are a number of factors that can lead to differences between two such populations, such as differences in species frequency (i.e. raw representation) within the sample population, the isotope values of the plants in the area where the animals were living, and interlaboratory differences in measurements. This often makes the disentangling of datasets very complex, as the factors are never exclusive and must always be considered in relation to one another.

Turning to the specific data presented here, the two sites have almost identical percentages of horse and deer samples. However, the percentages of cattle and sheep are almost exactly inverted, with Pocklington having 44% cattle and 19% sheep/goat to the Wetwang Slack breakdown of 23% and 38%, respectively. There are

differences in isotopic fractionation that often can be observed between species, especially when comparing larger population sizes. While horses and cows both consume grass, their digestive systems are very different, and where the animals can be isolated into reliable populations based on the geology on which they fed, a shift can often be observed in $\delta^{13}C$, with cows showing an enrichment of approximately 1‰ (Fig. 17.2; Hamilton *et al.* 2019, fig. 6). Ovicaprids (sheep/goat) will usually have higher variation in the isotopic values as the two species in this group have different typical diets, with sheep eating primarily grasses and goat also consuming tree and bush leaves and saplings. However, much of the overall variability observed is likely the result of differences in management practices between ovicaprids and other species.

If the differences observed between the measurements from the two sites are not the result of a biased weighting

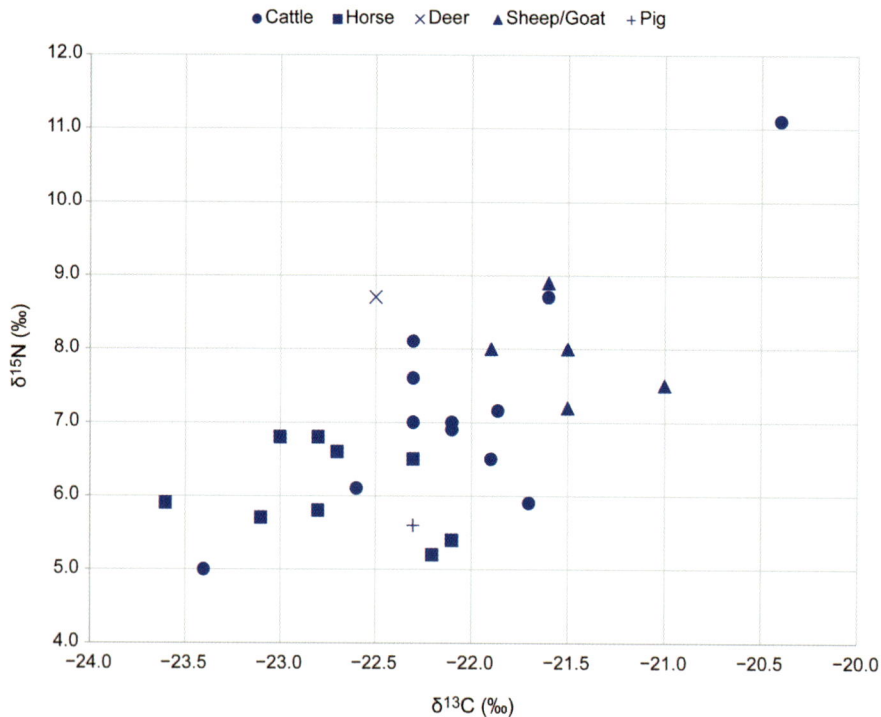

Figure 17.2 Plot of the δ¹³C and δ¹⁵N values for the animal teeth recovered from Burnby Lane

toward one species or another, then they are either the result of interlaboratory differences in measurements or actual differences in the base values for δ¹³C and δ¹⁵N in the plants in the different ecozones where the animals were raised. While currently there is no large international interlaboratory comparison that would allow an independent assessment of the performance of the laboratories whose measurements are included here, the laboratories are world-leaders in making isotope measurements and their processes use a combination of secondary standards to check and correct the measurements. As such, there is little reason to think the differences observed are the result of any systematic interlaboratory offsets. While the two sites are separated by only about 15km, this distance places them on different geologic formations and also in areas with different levels of agricultural productivity (Fig. 17.3, Natural England 2020). This could easily be the environmental difference that results in the isotopic difference observed between these two populations, and so it can be concluded there is a real, albeit subtle, difference in the δ¹³C and δ¹⁵N values of the plants growing in the vicinities where the Wetwang Slack and Pocklington animals were raised.

Summary of results

From archaeological and isotopic evidence, terrestrial herbivores appear to dominate the dietary protein of Iron Age people in Britain (Jay and Richards 2006; Albarella 2007). This trend is observed locally in the zooarchaeological records at the Hayton site, the currently nearest published contemporary settlement site, located approximately 4km south-south-east of the Burnby Lane, Pocklington cemetery site (Jaques 2015). Comparing the stable isotope values for the Iron Age humans with those from the terrestrial herbivores at Burnby Lane, Pocklington, the $\Delta^{15}N_{human-herbivore}$ value is 3.8‰, while the $\Delta^{13}C_{human-herbivore}$ value is 1.4‰. These data strongly suggest the Iron Age population buried at Burnby Lane had a diet almost entirely based on cereals and terrestrial herbivore protein, supporting the generally held belief that Iron Age Britons derived very little (if any) dietary protein from aquatic resources (Dobney and Ervynck 2007).

A similar exercise using the isotope values derived from terrestrial herbivores animals recovered from just over 15km to the north-east at the site of Wetwang Slack results in $\Delta^{15}N_{human-herbivore}$ = 6.1‰ and $\Delta^{13}C_{human-herbivore}$ = 0.9‰. This comparison between the Burnby Lane human population and the E YORKS Herbivore isotopes leads to a contradictory interpretation of the data and suggests either the exploitation of freshwater resources or increased consumption of higher trophic-level terrestrial animals, such as pig. These data highlight the importance of developing robust isotope baselines that can be assumed to represent the bioavailable isotope values

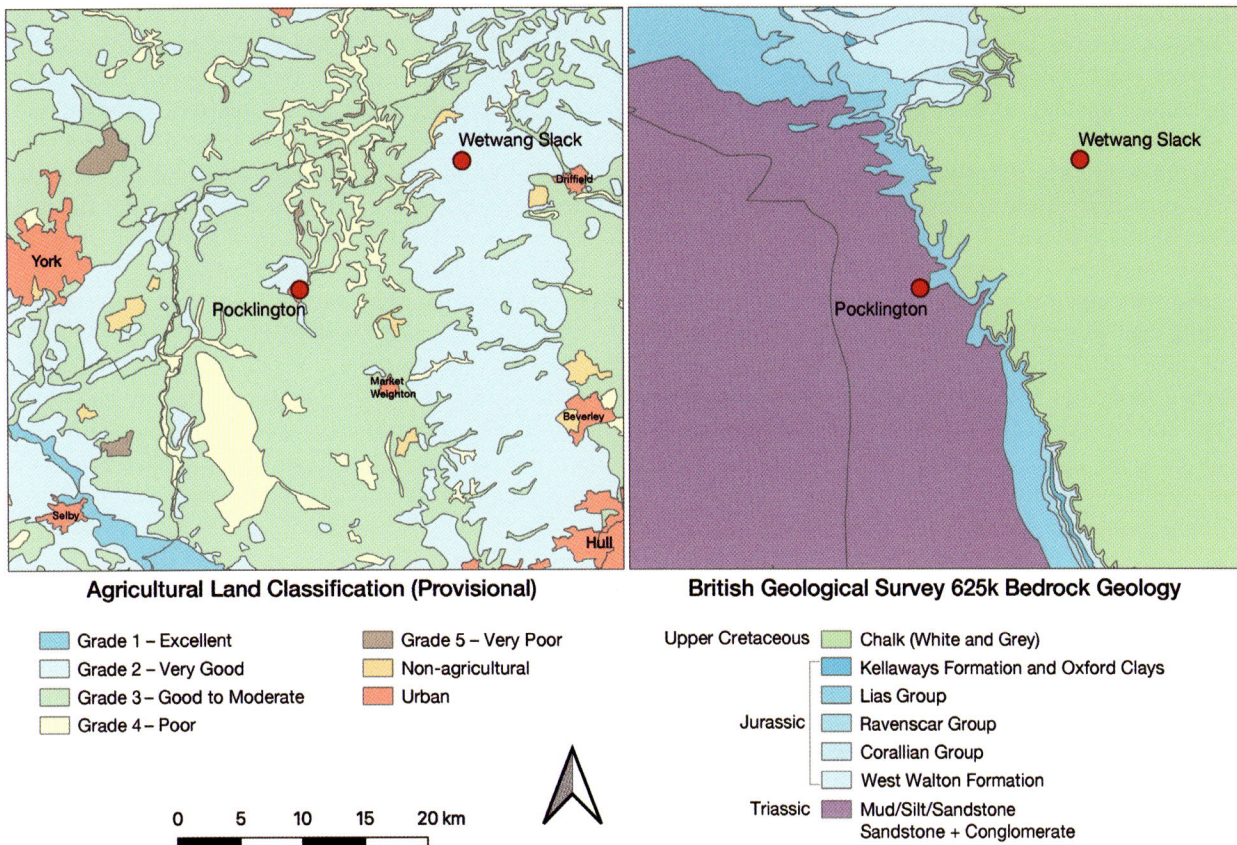

Figure 17.3 Maps showing the locations of Burnby Lane and Wetwang Slack against the data for the (left) Agricultural Land Classification (© Natural England copyright. Contains Ordnance Survey data © Crown copyright and database right 2020) and (right) British Geological Survey 625k Bedrock Geology (BGS © UKRI – contains OS data © Crown copyright 2020)

for the population – the isotope values of the food that was regularly consumed – otherwise there is a strong possibility the analyses could lead to spurious or even incorrect interpretations. With that in mind, a comparison between the isotopic values on terrestrial herbivores from the two sites will be important for understanding subtle yet significant changes in diet through time and how that might be related to shifts in economy, notably the scale of the animal economy but also of agriculture more generally.

Results: mobility stable isotopes

A total of 33 individuals dating to the Iron Age and buried at Burnby Lane (*n* = 31) and The Mile (*n* = 2) have had isotopic measurements made on skeletal tissues that can be used to investigate the movement and mobility of this population. In order to track the movement of individuals reliably it is important that robust baseline datasets exist or are developed for the local and surrounding geologies so that inferences can be made as to the areas from where people came or to which they

went. In addition to the carbon and nitrogen isotope data presented as part of the dietary study, sulphur isotopes were measured on the same samples, providing us with three isotopes that can be used together to determine more accurately the locations where each individual lived at various stages in their life prior to being buried at either Burnby Lane or The Mile.

Mobility baseline

Although the dietary baseline enabled the identification of subtle differences in the carbon and nitrogen isotope values for animals from Pocklington versus those from Wetwang Slack, the mobility determination is largely driven by the sulphur isotopes in the sample and relates those to the expected values for the different geologic packages in the region. Figure 17.3 shows the bedrock geology for Pocklington and the area covered by an approximate 20km radius, which includes Wetwang Slack. Two things are immediately clear from looking at the geologic age-based colour-coding: (1) the area is primarily covered by either the Upper Cretaceous chalk that surrounds Wetwang Slack or the Triassic mud/silt/sandstone that lies beneath Pocklington and extends to the west; and (2) Pocklington lies very near the edge of the Triassic geology, within 1km of the Jurassic-period Lias Group and 3km of the Upper Cretaceous chalk. This stands in contrast to Wetwang Slack that is nearly 8km south-east of the nearest Jurassic geology of the West Walton formation. This is important as it directly impacts how we must approach the dataset when determining the value of the 'local' geology. Additionally, it is important to remember that consumer isotope values will reflect the isotopes of all the animals they eat, such that the variability in the total faunal population must be taken into consideration in addition to the range that is inferred to be 'local'.

Animal isotopes: Pocklington vs. Wetwang Slack

The only other archaeological work on sulphur isotopes in East Yorkshire was undertaken by Jay *et al.* (2013), where they developed a δ^{34}S baseline using seven terrestrial herbivore samples from Wetwang Slack (13.0–16.5‰; Jay *et al.* 2013, table 1). This value is very similar to the range determined by Hamilton *et al.* (2019) of 12.9–18.8‰ for δ^{34}S on the same chalk geology over 300km away in Hampshire, though it must be pointed out that in the Hampshire dataset approximately 20% of the 71 animals were determined to have 'non-local' isotope values and would have been transported at least 20km to the sites, if they were to have been reared on a different geology. The δ^{34}S values for the 27 animal samples from Pocklington showed considerably variability (0.4–16.8‰). With an overall mean δ^{34}S value of 9.5±3.8‰ (range 1.9–17.1‰; 95% confidence), it was felt highly likely that they too demonstrated a population that comprised animals raised on different geologies. Therefore, the cosine similarity coefficient and the unweighted pair group method with arithmetic means cluster analysis methodology presented in Hamilton *et al.* (2019) was used here to determine the most likely range of δ^{34}S values for locally reared animals.

Three groups were identified and are presented from greatest to smallest number of members. Group 1 contains 17 animals (cattle = 7; horse = 6; sheep/goat = 2; red deer = 1; pig = 1) with a δ^{34}S = 8.2±1.7‰ (range 4.8–11.6‰ at 95% confidence). Group 2 contains 10 animals (cattle = 5; sheep/goat = 3; horse = 2) with a δ^{34}S = 13.5±1.7‰ (range 10.1–16.9‰ at 95% confidence). Finally, there are a horse and a pig in in Group 3, with δ^{34}S values of 0.4‰ and 0.5‰, respectively.

Following the 'criterion of abundance', we assign the range associated with Group 1 as representative of the 'local' δ^{34}S values. Although extending to smaller values, Group 2 almost certainly represents the chalk, with the lowest values that overlap with Group 1 (~10–12‰ range) possibly representing samples that

include collagen from a period in life living on two geologies. Given the differences highlighted above in the carbon and nitrogen isotope values of the Pocklington and Wetwang Slack faunal samples, these isotopes will be increasingly important for teasing apart the human data in this overlapping area. Finally, it is not possible to provide a potential geographic location for the two animals in Group 3. Unpublished data from the SUERC laboratory on Iron Age cattle (*n* = 52) from a site in Cambridgeshire on the West Walton and Kellaways Formation and Oxford Clays suggest these Jurassic-period lithologies have a δ^{34}S value of −16.9±7.4‰ (range = −31.8 to −2.0‰; 95% confidence), and so we might expect animals and people living some or all of their life on these Jurassic geologies to have extremely depleted δ^{34}S values.

Summary of results

The results are summarised in Table 17.2. The interpretation of the isotope values uses the Group 1 δ^{34}S values to define the expected sulphur isotope ratio for a person living on the geology surrounding Pocklington. Given that, there are nine Iron Age individuals, out of the 31 investigated at Burnby Lane, who have lived some part of their life off this geology. This is nearly one-third of the population in the Burnby Lane cemetery, and it fits well with the data of Jay *et al.* (2013) from Wetwang Slack where four of the 15 individuals studied appeared to have originated from off the chalk geology of that region.

Just as that dataset showed no correlation between burial type and movement, so the Burnby Lane dataset shows no correlation between the movement of a person and their burial type (e.g. central barrow, secondary barrow, or no barrow). Only four of the 20 individuals (20%) studied who were centrally interred in a barrow demonstrate significant movement in their lifetime (Sk 85, 113, 121, and 122). Given Sk 122 is nearly centrally located within the ditch defining what was originally presumed to be a Bronze Age round barrow, it may be this Iron Age individual is actually a secondary burial or perhaps was not actually buried within a barrow. Thus, the percentage could be considerably lower. Of the eight individuals studied who were not within a square barrow, three (38%) showed considerable movement at some point in their lifetime.

It is also worth considering the sex of an individual and movement. At Burnby Lane, five of the individuals were male (Sk 52, 67, 73, 85, and 113), while two were female (Sk 8 and 121). The other two individuals were a juvenile and unsexed adult. While both sexes appear to have been mobile, it is interesting to note that the three people who were locally raised and who moved away for their middle years were an unsexed adult and two males.

Table 17.2 Pocklington IA Mobility Results: results for the Iron Age burials at Burnby Lane and The Mile that were investigated for mobility using δ³⁴S measurements

Sk no.	Sex	Age	Child-hood	δ³⁴S (‰)	Mid-life	δ³⁴S (‰)	Near death	δ³⁴S (‰)	Interpretation
Burnby Lane									
2	?F	46+	P	11.3	P	10.2	P	9.9	
8	F	26–35	C	15.9	C	13.0	C	12.6	This woman lived her life on chalk geology but was buried at Pocklington. Potentially moved to the area very late in life as δ³⁴S of the femur is lower than the tooth and the rib is even lower than the femur, suggesting a slight move toward equilibration
13	U	36–45	P		P	4.3			
16	F	17–20	P	9.0	P	9.1	P	9.9	
20	?M	36–45?			P	9.7			
21		14.5–16.5			P	6.4			
27	M	36–45	P	7.9	P		P	8.0	
39	F	36–45?	P	10.5	P	8.9	P	7.4	
40	F	36–45?	P	9.7	P	10.7	P	10.2	
45	?M	18–25			P	8.5			
51	F	26–35	P	10.2	P	9.8			
52	?M	18–25	C	14.1	P	9.0			This ?man spent his childhood on chalk before moving to Pocklington geology. Given his age at death, it is likely he moved in his mid-teens, which would have enabled the bone collagen in his femur to equilibrate to the Pocklington geology values
54	M	26–35	P	7.1	P	7.7	P	7.7	
56	M	26–35	P	9.4	P	8.9			
58	?M	36+?	P	8.0					
67	M	18–35?	P	9.5	?	3.4 Femur 6.7 Tibia			This man spent his childhood on the Pocklington geology but moved away probably in his mid-teens. He potentially returned to the Pocklington geology in the decade prior to death, as the femur sample has δ³⁴S value that is considerably different from the tooth and the tibia appears to have equilibrated closer to the values of the local geology
73	M	36–45?	C	11.3	P	9.0	P	8.6	This man spent his childhood on chalk before moving to Pocklington geology. Given his age at death, he likely moved in his mid-teens or early 20s so that bone collagen in femur could equilibrate to the Pocklington geology values.
81	F	26–35?	P	8.3	P	7.0			
82	?F	25+			P	8.1	P	9.3	
83	?F	15–17	P	4.7					

(Continued)

Table 17.2 Pocklington IA Mobility Results: results for the Iron Age burials at Burnby Lane and The Mile that were investigated for mobility using $\delta^{34}S$ measurements (Continued)

Sk no.	Sex	Age	Child-hood	$\delta^{34}S$ (‰)	Mid-life	$\delta^{34}S$ (‰)	Near death	$\delta^{34}S$ (‰)	Interpretation
85	M	36+	P	8.9	?	0.9			This man was raised on the Pocklington geology but moved away after his mid-teens. The lack of stable isotopes on the rib makes it impossible to determine if he returned to the area at any point prior to death
89	U	18+			P	8.1			
113	M	26–35	?	3.2	P	6.0			This man was born and raised away from Pocklington and subsequently moved onto the geology in his teens or possibly early 20s
115	U	18+			P	8.8			
119	?F	46+	P	8.8	P	9.3	P	9.2	
120	?M	26–45	P	5.8	P	5.6			
121	F	25+	?	1.7	?/P	4.3	?/P	4.9	This woman was raised on a geology away from Pocklington and likely moved to the area within a decade of her death. The $\delta^{34}S$ values on her femur and rib are on the low side of the range for the local geology, which suggests the collagen in these bones was equilibrating
122		9.5–11			C	11.2			This juvenile was living on chalk geology probably until very near their death
129	?M	46+?	P	10.1	P	9.1	P	9.1	
139	U	25+	P	8.8	?	−6.5			This unsexed adult was raised on the Pocklington geology and moved away in their late teens or later
155	F	26–35	P	7.0					
The Mile									
303	M		C/P	12.2	C/P	11.6	C/P	10.1	This man appears to have $\delta^{34}S$ values from across the skeletal elements that suggest a mixed diet/residence across the chalk and Pocklington geologies. The trend is toward a movement from the chalk to Pocklington and so it is possible that move was made shortly before death
424	M		C	14.0			P	6.9	This man was raised on the chalk and lived on the Pocklington geology for probably at least 3 years prior to death so that the rib bone $\delta^{34}S$ value could be fully equilibrated

*Skeleton numbers in **bold** have $\delta^{34}S$ values that suggest the individual moved to the Pocklington geology at some point in their life, while those in **bold italics** have values that suggest they were raised on the Pocklington geology but subsequently moved away for a period before coming back to the area before or in death*

The isotope values for each individual interpreted as having moved are given in Figure 17.4. The two burials from The Mile are also shown here. Three individuals (Sk 8, 52, and possibly 73) would appear to have moved from sites on the chalk to the area around Pocklington, while Sk 113 and 121 were raised on a geology other than Pocklington that was not chalk. Additionally, Sk 122 has a single skeletal element that was investigated and the $\delta^{34}S$ value is at the very upper range for Pocklington, which is the very lowest range of the chalk geology (Group 2) and is included here as a potentially mobile individual.

Perhaps most interesting are the stories of the individuals that are possible when considering the isotope data of the separate skeletal elements in conjunction with the age of each person. We can begin to consider the life-story of the woman buried in an unenclosed grave in the western area of Burnby Lane (Sk 8) who was raised on the chalk geology east of Pocklington and appears to have come to the site a year or so before her death, since her femur and rib bones approach the local Pocklington $\delta^{34}S$ value, but the rib never fully equilibrates. Then there is the man buried in a square barrow in the northern portion of the site (Sk 85), who was raised around Pocklington and moved away after his mid-teens. While his rib bone repeatedly failed to produce suitable collagen, we know this man returned to Pocklington at the closing stage of his life or was brought here after death for his burial and that he was important enough within society to warrant burial within a barrow. Interestingly, aDNA analysis (Patterson *et al.* 2022) revealed his sister is the central interment in a barrow 25m to the west (Sk 82) and she lived her life on the local geology. Of note is the evidence that both individuals from The Mile were raised on the chalk of the Wolds. While Sk 424 (the chariot burial) has a $\delta^{34}S$ value on his tooth that is clearly indicative of a childhood spent on the chalk, Sk 303 (round barrow burial) has values for his tooth and femur that are borderline for the chalk and the local Pocklington geology. It is possible that the latter grew up in an area where his food was raised on both geologies. Or he regularly moved between the two areas throughout much of his life and settled in the Pocklington area in the final years before his death, as

the rib $\delta^{34}S$ value appears to reflect the local Pocklington geology more closely.

At present we do not know whether any of the individuals moved of their own volition and if so, what the motivation was for this movement. Explanations could include positive family alliances, childbearing and rearing, or the negative impact of violent strife or local stress. It is hoped that future researchers will use incremental analysis of the reserved dentine to determine the age at which the mobile individuals moved more precisely and compare this with other evidence that may indicate the impetus for the movement.

Finally, it is worth noting that while there is no data amongst these burials to suggest any individuals raised around Pocklington moved to the chalk and subsequently returned to Pocklington, that is not to say we should interpret Pocklington as a place to which people are being pulled westward from the chalk. Returning to the burials investigated by Jay *et al.* (2013), we can see that their four 'interesting' individuals likely originated from the geology around Pocklington (Fig. 17.5). Amongst those four burials one is a chariot burial. Despite the importance placed on chariot burials and the fact that the two individuals from The Mile, presented here in brief, were likely both raised on the chalk geology, one Wetwang Slack chariot burial (WWS-454) is of a female who likely grew up on the geology surrounding Pocklington.

The movement and mobility of the Iron Age people living in East Yorkshire and buried at sites such as Burnby Lane and Wetwang Slack was very much fluid and inclusive. There is no correlation between age of movement, sex of the individual, status (as inferred from burial type), or location. It would appear anyone has the potential to move at some point in their life and that the reasons are most likely personal and historically situated. Looking at other populations in this way and including other 'mobility' isotopes (e.g. $\delta^{18}O$ and $^{87}Sr/^{86}Sr$), higher-resolution sampling (e.g. sampling multiple teeth or incrementally within a single tooth), and aDNA studies will lead to the development of a robust wider social narrative about not just mobility in the Iron Age, but connectivity and the web of networked relations across East Yorkshire.

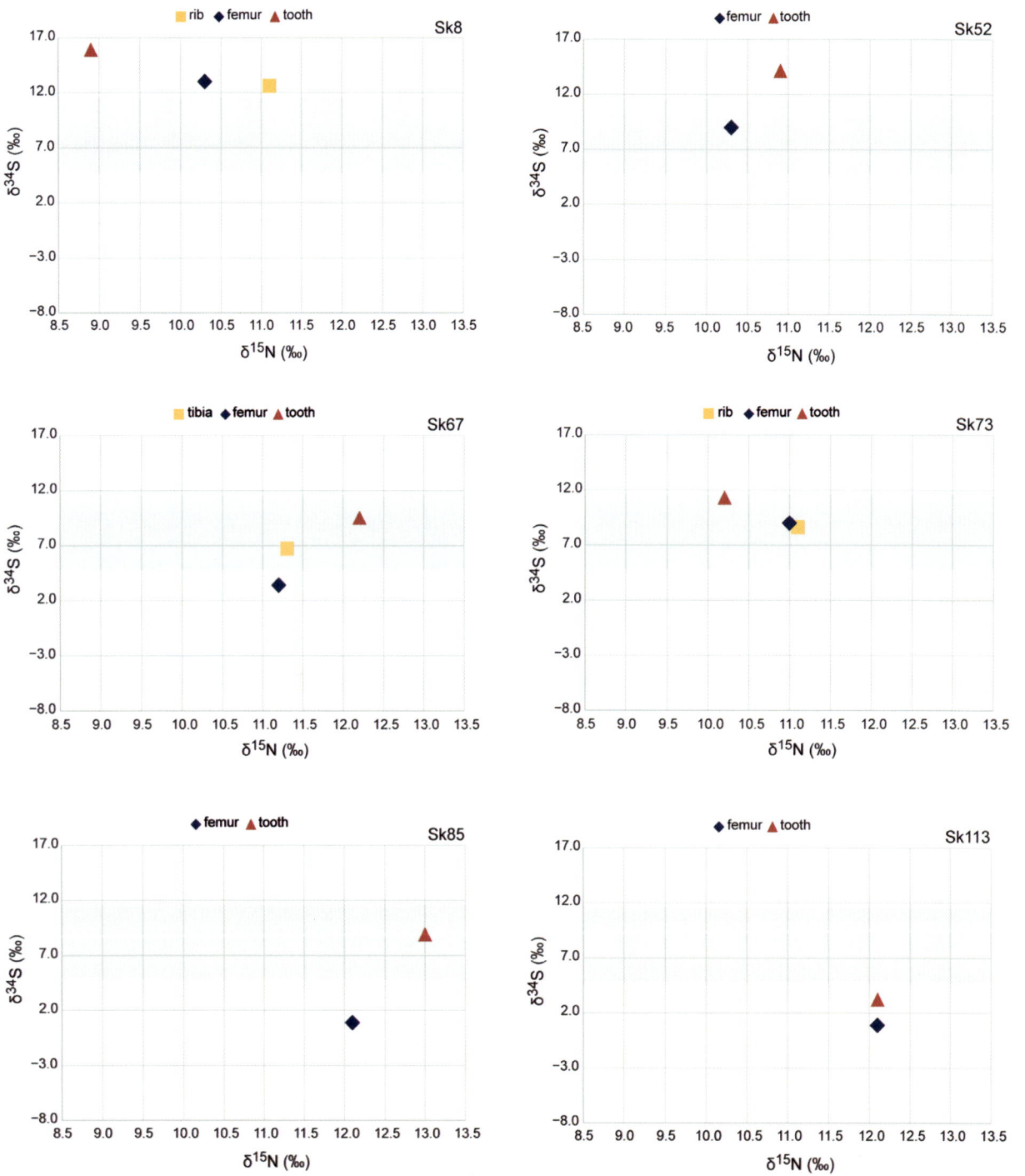

Figure 17.4 Plots of the δ³⁴S and δ¹⁵N values for the Iron Age burials from Burnby Lane and two burials from The Mile. The grey bar indicates the expected range of δ³⁴S values for individuals living on the geology of Burnby Lane, as defined in the text. The values greater than this range are most likely indicative of living on the chalk geology to the east, while the current understanding of δ³⁴S distributions across Britain limit the identification of locations for values lower than the Burnby Lane range

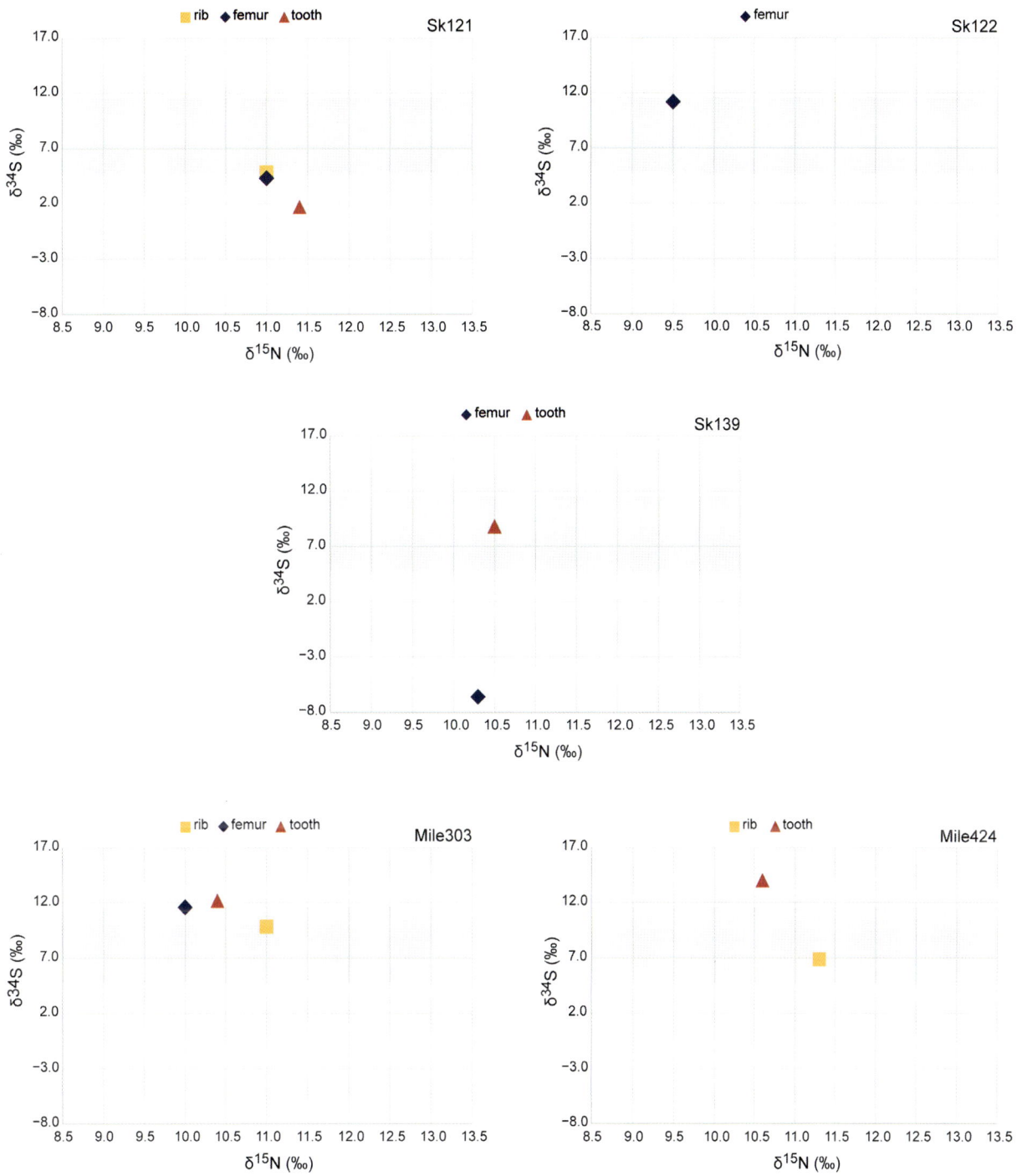

Figure 17.4 (Continued)

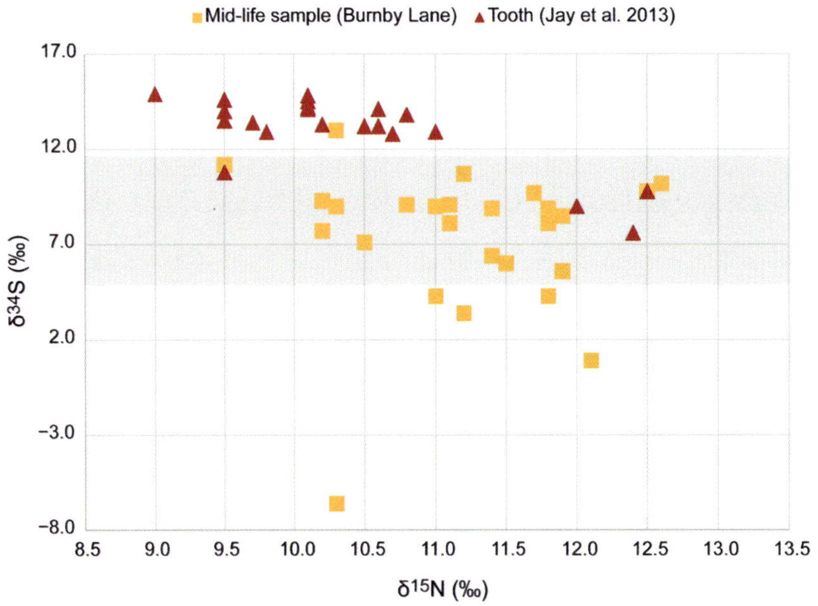

Figure 17.5 Plot of the δ³⁴S and δ¹⁵N values for the mid-life sample (femurs, with the exception of Sk 20 and 122 humerus and Sk 2 and 89 lower leg bone) of the Iron Age burials from Burnby Lane, the chariot burial from The Mile and the childhood sample (dentine) for the people recovered at Wetwang Slack (Jay et al. 2013)

The significance of circular barrows of the Arras culture – warrior graves or just a local tradition?

Paula Ware

The discovery at the Burnby Lane cemetery of five circular barrows surrounded by square barrows and flat burials triggered a desire to discover the significance of the circular form (Fig. 18.1). Why were these burials selected for a separate, distinctive burial rite? A further, single circular barrow at The Mile, Pocklington (Fig. 18.2) and three circular barrows at Burton Fleming (MAP 2013) added to the body of evidence and led to the production of this chapter.

Imagery plays a central role in studies of the middle Iron Age, and whilst examining the evidence my attention was drawn to the ring and dot pattern associated with so many objects of the period having more than a passing resemblance to the cropmark of a ploughed-out circular barrow. In the 19th century the characteristic burial rite of the East Yorkshire Iron Age cemeteries led to a belief that it was unique to a tribe of the region. In the 20th century, 'tribe' was replaced by 'culture', with Hawkes (1959) referring to the Arras *culture* in the late 1950s. Stead cited the markers for the Arras culture as '(i) large cemeteries of small barrows, (ii) some barrows defined by square-plan ditches and (iii) some barrows covering vehicle burials' (Stead 1979, 11).

On examination of the available evidence it was apparent that a small number of circular barrows could be found amongst the predominant square barrows in Arras culture cemeteries both on the continent and in East Yorkshire. In general, these circular barrows have been given scant attention within narratives of Arras culture cemeteries but their significance cannot be ignored, as they may provide evidence for the 'warrior grave' and the social movement of an elite band of males through the continent and to East Yorkshire.

Circular Iron Age barrows in East Yorkshire

History

The circular barrow form in the Iron Age has long been recognised (Sheppard 1939; Stead 1965; Collis 1973; Whimster 1979; Anthoons 2011), with Halkon narrating a comprehensive account of the history of square barrow investigations in East Yorkshire from the 18th century to the present day (Halkon 2013). It is clear that the distinction was being made between the square and circular form in these early excavations.

Aerial photographs confirmed Greenwell's 1906 observations on the ground that traces of ploughed-out barrows, both circular and square, could be seen as soilmarks south of Danes Graves Plantation, Nafferton parish, with Stoertz (1997, map 2) identifying more than a 100 square and circular barrows within the cemetery.

In 1938, construction works on a new airfield at Eastburn, Driffield revealed *c.* 50 barrows: when these were examined just before being covered with concrete, each tumulus was clearly indicated in the very white chalk by a circle representing a slight trench on the outside of the mound, and a dark, usually squarish place in the centre 3–4ft (*c.* 0.9–1.2m) across, which contained a skeleton (Sheppard 1939, 35).

Whilst the skeletons were never examined, the finds from the graves were collected, providing evidence for warrior burials including a spear, sword, shield parts and brooches. Unfortunately, like so many early barrow excavations, detailed analysis was not possible and many of the finds have since disappeared. In 1960, John Bartlett, the then Keeper of Archaeology at Hull museum, recorded five circular barrows at Rudston, all with diameters of 6m, containing single central graves with crouched burials; no details of grave goods are recorded (Whimster 1979, 244).

Figure 18.1 Burnby Lane: overall view of circular barrows (south at the top)

Form and burial rite

The majority of chariot burials have been located within square barrows, including the most recent ones excavated at Burnby Lane (Barrow 85) and The Mile (Barrow 485). However, descriptions of chariot burials by both Mortimer (1905a) and Stillingfleet (1846) reveal that these could also be contained within circular barrows. Stillingfleet described both the 'King's Barrow' and the 'Queen's Barrow' at Arras as circular. The dimensions for these barrows are much larger, at *c.* 8m diameter, and are therefore excluded from the group under discussion, the majority of which are *c.* 6m in diameter. While chariot burials are not wholly the preserve of one gender, the majority are occupied by males. Detailed analysis of the chariot burial rite is included in Anthoons' (2021) comprehensive publication.

The second half of the 20th century gave rise to the seminal works of Ian Stead, John Dent and Tony Brewster which developed the study of the Arras culture into a coherent narrative, with analysis of rites and material culture (Brewster 1980; Dent 1982; Stead 1991a). Stead also noticed a distinct burial rite associated with circular barrows: 'It is clear that many of these spearheads were buried not as grave goods in the usually accepted sense, but as the remains of a ritual carried out during the burial ceremony' (Stead 1991a, 33). The best examples are from the central graves of four small circular barrows at Garton Station.

The precise implications of the circular barrow enclosure are elusive, leading Halkon to conclude that 'not all the burial mounds were square, as some burials were enclosed by ring ditches, though the reason for this difference is now lost to us' (Halkon 2013, 71). The emerging picture highlights circular barrows as even more significant when the form is considered together with the grave goods. Whilst not exclusive to the circular form, the vast majority of circular ring ditches contain martial objects including some associated with the burial rite of spearing.

The absence of overall site plans and excavation records from many of these early excavations makes observations on the spatial distribution of circular Iron Age barrows within the cemeteries difficult. It is impossible to cover all excavation records in this chapter but thanks to the many detailed available sources and the latest discoveries, which add to the existing corpus of information, some tentative interpretations can be made. While the focus of previous research excavations has tended to look for potential barrows with possible chariots contained within square enclosures, perhaps more attention should be paid to the circular barrows.

Defining features of circular barrows

I would like to challenge the assumption that we may never know the reason behind the distinct circular form. Is it now possible to attempt to qualify the significance

Figure 18.2 The circular barrow at The Mile, facing north. Scales: 2m

of these circular barrows and indeed suggest why certain individuals were accorded this burial rite?

It is the ring ditch that is the defining feature of these monuments and this is clearly seen in both aerial photographs and on the ground. However, it is possible that some flat graves are misrepresented, as they may have originally had a ring ditch, particularly those with burials in deep rectangular graves. Shallow ditches would have been vulnerable to plough damage and without the evidence, such burials must be excluded from this assessment.

Statistically, the square barrow is the dominant form but if we look at the larger cemeteries, including Burnby Lane, a pattern emerges, with circular barrows comprising a small percentage (3–5%) of the overall total. Circular barrows appear in the majority of larger cemeteries in East Yorkshire including Danes Graves, Burton Fleming and Burnby Lane but they can also appear in isolation, as at The Mile. Unfortunately, they have largely been ignored in the archaeological record in both East Yorkshire and continental sites but the recent excavations have identified particular features that occur frequently, Barrow 37 at Burnby Lane being a good example (Fig. 18.3):

- a precise, circular barrow between 5.5m and 6.5m in diameter;
- a shallow U-shaped profile ring gully between 0.2m and 0.5m in depth;
- a deep rectangular grave of minimum depth 0.5m but often exceeding 0.8m;
- a male skeleton;
- either isolated or located within a cemetery;
- dated to the Middle Iron Age.

Additional features may include the following but are not exclusive to the circular barrow:

- skeletons with evidence of blunt force trauma;
- distinctive grave goods including swords, shields, spears, brooches and food deposits;
- evidence for the burial rite of spearing;
- secondary burials or flat graves in close proximity containing females;
- contains box/coffin;
- a causeway;
- possibility for a chariot, especially on the continent.

Figure 18.3 Burnby Lane: Barrow 37, Skeleton 78, facing north. Scales: 1m

Excavation records reveal that whilst the majority of circular barrows conform to the above criteria, at least 20% of circular barrows do not have the applicable features. Further research is required to establish how agricultural ploughing or robbing in antiquity has damaged or removed potential evidence.

Stead's work established a connection between the Arras culture of East Yorkshire and a continental tradition for wheeled-vehicle burials and square barrows (Stead 1961). The continental burial rite had its origins in the later Hallstatt period in central Europe and extended westward to Switzerland, Germany and the Champagne region of France. Stead states that 'the presence of cart burials on the continent implies that this aspect of the

Yorkshire cultures was due to immigration from abroad' (Stead 1965, 77). The Champagne area has the largest number of chariot burials, with others located in Austria, Czech Republic, Germany, Netherlands, Belgium and Switzerland. The debate over migration from the continent to East Yorkshire continued throughout the latter half of the 20th century as studies of material culture developed. Stead's opinion changed over time, later works (Stead 1979; 1991a) suggesting more an adoption and remodelling of some continental styles, since it was clear that certain elements were from a local tradition which included distinctive ceramics and brooches as well as the dismantling of chariots and crouched burials rather than the intact chariots and extended burials seen on the continent.

Continental circular barrows

Circular barrows dated to the middle Iron Age are found in cemeteries in both East Yorkshire and northern Europe. Much of the continental evidence from Switzerland, Germany and Czech Republic concentrates on the recovered artefacts, many providing evidence of warriors of the Early La Tène period including the life-size Glauberg stone sculpture depicting a warrior (Stollner 2014, 121). The shield boss portrayed on the sculpture has parallels with the shield in Barrow 485 at The Mile (see below). What is often lacking from these published reports is a description of the burial monument itself, with just the description of the grave being included, which is frustrating. A further issue that is highlighted by Anthoons is that 'on the continent, unlike East Yorkshire, barrows are considered to have been round, even when set in a square enclosure' (Anthoons 2021 106). All the examples cited below distinguish the circular form either in plan or aerial photographs. Recent research by Peter Ramsl (2020) provides a corpus of evidence from cemeteries in Slovakia, Eastern Austria and Moravia, with detailed descriptions of male burials, which has aided the narrative.

It is not possible to give a detailed account of all published sources from the continent but a perfunctory review of some of the easily accessible accounts allows a comparison between the two areas (Table 18.1). At Mannersdorf am Leithagebirge in Austria, detailed excavation plans reveal two circular barrows with a central grave surrounded by square barrows (Barrows 60 and 74) (Ginoux and Ramsl 2014, 279). In Barrow 60, a child and a man were buried together. The male was aged 17–25 and had a sword and broken spear. Another inhumation burial of a warrior (44) and a double grave (46) with the burial of a warrior and cremation remains in an urn were surrounded by circular trenches. The third, also circular, surrounded a child's grave (75) with rich equipment including a gold and silver wire ring and a vessel made of clay in the form of a shoe (Ramsl 2020, 30). France has an extensive archive of aerial photographs of cropmarks

Table 18.1 Continental cemeteries with circular barrows

Cemetery	Country	Circular	Weapons	Inhumation	Cremation	Male	Other grave goods	Reference
Palárikovo I	Slovenia	x	x	x		x	x	Ramsl 2020
Gemeinlebarn-Schneiderweg	Austria	x	x	x		x	x	Ramsl 2020
Herzogenburg Grave 2	Austria	x	x	x		x	x	Ramsl 2020
Inzersdorf	Austria	x	x	x	x	x	x	Ramsl 2020
Mannersdorf am Leithagebirge II	Austria	x	x	x		x	x	Ramsl 2020
Oberndorf	Austria	x	x	x		x	x	Neugebauerand Gattringer 1982; Neugebauer 1988; 1992; Megaw *et al.* 1989; Ramsl 2018b; 2020
Ossarn 25/1963	Austria	x		x		x	x	Engelhardt 1969; 1976; Neugebauer and Gattringer 1984; Megaw *et al.* 1989; Neugebauer 1992; Ramsl 2020
Pottenbrunn	Austria	x	x	x	x	x	x	Neugebauer and Ramsl 1998
Rassing Tumulus 2	Austria	x				x		Preinfalk 2005; Ramsl 2020
Walpersdorf	Austria	x	x	x	x	x	x	Neugebauer 1997; 1999
Glauberg	Germany	x	x	x		x	x	Ramsl 2020
Hochdorf	Germany	x	x	x		x	x	Biel 1985
Lavau	France	x	x	x		x	x	19 November 2015/ Actualité INRAP 16 June 2015/Actualité INRAP
Menil-Annelles	France	x	x	x	x	x	x	Stead *et al.* 2006
Quilly	France	x	x	x		x	x	Stead *et al.* 2006
Mairy-sur-Marne	France	x	x	x		x	x	Stead *et al.* 2006
Mont-Trote	France	x	x	x		x	x	Rozoy 1987
Witry-les-Reims	France	x						Whimster 1979
Vert-la-Gravelle	France	x						Whimster 1979
St Remy-sur-Bussy	France	x						Whimster 1979
Gravon	France	x						Whimster 1979
Allincourt	France	x						Stead *et al.* 2006
Bouy	France	x						Whimster 1979
Ville-sur-Retourne	France	x						Stead *et al.* 2006
Saulces-Champenoises	France	x						Stead *et al.* 2006

revealing cemeteries with both square and round barrows including 11 at Mairy-sur-Marne, Marne and three at Mont-Trote cemetery, Marne (Rozoy 1987). Further examples include Witry-les-Reims; Vert-la-Gravelle; St Remy-sur-Bussy; Gravon; Allonville; Bouy; Juniville; and Ville-sur-Retourne (Stead 1961, 54; Flouest and Stead 1974, 62; Stead *et al.* 2006) where square barrows are outnumbered by circular barrows.

Detailed descriptions are available from six French sites excavated in the 1970s, in which one particular barrow excavated at Quilly stands out (Stead *et al.* 2006, 24). Barrow C was circular and contained a single central grave; unfortunately, the inhumation had been disturbed in antiquity but was recorded as a male aged 35 years plus. The group of finds includes: four spearheads which were placed on the right side of the skeleton in line with or beyond the feet, pointing into the bottom of the grave; two fragments of a La Tène I iron two-coil spring brooch; four iron rings; and three iron toilet items including a razor, tweezers and nail cleaner. Such items are often found in (principally male) graves in the Champagne region and date to the late Hallstatt D and La Tène I graves (Stead *et al.* 2006, 199).

Differences between the East Yorkshire and continental cemeteries

Features of continental circular barrows:

- barrows are much larger, some exceeding 30m but on average *c.* 8–10m;
- burials are usually extended, with earlier ones orientated head to the south;
- early circular barrows may contain cremation rather than inhumation;
- frequently contain other grave goods such as ceramics and personal objects as well as weaponry;
- primary male burials maybe also occasionally be accompanied with either female or child.

Circular barrows from East Yorkshire

The most recent excavations at Burnby Lane and The Mile, Pocklington and at Burton Fleming provide detailed examples of circular barrows from East Yorkshire, with several having the benefit of radiocarbon dates. Further examples of circular barrows from earlier excavations are included in Table 18.2.

Burnby Lane Barrow 32

Barrow 32 (see Chapter 4) was circular with a diameter of *c.* 5.8m. The ditch had a broad-U profile, measuring between 0.25m and 0.30m in depth; the fill contained animal bone fragments. The rectangular central grave measured 2.18m from north to south, 1.38m from east to west and 0.64m deep.

The burial was an 18–25-year-old male (Sk 59), laid prone with head to the north, facing east. The lower legs were bent backwards and upwards towards the pelvis and the left arm folded under the torso. The body presented evidence for multiple blunt force trauma. Included within the grave was a curved iron riveted strip similar to the strips found in Barrow 37 relating to parts of a dismantled shield.

Burnby Lane Barrow 33

Barrow 33 was circular with an internal diameter of *c.* 5.2m. The ditch was 0.35m deep with a flat-based

V profile and contained Iron Age sherds. The rectangular grave measured 1.85m from north to south, 1.20m from east to west, and 0.8m deep.

The grave contained the skeleton of a 26–35-year-old male (Sk 56), laid in a part crouched and part prone posture, face downwards, with the limbs tucked under the torso, and the head to the north facing east. He had a fracture of the left clavicle and the grave fill contained a brooch (SF 66, see Chapter 11). Unfortunately, radiocarbon-dating failed due to poor preservation and lack of suitable collagen.

Burnby Lane Barrow 34

Barrow 34 was circular, measured *c.* 5.8m in diameter overall, with a shallow U-shaped ditch *c.* 0.30m deep, the fill of which contained animal bone fragments. The rectangular central grave measured 2.2m long, 1.4m wide and 0.5m deep and contained the skeleton of an 18–25-year-old crouched male (SK 57), laid on the left side, with the head to the north, facing east. The grave goods included an iron sword, five iron spearheads and an iron ferrule. Evidence indicates that the grave also contained a structure, suggesting some circular barrows do contain coffins/structures. This is important new information as Anthoons' detailed examination of East Yorkshire cemeteries had suggested that this feature was missing from circular barrows (Anthoons 2011, 52). A secondary burial placed in the barrow ditch was a crouched female aged 46+ years with head to the north, facing east.

Burnby Lane Barrow 35

Barrow 35 was a circular barrow and measured *c.* 5.2m in diameter with a shallow ditch 0.2m deep. The central grave, which was rectangular, measured 1.64m from north to south, 1.10m from east to west, and around 0.35m in depth. It contained the skeleton of a male (SK 61), over 26 years of age, placed prone in a flexed posture, with head to the north, facing east.

Burnby Lane Barrow 37

Barrow 37 was circular and measured 5.2m in diameter with a shallow ditch 0.20m deep which contained four calcite-gritted sherds (Fig. 18.3). The central grave was rectangular with a bowed southern side and measured 2.00m in length north to south, 1.35m in width from east to west, and was *c.* 0.40m deep. The grave contained the skeleton of an adult male, over 36 years of age (Sk 78), in a flexed posture, lying on the left side with head to the north, facing east and placed within a structure with the remains of a composite shield.

The Mile Barrow 485

The circular barrow had a diameter of *c.* 6m with a ditch 0.5m deep (see Chapter 6). A rectangular central grave which measured 1.84m long, 1.18m wide and 0.72m deep

Table 18.2 East Yorkshire warrior graves in known cemeteries

Cemetery	Circular	Male	Weapons	Inhumation	Trauma	Spears	Other finds	Position	Reference
Arras	x	x	x	x		x	x	crouched, extended, flexed	Stillingfleet 1846; Greenwell 1906
Bugthorpe	x	?	x	x			x		Mortimer 1905a
Burnby Lane, Pocklington	x	x	x	x	x	x	x	3 crouched, 2 flexed	Ware & Stephens 2020
Burton Fleming/ Bell Slack	x	x	x	x		x	x	Predominately crouched, head to north, 18 extended	Stead 1991a
Burton Fleming	x	x	?	x	x			crouched	MAP 2013
Cowlam				x			x		Stead 1986
Danes Graves	x	x	x	x		x	x	crouched, extended, flexed	Greenwell 1906; Mortimer 1905a
Driffield 1938	x		x	x		x	x	crouched	Sheppard 1939
Eastburn	x	x	x	x		x	x	crouched	Stead 1991a
Garton Station	x	x	x	x	x	x	x	Crouched, flexed	Stead 1991a
Grimthorpe	x	x	x	x		x	x	crouched	Mortimer 1905a
Kirkburn	x	x	x	x	x	x	x	crouched	Stead 1991a
North Grimston	x	x	x	x		x	x	crouched	Mortimer 1905a
Rillington	x								AP, Harding 2015
Rudston Makeshift	x		x	x	x	x	x	crouched, extended, flexed	Stead 1991a
Scorborough	x	x	x	x		x	x	crouched, extended, flexed	Stead 1961
Seamer Moor	x	x	x					crouched, cremations	Hinderwell 1811; Stead 1961
Skipwith Common	x		x	x			x	cremation	Procter 1855
The Mile, Pocklington	x	x	x	x	x	x	x	crouched	Ware & Stephens 2020
Wetwang Slack	x	x	x	x	x		x	crouched, extended, flexed	Brewster 1980; Dent 2010

was situated at the centre of the enclosed area. The grave contained the well-preserved skeleton (Sk 303) of a young adult male (18–25 years old) laid in a crouched position on his left side, facing east. The arms were bent at the elbows and both hands were drawn up in front of the face. The skeleton revealed evidence for blunt force trauma and the grave goods included the deliberately dismantled parts of a shield and five iron spears and three bone points (Fig. 18.4). The burial was radiocarbon-dated to 350–50 cal BC. Located *c.* 1m to the south-west of the above circular barrow was a deep rectangular grave containing the skeleton of a female aged 18–25 years (Sk 274), in a crouched position with head to the north, facing east.

Burton Fleming

Excavations in 2013 (MAP, 2013) in advance of the construction of a chicken shed located three largely complete barrows (two circular, one square) and four inhumations, all of which were fully excavated. A third, probably circular, barrow was only partially excavated as it continued beyond the area of excavation. All three largely complete barrows had central crouched inhumations and the grave of another inhumation cut into the northern ditch of the square barrow. The excavations were situated to the south of Ian Stead's earlier excavations (Stead 1991a, 17) and provide further evidence for the survival of barrows in the area.

Burton Fleming Barrow 89

Barrow 89 had a diameter of 5.9m with a shallow U-shaped ditch *c.* 0.2m deep. The central grave measured 1.60m long by 0.53m wide and 0.07m deep and contained the skeleton of an adult male, aged 18–25 and with a stature of 1.74m. The radiocarbon date on the tibia places his death in the period 360–50 cal BC (SUERC-63424).

Figure 18.4 The Mile circular barrow: central grave with shield and spears (warrior grave), facing north-east. Scales: 1m and 0.4m

Burton Fleming Barrow 90

Barrow 90 had a diameter of 6m with a narrow gap between two terminals in the south-west corner. The ditch was fairly shallow with a U-shaped profile measuring *c.* 0.2m deep (Figs 18.5 and 18.6).

The central grave was rectangular in plan and measured 1.62m long (north–south), 1.20m wide (east–west) and 1.05m deep. The grave had vertical sides and a flat base and contained a crouched inhumation burial which was laid on its left side, facing east and head to the north. The skeleton was an adult male, aged 46+ and with a stature of 1.63m. The radiocarbon date from his tibia places his death in the period 340 cal BC–cal AD 10 (SUERC-63429).

Other East Yorkshire sites

The following information is derived from Stead (1991a). Excavations at Garton Station located four circular barrows, all containing males with combinations of spear and/or shields (GS4 – 3 spears and shield; GS5 – 4 iron spearheads, 3 bone points and shield parts; GS7 – 11 spearheads; GS10 – 14 spearheads and shield). At Kirkburn, the two circular barrows K3 and K4 had causeways and K3 contained three spearheads. It is possible that other circular barrows have causeways but these have not been recognised if the ring gully has been partially truncated by later activity. The Rudston excavations located seven circular barrows (R51, R141, R154, R168, R175, R176 and R179). R154 included two spears within the grave.

Discussion

The juxtaposition of round and square barrows is a recurrent feature when discussing Iron Age cemeteries and often the circular form is described as utilising space between earlier square barrows, but it seems there is far more significance to the form than economy of space. Giles has developed the theory that 'the over-riding concern by the end of this era was *where* one was buried, next to *whom*. It suggests an obsession with relationships, whether these had a genetic basis or not: creating an architecturally self-evident claim of association' (Giles 2012, 77). The recent work of Patterson *et al.* (see Chapter 19) increases the likelihood of Giles's assumption that what mattered was relationships, in that cemeteries developed into spaces where positioning and type of barrow were prescribed by familial and status associations. It appears likely that who and what you were determined the style of burial. The importance of communal remembrance is revealed by the location of flat graves and secondary burials containing females within metres of a circular barrow containing a male with weapons (see Chapters 4 and 6). Evidence from the continent points to some females actually being interred in the grave at the same time. Burnby Lane provides crucial evidence for familial association between the circular barrows and flat graves with several associations identified through aDNA. Ongoing research may provide the elusive confirmation for a migratory elite.

A clear distinction was made at the time of burial as to which rite was to be assigned. The circular barrow appears to be the preserve of the male, but is there enough evidence to apply the label 'warrior burial'? There is little evidence to support a violent society, but it is clear that some male burials are a testimony to conflict. Giles effectively describes the burial rite:

> in a funerary setting weapons evoked qualities of power related to brute strength as well as martial skill: the cutting, splitting, stabbing and slicing actions of blades inflicting wounds, the strength required to withstand or deflect blows, the judgement of an opponent's moves and orchestration of a fight. They spoke the ideals related to masculine power, to both attack and defend, which may have been vital to the reproduction of the community's honour and the creation of a prestigious, armed ancestry. (Giles 2012, 168)

We are not simply dealing with elite graves, but with ritually significant burial rites that were important for the disposal of elite persons within the community. The individual was accorded a rite that separated them from the majority of the male population. I am prepared to say that the circular barrow can be assigned to the warrior.

Figure 18.5 Burton Fleming: Plan of Barrow 090

Figure 18.6 Burton Fleming: Barrow 090, facing north. Scales: 1m

Archaeological evidence indicates that the populations from lower Austria established significant westward connections with the Champagne area (eastern France) in the La Tène A period. Other connections seem to have occurred later, notably with populations from Switzerland, the Rhineland, and northern Italy. However, it has to be noted that all of these regions were inter-connected into a wider cultural network (Ramsl 2020, 20).

Is it possible that we are looking at a burial rite that represents, as Stollner suggests, 'a warrior ethos that apparently absorbed aspects of heroism from the *mos maiorum*, fitting for an elite, which had established itself by conflict and competition with the southern Hallstatt centres' (Stollner 2014, 133).

Small-scale migration by an influential elite which included warriors (perhaps even mercenaries) and farmers introduced burial rites from the continent that were adapted and incorporated into burial practices which included the circular barrow. Work by Patterson *et al.* on the DNA from the population at Burnby Lane cemetery appears to support this theory:

However, the East Yorkshire burials are distinctive in another way: regional differentiation in IA Britain, as measured by *F*ST [the index by which population differentiation is measured], is higher between East Yorkshire and other groups than it is between any other pair of IA populations in England and Wales in our dataset (Extended Data Table 2). Comparative data from the continent could make it possible to determine whether this is due to isolation of IA East Yorkshire from the rest of southern Britain, or later streams of migration specifically affecting East Yorkshire. (Patterson *et al.* 2022, 7)

The movement of people perpetuates a form of burial practice that recognises the status of the individual. The circular barrow distinguishes the interred individual by the distinctive burial rite, a pattern that emerges throughout the continent with the movement of people.

As Stollner suggests (2014, 122), status was indicated not only by single weapons but often individuals had complete armour, swords, shields and other war weapons placed within the grave, in contrast to the Hallstatt period of the 6th and early 5th centuries BC.

Are the circular barrows of East Yorkshire a recognition of an earlier continental tradition that perpetuates the symbol of the warrior within that society, possibly signifying a mercenary's grave? In order to explore this theory we need to look beyond the grave and examine the enclosures both in East Yorkshire and the continent and recognise that ephemeral ring ditches or remnants of them within cemeteries should not be ignored or dismissed. Flat graves in groups or isolation may once have had a circular enclosure that has been removed by ploughing. The position of such graves combined with radiocarbon dating and aDNA maybe key to understanding the chronology and morphology of the circular barrow.

This chapter is only a cursory examination of the evidence but we hope it gives some impetus to push forward research agendas. Academics and field archaeologists in collaboration can achieve remarkable results.

Synthesis of the Iron Age landscape

Mark Stephens

The Iron Age cemetery

Location

As we have seen, the Burnby Lane cemetery lay on the border between well-drained ground to the north and marshy terrain to the south. In the Iron Age this area was at the southern limit of a tractable gravel terrace bordering a watercourse that ran along the base of the western edge of the chalk Wolds. At this time, the pastures of the Wolds were likely given over to sheep farming, with Iron Age settlement concentrated along the Great Wold Valley and its tributaries (Fenton-Thomas 2005, 57–8). In the other direction, to the south-west of Pocklington, iron-working and smelting was carried out at many locations along the Foulness Valley and in an area that extended northwards from Bursea towards Holme on Spalding Moor, *c.* 7km south of the Burnby Lane site (Halkon 2011, illus. 5). Therefore, in broader landscape terms the Iron Age communities in the vicinity of Pocklington were well situated to exploit the environments, agricultural produce and industrial/craft output of three widely different zones, including the gravel plain on which they lived.

Returning to the immediate landscape of Burnby Lane, the Iron Age cemetery was established at the same location as the earlier hengiform feature and Bronze Age round barrows. This echoes the way in which the Wetwang Slack cemetery partly grew around a large Bronze Age barrow (Dent 1984, 21).

At Burnby Lane, square barrows were constructed around much of the circumference of the Bronze Age round barrow B71, indicating that its mound was still recognisable (see Fig. 3.1). It is possible that other square barrows may have been constructed within the centre of the putative mound of B71 but were destroyed by later ploughing. There were three Iron Age flat inhumations within the circuit of B71 (Sk 115 (16977), Sk 122 (17102) and Sk 139 (18133); Fig. 4.100); interestingly, two of these were buried with brooches (discussed further below) and one of these (Sk 139) had a relatively

early radiocarbon date (470–390 cal BC; SUERC-83081) suggesting that the barrow could have been an early focus of burial in the Iron Age. Enclosure E, to the north of B71, was overlain by the eastern group of square barrows; B30 and B38 directly overlay the enclosure ditch while B33, B34, B36 and B42 were constructed within the Enclosure. In the southern field, another large Bronze Age round barrow (B79) was respected by the distribution of square barrows, with B82 to the north, B78, B81, and B85 to the west, B83 to the south and B84 to the east. Giles has argued that the coincidence of square barrow cemeteries with 'ancient monuments' such as round barrows was to provide 'a connection to the ancestral dead' as well as using ancestors to 'negotiate access to resources' in the present (Giles 2012, 130), justifying claims in the present by a link, real or imagined, with the past.

The extensive Wetwang/Garton Slack square barrow cemeteries were located close to contemporary settlement, but that situation is so far unique, with no other parallels for the proximity of an Iron Age cemetery to large-scale settlement. It is perhaps due to the physical constraints of the relatively narrow valley in which the Wetwang/Garton settlement and burials lay. At Burnby Lane, the possible domestic structure represented by the oval ring gully (Fig. 5.2) and the (undated but pre-Roman) Enclosure H (Figs 4.2 and 5.3), along with a pit pre-dating B30 and a group of pits south-east of B84 (Fig. 5.4), are hints of Iron Age settlement activity on the eastern fringes of the cemetery, but the absence of settlement-type cropmarks in the field immediately to the east suggests that this was not extensive. Otherwise, the closest confirmed Iron Age settlement evidence comes from excavations at Cemetery Lane and Hodsow Lane on the west side of Pocklington, between 650m and 1.3km to the west of Burnby Lane. There are also undated cropmarks of probable settlements west of Primrose Wood (*c.* 250m to the south-west), and 1km to the south at South Moor (Fig. 1.4).

The excavation established the limits of both barrow groups at Burnby Lane, but how those limits were physically expressed on the ground is uncertain. The western group terminated cleanly on all sides, apart from the south-western corner, where a line of barrows stretched southward – perhaps this north–south line indicates the presence of an ancient boundary pre-dating the route represented by Burnby Lane. The western group respects both B79 and Enclosure E, although round barrow B71 was swallowed up by seven later Group 3 square barrows. Conversely, the eastern group appears to have been raised over Enclosure E from the outset. Ditch D passed between the two groups, and it is tempting to see this as the physical manifestation of an earlier, less formalised and/or permeable boundary. If that were the case, Ditch D must have been a long-standing feature that had been maintained through repeated recutting and the barrows would have been constructed along the boundary's southern edge, with only the final version of the boundary encroaching on the barrows. However, the way in which it cut across the corner of B1 makes this impossible as the boundary clearly truncates the barrow, showing that the boundary post-dated the barrow.

The limit of the eastern barrow group coincided with the western extent of the settlement-related activity suggested by the oval ring gully, which associated pottery suggests was contemporary with the Iron Age cemetery. The exact relationship of Enclosure H to the cemetery is uncertain as it was essentially undated (other than pre-dating the Roman Boundary C), but it could be more than coincidence that barrow construction did not extend into the area of the enclosure.

Each of the two separate barrow groups contained clusters of Group 2 and Group 3 barrows (see below for barrow groups); for the western group these filled in the space between Bronze Age round barrow B71 and six Group 1 barrows – B1, B2, B12 and B14 to the west and B69 and B72 to the east (Fig. 19.1). The distinguishing characteristic of the eastern group is the cluster of Group 3 circular barrows within it and it could be that the construction of these distinct barrows is an indication that the individuals buried here were seen as sufficiently 'separate' to dictate the location of their burial apart from others. In the same way, the chariot burial in B85, located as it was on the fringe of the western barrow group, might also have been regarded as standing apart.

In the western barrow group there is a suggestion that family links contributed to the positioning of burials within the cemetery (see Fig. 19.1). The two adult women buried in the adjacent barrows B49 and B50 had a 2nd-degree relationship, and the woman from B49 also had a 2nd- or 3rd-degree relationship with the late adolescent or young adult male buried within B47 (adjacent to the west) and the mature adult male buried in B65 (slightly further away to the east).

Typology and form of the barrows

Stead put forward a burial typology based on the form of burials that he identified during his excavation of cemeteries in and around the Great Wold Valley: Type A were crouched or contracted; B flexed or extended and often aligned east–west; C had unusual traits, e.g. buried with pork or unusual grave goods such as swords, mirrors or chariots (Stead 1991a, 170–80), to which Dent (1995, 74) added Type D – secondary burials cut into barrows, often of juveniles.

Dent's barrow typology, quoted by Halkon (Halkon 2013, 70), is based on the barrow form and size, recognising three main groups: (1) large enclosures, with no surviving central grave and occupying early positions within cemeteries (or otherwise isolated); (2) enclosures of varying sizes with graves of varying depth, usually within the early or middle stages of a cemetery; (3) small enclosures, often curvilinear, with deep (over 0.6m) central graves, at the latest stage of a cemetery. Such is the typology but applying it in practice might appear arbitrary in relation to some barrows.

Giles, while recognising regional trends within burial rites, is surely right in suggesting that 'individual cemeteries would have had their own distinct history of interment' (Giles 2012, 71). The following discussion of the details of the 82 Iron Age barrows, large, medium or small, and square, circular or sub-rectangular, along with the eight secondary and 41 flat Iron Age burials, pays heed to the typologies described above, while recognising that the Burnby Lane cemetery may have developed its own idiosyncrasies – after all, the gravel plain around Pocklington where Burnby Lane is situated is geographically distinct from both the High Wolds and the Great Wold Valley. (However, this does not mean that Burnby Lane was isolated in any way from the neighbouring Iron Age communities.)

Using the depth of the graves or barrow ditches to aid typology must be done cautiously, as the Burnby Lane cemetery was extensively plough-truncated, but not uniformly so. Another factor at Burnby Lane is that the cemetery was divided into two distinct groups, perhaps reflecting the priorities of two separate groups of people. This suggestion of separateness is supported by the fact that the known familial links do not overlap between the western and eastern barrow groups (Fig. 19.2).

To consider the western group first, the earliest barrows in Dent's typology are of Group 1, and there are examples of these relatively large barrows with no surviving grave: B1, B10, B14, B69 and B83, which are mainly situated in the north-western and western fringes of the western barrow group. However, the picture is blurred by the occurrence of barrows of similar size to the Group 1 barrows (B2 and B12) that have intact graves (albeit a very shallow grave in the case of B2 – a dubious explanation being that it might be secondary). Only B2 and B83, and B20, B69 and B72 (which had anomalous forms), are

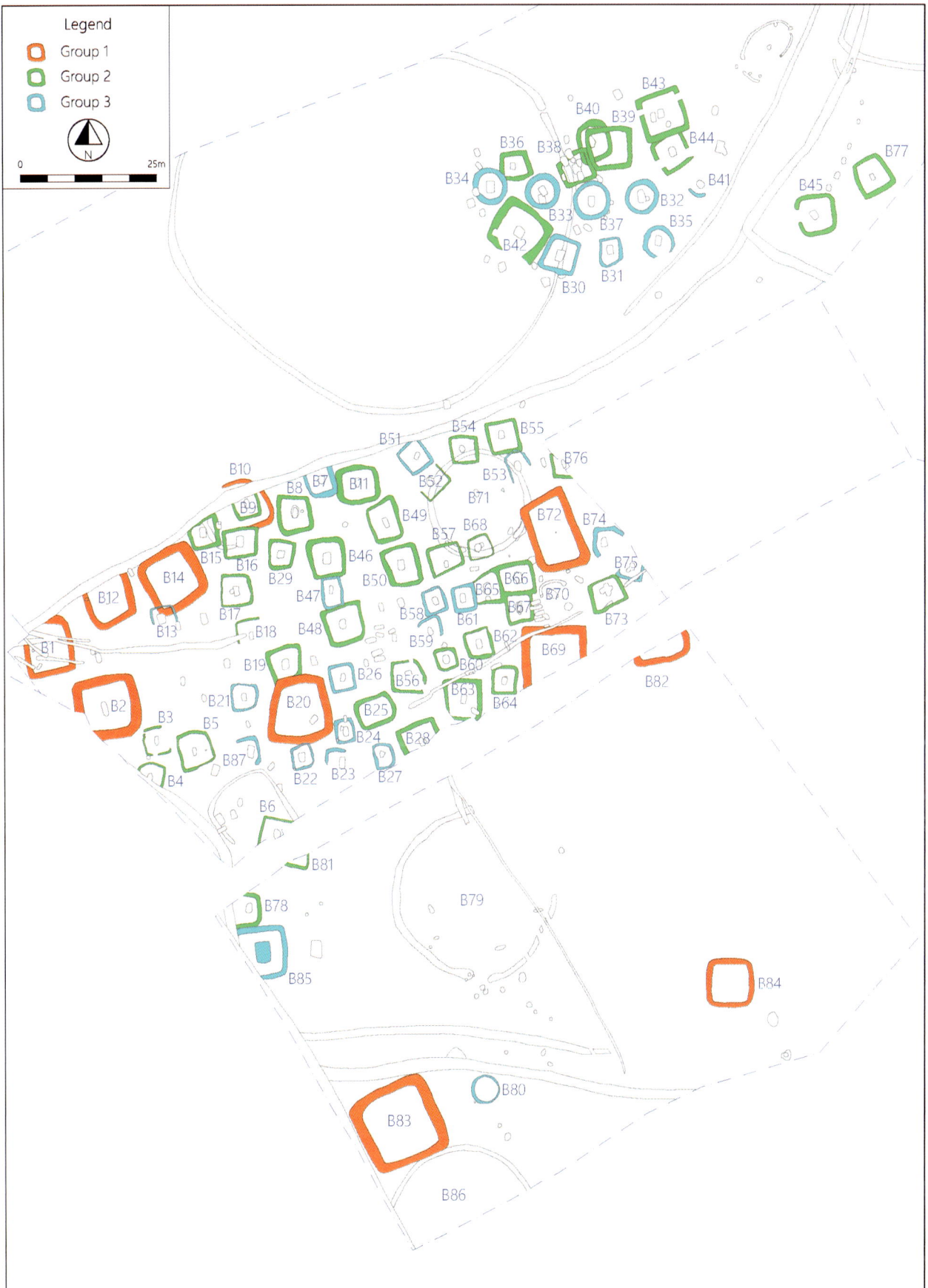

Figure 19.1 Distribution of barrow groups

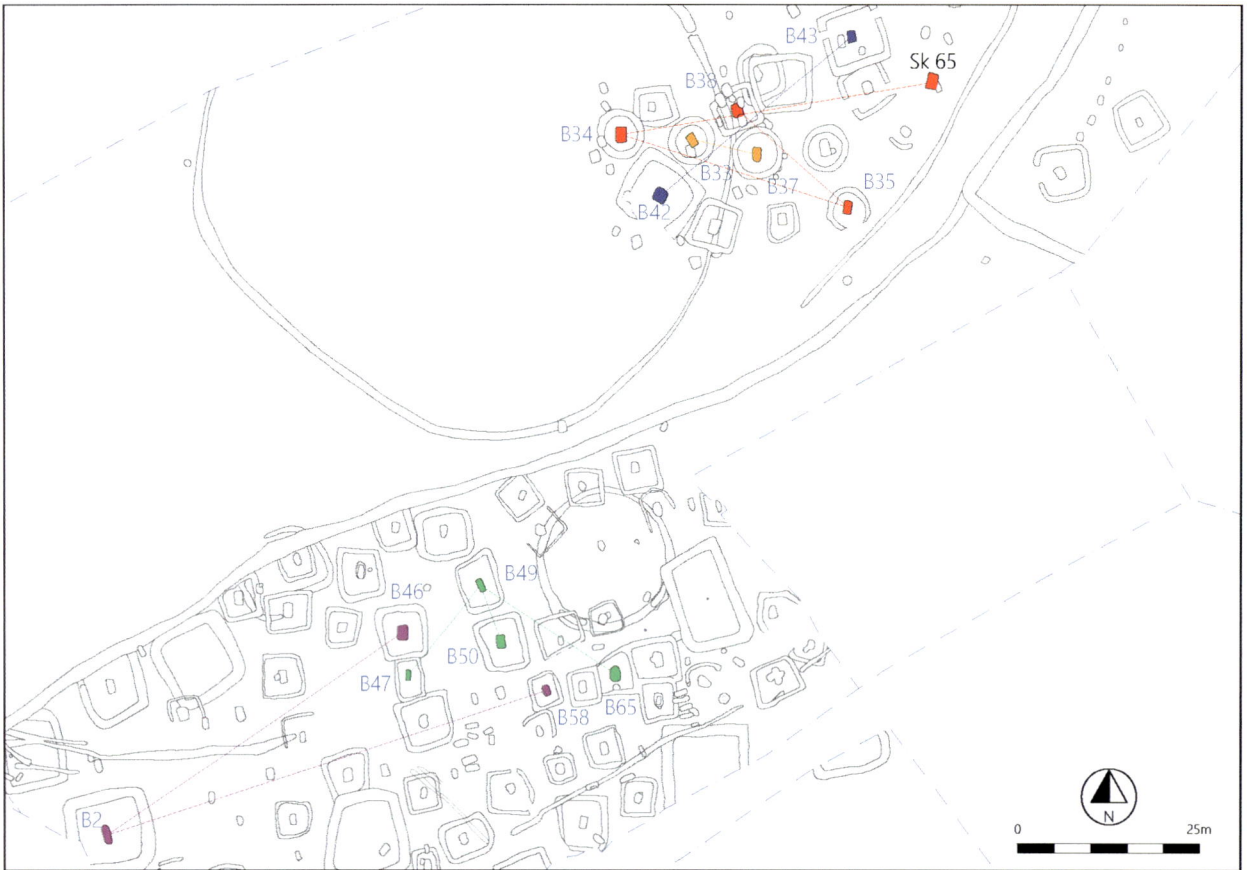

Figure 19.2 Familial relationships

within the 12–20m size range usual for Group 1 barrows. The scattered Group 1 square barrows excavated by On-Site Archaeology south-west of Burnby Lane (On-Site Archaeology 2015a) also had large enclosures and no surviving graves.

Most of the barrows in the western group at Burnby Lane conform to Group 2, that is moderately sized enclosures (4–7m wide) with central graves. These barrows are mostly square, with rounded corners, and alignments generally close to north–south, although there are distinct exceptions (B56 has a bowed eastern side).

The form of the Group 3 barrows varies widely, from rectangular (e.g. B24 and B47) to sub-oval (B53). These Group 3 barrows are distributed throughout the western barrow group. Where stratigraphic relationships exist, the Group 3 barrows are always the latest: B13 is later than B14 (Group 1), B47 later than B46 and B48 (Group 2), B22 later than B20 (Group 1), B61 later than B65 (Group 2), and B53 later than B55 (Group 2). The ditches of Group 3 barrows are often narrow and shallow (even allowing for truncation). It is possible that the unenclosed and evenly spaced burials between B3 and B18, if not the result of careful planning, were also once enclosed by ditches destroyed by ploughing. The circular enclosures of B32, B33, B34, B35 and B37 (plus the outlier B80) represent a distinct barrow form, worthy as being treated as a separate barrow group type and are discussed along with the eastern barrow group. This category of barrow is discussed in Chapter 18.

There are several anomalous traits within the eastern barrow group. The alignments of the square barrows here do not happily conform to the general north–south alignment of the western barrow group, with B30, B31 and B42 forming a radial pattern at the south-west margin. B40 appears to be the earliest barrow and had a distinctive form with a bow-shaped northern side, the ditches enclosing an area 4.7m across E–W and 5.4m from north to south. The slightly off-centre primary burial <16493> (Sk 89) had the earliest radiocarbon date obtained from a square barrow at Burnby Lane (720–390 cal BC, SUERC-78046). This early date is supported by B40 being the earliest in a sequence of three barrows, with B39 and B38. B39 had no surviving grave, and the Group 2 B38 had a deep primary grave with a structure, plus five secondary burials. Given the early date of B40, it is possible that the radial pattern of the barrows on its western side refers either to it, or to B38 with its cluster of 'reverential' secondary burials.

There were two other stratigraphical relationships between barrows in the eastern group. B43 was a relatively large square barrow (6.3m across) that was later than the smaller B44 (Group 2) to the south. At the north-west margin of the group, B36 – a square Group 2 barrow – pre-dated the circular B34.

B34 was one of five definite circular barrows in this area, with the truncated B41 perhaps also having originally had a round enclosure. These circular barrows appear to have been inserted into gaps between the existing square barrows. This recalls the location of the circular barrows (GS K and P, and GS S and W) at Garton Station (Stead 1991a, fig. 20).

The central graves of the circular barrows were between 0.36m and 0.89m deep, averaging at 0.64m. The enclosed areas were similar in size, between 4.2m and 4.5m in diameter. The associated central burials were all adult males, with ages ranging from 18–25 to 36–45, except for B41, which was female.

All six burials within the circular barrows (including B41) had rare traits associated with them; this is not a subjective statement, but it is borne out by fact. The only two Iron Age weapon burials at Burnby Lane were within circular barrows B34 and B37. Three of the seven Iron Age prone or semi-prone barrow-burials in the cemetery were central burials in circular barrows: B32, B35 and B41. Two (33.3%) of the six burials central to circular barrows were within structures (B34 and B37), compared to 12 (15.5%) from the remaining 77 Iron Age barrows, meaning that an individual buried centrally within a circular barrow was twice as likely to be placed within a structure than one buried at the centre of a square or rectangular barrow. Two of the circular barrows (B32 and B33) had extensive organic deposits at the base of their graves. Uniquely at Burnby Lane, the man buried prone within B32 had injuries from a bladed weapon (including probable defensive wounds), plus potentially fatal blunt-force injuries; the grave fill contained part of the binding-strip from the edge of a shield.

DNA analysis (Patterson *et al.* 2022) showed that each of the individuals buried within a circular barrow (excluding the possibly circular B41) had family links with at least one other person within another circular barrow: B35 2nd- or 3rd-generation links to B34, and B33 a similar link to B37 (Fig. 19.2). There were also 2nd- or 3rd-generation links between B34 to flat burial 16116 (Sk 65) situated on the eastern margin of the barrow group, and for B35 to the central burial of B38 (a square barrow).

It is also possible that all the 'special' traits associated with the central burials within circular barrows, contrasting as they do with those in square barrows, may be in part chronological (since Group 3 barrows appear to be late in the barrow sequence), as much as a desire to set them apart from contemporary square barrow rites. In either case, at Burnby Lane at least they stand out as a distinctive group, making an apparent statement about the individuals buried within them and establishing a firm distinction from those buried around them. In some cases, burial within a circular barrow might have been, in Parker Pearson's terms (1999a), a form of 'inversion' intended to divert the 'pollution' of inauspicious death. Certainly, at least one burial within a circular barrow,

the horrifically injured young man within Barrow 32, is readily interpretable as inauspicious.

The distinctive location of the circular barrows at Garton Station has been mentioned above. The grouping of circular barrows in other East Yorkshire cemeteries is also worth considering as a possible indication of 'separateness', examples being the pair of circular barrows (K3 and K4) on the southern side of the Kirkburn cart burial (Stead 1991a, fig. 23) and the clusters of circular barrows at the Eastfield, Rillington cemetery, which are part of a landscape that includes a long barrow as well as square barrows scheduled as MNY5250 (Stoertz 1997, map 1); other examples are the square and circular barrows south of Danes Graves Plantation, Nafferton (Stoertz 1997, map 2) and north of Cheesecake Hill, Norton (Stoertz 1997, fig.18.5).

Typologically, circular barrows have been included within Group 3 and they appear to represent the final stage of the Arras barrow burials. As we have seen above, the radiocarbon date for the circular barrow at The Mile centres firmly within the 2nd century BC and at Burnby Lane the circular B34 clipped the south-west corner of B36 (a square barrow with a central inhumation (Sk 63) dated to 180 cal BC–cal AD 10; SUERC-78041), all of which supports suggests the comparatively late date for circular barrows relative to square barrows.

Turning to barrow size at Burnby Lane, the majority (63) of the square and sub-rectangular barrow enclosures were less than 6m across, with 11 greater than 6m. (There were also two anomalous barrows: the trapezoidal B20 and the rectangular B72, as well as the six circular barrows). Group 1 barrows accounted for *c.* 10% of the total at Burnby Lane, with *c.* 68% of Group 2 and *c.* 21% of Group 3 (plus 1 of uncertain form). Only 15% of the square barrow enclosures at Burnby Lane were over 6m in size, compared to a 'majority' of barrows of that size at Cowlam, Arras, Danes Graves and Burton Fleming (Whimster 1979, 136). At Wetwang, *c.* 26% of barrow enclosures were over 6m in size (based on Dent 1984, app. 1.1). Therefore, unlike the other excavated East Yorkshire cemeteries, relatively small barrows, including those of Group 3 form, dominate at Burnby Lane. Smaller barrows are associated with the later phases of other cemeteries, so the preponderance of such barrows at Burnby Lane suggests that much of the funerary activity there falls within the later stage of Iron Age barrow burial.

The excavated barrow enclosures at Burnby Lane were only roughly square; many of the sides were not in fact parallel, and some barrows were markedly rectangular (e.g. B11, B16 and B25). The corners were usually rounded and a large majority of the enclosing ditches were continuous, with only one circuit (B45) being crossed by a causeway; other examples of discontinuous ditches are probably the result of later truncation. One of the barrows in the eastern barrow group (B40) had a distinctive sub-rectangular shape, with a bowed northern ditch. As we have already seen, B40 was the earliest in a sequence of three square barrows, and its distinctive form may be due to the relatively early date of the central burial.

Central burials

Seventy-one burials survived centrally within the Iron Age barrows, with the possibility of another severely truncated central burial within B72. There were 25 males and 18 females, with the remainder unsexed (of which six were pre-adult); however, the high number of unsexed burials means that the female/male ratio should be treated with caution. The majority (49) were buried with the head to the north; nine with the head to the south; one with the head to the south-west; and two uncertain. A large majority (85%) of these burials lay on the left side. The majority were laid in a crouched posture, with 11 flexed and two possibly contracted. Four of the central burials (B21, B32, B33 and B41) were prone.

Secondary burials

All eight Iron Age secondary burials at Burnby Lane were associated with three barrows (B34, B38 and B43) in the eastern barrow group, and the presence of these secondary burials is another distinguishing trait for that barrow group. One of the secondary burials cut into the western circuit of B34, three intruded into the ditches of B38, two were buried within the enclosure of B38, and two lay within the enclosure of B43. The mature adult female whose grave cut into the south-western side of B34's circular ditch appears to echo the female satellite burial on the south-west side of the circular barrow at The Mile (Chapter 6).

Seven of the secondary burials were buried with the head to the north, and one with the head to the south; all had crouched postures and lay on the left side. Five of these individuals were female or possibly female, two were possibly male and the other an unsexed child. Six were aged over 26 years, one was aged 15 to 17, and the other was aged between 4 and 6 years; there were no young adults. There is therefore a suggestion that the rite of secondary burial was biased towards mature women. Only one had a furnished burial – an adult woman in B38, who also was the only Iron Age individual at Burnby Lane to be buried with a pottery vessel. It is tempting to explain the cluster of secondary burials associated with B38 by the importance of the adult female central burial – could she have been a revered matriarch?

Overall, it is possible that many of the multiple secondary burials in the eastern barrow group are, like the circular barrows, a form of late-stage burial.

Flat burials

Forty of the Iron Age burials at Burnby Lane were 'flat burials' with no enclosing ditches (although it is possible that some originally were enclosed, as we have seen). There were concentrations of flat burials in the western part of the western barrow group, and on the fringes of the eastern barrow group, with others scattered throughout the cemetery. There were also three grave-like cuts with no obvious articulated human remains surviving: 15722 (which contained two beads) and 042 and 16699 (which contained fragments of long bone) (Fig. 4.101).

The majority of the flat burials were aligned north–south, with only six aligned south–north, and most were laid on the left side (22 of the north–south and all five of the south–north, the remainder being uncertain). The flat burials were mainly crouched (37), with two contracted and one flexed. Two individuals were prone. The sex of the flat burials was fairly evenly divided between 15 females, 13 males and 12 of unknown sex. There were four children aged between 9½ and 12½ years, which is a high proportion of the seven children in the entire Iron Age cemetery. The remainder of the flat burials were adults, with only three individuals aged over 46 years.

There was a distinct sub-group of five flat graves that had inhumations within structures. The grave cuts of this category were all relatively large, between 1.16m and 1.56m long, 0.62m and 1.06m wide, and 0.50m and 1.03m deep, with rectangular, or at least straight-sided, plans. All the associated burials were adults, two being female, one male and two unsexed. Four of the bodies were in crouched postures while one was flexed. Four had the head to the north and facing east, the other with the head to the south and facing west, so all were lying on the left side. These structures are discussed more fully below along with the other examples at the site.

The four radiocarbon dates obtained from flat burials all fall within the 4th to 2nd century cal BC, indicating that flat burials were being carried out alongside inhumation in barrows as an integral practice at the cemetery. One of the flat burials (Sk 62, 16116) was a 2nd- or 3rd-degree relative to the central burial in circular barrow B34.

Two flat burials from another Pocklington site (Canal Lane; Tabor 2009), with radiocarbon dates of 389–160 cal BC and 369–50 cal BC, are roughly contemporary with the flat burials at Burnby Lane; these indicate that unenclosed burial was being carried out not only in direct proximity to square barrows but within the wider landscape as well.

Multiple burials

There were no multiple burials at the Burnby Lane cemetery, other than the foetus/perinatal baby accompanying the central burial of the young adult woman in B12.

Burial orientation

The three significant factors associated with the orientation of the Iron Age burials at Burnby Lane are: the position of the head (north or south), the side on which a body was laid (left or right), and the direction in which the head was facing (east or west). These three factors vary throughout the cemetery (Fig 19.3).

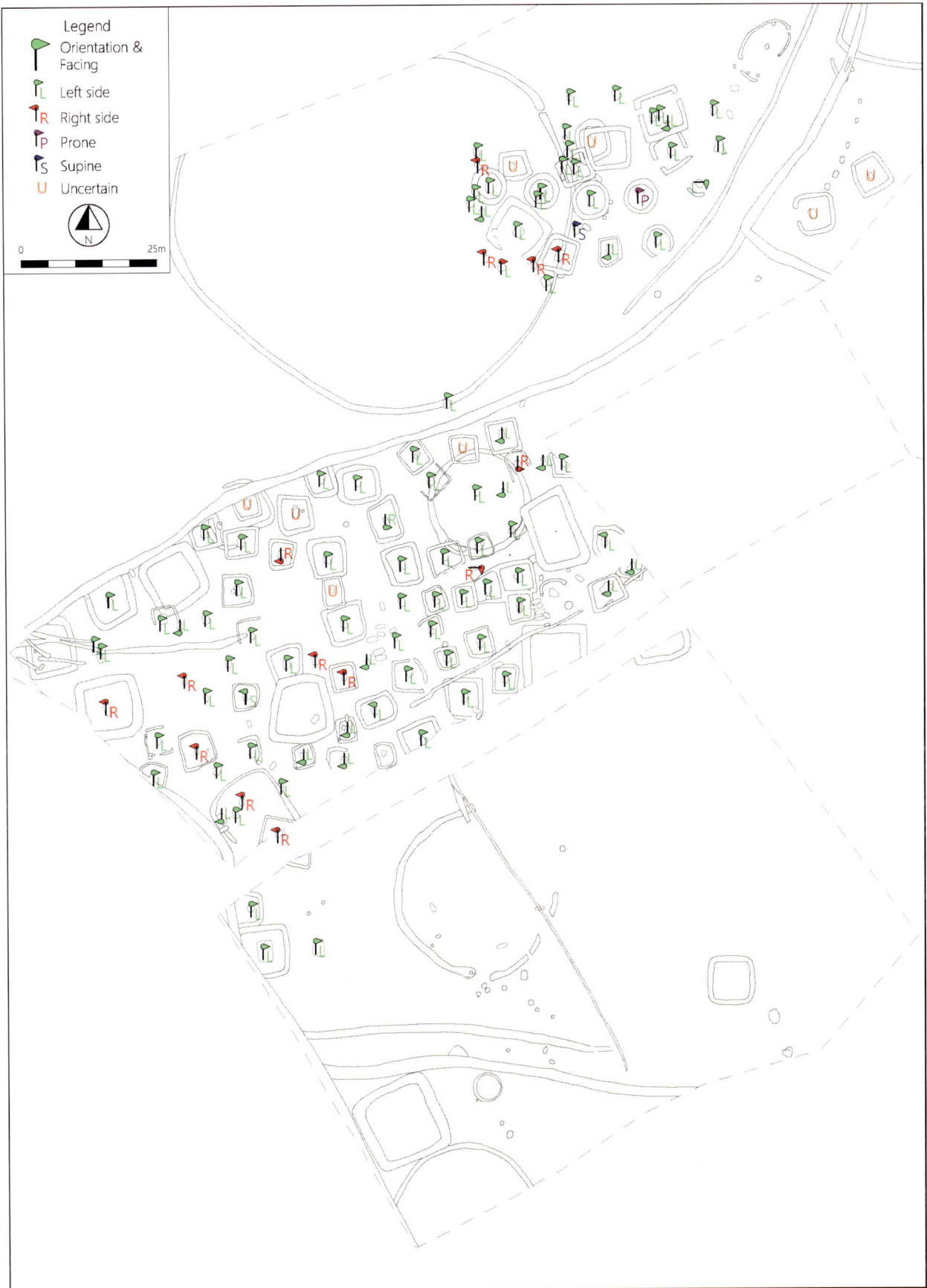

Figure 19.3 Distribution of orientation of Iron Age skeletons

The favoured orientation was with the head to the north and facing east. For those burials whose orientation was recoverable, the percentage buried centrally in barrows with the head to the north was 85%, leaving 15% with the head to the south. For individuals whose head position was recoverable, 85% buried in flat graves and 87.5% buried as secondary burials in barrows had the head to the north. For burials with heads to the south, the percentage breaks down as 15% of central barrow burials, 15% of flat grave burials, and 12.5% of secondary burials. Whimster examined the position of heads within the graves at the Scorborough, Danes Graves, Wetwang Slack and Burton Fleming cemeteries, calculating that at Danes Graves 63% had the head to the north and 25% to the south, and at Wetwang Slack 81% had the head to the north and 14% to the south, whereas of the 131 north–south-aligned skeletons at Burton Fleming, 73.3% had the head to the north, and 26.7% had the head to the south (Whimster 1979, 119). Thus the figure for Burnby Lane is broadly similar to that at Wetwang Slack.

The significance that north held is also shown by the orientation of the chariot burials, where all the examples excavated under modern conditions have the pole arranged from south to north, with the yoke end at the north. However, it is worth noting that not all the inhumations which accompany chariots have the head to the north.

There were 107 individuals where it was possible to be certain on which side they were laid: 88 (82.25%) of these were buried on the left side, leaving the remaining 19 (17.5%) on the right. (The side for the remaining Iron Age burials was uncertain, either because of later disturbance, poor preservation, or because their torsos were prone or supine). This 5:1 ratio is the same as that recorded by Whimster (1979). Breaking down the Burnby Lane burials into further categories, 85% of central barrow burials, 75% of flat burials and 100% of secondary burials were laid on the left side, although it must be borne in mind that the side could not be determined for 30% of central burials and 20% of flat burials. The adult woman buried at the centre of B74 lay on her right side, a position that exposed the iron bracelet on her left wrist and it is possible that a desire to display could influence the arrangement of some burials.

Parker Pearson (1999b, 56) considered that anomalous burials such as those buried on the right side and/or with the head to the south were another instance of 'inversion burial' designed to assuage the 'pollution' of an inauspicious death; however, one could also say that they might have gone no further than simply marking an inauspicious death. One suggestion is that east-facing burials were positioned in relation to the rising sun, the corollary being that west-facing burials faced the setting sun. The deliberate decision to place the head at the north or south end of a grave, or facing east or west, ultimately remains obscure, with a welter of cosmological, seasonal,

familial, ideological and/or hierarchical reasons all possible, but unproveable.

There could be firmer ground when considering the *date* of burials that had the head to the south. In the western barrow group, burials of this type were confined to flat graves or strongly associated with smaller Group 3 barrows (B18, B22, B23, B24, B29, B53 and B75). There is a cluster of 'south-headed' burials at the north-east margin of B71, and another immediately south of B20, plus a pair in small barrows (B73 and B75) south of B72. It is possible that these small clusters represent areas set aside for individuals who favoured a specific burial rite, or it could show that beliefs changed at the cemetery through time. As an example, the group of 'south-headed' burials in the central graves of the three Group 3 barrows (B22–B24) clustered at the south-east corner of B20, might relate to a possible increase in popularity of this rite in the later stages of the cemetery.

One suggestion is that the side on which an individual was buried depended on whether they were left- or right-handed, so a burial on the left side presented the favoured right side and *vice versa*. Around 10–12% of the modern population are left-handed and bearing in mind the likelihood that left-handedness was more common in the past (because of a lack of modern educational pressures), it could be speculated that the 16% of individuals at Burnby Lane who were buried on their right sides reflected their left-handedness. (Left-handedness is regarded as having significance in many societies, even being seen as 'profane' or, indeed, sinister.) However, it must be said that there appeared to be no connection among individuals at Wetwang Slack between the side they were buried on and their favoured hand, which was judged by the evidence of muscle development on the corresponding arm (Dent 1984, 85).

Posture

Stead illustrated five different burial postures in his report on Iron Age cemeteries in East Yorkshire: contracted; contracted on back; tightly crouched; crouched; and flexed (Stead 1991a, fig. 100). Dent took a more streamlined approach, which is followed in this report, with three categories: flexed; crouched; and contracted (Dent 1984, fig. 1.4). It could be argued that distinguishing between a burial at the less-extreme end of the scale of the crouched category and the upper end of the scale of flexed burials seems over ambitious, but there is an obvious difference between a posture where the chin is almost touching the knees and one where the legs are scarcely bent – such differences were surely the result of definite choice.

Overall, crouched burial was by far the preferred posture, representing 78% (94) of the Iron Age burials; 13 burials (10.8%) were flexed; five (4.2 %) contracted; and eight (7%) had uncertain postures. For individuals whose posture was certain, crouched burial seems to have been more common among the secondary and flat burials (both at 87.5%) than central barrow burials (73.2%), although the numbers may be skewed because the posture of only one individual buried in a flat grave was unknown, but there were more individuals with uncertain posture among the central (and secondary) burials.

Eleven Iron Age burials were flexed; nine were central to barrows (B13, B16, B18, B21, B35, B53, B55, B62 and B73) and two were flat burials (15274 and 16552). Six had the head to north and five had the head to south; most faced east, but the burials in B211, B55 and B73 faced west. The almost equal division of the head position for flexed individuals is anomalous to the proportion within the overall cemetery, as is the figure for the direction the heads were facing – 56% east, 46% west. Although this is a small sub-sample, the variant head-placing among the flexed burials could suggest a difference in the way these individuals were regarded. It is worth noting that only one of the flexed central barrow burials was demonstrably female, as opposed to five males. Both the flexed flat burials were females aged 26–35 years, and both were buried in deep rectangular graves, one of which contained a structure. Two of the flexed burials were adolescent, the remainder adult. One of the adults (B18, Sk 27, SF 24) and one of the adolescents (B55, Sk 126, SF 96) were buried with iron bow brooches.

The flexed burials in barrows were all in Group 3 barrows (B13, B18, and B21), smaller or rectangular examples of Group 2 (B16, B53, B55, B62 and B73), or circular barrows (B35). This suggests that flexed burial was increasingly popular during the later stages of the cemetery.

There were five contracted Iron Age burials at Burnby Lane, all of whom were placed with the heads to the north, two facing east, two facing west and one uncertain. There does not appear to be any correlation between contracted burial and sex (two were female, one male and two unsexed), or age (there was an adolescent, an adult, a middle adult and two middle/mature adults). There also does not seem to be any significance attached to the location of the contracted burials within the cemetery: two were central barrow burials (B25) and (B40), and three were flat burials. In all, contracted burial at Burnby Lane appears to represent simply one of the rites that was observed, albeit only occasionally, at the cemetery, with no other significance necessarily implied.

There were seven prone burials at Burnby Lane and it is worth bearing in mind that this posture was categorised as 'deviant' in the Anglo-Saxon period (Reynolds 2009). One of these burials (Sk 72, 16346) was both contracted and prone, four were crouched and two flexed. Six of the prone burials had the head to the north, four were facing east, two west and one was face downwards. There were four females, two males and one individual of unknown sex, hinting that there might be a relationship between

sex and this rite. The prone burials were all adults. There seems to be some significance in the distribution of the prone burials: there are three in the western barrow group, but of the four in the eastern group, three were central burials within circular barrows (B32, B33 and B41), which has already been identified above as one of the notable traits of this barrow form.

Grave structures

Definite traces of internal structures were recorded in 20 Iron Age graves at Burnby Lane; these were evidently intended to contain the burial (Fig. 19.4; Table 19.1). There were also two U-shaped deposits (in the central graves of B7 and B19) which might represent structures and two examples of thin lines of dark silt in the central graves of B31 and B40 that might also be structural remains. A further structure was present in the central grave of B23, extending for the entire height of the central grave along its western edge; this feature was too small to have accommodated a burial. It is possible that there were originally more graves with structures – there were examples of relatively large and deep rectangular graves that could have held structures – but structural traces were not recorded in these.

The exact nature of the grave structures is open to interpretation. Dent (1984, 25) referred to them as them as 'wooden coffins or cists': the term 'coffin' suggests a totally enclosed, portable wooden structure whereas 'cist' implies a structure constructed *in situ* within a grave. The term 'structure' has been used at Burnby Lane but 'cist' is equally appropriate.

Sixteen of the structures (the central burials in Barrows 6, 13, 22, 34, 37, 38, 42, 63, 66, 67 and 87, plus flat graves 007, 15275, 15427, 16104 and 16463) were rectangular. The widths of the structures ranged from 0.5m to 1.2m, the lengths from 0.9m to 1.8m, and the surviving heights from 0.02m to 0.40m.

The best-preserved and most complete grave structures (036 – flat grave 007; 16145–50 – flat grave 16104; 16457–61 – flat grave 16463) were recorded as lines of dark brown silt in three flat graves, giving the most accurate impression of the form. These structures measured 1.27m long by 0.84m wide by 0.40m high, 1.25m by 0.65m by 0.25m, and 1.56m by 1.06m by 0.15m respectively. The structure in grave 16104 had suggestions of a lid in the form of two 'planks' lying lengthways at the top of it, but as it appears that the north and east sides had collapsed, it is possible that the 'planks' were part of the collapsed sides. Two detached linear traces of wood were recorded within Structure 15262 (flat grave 15275), which could have been either from the collapse of the sides or a putative lid. The structure represented by deposits 16457–61 had also apparently partly collapsed, and there was a suggestion that this structure may have had several compartments.

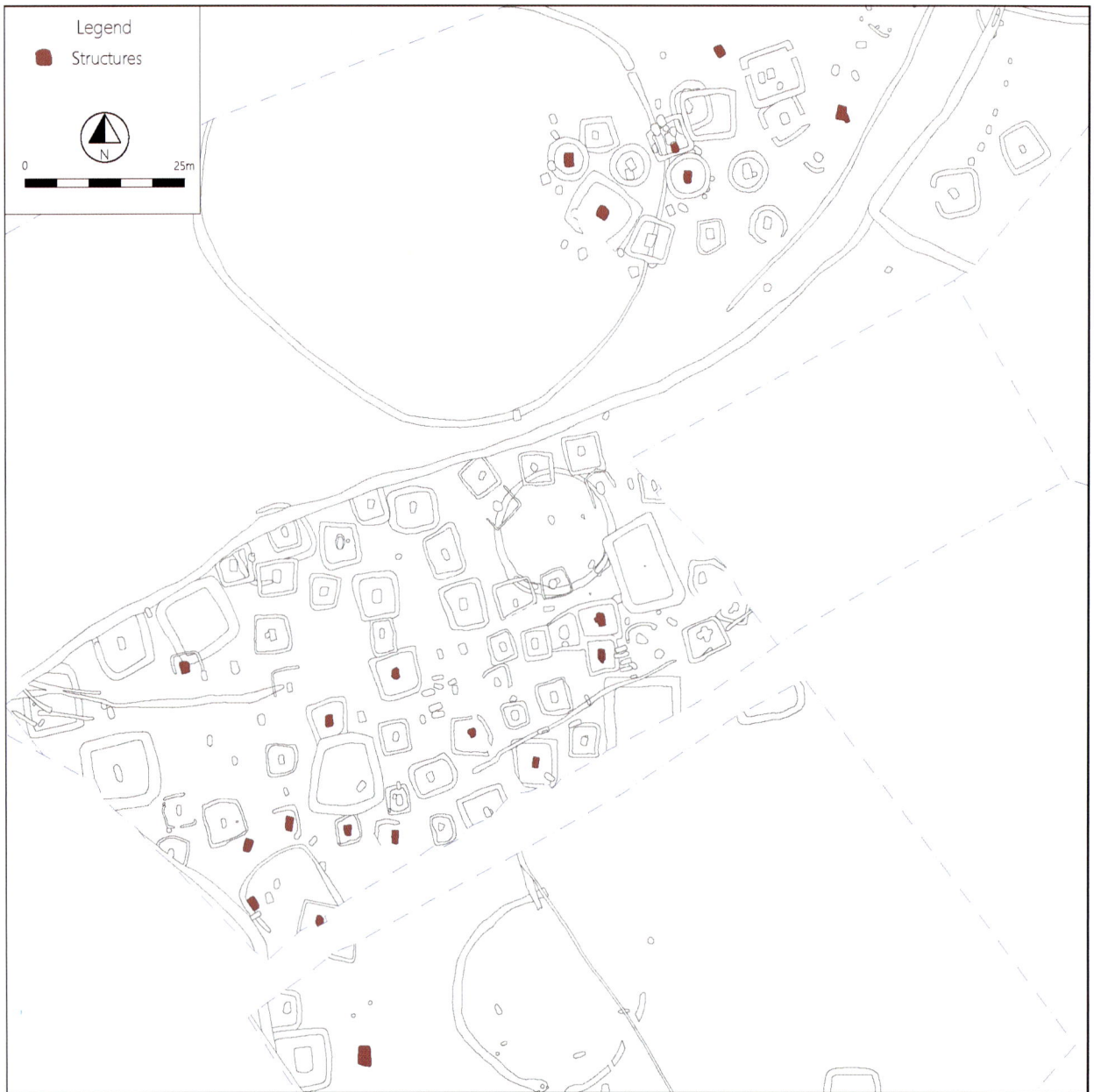

Figure 19.4 Distribution of burials with structures

Other grave structures were shown by shear lines within the grave fills, or distinct rectangular deposits that showed where the space inside the structures had infilled with soil different to that of the rest of the grave. One of these structures (15428 – flat grave 15427) appeared to have been made in three stages, although this might also be due to the collapse and shifting of the structure within the ground. From the meticulous excavation [by Peter Makey] of Structure 15428 it was possible to recover the form of the horizontal 'shuttering' from which it was made, the timbers being 120mm to 160mm high and 35mm thick. Interestingly, Structure 15428 incorporated transverse and lateral elements that could represent bracing. Transverse lines across Structure 16298 (B37, the Burnby Lane shield

burial) and Structure 16026 (B34, the sword/spear burial) strongly suggests that those structures were also braced.

An oval structure (16825) which surrounded the tightly crouched central burial of B56 measured 1.1m long and 0.6m wide. The curving form of the eastern side of this structure is reminiscent of a large basket, but it could also be the bowed remains of a collapsed timber structure. The semi-circular line of dark silt around the lower part of the central burial in B7 could be indicative of a similar structure to that in B56.

There were two instances of structures within graves that were too small to contain a burial. The first of these was an unusual example recorded in grave 15729 (the central grave of B23), which was shown by a distinct

Table 19.1 Graves with structures

B no.	Grave context	Str. no	Size (m)	Depth (m)	Burial context	Sk. no.	Sex	Age	Aligned	Facing	Posture	Comments
							Barrows with structures					
B6	15361	15358	1.25 × 0.52	0.10–0.12	15300	12	U	18–35	N–S	U	Flexed	
B13	15478	15478	1.02 × 0.52	0.02	15476	21	U	14.5–16.5	N–S	E	Cr.	
B15	15423	15497	0.4m wide	0.13–0.40	15496	25	M	36–45	N–S	E	Cr.	
B22	15711	15737	1.3 × 0.3	0.36	15710	33	U	36+	S–N	W?	Cr.	Bowed ends
B23	15729	15744	0.98 × 0.22	0.49	15728	35	M	36+	S–N	W	Flexed	Structure at S edge (not coffin)
B34	16029	16026	1.8 × 1.2	0.34	16027	57	M	18–25	N–S	E	Cr.	Sword/spear burial; round barrow
B37	16300	16298	1.6 × 1.2	0.1	16370	78	M	36+	N–S	E	Flexed	Shield burial
B38	16195	16374	>0.9 × 0.7	0.06–0.10	16773	80	F?	18+	N–S	E	Cr.	Pig bone
B42	16444	16455	1.6 × 0.99	0.24	16443	82	F?	26+	N–S	E	Cr.	Bronze brooch SF 84
B48	16591	16679	>0.4 × 0.7	0.08	16678	93	F?	46+	N–S	E	Cr.	
B56	16741	16825	1.1 × 0.5	0.09–0.25	16745	99	U	36+	N–S	E	Cr.	Oval structure
B63	18176	18174	1.1 × 0.5	0.22	18173	143	U	26–35	N–S	E	Cr.	
B66	18201	18226	1.7 × 0.7	0.09	18224	148	U	18–35	N–S	E	Cr.	
B67	18161	18163	1.1 × 0.5	0.2	18164	142	M?	36+	N–S	U	Flexed	
B87	15771	15770	1.82 × 0.65	0.21	15782	41	U	36+	N–S	E	Cr.	
							Flat graves with structures					
	7	36	1.27 × 0.84	0.84m	35	163	F	36–45	N–S	E	Cr.	
	15275	15262	1.20 × 0.62	1.03m	15274	11	F?	25–36?	S–N	N	Fl, Sup.	
	15427	15528	1.14 × 0.77	0.50m	15428	20	M?	36–45?	N–S	E	Cr.	
	16104	16145–50	1.25 × 0.65	0.60m	16166	65	F	26+	N–S	E	Cr.	E barrow group
	16463	16457–61	1.56 × 1.06	0.65m	16464	84	M?	36+	N–S	E	Cr.	E barrow group
							Possible structures					
B7	15342	15330	0.96 × 0.80	0.05–0.13	15371	7	U	6.5–8.5	N–S	E	Cr.	U-shaped
B19	15732	15371	1.30 × 0.80	0.47	15733	36	F	26–35	N–S	E	Cr.	U-shaped; bracelet SF 32
B31	16034	16055	1.10 × 0.03	0.01	16069	58	F	36+	S–N	W	Cr.	Single line only
B40	16247	16494	N: 0.03 × 0.18 W: 0.03 × 0.48	0.01 0.01	16493	89	F	Adult	N–S	?	Cr.	Thin lines of N and W sides?

rectangular deposit that ran down the whole depth of the grave's western edge, appearing to form a 'compartment' that butted up to the edge. The other example was the C-shaped ring around the head of the central burial for B15, which may have been a support for the head and neck of the body.

Such is the physical evidence for the grave structures, but were they coffins or 'cist-like' timber revetments around the burials? There were no iron dogs or nails that could have joined the structures together, but carpentered joints or glue may have been used instead. The structures could also have been self-supporting by the careful placing of horizontal timbers. As we have seen, evidence from two structures (15427 and 16298) suggests that the timbers may have been held in place by bracing with spars or laths of wood. Evidence for lids was very scant, but there was no evidence whatsoever that any of the structures had bases. The pelvis of the skeleton associated with Structure 15358 (B6) was tilted, suggesting that the decay of the body may have caused it to rotate within a void, such as that inside a 'coffin', but this could also have occurred within a structure that was temporarily left open (albeit for a considerable time). Generally, the skeletons within the grave structures were poorly preserved, making it difficult to judge if there had been any rotation of the bones that might have indicated the decay of the body within a void. All in all, the absence of evidence for bases, plus scant and ambiguous evidence for lids, makes it probable that the grave structures were not portable 'coffins', but timber 'revetments' or cists that were assembled *in situ*. Further support for this argument is found with the large structure in flat grave 16463, whose position flush with the edges of the grave suggests that it was constructed within the grave and not placed as a completed unit.

At the risk of speculating too far, open structures would allow a body to remain on display for a period of time without it being covered by spoil from the erosion of the grave's edges; it might also account for any movement of the bones as the body decayed. Such display could be related to a stage in which a corpse 'was still perceived to have a social agency, or a continual role in the community' (Giles 2012, 175). In any event, the upper parts of many of the graves containing structures were filled with deposits that were distinct from the material that both surrounded and filled the structures, suggesting that the graves were backfilled in three stages. The first stage would support the grave structure and leave it open, the second would cover the burial and fill the structure, and the third complete the backfilling of the grave. To provide a balance to this interpretation, Dent (1984, 26) asserted that two animal skeletons in a grave at Wetwang Slack (Burial 186) could not have occupied the position that they did if the grave had already been partly backfilled to support a timber framework, but it is possible that grave structures had variable forms, allowing for different configurations from grave to grave.

The size range for grave structures shows that there was considerable variation in the space available or required for the individual burials within them. In three cases (B13, B56 and B67), the body was tightly crouched within a relatively small structure. The two largest structures, which were within two of the circular barrows (B34 and B37), accommodated exceptional burials: the sword/spear burial and the shield burial respectively. In other grave structures (B63, B87 and flat graves 15427 and 16463) the burials were placed in an off-centre position, which could have allowed room for the inclusion of organic objects or material within the structure that have left no trace. In flat grave 16463, the burial was off-centre in the western part of the structure, and three sub-rectangular deposits of dark silt (16456) possibly represented decayed organic objects placed within the available space.

The location of structures within the individual graves also varied. Most structures were placed approximately centrally within the grave, but in B6 the structure was placed in the north-west part of the grave, and in B13 at the south-west corner of the grave, while in B42 the structure lay diagonally across the grave and in B63 the structure was also askew to the grave edges. These differences may have been due to the normal run of variation, but it is possible that the structures in B42 and B63 were placed at variance with the grave edges to ensure that the corpse had a particular alignment at the time the burial was carried out as opposed to accepting the alignment of the graves as originally prepared.

Grave structures were scattered throughout the cemetery. Any attempt at isolating specific groups is dubious as detecting the presence of a structure might depend on the pertaining hydrology, which varied across the site; it could be that structures were more easily detectable, through better preservation, in areas that were frequently waterlogged. With that in mind, grave structures were concentrated, though not exclusively, on the southern margins of the two barrow groups (where the impermeable Keuper marl was closest to the surface), and particularly within the deepest graves, whose bases were closest to the water table (and indeed waterlogged at the time of excavation).

In terms of the sex of individuals buried in structures, with three males/probable males, six females/probable females, and nine unknowns represented, it is not possible to make any meaningful comment. Apart from one adolescent (B13), the remainder were adults, seven of whom were over 36 years old.

Four of the graves with structures contained grave goods, all of which were within the eastern barrow group (B34, B37, B38 and B42). The grave goods consisted of the exceptional sword/spear burial (B34), the shield burial (B37), and a coral-decorated copper alloy brooch of probable 1st-century BC date (B42). A suckling pig (also exceptional) was placed with the central burial of B38. Accordingly, the provision of structures within these four graves can be seen to be another aspect that illustrates the effort lavished on these individuals. Two flat graves with structures were situated on the eastern fringe of the eastern barrow group, perhaps suggesting that this was a favoured location for burials of this type.

The two burials with structures can be dated to 370–160 cal BC (SUERC-81073; flat burial 15428) and 390–200 cal BC (mean Sk 21; SUERC-79413 and -78039; central burial B13). Considered along with the date of the brooch from B42, the likelihood is that graves with structures were current through the whole period of the cemetery's use, i.e. from the 4th to the 2nd century BC. While suggesting that the placement of structures in graves has no chronological significance, such a long period of use might explain the many different forms of grave structure in the Iron Age cemetery.

The 20 graves recognised with definite structures at Burnby Lane account for approximately 14% of the total of Iron Age burials at the cemetery, compared to 49 graves (from total of 446 – *c.* 11%) at Wetwang Slack (Whimster 1979, 130). At Burton Fleming there were 19 coffins, mostly in the later north–south-aligned graves.

The Iron Age population

The generally acidic soil conditions and seasonal waterlogging at Burnby Lane meant that most of the Iron Age skeletons were in poor and fragmented condition. Consequently, it was challenging both to sex the skeletons and make estimates as their age at death and stature. Full details, including pathology and dentition, are described in Chapter 13 and summarised in Table 19.2.

Of the 119 burials at Burnby Lane that can be confidently seen as Iron Age, 42 were of unknown sex, of which 13 were pre adult (younger than 18 years). There were 39 female, probably female or possibly female individuals, and 38 male, probably male or possibly male individuals. No great sex bias can therefore be seen in the Iron Age cemetery, but were the different sexes interred in specific locations in the cemetery?

Broadly speaking, no overall zones can be identified for males or females; however, it is likely that there are more localised clusters within the cemetery based on sex (Fig. 19.5). One cluster is a group of five females buried in flat graves between B6 and B87, towards the western edge of the western group. A further cluster can be seen in the nine adult females buried in eight adjacent barrows (B46, B48, B49, B50, B58, B60, B61 and B62) and a flat grave (Burial 16734) in the middle of the western group. In the eastern barrow group, there is a possible bias towards female burial at B38: three of the four secondary burials as well as the central burial were adult females.

The 13 pre-adults included a foetal/perinatal found with the young adult female buried in the centre of B12, and two individuals on the brink of adulthood (central burials in B47 and B55). There were three other pre-adults as

central barrow burials: B7 (6.5–8.5 years), B13 (14.5–16.5) and B57 (2–3 years), plus a secondary burial in B38 (4–6 years). The ages of the four flat burials ranged from 8 to 12.5 years, and three of these were 'satellite' burials on the western side of the eastern barrow group. The remaining individual was an older juvenile (Sk 122, 17102) buried within the circuit of Bronze Age barrow B71, from whom a 5th–4th-century cal BC radiocarbon date was obtained.

Four of the pre-adults at Burnby Lane were buried at the centre of square barrows, so some at least were given the same burial rite as adults, and presumably valued in the same way. (A very young child was buried in the off-centre grave of B57 and this slightly anomalous location raises the possibility that it was not the primary burial.) There is a possible tendency for the burial of pre-adults in smaller examples of Group 2 barrows (B7, B13, and B55), hinting that there might be a trend towards increased burial of children in barrows in the later stages of the cemetery.

At Wetwang Slack, the proportion of individuals below 17 years was 20.6% (Dent 1984, 85). Dent, referring to Stead, suggested that the paucity of infants below 2.5 years both at Wetwang and Burton Fleming was because they were buried within the barrow mounds (as secondary burials?), which were destroyed by later ploughing. The evidence for this at Burnby Lane, where pre-adults made up *c.* 11% of recorded burials, is inconclusive. The entirety of the barrow ditch fills, which were largely composed of back-fill from later ploughing/mound levelling, were excavated (and much of the spoil screened) without finding any pre-adult bones whatsoever that may have derived from putative burials within the barrow mounds, but it is possible that such fragile remains did not survive.

Approximately 20% of Iron Age individuals at Burnby Lane died between the ages of 18 and 25, 24% between 26 and 35, 25.6% between 36 and 45 and 6.6% over 46 years. A further 11.6% of adults could not be aged more closely. It is interesting to compare the proportion of males and females who died in the two categories of young middle adult (26–35) and older middle adult (36–45); a greater number of young middle adult females (*c.* 42% of the total, including unsexed) died than males (*c.* 31%) of a similar age, the higher percentage for females likely due to complications associated with pregnancy and childbirth. The situation is reversed among older middle adults, with more males of this age (54.8%) being buried in the cemetery compared to females (25.8%). Few individuals (6.6%) reached mature adulthood beyond the age of 46 years.

The average height for Iron Age people in Britain was 162cm for females and 168cm for males. The poor condition of the skeletons from the cemetery meant that the stature of only five individuals could be estimated. Four of these were female, two of whom were well above, one well below, and one close to the average height. The male, buried centrally in B18, was well above average height for the period.

Table 19.2 Pathology of the Iron Age burials

Burial context	Sk. no.	Barrow no.	Grave context	DDD	DJC	OA	CO	OP	EP	Lamellar bone	Pilasterism	Limb torsion	Limb bowing	Maxillary sinusitis	Dental health	Other
										Burnby Lane 5.37.12						
15092	1		15084												Calc.	
15176	2	B2	15172	Y	Y	Y		Y							Calc. car., AMTL	Potential neck aneurysm
15187	3	B3	15188		Y		Y		Y			Femora			Calc., DEH	Soft tissue trauma l. femur
15192	4		15191												DEH	
15219	5	B4	15220												Calc., car., AMTL	
15223	6	B5	15222												Calc.	
15331	7	B7	15332												Calc.	
15233	8		15234				Y		Y				Fibulae		Calc., car., PD, DEH	Stenosis; poss. trauma rt. tibia
15255	9		15256												Calc.	
15258	10		15259							Ribs, l. tibia			Femora		Calc.	Rib lesions
15274	11		15275				Y				Femora				Calc., DEH	
15300	12	B6	15361								Femora				Calc..	
15327	13	B9	15328								Femora	Femora			Calc.	Tibiae flattened
15341	14		15342												Calc.	
15394	16	B12	15395						Y						Calc., DEH	Sacroiliitis, Spondylolysis
15402	17	B12	15395													32–40 weeks foetus with 15394
15391/400	18/19	B8	15392													
15428	20		15427							Legs, endocranial	Femora		R. hum.		Calc., car., PD, DEH	
15476	21	B13	15478							Legs, endocranial					Calc.	
15494	24	B16	15495									Femora			Calc.	
15496	25	B15	15423				Y				Femora				Calc., DEH	
15514	26		15514		Y	Y				Endocranial	Femora				Calc., PD	Osteochondritis dissecans

(Continued)

Table 19.2 (Continued)

Burial context	Sk. no.	Barrow no.	Grave context	DDD	DJC	OA	CO	OP	EP	Lamellar bone	Pilasterism	Limb torsion	Limb bowing	Maxillary sinusitis	Dental health	Other
15622	27	B18	15623	Y	Y	Y				Tibiae			L. hum., ulnae		Caic., PD, DEH	Fracture T12
15630	28	B17	15629		Y						Femora				Calc., DEH	
15664	32		15665	Y	Y										4×AMTL, abscesses	R. Femur: fracture, soft tissue trauma
15710	33	B22	15711												Cal., car.	
15724	34	B21	15725												Calc.	
15733	36	B19	15732				Y								Calc.	Poss early HFI
15764	38		15765												Calc., car.	
15733	39		15774								Femora		Tibiae		2×AMTL, calc., car.	
15776	40		15777											Y	Calc., car., DEH	
15782	41	B87	15771												Calc.	
15795	42		15793							Endocranial					Calc., car.	
15846	43	B24	15847								Femora				Calc.	
15851	44B	B25	15854												Calc.	
15856	45	B26	15857				Y				R. femur		L. hum., tibiae	Y	Calc., car. PD	
15909	48	B28	15910												Calc., car., DEH	
15957	50		15958												DEH	
15960	51		15961		Y		Y			Endocranial Tibiae Fibulae					DEH, poss. abscess	Cyst r. os coxa
15963	52		15964							L. tibia					Calc.	Exc. muscle attachments both humeri
15966	53		15967												Calc, DEH	
15974	54	B29	15973						Y		Femora		Tibiae		Calc., PD Unusual tooth wear	

(Continued)

Table 19.2 Pathology of the Iron Age burials (Continued)

Burial context	Sk. no.	Barrow no.	Grave context	DDD	DJC	OA	CO	OP	EP	Lamellar bone	Pilasterism	Limb torsion	Limb bowing	Maxillary sinusitis	Dental health	Other
16001	55	B30	16002				Y		Y						Calc., car., PD, DEH	HFI
16018	56	B33	16019				Y						Humeri Tibiae	Y	Calc., PD	Fracture, l. clavicle
16027	57	B34	16029							R. tibia					Calc., car.	
16069	58	B31	16034											Y	Calc., car., DEH	Depression, l. orbit; HFI?
16072	59	B32	16073						Y	Femora L. tibia					Calc., PD, DEH	Extensive sharp & blunt force injuries
16092	60		16093							Endocranial			Tibiae		Calc., car., DEH	
16109	61	B35	16110							L. tibia	Femora				Calc., car.	
16116	62		16263												Calc., DEH	
16159	63	B36	16160												3× AMTL, abscess?	
16165	64	B34 (2nd)	16142	Y	Y	Y									Calc., car., PD 2 abscesses	
16166	65		16104	Y	Y	Y									Calc., car., PD	HFI
16278	66	B41	16279				Y		Y	Femora, tibiae					1×AMTL, calc., DEH	
16285	67		16287				Y				Femora				Calc., car., DEH	Lesions: ribs, face, jaw, cranium & neck
16289	68		16290	Y	Y					Endocranial, tibiae					4xAMTL, calc., car.	
16294	69	B38 (2nd)	16295												DEH	
16306	70		16307	Y	Y	Y	Y								Calc., car., PD, DEH prob. Abscess	Prob. gallstones
16334	71		16335	Y	Y	Y	Y	Potential			Femora			Y	1×AMTL, calc., car., DEH	Potential femoral neck fractures

(Continued)

Table 19.2 (Continued)

Burial context	Sk. no.	Barrow no.	Grave context	DDD	DJC	OA	CO	OP	EP	Lamellar bone	Pilasterism	Limb torsion	Limb bowing	Maxillary sinusitis	Dental health	Other
16346	72		16347				Y		Y						Calc., car., DEH	Unusual tooth wear, probable abscess
16355	73		16356		Y	Y	Y		Y						Calc.	Cysts on ox coxa
16358	74	B38 (2nd)	16327				Y								Calc., car. Unusual tooth wear	
16360	75		16361							Endocranial					Calc., DEH	
16363	76		16364						Y	L. tibia	Femora		Tibiae		1×AMTL, calc., car., PD	
16366	77	B38 (2nd)	16329		Y			Potential	Y		Femora				Calc., car.	
16370	78	B37	16300				Y		Y	Tibiae					Calc., car.	
16371	79	B38 (2nd)	16197				Y			Endocranial					Calc.	
16373	80	B38	16195		Y		Y	Y	Y	Endocranial					Calc., car.	HFI?
16403	81	B38 (2nd)	16193				Y		Y	R. tibia					Calc., car., PD,	
16443	82	B42	16444		Y				Y	Endocranial					2×AMTL, calc., car.	
16450	83	B43 (2nd)	16451							Femora Tibiae					Calc., DEH	
16464	84		16463		Y					Tibiae Metarsals					Calc., PD, DEH Prob. abscess	Healed fracture l. radius, exc. muscle attachment
16466	85	B43	16468	Y	Y	Y	Y		Y	Tibiae L. fibula					1× AMTL, calc., PD	
16470	86	B44	16471		Y						Femora				Calc., unusual wear, DEH	Healed fracture l. clavicle
16473	87	B43 (2nd)	16474							Endocranial	Femora		Tibiae		Calc.	Ex c. muscle attachment
16491	88	B45	16492													
16493	89	B40	16247													

(Continued)

Table 19.2 Pathology of the Iron Age burials (Continued)

Burial context	Sk. no.	Barrow no.	Grave context	DDD	DJC	OA	CO	OP	EP	Lamellar bone	Pilasterism	Limb torsion	Limb bowing	Maxillary sinusitis	Dental health	Other
16552	90		16559				Y			Endocranial					Calc, DEH	Early HFI
16606	92		16607								Femora				Calc, car., DEH	
16678	93	B48	16591	Y	Y			Potential				Femora	R. tibia		2×AMTL, calc., PD, DEH	
16701	94		16702					Y							3×AMTL, calc., PD	
16728	95	B58	16727												Calc, car, PD	Potential ossified haematoma
16733	96		16734		Y										Calc., car., PD, DEH	
16736	97		16737	Y	Y	Y		Y						Y	1×AMTL, calc., car., PD, abscess	HFI
16745	99	B56	16741		Y										Calc., PD	
16747	100	B60	16748							Endocranial					Calc.	Potential HFI
16780	101	B59	16781				Y								Calc.	
16783	102	B57	16785				Y			Endocranial					Calc.	
16883	107	B61	16851		Y										Calc., car.	Soft tissue trauma l. femur, Ossified haematoma r. Tibia
16896	109	B62	16880				Y								Calc.	
16990	113	B64	16991									Femora?	Femora		Calc., DEH	Spondylolysis
16997	115		16998													Badly truncated
17001	116	B47	17002												Calc., DEH	
17004	117	B11	17005												Calc.	
17078	118	B51	17079								Femora				Calc.	
17081	119	B46	17082	Y	Y	Y	Y				Femora	Femora			Calc., car., PD	
17087	120		17988							Endocranial Rt. tibia Rt. Femur	Femora		Humeri		Calc., car., PD, abscesses	Ectocranial porosity, united fractures of l. forearm

(Continued)

Table 19.2 (Continued)

Burial context	Sk. no.	Barrow no.	Grave context	DDD	DJC	OA	CO	OP	EP	Lamellar bone	Pilasterism	Limb torsion	Limb bowing	Maxillary sinusitis	Dental health	Other
17090	121	B50	17091								L. femur		L. femur Humeri	Y	Calc., car. PD	Trauma to r. clavicle, fracture r. rib Gout/cysts r. wrist,
17102	122		17101							Endocranial L. femur					Calc.	
17105	123	B52	17104		Y	Y				R. tibia					Calc, DEH	
17135	124	B53	17133							Tibiae	Femora				Calc., car.	Potential early *Hyperostasis frontalis interna*
17172	125	B54	17171													
17175	126	B55	17176													
18004	127	B72	18003												Calc.	
18013	129	B65	18012	Y	Y	Y	Y				Femora			Y	Calc., car., PD, DEH, abscess	Soft tissue trauma, rt. Femur Ossified haematoma, r. Femur
18123	136		18124				Y			Rt. Remur Rt. Tibia					Calc., car., PD	Inflamation of l. tempero mandibular joint
18133	139		18132		Y										Calc., car.	
18164	142	B67	18161		Y										Calc.	
18173	143	B63	18176													
18224	148	B66	18201							Endocranial						
18272	151	B68	18273		Y		Y								Calc., car., DEH	
18303	153	B73	18301		Y		Y				Femora				Calc., unusual tooth wear	Tibiae markedly flattened
18329	155	B75	18330		Y		Y							Y	Calc., car., DEH	
18346	157	B76	18343												Calc.	

(Continued)

Table 19.2 Pathology of the Iron Age burials (Continued)

Burial context	Sk. no.	Barrow no.	Grave context	DDD	DJC	OA	CO	OP	EP	Lamellar bone	Pilasterism	Limb torsion	Limb bowing	Maxillary sinusitis	Dental health	Other
18348	158	B74	18349												Calc., DEH	
18441	159	B77	18442													
4012	A	B49	4013				Y								Calc., DEH	Exc. muscle attachment r. hum. Spondylolysis
Burnby Lane 5.9.15																
16	161	B78	17		Y								Humeri Femora		Calc., car, PD	
7	163		35		Y		Y							Y	Calc., DEH	
394	165	B85	401				Y			Endocranial					Calc., poss. PD	Calcified pleura
The Mile 5.32.16																
274	274		275				Y								Calc., DEH	*Spina bifida occulta* Squatting facets
303	303		243											Y	Calc., PD, DEH	Nasal fractures, blunt force trauma to frontal bone, squatting facets
424	424		3613		Y										AMTL, Calc., PD, abscess	Trauma to l. femur, healing rib fracture, osteoporosis

Key: AMTL: ante mortem tooth loss, Calc.: calculus, Car.: caries, CO: *cribra orbitalia*, DDD: degenerative disc disease, DEH: dental enamel hypoplasia, DJC: degenerative joint condition, HFI: OA: osteo arthritis, OP: peridontal disease

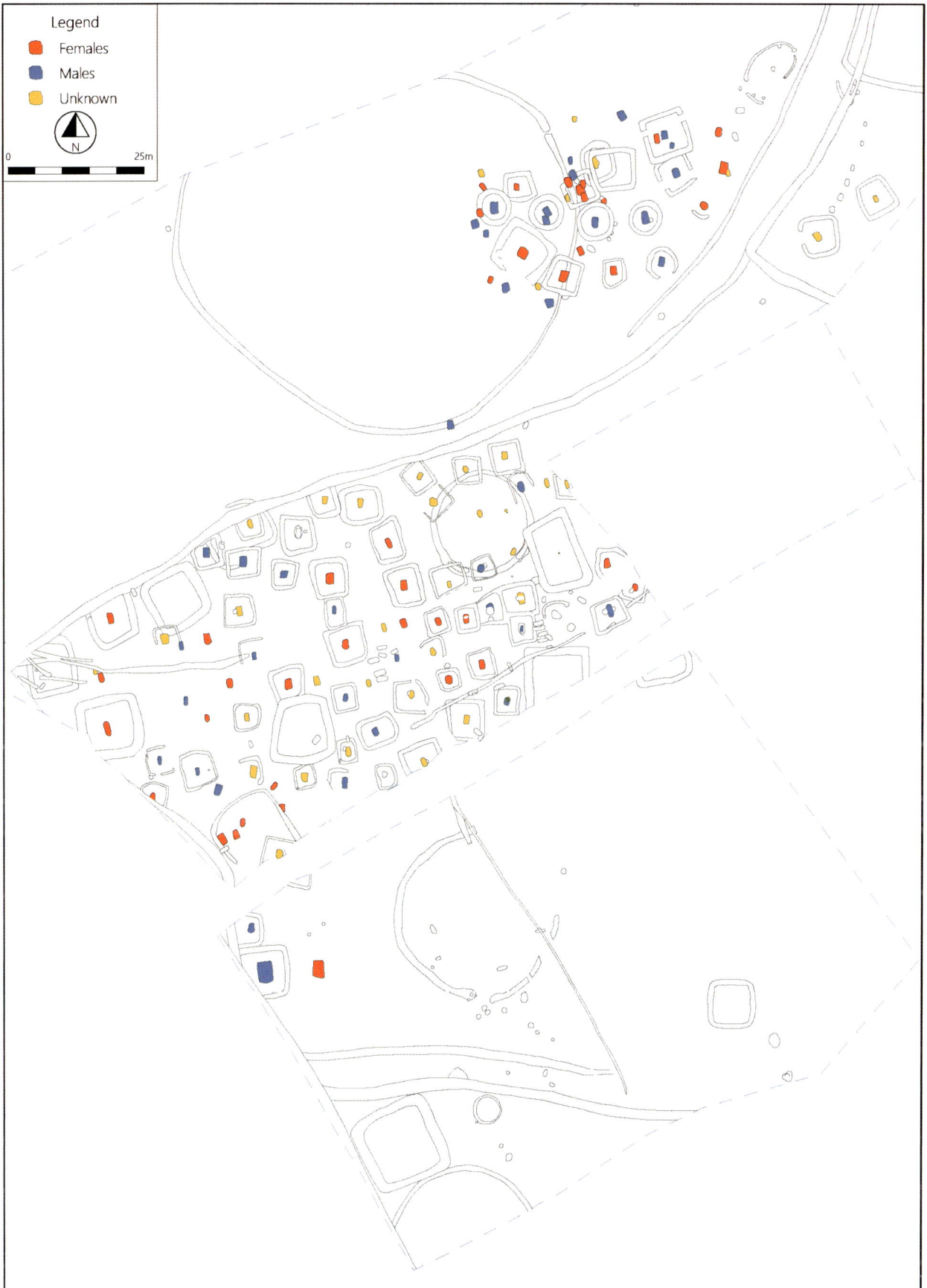

Figure 19.5 Burial location by sex

The health and pathology of the Iron Age population

Around 36.3% of the Iron Age individuals had enamel defects in their teeth (Dental Enamel Hypoplasia – DEH), which was caused by episodes of stress and/or poor health during their childhood. Twenty of these people were buried centrally within barrows (B3, B12, B15, B17, B18, B30, B31, B32, B41, B44, B47, B48, B49, B52, B56, B64, B65, B68, B74 and B75 – *c.* 31% of central barrow burials) and 21 were flat burials (50%), with two secondary burials (25%). Thus there is a hint that individuals who were buried centrally in barrows at Burnby Lane (less than a third of central burials) and secondary burials (a quarter of those) were less likely to have suffered childhood stress than those given flat burial (21 individuals or just under a half of all flat burials). This is only a tentative conclusion, given that isotope studies of the diet of a range of individuals from Wetwang Slack found no difference between high-status (chariot) burials and the rest of the population, as well as no other differences according to burial rite, age or sex (Jay and Roberts 2006).

Four of the non-adults had new bone formation on the inside of their skulls (endocranial new bone), which is associated with conditions such as chronic meningitis, trauma, anaemia, rickets, scurvy and tuberculosis. Twenty-six adults also had endocranial new bone formation, which may have been carried through from childhood. Half of the individuals from the cemetery with this condition were buried centrally within barrows (21% of all central burials), around one third were flat burials (27.5% of all flat burials), the remainder being secondary burials (50% of that category). Therefore, this stress-related condition also appears to have been less prevalent among those buried centrally within barrows, echoing the apparent situation for individuals with DEH.

Cribra orbitalia (CO), a condition related to scurvy (vitamin C deficiency) or resulting from severe infections, is another indicator of stress in agricultural populations. Thirty-three individuals had evidence of CO, or *c.* 39% of the Iron Age population. This figure may have been higher but has been obscured by poor bone preservation as well as the absence of the skull from some burials. The majority (20; nearly 61%) of individuals with this condition were buried centrally within barrows, where they represented just under one third of the total of central barrow burials. Nine flat burials suffered from CO (30.3% of the total of individuals with CO or 25% of the total of flat burials). The remaining three individuals were secondary burials to B38 (9.1% of the total; 37.5% of all secondary burials).

Even though there is an apparent hint that people buried centrally within barrows were less exposed or susceptible to the stresses that caused DEH and endocranial new bone formation, there is less distinction between those with CO, so perhaps we should be cautious in assuming that the central barrow burials represented a more favoured, or at least healthier, group of people.

There were 17 cases of bowing of the long bones: 016 (B78), 15233 (flat burial), 15255 (flat), 15428 (flat), 15622 (B18), 15733 (flat), 15856 (B26), 15974 (B29), 16018 (B33), 16092 (flat), 16363 (flat), 16473 (B38 secondary), 16678 (B48), 16990 (B64), 17087 (flat), 17090 (B50) and 18013 (B65). This may have been due to childhood rickets, or simply natural variation. Non-specific inflammation (possibly due to infection) was present among 24 individuals, although the original number may have been higher as some of the more ephemeral traces of this condition could have been destroyed by adverse soil conditions.

Inflammation of the sinuses caused by pollution such as smoke and dust, or exposure to pollen, was observed in 12 individuals. These affected more females (46.2%) than males (30.8%) and included central barrow burial and flat burial; all were adult and the majority were aged over 36 years, with only one below 25 years. Lesions on the ribs of three adults provided further evidence for respiratory tract infection. In the case of the Burnby Lane chariot burial (394), calcified pleura show that this individual had a severe lung disease.

Burial 16285 (Sk 67), which was stratigraphically earlier than the central burial of B33, had unusual lesions to his face, cranium, jaw and neck, along with rib lesions, all of which were consistent with, but not exclusive to, the presence of tuberculosis. The radiocarbon date shows that he died in the 4th or 3rd century BC, so this is possibly a rare Iron Age instance of tuberculosis.

Another infection was represented by the sacroiliitis (inflammation of the joints at the back of the pelvis) displayed by the late adolescent or young adult woman buried centrally in B12. This condition can develop as a result of pregnancy, and the late-term foetus found at her pelvis indicates that she was pregnant at the time of death. Sacroiliitis causes fever, lower back pain and impairment of movement and can only be treated by antibiotics; consequently, the infection probably played a major part in both her death and that of her baby.

Cysts were recognised in the hips of two individuals: 15960 (flat burial – female) and 16355 (flat burial – male). Large cysts in the right wrist of burial 17090 (B50 – female) were possibly the result of gout. While in modern populations gout is often related to a high-protein diet and excessive consumption of alcohol, it can also be associated with diabetes and heart disease.

Evidence of trauma was relatively widespread among the Iron Age population from Burnby Lane (Fig. 19.6). Two individuals – both central barrow burials – had broken their left clavicles: an adult male (B43) and an unsexed mature adult (B56). Broken clavicles usually arise from falls with the arm outstretched. A mature adult male (flat burial 16464) had a broken left radius, and another adult male (flat burial 17087) had broken both his left radius and left ulna. Breaks of both bones of the forearm are caused by considerable direct force, and when the ends of the bone either do not reunite properly, as was

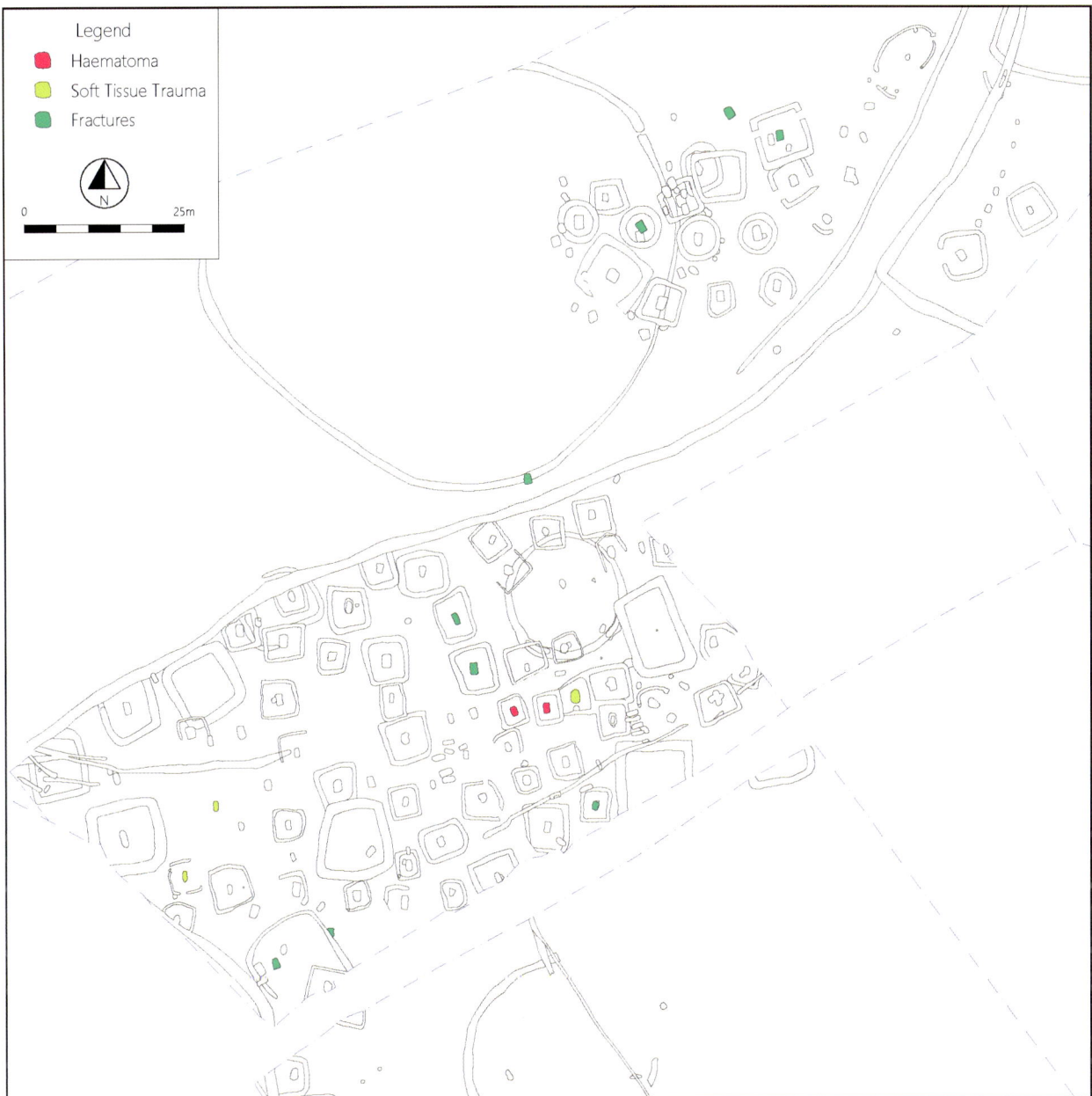

Figure 19.6 Distribution of burials with trauma

the case with 16464, or at all (as with 17087), reduced wrist movement results. The adult woman central burial of B50 (17090) had a healed rib fracture and a possible well-healed fracture to the right clavicle, while the middle-aged male central burial of B18 (15622) had a fractured thoracic vertebra.

Three individuals, all females, had ossified haematomae resulting from direct trauma to muscle tissue: the central burials of B58 (16728 – left femur), B61 (16883 – right tibia), and a flat burial (15255 – left femur). Further soft-tissue trauma was apparent on the lower limbs of another three individuals: 15187 (male central burial B3 – left femur), 15664 (male flat burial – right femur) and 18013 (male? central burial B65 – right femur). The

distribution of these individuals, all of whom were within the western barrow group, may have some significance. Barrows 58, 61 and 65 were adjacent barrows in a line in the central/eastern area of the group and the other three individuals were more loosely distributed in the western area, with 15187 (B3) and 15664 adjacent to each other and 15255 *c.* 25m to the south. If the distribution of individuals with bone fractures is also considered, this pattern seems to be continued: the two central burials of B49 and B50 both had fractures, these barrows continuing in a line northwards from B58 (although the 2nd-degree relationship between the two women in B49 and B50 may also be a factor). Burial 15233 had a potentially fractured tibia and was situated close to Burial 15255 in the south-west area of the cemetery. Another individual with fractures was also buried peripherally – Burial 17087 at the north of the western barrow group, and another with stress fractures (the central burial of B64) at the southern edge of the group. Assuming that the distribution of these burials is not simply coincidence, it is possible that the injuries (though not fatal) to these individuals marked them out in some way, perhaps being seen as inauspicious and leading to special treatment at death. To set against this suggestion, it is difficult to see any spatial pattern with the three individuals (the central burials of B33 and B43, plus flat burial 16464 to the north of B43) with fractures in the eastern barrow group, and the poor condition of many of the skeletons rendering identification of fractures difficult if not impossible.

The instance of inter-personal violence evidenced on the skeleton of the young adult male buried centrally to B32 has already been detailed above. This is an extraordinary record of a sustained attack that resulted in offensive and defensive injuries, by both bladed and blunt weapon(s), to the head, neck, arms, pelvis and left leg. Sharp force injuries to the leg are often the result of attempts to disable or 'bring down' an individual, whereas injuries to the pelvis/buttocks can be the result of attempts to humiliate.

As might be expected, joint disease was common among adults at Burnby Lane, particularly those aged over 35 years. The spine was affected by degenerative disc disease (DDD), degenerative joint change (DJC) and osteoarthritis (OA), all of which became more frequent with age and were commonest among mature adults. DJC and OA also affected other joints in the body, with OA more common in males. The mature adult female central burial of B2 (15176) had possible rheumatoid arthritis.

Six individuals had osteoporosis, which is most often associated with older adult females. Four of the individuals were female: 15176 (B2), 16373 (B38), 16678 (B48) and 16736 (flat burial), plus two males: 16334 (flat) and 16366 (B38 secondary). Male 16334 had compression fractures of both femoral necks, probably resulting from osteoporosis. Hyperostosis frontalis interna (HFI – bony deposits on the internal surface of the skull) is also associated with mature adults, particularly females. Seven individuals at Burnby Lane had clear signs of HFI – six females: 15391 (B8), 15733 (B19), 16001 (B30), 16166 (flat), 16373 (B38) and 16736 (flat), plus one possible example, a probable male 16069 (B31). There were two instances of probable early HFI: 16522 (unknown sex, flat) and 16747 (female – B60).

Gallstones are also more prevalent in old age, and a mature adult male flat burial (16306) had three probable gallstones in his torso. Due to a calcified structure in his neck, the same individual may have suffered from Eagle's disease, which causes sharp pain in the neck and lower head.

The dental health of the Iron Age population at Burnby Lane was poor, with a large majority of adults having periodontal disease caused by poor dental hygiene and resulting in heavy deposits of calculus. Ten adults had developed dental caries: 016 (B78 – male), 15630 (B17 – unknown sex), 15909 (B28 – unknown), 18123 (flat – unknown), 18133 (flat – unknown), 18164 (B67 – male), 18173 (B63 – unknown), 18224 (B66 – unknown), 18272 (B68 – unknown) and 18329 (B75 – female).

Isotope analysis

The isotope analysis of 55 individuals from Pocklington (53 from Burnby Lane and 2 from The Mile) is described in Chapter 17. Thirty-three samples (31 from Burnby Lane and two from The Mile) gave sufficient data for analysis, summarised here.

It appears that the diet for these people was dominated by cereals and terrestrial herbivore protein. In addition, the Pocklington samples, when compared with those from Wetwang, suggested greater consumption of either freshwater resources or pig meat.

Ten of the Burnby Lane individuals had lived part of their lives away from the Pocklington area. Three of these (two male) were raised locally but moved away in middle life, to return later. Three individuals grew up on areas of chalk geology before moving to the vicinity of Pocklington, and two were raised on areas of geology dissimilar from either the Pocklington area or the neighbouring chalk lands. Two individuals were raised around Pocklington and moved elsewhere before returning a relatively short time before they died.

Neither of the two analysed individuals from The Mile grew up in the immediate vicinity of Pocklington. The man buried with the chariot spent his childhood on the chalk and the younger man buried in the circular barrow was raised on the border between typical Pocklington geology and the chalk, possibly regularly moving between the two areas before coming to Pocklington near the end of his life. This illustrates a degree of mobility within the population, with movement to and from the Pocklington area to the chalk lands and *vice versa*, as well as two individuals who settled from elsewhere.

Material culture

Grave goods can entail the embellishment of the human burial itself, for instance with brooches for dress fastening and beads for decoration, and/or the inclusion of weapons, food offerings and pottery within the grave. The placing of a burial within a structure made of organic material is also a way of enhancing a burial, not least because of the effort involved and resources used. Textiles are another form of burial enhancement, but traces of these usually only survive where they have been in contact with metal. Traces of possible organic objects or material, other than textile, were recorded in some of the graves at Burnby Lane.

Giles quotes an overall figure of 34% for Iron Age burials with grave goods from East Yorkshire (Giles 2012, 161), but points out that this figure is for items that have been preserved in the archaeological record and excludes potential objects made of textile, wood and leather that generally leave no trace, and as we have seen, there were hints of such objects in some graves at Burnby Lane. Setting aside the possibility that all traces of organic grave goods have largely disappeared from the cemetery, the fact that only *c.* 18% of the Burnby Lane burials had grave goods represents a significantly lower percentage than the regional norm and may be due to the relatively high proportion of flat burials at the site, the presence and excavation of which was possibly under-represented at some other cemeteries. Considering central/primary burials alone, the proportion of individuals with grave goods rises to 25%, but this is still some way below Giles' figure. The percentages for secondary burials and flat burials buried with grave goods is much lower at Burnby Lane – 12.5% and 7.5% respectively. It could be that the figures for Burnby Lane are skewed by the paucity of burials with meat offerings – poor bone preservation may have removed much of the evidence at the site. All things considered, the proportion for burials with grave goods at Burnby Lane is closer to the 21.9% of burials at Wetwang Slack with 'dress fastenings, other ornaments, weapons, animal bones and pottery' (Dent 1984, 26).

Organic material and possible objects

Some form of organic 'lining' material was placed at the bases or edges of four central barrow graves (B6, B32, B43 and B65), plus flat grave 16287 (Fig. 19.7). It is unclear what these remains represented, but the uneven surface of the deposit in Grave 16287, and the fact that it included pottery sherds and charcoal fragments, suggests that turf had been gathered and used to line the base of this particular grave. Some of the less-substantial deposits in the other graves could have been matting or unprocessed plant material, such as straw, sedge or reed.

Organic material covered five central barrow burials (B15, B24, B34, B57 and B66), and four flat burials (15795, 16306, 16355 and 16358). Some of these organic deposits were amorphous, but the discrete rectangle over burial 15795, which left the head exposed, may be the traces of an organic object or mass of material laid to deliberately cover the torso and limbs and leave the head visible.

The ultimate expression of the covering of a burial was of course the shield burial in B37, but several other burials including B32 may hint at the presence of a shield with associated metal fittings. Equally, the possibility that

some graves with organic material but no associated metal fittings could represent the presence of a shield. The bark shield from Enderby, Leicestershire (Leicester University 2019), was constructed entirely from organic materials, showing that metal fittings are not necessarily diagnostic components for a shield.

Four other graves contained discrete patches of organic dark silt that suggest the inclusion of organic objects with the burial. The head of the central burial in B28 lay on an oval deposit that could have been intended as a headrest. A regular sub-circular deposit, 0.24m in diameter, was recorded at the base of flat grave 16307, and was perhaps the remains of a dish-shaped organic object. The three discrete sub-circular areas of organic silt found within the grave structure housing flat burial 16464 could also indicate the deliberate inclusion of organic material or objects with the burial, and a more amorphous area of dark silt, perhaps the remains of another organic object, was recorded adjacent to a B38 secondary burial (16366).

Meat offerings

In other cemeteries excavated in East Yorkshire (e.g. Wetwang/Garton Slack, Rudston and Burton Fleming) meat offerings, represented by pig and sheep bones, were found with some burials, although 'not in large numbers' (*c.* 5% at Wetwang Slack, Dent 1984, 27). These food offerings consisted of the fore or hind limbs of sheep, or whole or halved pig skulls, with or without the mandible, and often in the second year of age or younger. Based on the findings at the Makeshift cemetery at Rudston (Stead 1991a, 35–6), Stead proposed a variation to the placement of pig in graves, with his Type B flexed/extended east–west burials being associated with halved pig heads and often with fore limbs.

Meat offerings seem only very rarely to have accompanied Iron Age burials at Burnby Lane, with just one definite instance recorded (B38). Small amounts of animal bone were recovered with the human skeletons of six other primary burials (B2, B4, B6, B8, B31 and B45) and a secondary burial (B43) but whether these fragments represented token cuts of food or were accidental inclusions is uncertain. The rarity of meat offerings in the cemetery could be due to the soil conditions acting against the survival of animal bone and perhaps accounts for the fragmentary nature of the bone found with the seven additional burials listed above.

Pig bones were found with the central inhumation of B38, which was the crouched burial of a probable female adult who had parts of the left side of a juvenile pig's skull placed on her chest, with a left forelimb on her pelvis (Figs 4.41 and 19.7). The placement of the pig bone in this instance echoes Stead's Type B burials, but any further resemblance ends there because the B38 burial

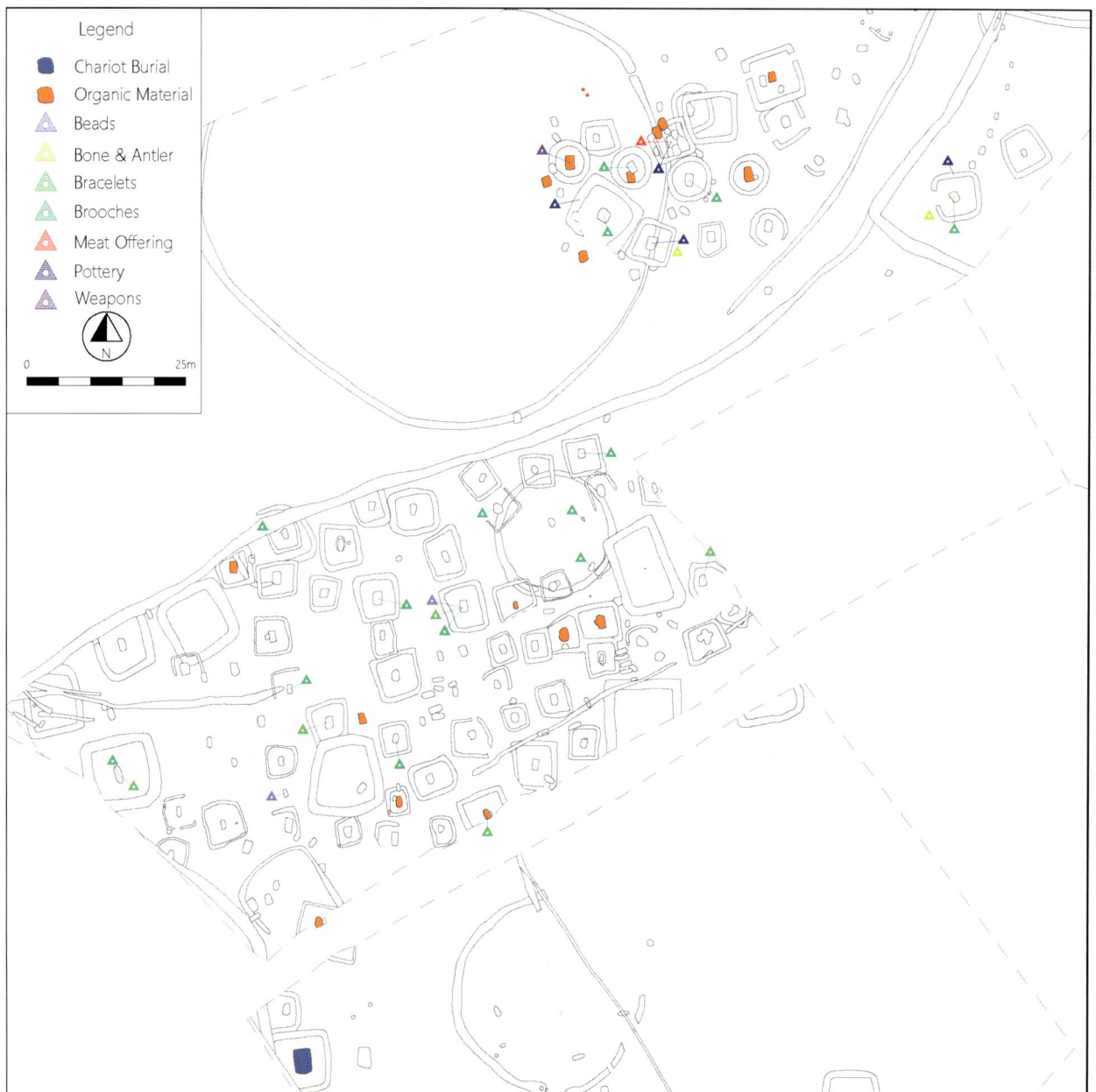

Figure 19.7 Distribution of burials with organic material and grave goods

was crouched, not flexed or extended, and aligned north to south rather than east to west.

The largest fragment of the remaining animal bone found with the burials at Burnby Lane was a piece of unidentified long bone in the grave for Burial 16473, a secondary burial within B43. As this bone was found up against the edge of the grave, off the grave floor and away from the crouched adult male human burial, it could have been an accidental inclusion. The remaining groups of animal bone that accompanied burials were too fragmentary to judge whether they were deliberate or accidental inclusions, although their proximity to the human bodies might suggest deliberate inclusion.

Returning specifically to pigs, their left sides were the favoured cuts included with inhumations at Rudston,

Burton Fleming (both Stead 1991a), Wetwang (Dent 1984), Melton (Stephens and Ware 2019), and The Mile (this volume), indicating that this was a widespread practice across the cemeteries serving the Iron Age communities of East Yorkshire. There was also an emphasis on the inclusion of the forelimbs and skull, which suggests these cuts were reserved for the dead, and if so, the implication is that the hind quarters were the preserve of the living – perhaps even being allotted for feasting at the burial sites.

More broadly, Parker Pearson (1999a, 46) attributed 'totemic significance' to the inclusion of pork with burials, stressing their importance as indicators of high status and this is certainly borne out by the profusion of pig bone buried with The Mile chariot.

The pig bone with The Mile chariot also showed a clear preference for cuts from young boars, which perhaps referenced their fierceness and vigour. All the pigs represented were young, high-value animals, giving prime, highly palatable cuts that demonstrated the generosity and importance of the people who placed them with the burial and perhaps also attributing the same qualities to the dead.

Bone and worked antler

Two pieces of worked antler were found with central burials – part of a beam in B45 and a tine in B30 (Fig. 19.7). Both pieces were cut or sawn across at the ends and had polished or smoothed surfaces. The example from B45 was found at the waist of the burial, so could conceivably had been a belt fastening. The tine from B30 was found in the fill near the top of the grave and so was not in direct association with the burial; it could have either been deliberately cast into the grave or accidentally included during backfilling.

Pottery

The only example of the inclusion of a ceramic vessel in an Iron Age grave at Burnby Lane was with an adult female secondary burial (16403) in B38 (Fig. 19.7). The vessel was a wide-mouthed jar which was badly crushed but complete (SF 83, Fig. 12.1). It was placed in front of the face of this eastward-facing burial, which elsewhere in East Yorkshire has been shown to be one of the less-favoured positions for pots buried with women of her age (26–35 years, Giles 2012, fig. 5.4). The inclusion of pots with a burial was perhaps a reference to the role of 'server-provider' (Parker Pearson 1999a, 53).

Pottery sherds were found in several graves but consisted mainly of single sherds from different vessels and were likely to have been accidental inclusions, as were the multiple sherds from flat graves 16093 and 16287. Other groups of pottery consisting of numbers of sherds from the same vessels within graves could perhaps point to deliberate deposition as it is likely that the vessels concerned were freshly broken at the time of backfilling. The overall fill of the central grave of B30 did, however, contain 11 sherds from three different jars, and an organic deposit resting on the shoulders of the adult woman whose grave this was contained four additional sherds. The fill of flat grave 16104 contained four sherds from a cylindrical jar and the fill of another flat grave (16463) included nine sherds from one vessel.

Graves of both men and women in other East Yorkshire cemeteries, e.g. Rudston (R6, 38 and 204), Burton Fleming (BF3, 8 and 20) and Wetwang Slack (WS154), contained sherds either in clusters or singly, but as with the pottery found within the graves at Burnby Lane, it is uncertain whether this represented vessels that were broken (deliberately or otherwise) during feasting, was background debris or had some deeper meaning.

Many of the barrow ditches also contained sherds, either single or multiple sherds from different vessels. However, the 80+ sherds of the same vessel in the north ditch of B45 (SF 88, Fig. 12.1), 11 sherds from a vessel in the base of the north ditch of B42, and 14 sherds from a wide-necked jar in the south-west corner of B83, could be the debris from feasting rather than the simple dumping of rubbish. The possibility that feasting was carried out in the cemetery is also shown by the shallow 'fire pit' cut into the initial silting of the east ditch of B45, so perhaps the sherds found in the barrow's northern ditch were debris from a feast.

Brooches

The brooches have been fully discussed and catalogued by Sophia Adams in Chapter 11; what follows here is a general review.

Fourteen Iron Age brooches were recovered from Burnby Lane, consisting of 12 iron or copper alloy bow brooches and two penannular examples (or parts of); two lone pins were also recovered. Typologically, the brooches were 3rd–2nd century BC in date, although Bayesian modelling suggests deposition in a time span from the 4th to the 2nd century BC (Chapter 16). The brooches are important because of their relatively good preservation and association with specific graves and burials. Two are of particular significance because of their rarity – the H-shaped brooch (SF 5) which accompanied the central burial in B2 (the first of this type to be recovered by excavation) and the arched bow brooch (SF 84) with the central burial of B42 (a type previously unknown in Yorkshire). Many of the brooch types are familiar from other East Yorkshire cemeteries (Garton/Wetwang, Burton Fleming and Rudston), while looking further afield, the brooch types are known from southern and eastern England, and Wales, where finds in a burial context are rare.

Any attempt to draw conclusions from the distribution of graves with brooches should be cautious because of the relatively small size of the sample (16 – including the lone pins). However, there is an apparent cluster of graves with brooches around Bronze Age barrow B71 (Fig. 19.7), consisting of the central graves of three adjacent Group 2 square barrows (B50, B52 and B55) and two flat burials (18133 and 16997). One of these burials was an adult woman; the remainder, three adults and one adolescent, were unsexed. The siting of these burials may have been an attempt to connect them with the earlier monument B71.

Brooch types from cemeteries in the Great Wold Valley are believed to show sex preference: arched, flat bow and decorated involuted for males, and long, flat and short involuted types for females. In addition, at Wetwang/Garton Slack there was a trend for females to have short involuted, penannular, inlaid bow and S-shaped brooch types. Again, with over a third of the Burnby Lane brooch burials being of unknown sex, it is difficult to detect preferences, but at least one of the short involuted brooches was buried with a woman, reflecting one of the trends noted at both the Great Wold Valley and Garton/Wetwang cemeteries. On the other hand, a man (B45) was buried with a penannular brooch, which is at variance to the female trend seen at Garton/Wetwang.

None of the burials in the five circular barrows had a brooch buried *directly* with them, but the central grave in B33 had a brooch within the grave fill *c.* 0.3m above the burial. It is possible that the complete brooch was cast into the grave during backfilling as part of the burial rite.

The radiocarbon dates available from the burials associated with brooches lay mainly within the 3rd century BC, with one date in the 4th century BC (18133 – a flat burial within the circuit of Bronze Age barrow B71) and two in the 2nd century BC (17081 – centrally buried within B46; and 16443 buried centrally within B42).

Bracelets

Six bracelets were recovered from Iron Age graves at Burnby Lane (Fig. 19.7), all from central barrow burials (B2 (two examples), B19, B28, B50 and B74) scattered throughout the western barrow group (see Chapter 11). The B2 burial had a copper alloy bracelet on each wrist; B19 an iron bracelet on the right wrist; B28 a fragmentary iron bracelet on the torso of a very badly preserved skeleton; B50 a copper alloy bracelet on the left wrist; and B74 an iron bracelet on the left wrist. All these burials were adult women, three being over 26 years old, apart from the unsexed adult from B28. The women from B2 and B50 were also buried with decorated copper alloy brooches, making these particularly rich instances of grave furnishings.

All the bracelets were unique but with strong similarities to both bracelets and decoration found on brooches in Arras cemeteries in East Yorkshire. There are no direct parallels with examples abroad, but the presence of inlaid coral and open-circle decoration is echoed by 4th-century BC examples from the Paris Basin.

Beads

Two of the Iron Age glass beads described in Chapter 12 were recovered from the base of a possible grave (15722) but these were the only examples expressly associated with an Iron Age burial at Burnby Lane. Three Anglian graves also contained Iron Age beads, two with single polychrome eye beads and another grave with two spiral-decorated barrel beads ('Meare Spiral', after examples from Meare Lake village) – one of which had the later, presumably Anglian, addition of a gold sleeve within the suspension hole. It is plausible that these beads were unearthed during the digging of later graves into the Iron Age cemetery and afterwards curated by Anglian women.

Glass beads with spiral and eye decoration are paralleled at other East Yorkshire sites including Garton/Wetwang and Arras (the 'Queen's' Burial). A single monochrome glass bead accompanied the adult woman buried at the centre of Barrow 50, its relative plainness contrasting with the richness of the brooch and bracelet that were also buried with her.

The chariots from Burnby Lane and The Mile

The chariots from Burnby Lane and The Mile were respectively the 21st and 23rd recorded examples from East Yorkshire (this total includes two examples – from Crambeck and the 22nd example, at Melton – that were discovered after the compilation of Halkon's list: Halkon 2013, table 2). There are two additional chariot burials from outside East Yorkshire (Newbridge, Edinburgh (Carter *et al.* 2013) and Ferry Fryston, West Yorkshire (Boyle *et al.* 2007)) and a further example has recently been excavated by the Dyfed Archaeological Trust in Pembrokeshire (*Current Archaeology* 2019). The British chariot burials known at the time of writing are summarised in Table 19.3.

The Burnby Lane chariot compares readily with other East Yorkshire chariot burials, although post-depositional damage had destroyed much of the evidence and presumably removed diagnostic fittings such as terrets and lynch pins. The placing of a central pole with the yoke end to the north and dismantled iron-tyred 12-spoke wheels to the south, with the inhumation resting on top of the pole, are all echoed to varying degrees at other East Yorkshire sites, even if they were not always arranged in the same pattern.

These vehicles were almost certainly not war chariots to be used as platforms for fighting, but rather 'used to transport privileged people' which might include the 'warrior travelling to and from the battlefield' (Greene 1972, 61–3, 70–1). Stead envisaged such vehicles as of simple construction, not designed to be driven at high speed, but 'capable of fairly stately progress' because there is no evidence that they had suspension (Stead 1991a, 61).

Apart from scantily recorded examples at Cawthorn Camps, Hunmanby (which also had a composite shield), and Pexton Moor (where chariot remains were found with upright wheels – Stead 1965), the closest parallel to The Mile chariot, that from Ferry Fryston, is perhaps ironically from outside East Yorkshire (Brown *et al.* 2007). Both The Mile and the Ferry Fryston chariots have distinctive pointed ends to the front of the body and were buried 'intact' with the wheels upright – so it appears that the entire vehicle was either still assembled, or perhaps that the box was detached from the axle. At Ferry Fryston it was pointed out that if the rear end of the box was designed to rest on the axle, the hind legs of the ponies ran the danger of striking the front of the box; allowing for this it was suggested that the box had been detached and moved forward from its original position when placed in the grave. It was also suggested that the box need not have been part of the actual chariot, but a separate container used expressly for the funeral, and further, as the iron tyres were mismatched, the vehicle may have been a composite. There is no doubt that those suggestions are entirely plausible; however, the fact that there are now two chariot burials of closely similar form surely makes it more likely that their arrangement in the grave reflects the configuration in which they were used (although of course it is possible that the chariot box and chassis were separated in the same way at both sites).

Table 19.3 British chariot burials

Site	Date of excav.	Sex	Chariot fittings	Terrets (no.)	Horse bits (no.)	Sword	Shield	Pig bones	Other objects	C¹⁴ date (cal BC)	Comments	Reference
Arras 1 (King's Barrow)	1815–17	M	2 iron tyres 2 nave hoops 2 lynch pins	5	2			2 skulls			2 horse skeletons	Greenwell 1877, 454–7; 1906, 284–6
Arras 2 (Charioteer's Barrow)	1815–17	M	2 iron tyres iron nave hoop 2 possible antler lynch pins	Y	2		bronze boss?	?	bronze case (pole cap?)			As above
Arras 28 (Lady's Barrow)	19th C	F	2 iron tyres 4 iron/bronze nave hoops	1 d-shaped bronze/iron	2 bronze/iron			Y	iron mirror bronze lid or cap			As above
Beverley Westwood	1875	?	2 iron tyres 4 iron nave hoops		2 iron							As above
Danes Graves 43	1897	?	1 iron tyre 1 iron nave hoop 2 iron lynch pins	5 (at least 2 bronze/iron)	2 iron			Y	Bronze/iron brooch; 2 bronze buttons		2 skeletons	Mortimer 1897; 1898
Cawthorn Camps	19th cent.	?	2 iron tyres 1 bronze nave hoop possible bronze harness rings		1 iron						possibly complete chariot	Mortimer 1905b, 361
Seamer Station	19th cent.	?	?								possible	Mortimer 1905a, 358
Huggate	19th cent.	?	2 iron tyres?								possible	Mortimer 1905a, 359
Middleton-on-the-Wolds	1888	?	?								possible	Mortimer 1905a, 359–60
Hornsea	1904	?	?								dubious	Stead 1965, 93
Hunmanby	1907	?	iron tyres iron nave hoops iron lynch pins?	1 bronze/iron	1 bronze		Y (bronze fittings)					Stead 1965, 94–5
Pexton Moor	1911/1936	?	iron tyre 2 iron nave hoops		1 bronze/iron							Kirk 1911, 62; Stead 1959, 214–16

(Continued)

Table 19.3 British chariot burials (Continued)

Site	Date of excav.	Sex	Chariot fittings	Terrets (no.)	Horse bits (no.)	Sword	Shield	Pig bones	Other objects	C¹⁴ date (cal BC)	Comments	Reference
Garton Slack	1970	M	2 iron tyres iron nave hoops iron pole cap (?)	5 bronze/iron	2 iron			Y	2 bronze slip buckles bronze 'pommel'			Brewster 1971, 289–92
Wetwang Slack 1	1984–85	M	2 iron tyres iron nave hoops	5 bronze/iron	2 iron	Y	iron spine; cover frags	Y	7 iron spear heads			Dent 1985, 85–92
Wetwang Slack 2	1984–85	F	2 iron tyres 4 bronze nave hoops	5 bronze	2 iron			Y	bronze container iron pin bronze mirror			Dent 1985, 85–92
Wetwang Slack 3	1984–85	M	2 iron tyres 4 iron nave hoops 2 antler lynch pins	5 bronze/iron	2 iron	Y	possible boss	Y				Dent 1985, 85–92
Garton Station (GS6)	1985	M	2 iron tyres 4 iron nave hoops 2 iron lynch pins	4 bronze	2 iron			Y			wheels put upright at grave edge	Stead 1991, 219, fig. 122
Kirkburn (K5)	1987	M	2 iron tyres 4 bronze nave hoops 2 bronze/iron lynch pins 2 bronze strap unions	5 bronze	2 iron/ bronze			Y	iron mail coat 2 bronze 'mini-terrets' 3 bronze toggles bronze 'lid'			Stead 1991, 224, fig. 127
Newbridge (Lothian)	2001	?	2 iron tyres	4 iron	2 iron					520–370	buried intact?	Carter *et al.* 2010
Wetwang Village	2001	F	2 iron tyres 2 bronze-coated iron lynch pins 2 bronze strap unions	5 bronze	2 bronze			Y	mirror brooch blue glass beads	350–120		Hill 2002, 410–12

(Continued)

Table 19.3 (Continued)

Site	Date of excav.	Sex	Chariot fittings	Terrets (no.)	Horse bits (no.)	Sword	Shield	Pig bones	Other objects	C¹⁴ date (cal BC)	Comments	Reference
Ferrybridge (West Riding)	2003	M	2 iron tyres 4 bronze-coated iron nave hoops 2 J-shaped iron lynch pins	5 bronze (hollow)	1 iron		iron and composite fittings	Y	composite brooch 3 decorated bronze strips	520–230; 400–200 (pig bones)	buried intact?	Brown *et al.* 2007, 121–50
Crambeck (Jamie's Crag)		?	iron tyre iron nave hoops iron lynch pin								wheels upright; not fully excav.	Wood 2018, 91–2
Burnby Lane (Pocklington)	2017	M?	iron tyre 2 iron nave hoops		1 iron, non-ferrous plating						2 ponies; grave truncated	This volume
Melton	2017	M	2 iron tyres 4 bronze nave hoops 2 iron lynch pins	3 bronze 1 bronze with iron core	2 iron				composite bronze/iron pole cap? 4 decorated sheet bronze 'clips'	330–204		Stephens and Ware 2019, 29–30
The Mile (Pocklington)	2017	M	2 iron tyres 4 bronze nave hoops 2 iron lynch pins	2 bronze 1 iron			decorative bronze plaques; ash board	Y	bronze brooch bronze bead	350–50	chariot intact? 2 upright ponies	This volume
Pembrokeshire	2018	?*	2 iron tyres 4 bronze nave hoops 2 bronze lynch pins bronze strap unions	1 bronze	2 bronze	Y			bronze horse brooch		wheels placed upright in slots mid–late 1st cent. AD	*Current Archaeology* 349, 355

?* = none surviving

The practicality of such long, narrow vehicles with the wheels and axle at the rear is shown by the 'curricles' which were fashionable in the Regency period. As for the problem caused by the ponies striking their hind legs against the edge of the box, this could be solved by training them to move at a restrained gait, or even by physical methods such as a breeching strap (although there is no surviving evidence for such). There is also no evidence for the chariots having suspension, so it follows that it would have been necessary to train the ponies to trot rather than canter or gallop in order to restrict their speed and hence lessen the risk of an accident. Finally, as the axle, pole, wheels and ponies at The Mile were apparently staged as if in life, it surely follows that the position of the box also reflected the position it had within the functioning chariot.

The Mile chariot appears to have been a usable vehicle in every respect, rather than being cobbled together for the purposes of the funeral. While it is true that the nave hoops for the eastern wheel were not identical, this does not mean that the chariot was assembled *ad hoc* for the funeral and the anomalous nave hoop can be interpreted as an addition or repair to a valued and purposeful vehicle. Repairs and possible wear to the other nave hoops point to a long period of use, the repairs having a parallel with the treatment of a nave hoop from Stead's K5 chariot (Stead 1991a, fig. 35, 3–4). The three surviving terrets are all different, although it could be argued that the two copper alloy terrets have a degree of stylistic integrity. The plated iron terret is potentially earlier and is of markedly different design, suggesting that it had a separate history before being combined with the other terrets. This accords with the strong argument that high-status objects such as swords and shields (and chariots) were augmented, not devalued, by additions and modifications (Chittock 2017). It could also fit with Lewis' suggestion that items of horse gear were handed down to emphasise the charioteer's lineage and/or show the 'approval or patronage' of senior members of the community (Lewis 2015, 182). The apparent 'mismatching' of the metal fittings from some other excavated chariots, e.g. Melton (Stephens and Ware 2019, 28), can also be interpreted as an expression of their long and valued histories. However, not all sets of chariot fittings should be viewed in the same light as there is a contrast between material from chariots such as The Mile and Melton and the stylistic unity of the sets of terrets from chariots such as Stead's K5 and GS6 (Stead 1991a, 227 and 221 respectively), Brewster's Garton Slack (Brewster 1980) and Dent's Wetwang 4 (Dent 1985), which suggests that different beliefs and approaches operated.

Both the Ferry Fryston and The Mile chariots can be seen as 'isolated' examples of burial, which (as Giles (2012) has suggested) possibly means that the 'charioteers' were seen as individuals who lay outside normal kinship or family groups, acting as protectors of others. This function might be echoed by the placing of a shield with The Mile charioteer in a direct allusion to protection.

In this respect it is worth noting that the Burnby Lane chariot was set at the edge of the main concentration of Iron Age burials. However, as chariot burial seems to have been carried out in the final stages of Arras-style barrow burial (Jay *et al.* 2012, more of which below), this may have inevitably led to the location of some chariot burials at the unoccupied margins of barrow groups and hence need not necessarily express any symbolism.

A shield is, of course, a physical expression of 'protection' (although shields can also have an offensive function, as discussed by Hitchcock 2018). The spectacular shield found with The Mile chariot was intact, like the chariot it was buried with, but unlike the dismantled shields from the adjacent circular barrow and from Burnby Lane. However, the shield was buried face-downwards, perhaps as a symbolic inversion that referred to the end of its physical use and drawing to a close the protection offered by the man buried with it.

Without overstating what might be expressed by the decoration and form of objects, it is believed that some chariot fittings (and other objects) carry symbolism associated with horses, who seem to have occupied a special place in Iron Age society as representatives of the two spheres of the wild and the domesticated (Lewis 2019, 113–16). In this light it is worth considering the symbolism of the dragonfly motif of The Mile charioteer's brooch. Dragonflies are fast-moving agile predators that are conspicuous in flight and range over long distances. Like horses, which appear to have been seen as existing on the border between the worlds of the domestic and wild (Lewis 2019, 115), dragonflies straddle two worlds – in this case water (as larvae) and the air (as adults) – and this liminality may have been perceived as having significance and power. It is tantalising to consider whether these attributes were seen by Iron Age people as appropriate to an individual associated with a chariot.

It is unfortunate that the truncation of the Burnby Lane chariot burial means that little can be said of this individual other than he was an adult male aged over 25 years, although the fact that he had calcified pleura from lung disease could mean that he was an older adult. As we have seen, the man buried with the chariot at The Mile was a mature adult over 46 years old who had led a long and active life, the physical strains of which had led to spondylolysis. Analysis of the isotopes (Chapter 17) suggests that he spent his early life on land underlain by chalk, presumably the Yorkshire Wolds (although it is worth bearing in mind that chalk outcrops southwards through Lincolnshire, into East Anglia, south-east England, then westwards as far as Dorset and eastwards to northern France and the Paris Basin).

The preceding paragraphs have touched on the possible roles and physical aspects of the two men buried with chariots. However, it has been suggested that there is not necessarily a direct link between a chariot and the individual buried with it (Lewis 2015, 268). Lewis points out that in burial contexts, chariot fittings have only been found in graves that contained the entire vehicle, as opposed to individual objects like weapons, items of personal adornment, pots and tools. Leaving aside the possibility that grave goods were not necessarily personal possessions, Lewis has suggested (2015, 182) that chariot burials were an expression of the wealth, power and connections of groups of people rather than having a direct connection to the individual buried with the chariot. The reverse could equally be the case, i.e. tht chariots were so intimately associated with an individual, as the personification of their status, function, purpose and character, that it followed that they were buried with *their* chariot.

The chariot from The Mile is unique in that the ponies were placed upright in the grave as if in movement. This can be interpreted as perpetuating the motion of the chariot and maintaining its power and even perhaps, as Lewis puts it, to continue 'to perform as a set of artefacts through which control over land and territory can be effected' (Lewis 2015, 261).

Furthermore, the chariots from both Burnby Lane and The Mile stand out due to the presence of ponies with the burial. Horses (or ponies) are believed to have been included in chariot burials at the King's Barrow at Arras and Hunmanby (Stead 1965, 77) and Seamer (Mortimer 1905, 38), although their presence at the last two sites is particularly unclear. It is conspicuous that of the ten chariot burials excavated under modern standards in East Yorkshire, the only two with ponies were found in the immediately vicinity of Pocklington. At the risk of stating the obvious, the arrangement of any individual chariot burial was a product of the desires of a specific group of people, with ideas differing from one community to another, albeit they were operating within the same broad tradition. Although the sample size of chariots from the Pocklington area is too small to be a reliable indicator, there might be a hint that the middle Iron Age communities around Pocklington favoured the inclusion of ponies with their chariot burials.

Speared burials

The young men buried with spears within the circular barrows at The Mile and Burnby Lane (B34) belong to the category of 'special' burials associated with the other circular barrows situated close to B34. These barrows have obvious parallels with the four small circular barrows at Garton Station (GS K, P, S and W – Stead 1991a, fig. 20) whose primary burials consisted of either young adult or young middle-adult males buried with iron spearheads. Like the man buried in The Mile circular barrow, the GS5 individual also had three bone points.

However, there are problems with identifying Skeleton 303 buried within the circular barrow at The Mile and the B34 burial as 'speared corpses' – that is burials that had spears directly cast at them. The spearheads within The Mile grave were distributed around the grave at varying

angles from vertical to horizontal, with four (SF 8, 14, 16 and 21) in a rough line between the torso and the legs, and three (SF 9, 13 and 15) away from the skeleton in the eastern part of the grave. The only spearhead that was actually in contact with the body (SF 7), lying on the lower right ribs, left no traces on the skeleton, showing that if the corpse had been speared, the spear cannot have had any forcible contact with the body.

At Burnby Lane, the B34 burial was accompanied by five iron heads from throwing spears, a ferrule and an iron sword – the latter intriguingly occupying the same relative position to the corpse seen with the shield fittings of The Mile spear burial. Four of the spearheads were laid out along the spine and so do not appear to have been thrust into the grave; the other one was in a more ambiguous position pointing away from the hip, but again with no evidence that it had been thrown into the grave. The ferrule lay over the tip of the sword. The sockets of the spearheads and the ferrule contained wood remains, suggesting that the shafts had been snapped off; as the shafts were likely to have been around 1.65m in length (a figure based on a multi-purpose spear from Lincolnshire – Inall 2019, 72) they would not have fitted into the grave if complete. There were also no signs on the skeleton of this man to suggest that any of the spears had been thrust at his corpse.

These factors do not easily support an argument that the spears were thrown or thrust towards the corpse as a ritual 'spearing' at either burial. However, it is necessary to bear in mind that, as Inall points out (quoting Milner – Inall 2019, 80), although wounds to the abdomen are often fatal, in one study only 2% of abdominal injuries left any marks on the skeleton, and only one third of wounds as a whole left any marks on the skeleton. It must be stressed that these figures were for arrow wounds in 19th-century America – not wounds from heavier spears in Iron Age East Yorkshire. The evidence, and absence of evidence, for this rite at The Mile and Burnby Lane is open to question.

As far as the two men buried at Burnby Lane and The Mile are concerned, the distribution of the spearheads around the body suggests more that they were deliberately laid, rather than thrown, into the grave. In this instance, the inclusion of spears with a burial can be interpreted as a 'martial salute' to these men and not necessarily as an attempt to either confine their spirit to the grave or ensure a warrior's death into the afterlife.

There could also be symbolism in the physical treatment of the spears. The presence of mineralised wood in the sockets of all the iron spearheads from the circular barrow at The Mile and B34 at Burnby Lane shows that the shafts must have been snapped off, rather than removed. This deliberate damage echoes the treatment of the shields from the circular barrow at The Mile and B37 at Burnby Lane and may represent the 'ritual killing' of these weapons. East Yorkshire examples of this process are uncommon but appear to be represented by the bent sword excavated by Northern Archaeological Associates on the Burstwick–Rimswell pipeline in 2016 (Current Archaeology 2018) and the late Iron Age Acklam Wold sword, which was deliberately bent within its scabbard before burial (Dent 1983, fig. 5.25). Other examples from Britain include the bent iron sword from a late Iron Age grave in Kelvedon, Essex (Sealey 2007) and the Mill Hill shield from Kent, which was apparently deliberately folded before it was placed in the grave (Parfitt 1995).

Iron-working residues

Nineteen Iron Age contexts at Burnby Lane contained iron-working residues or possible residues (Fig. 19.8).

Seven graves – the central graves of B12, B55 and B62, and flat graves 11093, 16104, 16307 and 19082 – contained definite smithing hearth fragments or undiagnostic slag, the remainder of the residues being found in barrow ditches (B8, B12, B14, B33, B39, B42, B43, B51 and B65) and the south-east quadrant of the oval ring gully. The residues were spread across the site and present in both the western and eastern barrow groups.

Clearly there was iron-working in the vicinity of Burnby Lane during the Iron Age and it is likely that the residues from this were deposited during natural silting into the barrow ditches, or re-deposited into the backfill

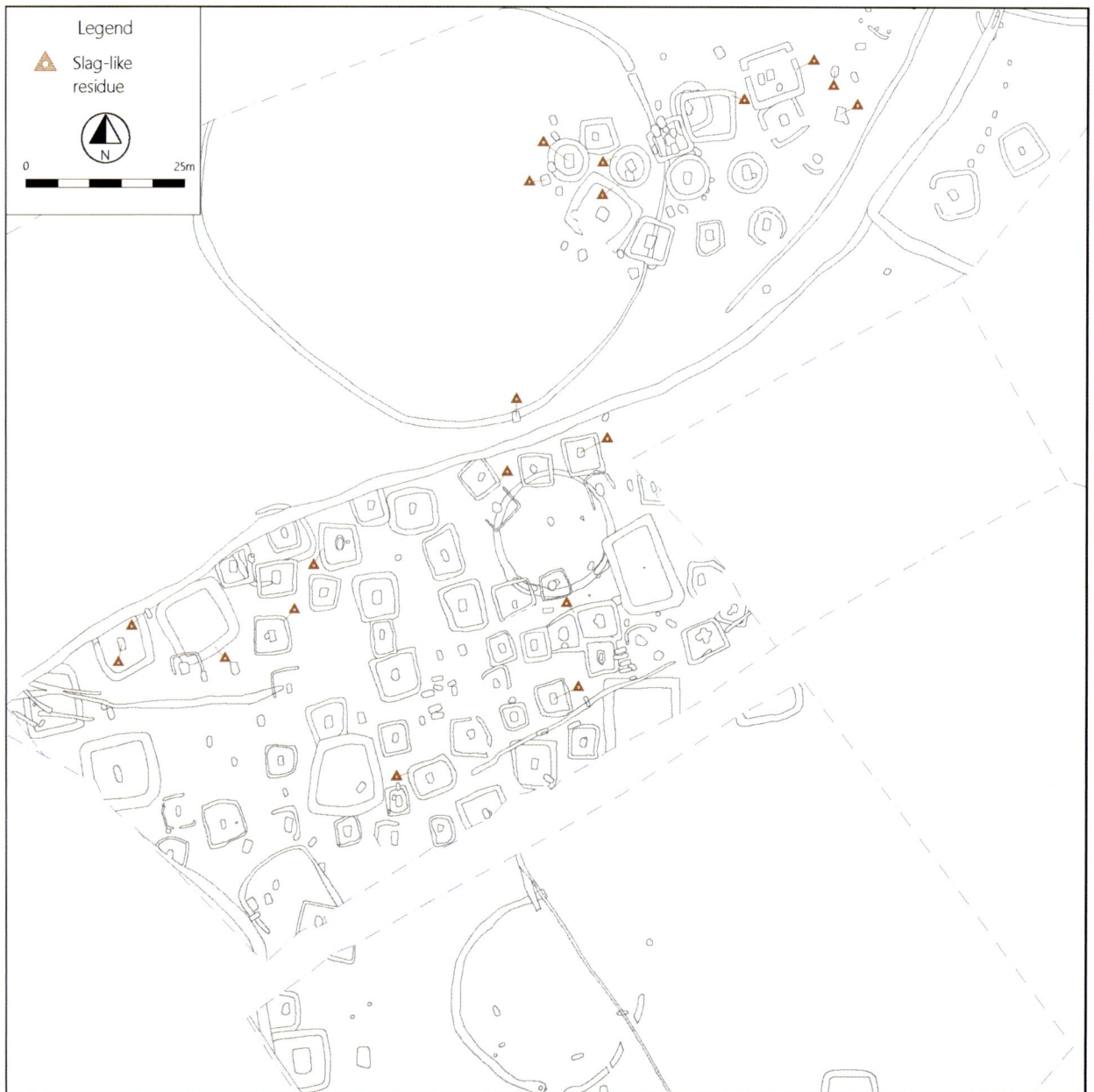

Figure 19.8 Distribution of slag-like residues

of certain graves from background material lying in the topsoil. However, the possibility remains that the inclusion of some of the residues into graves – particularly the large chunks of smithing hearth bottom and slag from flat grave 16104 – was deliberate and of significance to the woman buried there or her mourners.

Cow burials

The two cow burials situated on the eastern edge of the cemetery are another important element of the Iron Age funerary activity. While these two burials are assumed to be contemporary with the use of the cemetery, the only dating for the animals is that one the graves pre-dated a furrow. Attempts at radiocarbon-dating failed twice due to insufficient carbon, which is probably an indication of the relative antiquity of the cow burials and probable association with the cemetery.

The cattle concerned were adults, one senile and one a younger adult. The possibility that they represent the disposal of unwanted, perhaps diseased, carcases cannot be discounted, but given their location, close together on the south-eastern margin of the eastern barrow group, it is more likely that they are connected to the Iron Age funerary landscape. It could be that these cows were revered by their households as faithful providers of milk and cheese and so their graves were sited close to the human burials.

Cuts of meat from cattle were never included in Iron Age inhumations in East Yorkshire, only those from pig and sheep/goat. The burial of cattle during the Iron Age in circumstances other than prosaic was suggested by the skeleton of a calf buried in a pit beneath the floor of a roundhouse at Garton Slack which was interpreted as a 'foundation deposit' (Brewster 1980). The crouched 'ritualistic interment' of a cow excavated at Hodsow Lane, Pocklington has echoes of the Garton Slack cow burial as it was found close to the entrance of a possible late Iron Age/Roman roundhouse (OSA 2009). A great mass of cattle bone radiocarbon-dated to between the late 1st and early 4th century AD was found in the ditches of the Ferry Fryston chariot burial and probably represented feasting at the site, akin to Roman practice seen elsewhere in the country (Brown *et al.* 2007, 149). A complete cow burial excavated at Site M (*c.* 5km south of the Ferry Fryston chariot) was Iron Age in date (Brown *et al.* 2007). The Garton Slack, Hodsow Lane and Site M examples at least show similar special treatment of cattle after death to those at Burnby Lane.

20

Conclusion

Mark Stephens

The range of middle Iron Age burial rites, from chariot burial as an expression of 'aristocratic' status at one end of the scale, to unfurnished flat burials at the other, has been seen as illustrating a hierarchical society where social stratification was reflected by the comparative richness of individual burials. However, Parker Pearson articulated a degree of caution about this interpretation with his statement that 'the dead do not bury themselves' (Parker Pearson 1999b, 84), pointing to the fact that the character of any individual burial might reflect the status, beliefs and desires of those carrying out the funeral as much as those of the deceased. In addition, objects included with the dead might be designed more to aid the transition of the deceased from life to death than to maintain a direct link between the dead and their previous life.

However, as Giles points out, social differentiation in fact does appear to have been expressed through the differences in material culture represented in the variety of square barrow burials (Giles 2012, 27). Along with the variation in the richness of barrow burials, it is also worth considering as a possible indicator of social difference that some individuals at Burnby Lane were buried in unenclosed graves at the same time and at the same location as others were being buried at the centre of square barrows. That some of the unenclosed graves were arguably more richly furnished (with brooches and grave structures) than most of the central barrow burials means that flat burial could have been more the result of differences in belief and custom than social status.

A relatively short time span of anywhere between 5 and 130 years (*95% probability: Wetwang Slack*) and 10 and 75 years (*68% probability*) has been suggested for the Wetwang cemetery (Jay *et al.* 2012, 180). However, other cemeteries need not necessarily have followed the same pattern – indeed the dating of the brooches from Burnby Lane and radiocarbon dates from central barrow and flat burials there span the 4th and 3rd centuries BC, even perhaps into the 2nd century BC. If the period in which square barrow inhumation cemeteries operated was relatively short-lived, then other burial rites, not necessarily being confined to inhumation, must have existed before, after, and even at the same time (Champion 2019, 168–9). All of this has implications for any social differences implied by square barrow inhumation, as flat burial may have remained preferable to some groups of people.

Even with these considerations in mind, chariot burials clearly represented a great commitment of physical resources, and not simply of the chariot and its fittings. At Burnby Lane and The Mile, the 'disposal' by burial of the draught ponies, the upkeep of which had involved a lifetime's outlay in valuable fodder, stabling and training, represented a huge investment.

Chariots were, of course, in use in other areas of Iron Age Britain apart from East Yorkshire, but it was this area that was the focus of chariot *burial* as well as one of the main locations in Iron Age Britain where inhumation was practised. Differences in burial custom run alongside the 'subtle biological structure accompanying the regional character' of Iron Age Britain (Patterson *et al.* 2022); that study of the DNA also suggests that the Iron Age population of East Yorkshire stands out from all other British Iron Age populations, and harboured 'a large proportion of ancestry most likely from France'. The similarities of Arras-style burial customs (square enclosures, chariot burial) in East Yorkshire with those in the Champagne region may hint at ancestral links between the two areas, and the genetic association may be due either to the same middle–late Bronze Age influence from mainland Europe (followed by regional isolation) or, more tantalisingly, a separate migration from Europe to East Yorkshire during the Iron Age. The answer would hopefully be provided by studies of the relevant populations in France.

Chariot burials are generally held to have been carried out in a relatively short-lived period around 200 BC (although The Mile is a little earlier), coinciding with the final phase of regular Arras-type burial, after which there was a steep decline in decorated metalwork and, in broader terms, the occurrence of political and social changes throughout Europe (Jay *et al.* 2012, 184). From the middle to late Iron Age in East Yorkshire there was a trend away from open settlement towards habitation enclosed by ditches. That trend may be echoed by the growth of division within square barrow cemeteries, illustrated by the clustering of the later, smaller Group 3 barrows at Burnby Lane. For the Burnby Lane cemetery such changes ultimately mark the end of 'Arras' burial.

The results of the excavations described in described in this report are the largest group of Iron Age burials to be excavated in East Yorkshire since the 1980s. They are also the largest group, from what could be called a 'lowland' location (as opposed to the Arras heartlands of the higher Wolds), to be excavated under modern standards. Although there are many similarities with the large Wold cemeteries at Garton and Wetwang Slacks, Rudston and Burton Fleming (among others), not to mention physical links shown by the isotope study, there are also subtle differences in the expression of Arras-type burial from these sites. The Pocklington burials are, of course, part of a wider world and the research into genetic links that may exist between the Iron Age in East Yorkshire and mainland Europe will be an important next stage in exploring the origins and wider connections of the Arras culture. The study of any genetic connections among the individuals from Arras cemeteries also has great potential to illuminate the distribution of burials in a particular cemetery, as the preliminary study of the Burnby Lane and The Mile populations has shown. It follows that the Iron Age individuals buried at Pocklington have the potential to contribute greatly to this important strand of future research into the people of Arras East Yorkshire and beyond.

Bibliography

Adams, S., Booth, A., Haselgrove, C. and Joy, J. 2012 Iron Age brooches, coins and other copper alloy objects from Grandcourt Farm, Middleton, Norfolk. Sleaford: Archaeological Project Services unpublished report.

Adams, S.A. 2014 The First Brooches in Britain: from manufacture to deposition in the Early and Middle Iron Age. Unpublished PhD thesis, University of Leicester. http://hdl.handle.net/2381/28593.

Adams, S. 2017 Personal objects and personal identity in the Iron Age: the case of the earliest brooches, in T.F. Martin and R. Weetch (eds) *Dress and Society: contributions from archaeology*. Oxford: Oxbow Books, 48–68.

Albarella, U. 2007 The end of the Sheep Age: people and animals in Late Iron Age, in Haselgrove and Moore 2007, 389–402.

Aldhouse Green, M. 1996 *Celtic Art: reading the messages*. London: Everyman Art Library.

Allen, L. and Webley, L. 2007. Metalwork, in L. Webley, J. Timby and M. Wilson 2007 *Fairfield Park, Stotfold, Bedfordshire: Later Prehistoric Settlement in the Eastern Chilterns*. Bedford: Bedfordshire Archaeology Monograph 7, 94–6.

Almoujahed, M.O., Khatib, R. and Baran, J. 2003. Pregnancy-associated pyogenic sacroiliitis: case report and review, *Infectious Diseases in Obstetrics and Gynecology* 11, 53–7.

Anthoons, G. 2011 Contacts Between the Arras Culture and the Continent. Unpublished PhD thesis, University of Bangor.

Anthoons, G. 2021 *Iron Age Chariot Burials in Britain and the Near Continent*. BAR British Series 666. Oxford: Archaeopress.

Ashmore, P.J. 1999 Radiocarbon dating: avoiding errors by avoiding mixed samples. *Antiquity* 73, 124–30.

ASWYAS 2014 Land at Burnby Lane, Pocklington, East Yorkshire. Geophysical Survey. Unpublished report No. 2630.

Aufderheide, A.C. and Rodríguez-Martín, C. 1998. *The Cambridge Encyclopedia of Human Paleopathology*. Cambridge: Cambridge University Press.

Baray, L. 2016 *Les cimetières celtiques du Bassin parisien (VIIe IIe siècle av. J.C.). Systèmes typologique et chronologique*. Hors-Serie a Gallia. Paris: CNRS Editions.

Barnes, E. 1994. *Developmental Defects of the Axial Skeleton in Paleopathology*. Niwot CO: University Press of Colorado.

Barrett, J.C., Freeman, P.W.M. and Woodward, A. 2000 *Cadbury Castle Somerset. The later prehistoric and early historic archaeology*. English Heritage Archaeological Reports 20. London: English Heritage.

Barrett-Connor, E., Nielson, C., Orwoll, E., Bauer, D. and Cauley, J. 2010. Epidemiology of rib fractures in older men: osteoporotic fractures in men (MrOS) prospective cohort study. *British Medical Journal* 340, 1–8.

Beaumont, J. and Montgomery, J. 2015 Oral histories: a simple method of assigning chronological age to isotopic values from human dentine collagen. *Annals of Human Biology* 42, 407–14.

Beaumont, J., Gledhill, A., Lee-Thorp, J. and Montgomery, J. 2013 Childhood diet: a closer examination of the evidence from dental tissues using stable isotope analysis of incremental human dentine. *Archaeometry* 55, 277–95.

Biel, J. 1985. *Der Keltenfürst von Hochdorf*. Stuttgart: Konrad Theiss.

Bindal, M. and Krabak, B. 2007 Acute bacterial sacroiliitis in an adult: a case report and review of the literature, *Archives of Physical Medicine and Rehabilitation* 88, 1357–9.

Bishop, R.L., Rands, R.L. and Holley, G.R. 1982 Ceramic compositional analysis an archaeological perspective. *Advances in Archaeological Method and Theory* 5, 275–330.

Booth, A.L. 2015 Reassessing the long chronology of the penannular brooch in Britain: exploring changing styles, use and meaning across a millennium. Unpublished PhD thesis, University of Leicester. http://hdl.handle.net/2381/33157.

Boyle, A., Evans, T., O'Connor, S., Spence, A. and Brennand, M. 2007 Site D (Ferry Fryston) in the Iron Age and Romano-British Periods, in Brown *et al.* 2007, 121–60.

Brewster, T.C.M. 1980 *The Excavation of Garton and Wetwang Slacks*. East Riding Archaeological Research Committee Excavation Report 2. London: Royal Commission on Historical Monuments (England).

Brickley, M. and Ives, R. 2008 *The Bioarchaeology of Metabolic Bone Disease*. Amsterdam: Academic Press.

Brickley, M, and Smith, M. 2006 Culturally determined patterns of violence: biological anthropological investigations at a historic urban cemetery. *American Anthropologist* 108(1), 163–77.

Brickley, M.B., Moffat, T. and Watamaniuk, L. 2014 Biocultural perspectives of Vitamin D deficiency in the past, *Journal of Anthropological Archaeology* 36, 48–59.

British Geological Survey 2019a. https://www.bgs.ac.uk/Lexicon/lexicon.cfm?pub=MMG accessed 3 April 2019.

British Geological Survey 2019b https://www.bgs.ac.uk/Lexicon/lexicon.cfm?pub=POCKG accessed 3 April 2019.

Bronk Ramsey, C. 1995 Radiocarbon calibration and analysis of stratigraphy: the OxCal program. *Radiocarbon* 37, 425–30.

Bronk Ramsey, C. 1998 Probability and dating. *Radiocarbon* 40, 461–74.

Bronk Ramsey, C. 2001 Development of the radiocarbon calibration program. *Radiocarbon* 43, 355–63.

Bronk Ramsey, C. 2009 Bayesian analysis of radiocarbon dates. *Radiocarbon* 51, 337–60.

Brown, F., Howard-Davis, C., Brennand, M., Boyle, A., Evans, T., O'Connor, S., Spence, S., Heawood, R. and Lupton, A. (eds) 2007 *The Archaeology of the A1(M) Darrington to Dishforth DBFO road scheme.* Lancaster: Lancaster Imprints 12, Oxford Archaeology North.

Brunaux, J.P. and Rapin, A. 1988 *Gournay II: Boucliers et Lances, Dépôts et Trophées.* Paris: Revue Archéologique de Picardie, Éditions Errance.

Buck, C.E., Cavanagh, W.G. and Litton, C.D. 1996 *Bayesian Approach to Interpreting Archaeological Data.* Chichester: Wiley.

Bulleid, A. and Gray, H. St.G, 1911 *The Glastonbury Lake Village: a full description of the excavations and the relics discovered, 1892–1907.* Glastonbury: Glastonbury Antiquarian Society.

Byard, A. 2019 *50 Finds from Berkshire: objects from the Portable Antiquities Scheme.* Stroud: Amberley.

Caffell, A. and Holst, M. 2011 Osteological analysis, in C. Fenton-Thomas *Where Sky and Yorkshire and Water Meet*, On-Site Archaeology Monograph 2, 323–32. York: On-Site Archaeology.

Caffell, A. and Holst, M. 2013 Human remains, in L. Martin, J. Richardson & I. Roberts (eds), *Iron Age and Roman Settlements at Wattle Syke,* 201–27. Leeds: West Yorkshire Archaeological Society.

Caffel, A. and Holst, M. 2017 Preliminary osteological analysis Burnby Lane, Pocklington, East Riding of Yorkshire. York: York Osteoarchaeology Ltd unpublished report.

Cardwell, P. 2006 Watching Brief at Pocklington School, West Green, Pocklington, 2005. Barnard Castle: Northern Archaeological Associates unpublished Assessment & Evaluation Reports.

Carter, S., Hunter, F., Smith, A., Lancaster, S. *et al.* 2010 A fifth century BC chariot burial from Newbridge, Edinburgh. *Proceedings of the Prehistoric Society* 76, 31–74.

Champion, T. 2019 *A View from the South*, in Halkon (ed.) 2019b, 163–77.

Chisholm, M. 1962 *Rural Settlement and Land Use.* London: Hutchinson.

Chittock, H. 2017 An Iron Age patchwork: new evidence on the biography of the Grimthorpe shield. *Past* 81, 3–4.

Chittock, H. 2021 *Arts and Crafts in Iron Age East Yorkshire. A holistic approach to pattern and purpose, c. 400BC–AD100.* BAR (British Series) 660. Oxford: British Archaeological Reports.

Claypool, G.E., Holser, W.T., Kaplan, I.R., Sakai, H. and Zak, I. 1980 The age curves of sulphur and oxygen isotopes in marine sulphate and their mutual interpretation. *Chemical Geology* 28, 199–260.

Collis, J.R. 1968 Excavations at Owslebury Hants.: An interim report. *Antiquaries Journal* 48, 18–31.

Collis, J. 1973 Burials with weapons in Iron Age Britain. *Germania* 51, 121–33.

Congreve, A.L. 1938 *A Roman and Saxon site at Elmswell, East Yorkshire, 1937.* Hull: Hull Museums Publications 198.

Cook, G.T., Dunbar, E., Black, S.M. and Xu, S. 2006 A preliminary assessment of age at death determination using the nuclear weapons testing ^{14}C activity of dentine and enamel. *Radiocarbon* 48, 305–13.

Cowgill, J. 2001. Appendix IV. Slag, in Parry 2001, 18–19.

Cox, G. and Sealy, J. 1997 Investigating identity and life histories: isotopic analysis and historical documentation of slave skeletons found on the Cape Town foreshore, South Africa. *International Journal of Historical Archaeology* 1, 207–24.

Craig, O.E., Ross, R., Andersen, S.H., Milner, N. and Bailey, G.N. 2006 Focus: sulphur isotope variation in archaeological marine fauna from northern Europe. *Journal of Archaeological Science* 33, 1642–6.

Cranfield University 2019. *The Soils Guide.* Available: www.landis.org.uk. Cranfield University, UK. Accessed 1 May 2019.

Crowfoot, E. 1991. The textiles, in Stead 1991a, 119–25.

Current Archaeology 2018 Uncovering Bilton Water Main's 'Warrior Burial'. *Current Archaeology* 335.

Current Archaeology 2019 New finds from the Pembrokeshire chariot burial. *Current Archaeology* 355.

Dandy, D.J. and Edwards, D.J. 2003 *Essential Orthopaedics and Trauma.* Edinburgh: Churchill Livingstone.

de Buren, N. 1962 Causes and treatment of non-union in fractures of the radius and ulna. *Journal of Bone and Joint Surgery* 44B, 614–25.

DeNiro, M.J. and Epstein, S. 1978 Influence of diet on the distribution of carbon isotopes in animals. *Geochimica et Cosmochimica Acta* 42, 495–506.

DeNiro, M.J. and Epstein, S. 1981 Influence of diet on the distribution of nitrogen isotopes in animals. *Geochimica et Cosmochimica Acta* 45, 341–51.

Dent, J.S. 1982. Cemeteries and settlement patterns of the Iron Age on the Yorkshire Wolds. *Proceedings of the Prehistoric Society* 48, 437–57.

Dent, J.S. 1983 Weapons, Wounds and War in the Iron Age. *Archaeological Journal* 140, 120–8.

Dent, J.S. 1984 Wetwang Slack; an Iron Age Cemetery on the Yorkshire Wolds. Unpublished M.Phil. thesis, University of Sheffield, http://etheses.whiterose.ac.uk/1819/.

Dent, J.S. 1985 Three cart burials from Wetwang, Yorkshire. *Antiquity* 59, 85–92.

Dent, J.S. 1995 Aspects of Iron Age Settlement in Eastern Yorkshire. Unpublished PhD thesis, University of Sheffield.

Dent, J.S. 2010. *The Iron Age in East Yorkshire.* BAR British Series 508. Oxford: Archaeopress.

Dent, J.S. 2019 Excavations in Garton Slack and Wetwang Slack 1963–1989, in Halkon (ed.) 2019b, 33–47.

Dobney, K., Hall, A.R., Kenward, H.K. and Milles, A. 1992 A working classification of sample types for environmental archaeology. *Circaea* 9 (for 1991), 24–6.

Dobney, K. and Ervynck, A. 2007 To fish or not to fish? Evidence for the possible avoidance of fish consumption during the Iron Age around the North Sea, in Haselgrove and Moore 2007, 403–18.

Dunbar, E., Cook, G.T., Naysmith, P., Tripney, B.G. and Xu, S. 2016 AMS ^{14}C dating at the Scottish Universities Environmental Research Centre (SUERC) Radiocarbon Dating Laboratory. *Radiocarbon* 58, 9–23.

Engelhardt, K. 1969 latènezeitliche gräber aus Ossarn, p. B. St. Pölten, NÖ. *Archaeologia Austriaca* 45, 26–52.

Engelhardt, K. 1976 *Bronzezeitliche und latènezeitliche Gräber aus Ossarn.* [Festschrift r. Pittioni]. *Archaologia Austriaca.* Beih. 13. Wien, 362–96.

Felter, M. and Wilkinson, C. 2015 Burnby Lane, Pocklington: Report on the conservation and investigation of small finds. York: York Archaeological Trust unpublished conservation report.

Felter, M. and Wilkinson, C. 2020 The Mile, Pocklington. Report on the conservation and investigation of finds from a chariot burial and a separate burial with shield fittings. York: York Archaeological Trust unpublished conservation report.

Fenton-Thomas, C. 2005 *The Forgotten Landscapes of the Yorkshire Wolds.* Stroud: Tempus.

Fernandes, R. 2015 A simple (R) model to predict the source of dietary carbon in individual consumers. *Archaeometry* 58, 500–12.

Fitzpatrick, A. 2007 Dancing with dragons: fantastic animals in the earlier Celtic art of Iron Age Britain, in Haselgrove and Moore 2007, 339–57.

Flouest, J.L. and Stead I.M. 1974 Des tombes de La Tene II and III a Menil-Annelles et Ville-sur-Retourne (Ardennes). *Bulletin de la societe nationale archeologique chamenois* 67, 59–67.

Fontijn, D. 2019 *Economies of Destruction.* London: Routledge.

Foulds, E.M. 2014 Glass Beads in Iron Age Britain: a Social Approach. DPhil. thesis, University of Durham, ethese.dur.ac.uk/10523.

Foulds, E.M. 2017 *Dress and Identity in the Iron Age. A Study of Glass Beads and Other Items of Personal Adornment.* Oxford: Archaeopress.

Fowler, E. 1960 The origin and development of the penannular brooch in Europe. *Proceedings of the Prehistoric Society* 26, 149–77.

Fox, C. 1958 *Pattern and Purpose. A Survey of Early Celtic Art in Britain.* Cardiff: The National Museum of Wales.

Fraser, J. 2007 An Archaeological Evaluation on land at Cemetery Lane, Pocklington. Hull: Humber Field Archaeology unpublished report.

French, D.H. 1971 An experiment in water sieving. *Anatolian Studies* 21, 59–64.

Gaffney, C. 1995 Pocklington, Humberside: geophysical survey. Bradford: Geophysical Surveys of Bradford Report 95/43.

Gao, F., Kong, X-H., Tong, X-Y., Xie, D-H., Li, Y-G., Guo, J-J. and Tang, T-S. 2011. Tuberculous sacroiliitis: a study of the diagnosis, therapy and medium-term results of 15 cases. *Journal of International Medical Research* 39, 321–35.

Garrow, D., Gosden, C. and Hill, J.D. (eds) 2008 *Rethinking Celtic Art.* Oxford: Oxbow Books.

Garrow. D., Gosden, C., Hill, J.D. and Ramsey, C.B. 2010 Dating Celtic Art. A major radiocarbon dating programme of Iron Age and early Roman metalwork in Britain. *Archaeological Journal* 166 (1), 79–123.

Garrow, D. and Gosden, C. 2012 *Technologies of Enchantment. Exploring Celtic Art: 400 BC to AD100.* Oxford: Oxford University Press.

Gilbank, P. 2011 *'Bitesize' Project Archive 1514 – Pocklington School's Really Ancient History.* https://extranet.pocklingtonschool.com/WSDocs/Shared%20Documents/Pocklington%20500/Bitesize/BitesizeIssue4.pdf. Accessed 2 May 2019.

Giles, M. 2008 'Seeing red': the aesthetics of martial objects in the Iron Age of East Yorkshire, in Garrow *et al.* 2008, 59–77.

Giles, M. 2012 *A Forged Glamour: landscape, identity and material culture in the Iron Age.* Oxford: Windgather Press.

Giles, M. 2015 Performing pain, performing beauty: dealing with difficult death in Iron Age burials. *Cambridge Archaeological Journal* 25 (3), 539–50.

Giles, M., Green, V. and Peixoto, P. 2019 Wide connections: women, mobility and power in Iron Age East Yorkshire, in Halkon (ed.) 2019b, 47–66.

Ginoux, N.C. and Ramsl, P. 2014 Art and Craftsmanship in Elite-Warrior Graves: 'From BOII to Parisii and Back Again …' in C. Gosden, S. Crawford and K. Ulmschneider (eds) *Celtic Art in Europe: Making Connections,* Oxford: Oxbow Books, 274–85.

Greene, E.D. 1972 The chariot as described in Irish literature, in C. Thomas (ed.) *The Iron Age in the Irish Sea Province.* CBA Research Report 9. London: Council for British Archaeology, 959–67.

Greenwell, W. 1877 *British Barrows. A Record of the Examination of Sepulchral Mounds in Various Parts of England.* Oxford: Clarendon Press.

Greenwell, W. 1906 Early Iron Age Burials in Yorkshire. *Archaeologia* 60, 251–324.

Gresham, C.A. 1939 Spetisbury Rings, Dorset. *Archaeological Journal* 96, 114–31.

Halkon, P. 2008 *Archaeology and environment in a changing East Yorkshire landscape: the Foulness Valley c. 800 BC to c. AD 400.* BAR British Series 472. Oxford: Archaeopress.

Halkon, P. 2009 'Ceremony and carpentry?' Neolithic stone axeheads in an East Yorkshire (UK) lowland landscape. *Internet Archaeology* 26. https://doi.org/10.11141/ia.26.18

Halkon, P. 2011 Iron, landscape and power in Iron Age East Yorkshire. *Archaeological Journal* 168, 133–65.

Halkon, P. 2012 Iron landscape and power in Iron Age East Yorkshire. *Archaeological Journal* 168, 134–65.

Halkon, P. 2013 *The Parisi – Britons and Romans in Eastern Yorkshire.* Stroud: History Press.

Halkon, P. 2019a Recent research on the Arras Culture in its landscape setting, in D.C. Cowley, M. Fernández-Götz, T. Romankiewicz and H. Wendling (eds) *Relating Buildings, Landscape, and People in the European Iron Age.* Leiden: Sidestone, 57–69.

Halkon, P. (ed.) 2019b *The Arras Culture of Eastern Yorkshire. Celebrating the Iron Age.* Oxford: Oxbow Books.

Halkon, P. and Lyall, J. 2016 *The Archaeology of Nunburnholme Wold: An Interim Report 2016.* Hull: Nunburnholme Community Heritage project and University of Hull. http://www.nunburnholmewithkilnwickpercypc.co.uk/nunburnholmeexcavation2016.pdf

Halkon, P. and Millett, M. 1999 *Rural Settlement and Industry: studies in the Iron Age and Roman archaeology of lowland East Yorkshire.* Yorkshire Archaeological Report 4. Leeds: Yorkshire Archaeological Society.

Halkon, P., Lillie., M. and Lyall, J. 2014 *The Archaeology of Nunburnholme Wold: An Interim Report 2015.* Hull: Nunburnholme Community Heritage project and University of Hull. http://www.nunburnholmewithkilnwickpercypc.co.uk/nun2014interimwithcover.pdf

Halkon, P., Lillie., M. and Lyall, J. 2015 *The Archaeology of Nunburnholme Wold: An Interim Report 2015.* Hull: Nunburnholme Community Heritage project and University of Hull. http://www.nunburnholmewithkilnwickpercypc.co.uk/nunburnholmeexcavation2015.pdf

Halkon, P., Millett, M. and Woodhouse, H. 2015 *Hayton, East Yorkshire: Archaeological Studies of the Iron Age and Roman landscapes.* Yorkshire Archaeological Report 7. Leeds: Roman Antiquities Section, Yorkshire Archaeological Society.

Halkon, P., Manby, T.G., Millett, M. and Woodhouse, H. 2010 Neolithic settlement evidence from Hayton, East Yorks. *Yorkshire Archaeological Journal* 82, 31–57.

Halkon, P., Lyall, J., Deverell, J., Hunt, T. and Fernandez Gotz, M. 2019. Arras 200: revisiting Britain's most famous Iron Age cemetery. *Antiquity* Gallery 93, e11.

Halkon, P., Innes, J., Long, A., Shennan, I., Manby, T. Gaunt, G., Heath, A., Wagner, P., Schofield, J., Schreve D. and Roe, D. 2009 Change and continuity within the prehistoric landscape of the Foulness Valley, East Yorkshire. *East Riding Archaeologist* 12, 1–66.

Halstead, P. 1985 A study of mandibular teeth from Romano-British contexts at Maxey, in F. Pryor, C. French, D. Crowther, D. Gurney, G. Simpson and M. Taylor *Archaeology and Environment in the Lower Welland Valley Volume 1.* East Anglian Archaeology 27. Cambridge: East Anglian Archaeology, 219–24.

Hamilton, W.D. and Kenney, J. 2015 Multiple Bayesian modelling approaches to a suite of radiocarbon dates from ovens excavated at Ysgol yr Hendre, Caernarfon, North Wales. *Quaternary Geochronology* 25, 72–82.

Hamilton, W.D., Sayle, K.L., Boyd, M.O.E., Haselgrove, C.C. and Cook, G.T. 2019 'Celtic cowboys' reborn: Application of multi-isotopic analysis (δ^{13}C, δ^{15}N, and δ^{34}S) to examine mobility and movement of animals within an Iron Age British society. *Journal of Archaeological Science* 101, 189–98.

Harding, D.W. 2007 *The Archaeology of Celtic Art.* London: Routledge.

Harding, D. 2015 *The Iron Age in Lowland Britain.* London and New York: Routledge.

Harding, J. 2013 *Cult, Religion, and Pilgrimage: Archaeological Investigations at the Neolithic and Bronze Age Monument Complex of Thornborough, North Yorkshire.* CBA Research Report 174. York: Council for British Archaeology.

Harris, E., Sinha, B., Hoppe, P., Crowley, J.N., Ono, S. and Foley, S. 2012 Sulfur isotope fractionation during oxidation of sulfur dioxide: gas-phase oxidation by OH radicals and aqueous oxidation by H_2O_2, O_3 and iron catalysis. *Atmospheric Chemistry and Physics* 12, 407–24.

Haselgrove, C. and Moore, T. (eds) *The Later Iron Age in Britain and Beyond.* Oxford: Oxbow Books.

Haselgrove, C., Armit, I., Champion, T., Creighton, J., Gwilt, A., Hill, J.D., Hunter, F. and Woodward, A. 2001 *Understanding the British Iron Age: An Agenda for Action.* Salisbury: Trust for Wessex Archaeology.

Hattatt, R. 1982 *Ancient and Romano-British Brooches.* Sherborne: Dorset Publishing.

Hawkes, C.F.C. 1946 An unpublished Celtic brooch from Danes' Graves, Kilham, Yorkshire. *Antiquaries Journal* 26 (3–4), 187–91.

Hawkes, C. 1959 The ABC of the British Iron Age. *Antiquity* 33, 170–82.

Hedges, R.E.M., Clement, J.G., Thomas, C.D.L. and O'Connell, T.C. 2007 Collagen turnover in the adult femoral mid-shaft: modeled from anthropogenic radiocarbon tracer measurements. *American Journal of Physical Anthropology* 133, 808–16.

Henderson, J. 1991 The chemical analysis of the glass beads from Burton Fleming and Rudston, in Stead 1991a, 167–9.

Higgs, E.S. and Vita-Finzi, C. 1972 Prehistoric economies: a territorial approach, in E.S. Higgs (ed.) *Papers in Economic Prehistory.* London: Cambridge University Press, 27–36.

Hill, J.D. 1995 *Ritual and Rubbish in the Iron Age of Wessex: a Study on the Formation of a Specific Archaeological Record.* BAR British Series 242. Oxford: Archaeopress.

Hill, J.D. 2002 Wetwang Chariot Burial. *Current Archaeology* 178, 410–12.

Hinderwell, T. 1811 *The History and Antiquities of Scarborough and the vicinity* (2nd edn). Scarborough: William Blanchard.

Hitchcock, M. 2018 Reframing the Iron Age Shield. *Later Prehistoric Finds Group Newsletter* 12.

Hull, M.R. and Hawkes, C.F.C. 1987 *Corpus of Ancient Brooches in Britain: pre-Roman bow brooches.* BAR British Series 168. Oxford: Archaeopress.

Inall, Y. 2015 In search of the spear people: spearheads in context in Iron Age eastern Yorkshire and beyond. Unpublished PhD thesis, University of Hull.

Inall, Y. 2019 New Light on Iron Age Warfare in Britain, in Halkon (ed.) 2019b, 67–84.

Jacobsthal, P. 1944 *Early Celtic Art.* Oxford: Clarendon Press.

Jaques, D. 2015 The animal bones, in Halkon *et al.* 2015, 412–49.

Jay, M. and Roberts, M. 2006 Diet in the Iron Age Cemetery Population at Wetwang Slack, East Yorkshire, United Kingdom. Stable Isotope Evidence. *Journal of Archaeological Science* 33, 653–62.

Jay, M., Haselgrove, C., Hamilton, D., Hill, J.D. and Dent, J.S. 2012 Chariots and Context: new radiocarbon dates from Wetwang and the chronology of Iron Age burials and brooches in East Yorkshire. *Oxford Journal of Archaeology* 31(2), 161–89.

Jay, M., Montgomery, J., Nehlich, O., Towers, J. and Evans, J. 2013 British Iron Age chariot burials of the Arras culture: a multi-isotope approach to investigating mobility levels and subsistence practices. *World Archaeology* 45, 473–91.

Jope, J. 2000 *Early Celtic Art in the British Isles.* Oxford: Clarendon Press.

Joy, J. 2010 *Iron Age Mirrors: a biographical approach.* BAR British Series 518. Oxford: Archaeopress.

Jurmain, R. 1999. *Stories from the Skeleton.* London and New York: Routledge.

Kaenel, G. and Müller, F. 1991 The Swiss Plateau, in V. Kruta, O.H. Frey, B. Raftery and M. Szabó (eds), *The Celts.* London: Thames and Hudson, 251–9.

King, S. 2010 What makes War? Assessing Iron Age warfare through mortuary behaviour and osteological patterns of violence. Unpublished PhD thesis, University of Bradford.

King, S.J. and Bradley, R.I. 1987 *Soils of the Market Weighton District.* Sheet No. 106. Harpenden: Soil Survey of England and Wales.

Kipling, R. and Beamish, M. 2018 An Archaeological Excavation on land south of Soar Valley Way, Enderby, Leicestershire. Leicester: University of Leicester Archaeological Services Report 2018–108.

Kirk, J.L. 1911 The opening of a tumulus near Pickering. *York Philosophical Society* 1911, 62.

Kragten, J. 1994 Tutorial review. Calculating standard deviations and confidence intervals with a universally applicable spreadsheet technique. *The Analyst* 119, 2161–5.

Krouse, H.R. 1977 Sulphur isotope abundance elucidate uptake of atmospheric sulphur emission by vegetation. *Nature* 65, 45–6.

Lamb, A.L., Evans, J.E., Buckley, R. and Appleby, J. 2014 Multi-isotope analysis demonstrates significant lifestyle changes in King Richard III. *Journal of Archaeological Science* 50, 559–65.

Lamb, A.L., Melikian, M., Ives, R. and Evans, J. 2012 Multi-isotope analysis of the population of the lost medieval village of Auldhame, East Lothian, Scotland. *Journal of Analytical Atomic Spectrometry* 27, 765–77.

Legge, A.J. 1991 The animal bones, in Stead 1991a, 140–7.

Leicester University 2019 https://le.ac.uk/news/2019/may/23-enderby-iron-age-bark-shield.

Lewin, J. 1969 *The Yorkshire Wolds: A Study in Geomorphology.* Occasional Paper 11. Hull: University of Hull.

Lewis, A.S.G. 2015 Iron Age and Roman-era vehicle terrets from Western and Central Britain: An interpretive study. Unpublished PhD thesis, University of Leicester.

Lewis, A. 2019 Perpetual motion: a reading of the artistic and cultural significance of Iron Age terrets, in Halkon (ed.) 2019b, 111–21.

Lewis, M.E. 2000 Non-adult palaeopathology: current status and future potential, in M. Cox and S. Mays (eds) *Human Osteology in Archaeology and Forensic Science.* Cambridge: Cambridge University Press, 39–57.

Lewis, M.E. 2004 Endocranial lesions in non-adult skeletons: understanding their aetiology. *International Journal of Osteoarchaeology* 14, 82–97.

Lewis, M.E. 2007 *The Bioarchaeology of Children: Perspectives from Biological and Forensic Anthropology.* Cambridge: Cambridge University Press.

Lienhardt, R.G. 1961 *Divinity and Experience: the religion of the Dinka.* Oxford: Oxford University Press.

Lovell, N. C. 1997 Trauma analysis in paleopathology. *Yearbook of Physical Anthropology* 40, 139–70.

Macdonald, P. 2007 *Llyn Cerrig Bach: A Study of Copper Alloy Artefacts from the Insular La Tène Assemblage.* Cardiff: University of Wales Press.

McIntosh, F. 2010 DUR-8DF7F1: A Bronze Age Axe, https://finds.org.uk/database/artefacts/record/id/418905. Accessed: 24 April 2019.

MacKay, W.A. 1979 A discoidal knife from Kepwick and Neolithic finds from Pocklington. *Yorkshire Archaeological Journal* 51, 137–9.

Mackreth, D.F. 2011 *Brooches in late Iron Age and Roman Britain.* Oxford: Oxbow Books.

Makey, P. 2008 The flint assemblage, in J. Tabor, Pocklington Wastewater Treatment Works, East Riding of Yorkshire. Barnards Castle: Northern Archaeological Associates report 08/01.

Manby, T.G. 2021 The earlier prehistoric archaeology of the Vale of York, in A. Kershaw, P. Horne, D. MacLeod, and M. Oakey (eds) *'A perfect flat ...' Understanding the archaeology of the Vale of York.* Swindon: Historic England Research Report 272/2020 (online), 31–89.

Manby, T.G., King, A. and Vyner, B.E. 2003 The Neolithic and Bronze Ages: A time of early agriculture, in T.G. Manby, S. Moorhouse and P. Ottaway (eds) *The Archaeology of Yorkshire. An Assessment at the Beginning of the 21st century.* Yorkshire Archaeological Society Occasional Paper 3. Leeds: Yorkshire Archaeological Society, 35–116.

MAP 2013 West Hale Farm, Grindale Road, Burton Fleming, Driffield, East Yorkshire. TA 09495 71928. Archaeological Strip and Record. Unpublished assessment report MAP

10.21.2013. Report lodged at the Humber Historic Environment Record, Hull, also see this volume.

MAP 2014 Land at Burnby Lane, Pocklington, East Yorkshire: Archaeological Evaluation by Trial Trenching. Unpublished report. Report lodged at the Humber Historic Environment Record, Hull.

MAP 2015 Land at Burnby Lane, Pocklington, East Riding of Yorkshire. Archaeological Evaluation by Trial Trenching. Unpublished report. Report lodged at the Humber Historic Environment Record, Hull.

Marion S. 2004 *Recherches sur l'âge du Fer en Île-de-France. Entre Hallstatt final et La Tène finale. Analyse des sites fouillés. Chronologie et société*, BAR International Series 1231. Oxford: Archaeopress.

Marion, S., Bechennec, Y. and Le Forestier, C. 2008 Nécropole et bourgade d'artisans: l'évolution des sites de Bobigny (Seine-Saint-Denis), entre La Tène B et La Tène D. *Revue archéologique du Centre de la France* 45–6, 1–50. http://journals.openedition.org/racf/654

Matos, V. and Santos, A. L. 2006 On the trail of pulmonary tuberculosis based on rib lesions: results from the human identified skeletal collection from the Museu Bocage (Lisbon, Portugal). *American Journal of Physical Anthropology* 130, 190–200.

Mays, S. 1998 *The Archaeology of Human Bones.* London: Routledge.

Mays, S. A., Fysh, E. and Taylor, G. M. 2002 Investigation of the link between visceral surface rib lesions and tuberculosis in a medieval skeletal series from England using ancient DNA. *American Journal of Physical Anthropology* 119, 27–36.

Megaw, J.V.S. and Megaw, M.R. 1990 'Semper aliquid novum...' – Celtic dragon pairs re-reviewed. *Acta Archaeologica Hungaricae* 42, 55–72.

Megaw, J., Megaw, M. and Neugebauer, J. 1989 Zegnisse frühlatènezeitli- chen kunsthandwerks aus dem raum herzogenburg, Niederösterreich. *Germania* 67, 477–517.

Megaw, M.R. and Megaw, J.V.S. 1989 *Celtic Art from its Beginnings to the Book of Kells.* London: Thames & Hudson.

Moore, P. 2018 Pocklington Flood Alleviation Scheme (POCFAS), East Yorkshire. Archaeological trip, Map and Record Excavation. ASWAYAS Report no. 3201 (unpublished).

Moorhouse, S. 1973 Yorkshire archaeological finds register. *Yorkshire Archaeological Journal* 45, 200.

Moorhouse, S. 1978 Yorkshire archaeological finds register. *Yorkshire Archaeological Journal* 50, 9–10.

Morris, J. 2008 Associated bone groups; one archaeologist's rubbish is another's ritual deposition, in O. Davis, N. Sharples and K. Waddington *Changing Perspectives on the First Millennium BC.* Oxford: Oxbow Books, 83–98.

Mortimer, J.R. 1905a *Forty Years' Researches in British and Saxon Burial Mounds of East Yorkshire.* London: A. Brown & Sons.

Mortimer, J.R. 1905b Notes on the British remains found near Cawthorn Camps. *The Naturalist* 1905, 264–5.

Müldner, G., 2013. Stable isotopes and diet: their contribution to Romano-British research. *Antiquity* 87, 137–49.

Nadelhoffer, K.J. and Fry, B. 1994 Nitrogen isotopic studies in forest ecosystems, in K. Lajtha and R.H. Michener (eds) *Stable Isotopes in Ecology and Environmental Science.* Oxford: Blackwell, 22–4.

Natural England. 2020. *Provisional Agricultural Land Classification* (ALC). https://data.gov.uk/dataset/952421ec-da63-4569-817d-4d6399df40a1/provisional-agricultural-land-classification-alc. Downloaded 12/01/2021.

Nehlich, O., Boric, D., Stefanovich, S. and Richards, M.P. 2010 Sulphur isotope evidence for freshwater fish consumption: a case study from the Danube Gorges, SE Europe. *Journal of Archaeological Science* 37, 1131–9.

Nehlich, O., Fuller, B.T., Jay, M., Mora, A., Nicholson, R., Smith, C.I. and Richards M.P. 2011 Application of sulphur isotope ratios to examine weaning patterns and freshwater fish consumption in Roman Oxfordshire, UK. *Geochimica et Cosmochimica Acta* 75, 4963–77.

Neugebauer, J.-W. 1988 Neuere Forschungsergebnisse auf dem gebiet der hallstattkultur in Nordniederösterreich. *Archäologie Alpen Adria* 1, 85–108.

Neugebauer, J.-W. 1992 *Die Kelten im Osten Österreichs*. Wissenschaftliche Schrif- tenreihe Niederösterreich. St Pölten–Wien: Verlag Niederosterreichisches Presseshaus, 92–4.

Neugebauer, J.-W. 1997 rettungsgrabungen im Unteren Traisental in den jahren 1996 und 1997. *Fundberichte aus Österreich* 36, 451–632.

Neugebauer, J.-W. 1999 rettungsgrabungen im Unteren Traisental in den jahren 1998 und 1999. *Fundberichte aus Österreich* 38, 483–592.

Neugebauer, J-W. and Gattringer, A. 1982 die kremser Schnellstraße S 33. Zweiter vorbericht über die ergebnisse der archäologischen überwachung des groß- bauvorhabens durch die Abt. f. Bodendenkmale des Bundesdenkmalamtes im jahre 1982. *Fundberichte aus Österreich* 21, 66–7.

Neugebauer, J.-W. and Gattringer, A. 1984 rettungsgrabungen im Unteren Traisental im jahr 1984. vierter vorbericht über Aktivitäten der Abt. f. Bodendenkmale des Bundesdenkmalamtes nach der verkehrsfreigabe der kremser Schnellstraße S 33. *Fundberichte aus Österreich* 23, 97–142.

Neugebauer, J-W., Ramsl, A. 1998 die frühlatènezeitliche, birituelle Nekropole von Pottenbrunn, landeshauptstadt St. Pölten. Niederösterreiche. *Schriften des Bernischen Historischen Museums* 2, 255–64.

Newman, S. and Holst, M. 2016 Osteological Analysis, Melton Low Street Sherburn-in-Elmet. York: York Osteoarchaeology Ltd unpublished report

Norbeck, E.N. 1971 *Anthropology Today. An Introduction: Rites of Reversal.* Del Mar CA: CRM Books.

Novak, S. A. 2000 Battle-related trauma, in V. Fiorato, A. Boylston and C. Knüsel (eds) *Blood Red Roses: the archaeology of a mass grave from the Battle of Towton AD 1461.* Oxford: Oxbow Books, 90–102.

On-Site Archaeology 2009 Report on an Archaeological Evaluation at Broadhelm Park, Pocklington. York. On-Site Archaeology unpublished report.

On-Site Archaeology 2015a Phase 4, Land at The Balk, Pocklington, East Riding of Yorkshire. York: On-Site Archaeology OSA Report No. OSA15EV26.

On-Site Archaeology 2105b Land at Burnby Lane, Pocklington, East Yorkshire. Report on a Geophysical Survey. York: On-Site Archaeology npublished report.

Ortner, D.J. 2003 *Identification of Pathological Conditions in Human Skeletal Remains*. Amsterdam: Academic Press.

OxCal v4.2 (http:c14.arch.ox.ac.UK/)

Parfitt, K. 1995 *Iron Age Burials from Mill Hill, Deal.* London: British Museum Press.

Parker Pearson, M. 1999a Food, sex and death: cosmologies in the British Iron Age with particular reference to East Yorkshire. *Cambridge Archaeological Journal* 9 (1), 43–69.

Parker Pearson, M. 1999b *The Archaeology of Death and Burial.* Stroud: History Press.

Parry, J. 2001 Balk Field, Pocklington, East Yorkshire, Archaeological Watching Brief. Barnards Castle: Northern Archaeological Associates report 01/21.

Patterson, N., Isakov, M., Booth, T., Büster, L. *et al.* 2022. Large-scale migration into southern Britain at the end of the Bronze Age, *Nature* 601, 588–594. https://doi.org/10.1038/s41586-021-04287-4.

Payne, S. 1973 Kill-off patterns in sheep and goats: the mandibles from Asvan Kale. *Anatolian Studies* 23, 281–3.

Peterson, B.J. and Fry, B. 1987 Stable isotopes in ecosystem studies. *Annual Review in Ecology and Systematics* 18, 293–320.

Peterson, B.J. and Howarth, R.W. 1987 Sulfur, carbon, and nitrogen isotopes used to trace organic matter flow in the salt-marsh estuaries of Sapelo Island, Georgia. *Limnology and Oceanography* 32, 1195–213.

Plutarch 1961 *Moralia.,* trans. F.C. Babbit. London: Heinemann.

Ponce, P. and Holst, M. 2020 Osteological Analysis, Melton Business Park. York: York Osteoarchaeology Ltd unpublished report.

Preinfalk, F. 2005 grabhügeln am Ufer der Perschling. *Fundberichte aus Österreich* 2, 90–7.

Privat, K.L., O'Connell, T.C. and Hedges, R.E.M. 2007 The distinction between freshwater- and terrestrial-based diets: methodological concerns and archaeological applications of sulphur stable isotope analysis. *Journal of Archaeological Science* 34, 1197–204.

Procter, W. 1855 Report of the proceedings of the Yorkshire Antiquarian Club in the excavations of barrows from the year 1849. *Proceedings of the Yorkshire Philosophical Society* 1, 175–89.

Radley, J. 1967 New Bronze Age spear-heads from Yorkshire and a provisional list of Yorkshire spear-heads. *Yorkshire Archaeological Journal* 42, 15–19.

Radley, J. 1974 The prehistory of the Vale of York. *Yorkshire Archaeological Journal* 46, 10–22.

Raftery, B. 1983 *A Catalogue of Irish iron Age Antiquities.* Veröffentlichung des Vorgeschichtlichen Seminars Marburg, Sonderband 2. Marburg: Wasmuth KG.

Raftery, B. 1994 *Pagan Celtic Ireland: the enigma of the Irish Iron Age.* London: Thames & Hudson.

Ramsl, P. 2018 *Ein Beitrag zur Frage des Übergangs von der Hallstatt- zur Frühlatène- zeit in Nordostösterreich.* Annalen Naturhistorisches Museum Wien, Serie A. Wien, 493–502.

Ramsl, P. 2020 *Diversity of Male Identities in Early and Middle La Tene Period Cemeteries in Central Europe.* Archaeologica Slovaca Monographiae 32. Nitra: Archeologický ústav SAV.

Rees, C.E., Jenkins, W.J. and Monster, J. 1978 The sulphur isotopic composition of ocean water sulphate. *Geochimica et Cosmochimica Acta* 42, 377–81.

Reimer, P.J., Austin, W.E.N., Bard, E., Bayliss, A. *et al.* 2020 The IntCal20 Northern Hemisphere Radiocarbon Age Calibration Curve (0–55 cal kBP). *Radiocarbon* 62, 725–57.

Resnick, D. 2002. *Diagnosis of Bone and Joint Disorders.* Philadelphia PA: Saunders.

Reynolds, A. 2009 *Anglo-Saxon Deviant Burial Customs.* Oxford: Oxford University Press.

Richards, M.P., Fuller, B.T. and Hedges, R.E.M. 2001 Sulphur isotopic variation in ancient bone collagen from Europe:

implications for human palaeodiet, residence mobility, and modern pollutant studies. *Earth and Planetary Science Letters* 191, 185–90.

Richardson, J. 2013 Animal remains, in L. Martin, J. Richardson and I. Roberts *Iron Age and Roman Settlements at Wattle Syke*. Yorkshire Archaeology 11. Wakefield: West Yorkshire Archaeological Society, 228–51.

Richardson, J. 2019 Animal Bone assessment, in M.R. Stephens, 2019 Melton West Business Park, Wyke Lane, Melton, East Riding of Yorkshire. Archaeological Excavations 2017–19. Unpublished MAP report at Humber Historic Environment Record, Hull.

Rigby, V. 1991 The pottery, in Stead 1991a, 94–118.

Rigby, V. 2004 Pots in Pits. The British Museum Yorkshire Settlements Project. *East Riding Archaeologist* 11, 1–216.

Roberts, C.A. and Cox, M. 2003. *Health and Disease in Britain*. Stroud: Sutton.

Roberts, C.A. and Manchester, K. 2005. *The Archaeology of Disease* (3rd edn). Stroud: History Press.

Rogers, J. 2000 The palaeopathology of joint disease, in M. Cox and S. Mays (eds) *Human Osteology in Archaeology and Forensic Science*. Cambridge: Cambridge University Press, 163–82.

Rozoy, J.-G. 1987 *Les Celtes en Champagne: Les Ardennes au second Age du Fer: le Mont Troté, les Rouliers*. Memoires de la societe d'agriculture, commerce, science et artes du department de la Marne 4. Carleville-Meziers: Memoires de la Societe Archaeologique.

Salter, R. B. 1999. *Textbook of Disorders and Injuries of the Musculoskeletal System*. London: Lippincott Williams and Wilson.

Santos, A.L. and Roberts, C.A. 2001 A picture of tuberculosis in young Portuguese people in the early 20th century: a multidisciplinary study of the skeletal and historical evidence. *American Journal of Physical Anthropology* 115, 38–49.

Santos, A.L. and Roberts, C.A. 2006 Anatomy of a serial killer: differential diagnosis of tuberculosis based on rib lesions of adult individuals from the Coimbra Identified Skeletal Collection, Portugal. *American Journal of Physical Anthropology* 130, 38–49.

Sauer, N. J. 1998 The timing of injuries and manner of death: distinguishing among antemortem, perimortem and postmortem trauma, in K. Reichs (ed) *Forensic Osteology: Advances in the identification of human remains*. Springfield IL: Charles C Thomas, 321–32.

Sayle, K.L., Brodie, C.R., Cook, G.T. and Hamilton, W.D. 2019 Sequential measurement of $\delta^{15}N$, $\delta^{13}C$ and $\delta^{34}S$ values in archaeological bone collagen at the Scottish Universities Environmental Research Centre (SUERC): A new analytical frontier. *Rapid Communications in Mass Spectrometry* 33, 1258–66.

Sayle, K.L., Cook, G.T., Ascough, P.L., Gestsdóttir, H., Hamilton, W.D. and McGovern, T.H. 2014 Utilization of $\delta^{13}C$, $\delta^{15}N$, and $\delta^{34}S$ analyses to understand 14C dating anomalies within a Late Viking Age community in Northeast Iceland. *Radiocarbon* 56, 811–21.

Sayle, K.L., Cook, G.T., Ascough, P.L. Hastie, H.R., Einarsson, Á., McGovern, T.H., Hicks, M.T., Edwald, Á. and Friðriksson, A. 2013 Application of $\delta^{34}S$ analysis for elucidating terrestrial, marine and freshwater ecosystems: Evidence of animal movement/husbandry practices in an early Viking community around Lake Mývatn, Iceland. *Geochimica et Cosmochimica Acta* 120, 531–44.

Sayle, K.L., Hamilton, W.D., Cook, G.T., Ascough, P.L. Gestsdóttir, H., and McGovern, T.H. 2016a Deciphering diet and monitoring movement: multiple stable isotope analysis of the Viking Age settlement at Hofstaðir, Lake Mývatn, Iceland. *American Journal of Physical Anthropology* 160, 126–36.

Sayle, K.L., Hamilton, W.D., Gestsdóttir, H. and Cook, G.T. 2016b Modelling Lake Mývatn's freshwater reservoir effect: Utilisation of the statistical program FRUITS to assist in the re-interpretation of radiocarbon dates from a cemetery at Hofstaðir, north-east Iceland. *Quaternary Geochronology* 36, 1–11.

Schmidt, P.K. and Burgess, C. 1981 *The Axes of Scotland and Northern England*. Prahistorische Bronzefunde 9 (7). Munich: C.H. Beck.

Schoeninger, M.J. and DeNiro, M.J. 1984 Nitrogen and carbon isotopic composition of bone collagen from marine and terrestrial animals. *Geochimica et Cosmochimica Acta* 48, 625–39.

Schoeninger, M.J., DeNiro, M.J. and Tauber, H. 1983 Stable nitrogen isotope ratios of bone collagen reflect marine and terrestrial components of prehistoric human diet. *Science* 220, 1381–3.

Schweingruber, F.W. 1982 *Microscopic Wood Identification*. (2nd edn) Zurich: Verlag Kessel.

Schweingruber, F.H. 1990 *Anatomy of European Woods*. Berne and Stuttgart: Paul Haupt.

Scott, E.M. 2003 The Third International Radiocarbon Inter-comparison (TIRI) and the Fourth International Radiocarbon Intercomparison (FIRI) 1990–2002: results, analysis, and conclusions. *Radiocarbon* 45, 135–408.

Scott, E.M., Cook, G.T. and Naysmith, P. 2010 A report on phase 2 of the Fifth International Radiocarbon Intercomparison (VIRI). *Radiocarbon* 52, 846–58.

Sealy, J. 2001 Body tissue chemistry and palaeodiet, in D.R. Brothwell and A.M. Pollard (eds) *Handbook of Archaeological Sciences*. London: Wiley, 269–79.

Sealey, P.R. 2007 *A Late Iron Age Warrior from Kelvedon, Essex*. Chelmsford: East Anglian Archaeology 118.

Sefton, A. 2019 Exhibit: POC02. Pop-up Museum Catalogue Pocklington Beanfeast event.

Sharples, N.M. 1991 *Maiden Castle: excavations and field survey 1985–86*. English Heritage Archaeological Report 19. London: English Heritage.

Sheppard, T. 1907 Note on a British chariot burial at Hunmanby in East Yorkshire. *Yorkshire Archaeological Journal* 19, 482–8.

Sheppard, T. 1939 Excavations at Eastburn, East Yorkshire, *Yorkshire Archaeological Journal* 34, 35–47.

Silver, I.A. 1969 The ageing of domestic animals, in D. Brothwell and E. Higgs (eds) *Science in Archaeology*. London: Thames and Hudson, 283–302.

Skyrme, A.D., Selmon, G.P.F. and Apthorp, L. 2005. *Common Spinal Disorders Explained*. London and Chicago IL: Remedica.

Smith, P. 1937 *The Place-names of the East Riding of Yorkshire and York*. Oxford: English Place-name Society.

Smith, B.N. and Epstein, S. 1971 Two categories of $^{13}C/^{12}C$ for higher plants. *Plant Physiology* 47, 97–118.

Stace, C. 1997 *New Flora of the British Isles*. (2nd edn). Cambridge: Cambridge University Press.

Stacey, R. 2004. Evidence for the use of birch-bark tar from Iron Age Britain. *Past* 47, 1–2.

Stead, I.M. 1959 A chariot burial on Pexton Moor, North Riding. *Antiquity* 33, 214–16.

Stead, I. 1961 A distinctive form of La Tene Barrow in Eastern Yorkshire and on the Continent. *Antiquity* 41 (1–2), 44–62.

Stead, I.M. 1965 *The La Tene Cultures of Eastern Yorkshire*. York: Yorkshire Philosophical Society.

Stead, I. 1968. An Iron Age hillfort at Grimthorpe, East Yorkshire, England. *Proceedings of the Prehistoric Society* 34, 148–90.

Stead, I.M. 1976 La Tène Burials between Burton Fleming and Rudston, North Humberside. *Antiquaries Journal* 56 (2), 217–26.

Stead, I.M. 1979 *The Arras Culture*. York: Yorkshire Philosophical Society.

Stead, I.M. 1986 A group of Iron Age barrows at Cowlam, North Humberside. *Yorkshire Archaeological Journal* 58, 5–15.

Stead, I.M. 1991a *Iron Age Cemeteries in East Yorkshire: excavations at Burton Fleming, Rudston, Garton-on-the-Wolds and Kirkburn*. London: English Heritage and British Museum Press.

Stead, I.M. 1991b Many more Iron Age shields from Britain. *Antiquaries Journal* 71, 1–35.

Stead, I.M. 1995 The metalwork, in K. Parfitt (ed.) *Iron Age Burials from Mill Hill, Deal*. London: British Museum Press, 59–111.

Stead, I.M. 2006 *British Iron Age Swords and Scabbards*. London: British Museum Press.

Stead, I.M. and Rigby, V. 1999 *The Morel Collection. Iron Age antiquities from Champagne in the British Museum*. London: British Museum Press.

Stead, I.M., Flouest, J.L. and Rigby, V. 2006 *Iron Age and Roman Burials in Champagne*. Oxford: Oxbow Books

Stephens, M.R. 1986 *Interim Report on the Excavation of Devil's Hill, Heslerton*. Malton: East Riding Archaeological Research Committee.

Stephens, M.R. and Ware, P.A. 2019 The Iron Age cemeteries at Pocklington and other excavations by MAP, in Halkon (ed.) 2019b, 17–32.

Stillingfleet, E. 1847 Account of the opening of some barrows on the Wolds of Yorkshire. *Proceedings of the Archaeological Institute held at York 1846*, 26–32.

Stoertz, C., 1997 *Ancient Landscapes of the Yorkshire Wolds*. Swindon: Royal Commission on Historical Monuments (England).

Stollner, T. 2014 Between ruling ideology and ancestor worship: the *mos maiorum* of the Early Celtic 'Hero Graves', in C. Gosden, S. Crawford and K. Ulmschncidcr (cds) *Celtic Art in Europe: Making Connections*. Oxford: Oxbow Books, 119–33.

Stuart-Macadam, P. 1992 Anemia in past populations, in P. Stuart-Macadam and S. Kent (eds) *Diet, Demography and Disease: changing perspectives of anemia*. New York: Aldine de Gruyter, 151–70.

Stuiver, M. and Polach, H.A. 1977 Reporting of ^{14}C data. *Radiocarbon* 19, 355–63.

Sture, J. F. 2001 Biocultural Perspectives on Birth Defects in Medieval Urban and Rural English Populations. Unpublished PhD thesis, University of Durham.

Strauss, H. 1997 The isotopic composition of sedimentary sulphur through time. *Palaeogeography, Palaeoclimatology, Palaeoecology* 32, 97–118.

Tabor, J. 2005 Archaeological watching brief at Pocklington School, West Green, Pocklington, East Riding of Yorkshire. Barnards Castle: Northern Archaeological Associates report.

Tabor, J. 2008 Pocklington Wastewater Treatment Works, East Riding of Yorkshire. Barnards Castle: Northern Archaeological Associates report 08/01.

Tabor, J. 2009 Excavations at Canal Lane, Pocklington. *East Riding Archaeologist* 12, 127–66.

Taylor G, Young, D. and Mays, S 2005 Genotype analysis of the earliest known prehistoric case of tuberculosis in Britain. *Journal of Clinical Microbiology 43 (5) 2236–40*

Trust, B.A. and Fry, B. 1992 Stable sulphur isotopes in plants: a review. *Plant, Cell & Environment* 15, 1105–10.

Ubelaker, D.H., Bucholz, B.A. and Stewart, J.E.B. 2006 Analysis of artificial radiocarbon in different skeletal and dental tissue types to evaluate date of death. *Journal of Forensic Science* 51, 484–8.

van der Merwe, N.J. and Vogel, J.C. 1978 ^{13}C content of human collagen as a measure of prehistoric diet in Woodland North America. *Nature* 276, 815–16.

von den Driesch, A. and Boessneck, J. 1974 Kritische Anmerkungen zur Widerristhöhenberechnung aus Längenmassen vor-und frühgeschichtlicher Tierknochen. *Säugetierkundliche Mitteilungen* 22, 325–48.

Vyskocil, J.J., McIlroy, M.A., Brennan, T.A. and Wilson, F.M. 1991 Pyogenic infection of the sacroiliac joint: case reports and review of the literature. *Medicine* 70, 188–97.

Wadleigh, M.A., Schwarcz, H.P. and Kramer, J.R. 1994 Sulphur isotope tests of seasalt correction factors in precipitation: Nova Scotia, Canada. *Water, Air and Soil Pollution* 77, 1–16.

Walker, P. L., Bathurst, P. R., Richman, R., Gjerdrum, T. and Andrushko, V. A. 2009. The causes of porotic hyperostosis and cribra orbitalia: a reappraisal of the iron-deficiency-anemia hypothesis. *American Journal of Physical Anthropology* 139, 109–25.

Wheeler, R.E.M. 1943 *Maiden Castle, Dorset*. Report of the Research Committee of the Society of Antiquaries of London 12. Oxford: Society of Antiquaries.

Whitham, F. 1991 The stratigraphy of the Upper Cretaceous Ferriby, Welton and Burnham formations north of the Humber, north-east England. *Proceedings of the Yorkshire Geological Society* 48, 227–54.

Whimster, R.P. 1979 *Burial Practices in Iron Age Britain*. Unpublished PhD thesis, University of Durham etheses.dur. acuk/7999/.

Wood, R. 2018 Prehistory in the Crambeck landscape. Who cares about Romans anyway? *Prehistoric Yorkshire* 55, 91–2.

Yaldiz, M., Erdem, T., Dikicier, B. S. and Dilek, F. H. 2015 Lupus vulgaris mimicking hemangioma diagnosed 42 years after onset: a case report, *Journal of Medical Case Reports* 9, 215–17.

Younger, P.L. and McHugh, M. 1995 Peat development, sand cones and palaeohydrology of the spring-fed mire in East Yorkshire, UK. *The Holocene* 5, 59–67.

Zohary, D. and Hopf, M. 2000 *Domestication of Plants in the Old World* (3rd edn). Oxford: Oxford University Press.

Index

Numbers in *italic* denote pages with figures, those in **bold** denote pages with tables.